Interpersonal
COMMUNICATION

BUILDING REWARDING RELATIONSHIPS

D1081676

Kristen
**CAMPBELL
EICHHORN**
*State University of New York-
Oswego*

Candice
**THOMAS-
MADDOX**
Ohio University-Lancaster

Melissa
**BEKELJA
WANZER**
Canisius College

KENDALL/HUNT PUBLISHING COMPANY
4050 Westmark Drive   Dubuque, Iowa 52002

Book Team

Chairman and Chief Executive Officer   Mark C. Falb
President and Chief Operating Officer   Chad M. Chandlee
Vice President, Higher Education   David L. Tart
Director of National Book Program   Paul B. Carty
Editorial Development Manager   Georgia Botsford
Senior Developmental Editor   Angela Willenbring
Vice President, Operations   Timothy J. Beitzel
Assistant Vice President, Production Services   Christine E. O'Brien
Senior Production Editor   Mary Melloy
Permissions Editor   Renae Horstman
Cover Designer   Suzanne Millius
Web Project Manager   Sheena Reed

Cover contributions from Ben Dunkle
Cover Image © Handy Widiyanto, 2007, Shutterstock.
All Shutterstock images used under license from Shutterstock, Inc.

Dedication

Kristen Campbell Eichhorn
To Eric Eichhorn

Candice Thomas-Maddox
To Rick, Greyson, and Parker Maddox

Melissa Bekelja Wanzer
To Steve, Claire, and Ella Wanzer

Brief Contents

Contents

chapter **9**   **Terminating Relationships: Knowing When To Throw in the Towel**   238

chapter **13** **Health Communication: Managing Interpersonal
Interactions that Produce Anxiety**   **336**

Preface

BACKGROUND AND PHILOSOPHY

Throughout more than thirty-five combined years of teaching interpersonal communication (IPC), we have had the opportunity to use or review just about every IPC textbook published. In addition to our extensive teaching experiences, each of us has written and presented conference papers, book chapters, and journal articles in the area of interpersonal communication. While we agree that there are many excellent IPC texts on the market, something always seems to be missing. As we discussed the concepts, theories, research, and types of examples we would like to see included in an "ideal" IPC text, we discovered that we had several common themes on our textbook "wish lists." After countless discussions and over two years of researching and writing, the result is this textbook: *Interpersonal Communication: Building Rewarding Relationships.*

Our goal in writing this text is to provide students with a strong foundation combining both theory and research in the field of interpersonal communication. We feel that students need to understand the foundations of IPC and to explore how researchers in this field are employing empirical approaches to examine IPC concepts as they occur in everyday interactions. In essence, the field of interpersonal communication continues to evolve through its empirical approaches to examining relationships, and this book reflects those changes. It addresses a number of hot topics in IPC, including: the dark side of interpersonal communication (e.g., deception, jealousy, verbal aggression); development of the self and IPC; individual differences and IPC; intercultural differences; life span and health-related communication issues (e.g., communicating with persons with disabilities, communicating with health-care providers, and communicating about death); and current research concerning the role of computer-mediated communication in relationship development.

This text is intended for students wishing to improve their ability to relate to others and simultaneously improve their personal and professional relationships. This text is unique in that it:

- Provides a useful foundation for IPC students and extends the typical "basic communication" text by including a detailed discussion of IPC theory, individual differences, culture, media, IPC research, and technology.
- Includes in every chapter summaries of classic and contemporary IPC research conducted in the communication field. Most chapters also include examples of IPC-related research from fields such as psychology, sociology, anthropology, business, marketing, education, and computer technology.

- Discusses the impact of personality, culture, and personal transformation on relationships.
- Focuses on the evolution of communication in relationships across the life span and not simply on one particular point in time.
- Identifies potential challenges and pitfalls in interpersonal interactions and provides strategies for improving interpersonal communication competence.
- Emphasizes specific interpersonal skills needed to improve communication in all types of relationships. Provides examples of both effective and ineffective communication practices to help students understand these differences.
- Includes a discussion of interpersonal communication dynamics (conflict, conformity/conversational orientation, etc.) as they impact relationships in a variety of contexts (e.g., organizational, family, health). Discusses how these interpersonal communication dynamics can affect relationship satisfaction.
- Includes numerous popular culture examples from television, film, and music that illustrate interpersonal communication theories and concepts.
- Includes a number of self-report measures that students can complete to evaluate their communication skills and to pinpoint potential areas needing improvement.
- Includes a number of tables and charts that illustrate the concepts discussed in the chapters. Students are provided with multiple clear examples of theories, research, or concepts to help them organize and process course information.
- Includes a number of "how" and "why" questions throughout the chapters to stimulate students' thinking about the IPC concepts discussed.

ORGANIZATION OF THE TEXT

To assist instructors in guiding students on their interpersonal communication journey, this text is organized into three main areas.

Part One: The Basics of Interpersonal Communication

Part One provides an overview of the historical, conceptual, and theoretical foundations of this field and introduces the background, fundamentals, and key components of interpersonal communication. This section provides students with a fundamental framework and positions interpersonal communication within the general discipline of communication. For communication majors, this text provides reinforcement and consistency with introductory communication courses, and for nonmajors this section provides needed structure for the communication discipline.

More specifically, Part One provides an overview and introduction to interpersonal communication and continues toward an understanding of theories and concepts underpinning current trends in interpersonal communication research.

In Chapter One, IPC History and Foundation, we explore reasons for taking an interpersonal communication course, offer a definition of interpersonal communication and distinguish it from other types of communication, identify key interpersonal communication principles, and provide a brief overview of the history of interpersonal communication.

Chapter Two, Development of Self and Individual Differences, examines the process of identifying formation, the relationship between aspects of the self and IPC, and the impact of individual differences on IPC.

The goal of Chapter Three, Verbal Communication, is to explore verbal communication and how different types of messages (e.g., clear, ambiguous, powerful, powerless) affect the quality of our interactions and relationships.

Chapter Four, Nonverbal Communication, explains the types and functions of nonverbal communication and offers examples of how nonverbal messages impact social interaction.

In Chapter Five, Perception and Listening, we first explain the primary perceptual processes (e.g., selection, organization, interpretation) and how each affects the way we communicate with others. We discuss common perception errors (e.g., fundamental attribution error) and the relationship between perceptual processes and IPC. An important skill related to information processing is listening. In the final section of this chapter, we explore the complex process of listening and offer suggestions for improving listening skills.

Part Two: Dynamics of Interpersonal Relationships

This section addresses the dynamics experienced in interpersonal relationships. These chapters take a closer look at how relationships progress, as well as the challenges that are experienced in both romantic and platonic relationships.

By adopting a developmental approach to relationships, students are able to visualize the revolutionary process of relationships. In addition, they will gain an understanding of the key communication variables and patterns of behaviors that either strengthen or weaken our interpersonal relationships.

Beginning with Chapter Six, Initiating Relationships, we explore the dynamics of relationship initiation. We examine the role that attraction and similarity play in our decisions to initiate relationships and focus on the impact of self-disclosure and technology on relationships that are formed.

Realizing that rewarding relationships require time and energy, Chapter Seven, Relationship Maintenance and Conflict, focuses on strategies of maintenance and conflict resolution.

To assist students in understanding the potential dark side of relationships, Chapter Eight, The Dark Side, addresses issues such as jealousy, power, and compliance-gaining.

Chapter Nine, Terminating Relationships, focuses on understanding why and how to end relationships. In addition to exploring the stages of coming apart in relationships, the chapter provides strategies for managing the difficult process of relationship termination.

Part Three: IPC in Various Communication Contexts

Realizing that interpersonal communication is an essential part of all relationships that we experience, Part Three investigates IPC as it occurs in different communication contexts.

Beginning with Chapter Ten, Intercultural Communication, we explore the dynamics experienced when relationships are formed between people of different cultures. Concepts such as needs, values, and attitudes are addressed in this chapter, and strategies for enhancing intercultural relationships are provided.

One common context that all students can relate to is the family, and Chapter Eleven, Family Communication, applies concepts addressed in earlier chapters by exploring research that has examined relationship maintenance in families as well as addressing communication issues experienced in a variety of family relationships (e.g., parent-child, sibling, marital partners.)

Because organizations are an essential part of our everyday lives, Chapter Twelve, Organizational Communication, focuses on relationship dynamics experienced in the workplace (e.g., superior-subordinate, co-worker, romantic relationships, friendships). The presence of dialectical tensions in workplace relationships is addressed, and tips for effective socialization in organizations are provided.

Chapter Thirteen, Health Communication, explores effective communication in the health care context. Given that many people report anxiety when meeting with a doctor, this chapter includes research findings that help answer questions about communicating effectively with health care providers. This chapter also addresses why people experience anxiety when communicating with persons with disabilities and how to best approach these interactions. Finally, many people experience anxiety when discussing issues related to death and dying. In the final part of the chapter we introduce the difficult topic of death and dying and offer suggestions for communication in these situations.

Finally, Chapter Fourteen, From Face-to-Face to Cyberspace, focuses on the growing trend of online communication and how students build relationships via the Internet. Included in this chapter is a discussion of how face-to-face and online relationships differ, as well as strategies for safe cyberspace interactions.

In essence, this book offers a comprehensive view of interpersonal communication by providing a foundation for the interpersonal communication discipline; identifying key components that influence communication in relationships; identifying potential relationship pitfalls as well as skills and strategies to successfully overcome them; and discussing the implications of interpersonal communication across contexts.

STUDENT-ORIENTED PEDAGOGY

Because we recognize the importance of assessing student learning, we have included the following features in each chapter to facilitate student learning and help instructors measure learning outcomes.

Learning Objectives help students focus on the overall concepts, theories, and skills discussed in the chapter.

Key Terms, Theories, and Concepts are stated at the beginning of each chapter.

Bold-faced Key Words throughout the chapter include clear definitions for each term.

Real-world Examples or examples from the media illustrate chapter theories and concepts.

Summaries of classic and contemporary IPC scholarship are included throughout each chapter.

Discussion Activities at the end of each chapter help to stimulate discussion and increase understanding of chapter concepts.

Glossary of Terms serves as a helpful reference tool at the end of the text.

Sources detailed throughout the chapters and a comprehensive list of **references** at the end of each chapter document the extensive research cited.

INSTRUCTIONAL ONLINE ENHANCEMENTS

By using the web access code included in the textbook, both students and instructors are given access to online materials which are integrated chapter-by-chapter with the textbook to enrich students' learning.

    Look for the web icon in the margin to direct you to various interactive tools.

***Self Discovery Questions** are designed to understand student opinions, behavior, and attitudes towards course materials.

***Key Term Flashcards, Matching Exercises,** and **Drag and Drop Scenarios** reinforce concepts and assess comprehension.

***Sample Test Questions** can be used for practice and to assess retention.

***Short Video Clips** designed for use in or outside of class to facilitate class discussion.

Acknowledgements

We would first like to thank the Kendall/Hunt team who made this project possible. We are grateful to Paul Carty whose vision made this text a reality. To Angela Willenbring—words cannot express how much we value your support throughout this project. Not only did you demonstrate exceptional IPC skills, but you were always "in tune" with and supportive of the demands that we faced throughout this project. In addition, we would like to thank our Buffalo friends Ben Dunkle for his creative assistance with the cover and Megan O'Neil for her editing work on preliminary chapters of the text. To our communication colleagues whose research is cited in this text—thank you for continuing to explore the ways in which IPC touches our lives.

We gratefully acknowledge the constructive comments of the colleagues who provided reviews for individual chapters of this text. They include:

Jennifer Adams
DePauw University

Charlotte Amaro
Lake Superior State University

Brooks Aylor
La Salle University

Bryan Barrows
North Harris College

Marion Boyer
Kalamazoo Valley Community College

Ed Brewer
Murray State University

Rebecca Carlton
Indiana University Southeast

Ernest Doling
Ohio University

Thomas Feeley
SUNY Buffalo

Eric Fife
James Madison University

David Foster
University of Findlay

Elissa Foster
San Jose State University

Kari Frisch
Central Lakes College

Colleen Garside
Weber State University

Donna Goodwin
Tulsa Community College

Jo Anna Grant
California State University–San Bernardino

Rick Hogrefe
Crafton Hills College

Elaine Jenks
West Chester University

Gary Kuhn
Chemeketa Community College

Jennifer Knapp
Lycoming College

Sandra Lakey
Penn College of Technology

Betty Jane Lawrence
Bradley University

Phil Martin
North Central State College

Trudy Milburn
Baruch College–CUNY

Keri Moe
El Paso Community College

Bruce Montgomery
Milligan College

Sally Moore
Linn Benton Community College

Thomas Morra
Northern Virginia Community College

David Moss
Mt. San Jacinto College–San Jacinto

Kay Neal
University of Wisconsin–Oshkosh

Marshall Prisbell
University of Nebraska–Omaha

Kelly Rocca
St. John's University

Christine Shea
California Poly State University–San Luis Obispo

Alan Shiller
Southern Illinois University–Edwardsville

George Smith
University of Wisconsin–Platteville

Terri Sparks
Mesa Community College

Laurel Traynowicz
Boise State University

Jason Wrench
Ohio University Eastern Campus

To my husband Steve and daughters Claire and Ella—thank you for always making me laugh and for providing love and support while I worked on this project. A special thanks also to my two undergraduate research assistants, Ann Wojtaszczyk and Cara Cotter, for assisting with a variety of research-related tasks. This book would be a lot less interesting to college students if Ann and Cara were not around to help out with media examples, quotes, and IPC examples! Thank you also to my COM 204 and COM 630 students at Canisius College for offering suggestions on how to improve the textbook and providing encouragement while I was writing the textbook. Finally, a special thank you to Candice and Kristen for being great friends and colleagues, enduring my quirky humor attempts, and collaborating with me on this project!

Melissa Bekelja Wanzer

To Rick, Greyson, and Parker—thanks for being my guys. Your patience as I locked myself in my office for "just a while longer" and your hugs and smiles of encouragement as I finished each goal along the way made it possible for me to complete this project. Love you bunches and bunches! To my COMS 206 and 450 students at Ohio University-Lancaster—your brutal honesty and suggestions helped give this book an extra spark. You truly make my job fun. To Missy and Kristen—thanks for joining me on this adventure. The light at the end of the tunnel is finally here!

Candice Thomas-Maddox

To my dearest husband, Eric—thank you for your endless hours of support as I pushed forward to each new deadline. Your immeasurable patience, understanding, and words of encouragement fueled my personal drive to continue on this adventure. To all my unconditionally loving friends and my family—Mom, Dad, Laura, Shawn, and all the Eichhorns—thanks for providing me with great material and reminding me to drop my work once in a while to enjoy life along the way. To my colleagues and communication studies students at Towson University—thank you for all your feedback and suggestions, especially Holly Webb and Felicia Miller for your detailed recommendations. Finally, thank you to Melissa and Candice—you are amazing researchers, teachers, leaders, mothers, mentors, and friends.

Kristen Campbell Eichhorn

About the Authors

Kristen Campbell Eichhorn (Ph.D.—University of Miami) is an Assistant Professor in the Department of Communication Studies at the State University of New York at Oswego where she teaches introductory and advanced courses in interpersonal communication. She has also served on over a dozen masters theses which focused on interpersonal communication concepts. In addition, Dr. Eichhorn has taught a wide variety of other courses including, research methods, communication theory, organizational communication, nonverbal communication, persuasion, and business and professional communication. Her primary area of research is interpersonal communication in the organizational, instructional, and health settings. Her research has been published in a variety of journals including, *Communication Research Reports*, *College Student Journal* and *Public Relations Review*. Currently, Dr. Eichhorn serves as the Chair of the Interpersonal Interest Group for the Eastern Communication Association.

Candice Thomas-Maddox (Ed.D.—West Virginia University) is an Associate Professor of Communication Studies at Ohio University-Lancaster, where she also serves as Division Coordinator. Over the past fifteen years, she has taught a variety of courses focusing on interpersonal communication. In addition to teaching the introductory IPC course, Dr. Thomas-Maddox has taught IPC at the graduate level, as well as courses focusing on family, instructional, intercultural, and organizational contexts. She served on the editorial boards for *Communication Education*, *Communication Quarterly*, *Communication Research Reports*, and *Communication Teacher*. Dr. Thomas-Maddox currently serves as President for the Ohio Communication Association, and she will serve as President for the Eastern Communication Association in 2010.

Melissa Bekelja Wanzer (Ed.D.—West Virginia University, 1995) is a Professor in the Communication Studies Department at Canisius College. She teaches graduate seminars in interpersonal communication, research methods, persuasion, and small group communication. Dr. Wanzer also teaches undergraduate courses in family, gender, social problems, and basic and advanced interpersonal communication. Dr. Wanzer has researched the benefits of humor production in instructional, corporate, and health-care contexts. Her research appears in *Communication Education*, *Communication Teacher*, *Communication Quarterly*, *Health Communication*, *Journal of Health Communication* and *Communication Research Reports*. Dr. Wanzer received teaching and research awards from Syracuse University in 1992 and was the 2004 faculty recipient of the Dr. I. Joan Lorch Women Studies award at Canisius College.

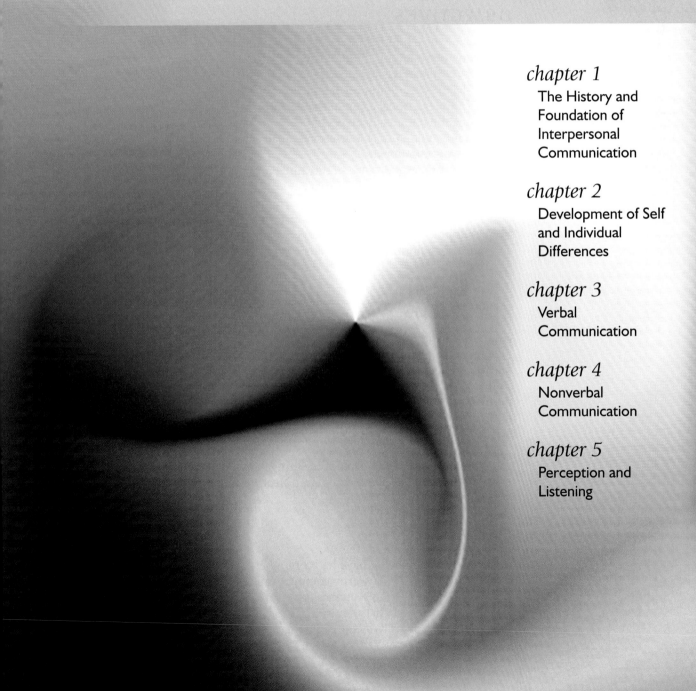

The Basics of Interpersonal Communication

The History and Foundation of Interpersonal Communication
Examining the Roots

OBJECTIVES

- Provide three important reasons for the study of interpersonal communication
- Discuss Spitzberg and Cupach's Components Model of communication competence
- Define interpersonal communication and distinguish it from other types of communication (e.g., intrapersonal, small group, organizational)
- Identify and explain each of the thirteen basic principles of interpersonal communication (INTERPERSONAL)
- Describe the pivotal research and historical events that contributed to the development of the field of interpersonal communication
- Define communication competence
- Define theory and explain the four goals of a theory

KEY TERMS

communication competence	intrapersonal communication	verbal and nonverbal component
knowledge	interpersonal communication	rules
skill	transactional	symbolic interactionism
motivation	content and relational components	Maslow's Hierarchy of Needs
mass communication		kinesics
organizational communication	process	proxemics
small group communication	shared meaning	Attribution theory
	metacommunication	theory

OVERVIEW

Chances are most people have had a number of frustrating experiences with communication. Whether we are communicating with someone face-to-face or are using our computer to send messages, our communication skills often falter and we ask ourselves what went wrong. For instance, have you ever talked on the phone with a family member, hoping to have a meaningful conversation, but as you hung up, you wondered why nothing really important was said? Have you ever taken your relationship partner out for a romantic anniversary dinner, anticipating the chance to reminisce about happy times together; but instead, the night was spent arguing and the date ended abruptly? Experiences such as these may be connected to either underdeveloped communication skills or a lack of awareness of the communication tactics and behaviors needed to negotiate these situations. Interpersonal skills can, and should, be continually evaluated and improved, reinforcing the importance of learning more about interpersonal communication. In this chapter we explore reasons for taking an interpersonal communication course, offer a definition of interpersonal communication, and distinguish it from other types of communication. Additionally, we identify key interpersonal communication principles, provide a brief overview of the history of interpersonal communication, and discuss the significance of communication theories.

Have you ever unexpectedly ended up in an argument over what you thought would be a good dinner conversation?

WHY STUDY INTERPERSONAL COMMUNICATION?

Researchers and practitioners from an array of disciplines often describe interpersonal skills as absolutely essential for success in their professional fields. Regardless of the profession you enter, it is very likely that effective communication skills are required for your success. For example, successful journalists note that there appears to be a strong relationship between a writer's conviviality and his creativity. Most individuals employed in this field agree that success at work is often contingent on one's ability to relate well to fellow journalists (Manssour 2003). Similarly, Steve Bauman (2003), an employee of NASA Glenn Research Center, notes that in a recent survey conducted in the engineering profession, oral communication skills were cited as one of the most important skills needed for recent engineering graduates. Individuals from all types of health care fields and services are encouraged to participate in interpersonal skills training to improve their ability to treat patients (see, for example, Rath et al. 1998). When health care providers communicate more effectively, patient satisfaction and motivation often increase (Thompson 1986; Wanzer, Booth-Butterfield and Gruber 2004). Not surprisingly, nurses of all levels of ability are expected to possess strong interpersonal communication skills in order to excel in their vocation (Crosby et al. 2003; Utley-Smith 2004). There are innumerable professions that demand strong interpersonal skills as a means of relating well to colleagues and clients, and to achieving and maintaining one's position within the organization. In fact, it is probably more difficult to identify a field or profession that does *not* demand strong interpersonal skills than it would be to list all those that do.

Developing strong interpersonal skills is more necessary than ever to negotiate in today's "bigger is better" business

Why would it be especially important for health care providers to have strong interpersonal skills?

environment (Myers and Tucker 2005). Organizations have undergone radical changes resulting in a more diverse workforce, a greater ability to obtain and process information through the Internet, and an expanding global marketplace which makes doing business with people from other cultures easier than ever before. According to management professors Laura Myers and Mary Tucker, as these changes occur, more emphasis is being placed on "people skills" in business programs across the nation and the specific "soft skills" which distinguish effective from ineffective managers. Effective managers must be able to deliver constructive criticism, manage conflicts between employees, persuade and influence individuals at all levels, provide support and guidance and exhibit appropriate leadership behaviors. Others, such as Daniel Goleman (1995), agree that in addition to possessing interpersonal communication skills, a strong sense of self and other awareness is what distinguishes successful from unsuccessful professionals.

What interpersonal skills are important to exhibit during a job interview?

© Kathye Killer, 2007, Shutterstock.

The job interview is an excellent example of a situation that demands effective interpersonal communication skills. A recent survey of personnel interviewers confirmed the importance of interpersonal communication skills during the interview process. The survey highlighted areas of improvement for potential job candidates (Peterson 1997). Marshalita Sims Peterson conducted a survey of approximately 500 personnel interviewers and found that while ninety percent of personnel interviewers indicate that strong communication skills are needed for success in corporate settings, only sixty percent feel that applicants exhibit effective communication skills during job interviews. The five most frequently identified verbal and nonverbal communication skill inadequacies exhibited during interview situations were: lack of eye contact, topic relevance, response organization, listening skills, and response clarity (Peterson 1997, 289). Several chapters in this textbook are intended to help you to become a more effective interviewee, particularly the chapters on verbal and nonverbal communication, perception and listening, and organizational communication.

Additional and equally important reasons for taking a course in interpersonal communication include the indisputable links between effective communication and health, and between effective communication practices and relationship satisfaction. Having rewarding communication and relationships with others is closely connected to both mental and physical health (Burleson and MacGeorge 2002; Omarzu, Whalen, and Harvey 2001). Knowing that others will "be there" for us during stressful or traumatic times in our lives offers us a sense of perceived social support, which correlates to mental well-being (Burleson and MacGeorge 2002). In his new book, *Social Intelligence: The New Science of Human Relationships,* Daniel Goleman (2006) provides additional support for the relationship between the quality of one's interpersonal relationships and one's mental and physical well-being. More specifically, this groundbreaking work focuses on the notion of a social brain that is biologically "wired to connect" with those around us. According to Goleman (2006) "our social interactions even play a role in reshaping our brain, through "neuroplasticity," which means that repeated experiences sculpt the shape, size, and number of neurons and their synaptic connections" (p. 11). Stated more simply, the ongoing relationships that we establish can shape the intricate "wiring" or neural circuitry of our brain. To further emphasize the link between our relationships and our health, Goleman describes unhealthy or abusive relationships as "toxic" to our social brain and healthy relationships are described as "vitamins." Thus, when we are around individuals that love and support us, this experience is analogous to taking vitamins that assist in the functioning of our social brain (Goleman 2006).

Many interpersonal communication scholars would agree that healthy communication is essential to achieving healthy relationships. When communication between individuals deteriorates or ceases to exist, relationships are often doomed for failure. A significant body of research focuses on the relationship between specific communication patterns or practices, such as emotional communication, and relationship satisfaction and longevity (see for example, Burleson and MacGeorge 2002; Burleson and Samter 1996; Metts and Planalp 2002; Noller and Feeney 1994; Roloff and Soule 2002). Interpersonal communication researchers have studied nearly all aspects of romantic and platonic relationships, including how people come together to form meaningful relationships (Knapp and Vangelisti 2000), how they maintain these relationships (Canary and Stafford 2001), the factors individuals consider when deciding to terminate a relationship, and the methods used to disengage these relationships (Baxter 1982; Cody 1982). Learning about effective communication practices can assist individuals throughout every stage of relationship development, from the beginning stages when individuals are uncertain about how to proceed, to the relational maintenance stage, or to the end of a romantic relationship. In this textbook we provide you with several chapters that focus on the stages of relationship development (initiating, maintenance, growing dark, and terminating) as well as the communication practices that both contribute to and detract from a relationship's reported "health."

The following sections of this chapter highlight the broad learning objectives to be addressed throughout this textbook. While there are specific learning objectives and key terms for each chapter, the following three primary objectives are the overall purpose of this textbook.

1. Students will be exposed to and become familiar with a wide range of communication concepts and theories that are central to the process of interpersonal communication.

In this chapter we define interpersonal communication and distinguish it from other forms of communication. Also, in an effort to better understand the "roots" of interpersonal communication, we discuss its history, with an emphasis on classic research and on the historical events that stimulated interest in this topic. Throughout the entire textbook you will see numerous boldfaced terms, concepts, and theories that we consider central to understanding the process of interpersonal communication. Our hope is that you will be able to define these terms and concepts and relate them to your own experiences.

2. Students will become more competent communicators.

We suspect that many of you are taking this course to improve your ability to send and receive messages from others, also known as communication competence. **Communication competence** is defined as the ability to send messages that are perceived as appropriate and effective (Spitzberg and Cupach 1984). The model most often used to describe communication competence is the Components Model advanced by Spitzberg and Cupach. This model highlights three key components of communication competence: knowledge, skill and motivation. The **knowledge** component of this model refers to understanding what reaction or action is best suited for a particular situation. Taking a class in interpersonal communication is the first step in acquiring knowledge and information about the process of forming relationships with others. The **skill** component of this model addresses one's ability to utilize the appropriate behaviors in a situation. It is important to remember that there is a difference between *knowing* how to do something (e.g., knowledge of interpersonal models, theories, and concepts) and actually *being able* to do it. For example, a person may understand the principles and concepts associated with managing conflict in relationships. However, when the time comes to put that knowledge to use, it may be difficult to engage in the appropriate behaviors. The final component of the model, **motivation,** refers to one's desire to achieve results in a competent manner. It is not enough to have knowledge and skills. You must also have a desire to achieve communication competence. To assess your current level of communication competence, we suggest you complete the Communication Competence Scale found in the final pages of this chapter at the onset of the course, and then again at the end of the semester.

While we can address the knowledge and skill aspects of communication competence, it is up to you to become more motivated and make attempts to achieve your interpersonal goals. Many of the chapters in this textbook offer valuable information about the communication process and emphasize specific communication behaviors linked to interpersonal communication competence. For example, in Chapters Three and Four we focus on the highly complex process of sending and receiving verbal and nonverbal messages. By calling attention to certain important aspects of nonverbal messages such as dress, body movements, gestures or eye contact, we hope students will hone in on the specific skills needed to communicate more effectively. Our chapter on perception and listening also highlights specific communication behaviors associated with effective communication. We often forget to focus on the process of message reception, which is why listening is often referred to as the "forgotten" communication skill.

3. Students will achieve rewarding personal and professional relationships.

People communicate and ultimately establish different types of relationships to satisfy three universal human needs: control, inclusion and affection (Schutz 1966). We communicate with others and establish relationships to control or manage our surroundings, to be part of a group, and to fulfill the need to feel liked. Virtually every chapter in this textbook explains interpersonal communication concepts and theories that will help you understand how relationships work. By teaching you the important communication concepts that are central to understanding the process of interpersonal communication, and by helping you acquire the skills needed to communicate more effectively, we are certain that our third and final goal will be met. And so we begin our journey by clarifying what we mean when we use the term interpersonal communication.

WHAT EXACTLY IS INTERPERSONAL COMMUNICATION?

Communication researchers continue to study many forms of communication, including

- Mass or mediated communication
- Organizational communication

We all want to successfully communicate with others and establish good relationships.

© Emiliano Rodriguez, 2007, Shutterstock.

- Small group communication
- Intrapersonal communication
- Interpersonal communication

Mass or Mediated Communication. The study of mediated or **mass communication** involves communicators that are typically separated in both space and time and who send and receive messages indirectly. Mass communication typically occurs when a small number of people send messages to a large, diverse and geographically widespread population (Cathcart and Gumpert 1983; Kreps and Thorton 1992).

Organizational Communication. Communication scholars also study **organizational communication,** which is recognized as communication that occurs within businesses or organizations. Organizational communication takes place between organization members within a clear hierarchical structure; individuals are typically encouraged to adhere to roles and rules established within this structure. In this text, we will examine the role of interpersonal communication in organizations, and different types of relationships in this context will be discussed.

Small Group Communication. **Small group communication,** another area frequently studied by communication scholars, is defined as "interaction among a small group of people who share a common purpose or goal, who feel a sense of belonging to the group, and who exert influence on one another" (Beebe and Masterson 1997, 6). Small group communication is complex and often occurs between three or more people who are interdependent and working to achieve commonly recognized goals or objectives.

What are some of the benefits of working in small groups?

Intrapersonal Communication. **Intrapersonal communication,** the most basic level of communication, takes place inside one's head and is silent and repetitive (Kreps and Thorton 1992). Many of us talk to ourselves which often affects our interpersonal communication decisions. Think about a time when you rehearsed a conversation in your mind before actually engaging in interpersonal communication. Perhaps it was a situation where you were building up the courage to ask someone on a date, or maybe you planned out a conversation with a colleague regarding a project at work.

Interpersonal Communication. **Interpersonal communication,** sometimes referred to as *dyadic* communication, is often loosely described as communication that occurs between two individuals. While most agree that interpersonal communication typically involves at least two people (Knapp, Daly, Albada and Miller 2002), there is great disparity in the actual definitions advanced by interpersonal communication researchers.

"In some respects, the construct of interpersonal communication is like the phenomenon it represents—that is, dynamic and changing" (Knapp et al. 2002, 8). It is not easy to develop a definition for this concept that is widely agreed upon, although there are certainly some similarities and overlap in the different ways interpersonal communication is typically defined by communication researchers. For example, Booth-Butterfield (2002) says "Interpersonal communication is when we interact on an individual-to-individual basis with someone, and we get beyond the roles in the situation" (p. 3). Similarly, DeVito (2001) defines interpersonal communication as "the

Interpersonal communication connects us in our relationships.

communication that takes place between two persons who have an established relationship; the people are in some way connected" (p. 5). Capella (1987) describes interpersonal communication as one person influencing another person's behavior, above and beyond that explained by "normal baselines of action" (p. 228). All of these definitions mention an exchange of some kind, typically between two individuals. These exchanges can potentially occur face-to-face, over the telephone or via the computer.

One area where there appears to be great variability in definitions of interpersonal communication is the "nature of interaction units," or type of interaction, where interpersonal communication typically occurs (Knapp et al. 2002, 9). Similar to Booth-Butterfield and DeVito, we argue that interpersonal communication typically occurs between individuals whose relationship has evolved beyond that of strangers or even acquaintances. Additionally, we agree with Miller and Steinberg (1975) who argue that the extent or degree of "interpersonalness" in a relationship often varies greatly, based on the type of information exchanged between the source and receiver. On any given day, you connect with a variety of people which may include business associates, family members, and relationship partners. We recognize that the communication occurring between a store clerk and a customer is less intimate, or personal, than the communication that occurs between a mother and daughter. For this reason, we note that interpersonal communication occurs along a continuum, with one end representing a type of interpersonal communication often described as "impersonal," and the other end representing a type of interpersonal communication described as "intimate." When we are able to adapt our messages to meet the specific attitudes, beliefs, values, or personality traits of the receiver, our communication is described as exhibiting a higher degree of intimacy. Alternatively, when we communicate with someone at a basic level and have only cultural or sociological information about the receiver, the communication is often described as less interpersonal or impersonal (Knapp et al. 2002). Thus, the communication that occurs in the relationship will often determine whether the relationship is described as impersonal or intimate, or something in between.

We define **interpersonal communication** as a process which occurs in a specific context and involves an exchange of verbal or nonverbal messages between two connected individuals with the intent to achieve shared meaning. While there is a wide range of definitions available, we chose one that emphasizes the importance of communication as a process that consists of both verbal and nonverbal components and results in shared understandings between the interactants. In the following section, we take a closer look at aspects of this definition and important principles of interpersonal communication.

AN OVERVIEW OF THE BASIC PRINCIPLES OF INTERPERSONAL COMMUNICATION

To help you remember some basic principles and terms associated with the process of interpersonal communication, we created the acronym, INTERPERSONAL.

Table 1.1	Basic Principles of Interpersonal Communication
I	Irreversible
N	Not communicating is difficult
T	Transactional
E	Evolving
R	Relational/content components
P	Process
E	Effectiveness important
R	Relationship building
S	Shared meaning/metacommunication
O	Other-oriented
N	Nonverbal messages
A	Abide by rules
L	Learned skill

Irreversible.   First, interpersonal communication is irreversible. This means that once you say something, you cannot take it back. It is permanent. You cannot recover by saying, "Oh, forget I said that." Do you remember the last time someone asked you, "How do I look?" The slightest pause or facial expression on your part cannot be taken back once it is detected by the receiver. Once we communicate something, verbally or nonverbally, we must build from it.

Not Communicating Is Difficult.   Communication scholars often say that one cannot not communicate because intentional messages are often perceived when sources exhibit nonverbal behaviors such as eye contact, gestures and body movements, facial expressions and touch. It is often the case that receivers perceive these nonverbal behaviors exhibited by sources as intentional nonverbal communication. Picture someone sitting in an apartment, staring straight ahead, her arms across her chest. Her friend walks into the room and asks why she is angry. The friend perceived the staring and crossed arms as the message "I am angry" when, in actuality, the person sitting was daydreaming about getting an extra-large cheese pizza.

Transactional.   Next, interpersonal communication is a transactional exchange of verbal and nonverbal messages. **Transactional** refers to the fact that even as we are sending messages, we are receiving them as well. When

Just by looking at their expressions and gestures, can you tell what these individuals are feeling?

you talk to your friend, she may smile at you and simultaneously nod her head to show that she is actively listening. At the same time, you notice her new glasses and raise your eyebrows while commenting, "Cool specs! I never knew you wore glasses!" As she listens to your comment, she glances at an attractive male walking past while responding, "I usually wear contacts, but I was too lazy to put them in this morning." In this simple conversation, several verbal and nonverbal messages are being sent and received simultaneously.

Evolving.

Since communication in interpersonal relationships is constantly evolving, each time we speak with someone, we are building on previous messages. We are developing a history with this person and, therefore, our communication reflects this change. Think about the conversations you have with your closest friends. Because you have probably spent countless hours discussing family, friends, career goals and other mutual topics of interest, it is not necessary to revisit these conversations in detail each time you see each other. Instead, you may make quick references to previously discussed events in your conversations. You may ask your friend questions such as "How is your brother recovering from his skateboarding accident?" or "Why do you think Bob ended your relationship by saying, 'Let's just be friends'?" Asking these types of questions illustrates how conversations and relationships evolve over time.

Relational/Content Components.

Each message exchanged between interactants is made up of two types of meaning: content and relational (Bateson 1951). The **content,** or informational component of a message, is the verbal message you send, the words you choose. The **relational component** of a message, which includes nonverbal messages such as eye contact, gestures, and vocal inflection, tells the receiver how you would like the message to be interpreted. Consider the following situation.

> A mother is waiting for her son to come home from an unexpected late night out with friends. She is quite angry because her son has been out two hours after his curfew. The mother is standing guard by the front door with her arms crossed and teeth clenched. As soon as her son comes home, he opens the door and sees her standing right inside the front door looking very frustrated. She says, "Where have you been? Why didn't you call me to tell me you were running late?"

The content information is simply her questions. The relational information is unique to the relationship between the mother and son. How does the speaker want the receiver to interpret the message? How do they feel towards each other? These feelings are conveyed through the nonverbal actions of the speaker such as the mother's clenched teeth, crossed arms, and angry tone of voice. In order to interpret messages accurately, it is important to pay close attention to both the content and relational components of messages.

Process.

Interpersonal communication is often described as a **process** because it is continuous, or ongoing (Berlo 1960). While verbal messages may have clear beginnings and endings, nonverbal messages do not. Whether or not we are aware of it, we constantly send messages to others about our attitudes, moods, and personalities through our clothing choices, facial expressions, bodily movements, and gestures. Communication is also described as a complex process that involves many different steps. For example, the listening process involves receiving the message, selecting components or aspects of the message to process, interpreting the message, responding to the message, and remembering important aspects of the message at a later date.

Effective Communication Is More Important than More Communication.

We must remember: we determine the effectiveness of our interactions based on the quality of our communication, not the quantity or amount of words exchanged between individuals. Sometimes it is important to adhere to the "less is more" principle when engaging in communication with others. Consider taking a road trip with a friend. Would you rather be driving with someone that never stops talking or with someone that does not speak as much, but when he does, tells a funny, meaningful story, or shares some interesting news? Being appropriate with our communication is much more important than talking all the time.

Relationship Building.

An essential function of interpersonal communication is relationship building. We use interpersonal communication to self-disclose, listen, build trust, and establish relationships. It is impossible to form healthy relationships without effective communication.

Shared Meaning.

Shared meaning is the goal of our interpersonal communication interactions. We do this by collaborating during the communication process in an effort to reduce ambiguity about what verbal and nonverbal messages mean. Although we may never share exactly the same understanding with someone, we work to find common experiences and, at the same time, increase our chances for successful interpersonal exchanges. Often people engage in what Gregory Bateson (1972) conceptualized as **metacommunication,** "communicating about communication," when they want to clarify a message's

Effective interpersonal communication builds trust and establishes relationships between people.

meaning. A friend might say to her roommate, "What did you mean when you said 'I am fine' in that tone of voice?" Or a man might ask his significant other, "I think we need to talk about why you've been so quiet lately." Metacommunication is used during social interaction to increase our shared meaning and to reduce uncertainty about the status of our relationships.

Other-Oriented.

Interpersonal communication should be other-oriented. We need to create messages in a way that ensures our audience will understand them. Using appropriate language in a given context is critical to our success as communicators. Have you ever had professors who lectured over your head? Perhaps they used terminology that was unfamiliar to the students, or moved quickly without considering whether students understood the material. Unfortunately, professors like this do not realize how important it is to alter their messages to accommodate the different perspectives and levels of student learning. Regardless of what a professor might intend to say, what matters most is what the students actually perceive. This is why feedback,

What can you learn about these people by reading their nonverbal messages?

listening, and dual-perspective taking are critical to effective communication. These concepts will be discussed in greater detail in Chapter Five.

Nonverbal Messages.   Communication is often defined as the process of sending verbal and nonverbal messages to a receiver. The **verbal component** consists of the words we choose. The **nonverbal component** comprises everything other than the words including, among other behaviors: eye contact, hand gestures, facial expressions, volume, and tone of voice. There are many times when the verbal component of our message suggests one idea, while the nonverbal component indicates a quite different message. When there is a contradiction between the nonverbal and verbal messages, we tend to believe the nonverbal message because it is often perceived as involuntary, or less controllable. Because we know that individuals place more weight on the nonverbal component of a message, we will often use nonverbal messages strategically to contradict the verbal message. For example, a person says sarcastically, "Yeah, I just loved the movie *Gigli* with Jennifer Lopez and Ben Affleck," while he rolls his eyes. The verbal message suggests he does indeed like the movie, while the nonverbal message suggests exactly the opposite.

Nonverbal Messages Are More Believable.   Nonverbal messages tend to be taken more seriously than verbal messages in our culture. The well-known phrase "actions speak louder than words" is based on this principle. Verbal and nonverbal messages are discussed in much greater detail in Chapters Three and Four.

Abide by Rules When Interacting with Others.   Another principle of interpersonal communication is that we abide by rules when interacting with others. In fact, much of our communication is governed by *rules*. What are some examples of appropriate guidelines, or **rules**, for communicating in the classroom? When we ask students this question, they often point out the importance of paying attention in class, not talking while the instructor is lecturing, and turning off cellular phones during class time. We learn rules like these through interacting with others, a trial and error process. While it may seem unlikely that the same rules apply to everyone regardless of individual differences such as sex, age, culture, and personality, it is important to realize that people are not completely random in their behavior. We recognize that there is no magic formula or single rule that will work with everyone in every situation; however, we are interested in the research findings that significantly contribute to the interpersonal communication literature. In this textbook, we identify common themes from interpersonal communication research that can help predict successful or unsuccessful communication outcomes.

Learned Skill. Finally, interpersonal communication is a learned skill. We are born with the capability to communicate, but we must work at improving our communication skills to reduce misunderstandings with others. It is through repeated social interactions, taking courses like this one, and reading about communication processes that we learn the most appropriate and effective ways to send and receive messages. Although some people may seem to be "naturals" when it comes to relating to others, virtually everyone struggles with certain types of communication situations. By completing this course you should develop a more sophisticated understanding of communication concepts, theories, and research, which are central to the study of interpersonal communication. Interpersonal communication students should be able to identify and implement communication skills associated with communication competence and to understand relationship development processes. It is also important for students to understand the history of this academic area and identify significant research and historical events that have contributed to this field. In the following sections, we present a brief overview of what some interpersonal scholars view as the history of interpersonal communication (Knapp, Daly, Albada, and Miller 2002).

HISTORY OF INTERPERSONAL COMMUNICATION

In order to completely understand an academic area, you must start at its roots. In the *Handbook of Interpersonal Communication*, Knapp, Daly, Albada and Miller (2002) provide an overview of the historical foundations of the field of interpersonal communication. The introductory chapter of the *Handbook* is dedicated to providing a framework for tracing the development of the field. Readers are presented with a timeline highlighting the accomplishments of scholars who have made prominent contributions to the understanding of relational communication.

According to Knapp and his colleagues (2002) one of the most influential studies for providing a framework for both interpersonal and organizational communication was the result of research conducted by Elton Mayo from 1927 until 1932 at the Western Electric Hawthorne Works in Chicago. Mayo, a professor at the Harvard Business School, originally designed the study to examine the impact of fatigue and monotony on work production. But while the study was designed to focus on one aspect of the work process, an interesting thing happened. Mayo discovered that social relationships and, more specifically, interactions between co-workers and supervisors, resulted in higher productivity. The Mayo study is an excellent example of how researchers sometimes stumble upon unexpected results that change the way we view phenomena.

During the 1930s, a series of research studies was conducted by scholars in other disciplines. These would provide the groundwork for the field of interpersonal communication. Researchers had begun to systematically study children's interactions to learn more about patterns of social interaction and role taking behavior (see, for example, Piaget 1926). Also during this time period, George Herbert Mead, a philosophy professor from the University of Chicago, studied the relationship between the meanings that result from our interactions with others and our sense of self. Mead is often credited with the theory which came to be known as symbolic interactionism.

Herbert Blumer, a colleague from the University of California-Berkeley, actually coined the term **symbolic interactionism** and described this concept as a "label for a relatively distinctive approach to the study of human group life and human conduct" (Blumer 1969, 1). One of the first premises of this theory is that people form meanings based on the symbols used in interactions. These symbols include words or messages, roles that people play, gestures, and even rules that exist for interactions. The theory of symbolic interaction is significant because it recognizes the importance of our responses to symbols or words and the impact this has on the development of self. Consider your current role as a college student. It is likely that you gained the self-confidence to pursue a college degree as a result of the encouragement you received from parents and teachers, as well as the expectations that you and your family members have for your future education. Perhaps when you were in high school, someone asked you which college you planned to attend. All of these symbols helped shape your perception of self.

Also during this period, Abraham Maslow, a psychology professor at Brooklyn College, strove to understand the forces that cause humans to engage in certain behaviors. Beginning in 1939, he conducted research that specifically focused on human needs, resulting in the pyramid that has become widely known as **Maslow's Hierarchy of Needs.** Many of these needs have been identified as forces which motivate people to form interpersonal relationships with one another. Once the basic physiological and safety needs have been fulfilled, humans seek to fulfill the love and belonging needs by interacting with other individuals. As a result of our interactions with others, self-esteem needs, the fourth level of Maslow's hierarchy are addressed. Messages received from others are influential in forming one's self-esteem and tackling issues of identity (Maslow 1943).

Progressing into the 1950s and 60s, new scholars produced significant research that began shaping and defining the field of interpersonal communication as it evolved into its own discipline. In the 1950s, anthropologist Ray Birdwhistell (1952) created the term **kinesics** to refer to the use of body movements and gestures as forms of communication. In the late 1950s and early 60s, anthropologist Edward T. Hall focused on the role of space, or **proxemics,** in shaping and influencing our interactions with others (1959). While the study of nonverbal behaviors has evolved as an intriguing aspect of interpersonal interactions, additional studies during this time contributed to our understanding of the role of self and others in relationships.

In 1959, sociologist Erving Goffman published *The Presentation of Self in Everyday Life.* His work has served as the foundation for communications scholars' understanding of the role that impression management plays in our interactions with others. Goffman's work has been influential in shaping many subsequent theories of self-versus-other perceptions in interpersonal relationships. During this same time, Fritz Heider, a psychologist who taught at the University of Kansas, published work that addressed how attributions shape our interactions with others (Heider 1958). **Attribution theory** has been influential in interpersonal studies because it addresses the judgments that we make when we communicate with others. Research on relationship initiation has drawn from Heider's work to explain the evolving process of attributions as we make decisions to pursue interactions.

While these prominent scholars provided a solid foundation for our current approaches to investigating interpersonal relationships, you may have noticed that they are not communication researchers. Scholars often cross boundaries and build on ideas initiated by researchers in other fields. Recognizing the contributions that scholars in the fields of psychology, sociology and anthropology have made to the communication discipline is critical to understanding the interdisciplinary nature of our work. It is fascinating to explore human relationships from such a variety of perspectives! In fact, as you take classes in other disciplines, you may learn about some of the same theories and concepts that were presented in your communication classes.

While the study of communication has existed for decades, it was not until the late 1960s and into the 70s and 80s that interpersonal communication scholars began to carve out their own niche in the study of human communication and to clearly define the study of interactions in relationships. Increasing political and social unrest in the late 60s and early 70s caused scholars to direct their attention to individuals and their relationships. Significant historical events like the Civil Rights movement and the Vietnam War stimulated research activity in such areas as group dynamics, decision-making, and conflict resolution. In 1967, *Pragmatics of Human Communication* was published (Watzlawick, Beavin, and Jackson) and was one of the first books to adopt an interactional approach to communication. In the first chapter of the book, the authors acknowledge that each communication situation involves a "frame of reference." Two key concepts that have become central to the study of interpersonal communication are addressed in this initial chapter–the relationship between communication partners and the function of the communication interaction. As a result of this groundbreaking text, colleges and universities added courses focusing specifically on the dynamics of interpersonal communication. Other textbooks soon followed (Keltner 1970; McCroskey, Larson, and Knapp 1971; Giffin and Patton 1971).

As the level of interest in interpersonal communication mushroomed, scholars in the discipline turned their attention to research studies designed to explain the dynamics of relationships. Professional associations at the international, national, and regional levels formed interest groups and divisions devoted to interpersonal topics. By the late 1970s, interpersonal communication had become firmly established as a prominent field of study. During the early 1980s, it was difficult to open an issue of any leading communication journal and not find an article pertaining to research on interpersonal communication. Scholars began directing their attention to developing and testing theories directly related to interpersonal interactions.

INTERPERSONAL COMMUNICATION THEORY

Many significant theoretical contributions are provided in the historical foundations of interpersonal communication. While you may experience a heightened sense of anxiety when your instructor mentions "theory," the concepts are actually quite simple and very useful. A **theory** is nothing more than a set of statements about the way things work. Julia Wood (2000) recognizes theories as "human constructions—symbolic ways we represent phenomena" (p. 33) and notes that we use theories to achieve one of four basic goals. The four widely recognized goals of a theory are: (1) to describe phenomena, (2) to explain how something works, (3) to understand, predict and control occurrences, and (4) to make social change (Wood 2000). As students of communication, you will find theories to be useful tools for explaining interactions or categorizing behaviors.

Over the past thirty years, interpersonal communication scholars have truly made their mark as a core focus in the field of communication studies. While the seeds for many of today's prominent interpersonal theories may have been planted by experts in the fields of psychology, sociology and anthropology, the discipline has grown into an area that interpersonal researchers have defined as their own. In fact, scholars who study communication in other contexts (i.e., instructional communication, organizational communication, intercultural communication) are now applying interpersonal theories as the foundation for studying interactions in other areas.

Many different theories will be discussed throughout this text as we explore key components of interpersonal communication in a variety of contexts. Here is an overview of some of the prominent theories and their corresponding chapter or chapters.

- Attachment Theory (2, 11)
- Attribution Theory (5, 9)
- Covariation Theory (5)
- Equity Theory (7, 9)
- Family Communication Patterns Theory (11)
- Interpersonal Deception Theory (8)
- Leader-member Exchange Theory (12)
- Nonverbal Expectancy Violation Theory (4)
- Relational Dialectics (12)
- Self-determination Theory (9)
- Social Comparison Theory (2)
- Social Exchange Theory (6, 9)
- Social Identity Theory (5)
- Social Penetration Theory (6)
- Symbolic Interaction Theory (11)
- Systems Theory (11)
- Uncertainty Reduction Theory (3, 6)

OVERVIEW OF THE TEXTBOOK

The organization of this book is three-fold. Part I provides an overview of the basic concepts and theories which are central to the understanding of interpersonal communication. Chapter One will introduce the background, fundamentals, and key components of interpersonal communication. In Chapter Two we will explore self identity formation and the role individual differences play in our communication style with others. Chapter Three discusses how verbal communication is used to shape meaning in others and examines how certain words provoke certain responses. Chapter Four identifies several dimensions of nonverbal communication and their functions. The last chapter in Part I, Chapter Five, provides an overview of perception (selection, organization and interpretation) and listening. This chapter also addresses the significance of listening as part of the communication process and offers suggestions for improving our listening skills.

Part II of the textbook will explore how relationships typically develop, discussing communication practices exhibited during the outlined stages that either facilitate or hinder relationship growth and development. Chapter Six identifies characteristics that draw us to others and examines how we communicate in initial interactions. In Chapter Seven, relationship maintenance strategies are offered and conflict management is discussed as a natural progression of relationships. If conflict is not managed properly, it may turn dark. Chapter Eight discusses the dark side of communication: jealousy, deception, power and obsession. The last chapter in Part II, Chapter Nine, provides a detailed overview of the relationship termination process. This chapter walks you through the process of relationship disengagement, decision making, and strategies for moving on.

Part III of our text is devoted to what Knapp and Daly (2002) identify in the *Handbook of Interpersonal Communication* as trends that communication scholars are paying increasing attention to in their research. Some of these trends include: an increased emphasis on the role of cultural differences in interpersonal interactions; an examination of interpersonal communication in applied settings such as health, family and organizations; and the impact of technology on interpersonal communication. Chapter Ten addresses communication with diverse populations and highlights important areas of miscommunication between individuals of different ages, sexes, races and/or cultures. Next, Chapter Eleven examines one area of applied communication research, family communication. The family communication chapter will discuss communication issues that occur across the family lifespan and across family relationships. Sibling, marital, and parent-child relationships will also be addressed in this chapter. In addition, Chapter Eleven will identify productive communication strategies and difficult communication situations that occur within the family. Communication in the workplace is another applied communication area that continues to be a popular research area for scholars. Chapter Twelve will introduce the unique aspects of organizational communication such as the development of superior-subordinate relationships, peer relationships, friendships, mentoring, and romantic relationships. Another type of applied communication that has received much attention in the literature is health communication. In Chapter Thirteen we identify situations that produce anxiety, typical responses to these health-related situations, and how we can improve our communication during these situations. Our final chapter will examine the impact of technology on our interpersonal relationships. Chapter Fourteen will provide an overview of the computer-mediated communication research. People rely heavily on various forms of online communication to form and maintain relationships with others. Consider the impact of technology on your own communication with friends and family members. Technologies such as the Blackberry and Pocket PCs have enabled colleagues to communicate with one another beyond the confines of the office walls. These and other computer-mediated communication issues will be addressed in the final chapter, Chapter Fourteen.

SUMMARY

This chapter provided a framework for the interpersonal communication discipline. We defined interpersonal communication and distinguished it from other types of communication. We identified key interpersonal communication principles and even developed an acronym to help you remember them! Finally, we provided an overview of the history of interpersonal communication to help you understand the roots of this discipline and contributions from scholars in others fields. Now it is time to embark on your interpersonal journey. As you read through the following chapters in Part I, you will explore other fundamental concepts of interpersonal communication. Part II will trace interpersonal relationships from initiation to termination. The final chapters, found in Part III, will examine interpersonal communication across contexts such as intercultural, family, organizational and computer-mediated communication. Bestselling author, Father John Powell said, "Communication works for those who work at it." Go work at it!

ACTIVITIES

Activity #1:   Complete the Communication Competence Scale

Place the number on the line that best describes your agreement with the items below, using the following scale:

Strongly Agree	Agree	Undecided	Disagree	Strongly Disagree
5	4	3	2	1

_____ 1. I find it easy to get along with others.

_____ 2. I can adapt to changing situations.

_____ 3. I treat people as individuals.

_____ 4. I interrupt others too much.

_____ 5. I am rewarding to talk to.

_____ 6. I can deal with others effectively.

_____ 7. I am a good listener.

_____ 8. My personal relations are cold and distant.

_____ 9. I am easy to talk to.

_____ 10. I won't argue with someone just to prove he/she is right.

_____ 11. My conversation behavior is not "smooth."

_____ 12. I ignore other people's feelings.

_____ 13. I generally know how others feel.

_____ 14. I let others know I understand them.

_____ 15. I understand other people.

_____ 16. I am relaxed and comfortable when speaking.

_____ 17. I listen to what people say to me.

_____ 18. I like to be close and personal with people.

_____ 19. I generally know what type of behavior is appropriate in any given situation.

_____ 20. I usually do not make unusual demands on my friends.

_____ 21. I am an effective conversationalist.

_____ 22. I am supportive of others.

_____ 23. I do not mind meeting strangers.

_____ 24. I can easily put myself in another person's shoes.

_____ 25. I pay attention to the conversation.

_____ 26. I am generally relaxed when conversing with a new acquaintance.

_____ 27. I am interested in what others have to say.

_____ 28. I don't follow the conversation very well.

_____ 29. I enjoy social gatherings where I can meet new people.

_____ 30. I am a likeable person.

_____ 31. I am flexible.

_____ 32. I am not afraid to speak with people in authority.

_____ 33. People can come to me with their problems.

_____ 34. I generally say the right thing at the right time.

_____ 35. I like to use my voice and body expressively.

_____ 36. I am sensitive to others' needs of the moment.

Note: Items 4, 8, 11, 12, and 28 are reverse-coded before summing the 36 items.

Source: From "Explication and Test of a Model of Communicative Competence" by J.M. Wiemann, *Human Communication Research*, 3, 195-213, 1977. Reprinted with permission of Blackwell Publishing, www.blackwell-synergy.com.

Evaluating Your Communication Competence

Activity #2:

Type: Self-Reflection Exercise

Recall the three components to communication competence: knowledge, skill, and motivation. Identify your strongest component and discuss why.
Identify your weakest component and discuss why.

Activity #3:   Exploring Interpersonal Communication across Contexts

Type: Class Discussion

Think about the different types of interpersonal communication relationships you have. Fill in the following chart by identifying specific interpersonal relationships that exist across the contexts. Then provide a sample dialogue of communication topics for each.

Interpersonal Context	Interpersonal Relationship	Dialogue Sample
Organizational (example)	Manager to employer	*"Denise, let's meet after lunch to discuss your progress."*
Health Communication		
Computer Mediated		
Intercultural		
Family		

REFERENCES

Bardwell, C. 2001. Making the transition from college to the world of work. *Black Collegian*, April, 1–2.

Barnlund, D. C. 1970. A transactional model of communication. In K. K. Sereno and C. D. Mortensen (Eds.), *Foundations of communication theory* (pp. 83–102). New York: Harper and Row.

Bateson, G. 1951. Information and codification: A philosophical approach. In J. Ruesch and G. Bateson (Eds.), *Communication: The social matrix of psychiatry.* New York: Wiley and Sons.

———. 1972. *Steps to an ecology of mind.* New York: Ballantine Books.

Bauman, S. 2003. Design engineers evaluate their education. *AIAA Bulletin*, B5.

Baxter, L. 1982. Strategies for ending relationships: Two studies. *The Western Journal of Speech Communication, 46*, 223–241.

Beebe, S. A., and J. T. Masterson. 1997. *Communicating in Small Groups (5th ed.).* New York: Addison-Wesley Longman.

Berlo, D. K. 1960. *The process of communication.* San Francisco: Rinehart.

Birdwhistell, R. L. 1952. *Introduction to kinesics: An annotation system for analysis of body motion and gesture.* Washington, DC: U.S. Department of State, Foreign Service Institute.

Blumer, H. 1969. *Symbolic interactionism: Perspective and method.* Englewood Cliffs, NJ: Prentice-Hall.

Booth-Butterfield, M. 2002. *Interpersonal essentials.* Boston, MA: Allyn & Bacon.

Burleson, B. R., and E. L. MacGeorge. 2002. Supportive Communication. In M. L. Knapp, and J. A. Daly (Eds.), *Handbook of Interpersonal Communication* (pp. 374–424). Thousand Oaks, CA: Sage.

Burleson, B. R., and W. Samter. 1996. Similarity in the communication skills of young adults: Foundations of attraction, friendship, and relationship satisfaction. *Communication Reports, 9*, 127–139.

Canary, D. J., and L. Stafford. 2001. Equity in the preservation of personal relationships. In J. H. Harvey and A. Wenzel (Eds.), *Close romantic relationships: Maintenance and enhancement* (pp. 133–151). Mahwah, NJ: Lawrence Erlbaum.

Cappella, J. N. 1987. Interpersonal communication: Definitions and fundamental questions. In C. R. Berger and S. H. Chaffee (Eds.), *Handbook of communication science.* Newbury Park, CA: Sage.

Cathcart, R., and G. Gumpert. 1983. Mediated interpersonal communication: Toward a new typology. *Quarterly Journal of Speech, 69*, 267–277.

Chelune, G. J., E. Waring, B. Yosk, F. Sultan, and J. Ogden. 1984. Self-disclosure and its relationship to marital intimacy. *Journal of Clinical Psychology, 40*, 216–219.

Cody, M. 1982. A typology of disengagement strategies and an examination of the role intimacy, reactions to inequity, and relational problems play in strategy selection. *Communication Monographs, 49,* 148–170.

Crosby, F. E., J. D. Dunn, M. D. Fallacaro, C. Jozwiak-Shields, and A. M. MacIsaac. 2003. Preadmission characteristics of advanced nursing practice students. *Journal of the Academy of Nurse Practitioners, 15,* 424–431.

DeVito, J. 2001. *The Interpersonal Communication Book (9th ed.).* New York: Addison Wesley Longman Inc.

Giffin, K., and B. R. Patton. 1971. *Fundamentals of interpersonal communication.* New York, NY: Harper & Row.

Goffman, E. 1959. *The presentation of self in everyday life.* Garden City, NY: Doubleday.

Goleman, D. 1995. *Emotional Intelligence: Why it can matter more than IQ.* New York: Bantam.

Goleman, D. 2006. *Social intelligence: The new science of human relationships.* New York, NY: Bantam Dell.

Gottman, J. 1979. *Marital interaction: Experimental investigations.* New York: Academic Press.

Hall, E. T. 1959. *The silent language.* Garden City, NY: Doubleday.

Heider, F. 1958. *The psychology of interpersonal relations.* New York, NY: Wiley.

Keltner, J. W. 1970. *Interpersonal speech-communication: Elements and structures.* Belmont, CA: Wadsworth.

Knapp, M. L., and A. Vangelisti. 2000. *Interpersonal communication and human relationships.* Boston: Allyn & Bacon.

Knapp, M. L., J. A. Daly, K. F. Albada, and G. R. Miller. 2002. Background and current trends in the study of interpersonal communication. In M. L. Knapp and J. A. Daly (Eds.), *Handbook of Interpersonal Communication* (pp. 3–20). Thousand Oaks, CA: Sage.

Kreps, G. L., and B. C. Thorton. 1992. *Health Communication: Theory & Practice.* Prospect Heights, Illinois: Waveland Press.

Manssour, A. B. B. 2003. Interpersonal communication and creativity in journalistic telework. *Cyberpsychology & Behavior, 6,* 41–48.

Maslow, A. H. 1943. A theory of human motivation. *Psychological Review, 50,* 370–396.

McCroskey, J. C., C. Larson, and M. L. Knapp. 1971. *An introduction to interpersonal communication.* Englewood Cliffs, NJ: Prentice-Hall.

Metts, S., and S. Planap. 2002. Emotional Communication. In M. L. Knapp and J. A. Daly (Eds.), *Handbook of Interpersonal Communication* (pp. 339–373). Thousand Oaks, CA: Sage.

Miller, G. R., and M. Steinberg. 1975. *Between people: A new analysis of interpersonal communication.* Chicago: Science Research Associates.

Montgomery, B. M. 1988. Quality communication in personal relationships. In S. Duck (Ed.), *Handbook of personal relationships: Theory, research, and interventions.* (pp. 343–362).

Myers, L. L., and M. L. Tucker. 2005. Increasing awareness of emotional intelligence in a business curriculum. *Business Communication Quarterly, 68,* 44–51.

Noller, P., and J. A. Feeney. 1994. Relationship satisfaction, attachment and nonverbal accuracy in early marriage. *Journal of Nonverbal Behavior, 18,* 199–222.

Omarzu, J., J. Whalen, and J. H. Harvey. 2001. How well do you mind your relationship? A preliminary scale to test the minding theory of relating. In Harvey, J. and A. Wenzel. (Eds.), *Close romantic relationships: Maintenance and enhancement* (pp. 345–356). Mahwah, NJ: Lawrence Erlbaum.

Peterson, M. S. 1997. Personnel interviewers' perceptions of the importance and adequacy of applicants' communication skills. *Communication Education, 46,* 287–291.

Piaget, J. 1926. *The language and thought of the child.* New York: Harcourt Brace.

Rath, D., P. Poldre, B. J. Fisher, J. C. Laidlaw, D. H. Cowan, and D. Bakker. 1998. Commitment of a cancer organization to a program for training in communication skills. *Journal of Cancer Education: The Official Journal of the American Association for Cancer Education, 13,* 203–206.

Roloff, M. E. and K. P. Soule. 2002. Interpersonal conflict: A review. In M. L. Knapp and J. A. Daly (Eds.), *Handbook of interpersonal communication* (pp. 475–528). Thousand Oaks, CA: Sage.

Rusbult, C. E., D. J. Johnson, and G. D. Morrow. 1986. Impact of couple patterns of problem solving on distress and nondistress in dating relationships. *Journal of Experimental Social Psychology, 19,* 274–293.

Schramm, W. L. 1954. *The process and effects of mass communication.* Urbana, IL: University of Ilinois.

Schutz, W. 1966. *The interpersonal underworld* (pp. 13–20). Palo Alto, CA: Science and Behavior Books.

Shannon, C. E., and W. Weaver. 1949. *The mathematical theory of communication.* Urbana, IL: University of Illinois.

Spitzberg, B. H., and W. R. Cupach. 1984. *Interpersonal communication competence.* Beverly Hills, CA: Sage.

Thompson, T. L. 1986. *Communication for health professionals.* Lanham, MD: University Press of America.

Utley-Smith, Q. 2004. Needed by new baccalaureate graduates. *Nursing Education Perspectives, 25,* 166–170.

Wanzer, M. B., M. Booth-Butterfield, and K. Gruber. 2004. Perceptions of health care providers' communication: Relationships between patient-centered communication and satisfaction. *Health Communication, 16,* 363–384.

Watzlawick, P., J. Beavin, and D. D. Jackson. 1967. *Pragmatics of human communication.* New York: Norton.

Wood, J. T. 2000. *Communication Theories in Action.* Wadsworth: Belmont, CA.

2

Development of Self and Individual Differences
Just Me, Myself, and I

OBJECTIVES

- Define the term self and explain why it is viewed as a complex process
- Define the term self-complexity and explain the benefits of high self-complexity
- Explain the three components of the self-system and discuss how each component affects interpersonal communication
- Discuss the development of the self with special emphasis on the individuals and groups of individuals that play important roles in the development of the self
- Explain attachment theory, including the three attachment styles that affect the way individuals view the self and others
- State the importance of direct definitions and identity scripts
- Discuss the significance of the self-fulfilling prophecy and social comparison processes for identify formation
- State the difference between state and trait approaches in studying communication
- Define communication apprehension and discuss its effects
- Discuss the way communication apprehension is typically measured and identify treatment options for individuals scoring high in communication apprehension
- Define willingness to communicate and distinguish it from communication apprehension
- Define and give examples of the two forms of destructive aggression
- Explain why some individuals are verbally aggressive
- Define and give examples of two forms of constructive aggression
- Define humor orientation
- Define affective orientation

KEY TERMS

self	reflected appraisal/	direct definitions
self-complexity	looking glass self	identity scripts
self-concept	attachment theory	attachment security
public self	secure	hypothesis
inner self	anxious-avoidant	social comparison
self-esteem	anxious-ambivalent	theory
self-regulation		

behavioral
  confirmation/
  self-fulfilling prophecy
similarity hypothesis
perpetual conflict
state approach
trait approach
personality
communication
  apprehension

willingness to
  communicate
systematic
  desensitization
cognitive modification
skills training
constructive and
  destructive forms of
  aggression

hostility
verbal aggressiveness
argumentativeness
independent-
  mindedness
assertiveness
humor orientation
affective orientation

OVERVIEW

In an excerpt from a song by the 1980s rock band, The Talking Heads, the burning question "How did I get here?" is raised. Most of us, at one time in our lives, have asked the same question. Another profound question, "Who am I?" fixates our culture. It is asked in song lyrics from rock

> *And you may find yourself living in a shotgun shack*
> *And you may find yourself in another part of the world*
> *And you may find yourself behind the wheel of a large automobile*
> *And you may find yourself in a beautiful house, with a beautiful wife*
> *And you may ask yourself—Well . . . **How did I get here?***

groups and Broadway alike, from No Doubt, Alanis Morisette, Will Smith, Elvis Presley, Seal, and the Smashing Pumpkins to the musical *Les Miserables*. The Talking Heads added another concern "How did I get to be this way?" The theme song of television's most popular show is "Who Are You?" and *CSI* and similar programs involve the audience in the weekly unraveling of someone's identity, seeking answers from his interactions with others. The preoccupying search for self is this chapter's concern. In the first half of this chapter we address these questions by discussing the process of identity formation. Special emphasis will be placed on the role that interpersonal communication and relationships play in this process. A definition of the term self is provided, along with an overview of relevant terms used to describe and explain various aspects of the self. Next, a detailed description of the development of the self is presented, with special attention given to those individuals and processes considered essential to identity formation.

© amygala imagery, 2007, Shutterstock.

In the second part of this chapter, we examine the impact of individual differences on interpersonal communication. When communication researchers want to learn more about the impact of individual differences on social interaction, they often turn their attention to communication-based personality traits. According to communication researcher John Daly (2002), "the greatest proportion of articles in our journals have explored topics directly or indirectly related to personality" (133). To learn more about how people differ in their communication patterns, we define the term personality, distinguish between trait and state approaches to interpersonal communication research, and provide explanations of a number of different communication based personality traits. While there are many traits that influence our communication with others, we focus on several that have been researched extensively. These have been identified as predispositions that can either hinder or facilitate communication with others. "Everyone thinks of changing the world, but no one thinks of changing himself," wrote Leo Tolstoy. By looking within instead of outwardly, we can choose to improve our ability to communicate.

DEFINITION OF SELF

While individuals use the term self frequently and with relative ease, it is quite challenging for researchers to offer a single consistent definition for the term (Baumeister 1998). The **self** has been defined as a psychological entity consisting of "an organized set of beliefs, feelings, and behaviors" (Tesser, Wood, and Stapel 2002, 10). Another way of understanding the **self** is as a complex system made up of a variety of interdependent elements that attain self-organization (Vallacher and Nowak 2000). In attempting to explain the self, theorists often emphasize the origins of self, noting that it emerges through communication and established relationships with others and is constantly developing and evolving (Epstein 1973; Park and Waters 1988). Take a moment to consider how your self-perceptions have changed over the years. Are you the same person you were five, ten, or fifteen years ago? You have probably changed and matured a great deal over the years and see yourself as being quite different from when you were younger. Thus, one's perception of self is often described as a process because it evolves and is largely determined by ongoing communication with significant others. This idea is further validated by social psychologist Arthur Aron (2003) who says, "What we are and what we see ourselves as being seems to be constantly under construction and reconstruction, with the architects and remodeling contractors largely being those with whom we have close interactions" (Aron 2003, 443). In later sections of this chapter we explore the specific individuals and processes that exert the greatest influence in shaping our self-perceptions.

The self is also recognized as highly complex and multidimensional. Researchers agree that there are numerous dimensions, or aspects, of the self that make up one overall perception of the self. While we might think of ourselves as relatively uncomplicated individuals, most of us are highly complex and can assume a variety of roles. For example, on any given day, you may assume the roles of student, employee, daughter, sister, friend, teammate, roommate, or resident comedian. This example illustrates how individuals vary in their **self-complexity** or number of self-aspects, also known as subselves. Individuals possessing higher levels of self-complexity reap a number of personal benefits. What does it mean to possess higher levels of self-complexity? Referring back to the example of the student, if she views her multiple roles (sister, teammate, friend, etc.) as separate or unique, and at the same time has encountered a number of life experiences associated with those roles, then she probably has a greater number of non-overlapping self-aspects, or higher self-complexity. On the other hand, a woman who views herself only in two closely-related roles, e.g., teammate and student, and has limited life experiences associated with these roles, will probably have fewer self-aspects, or lower self-complexity.

How does one benefit from higher levels of self-complexity? Individuals with higher self-complexity may be less prone to having mood fluctuations (Linville 1985) and may cope better with stress (Koch and Shepperd 2004). When individuals report lower self-complexity they are more likely to experience negative affect in response to a negative life event than someone who reports higher self-complexity. Individuals with lower self-complexity may not be able to separate the limited roles they assume and may experience what researchers call "spill over." Thus, a student athlete who has a bad game may not be able to separate her experience on the soccer field ("me as soccer player") from her experience in the classroom ("me as a student") and the negative affect from the soccer game will expand, or spill over, to other self-aspects (Koch and Shepperd 2004). The student athlete has a bad game, does not study for her chemistry exam because she is still angry about her performance on the field and, as a result, fails her chemistry test the next day.

Higher self-complexity may actually act as a buffer for people by allowing them to mentally separate themselves from painful life events (Linville 1987). Furthermore, the buffer effect has direct interpersonal, or relational, implications. The buffer effect was observed for those higher in self-complexity faced with relationship dissolution. Individuals higher in self-complexity thought about the relationship less and were less upset about their relationships ending than individuals lower in self-complexity (Linville 1987). Familiar fictional characters demonstrate instances of high and low

How could her performance on the soccer field affect other aspects of this girl's day?

self-complexity following relationship disengagement. For instance, *Gilmore Girls'* Rory Gilmore, whose roles of daughter, granddaughter, friend, and student are emphasized more heavily than that of girlfriend, dealt with the end of relationships with various boyfriends by spending more time with her mother and friends, and by increasing her involvement at school. These actions served as a buffer for Rory, which kept relationship concerns from dominating her thoughts or actions. In contrast, the popular show *The O.C.* exhibited the character Marissa Cooper, who fell into alcoholism and depression after her own breakup with central character Ryan Atwood. Marissa allowed the role of romantic relationship, which she found self-defining, to affect all other aspects of her self. While typically not as extreme as these two situations, instances of lower self-complexity, compared to high, are more likely to produce negative effects.

Importance of Studying the Process of Identity Formation

Why should interpersonal communication scholars study aspects of the self and the process of self development? Similar to other frequently studied concepts, research and perspectives on the self are vast and vary greatly (see, for example, Tesser, Felson, and Suls 2000; Tesser et al. 2002). There are a number of terms related to self in the literature and definitions for them are often inconsistent, making it difficult to integrate and interpret research on the self (Houck and Spegman 1999). But, before we can engage in a meaningful discussion of the self and related processes, we need to offer clear definitions of terms such as self-concept, self-esteem, and self-regulation. We also need to highlight distinctions between key terms and concepts. In addition, if we want to understand how and why individuals vary in attitudes, beliefs, values, mannerisms, security, psychological states, etc., we need to take a closer look at both how and why people perceive themselves in a particular way. Exploring the communicative and relational processes that affect the development of the self either positively or negatively is important because it helps us to understand who we are and why we are this way. Once we understand differences in how individuals develop a sense of self as well as the processes associated with the development of a more positive self-perception, we can train individuals to interact more competently with those around them. As Houck and Spegman (1999) argue, "Given its manifestation of social competence, the development of the self is of fundamental importance not only to the well-being of individuals, but also to the well-being of others with whom they associate" (2).

There are three constructs related to the self that typically emerge in discussions about the self and developmental processes. These three specific aspects of the self are: self-concept, or cognitions about the self; self-esteem, or affective information related to the self; and autonomy/self-initiative, or self-regulation, processes. In order to better understand the self-system and its related components, it is important to define and distinguish between these related constructs. In this chapter, we present a detailed definition of each of these three components, offer examples of related terms used to discuss each of these key areas, and provide a brief overview of the importance of these concepts to interpersonal communication and relationships.

The Self System

Terms such as self-concept, self-esteem, self-schema, and self-regulation are used in dialogues about the self and identity development. Some of these terms have been used interchangeably and yet, as we will see, they are very different constructs.

Self-Concept/Cognitions about the Self.

One term that often emerges in discussions about the self is self-concept. Houck and Spegman describe the **self-concept** as a cognitive construct which is a "descriptive reference to the self, or a definition of the nature and beliefs about the self's qualities" (Houck and Spegman 1999, 2). While there are a variety of other terms used when describing the self (self-cognition, self-image, self-schema, and self-understanding), self-concept is used most frequently. In the most basic sense, self-concept refers to what someone knows about himself.

Social psychologists and sociologists argue that people possess multiple perceptions of the self-concept, or different personas (Bargh, McKenna, and Fitzsimons 2002). For example, Goffman (1959) and Jung (1953) draw distinctions between a **"public" self,** or the self that we project during social interaction, and an **"inner" self** that we keep private and that may reflect how we really feel about ourselves. The public self is described as our "actual" self-concept while the inner self is presented as our "true" self. Psychologists note that individuals often project an actual self in public that is quite different from their true self. Individuals may not present their true selves for a variety of reasons. One reason could be the fear of evaluation from others. Or, in some instances, an individual may not yet fully know or understand his or her true self.

One place where individuals may feel more comfortable expressing their true selves is on the Internet (Bargh et al. 2002). According to researchers, the anonymity of the Internet gives people the chance to assume different personas and genders and to express aspects of themselves "without fear of disapproval and sanctions by those in their real-life social circle" (Bargh et al. 2002). Two different experiments were performed that used a reaction time task to access college students' perceptions of their true and actual selves. Researchers found that the true self-concept was more readily recalled during Internet interactions while the actual self was more accessible during face-to-face interactions. In a third related experiment, college students were randomly assigned to interact, either via the Internet or face-to-face. Students assigned to the Internet had an easier time expressing their true selves to their partners than those assigned to the face-to-face condition. If individuals feel more comfortable expressing their true selves during Internet exchanges, they are then more likely to establish relationships with individuals they meet on the Internet (McKenna, Green, and Gleason 2002). This research may provide some explanation for the fact that more individuals are using the Internet to establish romantic and platonic relationships.

© Zsolt Nyulaszi, 2007, Shutterstock.

Why do you think some people find it easier to express their "true" selves over the Internet?

An individual's self-concept influences how one views or interprets social interaction, and at the same time it regulates one's involvement in the interaction. Suppose the student council president is asked to speak to the superintendent of schools to discuss student views on proposed schedule changes. Her self-confidence in her role as a student leader causes her to assert herself in the interaction and offer suggestions for an alternative plan. Research on the relationship between self-concept and interpersonal processes has explored the effects of self-concept on social perception, the relationship between self-concept and selection of interaction partners, strategies individuals use to mold and interpret communication with others, and how individuals respond to feedback that is not consistent with their self-concept. Three of these areas of research—the relationship between self-concept and social perception, self-concept and partner choice, and self-concept and interaction strategies—are particularly interesting and relevant to understanding how and why our self-concept affects our communication with others.

Much of the research on the relationship between self-concept and social perception concludes that people are likely to view others as relatively similar to themselves (Markus and Wurf 1987). When you interact with your friends, family members, and co-workers, you perceive them to be more similar than dissimilar to you in attitudes, beliefs, values, goals, and behaviors. From an interpersonal communication perspective, similarity is an important variable that affects our interactions with others and, when used strategically as an affinity-seeking behavior, can potentially increase liking between interactants (Bell and Daly 1984).

The way one sees or defines one's self also affects both the choice of relationship partners and subsequent behavior in those relationships (Markus and Wurf 1987). Research on the relationship between self-perception and relationship satisfaction indicates that individuals report greater relationship satisfaction when they choose partners that validate views of themselves (Schlenker 1984; Swann 1985). In other words, individuals attempt to find a relationship partner who expresses similar or consistent views with their ideal or desired self. Much of the research on the role of the self in social interaction has examined the process of impression management during interpersonal encounters (Markus and Wurf 1987). Not surprisingly, individuals work diligently to present a particular image of themselves to both external

(Goffman 1959) and internal audiences (Greenwald and Breckler 1985). Using impression management techniques consciously and effectively is linked to heightened self-awareness (Schlenker 1985). While we may not always be aware of our impression management efforts, our day-to-day choice of dress, hairstyle, choice of words, and artifacts are selected strategically to project a specific desired image of ourselves to those around us. Think about the choices you make when deciding what to wear and how to style your hair in various social situations. It is highly likely that impression management played a role in your decisions.

Self-Esteem/Affect about the Self.

Another term used frequently when discussing the self is **self-esteem,** defined as the subjective perception of one's self-worth, or the value one places on the self (Houck and Spegman 1999). There are a number of related evaluative terms associated with self-esteem that include: self-affect, self-worth, and self-evaluation. All of these terms illustrate the evaluative nature of this concept with individuals typically experiencing either positive or negative feelings about themselves or their behavior. Self-esteem can be measured objectively, unlike self-concept. Research indicates that individuals typically vary in their reported levels of self-esteem. Those reporting higher levels of self-esteem feel more favorable about themselves and their behaviors than individuals with lower self-esteem.

How can a teacher influence a child's self-esteem?

According to researchers, self-esteem has become a "household" term today. Teachers, parents, therapists, coaches, and individuals that communicate regularly with children and have the potential to affect a child's self-esteem have been encouraged to focus on ways to help children see themselves more favorably (for an overview of this research, see Baumeister, Campbell, Krueger, and Vohs 2003). The previously held assumption driving these efforts was that individuals with higher self-esteem would experience a number of positive benefits and outcomes. More recently, Baumeister and his colleagues examined the extensive research on self-esteem with special attention on the relationship between self-esteem and performance, interpersonal success, happiness, and lifestyle choices (for an overview of this research, see Baumeister et al. 2003).

The findings from their extensive research were unexpected. Surprisingly, there was only a modest relationship between perceptions of self-esteem and school performance. Why? According to social psychologists, high self-esteem does not necessarily cause higher performance in school. Instead, researchers suspect that solid academic performance in school actually leads to higher self-esteem. When researchers investigated efforts to boost students' self-esteem, students did not improve in school and sometimes even performed at lower levels.

Similar to findings reported in the educational context, researchers concluded that occupational success may boost self-esteem rather than self-esteem leading to greater success in the workplace. The conclusions in this area are mixed, at best, with some research illustrating a positive relationship between self-esteem and occupational success and other research contradicting these findings (Baumeister et al. 2003). By this point, you might be asking yourself, "Are there any meaningful educational or occupational advantages associated with higher levels of self-esteem?" There *are* benefits to possessing higher self-esteem; they are just not as extensive as researchers initially estimated. For example, individuals with higher self-esteem seem to be more tenacious than those with low self-esteem. Social psychologists conclude that self-esteem may help individuals continue working on a task even after they failed initially (Baumeister et al. 2003).

What is the relationship between self-esteem and interpersonal communication and relationship success? Individuals self-reporting higher self-esteem typically indicate that they are well-liked and attractive, have better relationships, and make more positive impressions on others than those reporting lower levels of self-esteem. However, when researchers further investigated whether high self-esteem individuals were perceived this way by others using objective measures, the results were disconfirmed. The researchers further explain this finding by noting that while "narcissists are charming at first," they tend to eventually alienate those around them by communicating in ways that are perceived by others as inappropriate and ineffective (Baumeister et al. 2003, 1). The connection between self-esteem and the quality of romantic and platonic relationships is small to moderate, at best (Aron 2003). Some research indicates that there is a small consistent relationship between self-esteem and marital satisfaction and success over time (see, for example, Aube and Koestner 1992; Karney and Bradbury 1995). Based on research conducted thus far, couples' reported self-esteem does not appear to be a major predictor of marital satisfaction or persistence.

However, in addition to tenaciousness, there are some additional recognized benefits of having higher self-esteem. For example, higher self-esteem has been linked to feelings of happiness. Individuals reporting higher self-esteem are generally happier folks than individuals self-reporting lower self-esteem and are probably less likely to be depressed. Lower self-esteem has been repeatedly linked to greater incidence of depression under certain situations or circumstances. While it is disappointing to find that programs and initiatives created to boost individuals' self-esteem were generally ineffective in doing so, it is important to emphasize specific communication patterns that might be beneficial in helping others formulate positive self-impressions. Baumeister and his colleagues

Rewarding children for good behavior gives them a boost in self-esteem.

(2003) note that instead of giving children "indiscriminate praise" which may lead to excessive narcissism, parents and educators should focus on "using praise to boost self-esteem as a reward for socially desirable behavior and self-improvement" (1).

As you can imagine, there is a great deal of information available on how to boost one's self-esteem in order to avoid depression, increase tenaciousness, and relate more effectively to others. Perceptions of one's self-esteem can change over time because of significant life experiences. There are numerous websites, books, workshops, and even computer games available for individuals who want to address problems with low self-esteem. See table 2.1 for an example of the type of information currently available to help individuals combat self-esteem problems.

Table 2.1   Ways to Boost Your Self-Esteem

1. *Think back to when you tackled a task for the very first time.*
    Trying something for the first time can be a daunting experience. The next time you feel under-confident, recall the first time you tried something new—and succeeded! This will help you to overcome your fears.
2. *Do something you have been putting aside.*
    Once you complete this task, it will help you feel as though you can follow through on something.
3. *Work on your ability to relax.*
    There are a number of different ways to reduce anxiety and stress in your life. Consider taking exercise classes, meditating, or involving yourself in something that helps you relax.
4. *Recall all of your accomplishments.*
    Take a minute to reflect on all of the times you have succeeded at doing something that you set out to do (e.g., passing your driver's test, passing exams, putting money away for vacation).

Adapted from an article that appears on the Uncommon Knowledge website
www.self-confidence.co.uk/self/esteem/tips.

Research Brief   Playing Computer Games May Boost Self-Esteem

Mark Baldwin, a psychologist at McGill University in Montreal, argues that computer games offer another less conventional and interesting way to boost one's self-esteem. While these games are not recommended for individuals with serious self-esteem problems, Baldwin and his team of researchers found that the games helped people feel better about themselves and their relationships by focusing on the positive, not the negative (Dye 2004). Visit *http://abcnews.go.com/Technology/story?id=99532&page=1* to read the entire article.

Self-Regulation.   The third and final component of the self-system, self-regulation, is occasionally referred to in literature as self-determination, independence, self-assertion, self-control, or internalization. Self-regulation is regarded by some as a highly significant component of human existence (Bargh and Chartrand 1999). Why is self-regulation so important? Because **self-regulation,** defined as "the capacity to exercise choice and initiation" (Houck and Spegman 1999, 3), allows us to pursue and engage in goal-directed activity. It is important to study the process of self-regulation in order to understand how and why individuals are motivated and make choices. Research in this area examines aspects of initiative, motivation, and decision-making in relation to morality and developing a conscience. It also sets out to discover why some individuals are motivated to achieve goals and others are not. The significant process of self-regulation can occur at either a conscious or a subconscious level (Bargh and Chartrand 1999). You probably exert self-regulation, whether you are aware of the process or not.

What is the relationship between self-regulation and interpersonal communication and relationships? Baumeister and Vohs (2003) offer several examples of how the process of self-regulation is related to interpersonal communication and relationships. Problems such as interpersonal violence between relationship partners and extradyadic sexual relations are obviously linked in some way to failures in self-regulation. Self-regulation is closely related to successful maintenance of close romantic relationships (Baumeister and Vohs 2003). Related research by Finkel and Campbell (2001) indicated that individuals reporting higher levels of self-regulation were more likely to exhibit accommodating behaviors in their romantic relationships. Not surprisingly, most individuals prefer being in relationships with partners that are accommodating, or willing to compromise, to meet each other's needs.

The extent to which one communicates effectively and appropriately with others is also linked to self-regulation or initiative. Recall from Chapter One our discussion of Spitzberg and Cupach's (1984) model of communication competence and its three components. This model advances the significance of motivation or initiative in communicating effectively with others. While individuals may posses the skills and knowledge necessary for communicating effectively, if they are not motivated to do so, they will not enact the appropriate behavior. Thus, the process of self-regulation directly affects our communication abilities and the quality of interpersonal relationships.

Now that we understand the three main components of the self-system and their relationship to interpersonal communication, we move on to the discussion of the development of self. Two important questions to consider are: Which individuals or groups of individuals are most influential in forming or shaping our self-perceptions? And why? Exploring these questions in much greater detail will help to answer the questions: Who am I? And how did I become this way?

Interpersonal Communication and the Development of Self

Most scholars agree that the self emerges and develops through communication with those to whom we are close (see, for example, Aron 2003). What exactly does this mean? This statement implies that, as infants, we do not possess a sense of self, but that one develops through our interactions with significant others (Cooley 1902; Mead 1934). Cooley (1902) was the first to advance "the **looking glass self**" metaphor which describes the impact of interpersonal communication on the development of self. Researchers (Felson 1989) extended the concept of looking glass self to include the term **reflected appraisal,** referring to the tendency to view ourselves based on the appraisals of others. Who are these significant others that affect our self-perceptions? Researchers have generally studied the influence of family and other significant individuals such as peers and relationship partners as they affect the development of self. We review the importance of interpersonal communication with family, peers, and significant others as it relates to the construction and reconstruction of the self over time.

Family. Family plays a significant role in the development of one's identity. One theory that has received a great deal of attention from researchers studying the process of identity development is attachment theory. John Bowlby (1969, 1973) developed **attachment theory** in an attempt

© Losevsky Pavel, 2007, Shutterstock.

A child who feels secure in the family environment will naturally expect positive peer relationships.

to explain the strong bond children form with the primary caregiver and the stress which results from separation from one another. Communication plays a pivotal role in creating the security associated with this attachment. Other theorists have expanded on the original theory advanced by Bowlby (1969) and typically recognize three different types of attachment relationships—secure, anxious-avoidant, and anxious-ambivalent (Ainsworth, Blehar, Waters, and Wall 1978).

When the primary caregiver behaves in a loving, supportive, and nurturing way towards her child, the child is likely to develop a **secure** attachment. A secure attachment is often "characterized by intense feelings of intimacy, emotional security, and physical safety when the infant is in the presence of the attachment figure" (Peluso, Peluso, White, and Kern 2004, 140). Because children raised in a secure environment typically have a history of responsive and supportive caretaking from their caregivers (Ainsworth et al. 1978), these experiences lead the children to believe that others will act in a supportive and caring way as well. Children who develop secure attachment styles are confident in their interpersonal relationships with their peers (Park and Waters 1988). Why is this the case? Bowlby (1973) and others (see, for example, Sroufe 1988) hold that children's first exposure to relationships is in the family context and that this experience helps them formulate expectations for subsequent relationships. Secure children, whose previous relationship experiences are generally positive, expect people in future encounters to act similarly, and therefore behave accordingly. Some research indicates that secure children recreate communication patterns and practices they experienced with their primary caregivers when interacting with peers, ultimately leading to more positive peer relationships (Sroufe 1988).

Conversely, individuals experiencing an insecure or **anxious-avoidant** attachment relationship with their primary caregiver often report trauma or neglect from their parents and exhibit significant developmental deficits (Peluso et al. 2004). Mothers of children who develop this attachment style act emotionally distant and rejecting, behaving with anger towards their children. Not surprisingly, this style of parenting can have long-term negative psychological and relational effects on individuals (Peluso et al. 2004). Unlike secure children, insecure children experience difficulty in forming relationships with others. Working from Bowlby's original theory (1973), insecure children, whose previous relationship experiences were negative, often develop a more negative "working model" of relationships and recreate negative communication patterns among peers. Some research supports this premise, with insecure children behaving more negatively and aggressively toward both known and unknown peers than secure children (Lieberman 1977; Sroufe 1988).

The third attachment style, labeled **anxious-ambivalent,** develops as a result of inconsistent and irregular treatment from parents (Ainsworth et al. 1978). Compared to secure children, those with anxious-ambivalent attachment styles experience more developmental delays, exhibit an unusual amount of conflict and confusion associated with their relationship with the primary caregiver, and are more accident prone (Ainsworth et al. 1978; Lieberman and Pawl 1988; Sroufe 1988). Both the anxious-avoidant and anxious-ambivalent attachment styles are problematic because children typically internalize perceptions of the self that are negative, which affect subsequent relationships with peers and romantic partners (Park and Waters 1988).

Communication with family members also affects how we define our-selves. Many of you have probably heard your parents describe your talents, personality traits, or other attributes in detail to other family members, friends, or even total strangers. **Direct definitions** are descriptions, or labels, families assign to its members that affect the way we see and define ourselves (Wood 2001). A child whose nickname is "slugger" may perceive herself to be an outstanding softball player. Consider the impact that the nickname "trouble" would have on a child's perception. Most of us can recall the way our family members referred to us and it is likely that many of these refer-ences were internalized. Researchers point out the significance of direct defi-nitions by recognizing that positive labels can enhance our self-esteem while negative ones can have potentially deleterious effects on our self-perceptions (Wood 2001).

When you reflect back on your childhood, can you recall sayings or phrases that were repeated in your family? How about, "money does not grow on trees," "people who live in glass houses should not throw stones," "remember the golden rule," or "a family that prays together stays together?" Do any of these sayings sound familiar to you? Can you generate a list of phrases that were repeated in your family? These sayings are all examples of **identity scripts,** or rules for living and relating to one another in family con-texts. Identity scripts help individuals to define who they are and how to relate to others (Berne 1964; Harris 1969). These phrases, which most have probably heard more than once, influence the way we relate to others and also our self-perceptions.

Peer relationships.   While family relationships are important and clearly affect the development of the self, other relationships, such as peers, also play a significant role in identity development (Park and Waters 1988). The **attach-ment security hypothesis,** based on Bowlby's (1973) work, states that indi-viduals are attracted to and seek out peers and relationship partners that can provide them with a sense of security. Not surprisingly, peers, like parents, can also provide a sense of security and social support for one another. Some research indicates that attachment related functions are eventually transferred from parents to peers over time (Surra, Gray, Cottle, Boettcher 2004).

Research by Meeus and Dekovic (1995) supports the significance of peer relationships later in life and indicates that peers, to a certain extent, are even more influential than parents in the identity development of adolescents. According to researchers, as young children age and mature they also begin the process of separation and individuation from their parents. Children begin to socialize more frequently with their peers, and to protest when they are sep-arated from them. They begin to discover that most of their peer interactions are characterized by qualities such as equality and symmetry. Peer relation-ships, which tend to be more egalitarian, soon become more important than parental relationships and tend to influence child-parent relationship expecta-tions. As children grow and mature, they expect to form new relationships with their parents, also based on symmetry and equality. When these relation-ships do not progress as expected, adolescents become frustrated and perhaps even more bonded with their peers (Meeus and Dekovic 1995). While initially researchers suspected that peers were only influential in certain areas of iden-tity formation, research by Meeus and Dekovic (1995) illustrates the impact of peers on the formation of relational, educational, and occupational identity.

Not surprisingly, best friends exerted the greatest influence on one's development of relational identity while peers or colleagues exerted the greatest influence on occupational and educational identities.

Have you ever compared your talents to those of your friends?

Peer relationships are also important in defining the self because individuals often use peers as a means of personal assessment. It is not unusual for individuals to compare themselves to others to determine whether they are smart, attractive, athletic or successful. When individuals compare themselves to others in order to determine their abilities, strengths and weaknesses, they are engaging in the process of social comparison. Leon Festinger (1954) developed **social comparison theory.** This theory suggests that most individuals have a basic need, or drive, to evaluate and compare themselves to those around them. Festinger holds that one of the only ways of validating an evaluation of oneself is to find out if similar others agree with it (Tesser 2003). Thus, if a student wants to evaluate his ability in school, he will typically compare his abilities to those of his fellow similar classmates. How many of you immediately consult with your peers after receiving a test or paper grade?

Another way that relationships with others affect the development of self is through a phenomenon called **behavioral confirmation,** or self-fulfilling prophecy (Aron 2003). Aron (2003) defines **self-fulfilling prophecy** as a process in which people act to conform to the expectations of others (see, for example, Darley and Fazio 1980). One of the classic studies that illustrated self-fulfilling prophecy was conducted in the classroom with teachers who were randomly informed that their students were academic overachievers. Academic performances improved significantly for those average students whose teachers were told that they were high achievers. Why did the students improve academically? Because the teachers communicated with the students as if they were overachievers, the students internalized these perspectives and acted accordingly (Snyder, Tanke, and Berscheid 1977). Researchers also found that previous relationship experiences can influence our expectations of new relationship partners' behaviors (see, for example, Andersen and Berensen 2001). Thus, if an individual experienced problems in previous relationships, he or she may expect similar negative experiences in the future and may circuitously contribute to how the relationship progresses.

Relationship Partners.   Over time, the bond formed between partners in a romantic relationship is sure to affect the development of the self. One particularly interesting study provides further support for this statement. Researchers found that married couples come to look more alike over extended periods of time. Zajonc and his colleagues (1987) found students were more successful in matching pictures of couples married twenty-five years compared with pictures of the same couples, newly married.

Your intimate relationships have a major influence on how you view yourself.

Intimate relationships are also important to the development of the self because they influence how positively or negatively one views oneself (Aron 2003). Some recent research indicates that getting married and having children can actually increase an individual's feelings of self-worth (Shackelford 2001).

According to the **similarity hypothesis,** also related to Bowlby's research on attachment theory, we are most attracted to individuals that exhibit an attachment style similar to our own (Surra et al. 2004). Not surprisingly, researchers found that college students with secure attachment styles were more attracted to relationship partners that had also developed this attachment style. As the similarity hypothesis would predict, anxious-attachment individuals were also more likely to date anxious-attachment partners and to report being satisfied with these relationships (Surra et al. 2004). This research indicates that we often seek out individuals with similar attachment styles that also verify our perceptions of self-worth.

Relationships with family members, peers, and significant others affect the way we define ourselves and influence our evaluative perceptions of the self. Another way that we define ourselves, and simultaneously distinguish ourselves from others, is by describing our predominant personality traits.

In the second part of this chapter, we explore some of the ways people differ in how they communicate with others. While individual differences such as age, culture, ethnicity/race, sex/gender, and cognitive traits certainly affect the way we communicate. with others, interpersonal researchers have turned their attention to the powerful role that communication-based predispositions play in making sense of social phenomena (Daly 2002). In the next sections we discuss: (1) the impact of individual differences on social interaction, (2) differences between state and trait approaches to research, and (3) a number of personality traits that affect our communication with others. Because students are often interested in finding their scores on the communication-based personality instruments, we have included ways to measure many of the traits discussed in the chapter.

THE IMPACT OF INDIVIDUAL DIFFERENCES ON SOCIAL INTERACTION

Most of us have interacted with someone we might label "difficult" because of his or her communication behaviors. It is not unusual for students to share stories of the "difficult" or "less-than-popular" roommate who lives with them. This roommate is often described as difficult because he acts in a consistently problematic manner or manages regularly to offend others. Not surprisingly, this roommate's poor behavior not only impacts all of the housemates, but also affects relationship partners, friends, classmates and neighbors that must hear about and interact with the difficult roommate. A number of authors have written books about dealing with difficult people (see, for example, Keating 1984). Dealing with difficult personality types is an important and relevant topic for a number of reasons: (1) we all have to deal with difficult people, whether at home, school, or work, (2) we might be one of those "difficult people" because we have communication challenges linked to our personality, and (3) asking an individual to completely change his or her personality is unreasonable and can damage relationships. Social psychologist John Gottman (1999) describes **perpetual conflict** as disagreements between relationship partners that are often directly related to personality issues. This type of conflict is pervasive and not easily fixed because it often involves fighting over matters that cannot be easily resolved, like differences in couples' personality traits. It is very frustrating when someone tells you, matter-of-factly, to "completely change your personality" in order to become a better relationship partner. We know that this unproductive criticism is an unreasonable request.

When someone asks you repeatedly to change the same aspect of your personality, e.g., to talk more or to talk less, it is likely that this person is requesting a change in a personality trait. Much of the communication research conducted to date has adopted a trait approach to studying personality differences, which is quite different from a state approach.

A COMPARISON OF TRAIT AND STATE APPROACHES TO RESEARCH

When communication researchers investigate differences in communication behaviors, they clarify whether they are studying these behaviors from either a trait or a state approach. When they adopt a **state approach** to studying communication behaviors, they examine how individuals communicate in a particular situation or context. For example, an interpersonal communication researcher might examine how individuals feel right before they ask someone out on a date. Researchers might measure an individual's state anxiety to determine if this affects his or her ability to advance a request for a date. Thus, when researchers adopt a state approach to communication research they examine situationally specific responses (Daly and Bippus 1998).

When researchers adopt a **trait approach,** they attempt to identify enduring, or consistent, ways that people behave. If a researcher adopts a trait approach to studying communication behaviors, it means that he is interested in examining how individuals interact the majority of the time. Guilford (1959) defines a trait as "any distinguishable, relatively enduring way in which one individual differs from another" (6). Daly and Bippus (1998) identify several conclusions about traits: (1) they define ways in which people differ, (2) they can be broad or narrow in focus, (3) some address social characteristics while others emphasize cognitively-oriented variables, and (4) some can be measured using questionnaires while others are recognized by observing behaviors. Daly and Bippus comment on the distinction between state and trait approaches in research by stating, "The differences between trait and state are, in actuality, primarily differences in emphasis. Personality scholars tend to emphasize the trait over the state" (2).

Why are communication scholars so interested in studying personality traits? Communication scholars study traits because they are related to communication variables in a number of different ways. For example, in the following sections of this chapter we will learn about individuals who are highly apprehensive about communicating with others. These individuals are described as having trait-CA (Communication Apprehension) because they are consistently apprehensive about communication with others. Explained another way, high CA individuals tend to exhibit high levels of apprehension across a wide range of situations and with varied persons. Not surprisingly, research indicates that these individuals tend to exhibit a variety of behavioral disruptions when forced to interact with others (Allen and Bourhis 1996). This example illustrates the relationship between a trait (CA) and communication variables (behavioral disruptions, stuttering, pauses, etc.).

Because our **personality,** or predisposition to behave a certain way, is an important and relatively enduring part of how we see and define ourselves, interpersonal communication researchers are naturally interested in learning more about the impact of individual differences on social interaction. In addition, most researchers argue that communication behaviors linked to personality differences are explained, at least in part, by social learning; that is, we learn how to communicate by observing and imitating those around us. While a number of communication scholars have argued that one's genetic background best explains his or her personality predispositions (Beatty, McCroskey and Heisel 1998), it is still important to consider both explanations.

Finally, by learning more about how individuals with specific personality traits approach social interaction, we can advance some predictive generalizations about how they interact and plan our own behaviors accordingly. You might ask, why do communication researchers not just study self-concept? Unlike one's self-concept, which is subjective and could change from moment to moment, one's personality is relatively stable and consistent over time. For example, if you complete one of the communication-based personality measures in this chapter today and then complete the same one a year from now, it is very likely that your scores will be highly similar or even the same. Learning more about communication behaviors that are trait-based helps researchers understand the impact of individual differences across different contexts. In the remaining sections of this chapter, we review research that adopts a trait or personality approach to studying differences in communication behaviors.

© Yuri Arcurs, 2007, Shutterstock.

How is your communication affected by those around you?

COMMUNICATION APPREHENSION AND WILLINGNESS TO COMMUNICATE

In John Maxwell's (2002) book, *The Seventeen Essential Qualities of a Team Player*, he emphasizes communication as one of the most important skills needed for succeeding in teams. Other essential skills included in his list are adaptability, collaboration, enthusiasm, and the ability to establish relationships with team members. Not surprisingly, all of these qualities also require strong communication skills. Maxwell and countless other authors from a variety of academic and professional fields emphasize the relationship between communication skills and success at work. Throughout our own textbook we continually emphasize the link between communication and relationship stability and professional success. However, what if you are not comfortable communicating with others? If you or someone you know often avoids talking in most situations and with most people, it is likely that this individual would score high in communication apprehension and low in willingness to communicate. In the following sections, we examine these two related communication-based personality traits. For each communication-based personality trait we provide a general overview of the construct, describe ways to reliably measure the trait, and discuss research on the link between the personality trait and communication behaviors. Because high levels of communication apprehension can be extremely debilitating for individuals, treatment options are also discussed.

Approximately one in five individuals in the United States is considered high in communication apprehension (McCroskey 2006). For highly

Highly apprehensive individuals are more stressed and lonely than those who are low in communication apprehension.

apprehensive individuals, even anticipated communication with others evokes a significant amount of stress and psychological discomfort (McCroskey, Daly, and Sorensen 1976). James McCroskey (1977) conducted the seminal research in this area and defines **communication apprehension** as an "individual's level of fear or anxiety with either real or anticipated communication with another person or persons" (78). Communication apprehension (CA) can be measured in a variety of ways, but is frequently assessed using the Personal Report of Communication Apprehension (PRCA) developed by McCroskey (1978). The PRCA is a twenty-four-item five point Likert-type measure that assesses individuals' communication apprehension in general, as well as across four different areas: public, small group, meeting, and interpersonal/dyadic situations (see Applications at the end of this chapter). Individuals scoring high on the PRCA are generally quite anxious about communicating with others and will attempt to avoid interaction. Highly apprehensive individuals are less communicatively competent, less disclosive, and are more stressed and lonely than individuals low in communication apprehension (Miczo 2004; Zakahi and Duran 1985). Highly apprehensive college students are more likely to be considered "at risk" in college settings (Lippert, Titsworth, and Hunt 2005) and are less likely to emerge as leaders in work groups (Limon and La France 2005).

Willingness to communicate (WTC) is similar to communication apprehension because it also taps into an individual's propensity to avoid or approach communication with others. The willingness to communicate construct does not assess fear or anxiety, only one's tendency to approach or avoid communication in varied situations and with varied persons. McCroskey and Richmond (1987) coined the term willingness to communicate (WTC) and describe this construct as a person's tendency to initiate communication with others (McCroskey and Richmond 1998). WTC is further described as a "personality-based, trait-like predisposition which is relatively consistent across a variety of communication contexts and types of receivers" (McCroskey and Richmond 1987, 134). WTC can be measured via the WTC scale, which is a twenty-item measure that assesses an individual's willingness to interact with different individuals in different situations (see Applications section at the end of this chapter). Individuals completing the WTC scale indicate the percent of time they would choose to communicate in public, during a meeting, within a group, in a dyad, with a stranger, and in situations with acquaintances. For example, individuals are asked to indicate how often they would "talk with a service station attendant" or "talk with a physician." When individuals consistently indicate that they would not want to talk in most of the contexts listed, they are described as low in WTC. Conversely, individuals who indicate that they are willing to interact with others in a wide range of contexts are described as high in WTC.

Not surprisingly, highly apprehensive individuals are more likely to be low in WTC. Richmond and Roach (1992) summarize a significant body of research on the benefits and drawbacks for employees described as quiet, or low in WTC. First, they identify several positive factors associated with lower WTC. For example, individuals reporting lower WTC are typically less likely to initiate or perpetuate gossip and are also less likely to emerge as "squeaky wheels" within the organization. In addition, quiet individuals are less likely to take long breaks, unlike their more social high WTC counterparts. Finally, individuals with lower WTC are more likely to be discreet than more talkative individuals. Thus, organizations do not have to worry as much about quiet individuals sharing corporate secrets or new developments.

While there are some benefits of employing quiet individuals, Richmond and Roach (1992) note that, in general, quiet employees "are considered at risk in an organizational setting" for various reasons (Richmond and Roach 1992). More often than not, quiet individuals are perceived as less competent and intelligent because they do not contribute to discussions or share their accomplishments with others. Consequently, quiet employees are often mislabeled as incompetent and lacking business savvy. Research indicates that we tend to formulate negative impressions of employees who are quiet and, as a result, they are often less likely to get interviewed or considered for promotions. In research by Daly, Richmond, and Leth (1979), it was found that when individuals were described as quiet or shy in recommendation letters, they were less likely to be granted interviews than highly verbal individuals. Unfortunately, low WTC individuals may be more likely to experience the "last hired" and "first fired" syndrome than their high WTC counterparts (Richmond and Roach 1992).

What can be done to help individuals who are either high in CA or low in WTC? There is a significant amount of research that has identified treatment options for high CA individuals. Communication apprehension can be treated with methods similar to other types of phobias and neurotic anxieties (Berger, McCroskey, and Richmond 1984). According to McCroskey and his associates (1984), high levels of CA can be overcome or managed by applying three widely accepted treatment options. If these treatment options are not available, "there are other options available for individuals in the absence of these more formal treatments" (153). The three primary treatment options available for individuals high in communication apprehension are systematic desensitization, cognitive modification, and skills training.

One of the most effective means of treating high levels of CA is **systematic desensitization** (SD), a type of behavior modification derived from learning theory. Eighty to ninety percent of individuals who use systematic desensitization eliminate completely their high level or fear or anxiety. The basic premise behind systematic desensitization is that anxiety related to communication is learned and, as such, can be unlearned. **Cognitive modification,** also based on learning theory, is the second method of managing high levels of CA. "The underlying rationale for this treatment is that people have learned to think negatively about themselves, in this case, how they communicate, and can be taught to think positively" (Berger et al. 1984). The third and least successful way to treat high levels of CA is skills training. Skills training, when used as the sole method, is typically considered the least effective method for treating high levels of CA. Communication **skills training** might involve taking courses to help individuals learn to communicate more effectively. For example, individuals may take public speaking courses to improve their ability to design and deliver speeches. Experts recommend that persons with high levels of communication apprehension first employ systematic desensitization or cognitive modification as a means of reducing their anxiety and then participate in skills training courses to help manage

> *And I think that those who consider disabled people 'broken' fail to see that while some of us have disabilities that are physically obvious, in truth all people are disabled in one way or another—including disabilities of character and personality.*
>
> —Kyle Maynard

deficient communication skills. Whether you or someone you know is highly apprehensive about communication, it is important to note that the tendency to fear communication can be treated successfully.

AGGRESSIVE BEHAVIOR

Infante (1987a) recognizes a behavior as aggressive when it "applies force . . . symbolically in order, minimally to dominate and perhaps damage, or maximally to defeat and perhaps destroy the locus of attack" (58). He further explains that there are two types of aggressive behavior; he labels them destructive and constructive. **Destructive** forms of aggression are those that can potentially damage individual's self-esteem or, to use Infante's words "destroy the locus of attack." Two widely recognized types of destructive aggression are hostility and verbal aggression.

Hostility

Hostility is defined as "using symbols (verbal or nonverbal) to express irritability, negativism, resentment, and suspicion" (Infante 1988, 7). When someone expresses hostility, he or she might say, "I am so angry I did not get chosen for the lacrosse team and I blame the selection committee!" Individuals presenting hostile personalities generally devalue the worth and motives of others, are highly suspicious of others, feel in opposition with those around them, and often feel a desire to inflict harm or see others harmed (Smith 1994). One way to measure hostility is to use Cook-Medley Hostility Scale (Cook and Medley 1954) which is one of the most commonly used means of assessing trait hostility and appears to have construct, predictive, and discriminant validity (Huebner, Nemeroff, and Davis 2005; Pope, Smith, and Rhodewalt 1990). Sample items on the hostility measure are "I think most people will lie to get ahead," and "It is safer to trust nobody." Individuals completing the hostility measure indicate the extent to which they either agree or disagree with the statements using a five-point Likert scale.

Needless to say, feeling consistently hostile toward others affects the way one views the world and impacts relationships with others. Hostile individuals tend to be quite unhappy individuals who are more likely to report depression and lower self-esteem (Kopper and Epperson 1996). From a communication perspective, researchers try to accurately identify people or communication situations that evoke feelings of hostility in order to better understand this construct. If we can identify the types of situations or people that cause others to feel hostile, perhaps we can make attempts to modify or improve these situations. Recent research by Chory-Assad and Paulsel (2004) examined the relationship between students' perceptions of justice in college classrooms and student aggression and hostility toward their instructors. As expected, when students felt instructors were not fair in regard to course policies, scheduling, testing, amount of work, etc., they were more likely to feel hostile toward their teachers. Now that we know that perceptions of injustice in college classrooms leads to greater hostility in students, we can make recommendations on how to alter these situations and to reduce hostile reactions.

Hostile individuals are more likely to experience problems in committed romantic relationships. Rogge (2006) and his colleagues examined communication, hostility, and neuroticism as predictors of marital stability and found that couples were less likely to stay together when spouses reported higher levels of hostility and neuroticism. The researchers noted that while communication skills distinguished those who were married-satisfied and those who were married-unsatisfied, they did not always predict marital dissolution. It is important to note that hostility and neuroticism "contribute to a rapid, early decline in marital functioning" (Rogge et al. 2006, 146). In addition, an inability to empathize with relationship partners and manage conflict in a productive way may negatively impact future chances at relationship success. From an interpersonal communication perspective, it is important to determine the kinds of behaviors that elicit feelings of hostility from others, to then reduce or eliminate those behaviors, and to attempt to repair the damaged relationship using relationship maintenance strategies.

Verbally aggressive attacks can permanently damage relationships.

Verbal Aggression

Another personality trait labeled difficult, or problematic, during face-to-face encounters is verbal aggression. When individuals lack the ability to effectively argue, they often resort to verbally aggressive communication. Wigley (1998) describes **verbal aggressiveness** as the tendency to attack the self-concept of an individual instead of addressing the other person's arguments. Dominic Infante (1987; 1995) identified a wide range of messages that verbally aggressive communicators use. For example, verbally aggressive communicators may resort to character attacks, competence attacks, background attacks, physical appearance attacks, maledictions, teasing, swearing, ridiculing, threatening, and nonverbal emblems. On occasion, they might also use blame, personality attacks, commands, global rejection, negative comparison, and sexual harassment in their attempts to hurt others. As Wigley (1998) notes, "there seems to be no shortage of ways to cause other people to feel badly about themselves" (192).

Infante and Wigley (1986) developed the Verbal Aggressiveness Scale, which is a twenty item self-report personality test that asks people to indicate whether they are verbally aggressive in their interactions (found in Applications at the end of this chapter). Infante and Wigley were aware of the fact that people might not self-report their use of aggression. With this in mind, the researchers designed items on the measure to make it seem like they approved of aggressive messages. The researchers developed the Verbal Aggressiveness instrument to learn more about the behavior of people who were verbally aggressive.

For those of us who have ever interacted with someone who is highly verbally aggressive, one of the more common questions is why this person acts this way. There are a number of viable explanations for why some individuals possess trait verbal aggressiveness. Individuals may be verbally aggressive because they learned this behavior from others. Thus, social learning, or modeling effects explain why verbally aggressive parents have children that also become verbally aggressive. Another explanation for this trait is that verbally aggressive individuals lack the ability to argue effectively and, as a result, are more likely to become frustrated during arguments. The inability to defend one's position is frustrating and often causes the highly aggressive person to lash out at others. In this case, trait levels of verbal aggression are linked to argument skill deficiency (ASD). Researchers note that if verbal aggression is linked to ASD, then one way to combat this problem is to train individuals in effective argumentation (Wigley 1998).

There are a number of significant negative consequences for individuals who regularly communicate in verbally aggressive ways. Verbally aggressive individuals are more likely to use a variety of antisocial behaviors and, as a result, are less liked (Myers and Johnson 2003). Research by Infante, Riddle, Horvath, and Tumlin (1992) compared individuals who were high and low in verbal aggressiveness to determine how often they used different verbally aggressive messages, how hurtful they perceived these messages to be, and their reasons for using verbally aggressive messages. Individuals who were high in verbal aggressiveness were more likely to use a wide range of verbally aggressive messages (e.g., competence attacks, teasing, and nonverbal emblems). High verbal aggressives were less likely than low verbal aggressives to perceive threats, competence attacks, and physical appearance attacks as hurtful. When high verbal aggressives were asked to explain their behavior, they stated that they were angry, did not like the target, were taught to be aggressive, were in a bad mood, or were just being humorous. Wanzer and her colleagues (1995) found that verbally aggressive individuals are less socially attractive and more likely to target others in humor attempts than to target themselves. Their inappropriate use of humor may explain why acquaintances rate them as less socially attractive.

College students scoring high in verbal aggressiveness were more likely to be considered academically at risk in college settings than students scoring low in verbal aggressiveness (Lippert et al. 2005). Lippert and his colleagues (2005) call for more research to understand why verbally aggressive college students are more academically at risk. They suspect that verbally aggressive students' inappropriate classroom behavior may lead to negative evaluations from teachers and peers. Consistently negative experiences in the classroom may contribute to verbally aggressive students' at risk status.

What can be done to help high aggressives? From a communication perspective, it is important to recognize when we are being verbally aggressive with others and to attempt to eliminate these behaviors. Recognize that when you communicate in a verbally aggressive way, others may model your behavior. Have you ever had a younger sibling mimic your verbal or nonverbal messages? There is a substantial amount of research on this trait and the potentially negative effects of high amounts of verbal aggression on relationships in married (Infante, Chandler, and Rudd 1989), family (Bayer and Cegala 1992), and organizational contexts (Infante and Gorden 1991). If you are predisposed to using verbal aggression, enroll in courses that might help you improve your ability to argue. One of the most widely recognized ways to address or treat verbal aggression is to train individuals who are skill deficient in argumentation to defend their positions more effectively.

Next, we turn our attention to several communication-based personality traits that may help individuals communicate more effectively during social interaction. More specifically, we examine argumentativeness, assertiveness, humor orientation, and affective orientation.

CONSTRUCTIVE AGGRESSIVE BEHAVIOR

Argumentativeness and assertiveness are described by Infante as constructive forms of aggression. Both of these behaviors are considered **constructive** forms of aggression because they are more active than passive, help us achieve our communication goals, and do not involve personal attacks (Rancer 1998). For some individuals, arguing with friends, colleagues, or family members is considered enjoyable and challenging. For others, arguing leads to hurt feelings, confusion, or even anger.

Argumentativeness

According to Rancer, individuals vary extensively in their perceptions of argumentative behavior. Infante and Rancer (1982) define **argumentativeness** as "a generally stable trait which predisposes individuals in communication situations to advocate positions on controversial issues and to attack verbally the positions which other people hold on these issues" (72). When individuals are argumentative, they attack issues and positions. When individuals are verbally aggressive, they attack others by using competence or character attacks, or possibly even swearing. When someone exhibits high levels of argumentativeness, they are able to both advocate and defend positions on controversial issues. Infante and Rancer (1982) developed the Argumentativeness Scale, which is a twenty-item Likert-type scale that asks people to record how they feel about responding to controversial issues. Ten items on the scale assess motivation to approach argumentative situations and ten items assess motivation to avoid argumentative situations (see Applications section at the end of this chapter).

There are a number of benefits associated with argumentativeness. Highly argumentative individuals are more effective in their attempts to persuade others. They employ a wider range of persuasion and social influence tactics and tend to be more tenacious in their persuasion attempts (Boster and Levine 1988). Highly argumentative individuals are more resistant to compliance attempts from others and generate more counterarguments in response to persuasive encounters (Infante 1981; Kazoleas 1993). Argumentative individuals are viewed as more credible and competent communicators who are also more interested in communicating with others (Infante 1981; 1985). More recently, research by Limon and La France (2005) explored communicator traits associated with leadership emergence in work groups. As predicted by their hypotheses, college student participants low in CA and high in argumentativeness were more likely to emerge as leaders in work groups than students high in CA and low in argumentativeness. These findings illustrate the significance of this communication skill as it relates to one's potential to become a leader.

As mentioned previously, the inability to argue effectively is extremely problematic for individuals and for relationships. Research by Andonian and Droge (1992) linked males' reported verbal aggressiveness to date rape, which is an especially aggressive form of interpersonal behavior. They found that males' tendency to report acceptance of date rape myths, e.g., females might say no to sexual intercourse but really mean yes, was positively related to verbal aggressiveness and negatively related to argumentativeness. Again, this study, like others, emphasizes the constructive nature of argumentativeness and the destructive nature of verbal aggression. Similarly, in the organizational setting, the best conditions for organizational communication are when managers and employees are both high in argumentativeness and low in verbal aggression (Infante and Gorden 1987; 1989). Research on the benefits of argumentativeness in organizational contexts supports the notion of **independent-mindedness,** which refers to the extent to which employees can openly express their own opinions at work (Rancer 1998). The research on the benefits of argumentativeness in different contexts illustrates the significance of this skill.

Can we train individuals to argue more constructively? A number of programs have achieved successful results in training individuals to improve their ability to argue effectively. Anderson, Schultz, and Staley (1987) implemented cognitive training in argument and conflict management to encourage individuals to argue with one another. For individuals who are low in argumentativeness, this can be a daunting task. The researchers were pleased that they were able to see results from females who were low in argumentativeness. This study, as well as others, indicates that individuals can be trained to argue more effectively.

Assertiveness

How can assertive behavior contribute to individual success?

Another form of constructive aggression is **assertiveness,** which is defined as the capability to defend your own rights and wishes while still respecting and acknowledging the rights of others. When individuals act in an assertive way, they stand up for themselves and are able to initiate, maintain, and terminate conversations to reach interpersonal goals (Richmond and Martin 1998). One way to measure assertiveness is by using the Socio-Communicative Orientation Scale developed by Richmond and McCroskey (1990). This measure includes ten assertiveness items and ten responsiveness items. Individuals are asked to report how accurately the items apply to them when they communicate with others. Some examples of assertive characteristics include: defends own beliefs, independent, and forceful. Individuals use Likert-type responses to indicate whether they strongly agree or strongly disagree that these characteristics apply to them (see the Applications section at the end of this chapter).

There are innumerable benefits associated with the assertiveness trait. By acting in an assertive manner, individuals are able to defend themselves, establish relationships, and take advantage of opportunities. Richmond and Martin (1998) note that assertive communication is more beneficial than aggressive communication and can lead to "long-term effectiveness while maintaining good relationships with others" (136). Assertive individuals are perceived as more confident and self-assured and often rated as more effective teachers and managers than unassertive individuals. When it comes to practicing safe sex, sexually assertive males are more likely than unassertive males to use condoms to protect themselves (Noar, Morokoff, and Redding 2002). Researchers say that increasing sexual assertiveness in males may lead to long-term increases in safer sexual behaviors (Noar et al. 2002).

Humor Orientation

Booth-Butterfield and Booth-Butterfield (1991) developed the concept of **humor orientation** and define it as the extent to which people use humor as well as their self-perceived appropriateness of humor production. Humor orientation (HO) can be measured using the Humor Orientation Scale (found in the Applications section at the end of this chapter), which is a seventeen-item questionnaire that assesses how often people use humor in their day-to-day communication and how effective they are at enacting humorous messages. When developing the HO measure, M. Booth-Butterfield and

S. Booth-Butterfield (1991) examined the different types of humorous communication behaviors people used when they were attempting to be funny. They found that individuals scoring higher on the HO measure (also called high HO's) accessed more categories of humorous communication behaviors such as nonverbal techniques, language, expressivity, and impersonation. Persons who enacted humor frequently and effectively perceived themselves as funny, and utilized a variety of humorous communication behaviors across diverse situations. Wanzer, Booth-Butterfield, and Booth-Butterfield (1995) later confirmed that high humor-oriented people were perceived by others as funnier than low HO's when telling jokes. Thus, being humorous is not simply in the eye of the high HO.

There appear to be a variety of intrapersonal and interpersonal benefits associated with the humor orientation trait. For example, high HO's are typically less lonely (Wanzer et al. 1996a), are more adaptable in their communication with others, have greater concern for eliciting positive impressions from others, and are more affectively oriented, i.e., are more likely to use their emotions to guide their communication decisions (Wanzer et. al. 1995). Honeycutt and Brown (1998) found that traditional marital types, which usually report the highest levels of marital satisfaction (Fitzpatrick 1988), were also higher in HO than other types. When managers are perceived as more humor-oriented by their employees, they are also viewed as more likable and effective (Rizzo, Wanzer, and Booth-Butterfield 1999). Not surprisingly, there are a number of benefits for teachers who use humor effectively in the classroom. For example, students report learning more from instructors perceived as humor-oriented (Wanzer and Frymier 1999) and also report engaging in more frequent communication outside of class with humor-oriented teachers (Aylor and Opplinger 2003).

© Zsolt Nyulaszi, 2007, Shutterstock.

Humor can add more than just laughs to the work environment.

More recently, researchers have examined whether high humor-oriented individuals are more likely than low humor-oriented individuals to use humor to cope with stress and whether they benefit from this "built in" coping mechanism (Booth-Butterfield, Booth-Butterfield, and Wanzer 2006; 2005). In two different, yet similar studies, employed participants reported their HO, whether they used humor to cope with stressful situations, coping efficacy, and job satisfaction. The researchers speculated that individuals employed in highly stressful jobs, such as nursing, would: (1) benefit from the ability to cope using humor, and (2) would vary in this ability based on HO scores (Wanzer et al. 2005). Nurses who reported higher HO were more likely than low HO nurses to use humor to cope with stressful work situations and to perceive their coping strategies as effective (higher coping efficacy). In addition, humor-oriented nurses reported greater coping efficacy, leading to higher job satisfaction. Researchers found the same relationships between HO, coping and job satisfaction in a similar study of employed college students (Booth-Butterfield, Booth-Butterfield, and Wanzer 2006). These studies illustrate how humor can help individuals cope with difficult or stressful situations.

Can we train people to use humor more appropriately and effectively? Perhaps. We know that people often participate in improv classes and classes on stand-up comedy to improve their ability to deliver humorous messages. It seems likely that if people understand why certain messages are universally perceived as funny, they could be trained to improve their ability to deliver humorous messages with greater success. For now, researchers who study humor and the effects of humor recommend that individuals avoid using any type of humor based on stereotypes, or humor viewed as racist, sexist, ageist, or homophobic. Individuals need to be aware of audience characteristics that influence the way humorous content is interpreted and make attempts to use humor that is innocuous. For example, individuals who want to incorporate more humor into their day-to-day communication may use more self-disparaging humor, making certain not to overuse this type of humor as it may damage one's credibility.

Affective Orientation

Affective orientation refers to the extent to which individuals are aware of their own emotional states and use them when making behavioral decisions (Booth-Butterfield and Booth-Butterfield 1990). Individuals described as affectively oriented tend to be quite aware of their affective states and consult them before acting. Conversely, individuals described as low in affective orientation tend to be relatively unaware of their emotions and tend to reject their emotions as useful (Booth-Butterfield and Booth-Butterfield 1998). Affective Orientation (AO) can be measured via the Affective Orientation (AO15) Scale which is a fifteen-item instrument used to assess the extent to which individuals are aware of and consult their affective states and can be found in the Applications section at the end of this chapter. The revised fifteen-item measure "offers a more definitionally focused and concise operationalization of AO, exhibits minimal gender differences in mean scores and it is psychometrically more sound than the original AO scale" (Booth-Butterfield and Booth-Butterfield 1998, 180).

What are some of the benefits and/or drawbacks of higher AO? Individuals that exhibit higher levels of AO tend to be more nonverbally sensitive and better at providing comfort to others (Booth-Butterfield and Andrighetti 1993; Dolin and Booth-Butterfield 1993). Interestingly, individuals with higher AO also tend to utilize humor more frequently than lower AO individuals (Wanzer et al. 1995). The researchers suspect that higher AO individuals might use humor as one method of treating or managing negative affective states. From a relationship perspective, higher AO individuals tend to be more romantic and idealistic in their beliefs about intimate relationships (Booth-Butterfield and Booth-Butterfield 1994). More recent research on AO has examined the relationship between this trait and health behaviors.

© Serghei Starus, 2007, Shutterstock.

What kind of campaign might work to persuade this individual to quit smoking?

Specifically, researchers have been examining the relationships between AO and specific health practices such as smoking. Higher AO individuals are more likely to smoke than low AO's (Booth-Butterfield and Booth-Butterfield 1998). These findings are important and can be used to formulate successful persuasive campaigns. For example, the researchers note that since smokers are more affectively oriented, persuasive prevention campaigns should generate negative affective states (e.g., fear) and then connect them in some way to smoking (Booth-Butterfield and Booth-Butterfield 1998).

Individuals may reap a variety of personal and interpersonal benefits when they exhibit higher levels of argumentativeness, assertiveness, humor orientation, and affective orientation. While these traits are not the only ones that have proven to be beneficial for sources (e.g., cognitive complexity), they are studied frequently, and can be assessed via self-report instruments, and are linked to other positive traits and characteristics.

SUMMARY

The goal of this chapter was to help you learn more about the complex, evolving, and multidimensional nature of the self. To learn more about who we are and why we act a certain way, we explored the role of interpersonal communication and relationships in identity formation. Communication with family members, peers, and relationship partners influences how we see ourselves and how we relate to others. Our personality differences also affect the way we relate to others. In this chapter we discussed differences between state and trait approaches to studying personality and the connection between personality traits and communication behaviors. Communication based personality traits such as CA, WTC, hostility, verbal aggression, argumentativeness, assertiveness, humor orientation, and affective orientation were discussed in this chapter. Some of the behaviors associated with these communication traits can be problematic for both sources and receivers. We hope that after reading this chapter you now have a better understanding of these traits and how some can either hinder or facilitate our communication with others.

APPLICATIONS
Discussion Questions

A. Write about or discuss in small groups the person/persons that were most influential in your life. What other individuals play a role in the process of identity formation that were not identified in this chapter?

B. Visit several websites that offer suggestions for improving one's self-esteem. Critique these websites based on the following criteria: (1) Quality and quantity of information presented, (2) Inclusion of a discussion of both the pros and cons of high and low self-esteem, (3) Credentials of the individuals posting these sites, and (4) Ease of navigation of these sites. Based on your analysis of these sites, would you use these sites or send friends to these sites for information?

C. Complete one or more of the personality measures included in this chapter and score them. Recruit a friend that knows you quite well to complete the measure based on how the friend perceives your communication behaviors. Next, draw comparisons between self and other reports of the communication-based personality assessments. After examining the self and other reports closely, write about the following: (1) Are there similarities in the self and other reports, (2) Are there differences in the self and other reports, (3) Are these scores valid—do they accurately explain your communication tendencies, (4) After completing these assessments, do you feel it is necessary to change any aspect of communication behaviors? Why or why not?

ACTIVITIES

Activity #1:   **Personal Report of Communication Apprehension**

This instrument is composed of twenty-four statements concerning feelings about communicating with other people. Please indicate the degree to which each statement applies to you by marking whether you (1) strongly agree, (2) agree, (3) are undecided, (4) disagree, or (5) strongly disagree. Work quickly; record your first impression.

_____ 1. I dislike participating in group discussions.

_____ 2. Generally, I am comfortable while participating in group discussions.

_____ 3. I am tense and nervous while participating in group discussions.

_____ 4. I like to get involved in group discussions.

_____ 5. Engaging in a group discussion with new people makes me tense and nervous.

_____ 6. I am calm and relaxed when participating in group discussions.

_____ 7. Generally, I am nervous when I have to participate in a meeting.

_____ 8. Usually I am calm and relaxed while participating in meetings.

_____ 9. I am very calm and relaxed when I am called upon to express an opinion at a meeting.

_____ 10. I am afraid to "press" myself at meetings.

_____ 11. Communicating at meetings usually makes me uncomfortable.

_____ 12. I am very relaxed when answering questions at a meeting.

_____ 13. While participating in a conversation with a new acquaintance, I feel very nervous.

_____ 14. I have no fear of speaking up in conversations.

_____ 15. Ordinarily I am very tense and nervous in conversations.

_____ 16. Ordinarily I am very calm and relaxed in conversations.

_____ 17. While conversing with a new acquaintance, I feel very relaxed.

_____ 18. I'm afraid to speak up in conversations.

_____ 19. I have no fear of giving a speech.

_____ 20. Certain parts of my body feel very tense and rigid while I am giving a speech.

_____ 21. I feel relaxed while giving a speech.

_____ 22. My thoughts become confused and jumbled when I am giving a speech.

_____ 23. I face the prospect of giving a speech with confidence.

_____ 24. While giving a speech, I get so nervous I forget facts I really know.

SCORING: In order to compute the total score follow this formula: Total = 72 + (sum of the scores from items 2, 4, 6, 8, 9, 12, 14, 16, 17, 19, 21, 23) – (sum of the scores from items 1, 3, 5, 7, 10, 11, 13, 15, 18, 20, 22, 24)

The average score for college students is typically 65.6. Scores of 80 and higher indicate high levels of CA. Scores of 50 and lower indicate lower levels of CA.

Source: From *Communication Apprehension, Avoidance And Effectiveness, 5E* by Virginia P. Richmond & James C. McCroskey, Published by Allyn & Bacon, Boston, MA. Copyright © 1998 by Pearson Education. Reprinted by permission of the publisher.

Willingness to Communicate Scale (WTC)   Activity #2

Below are twenty situations in which a person might or might not choose to communicate. Presume you have *completely free choice*. Indicate the percentage of times you would choose *to communicate* in each type of situation. Indicate in the space at the left what percent of the time you would choose to communicate.

0=never, 100=always

_____ 1. Talk with a service station attendant.

_____ 2. Talk with a physician.

_____ 3. Present a talk to a group of strangers.

_____ 4. Talk with an acquaintance while standing in line.

_____ 5. Talk with a salesperson in a store.

_____ 6. Talk in a large meeting of friends.

_____ 7. Talk with a police officer.

_____ 8. Talk in a small group of strangers.

_____ 9. Talk with a friend while standing in line.

_____ 10. Talk with a waiter/waitress in a restaurant.

_____ 11. Talk in a large meeting of acquaintances.

_____ 12. Talk with a stranger while standing in line.

_____ 13. Talk with a secretary.

_____ 14. Present a talk to a group of friends.

_____ 15. Talk in a small group of acquaintances.

_____ 16. Talk with a garbage collector.

_____ 17. Talk in a large meeting of strangers.

_____ 18. Talk with a spouse (or girl/boyfriend)

_____ 19. Talk in a small group of friends.

_____ 20. Present a talk to a group of acquaintances.

SCORING: To calculate the total WTC score follow these steps:

Step 1:   Add scores for items 3, 8, 12, and 17; then divide by 4.
Step 2:   Add scores for items 4, 11, 15, and 20; then divide by 4.
Step 3:   Add scores for items 6, 9, 14, and 19; then divide by 4.
Step 4:   Add the final scores from steps 1, 2, and 3; then divide by 3.

>82 High overall WTC
<52 Low overall WTC

Source: Richmond, V. P. and J. C. McCroskey. 1995. *Communication: Apprehension, avoidance, and effectiveness. (4th ed.).* Scottsdale, AZ: Gorsuch Scarisbrick.

 **Activity #3:   Verbal Aggressiveness Scale**

This survey is concerned with how we try to get people to comply with our wishes. Indicate how often each statement is true for you personally when you try to influence others by using the following scale: (1) almost never true, (2) rarely true, (3) occasionally true, (4) often true, (5) almost always true.

_____ 1. I am extremely careful to avoid attacking individuals' intelligence when I attack their ideas.

_____ 2. When individuals are very stubborn, I use insults to soften the stubbornness.

_____ 3. I try very hard to avoid having other people feel bad about themselves when I try to influence them.

_____ 4. When people refuse to do a task I know is important, without good reason, I tell them they are unreasonable.

_____ 5. When others do things I regard as stupid, I try to be extremely gentle with them.

_____ 6. If individuals I am trying to influence really deserve it, I attack their character.

_____ 7. When people behave in ways that are in very poor taste, I insult them in order to shock them into proper behavior.

_____ 8. I try to make people feel good about themselves even when their ideas are stupid.

_____ 9. When people simply will not budge on a matter of importance, I lose my temper and say rather strong things to them.

_____ 10. When people criticize my shortcomings, I take it in good humor and do not try to get back at them.

_____ 11. When individuals insult me, I get a lot of pleasure out of really telling them off.

_____ 12. When I dislike individuals greatly, I try not to show it in what I say or how I say it.

_____ 13. I like poking fun at people who do things that are very stupid in order to stimulate their intelligence.

_____ 14. When I attack a persons' ideas, I try not to damage their self-concepts.

_____ 15. When I try to influence people, I make a great effort not to offend them.

_____ 16. When people do things that are mean or cruel, I attack their character in order to help correct their behavior.

_____ 17. I refuse to participate in arguments which involve personal attacks.

_____ 18. When nothing seems to work when trying to influence others, I yell and scream in order to get some movement from them.

_____ 19. When I am not able to refute others' positions, I try to make them feel defensive in order to weaken their positions.

_____ 20. When an argument shifts to personal attacks, I try very hard to change the subject.

SCORING: Sum the scores all the items after reversing scoring for items 1, 3, 5, 8, 10, 12, 14, 15, 17, and 20.

Average score for college students is 49. Scores of 59 and higher indicate higher levels of verbal aggression. Scores of 39 and lower indicate lower levels of verbal aggression.

Source: From "Verbal Aggressiveness: An Interpersonal Model and Measure" by D.A. Infante and C.J. Wigley, III, _Communication Monographs_, 1986, 53, 61-69. Reprinted by permission of Taylor & Francis.

Argumentativeness Scale

Activity #4:

This questionnaire contains statements about arguing about controversial issues. Indicate how often each statement is true for you personally by placing the appropriate number in the blank to the left of the statement. Indicate if the statement is; (1) almost never true for you, (2) rarely true for you, (3) occasionally true for you, (4) often true for you, or (5) almost always true for you. Remember, consider each item in terms of arguing controversial issues.

_____ 1. While in an argument, I worry that the person I am arguing with will form a negative impression of me.

_____ 2. Arguing over controversial issues improves my intelligence.

_____ 3. I enjoy avoiding arguments.

_____ 4. I am energetic and enthusiastic when I argue.

_____ 5. Once I finish an argument I promise myself that I will not get into another.

_____ 6. Arguing with a person creates more problems for me than it solves.

_____ 7. I have a pleasant, good feeling when I win a point in an argument.

_____ 8. When I finish arguing with someone I feel nervous and upset.

_____ 9. I enjoy a good argument over a controversial issue.

_____ 10. I get an unpleasant feeling when I realize I am about to get into an argument.

_____ 11. I enjoy defending my point of view on an issue.

_____ 12. I am happy when I keep an argument from happening.

_____ 13. I do not like to miss the opportunity to argue a controversial issue.

_____ 14. I prefer being with people who rarely disagree with me.

_____ 15. I consider an argument an exciting intellectual challenge.

_____ 16. I find myself unable to think of effective points during an argument.

_____ 17. I feel refreshed and satisfied after an argument on a controversial issue.

_____ 18. I have the ability to do well in an argument.

_____ 19. I try to avoid getting into arguments.

_____ 20. I feel excited when I expect that a conversation I am in is leading to an argument.

SCORING: To compute the Argumentativeness trait score, follow these steps:

Step 1:   Add the scores for items 2, 4, 7, 9, 11, 13, 15, 17, 18, and 20.
Step 2:   Add 60 to the sum obtained in Step 1.
Step 3:   Subtract the total from Step 2 from the total from Step 1.
Step 4:   To compute your argumentativeness score, subtract the total obtained in Step 3 from the total obtained in Step 2.

73–100   High in argumentativeness
56–72   Moderate in argumentativeness
20–55   Low in argumentativeness

Source: Reprinted by permission of Waveland Press, Inc. from *Arguing Constructively* by D.A. Infante. Long Grove, IL: Waveland Press, Inc., 1988. All rights reserved.

Assertiveness-Responsiveness Measure

The questionnaire below lists twenty personality characteristics. Please indicate the degree to which you believe each of these characteristics applies to you while interacting with others by marking whether you: (5) strongly agree that it applies, (4) agree that it applies, (3) are undecided, (2) disagree that it applies, or (1) strongly disagree that it applies. There are no right or wrong answers. Work quickly; record your first impression.

_____ 1. Helpful

_____ 2. Defends own beliefs

_____ 3. Independent

_____ 4. Responsive to others

_____ 5. Forceful

_____ 6. Has strong personality

_____ 7. Sympathetic

_____ 8. Compassionate

_____ 9. Assertive

_____ 10. Sensitive to the needs of others

_____ 11. Dominant

_____ 12. Sincere

_____ 13. Gentle

_____ 14. Willing to take a stand

_____ 15. Warm

_____ 16. Tender

_____ 17. Friendly

_____ 18. Acts as a leader

_____ 19. Aggressive

_____ 20. Competitive

SCORING: To score your responses, add what you marked for each item as follows:

Assertiveness: Add items 2, 3, 5, 6, 9, 11, 14, 18, 19, 20
Responsiveness: Add items 1, 4, 7, 8, 10, 12, 13, 15, 16, 17

Scores above 40 indicate high assertiveness or responsiveness, and scores below 20 indicate low assertiveness or responsiveness. Scores between 20 and 40 indicate a moderate level of either trait.

Source: From _Communication Apprehension, Avoidance And Effectiveness, 5E_ by Virginia P. Richmond & James C. McCroskey, Published by Allyn & Bacon, Boston, MA. Copyright © 1998 by Pearson Education. Reprinted by permission of the publisher.

Activity #6:   Humor Orientation Scale

Below are descriptions of how you may communicate in general. Please use the scale below to rate the degree to which each statement applies to your communication.

1=strongly disagree
2=disagree
3=neutral
4=agree
5=strongly agree

_____ 1. I regularly tell jokes and funny stories when in a group.

_____ 2. People usually laugh when I tell jokes or funny stories.

_____ 3. I have no memory for jokes or funny stories.

_____ 4. I can be funny without having to rehearse a joke.

_____ 5. Being funny is a natural communication style with me.

_____ 6. I cannot tell a joke well.

_____ 7. People seldom ask me to tell stories.

_____ 8. My friends would say I am a funny person.

_____ 9. People don't seem to pay close attention when I tell a joke.

_____ 10. Even funny jokes seem flat when I tell them.

_____ 11. I can easily remember jokes and stories.

_____ 12. People often ask me to tell jokes or stories.

_____ 13. My friends would not say that I am a funny person.

_____ 14. I don't tell jokes or stories even when asked to.

_____ 15. I tell stories and jokes very well.

_____ 16. Of all the people I know, I am one of the funniest.

_____ 17. I use humor to communicate in a variety of situations.

Step 1:   Flip the responses (5 = 1, 4 = 2, 2 = 4, and 1 = 5) for questions 3, 6, 7, 9, 10, 13, 14.

Step 2:   Once questions have been flipped, add up all items. Your score should fall somewhere between 17 and 85.

For college students the average on the HO measure is typically around 61.
If you score 71 or higher you are considered high in humor orientation (high HO).
If you score in the 50–70 range you are considered moderate in humor orientation.
If you score 49 and below you are considered low in humor orientation (a low HO).

Source: From "Individual Differences in the Communication of Humorous Messages" by M. Booth-Butterfield, & S. Booth-Butterfield, S., *Southern Communication Journal*, 1991, 56, 32-40. Reprinted by permission of Taylor & Francis.

Affective Orientation Scale

The following statements refer to the feelings and emotions people have and how people use their feelings and emotions to guide their behavior. There are no right or wrong answers. Also realize that emotions and feelings can be positive or negative. A person can feel anger; another can feel love and tenderness. Both cases, however, are emotion. Use the following 5-point scale to indicate whether you, (5) strongly agree, (4) agree, (3) are uncertain, (2) disagree, or (1) strongly disagree with each statement.

_____ 1. I use my feelings to determine what I should do in situations.

_____ 2. I listen to what my "gut" or "heart" says in many situations.

_____ 3. My emotions tell me what to do in many cases.

_____ 4. I try not to let feelings guide my actions.

_____ 5. I am aware of and use my feelings as a guide more than others do.

_____ 6. I won't let my emotions influence how I act most of the time.

_____ 7. I follow what my feelings say I should do in most situations.

_____ 8. Most of the time I avoid letting my emotions guide what I do.

_____ 9. I usually let my internal feelings direct my behavior.

_____ 10. Usually my emotions are good predictors of how I will act.

_____ 11. My actions are often influenced by my awareness of my emotions.

_____ 12. My emotions provide me solid direction in my life.

_____ 13. How I act often depends on what my feelings tell me to do.

_____ 14. Even subtle emotions often guide my actions.

_____ 15. When I am aware of my emotional response, I listen to it to determine what to do.

SCORING: To determine the score on this scale, complete the following steps:

Step 1.   Reverse the scores of 4, 6, and 8, and then add them together.
Step 2.   Add the rest of the scores together.
Step 3.   Total steps 1 and 2.

> 60 Higher affective orientation
< 44 Lower affective orientation

Source: From "Conceptualizing Affect as Information in Communication Production" by M. Booth-Butterfield & S. Booth-Butterfield, *Human Communication Research*, 16, 451-476, 1990. Reprinted with permission of Blackwell Publishing, www.blackwell-synergy.com.

REFERENCES

Ainsworth, M. D. S., M. C. Blehar, E. Waters, and S. Wall. 1978. *Patterns of attachment: A psychological study of the strange situation.* Hillsdale, NJ: Erlbaum.

Allen, M., and J. Bourhis. 1996. The relationship of communication apprehension to communication behavior: A meta-analysis. *Communication Quarterly, 44,* 214–226.

Andersen, S. M., and K. Berensen. 2001. Perceiving, feeling, and wanting: Motivation and affect deriving from significant other representations and transference. In J. P. Forgas, K. D. Williams, and L. Wheeler (Eds.), *The social mind: Cognitive and motivational aspects of interpersonal behavior* (231–256). New York: Cambridge University Press.

Anderson, J., B. Schultz, and C. Courtney Staley. 1987. Training in argumentativeness: New hope for nonassertive women. *Women's Studies in Communication, 10*, 58–66.

Andonian, K. K., and D. Droge. 1992. *Verbal aggressiveness and sexual violence in dating relationships: An exploratory study of antecedents of date rape.* Paper presented at the annual meeting of the Speech Communication Association, Chicago, IL.

Aron, A. 2003. Self and close relationships. In M. R. Leary and J. P. Tangney (Eds.), *Handbook of self and identity.* New York: The Guilford Press.

Aube, J., and R. Koestner. 1992. Gender characteristics and adjustment: A longitudinal study. *Journal of Personality and Social Psychology, 70*, 535–551.

Aylor, B., and P. Opplinger. 2003. Out-of-class communication and student perceptions of instructor humor orientation and socio-communicative style. *Communication Education, 52*, 122–134.

Bandura, A. 1986. *Social foundations of thought and action.* New York: Prentice Hall.

Bargh, J. A., and T. L. Chartrand. 1999. The unbearable automaticity of being. *American Psychologist, 54*, 462–479.

Bargh, J. A., K. McKenna, and G. M. Fitzsimons. 2002. Can you see the real me? Activation and expression of the "true self" on the Internet. *Journal of Social Issues, 58*, 33–48.

Baumeister, R. F. 1998. The self. In D. Gilbert, S. T. Fiske, and G. Lindzey (Eds.), *The Handbook of social psychology* (680–740). New York: Oxford Press.

Baumeister, R. F., and K. D. Vohs. 2003. Self-regulation and the executive function of the self. In M. R. Leary and J. P. Tangney (Eds.), *Handbook of self and identity.* New York: The Guilford Press.

Baumeister, R. F., J. D. Campbell, J. I. Krueger, and K. Vohs. 2003. Does high self-esteem cause better performance, interpersonal success, happiness or healthier lifestyles? *Psychological Science in the Public Interest, 4*, 1–44.

Bayer, C. L., and D. J. Cegala. 1992. Trait verbal aggressiveness and argumentativeness: Relations with parenting style. *Western Journal of Communication, 56*, 301–310.

Beatty, M. J., J. C. McCroskey, and A. D. Heisel. 1998. Communication apprehension as temperamental expression: A communibiological perspective. *Communication Monographs, 65*, 197–219.

Bell, R. A., and J. A. Daly. 1984. The affinity-seeking function of communication. *Communication Monographs, 49*, 91–115.

Berger, B. A., J. C. McCroskey, and V. A. Richmond. 1984. Communication apprehension and shyness. In W. N. Tinally and R. S. Beardsley (Eds.), *Communication in pharmacy practice: A practical guide for students and practitioners* (128–158). Philadelphia, PA: Lea & Febiger.

Berne, E. 1964. *Games people play.* New York: Grove.

Booth-Butterfield, M., and A. Andrighetti. 1993. *The role of affective orientation and nonverbal sensitivity in the interpretation of communication in acquaintance rape.* Paper presented at the annual convention of the Eastern Communication Association, New Haven, CT.

Booth-Butterfield, M., and S. Booth-Butterfield. 1990. Conceptualizing affect as information in communication production. *Human Communication Research, 16*, 451–476.

———. 1991. Individual differences in the communication of humorous messages. *Southern Communication Journal, 56*, 32–40.

———. 1994. The affective orientation to communication: Conceptual and empirical distinctions. *Communication Quarterly, 42*, 331–344.

———. 1996. Using your emotions: Improving the measurement of affective orientation. *Communication Research Reports, 13*, 157–163.

———. 1998. Emotionality and affective orientation (171–190). In McCroskey et al. (Eds.), *Communication and personality.* Cresskill, NJ: Hampton Press.

Booth-Butterfield, M., S. Booth-Butterfield, and M. B. Wanzer. 2006. Funny students cope better: Patterns of humor enactment and coping effectiveness. *Communication Quarterly.* (In Press)

Boster, F. J., and T. Levine. 1988. Individual differences and compliance-gaining message selection: The effects of verbal aggressiveness, argumentativeness, dogmatism, and negativism. *Communication Research Reports, 5*, 114–119.

Bowlby, J. 1969. *Attachment and loss: Vol. 1. Attachment.* New York: Basic Books.

———. 1973. *Attachment and loss: Vol. 3. Loss, sadness, and depression.* New York: Basic Books.

Chory-Assad, R. M., and M. Paulsel. 2004. Classroom justice: Student aggression and resistance as reactions to perceived unfairness. *Communication Education, 53*, 253–273.

Cook, W. W., and D. M. Medley. 1954. Proposed hostility and pharisaic-virtue scales for the MMPI. *Journal of Applied Psychology, 38*, 414–418.

Cooley, C. H. 1902. *Human nature and the social order.* New York: Scribner's.

Daly, J. A. 2002. Personality and interpersonal communication. In Knapp and Daly (Eds.), *Handbook of interpersonal communication* (133–180). Thousand Oaks, CA: Sage Publications.

Daly, J. A. and A. M. Bippus. 1998. Personality and interpersonal communication: Issues and directions. In McCroskey et al. (Eds.), *Communication and personality* (1–40). Cresskill, NJ: Hampton Press.

Daly, J. A., V. P. Richmond, and S. Leth. 1979. Social communicative anxiety and the personnel selection process: Testing the similarity effect in selection decisions. *Human Communication Research, 6,* 18–32.

Darley, J. M., and R. H. Fazio. 1980. Expectancy confirmation processes arising in the social interaction sequence. *American Psychologist, 35,* 867–881.

Dolin, D., and M. Booth-Butterfield. 1993. Reach out and touch someone: Analysis of nonverbal comforting responses. *Communication Quarterly, 41,* 383–393.

Dye, L. 2004. Researchers design games to boost self-esteem. Retrieved on 12/20/2006 from *abcnews.go.com/Technology/print?id.*

Epstein, S. 1973. The self-concept revisited: Or a theory of a theory. *American Psychologist, 28,* 404–416.

Felson, R. B. 1989. Parents and reflected appraisal process: A longitudinal analysis. *Journal of Personality and Social Psychology, 56,* 965–971.

Festinger, L. 1954. A theory of social comparison processes. *Human Relations, 7,* 117–140.

Finkel, E. J., and W. K. Campbell. 2001. Self-control and accommodation in close relationships: An interdependence analysis. *Journal of Personality and Social Psychology, 81,* 263–271.

Fitzpatrick, M. A. 1988. *Between husbands and wives: Communication in marriage.* Newbury Park, CA: Sage.

Goffman, E. 1959. *The presentation of self in everyday life.* Garden City, NY: Doubleday.

Gottman, J. M. 1999. *The marriage clinic: A scientific based marital therapy.* New York: Norton.

Greenwald, A. G., and S. J. Breckler. 1985. To whom is the self presented? In B. R. Schlenker (Ed.), *The self and social life* (126–145). New York: McGraw-Hill.

Guilford, J. P. 1959. *Personality.* New York: McGraw-Hill.

Harris, T. 1969. *I'm OK, you're OK.* New York: Harper & Row.

Honeycutt, J., and R. Brown. 1998. Did you hear the one about?: Typological and spousal differences in the planning of jokes and sense of humor in marriage. *Communication Quarterly, 46,* 342–352.

Houck, G. M., and A. M. Spegman. 1999. The development of self: Theoretical understandings and conceptual underpinnings. *Infants and Young Children, 12,* 1–16.

Huebner, D. M., C. J. Nemeroff, and M. C. Davis. 2005. Do hostility and neuroticism confound associations between perceived discrimination and depressive symptoms? *Journal of Social and Clinical Psychology, 24,* 723–740.

Infante, D. A. 1981. Trait argumentativeness as a predictor of communicative behavior in situations requiring argument. *Central States Speech Journal, 32,* 265–272.

———. 1985. Inducing women to be more argumentative: Source credibility effects. *Journal of Applied Communication Research, 13,* 33–44.

———. 1987. Aggressiveness. In J. C. McCroskey and J. A. Daly (Eds.), *Personality and interpersonal communication* (157–192). Newbury Park, CA: Sage.

———. 1988. *Arguing constructively.* Prospect Heights, Illinois: Waveland Press.

———. 1995. Teaching students to understand and control verbal aggression. *Communication Education, 44,* 51–63.

Infante, D. A., and W. I. Gorden. 1987. Superior and subordinate communication profiles: Implications for independent-mindedness and upward effectiveness. *Central States Speech Journal, 38,* 73–80.

———. 1989. Argumentativeness and affirming communicator style as predictors of satisfaction/dissatisfaction with subordinates. *Communication Quarterly, 37,* 81–90.

———. 1991. How employees see the boss: Test of an argumentative and affirming model of superiors' communicative behavior. *Western Journal of Speech Communication, 55,* 294–304.

Infante, D. A., and A. S. Rancer. 1982. A conceptualization and measure of argumentativeness. *Journal of Personality Assessment, 46,* 72–80.

Infante, D. A., B. L. Riddle, C. L. Horvath, and S. A. Tumlin. 1992. Verbal aggressiveness: Messages and reasons. *Communication Quarterly, 40,* 116–126.

Infante, D. A., and C. J. Wigley. 1986. Verbal aggressiveness: An interpersonal model and measure. *Communication Monographs, 53,* 61–69.

Infante, D. A., T. A. Chandler, and J. E. Rudd. 1989. Test of an argumentative skill deficiency model of interspousal violence. *Communication Monographs, 56,* 163–177.

Jung, C. G. 1953. *Psychological reflections.* New York: Harper and Row.

Karney, B. R., and T. N. Bradbury. 1995. The longitudinal course of marital quality and stability: A review of theory, methods, and research. *Psychological Bulletin, 118,* 3–34.

Kazoleas, D. 1993. The impact of argumentativeness on resistance to persuasion. *Human Communication Research, 20*, 118–137.

Keating, C. 1984. *Dealing with difficult people: How you can come out on top in personality conflicts.* New York: Paulist Press.

Koch, E. J., and J. A. Shepperd. 2004. Is self-complexity linked to better coping? A review of the literature. *Journal of Personality, 72*, 727–760.

Kopper, B. A., and D. L. Epperson. 1996. The experience and expression of anger: Relationships with gender, role socialization, depression and mental health functioning. *Journal of Counseling Psychology, 43*, 158–165.

Lieberman, A. F. 1977. Preschooler's competence with a peer: Relations with attachment and peer experience. *Child Development, 48*, 1277–1287.

Lieberman, A. F., and J. H. Pawl. 1988. Clinical applications of attachment theory. In J. Belsky and T. Nezworski (Eds.), *Clinical implications of attachment* (327–351). Hillsdale, NJ: Erlbaum.

Limon, S. M., and B. H. LaFrance. 2005. Communication traits and leadership emergence: Examining the impact of argumentativeness, communication apprehension and verbal aggressiveness in work groups. *Southern Communication Journal, 70*, 123–133.

Linville, P. W. 1985. Self-complexity and affective extremity: Don't put all your eggs in one cognitive basket. *Social Cognition, 3*, 94–120.

———. 1987. Self-complexity as a cognitive buffer against stress-related illness and depression. *Journal of Personality and Social Psychology, 52*, 663–676.

Lippert, L. R., B. S. Titsworth, and S. K. Hunt. 2005. The ecology of academic risk: Relationships between communication apprehension, verbal aggression, supportive communication, and students' academic risk. *Communication Studies, 56*, 1–21.

Markus, H., and E. Wurf. 1987. The dynamic self-concept: A social psychological perspective. *Annual Review of Psychology, 38*, 299–337.

Maxwell, J. C. 2002. *The seventeen essential qualities of a team player.* Nashville, TN: Thomas Nelson Publishers.

McCroskey, J. C. 1977. Oral communication apprehension: A summary of recent theory and research. *Human Communication Research, 4*, 78–96.

———. 1978. Validity of the PRCA as an index of oral communication apprehension. *Communication Monographs, 45*, 192–203.

McCroskey, J. C. 2006. Personal communication with the author.

McCroskey, J. C., and M. J. Beatty. 1984. Communication apprehension and accumulated communication state anxiety experiences: A research note. *Communication Monographs, 51*, 79–84.

McCroskey, J. C., J. A. Daly, and G. A. Sorensen. 1976. Personality correlates of communication apprehension. *Human Communication Research, 2*, 376–380.

———. 1995. Correlates of compulsive communication: Quantitative and qualitative characteristics. *Communication Quarterly, 43*, 39–52.

———. 1998. Willingness to communicate. In McCroskey et al. (Eds.), *Communication and personality* (119–132). Cresskill, NJ: Hampton Press.

McCroskey, J. C., and V. P. Richmond. 1987. Willingness to communicate. In J. C. McCroskey and J. A. Daly (Eds.), *Personality and interpersonal communication* (129–156). Newbury Park, CA: Sage.

McKenna, K. Y. A., A. S. Green, and M. E. J. Gleason. 2002. Relationship formation on the Internet: What's the big attraction? *Journal of Social Issues, 58*, 9–31.

Mead, G. H. 1934. *Mind, self, and society.* Chicago: University of Chicago Press.

Meeus, W., and M. Dekovic. 1995. Identity development, parental and peer support in adolescence: Results of a national Dutch survey. *Adolescence, 30*, 931–945.

Mizco, N. 2004. Humor ability, unwillingness to communicate, loneliness, and perceived stress: Testing a security theory. *Communication Studies, 55*, 209–226.

Myers, S. A., and A. D. Johnson. 2003. Verbal aggression and liking in interpersonal relationships. *Communication Research Reports, 20*, 90–96.

Noar, S. M., P. J. Morokoff, and C. A. Redding. 2002. Sexual assertiveness in heterosexually active men: A test of three samples. *AIDS Education and Prevention, 14*, 330–342.

Park, K. A., and E. Waters. 1988. Traits and relationships in developmental perspective. In S. Duck (Ed.) *Handbook of personal relationships: Theory, research, and interventions* (161–176). Chichester: John Wiley & Sons Ltd.

Peluso, P. R., J. P. Peluso, J. F. White, and R. M. Kern. 2004. A comparison of attachment theory and individual psychology: A review of the literature. *Journal of Counseling and Development, 82*, 139–145.

Pope, M. K., T. W. Smith, and F. Rhodewalt. 1990. Cognitive, behavioral and affective correlates of the Cook and Medley Hostility Scale. *Journal of Personality Assessment, 54*, 501–514.

Rancer, A. S. 1998. Argumentativeness. In McCroskey et al. (Eds.), *Communication and personality* (149–170). Cresskill, NJ: Hampton Press.

Richmond, V. P., and D. K. Roach. 1992. Willingness to communicate and employee success in U.S. organizations. *Journal of Applied Communication*, 95–115.

Richmond, V. P., and J. C. McCroskey. 1990. Reliability and separation of factors on the assertiveness-responsiveness measure. *Psychological Reports*, 67, 449–450.

Richmond, V. P., and M. M. Martin. 1998. Sociocommunicative style and sociocommunicative orientation. In McCroskey et al. (Eds.), *Communication and personality*. Hampton Press: Cresskill, NJ.

Rizzo, B., M. B. Wanzer, and M. Booth-Butterfield. 1999. Individual differences in managers' use of humor: Subordinate perceptions of managers' humor orientation, effectiveness, and humor behaviors. *Communication Research Reports*, 16, 370–376.

Rogge, R. D., T. N. Bradbury, K. Halweg, J. Engl, and F. Thurmaier. 2006. Predicting marital distress and dissolution: Refining the two-factor hypothesis. *Journal of Family Psychology*, 20, 156–159.

Schlenker, B. 1984. Identities, identifications and relationships. In V. Derlega (Ed.), *Communication, intimacy and close relationships*. New York: Academic Press.

———. 1985. Identity and self-identification. In B. R. Schlenker (Ed.), *The self and social life* (65–99). New York: McGraw-Hill.

Self-Improvement. (n.d.). Retrieved September 29, 2005, from *http://www.mygoals.com/content/self-improvement.html*.

Shackelford, T. K. 2001. Self-esteem in marriage. *Personality and Individual Differences*, 30, 371–391.

Smith, T. W. 1994. Concepts and methods in the study of anger, hostility, and health. In A. W. Siegman and T. W. Smith (Eds.), *Anger, hostility, and the heart* (23–42). Hillsdale, NJ: Erlbaum.

Snyder, M., E. D. Tanke, and E. Berscheid. 1977. Social perception and interpersonal behavior: The self-fulfilling nature of social stereotypes. *Journal of Personality and Social Psychology*, 35, 656–666.

Spitzberg, B. H. and W. R. Cupach. 1984. *Interpersonal communication competence.* Newbury Park, CA: Sage.

Sroufe, L. A. 1988. The role of infant-caregiver attachment in development. In J. Belsky and T. Nezworski (Eds.), *Clinical implications of attachment* (18–38). Hillsdale, NJ: Erlbaum.

Surra, C. A., C. R. Gray, N. Cottle, and T. M. Boettcher. 2004. Research on mate selection and premarital relationships: What do we really know? In A. L. Vangelisti (Ed.), *Handbook of family communication* (53–82). Mahwah, NJ: Lawrence Erlbaum.

Swann, W. R. 1985. The self as architect of social reality. In B. R. Schlenker (Ed.), *The self and social life* (100–126). New York: McGraw-Hill.

Tesser, A. 2003. Self-evaluation. In M. R. Leary and J. P. Tangney (Eds.), *Handbook of self and identity.* New York: The Guilford Press.

Tesser A., J. V. Wood, and D. A. Stapel. 2002. Introduction: An emphasis on motivation. In A. Tesser, D. A. Stapel, and J. V. Wood (Eds.), *Self and motivation: Emerging psychological perspectives* (3–11). Washington, DC: American Psychological Association.

Tesser, A., R. B. Felson, and J. M. Suls (Eds.). 2000. *Psychological perspectives on self and identity.* Washington, DC: American Psychological Association.

Vallacher, R. R., and A. Nowak. 2000. Landscapes of self-reflection: Mapping the peaks and valleys of personal assessment. In A. Tesser, R. B. Felson, and J. M. Suls (Eds.), *Psychological perspectives on self and identity* (35–65). Washington, DC: American Psychological Association.

Wanzer, M. B., and A. B. Frymier. 1999. The relationship between student perceptions of instructor humor and student's reports of learning. *Communication Education*, 48, 48–62.

Wanzer, M. B., M. Booth-Butterfield, and S. Booth-Butterfield. 1995. The funny people: A source orientation to the communication of humor. *Communication Quarterly*, 43, 142–154.

———. 1996. Are funny people popular? An examination of humor orientation, verbal aggressiveness, and social attraction. *Communication Quarterly*, 44, 42–52.

———. 2005. "If we didn't use humor, we'd cry:" Humorous coping communication in health care settings. *Journal of Health Communication*, 10, 105–125.

Wigley, C. J. 1998. Verbal aggressiveness. In McCroskey et al. (Eds.), *Communication and personality* (191–214). Cresskill, NJ: Hampton Press.

Wood, J. T. 2001. *Interpersonal communication: Everyday encounters. (3rd ed.)* Belmont, CA: Wadsworth Publishing Company.

Zajonc, R. B., R. K. Adelmann, S. B. Murphy, and R. N. Niedenthal. 1987. Convergence in the appearance of spouses. *Motivation and Emotion*, 11, 335–346.

Zakahi, W. R., and R. L. Duran. 1985. Loneliness, communication competence, and communication apprehension: Extension and replication. *Communication Quarterly*, 33, 50–60.

Verbal Communication
Words of Wisdom

© PhotoCreate, 2007, Shutterstock.

OBJECTIVES

- Define verbal communication
- Understand the characteristics of verbal communication
- Distinguish between connotative and denotative meaning
- Differentiate between relational and content levels of meaning
- Explain the difference between constitutive and regulative rules
- Describe the four functions of verbal communication
- Explain the Sapir-Whorf hypothesis
- Explore how uncertainty reduction is associated with verbal communication
- Discuss the difference between direct and indirect verbal communication styles
- Clarify the difference between informal and formal messages
- Distinguish between powerful and powerless language
- Provide examples of sexist language in our culture
- Define hate speech
- Understand verbal immediacy and how it contributes to confirming or disconfirming messages
- Identify how the life span factor impacts verbal communication
- Recognize gender differences in verbal communication
- Recall three verbal communication "Best Practices"

KEY TERMS

verbal communication	content level of meaning	clarity
rules	context	equivocation
constitutive rules	jargon	powerful language
regulative rules	cognitive function	powerless language
symbols	Uncertainty Reduction Theory	credibility
—concrete	self-disclosure	competence
—abstract	linguistic determinism	character
semantics	linguistic relativity	goodwill
denotative meaning	Sapir-Whorf hypothesis	status
connotative meaning	direct/indirect	sexist language
subjective	formal/informal	hate speech
relationship level of meaning		immediacy
		verbal immediacy

OVERVIEW

Like a drug, the words we use in our interpersonal interactions can alter and influence relationships. Depending on our goals,

> *Words are, of course, the most powerful drug used by mankind . . .*
> —Rudyard Kipling

verbal communication can be used to enhance our relationships or to destroy them. We have the power to make others feel competent, attractive, and strong. On the other hand, we know how to upset and annoy others, and to make them feel weak. This chapter discusses how the words we use impact our interpersonal relationships.

We begin by defining verbal communication and examining several of its distinct features and functions. We continue by examining factors that impact our verbal communication and how it is perceived by others.

DEFINING VERBAL COMMUNICATION

Verbal communication refers to the words we use during the communication process. We use words strategically to relate to the outside world and to create meaning. Have you ever played the game charades and attempted to convey a message to others without using words? Have you ever tried to communicate with someone who did not speak your language? These two examples illustrate how difficult it can be to express ourselves without relying on verbal communication. The words we use have a strong impact on our interpersonal relationships. What we say initially often determines whether we will have future interactions with others. There are four key characteristics of verbal communication. These include: rules, symbols, subjectivity, and context.

Rules

It is important to realize that there are certain rules we must follow when using language. **Rules** are agreed upon and provide a structure for what is socially acceptable communication in our culture. You follow certain rules when talking with your friends that are quite different than when you talk with your grandparents. There are two basic types of rules that relate to verbal communication: constitutive and regulative (Cronen, Pearce, and Snavely 1979; Pearce, Cronen and Conklin 1979). **Constitutive rules** help define communication by identifying appropriate words and behaviors. For example, how do you show respect in a classroom? Students follow constitutive rules in the classroom when they address their professors formally, using

© digitalskillet, 2007, Shutterstock.

What constitutive rules do parents and children have for communicating mutual respect?

What regulative rules do you practice in the classroom?

© Lorraine Swanson, 2007, Shutterstock.

Dr., Mr., or Mrs. Constitutive rules are also in effect when students avoid using slang or swear words. Failure to understand appropriate rules can be detrimental to a student's success as an appropriate and effective interpersonal communicator. Can you think of the constitutive rules you would follow during a business interview?

Regulative rules control our communication by managing communication interaction. Who are we supposed to talk with and how should we speak to this person? What topics are acceptable? For how long should we talk? Think about the regulative rules in the classroom. Students greet each other when they enter the classroom, they do not interrupt the professor, and they take turns speaking. These rules are context-bound, that is to say, the rules will change depending on the audience and context. Our verbal communication is governed by constitutive and regulative rules and through language structure. This makes it possible for us to create shared meaning and have a common understanding of appropriateness across contexts.

Symbols

A second feature of verbal communication is that it is symbolic. **Symbols** are socially agreed upon representations of phenomena and range between being concrete and abstract. **Concrete symbols** are more likely to resemble what they represent. **Abstract symbols** are arbitrary and nonrepresentational. For example, a chair is used to sit on and is a concrete symbol. However, the printed word "chair" is abstract and arbitrary. The more concrete (and therefore less abstract) a symbol is, the more it is associated with its meaning. Verbal communication is made up of abstract, arbitrary, and agreed upon concrete symbols or words.

It is difficult to discuss symbols without discussing **semantics,** or the meaning, we attribute to each word or symbol. When people interpret words they focus on both the denotative and connotative meanings. The **denotative meaning** refers to the universal meaning of the word, or the definition you would find in the dictionary. The **connotative meaning** refers to the personal meaning that the source has with that word. For example, the word "fireplace" connotes hospitality and warmth. Connotative meanings are difficult to explain because they can be different for everyone. This leads us to the third characteristic of verbal communication, subjectivity.

Subjectivity

Because everyone has a unique worldview, the way we use and interpret verbal communication is strongly influenced by individual biases. Verbal communication is **subjective** because we interpret the world through our own experiences, historical perspective and cultural upbringing, our physical environment, and the socio-emotional nature of relationships. Our perceptions are distinct and limited to our own personal field of experience and developed schema.

The subjective meanings we place on our verbal communication have relationship and content levels of meaning. The **relationship level of meaning** is highly sensitive to the people involved in the conversation and the process of communicating, whereas the **content level of meaning** is primarily related to the topic at hand.

Consider the following conversation:

Samantha: Do you want to come to my mom's birthday party?

Edgar: Well, it is in an hour and I am in the middle of working on the house.

Samantha: So, you don't want to come?

Edgar: Well, the contractor is coming tomorrow so I have to get this done.

Samantha: You missed my sister's birthday party, also. I am starting to think you just don't want to spend time with my family.

Edgar: That is not true. I just have to get this work done.

Samantha: I cannot believe you are going to miss the birthday party.

Edgar: Do you want me to drop everything and come?

Samantha: I shouldn't have to tell you what to do; you should know what the right thing to do is.

Edgar: I am sorry, but I have to finish this project before the contractor comes.

The conversation above illustrates a common problem in interpersonal relationships: one party is focused on the content level of meaning and the other is interested in the relationship level of meaning. Edgar is focused on the content or the information in the message, while Samantha is concerned with how the communication process is affecting the relationship. Edgar is determined to finish working on the house and cannot understand why Samantha would be upset. Samantha feels Edgar is not really listening to what she is saying and does not understand. The content level of meaning is found in the words we use and the relationship level of meaning is often interpreted through our nonverbal behaviors, through how something is said. Because of Edgar's past behavior and concern for the house, Samantha perceived his nonverbal behavior as insincere. Edgar, however, heard Samantha complaining about not going to the birthday party and offered a valid reason for not attending. When one individual is relying on content level of meaning and the other is focused on the relationship level of meaning, often a source of conflict is the result. Overall, verbal communication is widely subjective and a function of our personal associations and the meanings we place on words, situations, and experiences. In order to improve our communication with others, it is important to seek clarification of ambiguous messages, identify areas of miscommunication, and talk about ways to improve communication. Relationship partners need to engage in productive metacommunication, which means that they need to talk in greater detail about both the quality and quantity of messages exchanged.

Context

The final feature of verbal communication is the contextual framework. The **context** refers to the environment, situation, or setting in which we use verbal communication. The context may influence the interpretation, meaning and appropriateness of the communication. For example, we may use a particular greeting with our roommates such as, "What's up?", while we may choose alternative words when we are greeting our grandparents, such as "Good morning, Grandfather!" The interpretation of our words changes when we consider the context in which they are used. In the last section of this textbook, we will review five general contexts in which interpersonal communication occurs. These are: intercultural communication, family communication, organizational communication, health communication, and computer-mediated communication.

In the following section of this chapter we review three specific examples in which researchers have focused on the context of the verbal communication to better understand our overall communication behaviors. These contexts include: African American English or Ebonics, organizational jargon, and communicating affection.

The dialect known as Black English, or Ebonics, developed within the African American community. Robert Williams coined the term Ebonics by merging the words "ebony" and "phonics" in his 1975 book *Ebonics: The True Language of Black Folks.* The term was not widely known until 1996 when the Oakland Unified School District in California recognized the legitimacy of Ebonics, or African American English (AEE), starting a media frenzy (Weldon 2000). Weldon argues that dialects are socially constructed linguistic systems that are rule-governed and natural. Dialects are neither inferior, nor genetically constructed, rather, they are socially determined. Although the linguistic system Ebonics is well-defined and sound, individuals often place prejudices, biases, and value on this particular dialect. Although it is dismissed by some as "bad English," Ebonics has a well-documented and rich cultural and historical background (see Rickford 1999; 2000; Dillard 1972).

A person who doesn't work in the lab would have a difficult time understanding the scientists' jargon.

© Laurence Gough, 2007, Shutterstock.

Jargon is defined as a specialized vocabulary that is socially constructed and regularly used by members of a particular trade, profession, or organization. Jargon will differ greatly in different organizations and workplaces. Oftentimes jargon is used in technical and scientific fields to refer to concepts and terms in a universal manner. One category of jargon is the development of acronyms/abbreviations. Members of the military may use jargon such as MRE's, PCD's, MEO, and CDC when communicating with each other. What is the purpose or function of jargon? These verbal shortcuts can enhance communication by increasing precision and speed during social interaction (Hirst 2003). This specialized language may be abused when individuals use it with receivers who are not familiar with the vocabulary, and the speaker may be perceived as being pretentious (Nash 1993). For example, most of us prefer our health care providers to communicate clearly with us, avoiding the use of jargon and technical language. Organizational jargon or "shop talk" is contextually bound and may be considered rude or pretentious when communicating with individuals outside of the organization.

Another example of contextually bound verbal communication is expressing affection. Many of us reserve special terms for our most intimate relationships. Consider the last time you told someone "I love you." You may have contemplated these three little words for quite a while before actually saying them. That is because these few words have large implications. These expressions of affection often initiate or accelerate relational development (Floyd 1997). We often save particular words or phrases for special individuals that impact or influence us. Communicating affection is risky. When the receiver is not on the same page as the sender, the communicative attempt may have a negative outcome. It is important that the sender consider the trust level, reciprocity, and future interactions, as well as the length of the relationship. If the receiver does not feel the same way, he may feel manipulated or perceive the sender as imposing confusing relational boundaries (Ebert and Floyd 2004). Once again, our verbal communication is bound by the context of the situation.

Now that we have defined verbal communication and provided its features, we can discuss the functions verbal communication serves.

FUNCTIONS OF VERBAL COMMUNICATION

There are four functions that help explain how we use our verbal communication. They are: cognitive function, social reality function, group identity function and social change function. Each is discussed below.

Cognitive Functions

The **cognitive function** of verbal communication can be defined as how we use language to acquire knowledge, to reason, and to make sense of the world. The cognitive function of verbal communication maintains a strong connection with culture. The culture we are raised within greatly influences how we use language. Growing up in a small town versus a large city or as part of a quiet family versus a loud family, or being raised in the South versus the North will influence the type of language we use.

We use verbal communication to acquire information. One way we acquire information about our interpersonal relationships is through uncertainty reduction.

Charles Berger proposed that the main purpose of verbal communication is to "make sense" out of our interpersonal world (as cited in Griffin 2003). Berger developed **Uncertainty Reduction Theory,** which suggests that human communication is used to gain knowledge and create understanding by reducing uncertainty and, therefore, increasing predictability. The more we ask questions and learn about someone new, the more we are reducing our uncertainty about him. For example, when we are first introduced to people, there are high levels of uncertainty. We may ask ourselves: Who is this person? Where are they from? Are they like me? Consider the last time you met someone new. Chances are the conversation went something like the one found below.

> **James:** Hi, I'm James. What is your name?
>
> **Erica:** My name is Erica. Where are you from?
>
> **James:** I'm from New York, and you?
>
> **Erica:** I am from Florida, but I am here studying communication.
>
> **James:** That is my major also. Are you interested in broadcasting?
>
> **Erica:** No, I am studying communication studies. I am interested in going to law school.

This example demonstrates how we use verbal communication to acquire knowledge through uncertainty reduction. Through the process of **self-disclosure,** or purposefully revealing personal information about ourselves, we are able to decrease the ambiguity of a situation. This is an example of how our verbal communication serves the cognitive function of acquiring knowledge and making sense out of the world. We will examine the concept of self-disclosure and its role in relationship initiation more closely in Chapter Six.

Social Reality Function

"The language used in everyday life continuously provides me with the necessary objectifications and posits the order within which these make sense and within which everyday life has meaning for me. I live in a place that is geographically designated; I employ tools from can openers to sports cars which are designated in the technical vocabulary of my society; I live within a web of human relationships from my chess club to the United States of America which are also ordered by means of vocabulary. In this manner, language marks the co-ordinates of my life in society and fills that life with meaningful objects." (Peter L. Berger. The Social Construction of Reality. New York: Doubleday, 1966, p. 22.).

In this quote from *The Social Construction of Reality*, the authors suggest that reality is socially constructed through our language and vocabulary. In other words, what appears to be real in society is socially agreed upon through our communication with others. Consider the words that have evolved in the U.S. culture across previous decades. In the 1970s, the terms "Watergate," "test-tube baby," and "Rubik's cube" became words which were widely understood by members of the U.S. because of events or products that had been introduced during that time period. Similarly, the words "AIDS" and "compact disc" were added to dictionaries in the 1980s. As the reality of the culture evolved, new words were created to explain and describe the changing society. Thus, our verbal communication serves to create our social reality.

Two American linguists, Edward Sapir and Benjamin Lee Whorf, were interested in how humans used language as a tool to make sense of the world. They developed the concept of **linguistic determinism,** which suggests that "language *determines* thought" (Whorf 1956; Sapir 1956). Although this groundbreaking and extreme perspective has few supporters today, many do share the belief that thought *influences* language. Sapir and Whorf also conceptualized **linguistic relativity,** which states that distinctions encoded in one language are unique to that language alone, and that "there is no limit to the structural diversity of languages" (Whorf 1956; Sapir 1956). By comparing the vocabulary of Inuit and Aztec peoples they found that the Inuit have many different words for "snow." There are different words for falling snow, powdery snow, slushy snow, packing snow, and icy snow, and there are even more. On the other hand, in Aztec there is only one word for snow, one word for cold, and one word for ice. In addition, Sapir and Whorf were fascinated by the fact that the Hopi language did not distinguish between past, present, and future time. Time is not considered multidimensional in their culture, whereas time is a fundamentally critical concept in Western society. Think about how we use time in such fields as physics and engineering. Also, our culture is embedded with daily planners, calendars, and appointments that rely heavily on our shared meaning of time. The **Sapir-Whorf hypothesis** suggests that the language we learn, as well as the culture we are exposed to, is used to shape our entire reality.

Group Identity Function

Another function of verbal communication is to serve as a symbol of group solidarity. Because we have similarities in language at work, in our family, and throughout our interpersonal relationships, verbal communication provides an identity function. Think about the cliques that were formed in high school. There were students who played in the band, athletes, theater members, and student council members. Students often describe and define themselves based on their affiliations or social groups. Within the different groups, shared "codes" develop that only members understand. These codes may be in the form of inside jokes, nicknames, abbreviations, or other specialized vocabulary. Their purpose is to form a sense of group identity. In other words, this function of verbal communication serves to distinguish one group from others and to provide a sense of similarity for its members.

Families can be considered a type of group. Think about your family. Are there inside jokes that get repeated over and over? You may hear something like, "Remember the time that Mom made Julie walk across the kitchen to get an apple, because she did not believe she had a broken leg? Or the time Shawn lied to Mom and Dad about that 'hit and run' so he could get a new bike?" We choose to let others "in" on the joke when we allow new members to enter into the group. From outside the group, non-members may interpret the stories, jokes, and nicknames as inappropriate, inconsiderate and not humorous. However, group members who use verbal communication for this function feel a sense of belonging. Verbal communication that is used to form group identity is used to maintain the group's rituals and celebrate the history of the group.

This boy may describe himself as a baseball player because of his group identity.

Social Change Function

Language can "imprison us" or it can "set us free." This is how Ting-Toomey and Chung (2005) describe the social change function of language. In other words, language can inhibit our abilities to perceive the world in unique ways or it can dynamically change habits and prejudices. We often try to avoid offending others by using politically correct language. Political correctness stems from the convergence of several factors, three of which are the Sapir-Whorf hypothesis, the Civil Rights Movement, and language reform. The Sapir-Whorf hypothesis provided a theoretical framework that suggested language can be used to attempt social change and influence reality. In addition, the feminist and racial equality movements altered our language system by eliminating gender-based and racial-based terms from our vocabulary. It is suggested that a more sensitive language will reflect a more caring society.

The Global Language Monitor (GLM) is a San Diego-based company that tracks and analyzes trends in the English language. The GLM staff monitors the evolution and demise of language, word usage, word choices, and their impact on the various aspects of culture. GLM suggests that the September 11 attacks on America have changed forever the way we speak and interpret various words. Currently, they suggest, the numbers 9/11 are the official shorthand for the 2001 terrorist attacks and *ground-zero* stirs up thoughts of a sacred burial ground where the twin towers once stood. Also since the attacks, the word *hero* includes police, firefighters, EMTs, and any type of first responders who place their lives on the line for the public good. See table 3.1 for the Top Ten Words of 2005 reported by the GLM.

Table 3.1
Table 3.1   Verbal Communication: How Have These Words Influenced Your Meaning?

Global Language Monitor: The Top Ten Words of 2005

1. Refugee: Though the word was considered politically incorrect in the US, 'refugees' were often considered the lucky ones in streaming away from a series of global catastrophes unmatched in recent memory.
2. Tsunami: From the Japanese *tsu nami* for 'harbor wave,' few recognized the word before disaster struck on Christmas Day, 2004, but the word subsequently flooded media coverage.
3. Poppa/Papa/Pope: (Italian, Portuguese, English, many others). The death of beloved Pope John Paul II kept the words on the lips of the faithful around the world.
4. Chinglish: The new second language of China from the Chinglish formation: CHINese + EngLISH.
5. H5N1: A looming global pandemic that could dwarf the Bubonic Plague of the Middle Ages (and AIDS) boggles the contemporary imagination.
6. Recaille: A quick trip around the Romance languages (French jargon, *scum;* Spanish, *rabble* or *swine;* Italian, *worthless dregs*) illustrates the full freight of the word used to describe youthful French rioters of North African and Muslim descent.
7. Katrina: Name will become synonymous with natural forces responsible for the total and utter destruction of a city.
8. Wiki: Internet buzzword (from the Hawaiian *wiki wiki* for 'quick, quick') that describes collaboration software where anyone can contribute to the ongoing effort.
9. SMS: Short Message Service. The world's youth sent over a trillion text messages in 2005. Currently being texted are full-length novels, news, private messages and everything in between.
10. Insurgent: Politically neutral term used to describe enemy combatants.

*"Global Language Monitor: The Top Ten Words of 2005" from *Global Language Monitor*, www.languagemonitor.com, © 2006. Used by permission.

Now that we have explored the cognitive, social reality, group identity, and social change functions of verbal communication, we turn our attention to the different types of verbal communication styles.

VERBAL COMMUNICATION STYLES

Everyone has his own unique style of communicating. In this section, we have designated four common verbal communication styles. They have been labeled: direct-indirect, informal-formal, clarity-equivocality, and powerful-powerless. There are a number of different strengths and weaknesses associated with each of these verbal communication styles. These individual differences exist on a continuum and are not to be viewed as dichotomous groups. In other words, you will not necessarily be "one or the other" but you may be closer to one end of the spectrum than the other. While most people place themselves in the middle of the spectrum, you may be more likely to describe yourself as using a particular verbal style more consistently.

Direct/Indirect

Direct communication style explicitly verbalizes inquiries and comments in a straightforward manner, while the **indirect** communication style relies on a more roundabout or subtle method of communicating. Individuals who rely on indirect communication often use nonverbal communication such as facial expressions and eye contact, more often than verbal communication to convey a message.

What strategy do you think he is using to end this relationship?

© Liv friis-larsen, 2007, Shutterstock.

Leslie Baxter refers to the extent to which individuals are direct and indirect in her theory of relationship dissolution. She suggests individuals have different styles when it comes to ending relationships. Withdrawing, being annoying or hurtful, or suggesting "being friends" would be considered indirect strategies. But an individual may rely on direct strategies to end a relationship. A simple statement that "It is over" or a fight where each partner blames the other would be examples of direct strategies. Baxter suggests that apprehensive people are more likely to use indirect strategies (as cited in Littlejohn 1992). It is important to point out that individuals will often intentionally choose a more indirect communication style over a direct style to save face for the receiver. Picture yourself at a boring party. Instead of telling the host you are bored and are ready to leave, you may engage in a more subtle approach. Perhaps you start to yawn and hint that you did not get much sleep last night. Engaging in an indirect communication style is sometimes more considerate than expressing your true feelings directly.

Indirect
(subtle)   →←   Direct
(straightforward)

Informal/Formal

The formality of a communicated message refers to the extent to which it is official and proper. A **formal** style of communicating is typically used when you are communicating with someone of higher power, such as a parent, grandparent, teacher, boss, or health professional. It is used to show respect. **Informal** communication refers to using a relaxed, casual, and familiar verbal communication style. This is typically used with your peers and co-workers.

© Suhendri Utet, 2007, Shutterstock.

Informal communicative styles are most often used when speaking with peers and co-workers.

Choosing between informal or formal communicative styles can be tricky in intercultural situations. People who live in the United States, Canada, Australia, and Scandinavia tend to be more informal in their communication styles, whereas people of Asian and African cultures tend to be more formal. Adler and Rodman (2006) suggest that there are different degrees of formality for speaking with old friends, acquaintances, and strangers. The ability to use language that acknowledges these differences is the mark of a learned person in countries like South Korea. Whenever you are uncertain about a situation, it is better to be formal than informal, since most cultures value formality. Adopting a more formal communication style will demonstrate respect on your part.

Informal
(casual)   →←   Formal
(proper)

Clarity/Equivocation

Another aspect of verbal communication involves the extent to which you express yourself with clarity, as opposed to equivocality. While **clarity** refers to the simplistic, down-to-earth, and understandable nature of the communication, Bavelas and his colleagues (1990) define **equivocation** as "nonstraightforward communication . . . [that] appears ambiguous, contradictory, tangential, obscure, or even evasive" (28). In other words, equivocation involves communicating by choosing specific words that may not demonstrate the whole truth. Equivocation allows an individual the possibility to deny events after the fact. Former President Bill Clinton denied having "sexual relations" with Monica Lewinsky. Later, Clinton stated he interpreted the agreed upon definition of sexual relations to exclude his receiving oral sex. This example demonstrates how someone uses equivocation to protect themselves by intentionally not revealing the entire truth. However, like indirect communication, individuals may choose to act in an equivocal manner to protect someone else's feelings. For example, you may tell your date, "This lunch was very thoughtful," even though you have no intention of going on another date with this person. Be aware that sending mixed messages may lead to confusion and awkward discussions in the future.

Communicating in a clear manner obviously has many benefits. In the classroom, researchers found that students taught by teachers with a clear communication style learned more than those taught by teachers with a less clear communication style. Students reported less receiver apprehension, less fear of misinterpreting, and less fear of inadequately processing information. Finally, students indicated that they were more favorably disposed towards clear teachers and reported more positive affect for both the professor and the course material (Cheseboro 2003).

Clarity
(simple and
clear)

Equivocality
(ambiguous)

Powerful/Powerless Language

The final verbal communication style that we will discuss is the extent to which your language is powerful or powerless. In our society, **powerful language** is associated with positive attributes such as assertiveness and importance and it can be influential, commanding, and authoritative. Powerful language is a combination of using proper English, clear thoughts, organized ideas, and a persuasive structure. **Powerless language,** on the other hand, is associated with negative attributes such as shyness, introversion, timidity, nervousness, and apprehension. Avoiding linguistic features that suggest powerless language may positively impact the way we are interpreted. Types of powerless speech include hesitations, hedges, tag questions, polite forms, intensifiers, and disclaimers (see table 3.2).

Some researchers described powerless language as "feminine" or "women's language" (Lakoff 1973; 1974). In her work, Lakoff recognizes women's subordinate position in society by the language they use. She suggests women avoid powerless language if they want to move toward political and social equality. More recent research suggests that anyone who relies on powerless language, regardless of class or gender, should be aware of the judgments that might be attached (Rubin and Nelson 1983).

The use of powerful language has also been studied in the classroom. Haleta (1996) examined students' perceptions of teachers' use of powerful versus power-

Table 3.2	Powerless Language, Interpretation, and Examples	
Powerless Language	**Interpreted as**	**Example**
Hesitation	Uncertain, nervous, timid	*"I think . . . well, yeah . . . I saw someone take, errr, your notebook."*
Hedges	Less absolute, qualifying phrases	*"I guess that would be a good idea."*
Tag questions	Weak assertion, less absolute	*"That was a good idea, wasn't it?"*
Polite forms	Subordinate	*"Please pick up your dishes."*
Intensifiers	Unsuccessful attempt to make words sound stronger	*"It's really, really easy."*
Disclaimers	Diversion of responsibility, fault, truth	*"Remember, this is just what I heard . . ."*

Powerful ←——————————→ Powerless

less language. Findings suggest that students' initial perceptions of powerful teachers were significantly higher in perceptions of dynamism, status, and credibility than those teachers who used powerless language. Students' level of uncertainty was significantly higher with those teachers who used powerless language.

PERCEPTIONS AND VERBAL COMMUNICATION

Research has shown that we need to hear only ten to fifteen seconds of an individual's speech to form initial perceptions (Entwisle 1970). The next section is designed to give you some insight on some typical perceptions of verbal communication. First, we explore how language choices can impact perceptions of credibility and status. We then discuss types of communication considered biased. We also explore the concept of verbal immediacy as it relates to confirming and disconfirming messages. An overview of different types of message design logics is also included in this section.

Credibility and Status

We can demonstrate credibility in our interpersonal relationships through our verbal communication messages. **Credibility** or believability can be defined as having three dimensions: competence, character, and goodwill (McCroskey and Young 1981; McCroskey and Teven 1999). **Competence** refers to your knowledge or expertise, while **character** is the extent to which you are trustworthy. The third dimension, **goodwill,** refers to your ability to care or feel concerned.

Typically, we base our perceptions of credibility on the perceived status of an individual. **Status** refers to the level of position an individual has when compared with others. This may be social, socio-economic, and/or organizational status. In addition to nonverbal behavior, we can gain an understanding of credibility through an individual's verbal comments. The degree of formality, vocabulary, accent, rate of speech, fluency of language, and articulation all play a role in our perceptions of credibility and status. Our perceptions also affect our ability to listen. We tend to listen more attentively to persons of high status rather than to someone we perceive as having low status.

Bias Communication through Language

In the beginning of this chapter we said that the words we choose can be used to strengthen relationships or to destroy them. When we use biased, sexist, racist, and offensive language we are choosing to cause harm to others.

Recall the following riddle:

A doctor and a boy are fishing. The boy was the doctor's son, but the doctor was not the boy's father. Who was the doctor?

The answer is: The doctor is the boy's mother. The punch line of this riddle is relying on the fact that we would initially assume that the doctor was male. Researchers have agreed that sexist language ultimately reinforces a sexist community. **Sexist language** refers to any speech that is degrading to males or females. Most of the research examines how females are subordinate figures in the male-geared vocabulary, with words like chairman and fireman illustrating the masculine focus of our language structure. To avoid sexist language, researchers suggest using gender-neutral words. For instance, The National Council of Teachers of English (NCTE) suggests several guidelines (see table 3.3).

Table 3.3   Suggestions for Avoiding Sexist Language

National Council of Teachers of English Guidelines

Examples	Alternatives
mankind	humanity, people, human beings
man's achievements	human achievements
man-made	synthetic, manufactured, machine-made
the common man	the average person, ordinary people
man the stockroom	staff the stockroom
nine man-hours	nine staff-hours
chairman	coordinator, moderator, presiding officer, head,
businessman	business executive
fireman	firefighter
mailman	mail carrier
steward and stewardess	flight attendant
policeman/woman	police officer
congressman	congressional representative

EXAMPLE: Give each student his paper as soon as he is finished.
ALTERNATIVE: Give students their papers as soon as they are finished.
EXAMPLE: The average student is worried about his grade.
ALTERNATIVE: The average student is worried about grades.

Adapted from http://owl.english.purdue.edu/handouts/general/gl_nonsex.html.

Verbally attacking individuals on the basis of their race, ethnic background, religion, gender or sexual orientation is considered **hate speech** (Pember 2003). As with sexist language, hate speech is used to degrade others. Hate speech includes racist language or words that dehumanize individuals from a particular ethnicity. Anthony Hudson argues, "The use of language to achieve and or perpetuate the subordination of a group of people is well documented. Whether it be Jews in Nazi Germany, African Americans in the U.S., or slaves in Mauritania, language has been and continues to be a vital tool in the oppression and abuse of minority groups" (2003, 46).

We need to be aware that the words we choose to express ourselves with may have powerful implications. We all have a responsibility to have a zero tolerance for these types of speech acts. Bobbye Persing succinctly states, "Meanings are in people, not in words, and if certain words create negative images in the receivers, we should stop using these words. . . . If we deny the importance of words we are denying the very fiber of our stock . . . communication" (1977, 19).

VERBAL IMMEDIACY

It makes sense to say that we approach things we like and avoid things we do not. Albert Mehrabian and his colleagues used this approach-avoidance theory as a basis for the concept of immediacy in the late 1960s. Mehrabian describes **immediacy** as the process of using communication behaviors purposefully to reduce psychological and physical distance (1969). Researchers have found many benefits to engaging in immediacy behaviors, including increased perceptions of liking and attraction. Immediacy may be enacted verbally and nonverbally, but we will focus on the verbal features in this chapter.

Verbal immediacy refers to using specific word choices and syntactic structures to increase perceptions of psychological closeness. Something as simple as using words such as "we" and "our" are considered more immediate than "I" and "yours." Consider this the next time you confront your roommate about the apartment being cluttered. You might say, "We should clean this apartment before dinner. Our stuff is everywhere," instead of "You should clean the apartment. I cleaned last time."

Gorham (1988) examined verbal immediacy in the classroom. She suggests that instructors can gain a psychological closeness with their students and enhance their humanness by engaging in a variety of verbal immediacy behaviors such as using humor, self-disclosing, utilizing students' names and viewpoints throughout lecture, incorporating student suggestions into the course, and showing a willingness to work with students outside of the classroom. Teachers' use of verbally immediate messages was correlated with perceived cognitive and affective learning outcomes. Utilizing verbally immediate messages with friends, family members and co-workers has been proven to result in the benefits of both learning and the perceptions of liking and attraction.

One way to portray verbal immediacy is through confirming messages. Research suggests we discover and establish our identity through confirming

Table 3.4   Confirming Messages

Function of Confirming Message	Expresses	Example of Confirming Message	Outcome
To express recognition of the other's existence	*"To me, you exist."*	*"Certainly, that is upsetting."*	This recognizes and validates the speaker's feelings
To acknowledge a relationship of affiliation with the other	*"We are relating."*	*"Wow! That happened to me, too."*	This recognizes that you can relate to the speaker
To express awareness of the significance or worth of the other	*"To me, you are significant."*	*"What happened to you is terrible!"*	This suggests you are attentive to their situation
To accept or endorse the other's self-experience	*"Your way of interpreting the world is valid."*	*"Sure, I can see how you thought that."*	You are increasing perceptions of value and respect

messages in interpersonal relationships (Buber 1957). **Confirmation** is the process in which individuals feel recognized, acknowledged, valued, and respected (Laing 1961). Conversely, disconfirming messages communicate a sense of insignificance and worthlessness and act to invalidate the source (Watzlawick, Beavin, and Jackson 1967). Research in this area has found that our self-esteem is tied up in these confirming and disconfirming messages (Cissna and Keating 1979).

Cissna and Sieburg (1981) state that there are four functions of confirming messages: (1) to express recognition of the other's existence, (2) to acknowledge a relationship of affiliation with the other, (3) to express awareness of the significance or worth of the other, and (4) to accept or endorse the other's self-experience. In table 3.4 we have listed the four functions of confirming messages, stated what is being intrinsically expressed to the other person for each function, provided examples of how to verbalize the confirming messages in interpersonal relationships, and described possible outcomes of communicating in this manner.

Conversely, there are three groupings of disconfirming messages: indifference, imperviousness, and disqualification of the message or speaker. See table 3.5 for a complete list of types and examples of these messages. Be aware of the extent to which you may rely on these behaviors. It may be the cause of unsatisfying relationships and ineffective communicative patterns.

Message Design Logic (MDL)

Another way to portray verbal immediacy can be seen through our message design logics. In the late 1980s, Barbara O'Keefe linked cognitive complexity with communication and suggested people possess their own personal implicit theories of communication. There are three theories, known as **message design logics,** which individuals use to interpret how communication works (O'Keefe 1988). The message design logic you are working under will determine how you understand, and ultimately use, communication. Perceptions of message design logics also have great implications.

Individuals working within the **expressive** design logic believe that "language is a medium used for expressing thoughts and feelings" (O'Keefe

Table 3.5   Types of Disconfirming Messages

Disconfirming Message	Type	Example
Indifference response	Denying the presence of the other	Being silent when a response is expected, looking away, withdrawing, engaging in unrelated activities
	Denying the relation or involvement of the other	Using impersonal language by avoiding using the first person, avoiding feeling statements or disclosures, using nonverbal "distancing," avoiding eye contact and touch
	Rejecting the communication of the other	Talking "over" another, interjecting irrelevant comments
Imperviousness or lack of accurate awareness of others perceptions	Denial or distortion of others self-expression	*"You don't really mean that,"* or *"You are only saying that because . . ."*
	Pseudo-confirmation	*"Stop crying, there is nothing wrong with you,"* or *"Don't be silly, of course you are not scared."*
	Mystification	*"No matter what you say, I know you still love me,"* or *"You may think you feel that way now . . ."*
	Selective responses	Rewarding speaker with attention and relevant responses only when he communicates in an approved fashion, while becoming silent or indifferent when the communication does not meet the responder's approval
Disqualification	Messages that disqualify the other person by direct disparagement	Insult, name-calling, or indirect disparagement (verbal or nonverbal),
	Messages that disqualify another message by transactional disqualification or tangential response	Using the speaker's remark as a starting point for a shift to a new topic to accomplish your own agenda
	Messages that are self-disqualifying	Being unclear, incomplete, ambiguous, or sending incongruent verbal-nonverbal messages

1988, 85). These people will say whatever is on their mind and work under the premise that if everyone communicated openly and honestly we could understand and relate to each other better. Success, as defined by the *expressive*, is the extent to which individuals can disclose openly, clearly, and truthfully. Regardless of the situation, they feel that they have no choice but to express their genuine thoughts and feelings.

Individuals working within the **conventional** design logic suggest that communication is socially constructed, rule guided behavior. These people take into account the context of the situation and personal goals when deciding to go forward with what they consider is appropriate communication. They work under the premise that each circumstance has an appropriate response depending on what your goal is for the situation. Within the conventional design logic, O'Keefe (1988) suggests, "propositions one expresses are specified by the social effect one wants to achieve, rather than the thoughts one happens to have" (86). Success is defined by cooperativeness and appropriateness.

Individuals working within the **rhetorical** design logic believe communication is a function of co-constructing reality with the parties involved. These people view communication as "the creation and negotiation of social selves and situations" (O'Keefe 1988, 85). Success is defined by the extent to which you use your verbal behavior, character, and social setting to create a desired social reality. They create in-depth messages that serve multiple goals and are multi-dimensional in nature. They are truthful, appropriate, sensitive, harmonious, and unanchored by context.

Consider the following example:

It is your senior year and you live off-campus with a new roommate. After getting out of class early, you decide to meet your friends at the gym to burn some calories before dinner. You stop by your apartment to get your sneakers and after searching your entire apartment, you cannot find them anywhere. Where could they be? Your friends call your cell phone to find out where you are. You explain that you cannot find your sneakers. They laugh at you and say they just saw you wearing them yesterday. Annoyed, you hang up the phone and continue searching. Ten minutes later, the door of your apartment swings open and your roommate comes bouncing in wearing your sneakers.

How would you respond?

The *expressive design logic* individual may react by saying:

"You are so inconsiderate . . . what are you doing wearing my sneakers? I was supposed to meet my friends twenty minutes ago at the gym and I have been searching all over for them. I can't believe you would use my things without asking. Do not touch *anything* of mine ever again."

The *conventional design logic* individual may react by saying:

"Are those my sneakers? You cannot take my things without asking. I have been searching everywhere for those sneakers because I thought I misplaced them. When you want to use something that is mine, you need to ask me."

The *rhetorical design logic* individual may react by saying:

"I realize we are new roommates and I would really like us to continue out the year not only as roommates, but as friends. So, I think it is important for us to communicate if we are going to be borrowing each other's property. It is okay if you use my things, just text me or leave me a note, so I'll know."

Past research has shown **expressive** message producers have significantly more negative perceptions than the other message design logics. It is plausible to suggest that because they are more likely to be insensitive, inappropriate, threatening and offensive to their audience, they may be witness to more negative responses from them. O'Keefe and McCornack (1987) found that judges rated expressive messages as less effective and expressive sources less attractive than individuals that used conventional and rhetorical message design logics. More recently, research found expressives to be more cynical than people who use conventional and rhetorical message design logics

(Edwards and Shepherd 2004). Also, in the organizational setting, individuals in superior-subordinate relationships with expressive message producers tended to feel less supported, more burned out, and more stressed than when they are working with conventional and rhetorical message producers (Peterson and Albrect 1996). Both the conventional and rhetorical message design logics consider the context of the situation when communicating and this research reinforces the importance and positive outcomes of considering the contextual influences.

Factors such as age, sex, and context influence the words that we choose to use when communicating as well as how we interpret verbal messages from others.

FACTORS AFFECTING VERBAL COMMUNICATION

Life Span

One factor that influences how we choose to verbally communicate and how others interpret those communicative acts is age. This includes how our communication changes and is interpreted over time. From perceptions of control in mother-daughter relationships (Morgan and Hummert 2000) to the meaning of friendships (Patterson, Bettini, and Nussbaum 1993), our communicative patterns differ over our lifetime. The meaning behind any communicative act is inherently a function of the point in one's life in which this communicative act occurred (Nussbaum 1989). From infants to the elderly, Jon Nussbaum and his colleagues have conducted a considerable amount of research on the relationship between life span factors and communication behaviors (see Williams and Nussbaum 2001 for a more recent review). In the next section we offer three examples of how our verbal communication with different age groups has an impact on our lives.

How we respond to our children may impact how they view themselves. For example, those parents who are controlling and critical may threaten a child's self-esteem. As discussed in Chapter Two, self-esteem is the value we place on ourselves. Some research indicates that having high self-esteem has been associated with several positive attributes such as competence, assertiveness, and attractiveness. Although the concept is still developing, many parents struggle to establish environments where children have the opportunity to develop a heightened view of self. Some research has shown that children with low or unstable self-esteem levels reported significantly more instances of critical and psychologically controlling parent-child communication (Kernis, Brown, and Brody 2000). When parents are less likely to acknowledge their children's positive behaviors or show approval in value-affirming ways, children are more likely to develop low self-esteem. To improve children's perceptions of self, parents should attempt to occasionally use confirming messages and avoid disconfirming messages. Confirming messages will express recognition of the child's existence and the worth of the child. These findings suggest that parent-child verbal communication effectiveness can impact a child's level of self-esteem.

What parents choose to talk about with their teens and what they choose to ignore may have serious impact on their teen's behavior. Recent research

© iofoto, 2007, Shutterstock.

What kinds of confirming messages do parents give to their children?

on parent-child communication indicates that the extent to which parents communicate with their teens about sex, birth control, and sexually transmitted diseases will directly impact the teen's sexual behavior. Specifically, research by Whitaker and Miller (2000) found that parents who spoke to adolescents about sex reduced the associations the adolescents made about their own behavior with perceptions of their peers' sexual behavior. Whitaker and Miller also found that communicating to teens about condom use correlated with adolescents' safer sexual behavior.

Consider the following scenario.

Patrick goes to the nursing home to visit his only living grandmother. He typically goes with his mother, but since he was leaving for college the next day, he thought he would stop in to say goodbye before he left town. Patrick walks in the room and yells, "HELLO, GRANDMA!" His grandmother acknowledges his greeting by shaking her head and smiling. "How are you feeling today?" he asks slowly. She replies jokingly, "I would be feeling better if I could get some decent food." Patrick notices his grandmother has not eaten much from the lunch tray lying over her lap. "Grandma, you really should eat . . . it's good for you," he asserts. He proceeds to pick up her fork, "Here. . . . let me help you." She pushes his hand away, and snaps, "I am fine!"

How can intergenerational interactions be improved?

© absolut, 2007, Shutterstock.

Why does Patrick treat his grandmother like this? The **Communication Predicament of Aging Model** (Coupland, Coupland, and Giles, 1991; Ryan, Giles, Bartulucci, and Henwood, 1986; Ryan, Hummert, and Boich, 1995) suggests that when young people communicate with the elderly they often rely on negative stereotypes. These negative stereotypes imply that the elderly have declined in cognitive, perceptual, and emotional competence. As a result of these faulty perceptions, young people overcompensate by engaging in "patronizing communication" with the elderly. These patronizing communicative behaviors include: (1) speaking in short sentences, (2) using simple words, (3) using high volume, (4) speaking at a slow rate, and (5) exaggerating articulation. This patronizing talk may contribute to unsatisfactory intergenerational interactions.

Although it is important to be able to communicate across age groups, it is often difficult because of the lack of homophily, or similarity. These three examples offer some insight on the problematic symptoms and implications of verbally communicating outside of your age group.

Sex Differences in Verbal Communication

When it comes to communicating, are men really from Mars and women from Venus? Maltz and Borker (1982) theorize that the way in which girls and boys play at a young age impacts their speech later in life. Let us look at the type of games young children play.

Girls often enjoy games that rely on cooperative play, such as house, Barbie, or school. In these types of play there needs to be a negotiation of rules. Questions like who will be Barbie and who will be the teacher need to be answered.

After all, it would be difficult to play school if everyone wanted to be the teacher and no one wanted to be the students. During these childhood games, girls focus on their own and others' feelings, attitudes, and emotions. In addition, girls often discuss taking turns and decide on imaginary scenes. Therefore, girls encourage talk, collaboration, and sharing. They value cooperativeness and discourage aggressiveness.

Typical girls' games focus on feelings and sharing.

Boys, on the other hand, tend to be more competitive in their childhood games. Cops and robbers, war, sports, "king of the hill," and hide-and-seek are just a few examples of boy's games. Typically in these games, there are set rules, so there is less negotiation and, therefore, less talk. Discussions are usually driven by reiterating the rules or reinforcing them. Boys value competitiveness and aggressiveness because their games center on a clear winner and loser. They value assertiveness, direct communication, and having a clear purpose.

It is difficult to discuss sex differences without mentioning Robin Lakoff, one of the first women to publish theories on gender differences in communicating. In the early to mid 1970s she suggested that women lack a sense of humor, use senseless adjectives (divine, lovely), use more hedges, "sort of" or "kind of," use more polite forms of communicating ("Would you mind if . . ." or "I would appreciate it if you . . .") and have more words for things like colors. A student of Lakoff was Deborah Tannen, who became a professor at Georgetown University and the author of several best-selling books, including *You Just Don't Understand: Women and Men in Conversations.* Tannen proposes that women engage in **"rapport talk,"** or talking for the sake of talking. In other words, women talk for pleasure and to establish connections with others. In contrast, men engage in **"report talk,"** or talking to accomplish goals. Males talk to solve problems and are more instrumental in their approach to communication. Over the last twenty

Boys tend to favor games that end with a clear winner and loser.

years, Tannen has identified a number of differences in male and female perspectives in regard to communication and relationships. She emphasizes that no one approach or style of communication is better than the other, just different. To improve male-female communication, it is important to understand the differences in perspective as well as the reasons they exist.

This section provides some insight into how men and women may be socialized to communicate differently. This is not to say that throughout your experiences, you have not met males that engage in rapport talk and females that engage in report talk. We acknowledge that these are research generalizations and they certainly do not apply to everyone.

Contextual Differences

In addition to age and gender, the context of the verbal communication will impact the outcome of the message. We identified context as a characteristic of verbal communication in the beginning of this chapter. We believe this is a key feature when determining appropriate verbal communication. Therefore we have provided a more in-depth examination into how to communicate effectively within specific contexts, including within intercultural relationships (Chapter Ten), our families (Chapter Eleven), our co-workers and boss (Chapter Twelve), and with health care professionals (Chapter Thirteen).

Women's conversations often revolve around rapport talk.

Furthermore, we will discuss how appropriate communication is used in initiating (Chapter Six), maintaining (Chapter Seven) and terminating (Chapter Nine) friendships and romantic relationships.

BEST PRACTICES: AVOID VERBAL PITFALLS

Oftentimes our verbal communication is misinterpreted. This may be due to connotative meanings, sex differences, or varying verbal styles. Therefore it is important to be clear, appropriate, and concrete.

Clarity

When you are composing a message, keep in mind the KISS acronym: Keep It Short and Simple. Be clear and succinct. Often we think that by using large words, we will be perceived as more intelligent, but you do so at the risk of confusing your audience. Using ambiguous terms is risky. Direct and clear language will increase your chances of reaching shared meaning—your ultimate goal.

On the other hand, when you are on the receiving end of the message, it is important to ask questions to clarify verbal responses. Paraphrase, summarize, and ask direct questions to clarify, even when you think you understand what is being said. These concepts and others will be discussed in more depth in Chapter Five: Perception and Listening.

Appropriateness

Targeting your verbal responses will increase your communication competence. Ask yourself, "What is the best way to send this message to this particular receiver?" The only way to get better is to try different approaches and see how they work. Most people will appreciate your genuine effort to "reach" them.

Concreteness

Concreteness refers to being able to communicate thoughts and ideas specifically. In other words, choose your words wisely. By avoiding jargon and tangential words you will keep the receiver of your message "on track." Avoid superfluous words—they are not necessary. Intentionally choosing words your receiver will understand and relate to will increase your chances of being understood.

SUMMARY

Research on verbal communication dates back to Aristotle and continues to this day. We are fascinated with how individuals learn and use words because their impact is so powerful and significant. Catastrophes such as 9/11 and Katrina affect our language and change it forever. Television and movies also introduce new words and phrases, such as "Vote for Pedro" and "Welcome to Hollywood," into our vocabulary. In this chapter we presented definitions, features, functions, and perceptions of verbal communication. The goal of this chapter was to increase student understanding of verbal communication and how certain verbal styles are perceived by others. Heightening awareness of our own verbal communication as well as the verbal communication used by others will ultimately improve our understanding of interpersonal relationships.

APPLICATIONS

Discussion Questions

A. Gender Differences and Rules: Are there gender differences in regulative and constitutive rules? Do men and women follow different rules? When? Where? When is it socially acceptable for a male to violate a rule? What about a female?

B. Political Correctness: Has it gone too far?
Below are some proposed politically correct words:

Misguided Criminals vs. *Terrorist* (to strip away all emotions).

Thought Shower vs. *Brainstorming* (offensive to those with brain disorders).

Deferred success vs. *Fail* (to bolster self-esteem).

C. How do the words we choose affect our perceptions?

ACTIVITY

Instructional Findings: Confirming/Disconfirming

In the classroom, it was found that students felt more confirmed when they perceived their teacher engaging in confirmation behaviors (Ellis 2000).

DIRECTIONS: Complete the scale below by choosing the number on the line that most accurately describes the extent you believe the following statements about your instructor. This measures whether your instructor uses confirmation behaviors.

Strongly Agree	Agree	Neither agree nor disagree	Infrequently	Never
5	4	3	2	1

_____ 1. Spends time to thoroughly answer students' questions.

_____ 2. Tries to become acquainted with students.

_____ 3. Responds sarcastically to some students' remarks or questions in class.*

_____ 4. Makes it known that students' remarks or questions are welcome in class.

_____ 5. Pays attention to selected students only in class and ignores everyone else.*

_____ 6. Acts in a pompous manner.

_____ 7. Shows interest by listening closely when students offer remarks or ask questions in class.

_____ 8. When students ask for extra help from the teacher, he/she criticizes.*

_____ 9. Patronizes students.*

_____ 10. Bullies students.*

_____ 11. Says that he/she knows that the students are capable of succeeding in the class.

_____ 12. Mocks students in front of the class.*

_____ 13. Plays favorites.*

_____ 14. Is willing to answer questions outside of class.

_____ 15. Teaches by encouraging feedback from students.

_____ 16. Is willing to use different methods to help students comprehend concepts.

_____ 17. While lecturing, makes an effort to have eye contact with students.

_____ 18. He/she can improvise if needed to answer questions during a lecture.

_____ 19. Offers a smiling face in class.

_____ 20. Makes sure students comprehend material before continuing.

_____ 21. He/she asks students their opinion of how class is progressing, including homework.

_____ 22. Lectures integrate exercises if possible.

_____ 23. Students who don't agree get no response from the teacher.*

_____ 24. Assignments receive oral or written encouragement.

_____ 25. Tells the students that he/she can't spare the time to meet with them.

---

*Four aspects: instructor's response to student remarks/questions, apparent interest in student learning, method of teaching, absence of disconfirmation

Source: Adapted from: Ellis, K. 2000. Perceived teacher confirmation: The development and validation of an instrument and two studies of the relationship to cognitive and affective learning. *Human Communication Research, 26,* 264–291.

REFERENCES

Adler, R. B., and G. Rodman. 2006. *Understanding human communication.* New York: Oxford University Press.

Bavelas, J. B., A. Black, N. Chovil, and J. Mullett. 1990. *Equivocal communication.* Newbury Park, CA: Sage.

Berger, P. L., and T. Luckmann. 1966. *The social construction of reality: A treatise it's the sociology of knowledge.* Garden City, New York: Anchor Books.

Buber, M. 1957. Distance and relation. *Psychiatry, 20,* 97–104.

Cheseboro, J. L. 2003. Effects of teacher clarity and nonverbal immediacy on student learning, receiver apprehension and affect. *Communication Education, 52,* 135–147.

Cissna, K. N., and S. Keating. 1979. Speech communication antecedents of perceived confirmation. *The Western Journal of Speech Communication, 43,* 48–60.

Cissna, K. N., and E. Sieburg. 1981. Patterns of interactional confirmation and disconfirmation. In C. Wilder-Mott & J. H. Weakland (Eds.), *Rigor and imagination: Essays from the legacy of Gregory Bateson* (253–282). New York: Praeger.

Coupland, N., J. Coupland, and H. Giles. 1991. *Language, society and the elderly.* Oxford: Basil Blackwell.

Cronen, V. E., W. B. Pearce, and L. Snavely. 1979. A theory of rule structure and forms of episodes, and a study of unwanted repetitive patterns. Communication Yearbook III, Transaction Press (225–240).

Dillard, J. L. 1972. *Black English: Its history and usage in the United States.* New York: Random House, Inc.

Ebert, L., and K. Floyd. 2004. Affection expressions as face threatening acts: Receiver assessments. *Communication Studies, 55,* 254–270.

Edwards, A., and G. J. Shepherd. 2004. Theories of communication, human nature, and the world: Associations and implications. *Communication Studies, 55,* 197–208.

Ellis, K. 2000. Perceived teacher confirmation: The development and validation of an instrument and two studies of the relationship to cognitive and affective learning. *Human Communication Research, 26,* 264–291.

Entwisle, D. R. 1970. Semantic systems of children: Some assessments of social class and ethnic differences. In F. Williams (Ed.), *Language and Poverty,* New York: Sage.

Floyd, K. 1997. Communicating affection in dyadic relationships: An assessment of behavior and expectations.*Communication Quarterly, 45,* 68–80.

Gorham, J. 1988. The relationship between verbal teacher immediacy and student learning. *Communication Education, 37,* 40–53.

Griffin, E. 2003. *A first look at communication theory.* Boston: McGraw-Hill.

Haleta, L. 1996. Students perceptions of teachers' use of language: The effects of powerful and powerless language on impression formation and uncertainty. *Communication Teacher, 45,* 16–28.

Hirst, R. 2003. Scientific jargon: Good and bad. *Journal of Technical Writing and Communication, 33,* 201–229.

Hudson, A. 2003. Fighting words. *Index on Censorship, 32,* 45–52.

Kernis, M. H., A. C. Brown, and G. H. Brody. 2000. Fragile self-esteem in children and its associations with perceived patterns of parent-child communication. *Journal of Personality, 68,* 225–252.

Laing, R. D. 1961. *The self and others.* New York: Pantheon.

Lakoff, R. 1973. Language and woman's place. *Language in Society, 2,* 45–80.

Littlejohn, S. W. 1992. *Theories of communication (4th ed).* Belmont, CA: Wadsworth Publishing Company.

Maltz, D., and R. Borker. 1982. *A cultural approach to male-female miscommunication,* In J. Gumperz (Ed.), *Language and social identity,* Cambridge: Cambridge University Press (196–216).

McCroskey, J. C., and J. J. Teven. 1999. Goodwill: A reexamination of the construct and its measurement. *Communication Monographs, 66,* 90–103.

McCroskey, J. C., and T. J. Young. 1981.Ethos and credibility: The construct and its measurement after three decades. *Central States Speech Journal, 32,* 24–34.

Mehrabian, A. 1969. Some referents and measures of nonverbal behavior. *Behavioral Research Methods and Instrumentation, 1,* 213–217.

Morgan, M., and M. L. Hummert. 2000. Perceptions of communicative control strategies in mother-daughter dyads across the life span. *Journal of Communication, 50,* 49–64.

Nash, W. 1993. *Jargon: Its uses and abuses.* Oxford: Blackwell Publishers.

Nussbaum, J. F. 1989. *Life-span communication: Normative processes.* Hillsdale, NJ: Lawrence Erlbaum.

O'Keefe, B. 1988.The logic of message design: Individual differences in reasoning about communication. *Communication Monographs, 55,* 80–103.

O'Keefe, B. J., and S. A. McCornack. 1987. Message design logic and message goal structure: Effects on perceptions of message quality in regulative communication situations. *Human Communication Research, 14,* 68–92.

Patterson, B., L. Bettini, and J. F. Nussbaum. 1993. The meaning of friendship across the life-span: Two studies. *Communication Quarterly, 41*, 145–161.

Pearce, W. B., V. E. Cronen, and R. F. Conklin. 1979. On what to look at when studying communication: A hierarchical model of actors' meanings. *Communication, 4*, 195–220.

Pember, D. 2003. *Mass media law.* Boston: McGraw-Hill.

Persing, B. 1977. Sticks and stones and words: Women in the language. *Journal of Business Communication, 14*, 11–19.

Peterson, L. W., and T. L. Albrecht. 1996.Message design logic, social support, and mixed status relationships. *Western Journal of Communication, 60*, 291–309.

Rickford, J. 1999. *African American Vernacular English.* Malden, MA: Blackwell Publishers, Inc.

Rickford, J., and R. Rickford. 2000. *Spoken soul: The story of black English.* Hoboken, NJ: John Wiley.

Rubin, D. L., and M. W. Nelson. 1983. Multiple determinants of a stigmatized speech style: Women's language, powerless language, or everyone's language. *Language and Speech, 26*, 273–290.

Ryan, E. B., H. Giles, G. Bartolucci, and K. Henwood. 1986. Psycholinguistic and social psychological components of communication by and with the elderly. *Language and Communication, 6*, 1–24.

Ryan, E. B., M. L. Hummert, and L. H. Boich. 1995. Communication predicaments of aging: Patronising behavior towards older adults. *Journal of Language and Social Psychology 14*, 144–166.

Sapir, E. 1956. *Language, Culture and Personality.* D. G. Mandelbaum (Ed.). Berkeley and Los Angeles: University of California.

Ting-Toomey, S., and L. C. Chung. 2005. *Understanding intercultural communication.* Los Angeles, CA: Roxbury.

Watzlawich, P., J. H. Beavin, and D. D. Jackson. 1967. Pragmatics of human communication: A study of interactional patterns, pathologies, and paradoxes. New York, NY: W. W. Norton & Company.

Weldon, T. L. 2000. Reflections on the Ebonics controversy. *American Linguist, 75*, 275–278.

Whitaker, D. J., and K. S. Miller. 2000. Parent-adolescent discussions about sex and condoms: Impact on peer influences of sexual risk behavior. *Journal of Adolescent Research, 15*, 251–273.

Whorf, B. L. 1956. J. B. Carroll (Ed.), *Language, thought and reality.* Cambridge, MA: MIT Press.

Williams, A., and J. F. Nussbaum. 2001. *Intergenerational communication across the life span.* Mahwah, NJ: Lawrence Erlbaum.

Nonverbal Communication
It's Not *What* You Said; It's *How* You Said It

OBJECTIVES

© Anatoliy Babiychuk, 2007, Shutterstock.

- Define nonverbal communication
- State the differences between nonverbal and verbal communication
- Explain Nonverbal Expectancy Violation Theory
- State the similarities between nonverbal and verbal communication
- Explain the eight types of nonverbal communication
- Explain the four functions of nonverbal messages
- Describe three functions of facial communication
- Explain and provide examples of the five categories of kinesics
- Explain and provide examples of the four types of space
- Provide examples of personal and environmental adornment
- Explain and provide examples of the five categories of touch
- Distinguish between monochronic and polychronic time orientations
- Discuss how we use nonverbal communication to regulate our conversations
- Define the term immediacy
- Advance a definition of the direct effects model of immediacy
- Advance four suggestions for improving our ability to send and receive nonverbal messages
- Describe electronic paralanguage and discuss how it differs from verbal paralanguage

KEY TERMS

nonverbal communication	facial communication	functional-professional
continuous	oculesics	social-polite
multi-channeled	kinesics	friendship-warmth
constitutive rules	emblems	love-intimacy
Nonverbal Expectancy Violation Theory	illustrator	sexual-arousal
physical arousal	regulator	proxemics
cognitive arousal	affect displays	markers
culturally bounded	social referencing	paralanguage
	adaptors	physical appearance
	haptics	homophily

endomorph

mesomorph

ectomorph

artifacts

personal adornment

environmental
  adornment

environmental factors

chronemics

monochromic

polychromic

repetition

complementing

accenting

regulate

turn-yielding

turn-maintaining

back-channeling cues

turn-requesting

turn-denying

emotions

encoding

decoding

immediacy

communication
  apprehension (CA)

electronic paralanguage

emoticons

acronymns

flaming

OVERVIEW

Originally performed by Keith Whitley, the song "When You Say Nothing at All" captures the power of nonverbal communication, communicating to others without using words. The lyrics in this song illustrate that certain nonverbal behaviors create meaning for others. For example, to this particular person the smile communicates "you need me," and the eyes suggest "you will never leave me." Even the "touch of your hand" implies safety. Finally, the song suggests that these nonverbal behaviors are more significant than words by stating, "You say it best when you say nothing at all." We address these characteristics of nonverbal communication throughout this chapter. First, we define nonverbal communication and discuss how it is similar and dissimilar to verbal communication. Next, eight types of nonverbal communication and their functions are offered. In the final sections, we explore how to improve your nonverbal communication and identify potential pitfalls.

It's amazing how you can speak right to my heart.
Without sayin' a word you can light up the dark.
Try as I may I could never explain,
what I hear when you don't say a thing.
The smile on your face lets me know that you need me.
There's a truth in your eyes sayin' you'll never leave me.
The touch of your hand says you'll catch me if ever I fall.
You say it best, when you say nothin' at all.
All alone I can hear people talking about,
but when you hold me near you drown out the crowd.
Old Mr. Webster could never define
what's bein' said between your heart and mine.
The smile on your face lets me know that you need me.
There's a truth in your eyes sayin' you'll never leave me.
The touch of your hand says you'll catch me if ever I fall.
You say it best, when you say nothin' at all.

From "When You Say Nothing At All" by Don Schlitz. © 1988 by MCA Music Publishing, Don Schlitz Music. All rights administered by Universal Music Corp./ASCAP. Used by Permission. All Rights Reserved.

DEFINING NONVERBAL COMMUNICATION

Beyond these song lyrics, the popularity of nonverbal communication in today's culture is immense. There has been a vast amount of research done in this area. Scholars have examined everything from the importance of physical attractiveness on the job interview (Watkins and Johnston 2000) to the implications of creating positive impressions

© Galina Barskaya, 2007, Shutterstock.

How do you think these women feel about each other?

by using certain nonverbal behaviors during the physician-patient interaction (Street and Buller 1987). In addition, there are entire courses devoted to the awareness and impact of nonverbal communication at both the undergraduate and graduate levels. Furthermore, several hundred books and websites address the repercussions of using appropriate versus inappropriate nonverbal communication. We are fascinated by the impact nonverbal messages have on our day-to-day interactions. From something as obvious as our physical appearance to something as subtle as a pause during a conversation, we are captivated by the meanings created by others' nonverbal behaviors. While it is impossible to put a numerical value on the amount of meaning created through nonverbal and verbal communication, we know that the majority of meaning is created through nonverbal communication. Researchers have estimated that the nonverbal behaviors exhibited by a source (e.g., body movements, gestures, vocal qualities, etc.) can explain sixty-five (Hickson, Stacks, and Moore 2004) to ninety-three percent (Mehrabian and Ferris 1967) of any given message's meaning. This makes sense if you think about the amount of time you spend communicating nonverbally versus verbally. Even when we are not speaking we are constantly sending nonverbal messages to others. Consider all of the nonverbal messages you sent to your instructor today while you were sitting in class listening to the lecture.

The popular phrases "It is not *what* you said, it is *how* you said it," or "actions speak louder than words" are examples of the emphasis our culture places on the nonverbal portion of communicating. While verbal communication refers to the words we use to express ourselves, **nonverbal communication** refers to all aspects of communication other than the words we use, including but not limited to: facial expressions, body movements and gestures, physical appearance, and voice.

As explained in Chapter Three, each message we send has two components: the content level of meaning and the relationship level of meaning. While the content level of meaning is usually conveyed through the words we use, the relationship level of meaning is often created through *how* we say those words. Therefore, understanding nonverbal communication will play a critical role in understanding the relationship level of meaning in our messages.

Throughout the remaining sections of this chapter we isolate specific types of nonverbal communication and discuss relevant research findings. However, before we do this, it is necessary to first distinguish nonverbal communication from verbal communication.

HOW IS NONVERBAL COMMUNICATION DIFFERENT FROM VERBAL COMMUNICATION?

The first characteristic that is unique to nonverbal communication is that it is **continuous.** While there is a clear distinction between when we begin verbally communicating and when we stop, nonverbal communication continues beyond our words. Recall our discussion of the definition of communication provided in Chapter One and the statement; *you cannot not communicate.* We continuously send nonverbal messages which are being perceived by others. Even in the absence of others, we are sending nonverbal messages. For example, think about a high school friend you have not spoken to in a long time. She may perceive your silence and distance in several ways. Perhaps she thinks you are extremely busy or maybe that you are upset with her. What else might she think?

Our nonverbal messages may conflict with our verbal messages. We may say one thing, but behave inconsistently with our verbal message. For example, you might tell Aunty Lucy you liked the knit scarf she made for you. However, your facial expressions might tell another story as you pull the purple-and-red polka dot knit scarf out of the package. When our nonverbal and verbal messages contradict each other, research has shown that we tend to believe the nonverbal messages. Therefore, a second unique feature of nonverbal communication is that nonverbal is more believable than verbal communication. Although our nonverbal communication often supplements our verbal communication, such as raising our eyebrows to help stress or emphasize certain words, we tend to believe the nonverbal more than the verbal when there is a discrepancy between the two. While Aunt Lucy heard you say you liked the scarf, she will probably interpret your facial grimace as a stronger indicator of whether it will actually become a part of your wardrobe.

While verbal communication relies solely on the words we exchange with others, nonverbal communication has many different outlets. Therefore, a third distinct feature of nonverbal messages is they are **multi-channeled.** We can use several senses to communicate something nonverbally. Doctors dress professionally, maintain eye contact, listen attentively, and hang their diplomas on the wall in an attempt to establish credibility with their patients. Likewise, day spas manipulate lighting, music, and aroma to communicate a relaxing and calm atmosphere. Because we use multiple cues to send the same message, it makes sense that we will have a higher chance of nonverbal effectiveness. Although it may seem that nonverbal and verbal messages are quite different, they do have similar characteristics. Let us discuss three similarities between verbal and nonverbal communication.

HOW IS NONVERBAL SIMILAR TO VERBAL COMMUNICATION?

Just like verbal messages, nonverbal messages are rule-guided. As mentioned in Chapter Three, there are certain rules we must follow to be socially appropriate and these rules are culturally defined. In regard to nonverbal communication, **constitutive rules** refer to the behaviors we enact to help define the appropriateness of our communication. For example, if we asked you to generate a list of nonverbal behaviors that would communicate respect in a job interview, could you do this? We can demonstrate respect and professionalism in a job interview through our choice of clothing and use of certain gestures and facial expressions. Also, we adhere to specific rules when it comes to regulating or monitoring our communication with others. In the same way we use words to start, maintain, or end our conversations with others, we also use nonverbal communication to control or regulate our conversations. Eye contact (or lack of), specific hand gestures, paralanguage, and nods are all examples of nonverbal signals that we use to indicate turn-taking cues in conversation. Later in this chapter we will discuss three specific ways to use nonverbal communication to regulate our conversations.

Judee K. Burgoon (1978) developed **Nonverbal Expectancy Violation Theory** to help understand rule-guided behavior. The theory suggests that individuals hold expectancies for nonverbal behavior and when these expectations are violated (or the rules are not abided by) there are two common reactions, **physical arousal** and **cognitive arousal.** If you are in an elevator alone and the door opens and a stranger enters, the nonverbal expectancy is that they will stand as far away from you as possible (in order to maximize each other's personal space). If this stranger stood directly next to you, this would be a violation of the space rule. In response to this space violation you probably would consider stepping away (physical arousal) and also might consider the person odd (cognitive arousal) for not abiding by the "elevator rules."

Another similarity between nonverbal and verbal messages is that they are **culturally bounded.** The rules we follow during social interaction are socially constructed and are restricted to a specific culture. Nonverbal gestures in the United States that imply certain meanings are not universally understood. In the United States, when we touch our forefinger to our thumb to create a circle and spray the other three fingers upward we are signaling to others "okay." In France, this same gesture means "zero." In Japan it signals "money" and in Germany it is considered an obscene gesture. As with our verbal language, nonverbal messages are culturally bounded and do not necessarily translate to other cultures. Even within the United States, there are several subcultures that attribute their own distinct meanings to particular nonverbal behaviors. Consider gang members and their particular signs of inclusion, or social groups such as fraternities that have specific handshakes. Nonverbal communication can be unclear and confusing and may lead to many misinterpretations. Therefore, it is important to be aware of how we enact these behaviors and be sure to confirm their meaning by asking questions when messages are perceived as ambiguous.

Finally, both verbal and nonverbal messages are contextually restricted. As we previously mentioned, we must consider the situation, environment and setting we are in when deciding on appropriateness. Depending on the context of the nonverbal communication, it may influence the interpretation, meaning, and appropriateness of the communication. When we are pitching a new idea to our boss, we tend to dress more formally and manipulate our posture to appear more professional. However, can you imagine how surprised your friends would be if you continued this behavior while you were relaxing at home? Just like the words we use, our nonverbal behaviors should be modified to fit the situation. To gain a better understanding of these specific nonverbal behaviors we will introduce eight types of nonverbal communication.

EIGHT TYPES OF NONVERBAL COMMUNICATION

We have grouped nonverbal communication into eight types: facial communication, kinesics, haptics, proxemics, paralanguage, physical appearance, artifacts, and chronemics. In this section we will explain each type and provide insight on how the particular nonverbal behavior influences meaning during social interaction.

Facial Communication

Let us begin with **facial communication.** This includes any expression on the face that sends messages. Think about the thousands of different expressions you can make with your face by raising or lowering your eyebrows, shutting or

opening your eyes, wrinkling your nose, and protruding your lips. Three functions of facial communication are to *display emotion,* to *supplement the verbal communication,* and to *compliment the verbal communication.* Our face is the primary channel for expressing emotions. The most basic emotions displayed through our facial expressions are often referred to by the acronym SADFISH which stands for sadness, anger, disgust, fear, interest, surprise, and happiness.

The second function of facial expressions is to supplement the verbal communication. Individuals reveal their attitudes toward certain subjects through their facial expressions. Think about how we analyze facial expressions when someone opens a gift from us. We can typically tell if they like the gift by the type of facial expression revealed. In addition, we use facial communication to complement our verbal message. For example, when we want to emphasize a word we tend to raise our eyebrows and open our eyes wide. This type of facial display matches the verbal portion of the message. Overall, our facial movements communicate emotions, attitudes and motivation.

One type of facial communication that has received a great deal of attention in the literature is oculesics. **Oculesics** is the study of eye behavior. Researchers are fascinated by oculesics and how it influences meaning. Eye behavior in the United States is very particular and is often perceived as an important means of showing attention, interest and respect to others. We often encourage our students to engage in eye contact during interviews for internships or jobs. However, if someone provides too much direct eye

What is this emblem conveying?

© Juriah Mosin, 2007, Shutterstock.

contact, it can be interpreted as disturbing and frightening. Eye contact is a perfect example of a nonverbal behavior that is culturally defined. Direct eye contact in Asian cultures is considered rude, disrespectful, and intimidating while in the United States, eye contact during conversation is expected.

Kinesics

Another type of nonverbal communication often associated with facial expressions is **kinesics,** or body movements. Ekman and Friesen (1969) classify kinesics into five categories: emblems, illustrators, affect displays, regulators, and adapters. Let us examine each of these. **Emblems** are specific nonverbal gestures that have a particular translation. For example, extending your forefinger over your lips means to be quiet. Or if you wanted to signal to someone to "come here" you would wave your hand toward your body. Because these emblems are context-bound, they are often misinterpreted when communicating with individuals from other cultures. Kitao and Kitao (1988) explain that the emblem for "okay" in the United States is the emblem used for "money" in Japan. They write, "An American and a Japanese man wanted to meet some friends. The American called from a pay phone and signaled to the Japanese man the American emblem for "okay," indicating that the friends would be able to meet them. The Japanese man interpreted the emblem as meaning that more coins were needed for the pay phone and rushed over to put in more money" (89). Although this is a lighthearted example, you can imagine how misinterpretations during business exchanges might not be humorous and may even be costly.

Indicating something with a body gesture is an illustrator.

© Bartosz Ostrowski, 2007, Shutterstock.

Illustrator is the label used to indicate when you use your body to help describe or visually depict something. You have probably heard someone say, "I caught a fish this big!" while indicating the size of the fish with their hands. This is an example of an illustrator. We use illustrators to visually demonstrate how big our nephew is or to point someone in the right direction when he is lost. Illustrators are more universal and less ambiguous than emblems.

Regulators are any type of body movement that is used in conversation to control the communication flow. Sometimes one person is monopolizing the conversation and you want to signal to him that you have something to say. What would you do? You have many options such as leaning forward, opening your mouth, nodding, and using your hand to gesture.

We can demonstrate our emotions nonverbally through affect displays. **Affect displays** are overt physical responses to our emotions that can be either positive or negative. Positive affect displays are constructive and encouraging. Patting or rubbing a close friend on the back when he is sad is an example of an affect display. Hugging

Positive affect displays are constructive and encouraging.

© Miroslav, 2007, Shutterstock.

and kissing are additional ways to display positive affect towards another. What about negative affect displays? Recall the last time someone asked you why you were angry. Perhaps it was because you were clenching your teeth or glaring with your eyes. In what ways have you physically manifested feelings of boredom, frustration, or sadness?

It is amazing how quickly infants and young children pick up on these displays. These learned behaviors are typically modeled by the infant's parent or caregiver through a process called social referencing. **Social referencing** refers to the process by which individuals will rely on those around them to determine how to respond to unfamiliar stimuli (Campos and Stenberg 1988). For example, when an infant is introduced to someone or something new they look to the parent for reassurance. When the parent responds with a positive affect display, like a smile, she sends a message to the infant that this new stimuli is comforting and not threatening. It is not long before the child displays more complex emotions through nonverbal affect displays. He may roll his eyes because he is annoyed or stomp his feet and cross his arms in disgust.

Adaptors are body movements that are enacted at a low level of awareness and usually indicate nervousness, anxiety, or boredom. Individuals may display these types of behaviors in situations that evoke anxiety such as public speaking classes or other types of public performances. Sometimes students are not aware that while they are giving their speech they are also engaging in behaviors such as tapping a pen on the podium, cracking their knuckles, and fixing their hair. When they watch themselves on videotape later, they are surprised because they were often unaware that they were exhibiting these adaptors. Outside of the classroom, individuals who work in human resource departments are often trained to look for adaptors during interviews and screening processes. Interviewee behaviors such as a bouncing knee, playing with paper, and postural changes are examples of adaptors that are often exhibited during interviews and considered a sign of nervousness or weakness.

Do you have any nervous habits that you do unconsciously?

Haptics

An additional type of nonverbal communication is **haptics,** or touch. The amount of touch in interpersonal relationships is related to liking and status. Anderson and Sull (1985) suggest that individuals who like each other will touch more often than those who do not. In fact, if individuals are not fond of each other they will actively avoid touching. Individuals with higher status, such as your boss or professor, typically choose whether to initiate touch into the relationship. They also may use touch to maintain control. For example, a middle school teacher may lead a student by physically directing them towards the corner of the room while saying, "Let's move over here." This type of touch is considered role-bound because the teacher and student are working within specific positions. The type of touch and who it is by is determined by the level of the

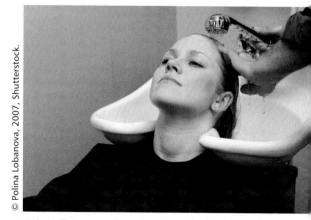

Hair stylists use a functional-professional touch in their work.

© Miroslav, 2007, Shutterstock.

Love-intimacy touches occur between family members and friends where there is affection and a deep level of caring.

interpersonal relationship. Thayer (1988) offers categories of touch based on people's roles and relationships. **Functional-professional** are touches that occur while accomplishing a specific task which is performed by those working within a specific role. For example, a barber, doctor, or nail technician will perform tasks which involve touch as part of their occupation. Functional touch also includes any touch that is done while trying to accomplish a goal. Helping a player off the ice when you are playing hockey or assisting an elderly woman across the street would both be situations employing functional touch. **Social-polite** are touches that occur between business partners, acquaintances and strangers. These include greetings and salutations, such as a handshake. **Friendship-warmth** are touches that occur between extended family members, close business associates, and friendly neighbors. This type of touch signals caring, concern and interest between interactants. A hug and a pat on the back are examples of this type of touch. There are some gray areas between this type of touch and the "love intimacy" category which may be a cause of great misinterpretation. **Love-intimacy** are touches that occur between family members and friends where there is affection and a deep level of caring. Extended hugs and holding hands are often examples of this type of touch. **Sexual-arousal** occurs within sexual/erotic contexts. Kissing is an example of this type of touch. Sometimes we use touch to initiate permission to enter into a "deeper" relationship with someone. If there is a discrepancy between the level of touch and your interpretation of the level of the relationship, it is important to be assertive and direct in your communication about this discrepancy with your relationship partner. Touch is the most intimate type of nonverbal communication and is also the most ambiguous. We interpret touch differently depending on the context. At a crowded club, party, elevator, or subway, touch is not interpreted as intrusive. However, within different contexts, when people intentionally enter our "space" we may view it as a violation. Now, let us discuss how our use of personal space contributes to nonverbal communication.

Proxemics

The fourth type of nonverbal communication is space, or **proxemics,** which refers to the invisible bubble we place around our bodies. Often this space is considered our "comfort zone." Americans are highly conscious of our space and our territory. We allow certain individuals into our space, depending on the context of the situation. Edward T. Hall (1966) defined four types of space as listed on the next page.

Although this chart provides us with a general idea of how individuals use space, perceptions of appropriate personal space differ among individuals. In the United States we are generally very concerned with others infringing on what we consider to be "our space" and are very protective of it. We may even go so far as to place physical objects, or **markers,** between ourselves and others. Similar to the ways in which animals mark their territory,

Table 4.1	Space, Context, and Nonverbal Communication	
Type of Space	**Distance**	**Individuals/Groups**
Intimate	0 to 18 inches	Reserved for those that are closest to us (e.g., boyfriend, girlfriend, spouse)
Personal	18 inches to 4 feet	Reserved for family members and close friends
Social	4 to 10 feet	The distance that we feel comfortable conducting everyday social situations with strangers, acquaintances, and business partners
Public	10 feet and farther	The distance reserved for large audiences

we may claim the territory around us by using markers to show others that this is our space. Think about all of the different ways that you may protect space that you consider yours. Have you ever spread out your books, bag, and articles of clothing in the library to purposefully take up more space? Have you ever spread out your belongings at the lunch table to discourage others from sitting next to you? Do you know anyone that intentionally takes up more than one parking space to deter anyone from parking "too close" to his vehicle? Males in our classes often admit they leave a seat between themselves and their friends at the movie theaters to increase their personal space. You may recall the popular *Seinfeld* "close-talker" episode; individuals who invaded someone's space while conversing were considered annoying and inappropriate. These are all examples of how our use of space influences meaning.

Paralanguage

The fifth type of nonverbal communication is **paralanguage,** which means everything beyond the words in the verbally communicated message. Paralanguage, or vocalic components of messages, includes pitch, rate, volume, pronunciation, inflection, tempo, accents, and vocal fillers such as ahh, ummm, and ya know. Hesitations and "sounds such as grunts, screams, laughs, gasps, sighs, and even silence fall under the purview of vocalics" (Hickson, Stacks, and Moore 2004, 258). Have you ever thought about the ways you use silence? You may use silence to show disgust, to keep a secret, to reveal a secret, or to enhance the importance of your message. As compiled by Knapp and Hall (2002), silence serves the following five functions: (1) to punctuate or emphasize certain words or ideas; (2) to evaluate or provide judgment of another's behavior (showing favor or disfavor, agreement, disagreement, attacking); (3) to hide or to reveal; (4) to express emotions: the silence of disgust, sadness, fear, anger or love; and (5) to engage in mental activity: show thoughtfulness, reflection, or ignorance (Bruneau 1973; Jaworski 1993; Jensen 1973). Because silence serves several functions, it is important to understand that it is often misunderstood. Can you recall a time when your silence was misconstrued?

Physical Appearance

The sixth type of nonverbal communication is **physical appearance,** which includes our body, clothing, make-up, height, size, and hair. Much of the literature on physical appearance examines the attractiveness of individuals. The literature (see, for example, McCroskey 1992) on this topic recognizes three different types of attraction: physical attraction (how visibly pleasing someone is), task attraction (how pleasing some is to work with), and social attraction (how pleasing someone is to interact with). We will focus primarily on physical attraction in this section.

What is perceived as attractive in the United States may be quite different from what is considered attractive in Thailand or Egypt. Likewise, what you might find attractive, your neighbor may find repulsive. However, we know that individuals are more attracted to physically attractive people than to physically unattractive people (Sprecher 1989). But perhaps this has more to do with **homophily,** or how similar we consider the target to be to ourselves. Although we cannot develop a global list of physically attractive attributes, we do know that there are benefits to being attractive. Watkins and Johnston (2000) found that when screening job applicants, attractiveness had no impact when the quality of the application was high. But attractiveness was a significant advantage when the application was mediocre. A more in-depth discussion of the three types of attraction will be examined in Chapter Six.

 **Research Brief**   **Physical Appearance**

In the early 1980s some scholars even examined female bust size as it relates to perceptions of physical appearance. Researchers found that women with large bust sizes were evaluated as being relatively unintelligent, incompetent, immoral, and immodest, while women with small bust sizes were evaluated as being more intelligent, competent, modest, and moral (Kleinke and Staneski 1980).

Body size is one aspect of physical appearance that has been studied by researchers and is linked to how we form impressions of others. Body size is the relationship between an individual's height, weight, and muscular build and has received considerable amount of attention in the nonverbal communication literature. In 1942, Sheldon and Stevens theorized that there was a link between a person's physical attributes and personality traits. After collecting data on male body types and temperament, they distinguished between three primary body types: endomorphs, mesomorphs, and ectomorphs (see Hickson, Stacks and Moore for a more in-depth discussion).

The **endomorph** body type is described as being short, round, and soft. Researchers have associated the endomorph body type with being lazy, better-natured, more old fashioned, less good looking, more agreeable, and more dependent on others compared to the other body types. One study found that self-perceived endomorphs had significantly stronger intentions to smoke cigarettes compared to the other body types (Tucker 1983). But are all individuals with this body type lazy? Certainly former NBA player Charles Barkley, who was at one time referred to as "The Round Mound of Rebound," is not described as lazy, dependent, or even overly agreeable. It is important to be aware of our tendency to inaccurately stereotype individuals based on their appearance.

The **mesomorph** body type is described as being physically fit, muscular, average height and weight, and athletic. Researchers have associated this body type with being stronger, better looking, more adventurous, younger, taller, and more mature compared to the other body types (Sheldon, Hartl, and McDermott 1949). The mesomorphic body type was perceived by college students as an ideal body type for both males and females (Butler and Ryckman 1993). Even professional clinicians have been found to stereotype based on body type. Fletcher and Diekhoff (1998) found that therapists judged more muscular males, or male mesomorphs, as more mentally healthy than endomorphs and ectomorphs.

The **ectomorph** body type is described as being tall, thin and frail. Characteristics associated with this body type include being more tense, nervous, quieter, taller, younger, introverted, more afraid of people, lacking confidence, and being less social when compared with the other body types (Sheldon, Hartl, and McDermott 1949). Not all perceptions of this body type are negative. For example, our culture certainly seems to value a thin or ectomorphic body shape, especially in women. The media has been criticized for only displaying images of thin women and contributing to the problem of eating disorders in young women. In an effort to reduce the number of eating disorders in young women, the modeling industry has adopted healthier standards for their models' body weight.

Portnoy (1993) examined whether perceptions of body types differed across the lifespan by measuring senior citizen perceptions of same-sex cohorts. The researcher found that endomorphs were rated significantly more negatively on measures of physical attraction, social attraction, task attraction, and communication desirability than the other body types. This research illustrated that perceptions of different body types are similar for both younger and older populations.

In addition to body type, height has also been examined as a physical characteristic that influences meaning. Are taller people perceived as more competent? To date, Judge and Cable (2004) have designed the most comprehensive analysis between physical height and work success. Their meta-analysis found that while controlling for sex, age, and weight, there were significant positive relationships between height and social esteem, leader emergence, performance, and income. Therefore, not only are taller people perceived as more competent, they actually get paid more. How much more? Their findings suggest that someone who is six feet tall earns, on average, nearly $166,000 more during a thirty-year career than someone who is five feet, five inches.

Artifacts

The seventh type of nonverbal communication is artifacts. **Artifacts** are defined as "the physical objects and environmental attributes that communicate directly, define the communication context, or guide social behavior in some way" (Burgoon, Buller, and Woodall 1994, 123). We can think about artifacts in terms of personal adornment and environmental adornment. **Personal adornment** refers to how we use artifacts on our bodies. Tattoos, jewelry, branding, scarring, painting, makeup, glasses, and body piercing are all examples of artifacts that can be considered personal adornment. Two popular personal adornment artifacts addressed in the literature are tattoos and body piercing.

Although tattoos and body piercing are becoming more mainstream, there are still negative perceptions associated with these artifacts. Some of these perceptions may be founded, since Carroll, Riffenburgh, Roberts, and Myhre (2002) noted that participants with tattoos and body piercings were more likely to engage in high risk-taking behaviors such as disordered eating behavior, gateway drug use, hard drug use, sexual activity, suicide, and violence. Forbes (2001) also found that tattoos and piercings in college students are associated with more risk-taking behavior, greater use of alcohol and marijuana, and less social conformity. Another study found individuals with body modifications (tattoos or body piercings other than earlobes) reported more symptoms of depression and trait anxiety than individuals without body modifications (Roberti and Storch 2005).

Environmental adornment refers to artifacts that we use in our environment to identify ourselves. Consider how much you can learn about someone just by walking through their bedroom. Think about the artwork on the wall, the cleanliness, the type of objects on the dresser, and the clothes hanging in the closet. The MTV show *Room Raiders* capitalized on this phenomenon. Contestants decided who to go out with based solely on the contents of the bedrooms of the prospective dates. In addition to our bedrooms, we often use artifacts in our cars, offices, and other personal spaces to reflect our identity. Try to identify the environmental adornment artifacts the next time you are in your professors' offices. Do they have any artwork? Do they have photos of their dog or children? Can you figure out their alma mater?

Closely related to those artifacts are additional **environmental factors,** such as the context, room layout, lighting, and/or color. Environmental factors will influence how we interpret meaning. Consider the environmental factors inside a McDonalds. Think about the lighting, seating and colors—do they encourage you to eat fast? Fast food restaurants are interested in high turnover and do not typically want you to become too comfortable while eating your burger and fries. In contrast, high-end restaurants are more concerned with having their patrons relax, order more food and drinks, and stay for a long time in their establishment. These types of restaurants will often use candlelight, comfortable seating, and soft music to create an environment that says "stay awhile." Around the holidays, department stores often play specific music and try to create a certain mood in the store to encourage shoppers to spend more money. Be aware of the setting and environment around you. Do you respond to certain colors? Is there a reason why most classrooms have white walls and very little artwork? Does certain music put you in a certain mood? What types of smells make you hungry? What scents make you calm? Heightened awareness of the impact of environmental factors is critical to your success as a competent communicator.

Chronemics

The final type of nonverbal communication is referred to as **chronemics,** or how we use and perceive time. Our subjective view of time is contingent on our personal/psychological orientation and our cultural influences. Edward T.

Hall (1976) suggests that each culture operates on a continuum from a mono-chronic orientation to a polychronic orientation to time. In general, Ameri-cans tends to be more **monochronic** because time is considered to be "linear" in nature. It spans across a "time line" and we can schedule appointments one after another in an orderly fashion. Think about how your daily planner is set up. (Or the fact that you *have* a daily planner.) You can segment time and schedule classes, appointments, and social events for each week, each day, and within each hour. Being punctual, scheduling appointments, and having strict adherence to starting times and ending times are all valued behaviors in the United States. During one of the authors' first day of graduate school, faculty stressed to the students, "Being on time is being late; being early is synony-mous with being on time." This example reinforces the monochronic orienta-tion that is valued in our culture. Being early in our culture is perceived as being organized, professional, prepared, and productive. Being late in our cul-ture is perceived as being lazy, disorganized, uninterested, and unprofessional.

In contrast to monochronic, **polychronic** cultures perceive time as circu-lar. This time orientation suggests that several things can be done at the same time. Polychronic cultures do not rely as heavily as monochromic cultures do on the clock. Meetings are viewed as time to cultivate relationships and it is more important to finish the conversation than to be "on time" for the next appointment. Time and activities are more fluid and things will "get done when they get done." Work time and personal time typically overlap in these cultures. Within the United States, this orientation has negative perceptions, such as being "nonambitious and a waste of precious time" (Hickson, Stacks, and Moore 2004, 316).

In addition to our cultural norms, we must also consider individual ori-entations. Consider how monochronic or polychronic your parents are. Did you grow up with a curfew? Did you have daily chores? Did you eat dinner at the same time each evening? Consider the extent to which you are mono-chronic. How punctual are you? Does it frustrate you when individuals do not accomplish tasks in an "appropriate" time? Do you consider "how long" things should take to accomplish?

FOUR FUNCTIONS OF NONVERBAL MESSAGES

Now that we have discussed the eight types of nonverbal communication, we will review four ways we use nonverbal behavior. The four functions of non-verbal messages are: (1) to facilitate our cognitive meaning, (2) to encode and decode emotions, (3) to express affection and support, and (4) to aid in impression formation/identity management.

Facilitate Cognitive Meaning

One primary function of nonverbal messages is aiding in cognitive meaning. We can use our nonverbal behavior in several ways to help create meaning. Ekman and Friesen (1969) specify five ways we aid our cognitive meaning. These include: repetition, contradiction, complementation, accent, and regu-lation. First, **repetition** refers to both verbal and nonverbal expressions made simultaneously to reinforce each other. The nonverbal message repeats the verbal message in order to increase the accuracy of the message. For example, when a police officer is directing traffic he may extend his hand and yell "Stop!" In this example, the cognitive meaning of the verbal message is repeated with the nonverbal emblem. We can use this function when we want to clarify or increase accuracy of the messages we send.

On the other hand, our nonverbal and verbal expressions may be contradictory. Oftentimes we say one thing and behave in a way that is inconsistent with our verbal message. When our nonverbal and verbal messages contradict each other, research has shown that we tend to believe the nonverbal messages. Once again, we refer to the heuristic, "It is not what you said, but how you said it." If someone says, "I really like your new car," you will determine the sincerity of the message by dissecting the nonverbal cues. Was it said sarcastically? What do their facial expressions reveal? After scrutinizing the nonverbal and verbal messages, we will determine whether the verbal portion of the message was genuine. If there are any discrepancies between the two messages, we will rely on the nonverbal portion of the message.

Thirdly, **complementing** is a process by which our nonverbal communication is used in conjunction with the verbal portion of the message. We can determine the attitudes people hold when we examine the extent to which the verbal and nonverbal messages are complementing each other. If you want to make sure that your relationship partner knows that you are angry with her, you may glare at her and say, "I am so angry with you!"

The fourth way we aid our cognitive meaning, according to Ekman and Friesen (1969), is through accenting. **Accenting** is used when we want to stress or emphasize a particular word or phrase in our verbal message. If a friend says, "Please, do not be *late* to the party", and stresses the word "late," her use of accenting implies that it is important to her that you are on time for the party. Accenting can change the meaning of the original message, as well as the emotion conveyed (Anderson 1999). Consider how the meaning and the emotion of the same sentence changes slightly when we accent different words in the following statements:

George, will you pick up fat-free milk from the store today?
George, will you pick up *fat-free* milk from the store today?
George, will you pick up fat-free milk from the store *today?*

The final way to aid our cognitive meaning is to **regulate** conversations. Duncan (1972) first introduced three ways we use nonverbal communication to regulate or negotiate our conversations. First, we engage in **turn-yielding** behaviors which signal to the listener that we are going to stop talking. Some examples of these signals include placing a drawl on the final syllable, placing emphasis on a final word, saying, "do you know what I *mean*?" displaying an open and direct body position, and leaning forward. Second, we can also engage in suppressing signals or **turn-maintaining** that suggest to the listener that we want to continue talking. These behaviors include talking more quickly and/or more loudly using hand gestures that suggest "wait a minute" or "one last point," and filling more pauses. **Back channeling cues** are used by listeners to signal that they are motivated to listen to us, they are not interested in "taking over the floor." Some nonverbal behaviors they may engage in include nodding their heads, and saying "I agree" or "ah huh." They are confirming interest in our message, but they are not interested in speaking themselves. Wiemann and Knapp (1975) added **turn-requesting** to the list of turn-taking cues. They suggest that listeners use buffers, short words or phrases such as, "But uhhh . . ." or "You know . . ." to signal to the speaker that they are interested in speaking. These buffers may be used while the speaker is talking or during a pause in conversation. If used properly, the speaker should finish his thought and relinquish the floor to them. Burgoon, Hunsaker, and Dawson (1994) identified an additional turn-taking cue referred to as **turn-denying.** Listeners use this cue when they are not interested in "taking over the floor." They may signal that they are not interested by increasing space between themselves and the speaker and/or avoiding direct eye contact with the speaker.

Encoding and Decoding Emotions

A second function of nonverbal communication is to display and interpret emotions. **Emotions** are subjective feelings such as happiness, anger, shame, fear, guilt, sadness, and excitement that produce positive or negative reactions that are physical, psychological and physiological. We often weigh the appropriateness of our outward reaction of emotion and judge whether it is desirable and/or acceptable (see Anderson 1999). Emotion is primarily communicated through nonverbal means. And typically, our most intense emotional experiences result from the formation, maintenance, and termination of our interpersonal relationships (Bowlby 1979).

Encoding emotions refers to an individual's ability to display feelings. Scholars have suggested as we get older we are better able to encode emotions such as happiness, anger, sadness, and fear (Mayo and LaFrance 1978). Furthermore, a seminal study found that regardless of gender, young children seem to express emotions quite similarly. However, as girls become older they become more accurate in detecting affective states in others and more expressive. Boys, on the other hand, are less accurate in detecting affective states in others and are less expressive encoders (Buck 1975). A more recent study revealed that women were more effective in encoding emotions than men (Wagner, MacDonald, and Manstead 1986). This research makes sense because it is more socially acceptable for women to express their emotions in the American culture. Men are more likely to suppress their feelings. In 1994, Kring, Smith, and Neale developed the Emotional Expressivity Scale (EES) to measure the extent to which individuals outwardly display their emotions. Complete the scale at the bottom of the next page to determine your own emotional expressivity (see Table 4.2).

Decoding emotions refers to the ability to accurately read and interpret the emotional states of others. Most scholars agree that individuals who are skilled encoders are also skilled decoders (see Burgoon, Buller, and Woodall 1994). Therefore women tend to be better decoders than men (Wagner, MacDonald, and Manstead 1986). However, research has shown that men tend to improve their sensitivity to facial expressions with individuals over time (Zuckerman, Lipets, Koivumaki, and Rosenthanl 1975). Test your decoding abilities by trying to interpret the emotions of the following facial expressions and vocalics.

What are these facial expressions saying?

Table 4.2   **Emotional Expressivity Scale**

Using the following scale, place the number on the line that best describes your agreement with the following statements.

5 = Strongly Agree   4 = Agree   3 = Neither Agree nor Disagree
2 = Disagree   1 = Strongly Disagree

_____ 1. I think of myself as emotionally expressive.

_____ 2. People think of me as an unemotional person.*

_____ 3. I keep my feelings to myself.*

_____ 4. I am often considered indifferent by others.*

_____ 5. People can read my emotions.

_____ 6. I display my emotions to other people.

_____ 7. I don't like to let other people see how I am feeling.*

_____ 8. I am able to cry in front of other people.

_____ 9. Even if I am feeling very emotional, I don't let others see my feelings.*

_____10. Other people aren't easily able to observe what I am feeling.*

_____11. I am not very emotionally expressive.*

_____12. Even when I am experiencing strong feelings, I don't express them outwardly.*

_____13. I cannot hide the way I am feeling.

_____14. Other people believe me to very emotional.

_____15. I don't express my emotions to other people.*

_____16. The way I feel is different from how others think I feel.*

_____17. I hold my feelings in.*

* = Recode these items (5=1; 4=2; 3=3; 2=4; 1=5)
After you recode the negative items, sum all the scores together.
Range = 17–85

From "Individual Differences in Dispositional Expressiveness: The Development and Validation of the Emotional Expressivity Scale" by A.M. Kring, D.A. Smith, & J.M. Neale. *Journal of Personality and Social Psychology*, 66, 934-949. Copyright © 1994 by the American Psychological Association. Reproduced with permission. No further reproduction or distributed is permitted without written permission from the American Psychological Association and Ann M. Kring.

Express Affection and Support

A third function of nonverbal communication is to provide affection and support. Oftentimes we will display nonverbal comforting strategies in our interpersonal relationship when someone is going through a difficult or stressful

Table 4.3	Nonverbal Communication: Comforting Strategies

Comforting Strategy	Examples
Attentiveness (Showing you care)	Active listening behaviors and head nodding
Eye contact	Maintaining direct eye contact with the person
Crying	Referencing crying or weeping, either the other person's or the comforter's
Vocalics	Using one's voice to show concern, references to tone of voice, intensity, and speaking softly
Instrumental activity (Doing something for the other person which may or may not be directly related to the distress)	Making dinner or running errands for the other person to show support
Facial expression (Showing emotional reaction through one's face)	Adapting facial features to show empathy or simply looking concerned or sad
Proxemics	Using proxemics to close up the space without touching
Gesturing	Using hand and arm movements to show empathy, anger, and/or agitation about what the person is saying
Hugs	Directly hugging the person, either a whole or half hug
Pats	Touching arm or shoulder
Increased miscellaneous touch	Any type of increase in touching that does not fall into hugging or patting category
Emotional distancing (Comforting avoidance response)	Behaviors that are self-oriented and avoidant, intended to keep distance or to remain uninvolved

time. Dolin and Booth-Butterfield (1993) identified twelve nonverbal comforting strategies that college students employ to lend support to others.

Their study revealed that females reported more nonverbal comforting strategies and more diverse comforting responses than males. This means that females not only use nonverbal comforting strategies more frequently, but they also use several different types of strategies. Males were more likely to use emotional distancing behaviors than females. This strategy was negatively related to all the other strategies and the authors suggest it could be considered a comforting avoidance response. See Table 4.3 above for a complete list of comforting strategies and messages.

Aid in Impression Formation/Identity Management

Another significant function of nonverbal communication is creating first impressions. Typically, our initial perception of someone is based on observing nonverbal behavior such as physical appearance, eye contact, and facial expressions. The information gathered through these first impressions is used to predict attitudes and opinions not yet revealed. This is referred to as proactive attribution. This information is also used for retroactive attribution, or to help explain the behavior of others in hindsight (Berger 1975). Although we gather this information quickly, it tends to remain stable over time—making these initial perceptions critical for future interactions. For example, research suggests that roommates whose initial impressions were positive had more satisfying subsequent interactions and used more productive strategies to solve conflict (Marek, Knapp, and Wanzer 2004). However, how often do you think our first impressions are inaccurate? We do not often provide second chances as we do not communicate long enough to find out if our first impressions were accurate.

BEST PRACTICES: AVOID COMMON NONVERBAL COMMUNICATION MISTAKES

To increase your effectiveness and appropriateness of receiving and displaying nonverbal communication in your interpersonal relationships, we offer suggestions in four areas. This section provides suggestions on how to monitor and adapt your nonverbal messages to your audience and context.

Common Areas of Miscommunication

First, nonverbal messages are often perceived as ambiguous and open for misinterpretation. The cultural barriers attached to many nonverbal behaviors can inhibit our interpretation of the meaning. Additionally, we do not usually have an extended period of time to create first impressions, which may have lasting results. Therefore, it is important to reinforce that nonverbal communication is not clear and is often misinterpreted. The more time we spend with others, the more we can interpret their nonverbal behavior accurately. Remember, nonverbal communication is multi-channeled and we can increase our chances of accurately interpreting others' behavior if we take all of the cues into consideration. Similarly, if we want to become more successful at getting our messages across to others, we will employ a number of different nonverbal behaviors that reinforce or clarify our verbal message. Therefore, if you want to make sure that your roommate knows that you are really angry with his behavior, you would look directly at him, fold your arms across your chest, lean forward, and accent certain words for emphasis while describing the reason you are angry.

Nonverbal Messages and Social Influence

Have you ever caused someone to change a behavior or attitude without intending to do so? Can you recall a specific time when you unintentionally influenced another person's attitudes or actions by displaying certain nonverbal behaviors? The two examples below illustrate how we can unintentionally influence others through our nonverbal behaviors.

1. Perhaps you broke eye contact with your sibling while she was telling you about something that happened to her at school. As a result of this behavior, your sister stopped talking and walked away from you. When

you asked her later why she walked away from you, she told you that she could tell that you were not interested in her story.

2. Several years ago a famous supermodel cut her long hair quite short and, as a result of this choice, many other women did the same. In an interview the model stated that she certainly did not intend to influence others to cut their hair short.

These examples illustrate how we may influence others' attitudes or behaviors through our nonverbal messages without intending to do so. Thus, it is important to monitor our nonverbal behaviors closely and consider how our actions may influence others. Be aware that we may unintentionally influence someone else's behavior or attitude through our nonverbal behaviors.

Of course there are also many times when we intend to influence others by exhibiting certain nonverbal behaviors. For example, each time you dress professionally for a job interview you attempt to influence the interviewer's perceptions of you as a viable job candidate. Communication researchers have had a longstanding interest in learning more about how certain verbal and nonverbal behaviors influence those around us. Much of the research in this area suggests that you can influence individuals by displaying nonverbal behaviors associated with power and authority or kindness and liking, or both. Individuals can give the impression of authority and expertise through nonverbal cues such as wearing uniforms (e.g., military), name tags which include titles (e.g., manager), and personal artifacts. Military personnel, police officers, doctors, or managers in a retail store all have control over certain resources, and have power to reward or punish. We are more likely to obey a police officer's suggestion to move our car than the suggestion made by a stranger on the street because the officer wearing the uniform has the power to give us a ticket. Other nonverbal messages that project an image of authority and power are eye contact, touch, voice, and space. We often can tell who has the most power in an organization by the size of his or her office. Other persuasive tactics involve liking and kindness. We can persuade others by our charismatic tone, physical attractiveness, and smile. Nonverbal immediacy behaviors have been shown to be associated with social influence.

Nonverbal Immediacy in the Classroom

Research Brief

Research on nonverbal immediacy has exploded in the last twenty-five years. McCroskey and his colleagues have specifically explored nonverbal immediacy in the educational context. They have found that a teacher's nonverbal immediacy behavior is highly related to student affect for the teacher (McCroskey and Richmond 1992; McCroskey, Richmond, Sallinen, Fayer, and Barraclough 1995), student affective learning (McCroskey, Fayer, Richmond, Sallinen, and Barraclough 1996), student cognitive learning (McCroskey, Sallinen, Fayer, Richmond, and Barraclough 1996) and student motivation toward studying (Christophel 1990; Richmond 1990). Therefore, it appears that teachers who enact nonverbal immediacy behaviors provide many benefits to their students.

Immediacy refers to the psychological and physical closeness we have with one another. Mehrabian (1971) developed this principle that suggests we are drawn to people and things that we like, prefer, and value highly. Nonverbal immediacy behaviors can indicate inclusion, approachability, involvement, warmth, and positive affect. Some examples of nonverbal immediacy behaviors that individuals might use during social interaction include: eye contact, decreasing distance, appropriate touch, positive facial expressions, open body positions, varying pitch and tempo, and spending time with another person. In general, nonverbal immediacy behaviors produce direct, positive effects on other people (Mehrabian, 1971, 207). This direct-effects model suggests that individuals who engage in immediacy behaviors are more likely to be perceived as warmer, friendlier, more intimate, and more attractive (Anderson 1999). Although immediacy behaviors seem to be ultimately a good thing, can you think of a circumstance where enacting nonverbal immediacy behaviors may be detrimental to your interpersonal relationships? In other words, can you think of a time when you might want to increase the psychological space between yourself and a relational partner? Anderson (1999) suggests that in less positive relationships immediacy behaviors can be perceived as suffocating and threatening.

Practice Sending and Receiving Nonverbal Messages

As mentioned previously, it is often quite difficult to interpret the nonverbal behavior of others. Therefore, we need to supplement our observations with questions. We can clarify our perceptions of other's nonverbal messages. Simply by asking questions such as: "Are you upset?" "Were you being sarcastic?" and "Are you serious?" are easy ways to clarify nonverbal signals from others. Remember that not all nonverbal communication is intentional. Typically, the intentional nonverbal signals are emphasized. Subtle nonverbal behaviors may not be intentional. To accurately interpret others' nonverbal messages it is important to pay attention to all of the behaviors exhibited and seek clarification when verbal and nonverbal messages are contradictory.

Furthermore, be aware of the potential impact of the nonverbal messages you send to others. Because the assumption is that all nonverbal messages are intentional, we must be aware of the nonverbal messages we send. How do others interpret your facial expressions, use of space, and touch? We may never find an answer to this question unless we ask others for feedback.

Recognize Differences in Nonverbal Communication Perceptions

Sometimes individual differences can influence an individual's nonverbal behavior. One example of this is the extent to which individuals have communication apprehension. Recall our discussion of **communication apprehension (CA)** in Chapter Two. **CA** refers to the level of fear or anxiety an individual has that is associated with real or anticipated communication with another person (McCroskey 1977). McCroskey (1976) proposes that high CA's avoid communication situations and actively try to decrease communication attempts. Therefore, he predicts that high CA's are more likely than low CA's to have increased space, to avoid eye contact, to be averse to being touched, to have less vocal variety, to have fewer kinesic movements, and to have longer pause times in conversation. The degree of CA an individual has will determine the nonverbal impact on their interpersonal communication situations.

Age is another factor that may impact how we interpret nonverbal behavior. Life span refers to how our communication changes over time. Just as our verbal communication changes over time, so does our nonverbal behavior. Because we learn most of our nonverbal communication through cultural exposure, it is common for children to lack knowledge in what is considered socially appropriate nonverbal expression. As adults, we have a good time laughing at young people when they make mistakes like making a disgusted face when they taste grandma's signature soup. We do not expect them to have mature social skills, since those skills are acquired over time, although research has shown that throughout our life span we tend to express emotions such as SADFISH, similarly. In other words, the way a child would act surprised is similar to how a ninety-year-old woman would—by opening her eyes, raising her eyebrows, and dropping her jaw. While initially we may have similar ways of expressing emotions, as we grow older we tend to engage in more self-monitoring techniques, become more aware of the rules regarding nonverbal behavior, and modify our behavior to fit these socially appropriate rules.

To send and receive nonverbal messages effectively, it is important to take into consideration the ambiguous nature of nonverbal messages. To make sure that the intended message is effectively communicated to your receiver, be sure that the verbal message is accompanied by multiple nonverbal behaviors that are consistent with the verbal message. Also, be aware of the fact that you can influence others both intentionally and unintentionally by exhibiting nonverbal messages. When you are confused about the nonverbal messages someone is sending, ask questions to clarify the message's meaning. Finally, when interpreting others' nonverbal messages, always consider the impact of individual differences such as personality, age, and culture on message delivery.

FUTURE DIRECTION FOR NONVERBAL COMMUNICATION: ELECTRONIC PARALANGUAGE

Current research has explored how we compensate for the lack of nonverbal cues during electronic communication. Nonverbal communication researchers know it is difficult to express emotions verbally. This is why in face-to-face situations we rely on a certain glance, smile, wink, or even tears to express our emotions. During computer-mediated communication we do not have the luxury of traditional nonverbal cues. Therefore we rely on electronic paralanguage to express emotions and regulate our conversations.

Electronic paralanguage includes emoticons, acronyms, abbreviations, and flaming. **Emoticons** are symbols made up of combinations of keyboard keys that convey emotions. For example, :) refers to a smiley face, while a :(refers to a frown face and ;) refers to someone winking. In addition, text messages and instant messages may insert actual artwork, such as ☺ or ☹.

Table 4.4	Nonverbal Communication: Electronic Paralanguage
Purpose	**Text Messaging Shorthand**
To express emotions	LOL, laugh out loud
	WYWH, Wish you were here
To regulate conversations	TTYL, talk to you later
	BRB, be right back
	L8R, later
	PMFJI, Pardon me for jumping in
	OMPL, one moment, please
	GGFN, gotta go for now
To provide feedback	IGTP, I get the point
	J/K, just kidding
	ISWYM, I see what you mean

Acronymns or text messaging shorthand are used to express a variety of non-verbal cues. Three functions are explored in Table 4.4 above.

Flaming refers to anti-social electronic behavior, such as swearing, firing insults, or shouting. Shouting or expressing anger in computer-mediated communication is usually indicated by typing in all capital letters (Krohn, 2004).

One difference between face-to-face nonverbal communication and engaging in electronic paralanguage is that emoticons are more deliberate and voluntary (Walther and D'Addario 2001). In traditional face-to-face situations, our nonverbal behavior is often unintentional. However, it is impossible to insert these emoticons without intent. Research has found that emoticons may serve the function of complementing the "written" statements, but they do not necessarily enhance them (Walther and D'Addario 2001).

SUMMARY

In this chapter we have introduced nonverbal communication and highlighted the importance of nonverbal communication in our everyday lives. We identified similarities to verbal communication and characterized the unique features of nonverbal behavior. Our hope is that you will heighten your awareness of how you use and interpret the eight types of nonverbal communication and understand how they function in your interpersonal relationships. By increasing your understanding of nonverbal communication, we hope you will avoid the communication problems that often accompany our nonverbal behavior. Remember that individuals are more likely to believe our nonverbal messages, regardless of intent. Therefore it is critical we understand the messages we are sending to others and how we interpret the nonverbal communication behaviors of others.

APPLICATIONS

Discussion Questions

A. Nonverbal Expectancy Violations: In what circumstances has someone violated your nonverbal expectancies? How did you respond? Under what circumstances would violating someone's expectations be considered favorable? Could there be benefits of violating someone's expectations?

B. Are our emotions innate or are they learned behaviors? This has been debated for the last 100 years. Charles Darwin's theory of facial expressions argues that our emotions are inherited (1965). This makes sense when we analyze babies and their expression of emotions. They have had little time to "learn" behavior and yet have universal signals (e.g., screaming) to express emotions. Other researchers suggest that our emotions have both genetic and biological origins because they are consistent among cultures (Ekman 1993; Izard 1992). What would you argue?

C. Discuss how instant messaging, text messages, email, and other computer–mediated methods of communication contribute to a polychronic culture.

D. Develop a list of regulative and constitutive rules for communicating online. How do you determine turn-taking? Is there such a thing as "interrupting" online? How do you demonstrate liking, professionalism, support, and/or anger? What is considered a rule violation online? How do you react to violations?

REFERENCES

Anderson, P. A. 1999. *Nonverbal communication: Forms and functions.* Mountain View, CA: Mayfield Publishing.

Anderson, P. A., and K. K. Sull. 1985. Out of touch, out of reach: Tactile predisposition as predictors of interpersonal distance. *Western Journal of Speech Communication, 49,* 57–72.

Berger, C. R. 1975. Proactive and retroactive attribution processes. *Human Communication Research, 2,* 33–50.

Bowlby, J. 1979. *The making and breaking of affectional bonds.* London: Tavistock.

Bruneau, T. J. 1973. Communicative silences: Forms and functions. *Journal of Communication, 23,* 17–46.

Buck, R. 1975. Nonverbal communication of affect in children. *Journal of Personality and Social Psychology, 31,* 644–653.

Burgoon, J. K. 1978. A communication model of personal space violation: Explication and an initial test. *Human Communication Research, 4,* 129–142.

Burgoon, J. K., D. B. Buller, and W. G. Woodall. 1994. *Nonverbal communication: The unspoken dialogue.* Columbus, OH: Greyden Press.

Burgoon, J., F. G. Hunsaker, and E. J. Dawson. 1994. *Human communication (3rd ed.).* Thousand Oaks, CA: Sage.

Butler, J. C., and R. M. Ryckman. 1993. Perceived and ideal physiques in male and female university students. *Journal of Social Psychology, 133,* 751–752.

Campos, J. J., and C. Stenberg. 1988. Perceptions, appraisals, and emotion: The onset of social referencing. In M. E. Lamb and L. R. Sherrod (Eds.), *Infant social cognition: Empirical and theoretical considerations.* Hillsdale, NJ: Erlbaum.

Carroll, S. T., R. H. Riffenburgh, T. A. Roberts, and E. B. Myhre. 2002. Tattoos and body piercings as indicators of adolescent risk-taking behaviors. *Pediatrics, 109,* 1021–1027.

Christophel, D. M. 1990. The relationship between teacher immediacy behaviors, student motivation, and learning. *Communication Education, 39,* 323–340.

Cortes, J. B., and F. Gatti. 1965. Physique and self description of temperament. *Journal of Consulting Psychology, 29,* 432–439.

Darwin, C. 1965. *The expression of emotions in man and animals.* Chicago: University of Chicago Press.

Dolin, D., and M. Booth-Butterfield. 1993. Reach out and touch someone: Analysis of nonverbal comforting responses. *Communication Quarterly, 41,* 383–393.

Duncan Jr., S. D. 1972. Some signals and rules for taking speaking turns in conversations. *Journal of Personality and Social Psychology, 23,* 283–292.

Ekman, P. 1993. Facial expression and emotion. *American Psychologist, 48,* 384–392.

Ekman, P., and W. V. Friesen. 1969. The repertoire of non-verbal behaviour: categories, origins, usage and codings. *Semiotics 1,* 49–98.

Fletcher, C., and G. M. Diekhoff. 1998. Body-type stereotyping in therapeutic judgments. *Perceptual and Motor Skills, 86,* 842.

Forbes, G. B. 2001. College students with tattoos and piercings: Motives, family experiences, personality factors, and perception by others. *Psychological Reports, 89,* 774–786.

Hall, E. T. 1966. *The hidden dimension,* NY: Doubleday.

Hall, E. T. 1976. *Beyond culture.* New York: Doubleday.

Hickson III, M., D. W. Stacks, and N. Moore. 2004. *Nonverbal communication* (4th *ed.*). Los Angeles, CA: Roxbury.

Izard, C. E. 1992. Basic emotions, relationship among emotions, and emotion-cognition relationships. *Psychological Review, 99,* 561–565.

Jaworski, A. 1993. *The power of silence: Social and pragmatic perspectives.* Newbury Park, CA: Sage.

Jensen, J. V. 1973. Communicative functions of silence. *ETC, 30,* 249–257.

Judge, T. A., and D. M. Cable. 2004. The effect of physical height on workplace success and income: Preliminary test of a theoretical model. *Journal of Applied Psychology, 89,* 428–441.

Kitao, S. K., and K. Kitao. 1988. Differences in the kinesic codes of Americans and Japanese. *World Communication, 17,* 83–103.

Kleinke, C. L., and R. A. Staneski. 1980. First impressions of female bust size. *Journal of Social Psychology, 110,* 123–134.

Knapp, M. L., and J. A. Hall. 2002. *Nonverbal communication in human interaction.* United States: Wadsworth.

Kring, A. M., D. A. Smith, and J. M. Neale. 1994. Individual differences in dispositional expressiveness: The development and validation of the emotional expressivity scale. *Journal of Personality and Social Psychology, 66,* 934–949.

Krohn, F. B. 2004. A generational approach to using emoticons as nonverbal communication. *Journal of Technical Writing and Communication, 34,* 321–328.

Marek, C. I, J. L. Knapp, and M. B. Wanzer. 2004. An exploratory investigation of the relationship between roommates' first impressions and subsequent communication patterns. *Communication Research Reports, 21,* 210–220.

Mayo, C., and M. LaFrance. 1978. *On the acquisition of nonverbal communication: A review.* Merrill-Palmer Quarterly, 24, 213–228.

McCroskey, J. C. 1976. The effects of communication apprehension on nonverbal behavior. *Communication Quarterly, 24,* 39–44.

McCroskey, J. C. 1977. Classroom consequences of communication apprehension. *Communication Education, 26,* 27–33.

McCroskey, J. C. 1992. *An introduction to communication in the classroom.* Edina, MI: Burgess Publishing Division.

McCroskey, J. C., J. M. Fayer, V. P. Richmond, A. Sallinen, and R. A. Barraclough. 1996. A multi-cultural examination of the relationship between nonverbal immediacy and affective learning. *Communication Quarterly, 44,* 297–307.

McCroskey, J. C., and V. P. Richmond. 1992. Increasing teacher influence through immediacy. In V. P. Richmond and J. C. McCroskey, (Eds.), *Power in the classroom: Communication, control and concern* (101–119). Hillsdale: NJ: Lawrence Erlbaum Associates.

McCroskey, J. C., V. P. Richmond, A. Sallinen, J. M. Fayer, and R. A. Barraclough. 1995. A cross-cultural and multi-behavioral analysis of the relationships between nonverbal immediacy and teacher evaluation. *Communication Education, 44,* 281–291.

McCroskey, J. C., A. Sallinen, J. M. Fayer, V. P. Richmond, and R. A. Barraclough. 1996. Nonverbal immediacy and cognitive learning: A cross cultural investigation. *Communication Education, 45,* 200–211.

Mehrabian, A. 1971. *Silent messages.* Belmont, CA: Wadsworth.

Mehrabian, A., and S. R. Ferris. 1967. Inference of attitudes from nonverbal communication in two channels. *Journal of Consulting Psychology, 31,* 248–252.

Portnoy, E. J. 1993. The impact of body type on perceptions of attractiveness by older individuals. *Communication Reports, 6,* 101–109.

Richmond, V. P. 1990. Communication in the classroom: Power and motivation. *Communication Education, 39,* 181–195.

Roberti, J. W., and E. A. Storch. 2005. Psychosocial adjustment of college students with tattoos and piercings. *Journal of College Counseling, 8,* 14–19.

Sheldon, W. H., and S. S. Stevens. 1942. *The varieties of temperament; a psychology of constitutional differences.* Oxford, England: Harper.

Sheldon, W. H., E. M. Hartl, and E. McDermott. 1949. *The variety of delinquent youth.* Oxford, England: Harper.

Sprecher, S. 1989. Premarital sexual standards for different categories of individuals. *Journal of Sex Research, 26,* 232–248.

Street, R. L., and D. B. Buller. 1987. Nonverbal response patterns in physician-patient interactions: A functional analysis. *Journal of Nonverbal Behavior, 11,* 234–253.

Thayer, S. 1988. Close encounters. *Psychology Today, 22,* 30–36.

Tucker, L. A. 1983. Cigarette smoking intentions and obesity among high school males. *Psychological Reports, 52,* 530.

Wagner, H. L., C. J. MacDonald, and A. S. R. Manstead. 1986. Communication of individual emotions by spontaneous facial expressions. *Journal of Personality and Social Psychology, 50,* 737–743.

Walther, J. B., and K. P. D'Addario. 2001. The impacts of emoticons on message interpretation in computer-mediated communication. *Social Science Computer Review, 19,* 324–347.

Watkins, L. M., and L. Johnston. 2000. Screening job applicants: The impact of physical attractiveness and application quality. *International Journal of Selection and Assessment, 8,* 76.

Wiemann, J., and M. Knapp. 1975. Turn-taking in conversation. *Journal of Communication, 25,* 75–92.

Zuckerman, M., M. S. Lipets, J. H. Koivumaki, and R. Rosenthanl. 1975. Encoding and decoding nonverbal cues of emotion. *Journal of Personality and Social Psychology, 32,* 1068–1076.

Perception and Listening
Do You Hear What I Hear?

© Elena Kouptsova-Vasic, 2007, Shutterstock.

OBJECTIVES

- Explain the reason humans are limited in their capacity to process information
- Distinguish between the three key perception processes
- Define the primary selectivity processes
- Describe the factors that affect the selective exposure, selective attention and selective retention processes
- Demonstrate an understanding of social identity theory
- Explain schemata and the types of information that it typically includes
- Describe the four schemata that we use to interpret communication events
- Define attribution theory and distinguish between internal and external attributions
- Explain covariation theory and the three types of information used to interpret people's behavior
- Define self-serving bias and explain how it is problematic
- Describe the fundamental attribution error
- Discuss three factors that influence our perceptions
- Distinguish between hearing and listening processes
- Identify the seven steps to effective listening
- Recall the four listening styles and identify the focus of each
- Explain the four motivations to listen and recall a potential pitfall of each
- Recognize the six common listening misbehaviors

KEY TERMS

perception	selective attention	personal constructs
limited capacity	novelty	stereotypes
processors	size	social identity theory
selection	concrete	scripts
selective exposure	selective retention	script theory
biased information	primacy and recency	interpretation
search	organization	attribution theory
proximity	constructivism	external attribution
utility	schemata	unintentionality
reinforce	prototypes	intentionality

internal attribution	BIG EARS	appreciative listening
covariation theory	paraphrasing	comprehensive
distinctiveness	positive feedback	listening
consistency	negative feedback	evaluative listening
consensus	dual perspective taking	empathetic listening
self-serving bias	noise	pseudo-listening
fundamental	listening styles	monopolizing
attribution error	people-oriented	disconfirming
rapport talk	action-oriented	defensive listening
report talk	content-oriented	selective listening
hearing	time-oriented listening	ambushing
listening	discriminate listening	

In the *Friends* episode "The One Where Ross and Rachel Take a Break," Ross becomes frustrated by Rachel's enthusiasm for her new job. To make matters worse, Ross has also been acting jealous over Rachel's relationship with her boss, Mark. Ross tries to explain to Rachel that he wants to have a relationship with her, that he is tired of always getting her answering machine and having dates cancelled because of her work. The situation becomes a bit heated when Rachel sarcastically asks Ross if he wants her to quit her job so she can be his girlfriend full-time, with no other obligations. Rachel gets very frustrated and tells Ross that they can't keep arguing about the same thing over and over again.

Finally, Rachel suggests that maybe they should take a break. Ross understands that to mean a moment to cool off and calm down; maybe do something that will take their minds off the problem. Rachel has something else in mind: a break from the relationship.

OVERVIEW

Just like Ross and Rachel, we have all encountered situations in relationships where our perceptions have caused us to interpret messages differently than they were intended. Ross perceived Rachel's request to take a "break" to mean that she needed a temporary time-out from their discussion. In Rachel's mind, the meaning of the word "break" was much different.

Imagine a world where we could completely eliminate misunderstandings between roommates, co-workers, relationship partners, parents, children, teachers, and students. Could such a world *ever* exist? In this chapter we explore the reasons our messages are sometimes partially interpreted, completely misinterpreted, or even ignored by others. Two processes that play a key role in how we send and receive messages in our relationships are perception and listening. In the first part of this chapter we examine the process of perception, paying special attention to the relationship between elements of perception and their relationship to interpersonal communication. We will then turn our attention to the process of listening and how it impacts our interpersonal relationships. Can you recall a time when someone accused you of not listening? Perhaps you *heard* what the person said but did not really *listen* to what they were saying. In the second part of this chapter we will distinguish between the terms *hearing* and *listening,* and advance a number of ways to improve listening, an extremely important, yet often neglected, communication skill.

Perception and listening are so closely intertwined that it is difficult to discuss one without addressing the other. As we form relationships, our perception impacts how we view the other person as well as how we interpret their messages and behaviors. In the opening scenario Ross perceived his relationship with Rachel to be solid. Rachel, on the other hand, perceived the relationship to be on rocky ground due to Ross' jealous behavior. It is not at all unusual for two people to perceive the same relationship in very different ways. Now consider the role that perception plays on your ability to listen. It should come as no surprise that if our perception differs, our listening skills will also differ. In fact, interpretation is a common factor present in both of the processes of perception and of listening. When Rachel commented that they needed a "break," Ross' perception of their relationship caused him to listen and interpret her message in a way that was very different from what Rachel intended. If you watch reality television shows such as *Survivor* or *Big Brother,* you see numerous examples of the link between perception and listening. Since these programs involve strategy, many of the players plant "seeds of doubt" in the minds of their competitors with the hope that it impairs their perception and ability to listen and interpret messages from others. Often, the winning contestant is the player who has succeeded in impairing the perception and listening skills of the competitors.

Our hope is that once you gain a better understanding of the relationship between these two concepts, you will gain a better understanding of why individuals view relationships, people, behaviors, and messages in different ways. An awareness of the impact of perception and listening in our relationships will increase the accuracy of our interpersonal communication. Let us first focus on the primary perceptual processes and examine the relationship between perception and interpersonal communication.

PERCEPTION AND INTERPERSONAL COMMUNICATION

Perception can be best described as the lens through which we view the world. Just as your view of color would be altered if you were to wear a pair of glasses with blue lenses, our perception impacts our view of people, events, and behaviors. One definition of **perception** is that it is the process of selecting, organizing and interpreting sensory information into a coherent or lucid depiction of the world around us (Klopf 1995). Stated more simply, perception is essentially how we interpret and assign meaning to others' behaviors and messages based on our background and past experiences. The word "experience" is important in understanding the overall process of perception. Consider the role that perception has played in your college experience. Perhaps you enjoy writing and have kept a personal journal. If your English professor assigned daily journal entries in her class, you might tell others that the class was one of the most enjoyable ones you have ever taken. Based on your experience—and your love for writing and journaling—you perceived the class to be easy and enjoyable, and you looked forward to communicating with your professor during her office hours to discuss how you could improve on your writing. But suppose there is another student who has struggled with writing throughout his academic career. He might report to others that the teacher was difficult to talk with and that her assignments were unfair. Based on his perception, their conversations during office hours may have been full of criticism and confusion, and he may describe the instructor as being "uncaring" and an "impossible perfectionist." Since each student brought a unique background and set of experiences to the class, the resulting perceptions of the teacher and class were very different.

Chances are that you have learned about perception in other classes, such as psychology or sociology. Researchers from a wide range of academic fields study perceptual processes. While psychologists conducted much of the initial research in the area of perception, communication scholars have focused specifically on the impact of perception on the meanings assigned to messages. From a communication perspective, perception is important because we often define ourselves based on our perceptions of how others see us. Recall our discussion in Chapter Two of reflected appraisal (or looking glass self) which explains how we form impressions of ourselves based on how we think others see us. If people respond favorably toward us, we may feel more self-assured and communicate in a more confident manner. Our perception also causes us to form impressions of others which impacts how we communicate with them. How would you feel if you approached one of your classmates at a party and she ignored you? Chances are you would perceive her to be rude and would avoid subsequent interactions with her when you see her in class or on campus. But take a moment to consider the factors that might have influenced your perception. Perhaps you, or maybe even your classmate, were nervous because you have not been to many parties on campus. Maybe your classmate did not recognize you due to the fact that there are many people in the class. There are a number of factors that could alter the perception each of you has of the interaction at the party. All of our interpersonal interactions are influenced by the perceptions we form of ourselves and others. In order to fully grasp the importance of perception, let us examine how we break down bits of information from our environment and form perceptions of ourselves and others.

Lyrics from a song made popular by the group The Police illustrate a common problem most of us have experienced in our lifetime—being inundated with too much information. Have you ever felt overwhelmed because it seemed as though your professor disseminated too much information in one lecture? Or have you experienced problems at work because your manager gave you too many instructions, tasks or responsibilities at once? Perhaps you have returned to your apartment after being away for a few days only to find that your inbox is overflowing with email and your answering machine is filled with messages. If any of these situations seem familiar to you, you are not

© Diego Cervo, 2007, Shutterstock.

Have you ever felt overwhelmed at work?

alone. On any given day, we encounter literally thousands of stimuli that bombard our senses and compete for our attention.

Social psychologist Robert Cialdini (2001) notes that we live in an extremely complicated society which he describes as "easily the most rapidly moving and complex that has ever existed on this planet" (7). Cialdini (2001) further states that we cannot analyze all aspects of our environment because "we haven't the time, energy or capacity for it" (7). If it is not possible to process and recall everything we see, hear, taste, touch, or smell, then how do we make sense of the world around us?

The way humans manage all of the stimuli encountered in the environment is to limit the amount and type of information taken in. This elimination process often occurs at a subconscious level. Thus, on any given day, we put limits on what we choose to see, hear, taste, touch, or smell. Because of the innate limitations in our ability to process information, humans are often described as **limited capacity processors.** Stated simply, we consciously and subconsciously make choices about the amount and type of stimuli we perceive. Think of a time when you were so focused on your homework that when your mother commented on how loud you were playing your music, you thought, "Wow, I can't even really hear it." To fully understand how people make sense of their environment, we need to take a closer look at three key perceptual processes: selection, organization and interpretation.

Selection

The first perception process is **selection.** While you might not always be consciously aware of the process of selection, we are continually making choices about the amount and type of information that we choose to notice. Remember our earlier discussion about our ability to be limited capacity processors? It is virtually impossible to pay attention to all the things we could possibly sense at any given time. These limitations in our ability to assimilate and interpret information prevent us from "taking it all in" and so we must select certain messages or stimuli over others. These selections we make are often done in a purposeful rather than random manner (Klopf 1995). Three primary selectivity processes which impact our perception include selective exposure, selective attention, and selective retention. The next sections provide an overview of each of these processes and discuss variables that affect them.

Selective exposure refers to the choice to subject oneself to certain stimuli. Choices regarding which messages and stimuli you will subject yourself to are made each day. You choose whether to expose yourself to the messages being sent by advertisers and newscasters when you decide whether to turn on your television or radio each morning. You choose whether to subject yourself to the messages left on your answering machine or via email. Often the choice to engage in selective exposure is based on our desire to seek information or stimuli that is comfortable or familiar to us. Culture plays a key role in determining what messages or stimuli we choose to expose ourselves to and those which we avoid. Consider the fact that some people avoid communicating with those from other cultural backgrounds. They engage in selective exposure by avoiding conversations with people from different cultures. Individuals may focus on the obvious differences of race or ethnicity and assume that they do not have anything in common with people who are

It's your choice to watch television and subject yourself to shows and advertising.

© Philip Date, 2007, Shutterstock.

so dissimilar. The choice to avoid communication may cause individuals to miss learning about all the beliefs and interests that are shared. According to Fischer and his colleagues (2005), we are most likely to seek out information consistent with our beliefs, values, and attitudes and to avoid information that is viewed as inconsistent. Our propensity to seek out certain types of information and avoid others is referred to as a **biased information search** (Fischer et al. 2005). While we might not consciously be aware of this process, each day we selectively choose to associate with particular individuals or groups of people and attend to certain types of messages in a variety of contexts. Perhaps today you chose to attend your communication class rather than going out to eat lunch with a friend. The decision to attend your communication class is yet another example of selective exposure.

There are a number of factors that affect selective exposure including, among others: proximity, utility, and reinforcement. Not surprisingly, we are most likely to selectively expose ourselves to messages that are nearby, or close in proximity. In fact, **proximity** is the number one predictor of whether we will develop a relationship with another person (Katz and Hill 1958). Consider the relationships that you formed with those who attended your high school. Proximity impacted your ability to selectively expose yourself to those in the same school and form relationships. While the Internet has changed the way we communicate and form relationships, most people still find it difficult to form relationships and communicate with those who are not physically close to them. Second, we are most likely to expose ourselves to messages that we perceive as being useful. **Utility** refers to the perception that particular messages are immediately useful; these messages have a much greater chance of being selected than those that are not seen as useful (McCroskey and Richmond 1996). Expecting an important message from your parents will influence your choice to selectively expose yourself to your email messages. If there are several messages in your inbox, a message from friend or family member is more likely to be viewed than one from the Department of Student Services at your university. Finally, most people expose themselves to messages that are consistent with their views, or **reinforce,** their attitudes and beliefs (Fischer et al. 2005). Thus, if you are strongly opposed to the death penalty, you will probably not attend a lecture delivered by a professor advocating capital punishment for convicted murderers.

Once we have made the decision to place ourselves in a position to physically receive a message, we then focus on certain aspects or elements of the message. **Selective attention** refers to the decision to pay attention to certain stimuli while simultaneously ignoring others. Factors which affect selective attention often include the novelty, size, and concreteness of the stimuli. **Novelty** refers to the tendency to pay attention to stimuli that are novel, new, or different. Novel aspects are more likely to capture our attention than those with which we are familiar. For example, we tend to notice a friend's new hairstyle almost immediately. In the *Friends* episode discussed at the beginning of the chapter, Rachel became more aware of and paid closer attention to changes in Ross' behavior. Previously, he had been secure and confident in their relationship, but as Rachel became more focused on her career, his messages communicated a new jealousy. Another factor that affects selective attention is the **size,** or magnitude, of the stimuli. We are more likely to pay attention to large items, objects, or people. It probably is not completely by chance that most Chief Executive Officers in U.S. companies are at least six feet tall and that virtually every U.S. President elected since 1900 has been the taller of the two candidates. Finally, we are more likely to pay attention to information that is **concrete,** or well-defined, than to information which is perceived as abstract or ambiguous. Individuals have an easier time attending to messages that are clear and straightforward. For example, if a manager tells an employee to "change her attitude and behavior," but does not provide specific or concrete information about how or why the attitude or behavior is problematic, the employee is likely to ignore this message (McCroskey and Richmond 1996).

What kind of an impression do you try to make in a job interview?

© Marcin Balcerzak, 2007, Shutterstock.

Once the decision has been made to expose and attend to stimuli, the final stage in the selectivity process involves **selective retention,** which refers to the choice to save or delete information from one's long term memory. Two factors affecting the propensity to retain information include primacy and recency effects, and utility. Researchers have identified a range of variables which affect an individual's ability to retain information. When studying the type of information people are most likely to retain, researchers note that arguments delivered first **(primacy)** and last **(recency)** in a persuasive presentation are more likely to be recalled and to be more persuasive (Gass and Seiter 2003). As we form relationships, we are often concerned with the first or last impression that we make. It has been estimated that we form our initial impression of others during the first three to five seconds. Recall the last job interview that you attended. Careful attention was paid to your clothing and appearance to ensure that you would make a positive first impression that the interviewer would remember. However, if you tripped and spilled the contents of your portfolio as you exited the interview, the recency of the last impression may be imprinted on the interviewer's memory. A second important factor related to retention is **utility,** or usefulness. Almost all of us have heard the phrase, "use it or lose it." Essentially what this phrase implies is that if we do not apply the information we obtain, we may not retain it later. For example, many of you might have received training in cardiopulmonary resuscitation (CPR) at one time in your life. But if one of your classmates needed CPR, would you remember the steps? The same principle is true of the information and skills discussed in this text. It is our hope that by providing you with examples of concepts and information, you will see the usefulness of the strategies and become more effective in your interpersonal interactions with others.

Organization

Once we have selected information, or stimuli, we then begin the process of placing it into categories in order to make sense of it. **Organization** "refers to our need to place the perceived characteristics of something into the whole to which it seems to belong" (Klopf 1995, 51). Organization is the process by which we take the stimuli and make sense of it so that it is meaningful to us. Remember the earlier example of the classmate who ignored you at a party? Some of the stimuli that caused you to form your perception included her lack of eye contact and her failure to reciprocate your greeting. In the organization process, you take each of these stimuli (eye contact and lack of communication) and put them together to form an impression.

One theory that is useful in understanding how individuals organize information in meaningful ways is constructivism. Kelly (1970) developed the theory of **constructivism** to explain the process we use to organize and interpret experiences by applying cognitive structures labeled schemata. **Schemata** are "organized clusters of knowledge and information about particular topics" (Hockenbury and Hockenbury 2006, 265). Another way to describe schemata is as mental filing cabinets with several drawers used to help organize and process information. Schemata are the results of one's experiences and, therefore, are dynamic and often changing as we encounter new relationships and life experiences. Suppose your first romantic relationship was a disaster. The initial schema you formed to organize information about romantic relationships (which may have been obtained from television shows or movies) was likely altered to include this negative experience you encountered. But suppose your next romantic partner is incredibly thoughtful and romantic. New information is incorporated to your schema that now enables you to evaluate various aspects of romantic relationships based on both the positive and negative experiences you encountered in the past. Thus, we apply schemata to make sense of our communication experiences. More specifically, we apply four different types of schemata to interpret interpersonal encounters: prototypes, personal constructs, stereotypes, and scripts (Fiske and Taylor 1984; Kelley 1972; Reeder 1985).

Have you ever thought of your ideal romantic partner? What would he or she be like? **Prototypes** are knowledge structures which represent the most common attributes of a phenomenon. These structures are used to help organize stimuli and influence our interactions with others (Fehr and Russell 1991). Prototypes provide us with a "benchmark" that is the standard used to evaluate and categorize other examples that fall into the same category. Recall your initial encounter with someone you dated recently. It is very likely that you evaluated this individual's behaviors based on whether this person fit your "prototypical," or best, example of a relationship partner. If you were to make a list of the characteristics you desire in the "ideal" romantic partner, these preconceived ideas and expectations represent your prototype and affect how you will perceive each potential romantic partner encountered in the future. Research by Fehr and Russell (1991) supports the idea that we have prototypes about love and friendship. They conducted six different studies in an attempt to identify participants' prototypical examples of different types of love (e.g., maternal love, paternal love, friendship love, sisterly love, puppy love, infatuation, and so on) and the factors associated with love. Characteristics such as caring, helping, establishing a bond, sharing, feeling free to talk, demonstrating respect, and exhibiting closeness were all associated with perceptions of love. In a related study, Fehr (2004) examined prototypical examples of interactions which led to greater perceived intimacy in same-sex friendships. Fehr (2004) found that interaction patterns which involved increased levels of self-disclosure and emotional support were perceived by friends as being more prototypical of expectations for intimacy than other types of practical support. Prototype theory is extremely useful in shedding light on how we organize our thoughts about interpersonal communication and relationships.

Personal constructs serve to help you evaluate others and influence your interactions.

A second type of schemata is **personal constructs** which Kelly (1955; 1970; 1991) describes as bipolar dimensions of meaning used to predict and evaluate how people behave. Personal constructs have also been described as the "mental yardsticks" that we use to assess people and social situations. Several examples of personal constructs include: responsible-irresponsible, assertive-unassertive, friendly-unfriendly, intelligent-unintelligent, and forthright-guarded. Personal constructs serve as another means of evaluating others and simultaneously influence how we approach interactions. For example, if you label your co-worker as "friendly" you may smile more at this person and share more personal information than you would with another co-worker labeled as "unfriendly." Raskin (2002) notes that we monitor our personal constructs closely and keep track of how accurately they predict life circumstances. When necessary, we revise them when we perceive them as unreliable. We tend to define situations and people based on the personal constructs that we use regularly. Thus, it is possible that we might not be aware of qualities some people possess or situations that we do not access regularly (Raskin 2002).

The third type of schema we use to help us organize information is stereotypes. **Stereotypes** are impressions and expectations based on one's knowledge or beliefs about a specific group of people which are then applied to all individuals who are members of that group. Stereotypes greatly influence the way messages are perceived. Some researchers argue that stereotypes are often activated automatically when an individual observes a member of a group or category (Carlston 1992) and we are likely to predict how that person will behave. For example, Hamilton and Sherman (1994) note that individuals' perceptions of different racial and ethnic groups are often "planted in early childhood by influential adults in their lives" (3). Influential individuals, such as family members, and the media play an important role in shaping how we define others and how we view the world.

Why do we categorize people, events, and objects? As mentioned previously, we are limited in our ability to process the sheer number of stimuli bombarding us at any given time. Thus, we identify ways to categorize and organize stimuli to enhance "cognitive efficiency," or to make information more manageable. A second explanation for our tendency to stereotype as described by Hamilton and Sherman (1994) is "categorization as self-enhancement" (6). Simply stated, we tend to evaluate those groups to which we belong more favorably than groups to which we do not belong. Recall the groups you associated with in high school. If you were a member of the student council, you may have viewed members as being strong leaders and very organized. Students who were not members of the student council may have created their own schema for evaluating its members—they may have labeled them as being "power-hungry," or aggressive. **Social identity theory** offers an explanation for our tendency to evaluate in-groups more

If you're on a sports team, you may identify more closely with other athletes.

positively than out-groups. According to social identity theory, an individual's self-esteem is often connected to membership or association with social groups (Hamilton and Sherman 1994; Turner 1987). In an effort to maintain a positive identity, we may overemphasize or accentuate differences between in-groups and out-groups.

Can placing people into groups or categories based on particular traits or characteristics be problematic? Absolutely! For example, individuals are often categorized based on whether they have some type of physical or mental disability. Braithwaite and her colleagues found that people without disabilities often assume that individuals with physical disabilities are helpless, while this is certainly not the case (Braithwaite and Harter 2000). They conducted a number of interviews with persons with physical disabilities and found that they often received a great deal of either unwanted or unsolicited help from persons without disabilities. This example illustrates the problem of inaccurately categorizing people. In this case, persons without disabilities inaccurately categorized persons with disabilities as helpless or needy, resulting in inappropriate "helping" behavior. Suggestions for managing these interactions more appropriately will be addressed in Chapter Thirteen when we discuss interpersonal communication in health-related contexts.

People form stereotypes about individuals based on race, culture, sex, sexual orientation, age, education, intelligence, and affiliations, among other characteristics. It is crucial that we realize that stereotypes are formed as a result of our perceptions of others and, as a result, can be accurate or inaccurate. When inaccurate or inflexible stereotypes are applied to individuals, they often divide rather than unite people. Is it possible to resist the temptation to stereotype or categorize people? While the research on changing stereotypes is not extensive, much of it is promising. Stereotyping is a normal tendency. Our desire to reduce our level of uncertainty about people and situations leads us into the stereotype "trap." We are uncomfortable in situations where we have little or no information about others, and our initial tendency is to open our schematic files in an attempt to locate any information that will help us figure out how to communicate. For example, one of the authors of your textbook is a native of West Virginia. Throughout her life, she has encountered stereotypes of people from West Virginia. When she lived in California, one of her college roommates commented, "You're nothing at all what I expected someone from West Virginia to be like!" When asked to describe her expectations, the roommate described some very negative stereotypes. The two became best friends and discovered that even though one was from Texas and the other was from West Virginia, they had more in common than they thought. If you have never communicated with a person from another culture, your first tendency may be to recall any information associated with the person's culture that you have read about or seen on television. Regardless of whether this information is accurate or inaccurate, it is often used as a "guide" for our expectations and communication. The key to overcoming the negative outcomes of stereotyping is to remain open-minded and flexible. While your tendency may be to look for something to help organize and make sense of stimuli, remember that the information used to form the stereotype may be incorrect. Fortunately, there is a growing body of scholarship which suggests that the stereotypes people form can be modified over time (Hamilton and Sherman 1994).

The last type of schema we use to organize is scripts. According to Abelson (1982), **scripts** are knowledge structures that guide and influence how we process information. Abelson (1982) describes scripts as an "organized bundle of expectations about an event sequence" (134). Simply stated, we adhere to a number of different scripts throughout a day, scripts that tell us what to do and say, as well as *how* to do and say it. Very often we never notice how scripted our day-to-day interactions are until someone deviates from the expected script. A comedian makes reference to the potential embarrassment caused by scripts in his description of an encounter he had when exiting a taxi cab at the airport.

Taxi Driver: Thanks! Have a nice flight!

Comedian: You too! *(then, realizing that the taxi driver is not flying)* I mean, the next time you fly somewhere.

Another scenario, a casual conversation between two co-workers at the copy machine in the workplace, illustrates the relevance of scripts to our day-to-day functioning.

Dominique: Hi Anthony!

Anthony: Hey Dominique, how are you?

Dominique: Not so good. My arthritis is acting up and it's making it impossible for me to get any work done on this report that is due at noon. Then my son's school just called to say he's not feeling well, and I can't get a hold of my sister to go pick him up at school. It's just been one thing after another.

Anthony: *(looking at his watch)* Wow, I didn't realize it was so late! Um, yeah, well, hey, nice talking to you. I've got to go!

Did Anthony respond appropriately to Dominique's explicit description of how she was feeling? Can you explain why Anthony had to go? **Script theory** explains Anthony's reaction to Dominique's description of her arthritis and problems with child care. According to script theory, we often interact with others in a way that could be described as "automatic" or even "mindless." Because we have repeated experience with these scripts, we are able to adhere to them in a manner described as "mindless," meaning that we are not consciously aware of the fact that we are following a script. Essentially, we rely on scripts to tell us how to proceed in situations and what to say. We enter into situations that we have been in before with a specific set of expectations and, when individuals violate our expectations by not adhering to the script, we are not sure what to do. From an interpersonal communication perspective, we use scripts to determine how to proceed during social interaction and form perceptions of others based on whether or not they are following the "script."

Interpretation

After we have selected and organized information, the final step in the perception process involves interpretation. **Interpretation** is the subjective process of making sense of our perceptions. The interpretation process is described as highly subjective because individuals' interpretations of communication events vary extensively and are influenced by a wide range of factors. The following sections serve as an overview of the dominant theory used to explain how people interpret information, discuss errors in interpretive processes, and identify factors that influence the ways we interpret information.

The dominant theory that explains how people explain their own and others' behavior is known as **attribution theory** (Heider 1958; Kelley 1967; 1971). This theory is also known as naïve psychology because people often try to connect observable behavior to unobservable causes (Littlejohn 1983). Can you recall a time when you have tried to explain a friend's unusual behavior? Perhaps she was supposed to phone you at a scheduled time, and the call never came. You may try to explain her lack of communication by theorizing that she overslept, the car broke down, or she had a fight with a significant other. All of these are causes that you have not directly observed, but they are used as potential explanations for the friend's behavior. Attribution theory is commonly applied to interpret the reasons for our own actions as well as the actions of others. According to Heider (1958) there are three basic assumptions to attribution theory: (1) that it is natural for people to attempt to establish the causes of their own and others' behavior, (2) that people assign causes for behavior systematically, and (3) that the attribution impacts the perceiver's feelings and subsequent behavior. Thus, the causes assigned to peoples' behaviors play a significant role in determining reactions to interpreted behaviors.

Maybe you visualize your friend standing by her broken-down car as a reason she didn't call you.

According to attribution theory, people assign causes to behaviors in a fairly systematic way and typically use different types of information to make these decisions. Generally, when individuals attempt to explain behaviors, they will choose among three different explanations: the situation, unintentionality or chance, and intentionality or dispositions (Heider 1958). A person's behavior may be best explained by considering the situation and how this factor may have influenced behavior. Situational factors are often referred to as **external attributions.** For example, perhaps you are normally talkative and outgoing when in social situations. However, you go to a party with some friends and see your former relationship partner with a new "love" interest. Because you still have feelings for this person, this situation is upsetting to you, and you spend the evening moping and avoiding conversations. Hence, your behavior at the party could be best explained by situational or external attributions. The second factor typically used to explain behavior is **unintentionality** or chance, which refers to one's inability to predict whether the behaviors will be consistent in the future (Kelsey et al. 2004). For example, someone may guess several answers on a difficult test and then claim that they may or may not be able to replicate their test performance again in the future. The third factor, **intentionality,** or disposition, is also referred to as an internal attribution. **Internal attributions** are typically described as being stable or persistent and often refer to behaviors that are likely to be exhibited repeatedly across a variety of contexts (Heider 1958). If your friend Sally acts quiet and reserved in almost all situations, then you would explain her quiet and reserved demeanor at your birthday party based on internal attributions or personality traits. When attempting to explain her behavior, you might say "Sally is just that way," or tell others that she is normally very shy.

Harold Kelley (1973) also developed a prominent theory of attribution which attempts to explain how we formulate perceptions of others. Kelley's **covariation theory** states that we decide whether peoples' behavior is based on either internal or external factors by using three different and important types of information: distinctiveness, consensus, and consistency. In order to apply Kelley's covariation principle, we must have multiple observations of individuals to accurately explain their behavior. **Distinctiveness** refers to whether or not a person typically behaves the same way with the target, or receiver, of the behavior. When distinctiveness is high, we tend to attribute others' behavior to external causes. When distinctiveness is low, we tend to attribute others' behavior to internal causes. For example, if Professor Munhall is always pleasant and helpful toward all students, he would be exhibiting low levels of distinctiveness. In this situation, Dr. Munhall's behavior would be attributed to internal factors (e.g., he is such a caring teacher). Suppose one minute Professor Munhall snaps at Alan during class and the next minute he responds calmly to Marcus' request for clarification. In this situation, his behavior would be described as highly distinctive since he does not normally behave this way toward students. External factors would be used to explain his highly distinctive behavior (e.g., he had a bad day).

The second type of information used to attribute causes to behaviors is consistency. **Consistency** refers to whether an individual behaves the same way across contexts and at various times. For example, would the person behave the same way regardless of whether she was at a party, at work, at school, or at a bar? It is important to keep in mind that the key element here is the context or situation. When an individual acts in a highly consistent manner, we tend to attribute the individual's behavior to internal rather than external causes. Very often, we ask whether the behavior is unique or consistent in the particular context. If your friend Kaia is always loud and outgoing in social situations, and you observe her acting this way at a party, you would explain her behavior based on internal rather than external factors. That is, Kaia acted in a loud, outgoing manner because this is the way she typically behaves with most individuals and in most situations (high consistency). Conversely, if Kaia was quiet, shy, and withdrawn at the same party, you might explain her behavior by saying that the party must not have been fun (external factor) because she was acting differently than the expected behavior in social situations (low consistency).

The final factor, **consensus**, considers whether the behavior is unique to the individual or if they are behaving in the way that would be typically expected of others. We say that consensus is high when a person acts the same way that others would behave. Recall our example from the beginning of the chapter. Did Ross behave in a way that was similar to the way Joey, Chandler, or several other men would respond? The key element in this factor is the actor, or source of behavior, (as opposed to the context, which is the focus of consistency). When consensus is high, we attribute peoples' behavior to external rather than internal factors. For example, the majority of Americans say that they do not enjoy giving speeches and typically experience anxiety prior to and during the event (high consensus). Thus, we attribute Jay's speech anxiety to external (everyone is nervous about public speaking) rather than internal factors. But suppose Jay actually looks forward to the prospect of public speaking. When someone actually enjoys giving speeches (low consensus), we might explain this person's unique behavior by saying this person is highly confident and self-assured (internal factors).

Not surprisingly, we often evaluate and explain our *own* behavior using standards that are very different from those used to evaluate and explain the behavior of *others*. The two most common attribution errors people make are known as the self-serving bias and the fundamental attribution error. The **self-serving bias** states that we tend to manufacture, or construct, attributions which best serve our own self-interests (Hamachek 1992). For example, when we excel in school or sports, we often explain our success based on internal factors or causes. We might think "I am smart" or "I am an incredible athlete," both of which are internal attributions. The self-serving bias provides us with a viable explanation for the sources of student motivation in the classroom. Research by Gorham and her colleagues (1992) indicates that students view motivation in school as a student-owned trait or characteristic. Thus, when a student feels motivated to do well in school, he or she credits this intention to do well on internal rather than external factors. On the other hand, when a student feels unmotivated, or is unwilling to work hard in school, he or she is more likely to attribute the cause of this lack of motivation to the teacher's behavior (external attributions—the teacher did not explain the assignment clearly) rather than to the self (internal attributions). Why do we avoid taking responsibility for our poor performance, mistakes, or shortcomings? One explanation for attributing our failures to external causes is to save face. While our tendency to protect our own self-image is understandable, it is important to realize that these distorted perceptions of self are problematic. Falsely taking credit for accomplishments and blaming others (or circumstances) for our failures can lead to distorted self-images and inaccurate representations of ourselves during social interaction (Hamacheck, 1992).

The next question to ask is whether we attribute others' failures and successes to external or internal factors? A second common attribution error often made during the interpretation stage of perception is the **fundamental attribution error.** When attempting to explain others' negative behaviors, we tend to overestimate the internal factors or causes and underestimate the external factors or causes. Conversely, when attempting to explain our *own* mistakes or shortcomings, we tend to overestimate the external causes and underestimate the internal causes. For example, if you are driving to school and see someone speeding by you, you might say to your friend, "What a reckless driver," (internal attribution). However, if you are speeding down the same road the next day and that same friend asks you why you are in such a rush, you might respond, "I am late for work," or "I need to get a parking space," both of which are external attributions. Kelsey and her colleagues (2004) recently used attribution theory to investigate the explanations students provided for their college instructors' classroom "misbehaviors." Examples of teacher misbehaviors include boring lectures, unfair grading, and providing too much information. The researchers found that students were more likely to attribute their teachers' inappropriate classroom behaviors to internal causes (e.g., he doesn't care about teaching) rather than to external causes (e.g., she's had a bad day). It is important to understand and acknowledge that while the way we make sense of our own and others' behaviors is less than perfect, it greatly affects how we interact with others. To improve the way we select, organize, and interpret information, it is also essential to consider our individual differences and how these differences impact our perception.

INDIVIDUAL DIFFERENCES AND PERCEPTIONS

While there are numerous factors that affect the way we perceive information, in this section we focus on three widely researched and acknowledged variables related to perception. Three variables that have been identified by scholars as impacting perception are sex, age, and culture. We begin our discussion by considering how sex differences affect perception and communication.

Do you think men and women view the world differently? Deborah Tannen, a noted gender scholar and linguist, would answer this question with an unequivocal "Yes!" Tannen (1986; 1990; 1994) notes that men and women hold different worldviews and philosophies regarding how they are expected to act in society which evolve from early interactions with family members, peers, and society. Tannen and other gender scholars (see, for example, Wood 1999) assert that men and women are socialized differently and, as a result, develop different perceptions of the world and their place within it. For example, women often perceive the world as a place to connect and form bonds with others. Men, on the other hand, view the world as a place to assert their independence and autonomy. These differences in perceptions affect the ways that men and women approach social interactions. Tannen says that women often engage in **rapport talk** which is analogous to small talk or phatic communication, while men often exhibit **report talk** which involves discussions about facts, events, and solutions. The following scenario illustrates the difference between rapport and report talk.

> *Elyse and Dave got a flat tire during their drive to work. As they discuss the event with colleagues, Elyse explains various details associated with the tire episode when speaking with her friends. "It was horrible! We were driving down the freeway when all of the sudden we heard a 'thump-thump' under the car. Of course, today would be the day that we left the cell phone at home on the table! Didn't you get a flat tire about a month ago, Janelle?"*

Typically, other females respond by sharing their similar stories and experiences. Dave, on the other hand, would provide the details of the morning's event differently.

> *"We got a flat tire on Interstate 270 this morning. We didn't have a cell phone, but the car behind us pulled over and let me use their phone to call AAA."*

It is important to note that not all men and women communicate this way. However, because men and women may see the world differently, it affects how they perceive themselves and others and ultimately impacts their interpersonal communication.

A second frequently studied variable that affects perceptions is age. Recall the last time you engaged in a conversation with older relatives, friends, or co-workers. Did you notice any differences in your perspectives on various issues? One student recently shared an example of a conversation held with her mother that illustrated the impact of age on perceptual differences. Because this female student does not like to cook or clean, her mother told her that "No man will want to marry her!" The daughter argued her "case" by explaining to her mother that times have changed and that women and men today often share domestic responsibilities in the home. This conversation between mother and daughter illustrates how age and experience impacts our perceptions. As we grow older, we tend to build on our diverse life experiences and our perceptions often change or, in some cases, become more firmly ingrained. Some research indicates that older individuals possess more consistent and stable attitudes and are more difficult to persuade (Alwin and Krosnick 1991). Other findings suggest that as people age they become more cognitively sophisticated and are better able to see the world from others' perspectives (Bartsch and London 2000). Thus, it is important to consider how age affects both our own and others' perceptions.

Finally, culture affects our perceptions of the world and simultaneously influences our communication with others. In Chapter Ten we discuss the impact of cultural differences on perceptions and interpersonal communication in greater detail. However, it is important to restate the powerful impact culture can have on our perceptions. One reason for examining cultural differences is to learn more about how socialization in different cultures affects peoples' perceptions and behavior. For example, researchers often study perceptual and behavioral differences in individualistic and collectivistic cultures. Collectivistic cultures emphasize group harmony and concern for others. An example of a collectivistic culture is found in China. Individualistic cultures, as found in the United States, tend to value individual rights, independence, and autonomy. Members of collectivistic cultures view the world much differently than individuals from highly individualistic cultures. There are numerous research examples which illustrate the difference between individualistic and collectivistic cultural beliefs, attitudes, behaviors, and values. One interesting study explored Chinese and U.S. managerial differences in attempts to influence employees (Yukl, Fu, and McDonald 2003). According to Yukl and his colleagues, "the cross-cultural differences in rated effectiveness of tactics were consistent with cultural values and traditions" (Yukl, Fu, and McDonald 2003, 68). Chinese managers rated informal strategies and strategies that emphasized personal relations as more effective than traditional Western strategies which emphasize being direct and task oriented. Swiss and American managers perceived more direct task-oriented tactics as being more effective than informal strategies and strategies that emphasized personal relations. In another study, Miller (1984) examined the impact of culture on the fundamental attribution error. She asked children and adults in India and the U.S. to provide possible explanations for pro-social (e.g., helping someone paint their house) and anti-social behaviors (e.g., engaging in aggressive behavior). Miller's findings provide valuable insight into how factors such as age and culture impact our perception. Children in both cultures offered similar attributions for the behaviors. However, adults in the U.S. were more likely than their Indian counterparts to explain events by attributing them to individual traits. Adults from India, on the other hand, focused on situational or contextual causes as possible explanations for behaviors. It is important to remember that most of us hold more favorable perceptions of the groups we belong to than those to which we do not belong. Thus, we should be cognizant of our tendency to be favorably disposed towards people, ideas, beliefs, and concepts from our culture and our inclination to be more critical of people, ideas, and concepts from other cultural perspectives.

THE LINK BETWEEN PERCEPTION AND LISTENING

By now you have a more sophisticated understanding of why some information is selected over others, how information is organized, and how messages are interpreted. Additionally, we have provided you with some information about common attribution errors that individuals make and variables that affect the process of perception. To further understand the potential implications of perception, we must consider how our different perspectives of people and messages influence and are influenced by listening. At the beginning of this chapter, we pointed out that perception and listening are closely related to one another. Our perception of others impacts both our ability and our desire to listen in social interactions.

In the *Friends* episode "The One the Morning After" Ross tries to explain to Rachel his reasons for sleeping with another woman on the same night that Rachel suggested that they take a "break" from their relationship. Ross pleads with Rachel to work through it. He tells her he can't even think of what his life would be like without her; without everything she is to him. Rachel just can't get beyond what Ross did to betray her. She tells him that he has become a completely different person to her, now that she's seen that he is capable of hurting her. Rachel believes there will never be anything he can say or do that will change the way she feels about him now.

Because her perception of Ross' commitment to their relationship has changed, so has Rachel's ability to listen to the messages he attempts to communicate. As we listen to messages communicated by others, new information is provided that may cause us to change existing perceptions or perhaps even form new ones. Listening is an essential part of effective interpersonal communication. Yet it is often understudied and underemphasized in communication courses. In the next section we make a distinction between hearing and listening, offer strategies to enhance your own listening skills, and describe the various listening styles employed by individuals.

Marge, it takes two to lie. One to lie and one to listen.

—Homer Simpson

The most basic of all human needs is the need to understand and be understood. The best way to understand people is to listen to them.

—Ralph Nichols

Listening, not imitation, may be the sincerest form of flattery.

—Dr. Joyce Brothers

Listening

These quotations illustrate the power and functions of listening in the communication process. Listening is a key element for acquiring information and developing and sustaining our relationships. Yet, communication practitioners often refer to listening as the "forgotten" communication skill. The fact that listening skills are often neglected or undervalued is surprising since most people engage in listening more than any other type of communication activity. For example, college students report that up to 50 percent of their time is spent listening, com-

Table 5.1	Daily Average Hours Devoted to Communication Activities	

Communication Activities	Total Number of Hours	Approximate Percentage of Time
Writing	1.82	8
Reading	1.40	6
Speaking	4.83	20
Listening*	5.80	24
Television*	2.12	9
Radio*	.86	4
CD/Tapes*	1.32	5
Phone*	1.87	8
Email	1.33	6
Internet	2.73	11
Total Listening Hours	**11.97**	**50**

Items marked with an * represent those activities which focus primarily on listening.

pared to speaking (20 percent), reading (6 percent), and writing (8 percent) (Janusik and Wolvin 2006). While colleges often require classes which emphasize competence in writing and speaking, few highlight listening as an important communication skill.

When we engage in effective listening behaviors we communicate a message that we comprehend and care about what the speaker has to say. Recall a time when you attempted to communicate with a friend or family member, only to receive a distracted response of "Yeah. Uh-huh. Mm-hmm." The lack of active listening behavior is extremely frustrating. A lack of awareness of ineffective listening behaviors has potential negative implications for both personal and professional relationships. Our goal in focusing on this topic is twofold: to assist you in understanding the listening process and to shed some light on how your own behaviors may be interpreted by others. Our hope is that after completing this chapter you will be able to evaluate your own listening skills and to implement some of our suggestions.

As stated earlier, individuals typically spend more time listening during their lifetime than any other communication activity. For many of you, this chapter will be the only formal training in appropriate and effective listening skills you will ever have. The implications of effective listening span a variety of interpersonal contexts. In the health care setting, Wanzer and her colleagues (2004) found that patients who perceived their physicians to employ effective listening skills were more satisfied with their doctor and the care provided. Research has also identified a link between one's career success and effective listening skills. Employers report that listening is a top skill sought in hiring new employees, and it plays a significant role in evaluations for promotion and incentives (AICPA 2006). As we begin our discussion of effective listening skills, it is important that we first distinguish between the concepts of "hearing" and "listening."

Gina was cooking dinner for Joni one evening after a long day at work. As she stirred the pasta sauce on the stove, she sighed, "I just don't understand why my manager doesn't see what's happening with our latest project. Half of the team is running around clueless, and I keep getting left with their messes to clean up."

Joni gave a half-hearted response while scanning her emails on her laptop. "Uh-huh," she said without breaking eye contact with the computer screen.

Gina stopped cooking and scolded Joni, "You never listen when I try to tell you about my day at work!"

Joni was shocked, "What do you mean? I heard every word you said!"

Gina countered, "Prove it! What did I just say?"

Joni dropped her head and apologized, realizing that while she had heard Gina talking, she hadn't really listened to a word she said.

Have you ever been involved in a situation similar to the one described above? Perhaps you have been the one who has heard the words but did not listen to what was being said. Perhaps one of the most common mistakes made in the listening process is making the assumption that hearing is the same as listening. In fact, listening and hearing are two distinct processes. **Hearing** involves the physical process of sound waves traveling into the ear canal, vibrating the ear drum and eventually sending signals to the brain. Although we often hear messages, we do not necessarily attend to them. This explains why you might be sitting in your room right now reading this text and hearing an air conditioner turn on, birds chirping outside, or friends yelling in the hallway. But while your brain has processed these sound waves, you may not have necessarily been listening for these stimuli. **Listening** not only involves the physical process of hearing, but it also involves the psychological process of attending to the stimuli, creating meaning and responding. Listening is often described as a dynamic and ongoing process in which individuals physically receive a message, employ cognitive processes to attribute meaning to the message, and provide verbal and/or nonverbal feedback to the source.

As you reflect on this definition, it should become quite apparent that listening is a highly complex process. First, listening is dynamic because it is an ongoing activity that requires an individual to be active and engaged. Unlike hearing, listening requires an individual to be mindful and aware of one's surroundings. After we physically receive the sound waves and hear the message, the next step involves employing cognitive processing to attribute meaning to the information that was received. Hopefully the steps involved in this cognitive process are familiar to you. They include: selection, organization, and interpretation. Do you recall our earlier discussion of these stages as part of the perception process? These same elements are involved in listening. We are selective in the information we expose ourselves to and attend to in the perception process; the same is true in listening. We select what sounds and messages we will listen to and which we will ignore. Have you ever encountered a mother who can carry on a phone conversation and never become

Table 5.2	Key Strategies for Effective Listening (BIG EARS)	
B		Be open and receptive to the message
I		Interpret the message
G		Give feedback
E		Engage in dual perspective
A		Adapt your listening style
R		Reduce noise
S		Store the message

distracted while children are screaming and playing in the background? The mother has selected what sounds to focus her attention on in the listening process—she has selected the message that is being received via the telephone. Just as we organize stimuli during the perception process, information is also organized as a part of the listening process. Finally, we must interpret information and assign a meaning to what we have heard while listening. The relationship between perception and listening should be even clearer—the similarities between both processes are nearly identical. The final stage of the listening process involves formulating a response, or feedback, to send to the source via verbal and/or nonverbal channels. Examples of verbal feedback may include, "You look sad," "Tell me more," or "What do you plan to do?" Some examples of nonverbal responses could include nodding your head, making eye contact, or even giving a hug.

To help you remember some of the key strategies involved in effective listening, remember the following acronym: **BIG EARS.** Each of these strategies is discussed in the paragraphs that follow.

Be Open to the Message.

Listening is difficult enough to begin with, but when we fail to prepare ourselves to receive messages, it becomes even more so. Effective listening requires you to employ effective nonverbal listening behaviors, control message overload, and manage your preoccupations and other distractions.

First, we need to be aware of our nonverbal listening behaviors. The next time you are sitting in class listening to a lecture, take a moment and consider the role your nonverbal behaviors play in the listening process. Do you look like you are open to receiving messages? Maintaining an open body position, engaging in eye contact, and responding to the lecture by nodding your head are all examples of nonverbal behaviors that communicate a willingness to listen.

Next, focus on ways to manage the multiple sources of information that are competing for your attention. Remember our discussion of perception and the role of selective attention and exposure? Effective listening behaviors require you to dedicate your attention to a particular message. The next time you are tempted to watch *Grey's Anatomy* while carrying on a phone conversation with your mother, think twice. One of the sources will ultimately win out over the other—will it be the television show or your mother?

© Anita, 2007, Shutterstock.

How can you keep yourself from daydreaming during a long lecture?

Finally, identify ways to manage the multiple preoccupations and distractions that can impair your ability to listen. Look beyond superficial factors that may be hindering your ability to focus on the message. While a professor's distracting delivery style or prehistoric clothing choices may cause your attention to focus away from the lecture being delivered, these are not excuses to disregard the source's message. Remain focused on the content of the message. On average, Americans speak at a rate of 125 words per minute. However, the human brain can process more than 450 words per minute (Hilliard and Palmer 2003) and we can think at a rate of 1000–3000 words per minute (Hilliard and Palmer 2003). So what happens with all that extra time? Often we daydream or we become bored because our brain can work faster than the speaker can talk. Therefore, it is important to dedicate yourself to relating the information to existing information that you already know. While this can be challenging at times, chances are that it will prove to be extremely useful. Ask yourself questions during a conversation or lecture such as, "How will this information benefit me?" or "How will this information benefit my relationship with the source?" Being open to receiving messages is the first step to ensuring an effective listening experience.

Interpreting the Message.   Interpretation refers to the cognitive processes involved in listening. Recall our discussion of the role of interpretation in perception. We pointed out that associations are often made between stimuli and things with which we are already familiar. Interpretation is also a key element in listening, and in verifying that the meaning we assigned to the message is close to that which was intended by the source. Some strategies to assist in interpretation of messages include asking questions, soliciting feedback, and requesting clarification. These strategies will help you interpret the source's message more accurately. Consider the following interaction between Maya and Raj:

Maya: I hate biology.

Raj: Why?

Maya: Well, I guess I don't hate it, but I am upset I did poorly on the first exam.

Raj: Why did you do poorly?

Maya: Because I studied the wrong chapters.

Raj: So, do you dislike the material?

Maya: Well, no, I actually enjoy the teacher and the book.

Raj: So, you like biology but you are upset you studied the wrong material?

Maya: Yes, I actually like the course; I am just mad because I know I could have received an A if I had studied the right material.

Because Raj asked Maya to provide additional information to help clarify why she hated biology he was able to interpret Maya's situation more clearly. In fact, it changed the meaning of the message entirely. Maya's initial message was that she hated biology and it turns out that she actually enjoys biology. Raj was able to accurately interpret the message because he asked questions and solicited feedback. But soliciting feedback is not the only element involved in listening. **Paraphrasing** is another useful strategy for clarifying meaning and ensuring that you have accurately interpreted a message. Paraphrasing involves restating a message in your own words to see if the meaning you assigned was similar to that which was intended. But this is still not enough. Effective listening also requires you to provide the source with feedback to communicate that you have both received and understood the message.

Give Feedback. Feedback serves many purposes in the listening process. By providing feedback to the source, we are confirming that we received the message and were able to interpret and assign meaning to what was being communicated. Feedback can be either positive or negative and communicate its own message. **Positive feedback** includes verbal and nonverbal behaviors that encourage the speaker to continue communicating. Examples of positive feedback include eye contact, nods, and comments such as, "I see," and "Please continue." **Negative feedback** is often discouraging to a source. Examples of negative feedback would be disconfirming verbal comments such as "You are over-reacting" or "I don't know why you get so upset," or negative nonverbal responses such as avoidance of eye contact, maintaining a closed body position (e.g., crossed arms), or meaningless vocalizations such as "Um-hmm." Positive feedback communicates interest and empathy for the speaker, whereas negative feedback often results in feelings of defensiveness.

© Phil Date, 2007, Shutterstock.

What kinds of positive feedback show that you are interested and listening?

Engage in Dual-Perspective Taking. **Dual-perspective taking,** or empathy, refers to the attempt to see things from the other person's point of view. The concept of empathy has been a primary focus of the listening process required of social workers and counselors. Norton (1978) explains this by theorizing that all people are part of two systems— a larger societal system and a more immediate personal system. While it is often possible to gain insight into an individual's societal system, truly understanding someone's personal system is often a more difficult task. Consider the phrase, "Put yourself in another person's shoes." Do you think it is possible to truly put yourself in another person's shoes? This would require us to be able to tap into their unique background and experiences in order to perceive things exactly as they do. But is this ever really possible? Our position is that it is not. This may help explain why we find it difficult to respond to a friend who

© Galina Barskaya, 2007, Shutterstock.

Empathetic listening requires an attempt to see things from your friend's point of view.

is going through a difficult break-up. Our initial response may be to respond with a statement like, "I know exactly how you feel. I've been through dozens of broken relationships." But this is not necessarily the best response. There is a unique history to your friend's relationship that you can never truly understand. While you cannot fully put yourself in her shoes, you can communicate empathy by attempting to see things from her point of view. Reaching into their "field of experience" (as discussed in Chapter One) and trying to understand the framework which they use to interpret the world can influence your ability to effectively listen. Dual-perspective taking requires a receiver to adapt his listening style to accommodate a variety of situations.

Adapt Your Listening Style.   Effective communicators are flexible in their communication style and find it easy to adjust both their speaking and listening styles, based on the unique demands of the receiver, the material, or the situation. Duran (1983) defines communicative adaptability as a cognitive and behavioral "ability to perceive socio-interpersonal relationships and adapt one's interaction goals and behaviors accordingly" (320). Duran and Kelly (1988) developed the Communicative Adaptability Scale. Their scale suggests we can adapt our communication in six different ways which include: social composure (feeling relaxed in social situations), social experience (enjoying and participating socially), social confirmation (maintaining the other's social image), appropriate disclosures (adapting one's disclosures appropriately to the intimacy level of the exchange), articulation (using appropriate syntax and grammar), and wit (using humor to diffuse social tension). You can determine the extent to which you are adaptable on these six dimensions by completing the Communication Adaptability Scale on page 135.

Reduce Noise.   **Noise** refers to anything that interferes with the reception of a message. Recall the various types of noise that were discussed in Chapter One: physical, psychological, and physiological noise. Our job as listeners is to focus on ways to reduce the noise that interferes with the reception of messages.

Oftentimes, this is easier said than done. While we are able to control some forms of physical noise that interfere with listening (e.g., cell phones or radios), other types of physical noise may be more difficult to manage (e.g., a neighbor mowing her yard). Obviously, the less noise there is, the better our chances of effectively receiving the message. Reducing psychological and physiological noise may be more difficult. Sometimes it is difficult to listen to a professor's lecture knowing that you have a big midterm exam in the class that follows, and gnawing hunger pains that begin during your 11:00 A.M. class can impair listening as well. Consider ways to manage these potential distractions and maximize listening potential—be prepared for that exam, be sure to eat something before leaving for class. Planning ahead for potential distractions to listening can ultimately assist you in receiving a message that you can store in memory for future reference.

Store the Message.   A final strategy in the listening process involves storing what we have received for later reference. This process involves three stages: remembering, retention, and recall. Have you ever been impressed with a doctor or a professor because they remembered, retained, and recalled your name? This is not an easy task. Nichols (1961) demonstrated that immediately after listening to a ten-minute lecture, students were only able to remember about fifty percent of what they heard. As time passes, so does our ability to remember. Nichols' study suggested that after two weeks, most listeners were only able to remember about twenty-five percent of what they had heard. The following are strategies that can be used to enhance message retention.

1. Form associations between the message and something you already know.
2. Create a visual image of the information you want to remember.
3. Create a story about what you want to remember to create links between ideas. *Suppose your mother asks you to go to the store to pick up soda, laundry*

Communicative Adaptability Scale

The following are statements about communication behaviors. Answer each item as it relates to your general style of communication (the type of communicator you are most often) in social situations. Please indicate the degree to which each statement applies to you by circling the appropriate number (according to the scale below) for each item.

5	4	3	2	1
Almost always true of me	*Often true of me*	*Sometimes true of me*	*Rarely true of me*	*Never true*

1. I feel nervous in social situations.	5	4	3	2	1
2. People think I am witty.	5	4	3	2	1
3. When speaking, I have problems with grammar.	5	4	3	2	1
4. I enjoy meeting new people.	5	4	3	2	1
5. In most social situations, I feel tense and constrained.	5	4	3	2	1
6. When someone makes a negative comment about me, I respond with a witty comeback.	5	4	3	2	1
7. When I embarrass myself, I often make a joke about it.	5	4	3	2	1
8. I enjoy socializing with various groups of people.	5	4	3	2	1
9. I try to make the other person feel important.	5	4	3	2	1
10. At times, I don't use appropriate verb tense.	5	4	3	2	1
11. I often make jokes when in tense situations.	5	4	3	2	1
12. While I'm talking, I think about how the other person feels.	5	4	3	2	1
13. When I am talking, my posture seems awkward and tense.	5	4	3	2	1
14. I disclose at the same level that others disclose to me.	5	4	3	2	1
15. I find it easy to get along with new people.	5	4	3	2	1
16. I know how appropriate my self-disclosures are.	5	4	3	2	1
17. When I self-disclose, I know what I am revealing.	5	4	3	2	1
18. I try to be warm when communicating with another.	5	4	3	2	1
19. I am relaxed when talking with others.	5	4	3	2	1
20. When I am anxious, I often make jokes.	5	4	3	2	1
21. I sometimes use one word when I mean to use another.	5	4	3	2	1
22. I do not "mix" well at social functions.	5	4	3	2	1
23. I am aware of how intimate the disclosures of others are.	5	4	3	2	1
24. I am verbally and nonverbally supportive of other people.	5	4	3	2	1
25. I sometimes use words incorrectly.	5	4	3	2	1
26. I have difficulty pronouncing some words.	5	4	3	2	1
27. I like to be active in different social groups.	5	4	3	2	1
28. I am aware of how intimate my disclosures are.	5	4	3	2	1
29. My voice sounds nervous when I talk to others.	5	4	3	2	1
30. I try to make the other person feel good.	5	4	3	2	1

*Reverse coded items = 1, 3, 5, 10, 13, 21, 22, 25, 26, 29

Social Composure = 1 + 5 + 13 + 19 + 29
Social Confirmation = 9 + 12 + 18 + 24 + 30
Social Experience = 4 + 8 + 15 + 22 + 27

Appropriate Disclosure = 14 + 16 + 17 + 23 + 28
Articulation = 3 + 10 + 21 + 25 + 26
Wit = 2 + 6 + 7 + 11 + 20

Source: From "An Investigation into the Cognitive Domain of Competence II: the Relationship Between Communicative Competence and Interaction Involvement" by R.L. Duran and L. Kelly, *Communication Research Reports*, 1988, 5, 91-96. Reprinted by permission of Taylor & Francis Ltd., www.informaworld.com.

detergent and paper cups. You can enhance your ability to remember the information by creating a story which links the ideas such as, "Sam dropped a paper cup full of soda on her jeans and now they need to be put in the laundry machine."

4. Create acronyms by using the beginning letters of a list of words to assist your recall. BIG EARS is an example of this tool.
5. Rhyme or create a rhythm to organize information. Creating a song or rhyme that is unusual or humorous typically helps trigger recall.

Listening Styles

Reflecting on your own interpersonal relationships, did you ever notice that individuals have different listening styles? Or perhaps you have noticed that an individual's listening style changed when the topic changed. Have you considered your own listening style and how it may change with the person or topic? For example, with our friends we might pay more attention to their feelings and when we listen to co-workers we may be more focused on the content of the message. Research has identified four predominant listening styles (Watson, Barker, and Weaver 1995). **Listening style** is defined as a set of "attitudes, beliefs, and predispositions about the how, where, when, who, and what of the information reception and encoding process" (Watson, Barker, and Weaver 1995, 2). This suggests that we tend to focus our listening. We may pay more attention to a person's feelings, the structure or content, or particular delivery elements, such as time. The four listening styles are people-oriented, action-oriented, content-oriented, and time-oriented. There is no optimal listening style. Different situations call for different styles. However, it is important to understand your predominate listening style. Let us take a closer look at each of these listening styles.

People-Oriented.   First, **people-oriented** listeners seek common interests with the speaker and are highly responsive. They are interested in the speaker's feelings and emotions. Research shows a positive relationship between the people-oriented listening style and conversational sensitivity (Cheseboro 1999). This makes sense since people-oriented listeners try to understand the speakers' perspective and therefore are more sensitive to their emotional needs. They are quick to notice slight fluctuations in tone and mood. For example, they may comment, "You really look upset," or "You smile every time you say her name." Although you must consider the individual and the situation, this style may work best when we are communicating with our friends or family about sensitive issues.

Action-Oriented.   An **action-oriented** listener prefers error-free and concise messages. They get easily frustrated with speakers who do not clearly articulate their message in a straightforward manner. They tend to steer speakers to be organized and timely in their message delivery. They grow impatient with disorganized speakers that use ambiguous descriptions or provide unrelated details. For example, an action-oriented listener may use the phrase "Get to the point," when the speaker is telling a lengthy story or may interrupt a speaker and say, "So. . . . what did you do?" The action-oriented listening style may work best when there is little time for extra details and decisions need to be made quickly.

Content-Oriented.   Unlike the people-oriented listener, the **content-oriented** listener focuses on the details of the message. They pick up on the facts of the story and analyze it from a critical perspective. They decipher between credible and noncredible information and ask direct questions. They try to understand the message from several perspectives. For example, they may say, "Did you ever think they did that because . . ." or "Another way to think about the situation is . . ." Because they analyze the speaker's content with a critical eye, the speaker may feel reluctant to share information because they do not want to hear alternative perspectives. Additionally, they may feel intimidated by the criticalness of content-oriented listeners since they are engaged by challenging and intellectual discussion. The content-oriented listening style works best in serious situations that call for vital decision-making.

Time-Oriented.   Finally, **time-oriented** listeners are particularly interested in brief interactions with others. They direct the length of the conversation by suggesting, "I only have a minute," or they send leave taking cues (such as walking away or looking at the clock) when they believe the speaker is taking up too much of their time. This type of listening is essential when time is a limited commodity. Usually, time is precious in the workplace. A day can be eaten up by clients, co-workers, supervisors, and other individuals needing our attention. Time-oriented individuals protect their time by expressing to others how much effort they will devote to their cause.

Gender and Cultural Differences in Listening Styles

Some researchers suggest there are gender differences when it comes to listening styles. In the mid-1980s, Booth-Butterfield reported that "males tend to hear the facts while females are more aware of the mood of the communication" (1984, 39). Just about twenty years later, researchers' findings were consistent in indicating that men score themselves higher on the content-oriented listening style and women score themselves higher on the people-oriented listening style (Sargent and Weaver 2003). In addition, Kiewitz and Weaver III (1997) found that when comparing young adults from three different countries, Germans preferred the action style, Israelis preferred the content style, and Americans preferred the people and time styles.

Although no listening style is best, it is imperative to understand your own listening style and to recognize the listening styles of others. Depending on the situation and the goals in communicating, you may need to adjust your listening style. In addition, recognizing the listening style in others will help direct your responding messages. For example, if you notice your boss is engaging in action-oriented listening style, you may want to produce a clearly articulated message. He may become irritated if you include miscellaneous information or use confusing vocabulary.

Motivation to Listen and Potential Pitfalls

When we do anything, we have some kind of motivation, or purpose. Sometimes this motivation is driven by our goals, dreams, and interests. Other

Table 5.3   Guidelines for Effective Listening

Effective listeners do their best to avoid these behaviors:

1. Calling the subject uninteresting
2. Criticizing the speaker and/or delivery
3. Getting overstimulated
4. Listening only for facts (bottom line)
5. Not taking notes or outlining everything
6. Faking attention
7. Tolerating or creating distractions
8. Tuning out difficult material
9. Letting emotional words block the message
10. Wasting the time difference between speed of speech and speed of thought

Source: Nichols, R. G., and L. A. Stevens. 1957. *Are you listening?* New York: McGraw-Hill.

times motivation may be a result of guilt, responsibility, or shame. Consider your motive for attending school. Perhaps you are a student because you have set a goal to graduate or maybe you are motivated out of a sense of responsibility to your parents. Either way, motivation drives behavior. Have you ever considered your motivation for listening? Researchers have identified five listening motivations (Wolvin and Coakley 1988). Certain motivations for listening lend themselves to particular listening barriers. Therefore, let us examine each of these motivations independently and offer potential pitfalls for each. Table 5.3 presents some guidelines for effective listening.

Discriminate Listening.   First, we may listen for the purpose of discriminating. The purpose of **discriminate listening** is to help us understand the meaning of the message. In certain situations we want to discriminate between what is fact and what is an opinion. Or perhaps we try to discriminate between what is an emotionally-based argument and what is a logically-based argument. One example of a situation in which we might engage in discriminate listening is in the workplace when we attentively listen to how a co-worker responds to our new recommendation. Here we are trying to determine if they agree or disagree with us. Another example is engaging in listening in the classroom when the teacher suggests that portions of the lecture will be on the exam. In this example, we are discriminating between what the teacher believes is important material for the exam and what is not going to be on the exam. Furthermore, we tend to use discriminate listening when we are trying to determine whether someone is lying to us.

Potential Pitfall.   Often when we are trying to discriminate between messages, we **selectively listen** to certain stimuli while ignoring others. For example, if someone does not maintain eye contact with us, we may jump to conclusions regarding her trustworthiness. If discrimination is your motivation, it is important to *keep an open mind and attend to the entire message.*

Appreciative Listening.   Another motivation we have for listening is **appreciative listening.** The purpose of appreciative listening is for the pure enjoyment of listening to the stimuli. This may be listening to your favorite tunes on your iPod, attending the opera, a musical or the movies, or listening to the sounds of the waves crashing on the shore.

Potential Pitfall.   With appreciative listening it is important to be proactive. In order to be successful in appreciate listening you must *decrease noise.* You can do this by controlling distractions. For example, turn off your cell phone. Sometime you can even choose your physical environment. If you are going to the movies, you can choose a particular seat away from potentially "loud" patrons. Or you may choose to go to the movies with a partner that will not inhibit your pleasure-seeking experience by talking or asking questions throughout.

Comprehensive Listening.   We also may be motivated to listen in order to grasp new information. **Comprehensive listening** involves mindfully receiving and remembering new information. When our boss is informing us of our new job duties or a friend is telling you when they need to be picked up at the airport we are engaging in comprehensive listening. Our goal is to accurately understand the new information and be able to retain it.

Potential Pitfall.   Often there are several messages that the speaker is sending and it is the job of the listener to determine which messages are the most important. With comprehensive listening it is critical to *recognize the main ideas and identify supportive details.* If you are unsure, *seek feedback or paraphrase the message.* For example, you may ask, "So you are flying Southwest and you need me to pick you up at baggage claim at 10:00 P.M., correct?"

Evaluative Listening.   When our motivation goes beyond comprehending messages to judging messages we are engaging in evaluative listening. **Evaluative listening** involves critically assessing messages. This occurs when a salesperson is trying to persuade us to buy a product or when we listen to political speeches. We are evaluating the credibility and competency of the speaker and the message. Our goal here is to create opinions and sound judgments regarding people and information.

Potential Pitfall.   Prejudices and biases may interfere with our listening ability when we are motivated to listen for evaluative purposes. For example, individuals who identify with a particular political party are quick to judge the messages of an individual representing an alternative party. It is important to *be aware of your own preconceived notions* and not let that impede on your ability to effectively interpret the speaker's message.

Empathetic Listening.   The last motivation to listen is for empathetic reasons. The purpose of **empathetic** (or therapeutic) **listening** is to help others. For example, we may meet up with our friends to discuss their most recent romantic episodes or we may help our family members make tough financial decisions. Our goal is to provide a supportive ear and assist in uncovering alternative perspectives. Often, just by listening our friends will identify their own issues or our family members will uncover their own solutions to their problems. Other times, they may ask for suggestions or recommendations.

Potential Pitfall.   It is critical to distinguish if the speaker indeed wants you to be an active participant in offering solutions or if he wants you "just to listen." Sometimes we assume that solutions are being sought, but what is really wanted is someone to act as a "sounding board."

Common Listening Misbehaviors

There can be severe consequences when we choose not to listen effectively. One study found that the second most frequently occurring mistake made by education leaders deals with poor interpersonal communication skills and that the most frequent example given for this type of mistake was *failure to listen* (Bulach, Pickett, and Booth 1998). The perception that we are not listening may be because we lack appropriate eye contact with the speaker, we appear preoccupied or distracted with other issues, or because we do not provide the appropriate feedback. When we send these signals, the speaker interprets our behavior as not caring. This can damage internal and external business relationships. These behaviors can have severe consequences. Another study examined the top five reasons why principals lost their jobs (Davis 1997). The results of this study found that the most frequently cited response by superintendents focused on failure to communicate in ways that build positive relationships. The results of this study can be applied to situations outside of the educational setting. So, how do people communicate in ways that do not build positive relationships? This section will identify the six common listening misbehaviors.

Pseudo-Listening.   **Pseudo-listening** is when we are pretending to listen. We look like we are listening by nodding our head or providing eye contact, but we are faking our attention. This is a self-centered approach to listening. Let us be honest, when we are pseudo-listening we are not "fooling" anyone. We are not able to ask appropriate questions and we are not able to provide proper feedback.

Monopolizing.   Listeners that engage in **monopolizing** take the focus off the speaker and redirect the conversation and attention to themselves. Often, monopolizers interrupt the speaker to try to "one up" the speaker. They may try to top his story by saying "That reminds me . . ." or "You think that is bad–let me tell you what happened to me. . . ."

Disconfirming.   Listeners that deny the feelings of the speaker are sending **disconfirming** messages. Recall our discussion in Chapter Four regarding the implication of sending disconfirming messages. Examples of disconfirming messages include: "You shouldn't feel bad . . ." or "Don't cry . . . there is no need to cry." This misbehavior discourages the source to continue speaking and decreases perceptions of empathy.

Defensive Listening.   An individual who engages in **defensive listening** perceives a threatening environment. Defensive communication has been defined as "that behavior which occurs when an individual perceives threat or anticipates threat in the group" (Gibb 1961, 141). Defensiveness includes "how he appears to others, how he may seem favorable, how he may win, dominate, impress, or escape punishment, and/or how he may avoid or mitigate a perceived or anticipated threat" (141). In other words, defensiveness is a process of saving "face." The issue of face is associated with people's desire to display a positive public image (Goffman 1967). An example of defensive listening is, "Don't look at me, I did not tell you to do that. . . ."

Selective Listening.   **Selective listening** happens when a listener focuses only on parts of the message. She takes parts of the message that she agrees with (or does not agree with) and responds to those particular parts. We reduce cognitive dissonance or psychological discomfort, screening out messages that we do not agree with, to remain cognitively "stable." For example, if we recently bought a new SUV, we may choose not to pay attention to messages suggesting that SUV's are not environmentally sound. We would, however, choose to pay attention to messages that suggest SUV vehicles rated higher on safety tests.

Ambushing.   Ambushers will listen for information that they can use to attack the speaker. They are selectively and strategically listening for messages that they can use against the speaker. Often ambushers interrupt the speaker. They do not allow the speaker to complete his thought and jump to conclusions. Ambushers make assumptions and get ahead of the speaker by finishing his sentences. They are self-motivated and lack dual perspective.

SUMMARY

In this chapter, we explained the perception process: selecting information, organizing information and interpreting information. Additionally, we identified and explained factors related to each of the three primary selectivity processes. At this point, you should have a more detailed understanding of why certain messages or information gets selected over others. We also learned more about the four types of schema that affect interpersonal communication. Once information has been selected and organized, the final step is interpretation. The primary theory that explains how we make sense of our own behavior and that of others is attribution theory. The way that we make sense of our own and others' behavior is quite different and flawed. In the final sections we discussed the two primary attribution errors as well as factors that affect our interpretation process.

In the last section of this chapter, we explained the difference between hearing and listening. Remember, listening refers to the dynamic process in which individuals physically hear a message, employ cognitive processes to attribute meaning to the message, and provide verbal and/or nonverbal feedback to the source. Afterwards, we identified the seven steps to effective listening by using the acronym BIG EARS: Be open to the message, Interpret the message, Give positive feedback, Engage in dual perspective, Adapt your listening style, Reduce noise, and Store the message. Not only is it important to increase your listening skills, it is also crucial to recognize different listening styles. We discussed four different types of listening styles: people-oriented, action-oriented, content-oriented, and time-oriented. Then we explained why people are motivated to listen. Four motivations to listen are to discriminate, appreciate, comprehend, and evaluate. By identifying potential pitfalls for each motivation, our hope is that you can adapt your communication to the message recipient and also be aware of your own shortcomings. Finally, we recognized six common listening misbehaviors including: pseudo-listening, disconfirming, defensive listening, monopolizing, selective listening, and ambushing.

EXERCISES

Activity #1:   "Chatter Matters"

Youngsters are encouraged to become little chatterboxes to promote better communication skills. Children aged three to five at Hardwick Primary School, Stockton, will receive a Chatter Matters bag each week, containing a game, book, toy, and CD designed to improve their talking, listening, and reading. Teacher Linda Whitwell said each week the children will swap bags, so they get to use a number of different devices to develop their talents. She said: "The children will be taking the bags home each week, so we are hoping to encourage parents to work with their children to improve their reading, writing, and speaking ability. It will be something fun and different for everyone to use, and hopefully it will have the desired affect." (p. 6). *This excerpt was taken from "The Northern Echo" on February 22, 2006.*

Discussion Questions:

1. What are some advantages of this endeavor?

2. What might be some limitations?

3. If you were coordinating "Chatter Matters," what would you emphasize?

From *The Northern Echo, February 22, 2006.* Reprinted with permission.

Activity #2:   Practice Responding

Complete the conversation below using the prompts in parentheses.
Sample: Erica: I am really sad.
            You: *What's the matter?* (Probe to find out more.)

1. Erica: My mom just called and she sounded awful.

   You: _____ (Probe to get an example.)

2. Erica: She said that my dad is leaving her.

   You: _____ (Paraphrase what Erica just said.)

3. Erica: Well, they have not been getting along lately.

   You: _____ (Probe to find out more.)

4. Erica: I noticed they were fighting more often over Thanksgiving.

   You: _____ (Empathize with Erica.)

5. Erica: Yeah. I am totally miserable.

Listening Responses

Activity #3:

Identify which listening responses are positive and which are negative by placing a "P" or an "N" on the line before the response.

_____   There is no reason to get upset.

_____   This happens to everyone.

_____   Can you give me an example? / What do you mean?

_____   Don't feel bad.

_____   So you're not getting along? / Do you mean you're arguing a lot?

_____   You're tougher than this.

_____   Snap out of it.

_____   What makes you think that? Tell me more.

_____   You must be really upset. That's terrible.

_____   She is not worth it.

_____   Get over it.

_____   It's not that bad.

Listening Is Work: Willingness to Listen

Activity #4:

Often, it is not a lack of skill that makes someone a poor listener; rather it is a lack of effort on the listener's part (Richmond and Hickson 2001). Determine the extent to which you do or do not make an effort to listen to speakers by completing the Willingness to Listen Measure on the next page. This measure tells you how well you listen in public speaking situations.

Willingness to Listen Measure

The following twenty-four statements refer to listening. Please indicate the degree to which each statement applies to you by marking whether you:

Strongly Disagree = 1; Disagree = 2; Neutral = 3; Agree = 4; Strongly Agree = 5

_____   1.   I dislike listening to boring speakers.

_____   2.   Generally, I can listen to a boring speaker.

_____   3.   I am bored and tired while listening to a boring speaker.

_____   4.   I will listen when the content of a speech is boring.

_____   5.   Listening to boring speakers about boring content makes me tired, sleepy, and bored.

_____   6.   I am willing to listen to boring speakers about boring content.

_____   7.   Generally, I am unwilling to listen when there is noise during a speaker's presentation.

_____   8.   Usually, I am willing to listen when there is noise during a speaker's presentation.

_____   9.   I am accepting and willing to listen to speakers who do not adapt to me.

_____ 10.   I am unwilling to listen to speakers who do not do some adaptation to me.

_____ 11.   Being preoccupied with other things makes me less willing to listen to a speaker.

_____ 12.   I am willing to listen to a speaker even if I have other things on my mind.

_____ 13.   While being occupied with other things on my mind, I am unwilling to listen to a speaker.

_____ 14.   I have a willingness to listen to a speaker, even if other important things are on my mind.

_____ 15.   Generally, I will not listen to a speaker who is disorganized.

_____ 16.   Generally, I will try to listen to a speaker who is disorganized.

_____ 17.   While listening to a non-immediate, non-responsive speaker, I feel relaxed with the speaker.

_____ 18.   While listening to a non-immediate, non-responsive speaker, I feel distant and cold toward that speaker.

_____ 19.   I can listen to a non-immediate, non-responsive speaker.

_____ 20.   I am unwilling to listen to a non-immediate, non-responsive speaker.

_____ 21.   I am willing to listen to a speaker with views different from mine.

_____ 22.   I am unwilling to listen to a speaker with views different from mine.

_____ 23.   I am willing to listen to a speaker who is not clear about what he or she wants to say.

_____ 24.   I am unwilling to listen to a speaker who is not clear, not credible, and abstract.

SCORING:

Scores can range from 24 to 120. To compute the score on this instrument, complete the following steps:

Step 1: Add scores for items 2, 4, 6, 8, 9, 12, 14, 16, 17, 19, 21, and 23

Step 2: Add scores for items 1, 3, 5, 7, 10, 11, 13, 15, 18, 20, 22, and 24

Step 3: Total score = 72 – Total from Step 1 + Total from Step 2.

Scores above 89 indicate a high willingness to listen. Scores below 59 indicate a low willingness to listen. Scores between 59 and 89 indicate a moderate willingness to listen.

Source: From *Going Public: Practical Guide To Public Talk* by Virginia Richmond & Mark Hickson III. Published by Allyn & Bacon, Boston MA. Copyright © 1995 by Pearson Education. Reprinted by permission of the publisher.

REFERENCES

Abelson, R. P. 1982. Three modes of attitude-behavior consistency. In M. P. Zanna, E. T. Higgins, and C. P. Herman (Eds.), *Consistency in social behavior: The Ontario symposium* (Vol. 2, 131–146). Hillsdale, NJ: Lawrence Erlbaum Associates.

AICPA. 2006. *Highlighted Responses from the Association for Accounting marketing survey: Creating the Future Agenda for the Profession—Managing Partner Perspective.* Retrieved December 22, 2006, from *http://www.aicpa.org/pubs/ tpcpa/feb2001/hilight.htm.*

Alwin, D. F., and J. A. Krosnick. 1991. Aging, cohorts, and the stability of sociopolitical orientations over the lifespan. *American Journal of Sociology, 97,* 169–195.

Bartsch, K., and K. London. 2000. Children's use of state information in selecting persuasive arguments. *Developmental Psychology, 36,* 352–365.

Booth-Butterfield, M. 1984. She hears . . . he hears; What they hear and why. *Personnel Journal, 63,* 36–43.

Braithwaite, D. O., and L. M. Harter. 2000. Communication and the management of dialectical tensions in the personal relationships of people with disabilities. In D. O. Braithwaite and T. L. Thompson (Eds.), *Handbook of communication and people with disabilities.* Mahwah, NJ: Lawrence Erlbaum Associates.

Bulach, C., W. Pickett, and D. Boothe. 1998. *Mistakes educational leaders make.* ERIC Digest, *122.* ERIC Clearinghouse on Educational Management, Eugene, OR.

Carlston, D. E. 1992. Impression formation and the modular mind: The associated systems theory. In L. L. Martin and A. T. Tesser (Eds.), *The construction of social justice* (pp. 301–341).

Chesebro, J. L. 1999. The relationship between listening and styles and conversational sensitivity. *Communication Research Reports, 16,* 233–238.

Cialdini, R. B. 2001. *Influence: Science and practice.* Boston, MA: Allyn and Bacon.

Davis, S. H. 1997. The principal's paradox: Remaining secure in precarious position. *NASSP Bulletin, 81, 592,* 73–80.

Duran, R. L. 1983. Communicative adaptability: A measure of social communicative competence. *Communication Quarterly, 31,* 320–326.

Duran, R. L., and L. Kelly. 1988. An investigation into the cognitive domain of competence II: The relationship between communicative competence and interaction involvement. *Communication Research Reports, 5,* 91–96.

Fehr, B. 2004. Intimacy expectations in same-sex friendships: A prototype interaction-pattern model. *Journal of personality and social psychology, 86,* 265–284.

Fehr, B., and J. A. Russell. 1991. The concept of love viewed from a prototype perspective. *Journal of Personality and Social Psychology, 60,* 425–438.

Fischer, P., E. Jonas, D. Frey, and S. Schulz-Hardt. 2005. Selective exposure to information: The impact of information limits. *European Journal of Social Psychology, 35,* 469–492.

Fiske, S. T., and S. E. Taylor. 1984. *Social cognition.* Reading, MA: Addison-Wesley.

Gass, R. H., and J. S. Seiter. 2003. *Persuasion, social influence and compliance gaining.* Boston, MA: Allyn and Bacon.

Gibb, J. R. 1961. Defensive communication. *Journal of Communication, 11,* 141–149.

Goffman, E. 1967. *Interaction ritual: Essays on face-to-face behavior.* New York: Pantheon Books.

Gorham, J., and D. M. Christophel. 1992. Students' perceptions of teacher behaviors as motivating and demotivating factors in college classes. *Communication Quarterly, 40,* 239–252.

Hilliard, B., and J. Palmer. 2003. Networking like a pro!: 20 tips on turning the contracts you get into the connections you need. Agito Consulting.

Hamachek, D. 1992. *Encounters with the self (3rd ed.).* Fort Worth, TX: Harcourt Brace Jovanovich.

Hamilton, D. L., and J. W. Sherman. 1994. Stereotypes. In R. Wyer and T. Srull (Eds.), *Handbook of social cognition (2nd ed.).* (1–68). Hillsdale, NJ: Lawrence Erlbaum.

Heider, F. 1958. Attitudes and cognitive organization. *Journal of Psychology, 21,* 107–112.

Hockberg, J. E. 1978. *Perception (2nd ed).* Englewood Cliffs, NJ: Prentice Hall.

Hockenbury, D. H., and S. E. Hockenbury. 2006. *Psychology (4th ed.).* New York, NY: Worth Publishers.

Janusik, L. A., and A. D. Wolvin. 2006. *24 hours in a day: A listening update to the time studies.* Paper presented at the meeting of the International Listening Association, Salem, OR.

Katz, A. M., and R. Hill. 1958. Residential propinquity and marital selection: A review of theory, method, and fact. *Marriage and Family Living, 20,* 27–35.

Kelley, H. H. 1967. Attribution theory in social psychology. In D. Levine (Ed.), *Nebraska Symposium on Motivation* (Vol. A5, p. 192–238). Lincoln: University of Nebraska Press.

———. 1971. *Attribution in social interaction.* Morristown, NJ: General Learning Press.

———. 1972. Causal schemata and the attribution process. In E. E. Jones, D. E. Kanouse, H. H. Kelley, R. E. Nisbett, S. Valins, and B. Weiner (Eds.), *Attribution: Perceiving the causes of behavior* (151–174). Morristown, NJ: General Learning Press.

———. 1973. The process of causal attribution. *American Psychologist, 28,* 107–128.

Kelly, G. A. 1970. A brief introduction to personal construct psychology. In D. Bannister (Ed.), *Perspectives in personal construct psychology* (1–30). San Diego: Academic Press.

———. 1991. *The psychology of personal constructs: Vol. 1. A theory of personality.* London: Routledge. (Original work published in 1955.)

Kelsey, D. M., P. Kearney, T. G. Plax, T. H. Allen, and K. J. Ritter. 2004. College students' attributions of teacher misbehaviors. *Communication Education, 53,* 40–55.

Kiewitz, C., and J. B. Weaver III. 1997. Cultural differences in listening style preferences: A comparison of young adults in Germany, Israel and the United States. *International Journal of Public Opinion Research, 9,* 233–247.

Klopf, D. 1995. *Intercultural encounters: The fundamentals of intercultural communication.* Englewood, CA: Morton.

Littlejohn, S. W. 1983. *Theories of human communication.* Belmont, CA: Wadsworth.

McCroskey, J. C., and V. A. Richmond. 1996. *Fundamentals of human communication.* Prospect Heights, Illinois: Waveland Press.

Miller, J. 1984. Culture and the development of everyday social explanation. *Journal of Personality and Social Psychology, 49,* 961–978.

Nichols, R. G. 1961. Do we know how to listen? Practical helps in a modern age. *Speech Teacher, 10,* 118–128.

Norton, D. 1978. *The dual perspective.* New York: Council on Social Work Education.

Raskin, J. D. 2002. Constructivism in psychology: Personal construct psychology, radical constructivism, and social constructivism. In J. D. Raskin and S. K. Bridges (Eds.), *Studies in meaning: Exploring constructivist psychology* (1–25). New York: Pace University Press.

Reeder, G. D. 1985. Implicit relations between disposition and behavior: Effects on dispositional attribution. In J. H. Harvey and G. Weary (Eds.), *Attribution: Basic issues and application* (87–116). New York: Academic Press.

Richmond, V. P., and M. Hickson, III. 2001. *Going public: A practical guide to public talk.* Boston: Allyn & Bacon.

Sargent, S. L., and J. B. Weaver III. 2003. Listening styles: Sex differences in perceptions of self and others. *International Journal of Listening, 17,* 5–18.

Tannen, D. 1986. *That's not what I meant.* New York: Ballantine Books.

———. 1990. *You just don't understand: Women and men in conversation.* New York: Ballantine Books.

———. 1994. *Gender and discourse.* New York: Oxford University Press.

Turner, J. C. 1987. *Rediscovering the social group: A self-categorization theory.* New York: Basil Blackwell.

Wanzer, M. B., M. Booth-Butterfield, and M. K. Gruber. 2004. Perceptions of health care providers' communication: Relationships between patient-centered communication and satisfaction. *Health Communication, 16,* 363–384.

Watson, K. W., L. L. Barker, and J. B. Weaver III. 1995. The listening styles profile (LSP-16): Development and validation of an instrument to assess four listening styles. *International Journal of Listening, 9,* 1–13.

Wolvin, A. D., and C. G. Coakley. 1988. Listening. Dubuque, IA: William C. Brown, Publishers.

Wood, J. T. 1999. *Gendered lives: Communication, gender, and culture (3rd ed.).* Belmont, CA: Wadsworth Publishing Co.

Yukl, G., P. P. Fu, and R. McDonald. 2003. Cross cultural differences in perceived effectiveness of influence tactics for initiating or resisting change. *Applied Psychology: An International Review, 52,* 68–82.

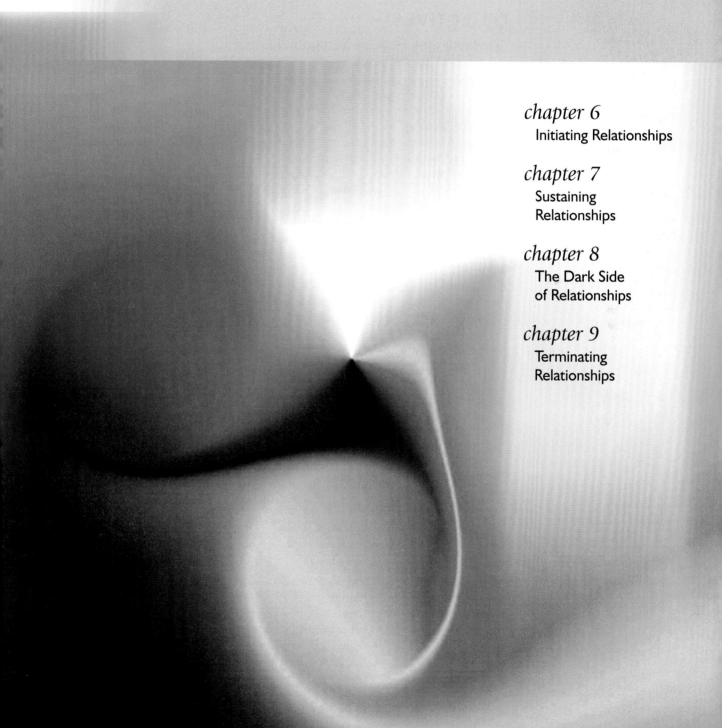

Dynamics of Interpersonal Relationships

Initiating Relationships
You Had Me at Hello

OBJECTIVES

- Identify three categories used to describe the nature of our relationships with others
- Explore four primary reasons people initiate interpersonal relationships
- Identify three types of attraction: physical, social, and task
- Understand the impact of age, gender, and culture on differences in perceptions of attraction
- Distinguish among social and task goals for relationship initiation
- Understand the three dimensions of similarity and four considerations that individuals make in assessing similarity to self
- Explore goals sought on a first date
- Understand the role of disclosure and reciprocal disclosure on relationship initiation
- Explore the relationship between social penetration and self-disclosure
- Identify the role of question-asking in reducing uncertainty in relationship initiation
- Explore the use of affinity-testing strategies in relationship initiation
- Identify five stages in the process of forming relationships
- Understand the impact of context on relationship initiation
- Explore the impact of technology on communication during relationship initiation
- Understand the four stages experienced by interracial couples in the relationship initiation process

© MaxFX, 2007, Shutterstock.

KEY TERMS

relationship	rules	impression
obligatory/involuntary	role	management
voluntary	interpersonal attraction	self-monitoring
duration	physical attractiveness	task attractiveness
context	social attractiveness	proximity

similarity/homophily	social goals	liking
demographic similarity	task goals	affinity-seeking
background similarity	self-disclosure	strategies
attitude similarity	reciprocal	social exchange theory
similarity to current self	self-disclosure	rewards
complementarity	social penetration	costs
attachment security	theory	initiation
similarity to ideal view	uncertainty reduction	experimenting
of self	theory	intensifying
false homophily	predicted outcome	integrating
goals	value theory	bonding

OVERVIEW

Many of you have probably heard of the movie *Jerry McGuire* and the line made famous by Renee Zellweger's character, "You had me at 'Hello.' " If only the process of initiating relationships with others was usually that easy! All of our relationships require a significant amount of time and energy. Consider the fact that *every* relationship we are involved in had to start somewhere. In this chapter we take a close look at how we define the term relationship, and how and why relationships are initially established. We also look at the communication behaviors and strategies used early in a relationship's development.

THE ROLE OF COMMUNICATION IN RELATIONSHIP DEVELOPMENT

The decision to begin a new relationship is filled with a myriad of emotions—confusion, excitement, anxiety, and anticipation. Consider the role played by many of the elements of interpersonal communication we have discussed up to this point. First, a person must decide whether to approach another person to initiate a relationship. Then the challenge involves figuring out how to make the initial approach. What opening line or verbal message should be used to make the all-important first impression? Let us not forget the impact of nonverbal messages as well; they have a tremendous impact on every stage of the relationship initiation process. We form assumptions about others based on such nonverbal clues as how they are dressed, whether they are standing with their arms crossed to communicate a closed body position, and whether they engage in eye contact with us. Of course, we also need to consider the role that self perception plays in the process. As discussed in Chapter Two, someone with a low level of self-esteem will face unique challenges when engaging in the relationship initiation process, as opposed to a person who has a positive self image.

As we begin our discussion of relationship development, it is important to first define what we mean by the term relationship. If you are involved in a relationship at this very moment, please raise your hand. Do you have your hand up? If not, you should probably reconsider how you define this term. When we have asked this question in our interpersonal communication classes, only a few students initially raise their hands. But after much prompting with questions such as, "Are you *sure* you're not involved in *any* relationships right now?" every member of the class has a hand up in the air. Our culture causes us to formulate stereotypes about what it means to be "in a relationship." Immediately, most people think of a "relationship" as involving romance. However, we are all involved in a number of different types of relationships at any given time.

RELATIONSHIP DEFINED

Messages about relationships surround us. A trip to the magazine section of a grocery store often involves exposure to multiple statements about the status of celebrity relationships. In the last two years writers for magazines have provided the public with the intimate details of budding relationships referred to only as, "TomKat" (Tom Cruise and Katie Holmes) and "Brangelina" (Brad Pitt and Angelina Jolie). The magazines *Cosmopolitan, People, Oprah,* and *Entertainment Weekly* also beckon you to learn how to attract members of the opposite sex with a sensuous new hairstyle, hip outfit, or clever banter. Even if you do not venture near the magazine sections or notice the magazine covers as you check out, take a moment to consider the most common themes of the songs played over the store loudspeakers while you shop. Many popular songs contain references to relationships. Messages about relationships are everywhere! While numerous magazine articles, movies and Web sites devote a lot of attention to romantic relationships, we encounter a variety of relationships throughout our lifetime. From family relationships to friendships and even work relationships, we form communicative bonds with people across a variety of contexts. But how exactly do we define the term relationship? A **relationship** is a connection between two individuals that results in mutual interaction with the intent of achieving shared meaning. In this chapter, we focus primarily on voluntary relationships, which differ greatly from those described as either obligatory or involuntary. Relationships with family members and co-workers are often defined as **obligatory/involuntary** because they often occur by chance and not by choice. Our relationships with friends, roommates, and romantic partners are considered **voluntary** because we enter into them of our own volition. Some relationships, like those we form with co-workers, may start out as obligatory and transform into voluntary ones. We begin by describing important elements of voluntary relationships.

Could this work relationship transform into a voluntary friendship?

© Yuri Arcurs, 2007, Shutterstock.

The Nature of Relationships

We often use referents to describe the numerous relationships in which we are involved. Three categories often used to describe the nature of a relationship include references to duration, context, and roles.

Duration.   **Duration** references are used to describe the length of time we have known the other person. Statements such as, "my friend from kindergarten," "my new co-worker," and "an acquaintance I met last week" are used to describe the duration of the relationship. These terms provide insight as to the amount of time that the relational partners have had to share information about one another.

Context. In some instances, relationships are described by referring to the **context**, or setting, in which the relationship was initiated. "Friends from the soccer team," "committee members from the PTO," or "co-workers on a project team," provide information about the environment in which the relationship exists. By making reference to the relationship context, clues are offered with regard to the **rules** or expectations for communication. Rules may be explicitly stated. A boss may openly state to employees that there is an "open door" policy in the office, indicating that employees should feel comfortable walking in without an appointment to discuss issues. Some rules are implicitly understood. Teammates have a mutual understanding that emotions have an impact on how messages are created and interpreted on game day. If a teammate has a bad game, the unspoken rule is that it is probably not wise to discuss the errors that were made. It is important to note that rules regarding the appropriateness of topics and the acceptable depth of discussions may differ from context to context. While an individual may be comfortable disclosing her intimate feelings about her newest romantic partner with a family member, such information could be viewed as highly inappropriate in the workplace.

Role. Finally, references to a person's **role** may be used to describe the nature of a relationship. Terms such as *mother, teacher, supervisor, colleague,* or *coach* are used to describe the role an individual plays in a particular relationship. It is important to note that role terms can also provide insight into the contextual nature of the relationship, and to shed light on the rules and expectations for interactions. More formality is needed when a student engages in an interaction with a teacher than when calling up a family member to discuss a bad grade on an assignment. By making reference to our relationships in terms of duration, context, or roles, we let others know what our initial expectations are for communication.

© Suzanne Tucker, 2007, Shutterstock.

What role does the coach play on the team?

Deciding to Make the First Move: *Why* We Initiate Relationships

Think back to your first day in this class. As you walked through the door, you scanned the classroom and were faced with the decision of where to sit. Were there any familiar faces in the room? If not, you ended up sitting next to someone you had never met before. At that point, you had two decisions to make. Should you (a) initiate a conversation with that person, and if so, (b) how should you begin the interaction? As you reflect on that first day of class, consider how quickly some of these decisions were made. Even if the decision of where to sit was influenced by the fact that there were a limited number of seats available, you still had to choose whether to initiate a conversation, and thus, initiate a relationship with a fellow classmate. Every

© Simone van den Berg, 2007, Shutterstock.

Will these two students more likely become friends because they sit near each other in class?

relationship has a unique history that includes an explanation of why we chose to initiate the relationship in the first place.

Over the years, scholars in the fields of communication, psychology and sociology have been fascinated by the question of *why* we initiate relationships. For example, when writing about why people initiate long-term romantic relationships, interpersonal communication researcher Anita Vangelisti (2002) describes the number of factors that contribute to mate selection as "daunting." Some research even indicates that the process of mate selection occurs by chance (Lykken and Tellegen 1993). While there appear to be many different reasons, years of research have identified four common explanations for why humans begin relationships. The four primary reasons we establish relationships with others are attraction, proximity, similarity, and purpose.

Not surprisingly, many decisions to initiate relationships are based on the attractiveness of another person. Second, scholars have discovered that we tend to initiate relationships with others on the basis of proximity. After all, it is much easier to begin a conversation with those who are physically close to us as opposed to those who are geographically distant. Third, relationships are typically initiated with those we perceive to be similar to us in some way. How we define similarity may differ from person to person. Relationships between adults may form because their children play on the same sports team. Students may form relationships because they are taking the same class or are in the same major. Finally, some relationships are initiated because they fulfill a purpose or a need. Consider the relationships that you have formed with co-workers or clients to fulfill a need at work. In the next sections, we take a closer look at each of the reasons for beginning a relationship.

DEFINING INTERPERSONAL ATTRACTION

Identifying the reasons for being attracted to one person and not to another is perhaps one of the greatest mysteries in life. Researchers have dedicated countless studies to exploring the phenomenon of initial attraction. After all, attraction is perhaps one of the most influential factors in setting the relationship initiation process into motion. While references to attractiveness are often assumed to be directed toward physical characteristics, **interpersonal attraction** refers to a general feeling or desire that impacts our decision to approach and initiate a relationship with another person. Many different forms of attraction influence our decision to begin relationships.

Attraction is one of the primary determining factors for choosing to initiate relationships, and it is the basis for forming initial impressions of others. While most people are quick to argue that forming first impressions of others based on their appearance is superficial and trivial, the fact remains that in the U.S. many of our decisions to initiate romantic relationships are rooted in our perceptions of the physical attractiveness of the other person. Consider a time when you were told that someone was beautiful. While you could argue that this could refer to either physical attractiveness or inner beauty, our first instinct is to assume that the statement is being made in reference to the individual's physical characteristics.

When asked to define attractiveness, most people tend to list physical characteristics associated with perceptions of attraction. While our initial impressions typically focus on the physical features associated with attractiveness, other factors can come into play as well. McCroskey and McCain (1974) identified three dimensions of attractiveness used when deciding whether to initiate relationships. These dimensions include: physical, social, and task attractiveness.

Physical Attractiveness

The dimension of attractiveness most often used in deciding whether to pursue a relationship is physical attractiveness. More often than not, we decide whether to initiate conversations with a potential relationship partner based on our perceptions of the partners' physical attractiveness (Vangelisti 2002). According to research by Reis and his colleagues (1980), we are more likely to perceive interactions as pleasant when we view the person we interact with as physically attractive. How do we determine whether someone is physically attractive? Judgments about what constitutes physical attractiveness are often answered by asking the question, "What do I think makes someone pretty or handsome?" When characteristics such as body shape or size, hair color or length, and facial features are used in making a determination of whether to initiate a relationship, this dimension is referred to as **physical attractiveness.** Aristotle recognized the value of physical attractiveness when he stated, "Personal beauty is a greater recommendation than any letter of reference."

Recall the discussion of perception in Chapter Five. The phrase "beauty is in the eye of the beholder" addresses the perceptual nature of physical attraction and provides insight as to why one person may be attracted to blondes while another is attracted to brunettes. Sometimes we are baffled as to how individuals who appear to be so completely opposite with regard to their physical appearance, could be attracted to one another. Our perception causes us to view physical characteristics in unique ways. Extensive research has concluded that romantic attraction is frequently related to the extent to which partners are physically attracted to one another initially (Curran and Lippold 1975; Goode 1996; Walster, Aronson, Abrahams, and Rottman 1966; Wilson, Cousins, and Fink 2006; Woll 1986). While some studies report that men may value physical attractiveness more than women (Buss 1989; Sprecher, Sullivan, and Hatfield 1994), it is clear that both men and women report physical attractiveness as a factor influencing their decision to initiate relationships (Hatfield and Sprecher 1986).

But why does physical attractiveness play such an important role in the early stages of relationship development? One explanation is that people tend to associate other positive and favorable characteristics with physical attractiveness. Take a moment to think about how much emphasis our culture places on physical attractiveness. An overwhelming amount of research (see, for example, Eagly et al. 1991) seems to support the bias that individuals have towards those perceived as physically attractive. One study found that people described as attractive were also perceived as kind, sexual, responsive, social, and sensitive (Dion, Berscheid and Walster 1972). In this same study,

Why is physical attractiveness important early in a relationship?

participants predicted that physically attractive individuals would experience more success in life, both personally and professionally. Other factors, such as age, gender and culture, influence our perceptions of physical attractiveness.

Age and Attractiveness.   Beginning at a very young age, we are taught that physical attractiveness is often rewarded or valued. After all, the princesses in Disney movies are always beautiful young women, while the evil characters are portrayed as being ugly. Hasbro's Barbie doll is presented to young children as an ideal image of female attractiveness. She has long, blonde hair and blue eyes, is big-breasted, tall and thin. Young children are able to identify her and many idolize her. But let's get real. Barbie's bra size has been estimated to be a DDD compared to the average C cup size of most women, and her body dimensions have been translated to the equivalent of 38-18-34 if she were a real woman. In fact, her tiny feet would not be able to support her busty upper body if she were a real woman. Nonetheless, young girls adore Barbie! They receive the message that being physically attractive, like Barbie, is associated with having friends and receiving more attention, not to mention a host of other rewards: cool clothes, cars, beach houses, and a "cool" life-style.

Even in the classroom, children receive messages regarding the importance of physical attractiveness. Research has shown that attractive children are perceived as being more popular with both classmates and teachers. Richmond (1992) states that elementary age students who are perceived as being physically attractive receive more attention from their teachers, while attractive high school and college age students receive higher grades than those who are perceived to be less attractive. Studies show that teachers provide higher evaluations and establish higher expectations for attractive students. Attractive people are perceived as being happier, more likeable, popular, and friendly (Berscheid and Reis 1998).

Even as we get older, physical attractiveness impacts our perception as well as the perceptions others have of us. Research has found that people under the age of thirty have been rated as being more physically attractive than people over the age of fifty (McClellan and McKelvie 1993), and faces perceived as being younger have been judged as being more pleasant compared to faces viewed as being older. Johnson and Pittinger (1984) discovered that physically attractive males and females aged 60 to 93 were rated more positively than those in the same age group who were perceived to be less attractive. Another study grouped males and females into age categories. These categories included participants aged 20 to 29, 30 to 39, 40 to 49, 50 to 59, and 60 to 69 years. Participants in the study were shown photographs of members of the opposite sex from the same age range categories and were asked to rate their physical attractiveness. Results of the study indicated that as males increased in age, they rated younger women as being more attractive than older women. However, the same was not true for women. Women in the older age categories rated males similar in age to be more physically attractive (Mathes, Brennen, Haugen, and Rice 1985).

Gender and Attractiveness.   While both men and women indicate that they view physical attractiveness as important in the initiation of romantic relationships, the intensity that each sex values attractiveness differs. For example, in a study by Hewitt and German (1987), women indicated a strong preference for men who were dressed more formally compared to those who were dressed informally. In the reality show *Queer Eye for the Straight Guy*, male participants receive a significant makeover that might include a new haircut, body waxing, grooming tips, a new wardrobe, and an apartment makeover. Friends, family members, and co-workers are asked to comment on the participant's new look. At the end of the show, relationship partners, who also happen to be women, typically respond very favorably to their partner's new hip, stylish and more formal clothing.

While many research studies point to the positive aspects of physical attractiveness, others have discovered potential pitfalls. In the workplace, physically attractive women often encounter biases *against* them when applying for administrative or executive positions (Zebrowitz 1997). The same is true of women who run for political office. While physically attractive women are often penalized for their appearance in these situations, the opposite was found to be true for attractive males seeking similar opportunities. Because of the increased attention on women's voting behavior in political elections, Lewis and Bierly (1990) examined the impact of female perceptions of male political candidates' attractiveness. Women rated physically attractive political candidates as being more competent than less attractive candidates.

Decisions to initiate dates are most often based on physical attractiveness. In a content analysis of more than 800 personal ads, Harrison and Saeed (1977) found that males are more likely to include descriptors of physical attractiveness as criteria for potential dates. In addition, men tend to indicate a strong preference for women who are younger than themselves. While women also included criteria such as *athletic*, *tall* or *attractive* in personal ads, references to a partner's status were included more often and emerged as a stronger predictor of attraction (Davis 1990).

To examine the impact of physical attractiveness in homosexual relationships, Sergios and Cody (1985) matched 100 men in dyads (pairs), based on ratings of physical attractiveness. Participants were told that they were being sent on a blind date that was matched through a computer. Physical attractiveness was the biggest predictor of liking and desire to seek a future date. This research is consistent with research on how heterosexual relationship partners select mates. Regardless of whether the relationship is a heterosexual or homosexual one, physical attraction plays a significant role in one's choice of a relationship partner.

Culture and Attraction.   Culture is an influential factor in our perception of physical attractiveness. Within our culture, media depict the accepted standards of beauty. Consider the appearance of typical movie villains such as the Joker or the Penguin from the *Batman* movies, and Ursula, the sea witch from *The Little Mermaid*. They are ugly and unattractive, whereas the hero is always handsome or beautiful. As the main characters in *The Exorcist* and *The Fly* turn evil, their external appearances transform from normal to unattractive. The timing of these changes seems to insinuate that there is a direct correlation between turning bad and turning ugly. We do not have to look that far or long to find messages about physical beauty in our culture. Images are found on television and billboards, in magazines, movies and books, and on the Internet.

Perceptions of physical attractiveness can differ across ethnic groups. A very curvaceous figure is often considered to be unattractive among

Caucasian women, but African American women may not agree (Hebl and Heatherton 1998). In fact, African American women are perceived as more attractive by African American males if they have a curvaceous bottom, as opposed to being able to fit into a pair of size four jeans.

As we cross cultural boundaries, it becomes apparent that there are universal perceptions of beauty as well. One particular physical feature that has been judged across cultures as a focal point for physical attraction is the human face. In particular, the more "feminine" a face appears the greater its perceived level of attractiveness. In a study comparing the attractiveness of men and women by looking at close-up photographs of their faces, both Caucasian and Japanese participants rated pictures of men and women whose facial features had been "feminized" or softened as being more attractive (Perrett, Lee, and Penton-Voak 1998).

What questions do you ask to determine your level of social attraction to someone?

© Galina Barskaya, 2007, Shutterstock.

Social Attractiveness

Once we initiate a conversation with another person, it is likely that our attention shifts from the physical attributes, which drew us to start talking in the first place, to identifying commonalities. **Social attractiveness** can be defined as common interests or similar patterns of communication that cause individuals to perceive one another as someone they would like to spend time with. Questions used to identify the level of social attraction with another person might include, "Would I like to hang out with this person?" and "Is this someone who would fit in with my friends?"

While physical attraction has a substantial impact on our decision to initiate relationships with others, social attraction is equally important. Some people exert considerable effort to ensure that others perceive their social behavior favorably. **Impression management** is defined as the process of maintaining a positive image of self in the presence of others. Consider the time and energy dedicated to making sure our physical appearance is "just right" when we meet or approach someone for the first time. When interviewing for a job, it is essential that the suit is pressed, the shoes are polished, and the hair is neat and clean.

Individuals vary greatly in the extent to which they are self-aware. **Self-monitoring** refers to a personality construct that causes a person to respond to social and interpersonal cues for appropriate communication behaviors in a variety of situations. High self-monitors are constantly aware of behaviors others perceive to be appropriate in interpersonal situations, and continuously strive to control how they are portraying themselves. By contrast, low self-monitors dedicate little, if any, energy to responding to the cues of social appropriateness. They do not spend a lot of time worrying if they break the social rules by wearing jeans to an event where everyone else is dressed more formally, or by belching in front of a potential romantic partner. To examine the relationship of self-monitoring and relationship initiation, participants were given file folders containing photographs and descriptions of personal attributes of potential dates. High self-monitors dedicated more time to reviewing the photographs in the folders, while low self-monitors spent more time reviewing the personal descriptions (Snyder, Berscheid, and Glick 1985). Thus, it appears that high self-monitors place more emphasis on physical attraction when selecting a potential partner for a date, while low self-monitors focus more on social attractiveness.

Task Attractiveness

While physical and social attributes may be influential in the initiatory phase of relationships, as individuals pursue their professional goals, decisions based on attractiveness may take on a much different perspective. **Task attractiveness** refers to the characteristics or qualities that are perceived as appealing when initiating relationships in which the goal is to complete a task or assignment. Suppose your professor allows you to select the team members you wish to work with on a huge term project. Are you going to select the most physically attractive person to work with on this assignment? Possibly, if your goal is to get a date for Saturday night. Are you going to choose the funniest or most social person in the class to be on your team? Maybe, if your goal is to have plenty of laughs as you work on the project. Most likely, you will seek out people with characteristics and qualities that you know are essential to getting the job done. A question used to identify perceived task attractiveness might be, "Does this person have what it takes to help get the job done?" Depending on the task, the list of qualities used to assess task attractiveness might be very different. If you consider yourself to be "technologically challenged," you may seek someone who you consider to be proficient with computers. Suppose there is a strict timeline for the project. In such a situation, you will probably seek a person who is dependable and organized.

Proximity

Consider our earlier question regarding your decision to initiate a relationship with the person seated next to you in this class. In essence, the decision to begin the relationship was influenced by proximity. **Proximity** refers to the physical distance between two people. The fact that you sit next to the same person for an entire semester increases the chance that you will choose to form a relationship with one another. Segal (1974) supported this notion in a study that examined friendships formed in a college classroom. At the beginning of the term, students were given seat assignments. When asked to indicate the persons whom they considered to be friends in the class, most students reported that they were friends with those who were seated next to them.

So why is proximity such a strong predictor of interpersonal attraction? One explanation may be found in the decreased effort that is required to establish relationships with those who are close in distance. It is just easier to strike up a conversation with the person seated next to you in class, or to share stories with the co-worker whose cubicle is directly adjacent to yours. Much more effort is required to start relationships with those who sit on the other side of the room or who work on different floors. Many people believe that long-distance relationships are doomed, simply based on the physical distance separating relationships partners.

Similarity/Homophily

These childhood friends grew up together and share the same background.

© Monika Wisniewska, 2007, Shutterstock.

After initiating a conversation, identifying potential topics to discuss can be the next hurdle to overcome. The goal of our discussions at this phase in a relationship is to identify common interests between ourselves and the other person. Remember the phrase, "Birds of a feather flock together?" This phrase refers to an important element of interpersonal attraction known as **similarity,** or **homophily.** Research confirms that we seek out relationships with those who have common interests, backgrounds, and goals, and who are similar in appearance (McCroskey, Richmond, and Daly 1975). This phenomenon might explain why friendships are formed among people who go to the same gym to work out, or how romantic relationships begin between two people who meet in an Internet chat room dedicated to discussions of reality television. Both of these situations provide common topics for discussion. Our similarity with others can be categorized based on demographic, background, or attitude commonalities. **Demographic similarity** is based on physical and social characteristics that are easily identifiable. Consider the relationships that you have initiated with others who are of a similar age or are the same sex. **Background similarity** refers to commonalities that we share as a result of our life experiences. Chances are that many of your friendships began as a result of experiences that you had in common with others—going to the same summer camp, playing on the same athletic team, working in the same organization, or simply growing up in the same hometown. Finally, **attitude similarity** focuses on our perception of the attitudes, beliefs, and values that we hold in common. Some relationships are formed as a result of our cultural, religious or political affiliations. When two friends express similar attitudes towards music, movies, or sports, they are exhibiting attitude similarity.

In their examination of interpersonal attraction and similarity, Klohnen and Luo (2003) identified four dimensions of similarity that individuals consider in initial attraction. These include:

- Similarity to current self
- Complementarity
- Attachment security
- Ideal-self similarity

Similarity to current self refers to the belief that individuals are attracted to those who are similar to themselves. The dimensions we use to identify the congruence between ourselves and others differ from person to person. You may seek someone whose sense of humor is similar to your own, while another person may view similar levels of intelligence as being more important. The **complementarity** hypothesis explains the saying "opposites attract." It predicts that people will be more attracted to those whose personality characteristics complement their own. This may explain why persons who have a high level of communication apprehension seek romantic relationships with those who have low levels of apprehension. To someone who is apprehensive about communicating, it is attractive to have someone who will initiate and carry out interactions. **Attachment security** predicts that individuals will be most attracted to those who are secure. Thus, we find individuals who are confident and trusting more attractive than individuals who are preoccupied by emotions of jealousy, neediness, or worry. Finally, some individuals are most attracted to those whom they perceive to be **similar to the ideal view of self** (as opposed to their actual or current self). Those who are similar to our view of how we would ultimately like to be are rated more favorably.

While creating a favorable impression is a primary conversational goal during the initiation phase of a relationship, it is important to establish realistic expectations. Have you ever experienced the "Me, too!" phenomenon in a romantic relationship or friendship? In a recent episode of the situation comedy *'Til Death*, Jeff is angry with his wife Steph because she lied to him about her interest in ice hockey. Steph finally reveals that she does not like ice hockey and does not want to go to ice hockey games with him anymore. Jeff is angry and wonders what else Steph has lied about and whether he really knows her at all. In one scene, Jeff enters the kitchen and says, "Hi Steph—if that is your real name!" Steph realizes that Jeff is upset about the lie and tries to explain her actions. She tells him that when he asked her out for the first time he also questioned whether she liked ice hockey, to which she enthusiastically replied "Yes!" Steph explains that if she had not said yes, they may have never dated at all because he might prefer someone with more similar interests. Rather than continue to perpetuate the lie, Steph chose to tell Jeff the truth. How often does a situation like this occur in relationships?

When we attempt to portray ourselves as being more similar to the other person than we really are simply to appear more attractive, we run the risk of encountering a relationship pitfall known as false homophily. **False homophily** refers to the presentation of a deceptive image of self that appears to be more similar than it actually is. Claiming that you have interests or beliefs in common with another person just to appear more attractive creates unrealistic expectations in the relationship. While this strategy may be effective for gaining attention in the initial stages of the relationship, eventually the differences will emerge and could cause potential problems, as illustrated in the Steph and Jeff example from *'Til Death*.

One interpersonal context that places considerable emphasis on similarity as a reason for initiating relationships is the Internet. In the absence of the more obvious physical clues that are often used to decide whether to initiate a relationship, information about commonalities is sought to decide whether to interact with the other person. Baker (2005) points out that couples who initially meet via the Internet are explicit in delineating their interests in an attempt to find others with common interests. Typically they go to virtual chat rooms which focus on a specified topic to ensure that they will have something in common with others in the online community. Think about the process of posting information in an online personal ad. Match.com *(www.match.com)* provides several options to search for the ideal partner. Of course, some of the criteria that can be used to search for the ideal mate include physical characteristics, but additional criteria are available to narrow the focus on the basis of similarities. Questions regarding interests (sports, hobbies), lifestyle (job, smoking, drinking), and personal values (faith, education, politics) are included to identify similarities in relational partners.

What social and task goals do you find in classroom relationships?

© PhotoCreate, 2007, Shutterstock.

Goals

A fourth reason people choose to initiate relationships with others is to fulfill a purpose, or goal. Charles Berger (1995) defines **goals** as "desired end states toward which persons strive" (143). Many of our interpersonal interactions are initiated to fulfill two primary goals: social and task. **Social goals** refer to desired end states that fulfill the need for inclusion or affection. Both parties involved in the initial relationship can experience the fulfilled need. Consider the new kid in school. In order to ease some of the anxiety of starting a new school, the student might approach a table of students in the cafeteria and ask, "Is this seat taken?" One explanation for the initiation of this interaction is to fulfill a social goal—the student seeks to fulfill the need for inclusion at school. **Task goals** are defined as desired end states that fulfill the need for the completion of a task. Consider your current relationship with your hair stylist or barber. You initiated the relationship because the task of getting your hair cut needed to be fulfilled. A phone call was made to a local hair salon with the goal of finding a competent stylist to complete the task. As you initiated a conversation with the stylist, the initial task goal was to describe the hair cut you desired. Consider all of the relationships you have initiated to fulfill task goals. Relationships are initiated with teachers to fulfill the task goal of achieving your educational objectives, and teachers form relationships with colleagues to accomplish tasks associated with the job. Interpersonal communication is instrumental in achieving our goals.

Dillard (1990) points out that our goals serve three functions in interpersonal relationships. First, goals are used to take action and fulfill an interpersonal need. Individuals determine what need to fulfill, and the goal prompts the initiation of the relationship. If your social goal is to form new friendships at school, you will introduce yourself in an attempt to take action to fulfill the need. Second, goals assist us in defining the purpose for the interaction or behaviors. Suppose a woman asks a colleague to join her for a cup of coffee to discuss the upcoming presentation for an important client. She realizes that the purpose for the interaction is to accomplish a task goal. However, if she had a romantic interest in the colleague the ulterior motive for the meeting may have been prompted by social goals. Finally, goals provide us with a standard to judge the behaviors and outcomes of interpersonal interactions. We evaluate our interpersonal interactions with others and judge their effectiveness based on whether or not we accomplish our goals. After a blind date we typically evaluate the date as being *good* or *bad*, based on the interaction that took place. If conversation was forced and awkward, we are likely to evaluate the date negatively.

In a study of first date goals, college students identified eight primary reasons for going on a first date (Mongeau, Serewicz, and Therrien 2004). Table 6.1 compares the responses offered by men and women for their decision for first dates.

It is interesting to note the gender differences in the goals behind asking a person out for a first date. Males were more likely than women to pursue the goal of sexual activity during a first date, while women exclusively

Table 6.1	Frequencies of Goals for First Dates		
Goal	Females	Males	Total
Reduce uncertainty (Get to know the other person better)	52	36	88
Relational escalation (Explore the possibility of pursuing a more intimate relationship)	48	25	73
Have fun (View dating as an enjoyable experience)	40	26	66
Companionship (Have someone to do things with)	16	7	23
Ego booster (Feel better about themselves)	6	6	12
Sexual activity	2	8	10
Hedonistic (Get something "free" from the date— concert ticket, fancy dinner)	8	0	8
Guilt (Avoid hurting the other person's feelings)	5	0	5

Source: From "Goals for Cross-Sex First Dates: Identification, Measurement and the Influence of Contextual Factors" from *Communication Monographs*, 2004, 71, 121–147. Reprinted by permission of Taylor & Francis.

reported that their goal for going on the date was due to hedonistic reasons or guilt. Overall, women appeared to focus more attention on relational goals for the first date compared to men. In the past, our culture taught us that first dates should be initiated by men. "Nice girls" were supposed to sit patiently and wait for the male to contact them and arrange for a date. But this trend is changing. Mongeau and his colleagues (1993) reported that approximately eighty percent of men and sixty percent of women went on a date initiated by the female.

Online interactions can also be initiated to fulfill goals. Katz and Rice (2002) pointed out that sometimes Indian parents use the Internet as a source to seek suitable mates for their children as a modern extension of their traditional matchmaking processes. Signing up to post and browse online personal ads signals a social goal—the intent to form a romantic relationship.

INTERPERSONAL COMMUNICATION THEORIES: *HOW* WE INITIATE RELATIONSHIPS

While the decision to initiate a relationship may be based on attraction, proximity, similarity, or purpose, one of the key factors in beginning the interaction and taking the relationship to the next level can be explained by examining prominent communication theories. Theories and concepts such as social penetration theory, uncertainty reduction theory, predicted outcome value theory, liking, and social exchange theory address *how* we initiate relationships with others. Before we address relevant interpersonal theories and concepts, we address the importance of initial impressions and self-disclosure in establishing a relationship.

Starting the Conversation

To identify commonalities, we must first initiate a conversation. For some people, this is one of the most difficult tasks in a relationship. After all, we are often reminded that, "You never get a second chance to make a good first impression." Consider the last time you attempted to start a conversation. Figuring out the most appropriate way to break the ice and create a positive initial impression can be intimidating. Over the years, many of our students have shared "pick-up lines" or relational openers that have been used to initiate conversations with a potential romantic partner. Table 6.2 includes a list of the most interesting. It is important to note that they are not necessarily the most effective conversation starters, although they do succeed in getting one's attention. Our advice is that the next time you think about using one of these pick-up lines to begin a conversation, don't. Informal surveys of our students have revealed that the vast majority feel a simple and sincere introduction is the most effective way to initiate a conversation.

Table 6.2   Notorious Pick-Up Lines/Relational Openers

Excuse me, do you have a quarter? I want to call my mother and tell her I just met the girl of my dreams.

Do you have a map? Because I keep getting lost in your eyes.

You must be tired because you've been running through my mind all night!

Your eyes are blue like the ocean and I'm lost at sea!

Do you know karate because your body is really kickin'!

Is there a rainbow today? I've just found the treasure I've been searching for.

Are you from Tennessee? Cause you're the only "ten" I see!

Do you believe in love at first sight or should I walk by again?

Hey, I like a girl with some meat on her! **(We STRONGLY discourage use of this relational opener!)

Somebody better call God because he's missing an angel.

If I could rearrange the alphabet I'd put U and I together.

You must be a Snickers because you satisfy me.

Your lips look so lonely. Would they like to meet mine?

Do you know how much a polar bear weighs? Enough to break the ice. Hi! My name is _____.

Were you in the Boy Scouts? Because you've sure tied my heart in a knot.

You're so sweet, you could put Hershey's out of business.

Apart from being beautiful, what do you do for a living?

Are you a parking ticket? Cause you've got "fine" written all over you.

So how does it feel to be the most beautiful girl in this room?

You must be a broom because you just swept me off my feet.

Self-Disclosure.   While it is difficult to determine which opening line should be used to initiate a conversation, taking the next step in the conversation can be an even greater challenge. Deciding what information to share about yourself, and what information you should seek from the other person can be viewed as a daunting task. During the early stages of relationship formation, partners will often self-disclose information in an effort to increase intimacy (Reis and Shaver 1988; Reis and Patrick 1996; Sprecher and Hendrick 2004). **Self-disclosure** is "the process of revealing personal information about oneself to another" (Sprecher and Hendrick 2004, 858). Self-disclosing is essential to relationship success and stability because it helps others learn who we are and what we want in a relationship. Aron (2003) validates this statement by noting that much of the process of becoming intimate with others involves disclosing information about the self and connecting the self to relevant others.

Typically, we disclose information more freely to those with whom we feel we have a close relationship. We are most likely to divulge information about ourselves to individuals we like and, as a result of this, tend to come to like those individuals even more (Kowalski 1999). However, in initial interactions the rules for disclosure are a bit more restrictive; we are more guarded in our disclosures. The task involves deciding what, and how much, information we should share. Have you ever heard a horror story of a first date where one person disclosed their deepest secrets or declared their undying affection for the other person? Needless to say, the recipient typically reports being turned off by such intimate disclosures so early in the relationship. Consider what topics are "safe" when initiating a relationship. Would it be best to discuss and make comparisons to your most recent romantic relationship on a first date? Probably not. Similarly, discussing how much money you earn or asking the other person to discuss their greatest fears in life would be viewed as highly inappropriate. As a general rule, **reciprocal self-disclosure**, the notion that disclosure of information between two people, is best when it is similar in terms of topics discussed and depth of disclosure. Disclosures of information in the initial stages of a relationship are often met with similar disclosures. Consider the following initial disclosures between two classmates on the first day of class:

© Darren Green, 2007, Shutterstock.

How much information do you feel comfortable disclosing in a new relationship?

> **Sabina:** Hi, I'm Sabina. Have you ever taken a class with Dr. Yost before?
>
> **Natalie:** Hey Sabina, I'm Natalie. No, I haven't had a class with her, but my roommate took it last semester.
>
> **Sabina:** Really, what did he say about it?
>
> **Natalie:** He said she's tough but fair.
>
> **Sabina:** Ouch! That's what I was afraid of. I have to take this class for my major and this is the only time that it fit into my schedule. If she's a difficult teacher then why did you take this class?
>
> **Natalie:** Well, even though she's tough, I've also heard that you learn a lot that will help you down the road in other classes in the major.
>
> **Sabina:** Oh, are you a communication major?
>
> **Natalie:** Yes, this is my second year. What year are you?

Sabina: I'm a junior, but I just transferred into the major at the beginning of the semester. I feel like I'm so far behind. Everyone else has their schedules all planned out and they know exactly who and what to take.

Natalie: Don't stress yourself out about it. We've all been there before. If you have any questions about who you should take, just ask me. Have you met with your advisor yet? They're pretty good about helping you map out your long-term schedule.

Consider the reciprocity of disclosure in this initial interaction. Both women share information about their majors as well as their fears about the class. As one asks a question, the other answers it. When one woman discloses information, so does the other. In situations where others fail to disclose similar information, we become uncomfortable and may perceive them to be hiding something, or engaging in deceptive communication.

Cultural Differences in Disclosure.   Not all cultures approach or perceive self-disclosure in the same way. Nakanishi (1986) found that Japanese view limited levels of self-disclosure as being more appropriate in initial interactions with others. Most research supports the notion that Japanese individuals tend to engage in less self-disclosure than those from Western cultures. In a study comparing the disclosures of Japanese compared with Americans across a variety of relationships, Japanese were found to engage in fewer disclosures than their American counterparts. However, both Japanese and American students reported they preferred to disclose information to their same-sex friends as opposed to their opposite-sex friends, and members of both cultures reported engaging in more in-depth disclosures in romantic relationships than in friendships (Kito 2005). Consider the rules that your culture has for disclosure. These cultural norms may cause frustration when interacting with a person from a different culture. Recall the earlier discussion of reciprocal disclosures. If a person from the United States was disclosing information about financial difficulties with a friend from Japan, expecting similar disclosures, the result would likely be frustrating for the American. Whereas members of the U.S. culture tend to be very open in disclosures, those from Asian cultures tend to be more reserved.

Even within a particular culture, personal preferences for disclosure exist, depending on how familiar we are with the other person. In particular, bartenders and hair stylists report receiving surprising numbers of unsolicited self-disclosures from their clients. A recent *Newsweek* article described the tendency for individuals to disclose personal information to their hair stylists (Silver-Greenberg 2005). Twanda Hamilton, a cosmetologist from Wichita, Kansas was quoted as saying, "You get a client in the shampoo bowl and they just open up and tell us that they are being beaten. We hear so much in the salon that no one else hears." In response to these unsolicited disclosures, a program called Cut-it-Out was launched to train stylists to recognize the signs of domestic abuse.

Social Penetration Theory

Altman and Taylor (1973) created **social penetration theory** to address how information is exchanged during relationship development. This theory focuses on how self-disclosure changes as relationships move from one level to the next. In essence, their theory explains how and why we move from superficial topics of conversation in the initial stages of relationships to more intimate conversations as the relationship progresses. In the movie *Shrek*, Shrek uses the analogy of an onion to explain to Donkey that even though he is an ogre, he possesses many layers of feelings and emotions that need to be taken into consideration.

Shrek: Ogres are like onions.

Donkey: They stink?

Shrek: Yes. No.

Donkey: Oh, they make you cry.

Shrek: No.

Donkey: Oh, you leave 'em out in the sun, they get all brown, start sproutin' little white hairs.

Shrek: NO. Layers. Onions have layers. Ogres have layers. Onions have layers. You get it? We both have layers. *(sighs)*

Donkey: Oh, you both have layers. Oh. You know, not everybody like onions. (*Shrek* directed by Andrew Adamson and Vicky Jenson, 1 hr. 30 min., DreamWorks Animation, 2001.)

This analogy helps to illustrate Altman and Taylor's explanation of the levels of information we reveal as we move from one stage of a relationship to the next. There are three primary levels of information that we reveal as we progress. These include superficial, personal, and intimate. Superficial information is revealed in initial interactions. Communication focuses on safe topics such as one's major, occupation, or hometown. As the relationship intensifies, a layer of the onion is "peeled" away and more personal information is revealed. Personal communication focuses on topics of a more personal nature such as likes, dislikes, and experiences. As the relationship progresses to a more intimate level, so does the communication. Intimate communication focuses on topics that are personal and private. In order to reveal intimate information, a level of trust must be present. At this innermost core of the onion, topics of discussion include goals, challenges, values, and motivations.

As mentioned previously, it is important to adhere to self-disclosure norms or expectations when sharing information with a potential relationship partner. Some research indicates that individuals who self-disclose inappropriately by sharing private information early in a relationship are perceived as odd, deviant or even dislikable (Werner and Haggard 1985). Table 6.3 on page 166 offers some suggestions for both providing self-disclosure and receiving self-disclosure from others competently.

Uncertainty Reduction Theory

Consider the extensive use of questions throughout the interaction between Sabina and Natalie. **Uncertainty reduction theory** (Berger and Calabrese 1975) identifies questions as a primary communication strategy used for encouraging reciprocal disclosure and reducing levels of uncertainty. To test the relationship between initial attraction and the use of questioning or disclosure, Douglas (1990) asked pairs to engage in a six-minute initial interaction. He found that the majority of questions were asked in the initial two minutes of

Table 6.3	Suggestions for Delivering and Receiving Self-Disclosures

DELIVERING

Begin by self-disclosing information on safe or neutral topics.

During initial conversations, talk about where you went to school, hobbies, talents, etc., before sharing any private information.

If possible, attempt to match your partner's disclosures in depth.

If your partner shares intimate information (e.g., fears, future goals, insecurities), he may expect you to reciprocate. Remember that reciprocal disclosures between partners often indicates trust and liking.

Before disclosing private information, ask yourself if this is someone you can trust.

If you feel you cannot trust this person or feel this person will share this information with others, it is probably not a good idea to share private information.

RECEIVING

Do not overreact when someone shares personal information with you.

Try not to become overly emotional or provide judgmental feedback when someone shares private information with you. For example, screaming, "YOU DID WHAT?" when a friend shares information is not recommended.

Provide verbal and nonverbal support.

Make an attempt to display warm receptive nonverbal cues during your conversation by maintaining eye contact, sitting near the person, nodding your head to indicate listening and, if appropriate, smiling. Engage in active listening behaviors which might include paraphrasing and appropriate empathic responses (e.g., I can see why you would be upset).

If you do not feel comfortable discussing a topic or issue, tell your friend or relationship partner.

Rather than avoid the person and risk damaging your relationship, tell the person why you are uncomfortable discussing the topic.

---

the conversation, and greater disclosures were made in the final two minutes of the conversation. Partners asked each other fewer questions as their answers required more detailed responses. Question-asking decreases as the questions require more in-depth responses. In the process of reducing uncertainty about the other person, individuals engage in a "strategy selection" process. This procedure requires them to maximize efficiency in gaining information about the other person while utilizing behaviors that are viewed as socially appropriate.

Predicted Outcome Value Theory

Once we have reduced our level of uncertainty about a new relationship, the next step involves deciding what we expect or want from the new relationship. **Predicted outcome value theory** focuses on the perceived rewards or benefits associated with the new relationship (Sunnafrank 1986). There is a shift from focusing on the need for more information about the other person to an analysis of the value obtained from the relationship. Consider when you meet someone for the first time. You probably engage in an analytical process to evaluate the potential for the future of the relationship. At that point a decision is made regarding whether to pursue the relationship, how the relationship should progress, and what type of relationship we should seek with the other person (e.g., friendship, romantic).

Liking

Our earlier discussion of uncertainty reduction theory discussed the strategy of information-seeking to decrease our level of uncertainty about the other person. However, an additional benefit of reducing our uncertainty is to increase liking between individuals. The more we know about a person, the greater the possibility that we will like one another. **Liking** is defined as the level of positive affect, or affinity, we feel toward another person. A critical factor in deciding to initiate a relationship is reciprocal liking—each partner must perceive the other as having mutual positive affect. However, the trick often rests in obtaining information as to whether mutual liking is present. Douglas (1987) conducted a study to identify affinity-testing strategies used to identify the presence or absence of mutual liking. Participants in the study were asked to describe the things they do to find out how much somebody of the opposite sex likes them, being reminded to focus specifically on strategies they would use in initial encounters. Eight different affinity-testing strategies were identified in this study: confronting, withdrawing, sustaining, hazing, diminishing the self, approaching, offering, and networking. Participants were also asked to rate the efficiency and appropriateness of each of the affinity-testing strategies. Confronting, which involved asking the individual direct questions, was viewed as the most efficient strategy followed by approaching and sustaining; in the interest of time, it is best to be up front and direct when determining whether reciprocal liking is present. With regard to appropriateness, sustaining was rated as the most socially appropriate strategy. When individuals used the sustaining strategy they made active attempts to keep the conversation going by getting others to reveal information about themselves. This research supports the use of questions to reduce uncertainty. Hazing and diminishing the self were viewed as socially inappropriate. Both strategies involve "playing games" or using manipulative tactics to determine the level of interest in a relationship. When individuals use these affinity-testing strategies, they may be perceived as deceptive and unacceptable.

While Douglas (1987) examined how individuals determine whether mutual liking exists in romantic relationships, research by Bell and Daly (1984) identified the wide range of strategies used in platonic relationships to gain liking. Bell and Daly describe **affinity-seeking strategies** as verbal and nonverbal communication behaviors that are often used strategically to gain liking from others. In their seminal research they asked college students to identify all of the different tactics they used to gain liking from peers. A total of twenty-five different affinity-seeking strategies were identified from the students' descriptive responses. Examples of affinity-seeking strategies included: altruism, physical attractiveness, facilitate enjoyment, comfortable self, inclusion of other, nonverbal immediacy, and openness. Not surprisingly, affinity-seeking strategies are used in all types of relationships to increase liking. For example, a number of studies indicate that both students and professors use affinity-seeking strategies to improve their relationships (see, for example, Frymier 1994; Wanzer 1995; 1998).

Social Exchange Theory

Have you ever heard the phrase "on the market" to refer to a person who is single and searching for a new romantic relationship? While at first this reference may seem degrading, it actually fits quite well with the strategies used when considering new relationships. The process one experiences when evaluating the pros and cons of initiating a relationship is actually quite similar to shopping—we examine the options available and seek the best "deal" available. **Social exchange theory** (also known as interdependence theory) refers to an assessment of costs and rewards in determining the value of pursuing or continuing a relationship (Thibaut and Kelley 1959). **Rewards** consist of behaviors or things that are desirable, which the recipient perceives as enjoyable or fulfilling. By contrast, **costs** are perceived as undesirable behaviors or outcomes. As we exchange information in the initial stages of a relationship, decisions are made regarding the relative value of continuing to pursue the relationship further. While your initial conversation with the person seated next to you on an airplane may be rewarding in the sense that you felt comfortable discussing topics of interest and it helped pass the time on a three-hour journey, the costs of maintaining the relationship (effort involved in emailing and calling the person) may outweigh the benefits. Thus, you decide to shake hands at the end of the flight, exchange pleasantries, and go your separate ways. But suppose the person seated next to you is employed at the company you've always dreamed of working for. In that instance, the costs involved in continuing to communicate across the distance are minimal compared to the potential reward of having an inside connection when you apply for employment at the company in the future.

Stages of Relationship Development

Now that we have explored the reasons why we initiate relationships and some of the theoretical explanations for how we use communication, we turn our attention to understanding the process of progressing from one stage of a relationship to another.

Mark Knapp (1978) proposes a "staircase" model depicting the interactive stages of relationship development and dissolution. The first five steps of this model, known as Coming Together, will be discussed here. Chapter Nine will discuss Knapp's (1978) stages of relationship disengagement or, Coming Apart. Before discussing the stages of relationship initiation and development, it is important to note the following caveats about the movement from one stage to the next (Knapp and Vangelisti 2003):

- Movement from one stage of the model to the next is typically sequential. Moving sequentially allows us to make predictions regarding the future of the relationship.
- Movement may progress from one stage forward to the next. This movement involves an analysis of the potential benefits of continuing the relationship and increasing the level of intimacy in communication.
- Movement may revert to a previous stage. This is often due to a decline in the communication behaviors prescribed in the present stage.
- Movement through the stages occurs at different paces for each unique relationship. While one relationship may move very quickly from one

stage to the next, another relationship may stall at one stage while the partners work through the communication challenges of the phase and make the decision of whether to progress to the next level.

Initiation.   **Initiation** occurs when one party decides to initiate conversation with another person. Communication during this phase typically consists of the polite formalities of introduction. Statements such as "How are you?" or "Is anyone sitting here?" are used to break the ice. Consider the role that variables discussed earlier in this chapter play in our decision to approach someone and initiate a conversation. For instance, we evaluate the person's attractiveness and scramble to come up with the perfect opening line. During this phase, impression management is essential. After all, we want to present ourselves in the most positive way possible. While some people may be tempted to use one of the pick-up lines discussed earlier in this chapter, the best strategy for making a good first impression is to be confident and sincere.

Experimenting.   You know that you have reached the **experimenting** phase when the communication involves excessive questions and discussions about topics such as classes, hobbies, or other demographic information. Whereas physical attraction has a strong influence on the decision to engage in the initiation phase, social attraction is discovered during the experimenting phase. Reciprocal disclosures are common, with one person asking questions such as, "So have you lived in Los Angeles your entire life?" and the other person responding with "No, I grew up in Chicago and moved to L.A. last year to escape the cold winters. Did you grow up in California?" Uncertainty reduction is the primary goal of this stage of relationship development.

Intensifying.   As we progress to the **intensifying** stage of the staircase model, our disclosures with one another increase in depth. Whereas in the experimenting stage we disclosed information on a variety of topics (breadth), during this phase the information shared becomes more personal and private (depth). Messages communicated between partners involve a lot of "tests" to determine the intensity or commitment felt by one another. Knapp and Vangelisti (2003) identify specific verbal characteristics that are common during the intensifying stage. These include using nicknames or terms of endearment to refer to one another (think "Hunny" or "Babe"), referring to one another through the use of first person plural pronouns ("*We* should go to the movies with Joe and Cara on Friday,") and making explicit references to the commitment like "I think about you all the time when you're not here."

Integrating.   The **integrating** stage is marked by a merging of personalities and identities. Not only do the partners see themselves as a couple, but others recognize and refer to them as a unit as well. Relationship rituals that occur during this stage include exchanging personal items such as clothing, pictures, and rings that can be worn or displayed to communicate their identity as a couple to others, engaging in similar verbal and nonverbal behaviors, and identifying common "property" that is identified as special to the relationship ("our" song or purchasing a pet together).

Getting married demonstrates commitment to a long-term relationship.

© iofoto, 2007, Shutterstock.

Bonding.   **Bonding,** the final stage of coming together, is viewed as a formal contractual agreement that declares to the world that the couple has made a serious commitment to one another. This stage can be marked by performing public rituals such as exchanging class rings to show that you are "going steady," or getting engaged, or that you have gotten married. It is important to note that while bonding can be viewed as a contract at any stage of the relationship, the message communicated between a couple during this stage is that there is a serious commitment that implies the goal of pursuing a long-term relationship.

Relationship Initiation Contexts

Another factor impacting the decision to initiate a relationship focuses on the setting in which the initial interaction takes place. In a study of college women, the actual settings where significant relationships began were examined (Jason, Reichler, and Rucker 1981). Five settings were identified by single women as the location where their significant relationships were initiated (see Table 6.4 below). Given that the women were currently enrolled in college classes, it should come as no surprise that they listed school as the place where their most important relationships began. While many would question the quality of a relationship that is initiated in a bar, women reported this as the initial location for nine percent of their significant relationships. In a study of relationship initiation in singles bars, researchers noted that a woman was approached by a man once every ten to twenty minutes. However, the average length of the interaction was approximately seven seconds (Glenwick, Jason, and Elman 1978). So while women may have many opportunities in single bars, it appears as though they choose not to pursue the majority of relationships initiated by men.

A study of preferred meeting places for gays and lesbians reveals a slight difference in setting choices. Gay bars are a popular place for initiating relationships given the fact that patrons of the bars are similar in terms of their sexual preference. Among lesbians, the second most preferred meeting place is at political functions, such as feminist or lesbian rallies (Huston and Schwartz 2003). It is important to note that some environments are not open

Table 6.4	Settings Where Most Important Relationships Began
Setting	**Percentage**
School	25
Work	20
Through friends	14
Bar	9
Party	9

Source: From "Characteristics of significant dating relationships: Male versus female initiators, idealized versus actual settings" by L.A. Jason, et al., *The Journal of Psychology*, 109, 185–190, 1981. Reprinted with permission of the Helen Dwight Reid Educational Foundation. Published by Heldref Publications, 1319 Eighteenth St., NW, Washington, DC 20036-1802. Copyright © 1981.

or welcoming to the initiation of homosexual relationships. Thus, frustration in locating a common place to meet similar others is often reported by gay men and lesbians.

The Role of Technology in Relationship Initiation

Online Relationship Initiation. As the number of people who form relationships online continues to grow, there is a greater need to understand the unique nature of interactions in cyberspace. In face-to-face interactions, the initial decision to approach another person is often based on physical characteristics. We see the person, make a decision of whether or not to approach him, and subsequently spend time getting to know one another by progressing through the relationship stages identified by Knapp and Vangelisti (2003). Online relationship initiation differs because of the absence of physical cues, which can affect the course of the relationship. Individuals meet via written messages or text. From there, they decide whether to talk with the other person via phone and, ultimately, in person. In essence, online relationship initiation could be considered a "test drive"—we can dedicate as little or as much time as we want getting to know the person before deciding if we want to meet face-to-face.

Baker (2005) developed a model delineating the characteristics of successful versus unsuccessful relationships which were initiated online (see Table 6.5).

While we might doubt the sustainability of relationships that are initiated online, research suggests otherwise. One study examined the stability of a variety of online relationships (acquaintances, friends, and romantic partners) over a two-year period and found seventy-five percent of respondents indicated that they were still involved in a relationship that had initiated online (McKenna, Green, and Gleason 2002).

Table 6.5   **A Model for Successful versus Unsuccessful Online Relationships**

Factor	Positive/Successful	Negative/Unsuccessful
Place met	Sites focused on specific interests	Sites focused on general interests
Physical appearance, degree of importance	Not viewed as being important	Considered very important or crucial
Hyperhonesty	Very honest online	Not honest in online interactions
Cybersex	Never or rarely engaged in cybersex	Frequently engaged in cybersex
Long-time communication before they met in person	Considerable time spent communicating online prior to face-to-face meeting	Little time spent interacting online prior to meeting
Relocation	At least one person willing to relocate	Neither partner is willing to relocate

Source: From *Double Click: Romance and Commitment Among Online Couples* by A. Baker, 2005, Cresskill, NJ: Hampton Press. Reprinted with permission of the publisher.

Will this on-line relationship last?

Text-Messaging.   If you are a fan of *American Idol,* you have probably seen the commercials for AT&T Wireless in which Ryan Seacrest sends a text message to a woman named Jeanette, across a crowded bar to inquire if she is interested in meeting his friend, Dave. In the end, Jeanette declines the offer to initiate a relationship, but the scene depicted in the commercial is one that is all too familiar to those currently experiencing the dating scene. A popular channel for communicating in Europe and Asia for several years, text-messaging has achieved growing popularity in the United States as a means to communicate with others in relationships. When initiating new relationships, text messaging serves as a "safe" channel for reducing uncertainty and gaining information about the other person before meeting again face-to-face. The term *silent dating* has been used to discuss the strategy of exchanging text messages for a week or more in the initial stages of a relationship *(http://thescotsman.scotsman.com/index.cfm?id=290812004)*. Anna Close, a twenty-eight-year-old teacher from Glasgow, describes the value of text messages in initial relationships as: "Before text-messaging I'd meet someone and then not hear from him because he'd be too scared to actually go through the process of picking up the phone and having a conversation. But now, if a man is interested in you, he won't call, but he'll definitely text."

Relationship Initiation and Culture

While you might think that perceptions with regard to relationship initiation differ across cultures, you might be surprised to find out that we are more alike than different. Pines (2001) examined the role of gender and culture in initial romantic attraction by comparing Americans with Israelis. She asked participants to describe how they met their romantic partner and indicate what attracted them to the other person initially (see Table 6.6).

Table 6.6	**Attraction Variables (percent) by Country**	
Attraction Variable	**USA**	**Israel**
Appearance	63	70
Status	8	0
Personality	92	94
Need filled	54	6
Propinquity	63	46
Mutual attraction	41	40
Arousal	22	25
Similarity	30	8

Source: From "The Role of Gender and Culture in a Romantic Attraction" by Ayala Malach Pines. Reproduced with permission from *European Psychologist*, Vol. 6, (2), pp. 96–102. © 2001 by Hogrefe & Huber Publishers.

The only significant differences occurred when comparing U.S. and Israeli responses to questions relating to status, propinquity, and similarity. Eight percent of Americans reported that they were attracted by the status of their relational partner, while none of the Israeli respondents indicated this was a factor. Propinquity, or the proximity between partners, was listed as being more influential to Americans. Americans report being more attracted to partners who lived, worked, or studied at the same place, as compared to Israeli respondents. Similarity of partners was found to be more important to Americans. Having similar experiences, values, interests, attitudes, and personalities was rated as being far more important to Americans than to Israelis.

Interracial Dating.   As the number of interracial relationships increases, so does our need for understanding the stages of progression that are unique to this relationship context. Foeman and Nance (2003) enhance our understanding of these phases by presenting a model of interracial development. In this model, four stages are encountered by the couple. These include:

- Stage 1—Racial awareness
- Stage 2—Coping with social definitions of race
- Stage 3—Identity emergence
- Stage 4—Maintenance

Racial awareness focuses on the existence of multiple perceptions regarding the new relationship. In addition to each partner's perception of the relationship, interracial couples must also deal with the perceptions of the members of one another's racial groups. If the couple decides to move beyond the initiation phase and awareness, the next stage involves coping with society's definitions and reactions to the racially mixed relationship. Several communication strategies are considered during this phase. In addition to identifying how to respond to questions and statements regarding racial differences, the couple needs to decide when to avoid potentially negative interactions with others and when to confront them. During the third stage, identity emergence, the couple begins to define how they see themselves as an "interracial" couple. They work together to develop strategies and skills for addressing problems and often view themselves as being unique or trendsetting. Maintenance, the final stage of the model, involves occasional recycling through the stages of the model as new life events occur (such as the addition of children to the family) that generate new reactions to their status as an interracial couple.

SUMMARY

In this chapter we have answered some of the questions regarding *why* we form interpersonal relationships with others and *how* we use communication to initiate them. While each relationship is unique, the reasons we choose to interact with others are fairly similar. Our hope is that you have gained both an understanding of, and the confidence for, using effective communication behaviors to pursue new relationship journeys. Perhaps the most important piece of advice we could offer as you begin a relationship with another person, whether it is platonic or romantic relationship, is to just be yourself.

APPLICATIONS

Discussion Questions

A. Recall a time when you were successful at initiating a romantic relationship. Offer several suggestions or guidelines for individuals that want to be successful when initiating conversations or beginning a romantic relationship. What types of things should you avoid saying or doing during this critical time period?

B. Based on your experience, how prevalent is the silent dating phenomenon? Discuss several pros and cons of silent dating.

C. In what context or under what circumstances did most of your important relationships begin? Do you initiate different types of relationships in different contexts? Are there similarities and differences in the questions asked/strategies employed during the initiating stages of platonic and romantic relationship development?

D. In your opinion, what is the best way to gain liking from another individual? Bell and Daly identified twenty-five affinity-seeking strategies that individuals use to gain liking. Can you identify at least ten strategies?

REFERENCES

Altman, I., and D. A. Taylor. 1973. *Social penetration: The development of interpersonal relationships.* New York: Holt, Rinehart, & Winston.

Aron, A. 2003. Self and close relationships. In M. R. Leary and J. P. Tangney (Eds.), *Handbook of self and identity.* New York: The Guilford Press.

Baker, A. 2005. *Double click: Romance and commitment among online couples.* Cresskill, NJ: Hampton Press.

Bell, R. A., and J. A. Daly. 1984. The affinity-seeking function of communication. *Communication Monographs, 51,* 91–115.

Berger, C. 1995. A plan-based approach to strategic interaction. In D. E. Hewes (Ed.), *The cognitive bases of interpersonal interaction* (141–180). Hillsdale, NJ: Lawrence Erlbaum.

Berger, C. R., and R. J. Calabrese. 1975. Some explorations in initial interaction and beyond: Toward a developmental theory of interpersonal communication. *Human Communication Research, 1,* 99–112.

Berscheid, E., and H. T. Reis. 1998. Attraction and close relationships. In D. Gilbert, S. Fiske, and G. Lindzey (Eds.), *Handbook of social psychology (4th ed.)* (193–281). New York: McGraw-Hill.

Buss, D. M. 1989. Sex differences in human mate preferences: Evolutionary hypotheses tested in 37 cultures. *Behavioral and Brain Sciences, 12,* 1–49.

Curran, J. P., and S. Lippold. 1975. The effects of physical attraction and attitude similarity on attraction in dating dyads. *Journal of Personality, 43,* 528–539.

Davis, S. 1990. Men as success objects and women as sex objects: A study of personal advertisements. *Sex Roles, 23,* 43–50.

Dillard, J. P. 1990. A goal-driven model of interpersonal influence. In J. P. Dillard (Ed.), *Seeking compliance: The production of interpersonal influence messages* (41–56). Scottsdale, AZ: Gorsuch-Scarisbrick.

Dion, K. K., E. Berscheid, and E. Walster. 1972. What is beautiful is good. *Journal of Personality and Social Psychology, 24,* 285–290.

Douglas, W. 1987. Affinity-testing in initial interactions. *Journal of Social and Personal Relationships, 4,* 3–15.

———. 1990. Uncertainty, information seeking and liking during initial interaction. *Western Journal of Speech Communication, 54,* 66–81.

Eagly, A. H., R. D. Ashmore, M. G. Makhijani, and L. C. Longo. 1991. What is beautiful is good, but . . . A meta-analytic review of research on the physical attractiveness stereotype. *Psychological Bulletin, 110,* 109–128.

Foeman, A., and T. Nance. 2003. From miscegenation to multiculturalism. In K. M. Galvin and P. J. Cooper (Eds.), *Making connections: Readings in interpersonal communication (3rd ed.)* (pp. 166–170). Los Angeles, CA: Roxbury.

Frymier, A. B. 1994. The use of affinity-seeking in producing liking and learning in the classroom. *Journal of Applied Communication Research, 22,* 87–105.

Glenwick, D. S., L. A. Jason, and D. Elman. 1978. Physical attractiveness and social contact in the singles bar. *Journal of Social Psychology, 105,* 311–312.

Goode, E. 1996. Gender and courtship entitlement: Responses to personal ads. *Sex Roles, 34,* 141–168.

Harrison, A. A., and L. Saeed. 1977. Let's make a deal: An analysis of revelations and stipulations in lonely hearts advertisements. *Journal of Personality and Social Psychology, 35,* 257–264.

Hatfield, E., and S. Sprecher. 1986. *Mirror, mirror: The importance of looks in everyday life.* Albany, NY: SUNY Press.

Hebl, M. R., and T. F. Heatherton. 1998. The stigma of obesity in women: The difference is black and white. *Personality and Social Psychology Bulletin, 24,* 417–426.

Hewitt, J., and K. German. 1987. Attire and attractiveness. *Perceptual and Motor Skills, 42,* page 558.

Huston, M., and P. Schwartz. 2003. The relationships of lesbians and of gay men. In K. M. Galvin and P. J. Cooper (Eds.), *Making connections: Readings in interpersonal communication (3rd ed.)* (171–177). Los Angeles, CA: Roxbury.

Jason, L. A., A. Reichler, and W. Rucker. 1981. Characteristics of significant dating relationships: Male versus female initiators, idealized versus actual settings. *The Journal of Psychology, 109,* 185–190.

Johnson, D. F., and J. B. Pittinger. 1984. Attribution, the attractiveness stereotype, and the elderly. *Developmental Psychology, 20,* 1168–1172.

Katz, J. E., and R. E. Rice. 2002. *Social consequences of Internet use: Access, involvement and interaction.* Cambridge, MA: The MIT Press.

Kito, M. 2005. Self-disclosure in romantic relationships and friendships among American and Japanese college students. *The Journal of Social Psychology, 44,* 181–199.

Klohnen, E. C., and S. Luo. 2003. Interpersonal attraction and personality: What is attractive—self similarity, ideal similarity, complementarity, or attachment security? *Journal of Personality and Social Psychology, 85,* 709–722.

Knapp, M. L. 1978. *Social intercourse: From greeting to goodbye.* Boston: Allyn & Bacon.

Knapp, M., and A. Vangelisti. 2003. Relationship stages: A communication perspective. In K. M. Galvin and P. J. Cooper (Eds.), *Making connections: Readings in interpersonal communication (3rd ed.)* (158–165). Los Angeles, CA: Roxbury.

Kowalski, R. M. 1999. Speaking the unspeakable: Self-disclosure and mental health. In B. R. Kowalski and M. R. Leary (Eds.), *The social psychology of emotional and behavioral problems* (225–248). Washington, DC: The American Psychological Association.

Lewis, K. E., and M. Bierly. 1990. Toward a profile of the female voter: Sex differences in perceived physical attractiveness and competence of political candidates. *Sex Roles, 22,* 1–12.

Lykken, D. T., and A. Tellegen. 1993. Is human mating adventitious or the result of lawful choice? A twin study of mate selection. *Journal of Personality and Social Psychology, 65,* 56–68.

Mathes, E. W., S. M. Brennan, P. M. Haugen, and H. B. Rice. 1985. Ratings of physical attractiveness as a function of age. *The Journal of Social Psychology, 125,* 157–168.

McClellan, B., and S. J. McKelvie. 1993. Effects of age and gender on perceived physical attractiveness. *Canadian Journal of Behavioral Science, 25,* 135–142.

McCroskey, J. C., and T. A. McCain. 1974. The measurement of interpersonal attraction. *Speech Monographs, 41,* 261–266.

McCroskey, J. C., V. P. Richmond, and J. A. Daly. 1975. The development of a measure of perceived homophily in interpersonal communication. *Human Communication Research, 1,* 323–332.

McKenna, K. Y. A., A. S. Green, and M. E. J. Gleason. 2002. Relationship formation on the Internet: What's the big attraction? *Journal of Social Issues, 58,* 9–31.

Mongeau, P. A., J. L. Hale, K. L. Johnson, and J. D. Hillis. 1993. "Who's wooing whom?" An investigation of female-initiated dating. In P. J. Kalbfleisch (Ed.), *Interpersonal communication: Evolving interpersonal relationships* (51–68). Hillsdale, NJ: Lawrence Erlbaum.

Mongeau, P. A., M. C. M. Serewicz, and L. F. Therrien. 2004. Goals for cross-sex first dates: Identification, measurement, and the influence of contextual factors. *Communication Monographs, 71,* 121–147.

Nakanishi, M. 1986. Perceptions of self-disclosure in initial interaction: A Japanese sample. *Human Communication Research, 13,* 167–190.

Perrett, D. I., K. J. Lee, and I. Penton-Voak. 1998. Effects of sexual dimorphism on facial attractiveness, *Nature, 394,* August, 27, 884–886.

Pines, A. M. 2001. The role of gender and culture in romantic attraction. *European Psychologist, 6,* 96–102.

Richmond, V. P. 1992. *Nonverbal communication in the classroom.* Edina, MN: Burgess.

Reis, H. T., and B. C. Patrick. 1996. Attachment and intimacy: Component processes. In E. T. Higgins and A. W. Kruglanski (Eds.), *Social psychology: Handbook of basic principles* (523–563). New York: Guilford Press.

Reis, H. T., and P. Shaver. 1988. Intimacy as interpersonal process. In S. Duck (Ed.), *Handbook of personal relationships: Theory, research, and interventions* (367–389). Chichester: John Wiley & Sons Ltd.

Reis, H. T., J. Nezlek, and L. Wheeler. 1980. Physical attractiveness in social interaction. *Journal of Personality and Social Psychology, 38,* 604–617.

Segal, M. W. 1974. Alphabet and attraction: An unobtrusive measure of the effect of propinquity in a field setting. *Journal of Personality and Social Psychology, 30,* 654–657.

Sergios, P., and J. Cody. 1985. Importance of physical attractiveness and social assertiveness skills in male homosexual dating behavior and partner selection. *Journal of Homosexuality, 12,* 71–84.

Silver-Greenberg, J. 2005. Dying to know. *Newsweek, 146,* September, 11.

Snyder, M., E. Berscheid, and P. Glick. 1985. Focusing on the exterior and the interior: Two investigations of the initiation of personal relationships. *Journal of Personality and Social Psychology, 48,* 1427–1439.

Sprecher, S., and S. Hendrick. 2004. Self-disclosure in intimate relationships: Associations with individual and relationship characteristics over time. *Journal of Social and Clinical Psychology, 23,* 857–877.

Sprecher, S., Q. Sullivan, and E. Hatfield. 1994. Mate selection preferences: Gender differences examined in a national sample. *Journal of Personality and Social Psychology, 66,* 1074–1080.

Sunnafrank, M. 1986. Predicted outcome value during initial interactions: A reformulation of uncertainty reduction theory. *Human Communication Research, 13,* 3–33.

Thibaut, J., and H. Kelley. 1959. *The social psychology of groups.* New York, NY: Wiley.

Vangelisti, A. L. 2002. Interpersonal processes in romantic relationships. In M. L. Knapp and J. A. Daly (Eds.), *Handbook of interpersonal communication* (643–679). Thousand Oaks, CA: Sage.

Walster, E., V. Aronson, D. Abrahams, and L. Rottman. 1966. Importance of physical attractiveness in dating behavior. *Journal of Personality and Social Psychology, 4,* 508–516.

Wanzer, M. B. 1995. *Student affinity-seeking messages and teacher liking: Subordinate initiated relationship building in superior-subordinate dyads.* Unpublished doctoral dissertation, West Virginia University, Morgantown, WV.

Wanzer, M. B. 1998. An exploratory investigation of student and teacher perceptions of student-generated affinity-seeking behaviors. *Communication Education, 47,* 373–382.

Werner, C. M., and L. M. Haggard. 1985. Temporal qualities of interpersonal relationships. In M. L. Knapp and G. R. Miller (Eds.), *Handbook of interpersonal communication* (59–99). Beverly Hills, CA: Sage.

Wilson, G. D., J. M. Cousins, and B. Fink. 2006. The CQ as a predictor of speed-date outcomes. *Sexual and Relationship Therapy, 21,* 163–169.

Woll, S. 1986. So many to choose from: Decision strategies in video dating. *Journal of Social and Personal Relationships, 3,* 43–52.

Zebrowitz, L. A. 1997. *Reading faces: Window to the soul?* Boulder, CO: Westview Press.

Sustaining Relationships
Relationship Maintenance Strategies and Conflict Management

OBJECTIVES

- Discuss the four goals of relationship maintenance
- Explain the four essential components of successful relationships
- Explain equity theory and discuss how it is related to the process of relationship maintenance
- Explain the skill similarity model and relate it to the process of maintaining our relationships with others
- Describe the five most common relationship maintenance strategies
- Offer a definition of relationship maintenance

© Kuzma, 2007, Shutterstock.

- Provide examples of additional types of relationship maintenance strategies (positive and negative) that emerge when relationship maintenance behaviors were studied in different types of relationships
- Identify the individual differences that affect relationship maintenance strategy choices
- Define CMC. Discuss the benefits and drawbacks of CMC as a means of maintaining our relationships
- Define conflict
- Identify the five key aspects of conflict episodes
- Differentiate between escalatory and de-escalatory conflict spirals
- Discuss the concept of conflict metaphors. Recognize examples of problematic conflict metaphors
- Distinguish between the three most common conflict management styles
- Describe the advantages and disadvantages for each conflict management style
- Explain the four most typical conflict responses
- Differentiate between productive and unproductive responses to conflict situations
- Identify examples of productive communication patterns that can be used during conflict episodes
- Recognize behaviors that should be avoided during conflict episodes

KEY TERMS

control mutuality
trust
liking or affinity
commitment
equity theory
skill similarity model
comforting skills
ego support
empathy
face-management skills
self-disclosure
relationship
  maintenance
  strategies
prosocial behaviors
ceremonial behaviors
communication
  behaviors
togetherness behaviors
positivity
openness
assurances

social networks
sharing tasks
joint activities
mediated
  communication
advice
humor
no flirting
avoidant
antisocial behaviors
computer-mediated
  communication
  (CMC)
exclusively Internet-
  based relationships
  (EIB)
primarily Internet-
  based relationships
  (PIB)
conflict
expressed struggle
interdependence

goal incompatibility
perceived shared
  resources
interference
escalatory conflict
  spirals
de-escalatory conflict
  spirals
conflict metaphors
conflict management
  styles
avoidance
competitive/distributive
collaborative/
  integrative
verbal aggression
exit
neglect
loyalty
voice
fair fighting

OVERVIEW

Relationships, like sharks, must constantly move forward or they will cease to exist. In Chapter Six we examined the process of initiating relationships. In this chapter we will examine how individuals maintain their relationships with others. While the process of *establishing* relationships is not without its own set of challenges, some people seem to have more trouble staying together. The difficulty in staying committed is best illustrated by the current divorce rate in the United States; approximately fifty percent of marriages will fail, and, sadly, most second

> *A relationship, I think, is like a shark, you know? It has to constantly move forward or it dies. And I think what we got on our hands is a dead shark.*
>
> *Annie Hall* directed by Woody Allen, 1 hr. 33 min., Rollins-Joffe Productions, 1977.

marriages have an even greater chance of ending. Why is it so difficult to maintain lasting relationships with others? What are some of the most effective ways to sustain our relationships? We will address these questions and take a closer look at some of the reasons it is often a struggle for individuals to maintain their romantic and platonic ties. Relationship maintenance strategies vary significantly depending on the relationship type. We use different strategies to maintain relationships with our romantic partners, friends, family members, and with colleagues at work. In this chapter we will explore the use of different strategies and examine their effect on relationship maintenance.

Computer-mediated communication, hereafter referred to as CMC, has emerged as a popular means for interacting with others. The majority of college students have access to computers. This enables them to interact with friends, roommates, romantic partners and family members via instant messaging, emails, or chat rooms. CMC is an important and frequently used means of maintaining relationships with others. In this chapter we will examine recent research that explores CMC as a means of sustaining relationships.

So what is the key indicator that a relationship is in trouble? Oftentimes it is the result of a poorly-managed conflict between relational partners. Conflict is inevitable, and in fact, all of us experience it at one time or another in our interpersonal relationships. To maintain relationships with those we care about, it is important to manage conflict appropriately. In the third section of this chapter, we present information on conflict in order to help you: (1) understand how conflict can be both good and bad in relationships, (2) approach and respond to conflict situations appropriately, and (3) consider how individual differences affect the way we manage conflict in our lives.

SIGNIFICANCE OF RELATIONSHIP MAINTENANCE

According to Steve Duck (1988), individuals involved in committed relationships spend much more time maintaining a relationship than in any other phase of the relationship. Relationship maintenance is not an easy task. It often takes a great deal of time, effort, and skill. To better understand the process of relationship maintenance, let us consider four common relationship maintenance goals as proposed by Dindia and Canary (1993). They state that individuals who are focusing on relationship maintenance have one of the following four goals in mind: (1) maintaining the existence of the relationship, (2) maintaining a desired state or condition in the relationship, (3) maintaining a satisfactory state in a relationship, or (4) repairing a relationship in an attempt to either restore it or sustain it in a satisfactory state (1993, 163). Let's consider each one of these definitions.

Maintaining the Existence of the Relationship

Have you ever had a friend whom you call only once or twice a year? Or perhaps there are friends or family members who send you an annual holiday card with a letter updating the events of the past year, and that is the only communication you have with them until the next Christmas card arrives. In both of these examples, the goal of relationship maintenance is to keep the relationship in existence, or to keep it from dying.

Maintaining a Desired State in the Relationship

The second goal, which focuses on maintaining the desired state of a relationship, can be explained by the relationship between characters in the television show *The Office*. Jim is attracted to his engaged co-worker, Pam. Rather than risk losing her friendship by revealing his true feelings, Jim communicates with Pam in "safe" ways to ensure that the current state of their relationship is maintained. This strategy of regulating the state of the relationship enables one partner to keep the relationship at a level that is satisfactory rather than dissolving the relationship altogether.

Maintaining a Satisfactory State

A third goal focuses on attempts made by both partners to maintain a level of relationship satisfaction that they find to be mutually agreeable. Depending on the type and status of the relationship, what partners define as "mutually satisfying" can differ from one relationship to the next. In the *Seinfeld* episode "The Deal," Jerry and Elaine are friends who consider engaging in a sexual relationship. In an attempt to maintain their current satisfactory relationship as friends, they agree on a set of rules that will enable them to enjoy being friends while enjoying a sexual relationship. However, Elaine soon becomes upset when Jerry gives her a birthday gift that she perceives as being insignificant. They soon discover that they are better off as friends, and they go back to the joking and sarcasm that were an essential part of their friendship in the first place. Thus, their focus is on maintaining the friendship that they both perceived as being satisfactory, abandoning their sexual relationship.

Repairing a Relationship

Dindia and Canary (1993) point out that relationship maintenance is often an ongoing task. Just as you would seek routine maintenance to repair any issues that might keep your car from running smoothly, individuals engage in relationship maintenance to make sure that relationships run smoothly. Perhaps you realize that your relationship with a friend has become more distant since you started a new romantic relationship. In an attempt to maintain your friendship, you realize that you have to fix some things—namely, spend more time together and engage in more communication with one another. Dindia and Canary (1993) note that it is important to remember that some aspects of these four goals can overlap with one another. Further, they point out that a relationship can be maintained even though one or both partners find it to be unsatisfactory, and even satisfactory relationships end for a number of reasons.

© mihaicalin, 2007, Shutterstock.

Spending time together helps friends reconnect and maintain their relationship.

WHY WE MAINTAIN SOME RELATIONSHIPS AND NOT OTHERS

So why is it that we choose to maintain some relationships and not others? There are numerous factors that are central to interpersonal communication and relationship maintenance, including: intimacy, immediacy, investment, attraction, similarity, liking, commitment, and affection (see, for example, Burgoon and Hale 1984). Rather than providing an exhaustive list of all of the characteristics that have been identified as relevant to sustaining relationships, interpersonal scholars have narrowed the list to the four relational characteristics that are generally perceived as universal to most relationships: control mutuality, trust, liking, and commitment (Canary and Stafford 1994). Research has shown that relationships without these characteristics often lack substance, and as a result may not be able to be maintained. **Control mutuality** is defined as "the extent to which couples agree on who has the right to influence the other and establish relational goals" (Canary and Stafford 1994, 6). Relationships in which partners experience a high level of control mutuality are the result of both partners agreeing on who takes control in decision-making situations. Suppose two friends are planning a vacation to celebrate the end of the school year. If one of them is extremely organized, both friends may agree that he should be the one to plan their itinerary for the trip. Another example would be a couple agreeing that one partner should be in control of their finances since the other is not particularly savvy with money issues. **Trust** has emerged as an equally important relationship characteristic. Individuals are often reluctant to reveal information to those they do not trust, and a lack of trust in a relationship can be devastating. Recall the example of the *Friends* episode discussed in Chapter Five. Ross violated Rachel's trust when he decided to sleep with another woman on the same night that he and Rachel broke up. Regardless of the numerous apologies and promises that Ross offered, Rachel declared that she could no longer trust him and, as a result, they were unable to maintain their relationship. Another characteristic required for sustaining a relationship is **liking,** or **affinity.** Mutual liking, or expressed affect, is a universal feature of relationships. We prefer to be around individuals who know and like us. Not surprisingly, it is often very difficult for us to say no to requests that come from individuals we like (Cialdini 2003). Sometimes a friend or family member asks you for a favor and you really are too busy to help, but you do so anyway. You accept their request because you like them and want to maintain a pleasant relationship. A fourth and final characteristic of successful relationships is **commitment,** which refers to our desire to continue a relationship. When we say we are committed to a relationship, this is usually interpreted to mean that we are in it "for the long haul" and "for better or for worse." While commitment is important in romantic relationships for obvious reasons, it is also relevant to familial and platonic relationships. Can you remember a time when you became upset or frustrated because you felt that you were more committed to maintaining a friendship or family relationship than the other person? Commitment, trust, control mutuality and liking are characteristics that most of us desire in our communication and relationships.

In addition to understanding these relational characteristics, it is also important to recognize the theoretical explanations for why we choose to maintain relationships. **Equity theory** offers perhaps one of the most widely understood explanations for why some individuals engage in relationship maintenance activity and others do not (Canary and Stafford 1992, 2001). According to this theory, a relationship is considered equitable when the ratio of inputs to outputs is equal for both individuals involved. If, for example, you contribute more inputs compared to the outputs you receive from your partner,

© Galina Barskaya, 2007, Shutterstock.

Committed relationships are in it "for the long haul."

you will feel underbenefited in the relationship, possibly resulting in anger at getting less than you deserve. In the movie *The Break Up*, the character Brooke (Jennifer Aniston) becomes frustrated when her boyfriend, Gary (Vince Vaughn), spends more time watching television and playing video games than with helping her do various household chores. Her frustration with the inequity in their relationship becomes apparent toward the end of the movie when Brooke lists for Gary all the things that she has contributed to the relationship. Surprisingly, she states that she does not expect him to contribute equally to the relationship, but simply wishes that he would recognize the effort that she has made. Conversely, if your output to input ratio is greater than that of your relationship partner, then you will feel overbenefited. Some of you may wonder why those who are overbenefited in relationships report feeling dissatisfied. Is it possible that individuals who receive too much attention, affection, or gifts could possibly be unhappy in a relationship? Absolutely! Overbenefited individuals may be less satisfied in their relationships because they feel guilty about not contributing equally to the relationship. Can you recall a time when you felt guilty because you were not dedicating as much effort to a relationship as the other person? Perhaps you have a friend who is always the one who calls or writes. Eventually, you may feel so guilty that you fail to return their phone calls or email messages because you have failed at contributing equally to the relationship.

If we rank, in order, the level of satisfaction experienced in relationships, it is not surprising that partners who are in equitable relationships report the greatest level of satisfaction. Those who feel overbenefited are the next most satisfied, and the least satisfied individuals are those who report feeling underbenefited. Consider these questions: Are relationships perceived as equitable because both partners engage in relationship maintenance strategies equally? Or do relationship partners who already perceive their relationships as equitable engage in more maintenance behaviors? Researchers Dan Canary and Laura Stafford (2001) argue that individuals in equitable relationships are more likely to use relationship maintenance behaviors than those involved in a relationship that is perceived to be inequitable.

HOW WE MAINTAIN RELATIONSHIPS: THE ROLE OF COMMUNICATION

Now that you have a better understanding of the four relational characteristics associated with maintenance and the role that theory plays in explaining why we choose to sustain relationships, let us examine how we use communication to maintain our relationships.

Brant Burleson and Wendy Samter (1994) emphasize the importance of similarity in communication skills in maintaining relationships. They state, "similarity in the nature and level of partners' social skills may be more important to relationship maintenance than the absolute level of skill sophistication of the partners" (62). They propose a **skill similarity model** that portrays relationship maintenance as a process requiring the involvement of both partners. In particular, they note that while what one individual does for another is important, it is also necessary to examine what the partners do with one another. Consider the married couple whose lives have become so

How do you comfort those who are close to you?

© Lisa F. Young, 2007, Shutterstock.

consumed with their children's activities that they fail to spend time alone. Perhaps they constantly do favors for one another to ensure that they can maintain their busy schedules, and they possibly even text message each other throughout the day. Eventually, they may discover that while they do things for each other, the lack of quality time with one another puts a strain on the relationship.

Burleson and Samter (1994) also argue that maintaining relationships with others is a skill that typically involves mastery of specific types of communication. Those who are able to master the communication skills that are viewed as valuable in a relationship are more likely to experience success. One communication skill that is valuable is labeled **comforting skill,** which is the ability to reduce another's emotional distress. Comforting can be communicated verbally ("I completely understand why you're so upset about this!") or via nonverbal channels, such as with a hug or an encouraging look. Another communication skill that is essential to relationship maintenance is **ego support,** which is described as the ability to make others feel positive about themselves. **Empathy** involves the ability to see things from the other person's point of view. Employing empathy communicates to others that their perspective is important in maintaining the relationship. Consider the relationship in which one partner is devoted to his religious beliefs, but the other partner may not have been raised to value religion. By respecting one another's differences in values and beliefs, maintenance is achieved. Perhaps they agree to attend church services together for particular events, and also agree not to force their beliefs on one another. **Face-management skills** are an essential part of relationship maintenance. In an earlier chapter, we defined face as one's self-perception that one wishes to present when interacting with others. Avoiding communication that could be perceived as face-threatening can strengthen a relationship. Examples of communication facework include: being polite, avoiding topics that could potentially cause embarrassment to another, and using disclaimers to help manage the other's perception of self (e.g., "I know I may be crazy to think that this means that you don't care . . ."). A final skill that is important to sustain relationships is **self-disclosure.** By engaging in appropriate disclosure and sharing our thoughts and feelings, we contribute an element that is valuable to the future of the relationship. Take a moment to consider your own relationships. Think about the role that each of these communication skills plays in their maintenance, and consider how different your relationship would be if the other person ceased to engage in these behaviors. Next, we will explore specific strategies that are necessary to help keep relationships going.

RELATIONSHIP MAINTENANCE STRATEGIES

When relationships possess the four qualities discussed earlier (control mutuality, trust, liking, and commitment) and are perceived as rewarding and equitable, individuals will seek out various ways to maintain these connections. Because our relationships cannot sustain themselves, it is up to us to engage in behaviors that will prolong them. **Relationship maintenance**

strategies are defined as the behaviors and activities used strategically "to sustain desired relational qualities or to sustain the current status of the relationship" (Canary and Stafford 2001, 134).

What are the most common relationship maintenance strategies that people use? Dindia and Baxter (1987) initially identified forty-nine different relationship maintenance strategies used by married couples. With these results they identified four categories of strategies: prosocial behaviors, ceremonial behaviors, communication behaviors and togetherness behaviors. **Prosocial behaviors** include being polite and cooperative in the relationship, while avoiding face-threatening communication. Recognizing the importance of rituals in sustaining relationships is the focus of **ceremonial behaviors.** Sharing Sunday dinner at Grandma's house, saying prayers with the

A big Sunday dinner is one ceremonial behavior for many families.

children before going to bed every night, and bringing your friend her favorite Dairy Queen ice cream cake every year to celebrate her birthday are all examples of ceremonial behaviors. **Communication behaviors** involve the exchange of open and honest information. Telling your significant other that his or her recent behavior has disappointed you, or sending a text message to a friend when you hear a song that reminds you of the fun you had on summer vacation are examples of behaviors that sustain relationships. Finally, partners expect one another to dedicate time and energy to **togetherness behaviors** as a strategy of relationship maintenance. Watching a favorite television show together or sharing a cup of coffee while you catch up on one another's activities are examples of togetherness.

Researchers Laura Stafford and Dan Canary (1991) examined all of the studies that had focused on how partners maintain relationships, and identified the five most common types of relationship maintenance strategies: positivity, openness, assurances, social networks, and sharing tasks. **Positivity** involves being polite, acting cheerful and upbeat, and avoiding criticism. Is it not easier to maintain a relationship with someone who has a positive outlook on life and on the relationship than with someone who is always pessimistic? **Openness** refers to the open and ongoing discussions that partners have about the status of the relationship. When individuals employ openness, they share their thoughts and feelings about the relationship. **Assurances** refer to the expression of love and commitment as well as making references to the future of the relationship. Relationship partners also sustain relationships by spending time with the mutual friends and family members who create a **social network.** The fifth and final strategy, **sharing tasks,** focuses on the extent to which partners share the chores and responsibilities associated with the relationship. Depending on the type of relationship, these tasks could include sharing responsibility for exchanging emails or phone calls, or allotting household tasks. Recall our earlier example of the frustration experienced by Brooke and Gary in *The Break Up*. In one scene, Brooke is cleaning dishes after a dinner party while Gary plays PlayStation and "unwinds." When Brooke becomes frustrated, Gary points out that she said that she does not want him to help with the dishes. Brooke replies that she wants him to want to help with the dishes—thus the role of sharing tasks becomes apparent to the maintenance of their relationship.

Sharing different household tasks helps maintain a relationship.

Since Stafford and Canary's initial investigation, there have been a number of follow-up studies exploring relationship maintenance strategies employed in a variety of relationships. For example, researchers have examined relationship maintenance in married adults (Dainton and Stafford 1993; Dainton and Aylor 2002; Ragsdale 1996), in gay and lesbian relationships (Haas and Stafford 1998), in dating couples (Dainton and Aylor 2002), in same sex (Canary et al. 1993) and cross-sex friendships (Messman, Canary, and Hause 2000) and in family relationships (Canary et al. 1993; Myers 2001; Myers and Weber 2004). Once researchers began investigating the use of maintenance strategies in the various types of relationships listed above, it became apparent that there were a number of taxonomies, or ways of classifying, relationship maintenance behaviors.

At this point, you will probably be happy to know that we are not going to cover all of the relationship maintenance strategies that exist. However, we will provide a brief overview of some of the additional maintenance strategies individuals might use with friends, romantic partners, family members, or co-workers such as: joint activities, mediated communication, advice, humor, no flirting, avoidance and antisocial behaviors (Canary et al. 1993). **Joint activities** refer to those behaviors relationship partners do together: "hanging out" with one another, watching television together, and going on trips with each other. Later in this chapter we will address the role that **mediated communication** plays in sustaining relationships. These behaviors include the exchange of email messages, letters, text messages, or phone calls to ensure a satisfying relationship. **Advice** typically involves disclosing personal information to the relationship partner or giving or seeking advice on some issue. **Humor** is also sometimes used as a means of maintaining relationships and might include the use of jokes and sarcasm in either positive or negative ways. A positive example of using humor would be "trying to make each other laugh," (Canary et al. 1993, 11) while a negative example of using humor might include being sarcastic or making fun of someone's appearance or personality.

Interestingly, there are also strategies individuals use to reduce the amount of intimacy in a relationship. One such strategy is labeled **no flirting** and includes behaviors such as "avoid flirting with him/her." Why do you believe this would be included under maintenance? The authors suggest that by not encouraging "overly familiar behaviors" we are able to help maintain relationships. How do you believe this works? The relationship maintenance strategies labeled avoidance and antisocial behaviors would initially appear to be antithetical to prolonging any type of relationship. When do individuals employ these types of "maintenance" behaviors? Strategies labeled **avoidant** include avoidance of "sore," or difficult, subjects that we should avoid discussing with our romantic partners, family members or friends, to steer clear of conflict. To maintain the quality of a relationship and, at the same time, preserve a sense of autonomy, it might also be necessary to establish times when we are away from our partners. Hence, relationship partners might have a "girls' night" or "boys' night" out. Partners also engage in either direct or indirect **antisocial behaviors,** which are described as behaviors which might seem unfriendly or coercive (Canary et al. 1993). To gain a relationship partner's attention or to signal that something is wrong in the relationship, one partner might act moody or difficult (indirect strategy) to gain the other person's attention. (Recall Brooke's behavior in *The Break Up.*) Olsen's (2002) research indicates that individuals might use verbally aggressive messages during conflict episodes to indicate that there is a significant relationship problem. Canary and his colleagues would describe this strategic use of aggressive communication as an antisocial behavior. Similarly, relationship partners might try to be more direct in their antisocial behaviors by being rude or mean to their partners' friends or family. These strategies may reduce the amount of closeness between relationship partners temporarily, and habitual use of these strategies might be detrimental to a relationship. However, for some individuals, avoidant and antisocial behaviors are perceived as valid ways of maintaining the relationship's health (Canary et al. 1993). See Table 7.1 for additional examples of relationship maintenance strategies.

As relationship partners become more connected, or interdependent, the use of relationship maintenance strategies generally increases (Canary and Stafford 2001). Not surprisingly, decreases in relationship maintenance behaviors by one or both partners often signals that a relationship is in trouble (Ayres 1983). Canary and Stafford's (1994) research indicates that the

Table 7.1   Relationship Maintenance Strategies

Strategy	Examples
1. Positivity	Engage in cheerful communication; Ask "How was your day?"
2. Openness	Solicit discussion on status of relationship; Ask partner to share feelings about the relationship
3. Assurances	Emphasize commitment to one another; Say "I love you" to one another
4. Social network	Express interest in spending time with mutual friends; Focus on building friendships that are mutual/shared
5. Sharing tasks	Help partner with various tasks, or household chores such as cooking and cleaning
6. Joint activities	Spend time hanging out with one another Go to the movies, football game, dinner
7. Mediated communication	Use email to communicate Call partner on the phone Send partner a card
8. Avoidance	Avoid talking about certain issues Avoid the relationship partner
9. Antisocial behaviors	Be mean or rude to him/her Act moody when around him/her
10. Humor	Call him/her a funny or silly name Use sarcasm when communicating
11. No flirting	Do not flirt with him/her Do not show any sign of romantic interest
12. Advice	Give/seek advice on variety of issues (e.g., love, relationships, school, future)

Source: Adapted from Canary and Stafford 1994; 1992; 2001, Canary et al. 1993; Messman et al. 2000.

"use of positivity, sharing tasks, and offering assurance help sustain control mutuality, trust, liking and commitment" (19). They also note that not all relationships will benefit equally from the use of these five strategies (positivity, assurances, etc.). Thus, it is important to examine research that summarizes how these strategies function in different types of relationships, paying special attention to the outcomes of their use.

RELATIONSHIP MAINTENANCE IN DIFFERENT TYPES OF RELATIONSHIPS

Are the tactics, or behaviors, that you use to maintain your friendships different from those you use to sustain your relationship with your romantic partner? They probably are. Researchers found that the use of relationship maintenance strategies differs depending on relationship type. While there is a vast amount of research available on relationship maintenance in different types of relationships, we will overview a small portion of it to understand how the frequency of relationship maintenance strategy use varies in different relationships. We also discuss the outcomes associated with the use of these strategies.

Relationship maintenance has been studied extensively in different types of romantic relationships (see, for example, Canary and Stafford 1992; 1993; Dainton 2000; Dainton and Stafford 1993). Researchers have investigated how relationship maintenance strategies differ based on (1) relationship length, (2) type of commitment, e.g., married or dating, (3) cultural differences, and (4) sexual preferences. Romantic partners use relationship maintenance strategies (e.g., positivity, openness, assurances, sharing tasks and cards/letters) more than friends (Canary et al. 1993). This finding is not particularly surprising since most of us put more energy into maintaining our romantic relationships. In another related study on married couples' use of relationship maintenance strategies, researchers found that married couples' use of relationship maintenance behaviors decreased over time (Dindia and Baxter 1987; Ragsdale 1996). Additionally, the use of relationship maintenance strategies in romantic relationships tends to become more routine and less strategic over time. In essence, we become comfortable with our partner and fall into a routine in which we use the same behaviors that have been proven to work in the past. In newer relationships, partners usually have to devote more time and energy to thinking about how they will strategically use assurances, positivity, or even openness as a means of stabilizing their relationship. Conversely, for individuals in long-term relationships, the use of these behaviors becomes part of the daily routine and is not something partners are always cognizant of doing. One example of this is the routine expression of affection through phrases such as "I love you." The husband of one of your authors routinely ends every phone conversation with her by stating, "Love you!" This phrase became such a routine part of their conversations that he inadvertently used it by mistake with a colleague at work. As he waited to leave a voicemail for the colleague, he thought about phoning his wife to discuss

Do you think this couple's relationship has become routine?

© Simone van den Berg, 2007, Shutterstock.

dinner plans. After the beep he left his message for the colleague, and absent-mindedly said, "Love you!" before hanging up. He quickly called back to leave a follow-up message explaining his behavior.

Are some strategies more effective than others? It depends on the type of relationship and the individuals involved. Relationship partners' use of assurances has been linked repeatedly to relationship satisfaction and commitment (Dainton and Aylor 2002; Stafford and Canary 1991). There are very few of us who do not like to hear our relationship partner say, "I love you." When comparing relationship maintenance behaviors of married couples to dating couples, married partners use more assurances and social networks, while dating couples engage in more openness (Stafford and Canary 1991). Because partners in dating relationships are still getting to know one another, individuals must be more open and willing to share information with one another for the relationship to move from the experimenting to the intensifying stage of relationship development.

Is it possible that culture plays a role in the types of relational maintenance strategies we employ? If you answered yes to this question, then you are correct. When comparing impact of culture for marital partners, African American couples indicated using task-sharing as a maintenance strategy less often than European American couples (Diggs and Stafford 1998). Researchers explain this result by pointing out that, generally, African American males and females tend to be more focused on adopting egalitarian roles in their relationship when compared to their European American counterparts. The researchers speculate that task-sharing might be discussed more frequently by European American couples because they have struggled historically with creating more equity in their romantic relationships. This study illustrates that partners' individual differences, which might include factors such as culture, personality, age, or even maturity, may also affect the types of relationship maintenance strategies used.

In an attempt to examine strategies used by gay and lesbian couples, Haas and Stafford (1998) discovered that heterosexual and homosexual couples employ many of the same strategies in their relationships. Two strategies that are unique to gay and lesbian relationships include (1) being "out" as a couple when communicating with their social networks, and (2) seeking out social environments that are supportive of gay and lesbian relationships. Additional research by Eldridge and Gilbert (1990) points to the importance of perceived equity in relational power and high levels of emotional intimacy in enhancing relationship satisfaction in lesbian relationships. Gay men indicate a preference for low levels of conflict and high levels of cooperation as factors that help maintain a satisfying relationship (Jones and Bates 1978).

Relationship maintenance has also been studied in different types of platonic relationships. For example, in opposite sex friendships, partners might see potential for romantic connection but want to keep the relationship platonic. In such a situation, individuals employ maintenance behaviors strategically in order to stay friends. More specifically, research by Messman, Canary and Hause (2000) indicates that opposite sex friends frequently employ the strategies of giving/seeking advice, assurances, positivity, cards/letters, sharing activities, and openness in an effort to stay friends. One surprising finding was that opposite sex friends were least likely to use the strategies labeled no flirting and avoidance. When opposite sex friends flirted with one another, they often did so in a teasing and non-sexual way to send the message that the relationship was a platonic one. The researchers also noted that opposite sex friends seem to use strategies that express support and acceptance of one another (Messman et al. 2000).

More recently, researchers investigated relationship maintenance in family contexts. Scott Myers (2001) studied how siblings use maintenance strategies with a specific focus on the relationship between use of maintenance behaviors and sibling liking. Myers asked 257 college students to indicate how often they used the relationship maintenance strategies of positivity, openness, sharing tasks, assurances and networks with their siblings. Students indicated that sharing tasks was used the most often and openness was used the least. Additionally, this study explored potential differences in male and female sibling use of relationship maintenance behaviors. Myers found that female siblings engaged in relationship maintenance behaviors more often than either cross-sex or male dyads. He also noted that, in general, women often report feeling closer to their siblings and receiving more affection and intimacy in their sibling relationships. In a study examining the maintenance strategies employed by fathers and daughters, 250 college women and their fathers completed a survey asking them to indicate the degree to which they use various maintenance strategies (Punyanunt-Carter 2006). Results indicated that fathers are more likely than their daughters to use various maintenance strategies, with the exception of social networks.

As researchers continue to explore the different ways that partners attempt to sustain a variety of relationships, they are also turning their attention to the increasing role that technology is playing in how people maintain these associations.

COMPUTER-MEDIATED COMMUNICATION AS A MEANS OF MAINTAINING RELATIONSHIPS

Consider this—if you use email or chat programs such as AOL or instant messenger to communicate regularly with family members, friends, co-workers or a romantic partner, you are using one of the relationship maintenance strategies discussed earlier in this chapter—**computer-mediated communication (CMC).** Not surprisingly, many Americans use CMC to meet new people or to sustain current relationships. In fact, a recent study found that nearly ninety million Americans engage in communication with others through an online group or social network (Fox et al. 2001). Among those using the Internet as a channel for interaction, the majority felt that it was a useful way to establish new connections and maintain current relationships (Fox et al. 2001). From a communication perspective, it is important to examine how CMC differs from traditional face-to-face interaction and to consider both the benefits and drawbacks of CMC.

Why has CMC become more popular as a means of establishing and maintaining relationships with others? First and foremost, more people have access to computers today and use them regularly for a variety of purposes. Also, because individuals spend more time on their computers for work or school, they also use them as a means of forming new relationships and maintaining their current ones. For individuals in established relationships who want to communicate with friends, family members and relationship partners, CMC is often less expensive and time-consuming than using the telephone or writing letters. Features of CMC which can affect interpersonal perceptions and, at the same time, alter the communication process include: limited access to nonverbal behaviors, delayed feedback, and editing ability. With CMC, there is limited exposure to nonverbal cues which shed additional insight as to the true meaning of a message. Can you recall a time when you perceived someone as being angry with you simply because his email response was short and to the point? The lack of nonverbal cues may cause you to misperceive the fact that he was in a hurry and wanted to send a quick response. Because of the asynchronous nature of email, individuals have time to formulate messages and

© Margot Petrowski, 2007, Shutterstock.

How might this conversation be different via CMC rather than in person?

respond to incoming messages at their own convenience. In addition, individuals who use email or chat programs can edit their messages before sending them, unlike live communication.

A benefit of CMC is that it is often used to sustain long-distance relationships. The number of individuals in long distance relationships (LDR) has been steadily climbing over the years (Rohlfing 1995). For college students who might be struggling financially, email and chat programs are a relatively inexpensive means of communicating regularly with one's long-distance relationship partner. Individuals in LDRs can use CMC as a means of communicating many of the relationship maintenance behaviors identified in this chapter—positivity, assurances, and even openness.

While the majority of relationship maintenance research conducted thus far examines the use of these strategies in face-to-face relationships, researcher Kevin Wright studied the use of relational maintenance strategies in different types of Internet relationships. Wright investigated the use of online relational maintenance strategies of college students in exclusively Internet-based and primarily Internet-based relationships (2004). "**Exclusively Internet-based (EIB) relationships** refer to relationships that are developed without any face-to-face interaction or interaction through traditional media, such as the telephone, letters, etc." (Wright 2004, 239). Conversely, **primarily Internet-based (PIB) relationships** may initially be formed online or through face-to-face interaction, could include acquaintances, friends, co-workers, or family members and often communicate through emails or instant messaging. While PIB relationships are more common than EIB relationships, the number of EIB relationships has increased dramatically as more Americans use the Internet to establish relationships.

To study differences in relationship maintenance behaviors in different types of online relationships, Wright surveyed 178 undergraduate students and asked them to report on their perceptions of the quality of communication that occurred online, frequency of relationship maintenance strategies, and type of online relationship. He found that openness and positivity were the most frequently used strategies in both EIB and PIB relationships. These strategies might be used more frequently because they are easier to employ over the Internet, or because they are perceived as more effective than other strategies (Wright 2004). Interestingly, Wright also found that individuals in EIB and PIB types of relationships did not differ significantly in the types of relationship maintenance behaviors they used. He indicates that it is difficult to tell whether individuals in these types of relationships actually prefer to use the same strategies to sustain their relationships. Perhaps, he says, the computer hinders individuals from using certain strategies online. This exploratory investigation illustrates the increased popularity of CMC as a means of sustaining interpersonal relationships.

CONCLUSIONS ABOUT RELATIONSHIP MAINTENANCE

There is an extensive body of research on strategic and routine relationship maintenance behaviors. Below, we highlight a number of significant conclusions from the relationship maintenance literature.

- Relationships are not self-sustaining and, as such, require a significant amount of time and effort.
- Individuals are most motivated to maintain relationships in which partners exhibit high amounts of trust, commitment, control mutuality and liking.
- Most individuals want to be in relationships that are perceived as equitable (inputs=outputs).
- Both routine and strategic relationship maintenance behaviors are used most frequently in equitable relationships.
- Five relationship maintenance strategies are used consistently regardless of the type of relationship, or whether the interactants communicate face-to-face or online: positivity, assurances, openness, sharing tasks, and social networks.
- Individual's use of assurances, networks and sharing tasks are consistently recognized as significant predictors of relationship commitment.
- When researchers further examined relationship maintenance behaviors in other types of relationships, additional strategies emerged, including, among others: humor, avoidance, antisocial behaviors, CMC, advice, conflict management.
- Effectiveness and frequency of strategy use depends on the type of relationship being investigated.
- Female siblings use more relationship maintenance strategies with one another than male siblings and male-female siblings.
- Individual differences such as culture affect the types of strategies used in relationships.

CONFLICT: A NATURAL COMPONENT OF ALL RELATIONSHIPS

The key to sustaining our relationships often rests in our ability to manage the conflicts that arise from time to time. To maintain stability in our relationships, it is necessary to manage conflict appropriately. Many relationship scholars have identified conflict management as an important maintenance behavior. Have you ever heard someone say, "We get along perfectly and agree on everything?" Chances are that the person wants to create a positive image of the relationship. The truth is that conflict is an inherent component of all relationships. Denying the presence of conflict in a relationship does not always indicate that the relationship is a healthy one. While our initial tendency is to view conflict as the ugly three-headed monster that destroys relationships, we need to take a step back and consider the benefits of conflict for both individuals and relationships. In the following sections we take a closer look at what conflict is, how it can be both productive and unproductive for individuals and relationships, and ways it can be effectively managed.

Definition of Conflict

Watch one episode of *Everybody Loves Raymond*, and, chances are, you will see conflict in action. But as you learn more about the characters on the show and their relationships with one another, you will soon understand that they are able to maintain the status of their relationships as a result of their ability to manage their disagreements. Regardless of whether disagreements occur between two co-workers, between husband and wife, or between two neighbors, there are aspects that all conflict episodes share. A number of definitions for conflict exist in the literature; however, we want to focus on one that approaches conflict from a communication perspective. Hocker and Wilmot (1991) define **conflict** as "an expressed struggle between at least two interdependent parties who perceive incompatible goals, scarce resources, and interference from the other party in achieving their goals" (12). To understand how and why conflict occurs, it is important to examine the main components of this definition in detail. There are five consistent aspects, or components, of conflict episodes, as listed below.

- Conflict involves an *expressed struggle.*
- Conflict parties are *interdependent.*
- Conflict parties perceive *incompatible goals.*
- Conflict parties *perceive shared resources.*
- Conflict parties perceive *interference* from one another in achieving goals.

Expressed Struggle.   The first consistent component of conflict is that it typically involves **expressed struggle** or open communication about the issue or problem. How do we know if a conflict with a friend, co-worker, or family member is really a conflict? From an interpersonal communication perspective, it is important to consider the communicative interchanges that make up the conflict episode (Hocker and Wilmot 1991).

Consider this dialogue between two roommates, Molly and Tiona:

Molly: Hey Tiona, do you want to go and get some coffee after you're done studying?

Tiona: No, thanks *(Makes no eye contact, stares at her book).*

Molly: Is something wrong, you seem a little annoyed? I thought you said you wanted to go and get coffee later this evening?

Tiona: I did, but now I don't.

Molly: Fine, don't tell me what is wrong!

Do you think both roommates are aware that there is a problem? It is no wonder that Molly is confused! This example illustrates the importance of expressing conflict openly. When there are joint communicative representations of conflict, that is, both partners openly express their concerns or emotions, we typically say that conflict has occurred. Some individuals might feel angry or frustrated with a relationship partner but choose not to express their concerns openly. Once people openly communicate their feelings or concerns with their relationship partners, interpersonal conflict has occurred. Interpersonal communication scholars agree that communication is an essential element in all interpersonal conflict. Additionally, they stress that communication both affects, and is affected by, aspects of relationships (Canary, Cupach, and Messman 1995; Hocker and Wilmot 1991).

Interdependence.   The second key element of conflict addresses the significance of partner **interdependence.** Stated simply, if individuals rely on one another and are aware of how their decisions or behaviors affect one another, they are more likely to experience conflict than individuals who do not rely on one another. For example, on *Everybody Loves Raymond,* Debra often gets upset with her mother-in-law, Marie, for her critical comments regarding Debra's parenting style and housekeeping abilities. But Debra realizes that Marie is an important part of her husband and children's lives, and deep down she probably seeks Marie's approval. The interdependence between Debra and Marie makes it more likely that they will engage in conflict over these critical comments. If a stranger were to make the same comments, it probably would not matter to Debra. The more interdependent relationship partners are, the greater the chances are for conflict to occur (Braiker and Kelley 1979).

Goal Incompatibility.   A third factor of conflict is **goal incompatibility.** According to Hocker and Wilmot (1991) people are most likely to "engage in conflict over goals they often deny as being important to them" (17). All of us, at one time or another, will experience opposition in trying to reach a goal. Hocker and Wilmot describe two common types of goal incompatibility that can lead to conflict. One type of goal incompatibility occurs when relationship partners want the same thing. Think about two basketball players who are both competing for the same position on the team or two employees who are both contending for the same position in a company. Another type of goal incompatibility occurs when two individuals want different things. Recall the last time you and your relationship partner disagreed on the restaurant you would go to for dinner. How long did you argue about this? Do you remember how you finally decided where you would eat? Sometimes conflict is about actual differences in restaurant choices while other times it is about who gets to choose the restaurant. Whether individuals perceive their goals as similar or different, perceived incompatibility in objectives is a consistent aspect of conflict episodes (Hocker and Wilmot 1991).

Perceived Shared Resources.   A fourth component of conflict is **perceived shared resources.** Resources refer to anything that an individual identifies as valuable or meaningful and can include, among other things: people, relationships, opportunities, material objects, or time. Hocker and Wilmot

(1991) point out that "The resources might be real or perceived as real by the person. Likewise, the perception of scarcity, or limitation, may be apparent or actual" (19). This is illustrated when an only child protests the addition of another sibling in the family and argues that the parents cannot possibly have enough love to go around for both children. Conflict experts say the best route to take in this situation is to try to change the child's perception of the available resource by assuring the child that there is more than enough love available for two children. Most interpersonal struggles revolve around perceived scarcity in power and self-esteem. As illustrated in the example above, the child was worried about receiving confirmation from the parents that would directly affect his or her self-esteem. Not surprisingly, when people fight or disagree, they often express sentiments which illustrate power and self-esteem struggles (Hocker and Wilmot 1991).

Interference.   The fifth and final component of conflict is **interference.** Is it possible for individuals who depend on one another and perceive incompatible goals and resources to not experience conflict? Yes it is. Hocker and Wilmot (1991) point out that even when incompatible goals and limited resources are present, individuals must perceive interference from the other in their attempt to achieve a goal. As soon as someone interferes with, or blocks, your goals, it is likely that you will experience conflict. In the *Home Improvement* episode "Back in the Saddle Shoes," Jill decides to go back to college and pursue her master's degree in counseling. Tim is less than supportive of the idea and actually presents arguments for why Jill should not go back to school. His attempts to interfere with Jill's goal of pursuing her degree lead to conflict. Eventually the truth comes out—Tim is afraid that Jill will fall for a more intelligent man if she goes back to school. When we feel like someone is trying to stand in our way of accomplishing a goal, conflict is likely to emerge.

Remember, in order for conflict to occur between individuals, the following criteria must be evident: (1) differences must be expressed openly and recognized by both partners, (2) partners must be interdependent, (3) partners must have incompatible goals, (4) partners must perceive competition for scarce resources, and (5) partners must perceive interference in goal achievement. Next, we examine how conflict can be beneficial or detrimental to maintaining stability in a relationship.

CONFLICT CAN BE PRODUCTIVE OR UNPRODUCTIVE IN RELATIONSHIPS

Depending upon how it is managed in interpersonal relationships, conflict can be productive or unproductive. When conflict is managed effectively, it can be good for both the relationship and the individuals involved. First, to establish meaningful relationships with others and survive in a social world, you must understand both the role of emotions (both your own and others') and the social and cultural norms for conflict situations. By doing so, conflict actually becomes an important part of your personal development and growth. A second benefit of experiencing and managing conflict in interpersonal relationships is that it tests the strength and character of relationships more vigorously than other types of social interaction (Canary, Cupach and Messman 1995).

When couples learn how to manage conflict effectively, they can strengthen their bond with one another and increase relationship satisfaction. Hence, individuals involved in the most rewarding relationships are able to manage conflict by using productive communication practices. For example, couples who manage conflict effectively and report higher relationship satisfaction refrain from aggression and focus more on confrontational (Cahn 1992) and collaborative communication (Sillars and Wilmot 1994).

Another way that conflict can be good for individuals is that it exposes them to different perspectives. For example, think about the last time you and your roommate argued about politics, religion, or even your favorite band. The process of actively disagreeing with another person can be personally beneficial because it exposes us to views that are different from our own. When we encounter views or perspectives that are different from ours, we usually re-examine our perspectives and reflect on why we feel or think a certain way in order to defend our views. This process of self-reflection can help individuals to either (1) develop a better understanding of their current perspective, or (2) develop a new perspective linked to the interaction with the relationship partner. Conflict can benefit individuals and relationships in a number of different ways.

When is conflict unproductive or destructive for individuals and relationships? Conflicts are typically described as unproductive, or destructive, when individuals walk away feeling frustrated or cheated by the end result. One type of destructive conflict is known as **escalatory conflict spirals.** This type of conflict is "characterized by a heavy reliance on overt power manipulation, threats, coercion and deception" (Hocker and Wilmot 1991, 34). In escalatory spirals, the conflict intensifies each time individuals communicate with one another and the conflict escalates with more destructive communication occurring each time individuals encounter each other. Individuals might also engage in unfair fighting tactics and make attempts to "get even" with one another. If you have ever watched the movie *War of the Roses,* you may recall how Oliver Rose and his wife, Barbara, focus all of their energy on increasing the intensity of the conflict surrounding their divorce. Each conflict episode builds on previous ones. At one point in the movie, Barbara decides she wants to start her own catering business. She asks Oliver to review a contract, which he berates and uses to swat a fly. Annoyed by his response, Barbara gets back at him by turning on all the appliances while Oliver is on the phone with an important client. Even their nonverbal behaviors indicate the escalating conflict experience in their relationship—during dinner they are relatively silent, but their body language speaks volumes.

When it comes to conflict situations, not everyone likes to fight it out. Rather than fight, some individuals might engage in **de-escalatory conflict spirals** that often involve flight responses (Hocker and Wilmot 1991). Some individuals avoid volatile situations and instead adopt withdrawal types of behaviors. Why do individuals avoid or withdraw from conflict situations? As we stated earlier in this section, individuals who are highly interdependent are more likely to experience conflict. Conversely, individuals who are not dependent on one another are less likely to engage in conflict. Perhaps relationship partners become bored with one another, apathetic about the relationship, or experience other problems in their relationship. If this is the case, then individuals might lose faith in the relationship, withdraw from interaction, and invest less time and effort into maintaining the relationship. Conflict in escalatory spirals is overt while conflict in de-escalatory spirals is covert. Individuals might avoid one another, or, when confronted, deny that there is a problem. When conflict is not out in the open, it cannot be addressed or managed. Thus, expressing conflict in a covert or indirect way is clearly unproductive.

TALKING ABOUT CONFLICT

The only way to improve conflict situations is to examine how we approach and communicate about them. Individuals often have difficulty managing conflict productively or collaboratively because they tend to think and talk about conflict in negative ways. People often talk about conflict using metaphors. What are some **conflict metaphors?** Examples would be using words like "explosive" or "a war" when describing the conflict process. Using these terms affects individuals' perceptions of conflict as well as their behaviors during conflict situations. Other negative metaphors used to describe conflict processes are: "conflict is a trial," "conflict is an upward struggle," "conflict is a mess," and "conflict is a game" (where one person is the winner and the other is the loser). All of these metaphors are problematic because they foster negative images of conflict, preventing people from collaborating, or working together, to manage difficult situations.

Hocker and Wilmot encourage individuals to use more positive terms to describe conflict to facilitate collaboration among individuals. For example, they suggest describing conflict as "a bargaining table," "a dance," "a balance," or a "tide." Talking about conflict using the more positive labels is productive because they emphasize collaboration among participants. Ideally, an individual will formulate the same productive images of conflict and approach conflict in the same way as the other individual involved. Thus, if you and your roommate both view conflict as a "balancing act," you recognize how important it is for the two of you to work together and keep your eye on the goal. If, however, you view conflict as a balancing act and your roommate views it as "war," you may not be able to work collaboratively toward a common goal.

CONFLICT MANAGEMENT STYLES

So if conflict can actually be healthy and productive in relationships, what are some ways to ensure that we are effective in managing it? Researchers have identified a variety of strategies that are used by individuals. The strategies can be pictured placed on a continuum, with violence at one end and collaboration at the other (Hocker and Wilmot 1991). When a conflict occurs, individuals typically decide whether they will avoid or confront it. Essentially, we make a decision to adopt various **conflict management styles** or habitual responses to conflict situations. The three most common conflict management styles individuals use to manage conflict are labeled: avoidance, competition (distributive), and collaboration (integrative). Each of these conflict management styles has unique advantages and disadvantages, depending on how and when they are used.

Avoidance

Avoidance is often used by partners who deny having a problem in the first place, or by someone who is uncomfortable at the prospect of engaging in conflict. In an effort to avoid conflict with another person, relationship partners might directly or indirectly deny there is a problem, use equivocation or evasive comments to avoid discussing issues, change topics, act noncommittal on an issue, or use jokes or humor. While occasionally avoiding conflict might not be problematic for relationships, consistently avoiding conflict has been found to be counterproductive for individuals in any type of relationship. Recall the recent conflict between former best friends Paris Hilton and Nicole Richie. Stories reported that the two stopped speaking to each other, avoided attending events where they knew the other would be, and even decided to end relationships with people who had previously been mutual acquaintances. Avoidance styles of conflict management are generally not productive because they often indicate a low concern for self, others, and the relationship, and are perceived as ineffective (Hocker and Wilmot 1991). What are some of the advantages and disadvantages of avoidance as a tactical strategy? See Table 7.2 below for an overview of the advantages and disadvantages of this strategy.

It is important to think about the benefits and drawbacks of using avoidance as a means of managing conflict. There are times when conflict should not be addressed because it is not the right time or place to discuss an issue with someone. Also, depending on an individual's culture, they may be more or less predisposed to avoid conflict with others. Finally, avoiding a conflict does not make it go away. Perhaps you can recall a time when avoiding an issue with someone actually made the situation worse.

If you consistently avoid conflict, will the problem go away by itself?

© Philip Date, 2007, Shutterstock.

Competitive/Distributive

The second conflict management style is described as **competitive** or **distributive**. It involves the use of aggressive and uncooperative types of behaviors. Individuals using this style pursue their own goals and objectives at the

Table 7.2   Avoidance as a Tactical Strategy

Sample Messages	Advantages	Disadvantages
Direct denial *"There is no issue here, really."*	Buys time to think about issues	Shows you do not care about relationship
Topic shift *"Let's not talk about that right now and instead focus on dinner."*	Best to use with trivial issues (don't sweat the small stuff)	Problem will not get solved
Noncommittal questions *"What do you want to do about this?"*	Can keep you from hurt feelings	Situation can get worse

Source: Adapted from Hocker and Wilmot 1991.

Table 7.3   Competitive/Distributive as a Tactical Strategy

Sample Messages	Advantages	Disadvantages
Criticism *"You have no sense of humor."*	Good in emergency situations	Can harm relationships
Hostile questions *"Who works the hardest in this relationship?"*	Can generate creative ideas	People get entrenched in positions
Rejection *"You have no idea what you are talking about."*	Useful in short-term situations	Can lead to covert conflict/games
Denial of responsibility *"It is not my fault that you can't communicate with me."*	Can show importance of issue	Not good if one party avoids conflict

Source: Adapted from Hocker and Wilmot 1991.

expense of others (Hocker and Wilmot 1991). The primary goal when adopting this style is to win the argument using whatever means necessary. Individuals using this style view conflict as a battle or competition and address conflict situations in either assertive or aggressive ways. When individuals use a competitive style of conflict they might offer personal criticism, rejection statements, hostile remarks, jokes or questions, presumptive remarks, or denial of responsibilities. Recently, Rosie O'Donnell criticized Donald Trump on her television show *The View* for his decision to allow Miss USA 2006 to retain her crown after allegations of alcohol abuse. O'Donnell referred to Trump as a "snake oil salesman" and mocked his hairstyle by flipping her hair to one side and mocking his voice. Trump retaliated by commenting that O'Donnell is "disgraceful" and referred to her as a "loser." As you can see, both O'Donnell and Trump engaged in a competition to see who could "one-up" the other. However, this style of managing conflict is not always unproductive. What are the advantages and disadvantages of using this style to manage conflict situations?

As we can see in Table 7.3 above, there are situations when using competition as a means of managing can be beneficial. For example, when an individual in a work setting is in a time crunch, lacks the time to debate all available alternatives, and feels strongly about his or her position, adopting a competitive stance to "win" an argument may be necessary. Or, if an issue has been discussed extensively and the individuals experiencing conflict have not made any progress toward resolving the disagreement, adopting a competitive stance may facilitate conflict resolution. Also, when individuals compete they often exert a great deal of energy, which sends a metamessage that the topic is important to the parties involved. However, competition can also damage relationships and isolate individuals who tend to avoid conflict situations. Unassertive or highly reticent individuals may avoid conflict situations when others adopt a competitive stance. Use of this style depends largely on the context and unique characteristics of the individuals involved.

Table 7.4	Collaborative/Integrative as a Tactical Strategy	
Sample Messages	**Advantages**	**Disadvantages**
Supportive remarks *"I can see why you would want to do that."*	Best when solutions must be mutually satisfying	Sometimes not worth time and effort
Concessions *"I promise to not interrupt you."*	Good for coming up with new and creative ideas	Can be used manipulatively
Soliciting criticism *"What are my communication weaknesses?"*	Preserves relationship	Everyone involved must embrace this style
Disclosive statement *"I was in a bad mood last night."*	Can lead to increased relationship satisfaction	Requires fairly strong communication skills

Source: Adapted from Hocker and Wilmot 1991.

Collaborative/Integrative

The final conflict management style, **collaborative** or **integrative,** is often described as a productive means of managing conflict because it requires open and ongoing communication. When relationship partners adopt this style, they offer descriptive and disclosive statements and, at the same time, make attempts to gain similar information from others (Hocker and Wilmot 1991). Partners work together to develop solutions to their disagreements that are mutually satisfying. Collaboration is often described as a "win-win" approach to solving relationship issues because both parties walk away satisfied with the outcome. See Table 7.4 for an overview of this strategy.

This style of conflict management is not without its own set of constraints. For example, there are times when decisions need to be made quickly. Think about a football coach arguing with his assistant coaches about which play to run to win the game; it would not be realistic for him to consult each coach before sending out the final play. Another challenge with this approach is that because it takes time and effort, people may be reluctant to use it. Also, people might feel that by soliciting feedback from everyone and getting issues out in the open, it might "open a whole other can of worms." Collaboration, by nature, encourages open expression of multiple perspectives. Sometimes encouraging others to openly express concerns can result in "tangents," lengthy discussion of unimportant or unrelated issues, and poor use of time. In other words, this approach could be viewed as time-consuming and challenging.

However, there are many benefits to using the collaborative/integrative approach to manage conflict management situations. When partners in romantic relationships report increased use of integrative styles of conflict management, relationship satisfaction increases (see, for example, Canary and Cupach 1988; Canary and Spitzberg 1989). Conversely, when partners in romantic relationships employ more distributive or avoiding styles of conflict, relationship satisfaction decreases significantly (Canary and Cupach 1988; Canary and Spitzberg 1989; Rands et al. 1981; Spitzberg et al. 1994; Ting-Toomey 1983). It should come as no surprise that those individuals who employ integrative conflict management strategies with relationship partners are generally perceived as more communicatively competent (Canary and Spitzberg 1989). Perceptions of relationship partners' competence mediate the relationship between conflict messages and relational outcomes. More specifically, Canary and Spitzberg (1989) note that "conflict messages are assessed as more or less appropriate, effective, and globally competent, and these assessments then affect relational features of trust, control mutuality, intimacy and relational satisfaction" (644). Thus, use of integrative conflict management styles, which are generally perceived as more appropriate and effective, increase relationship partners' reported satisfaction and trust.

THE DARK SIDE OF CONFLICT: VERBAL AGGRESSION

When partners lack communication skills, they are more likely to employ verbally aggressive communication behaviors, often resulting in violent episodes (deTurck 1987; Infante, Chandler and Rudd 1989; Infante, et al. 1990). **Verbal aggression** involves assaulting or criticizing another person's sense of self and typically involves attacks on one's character, competence, background, or appearance. These types of messages not only damage an individual's perceptions of self-worth, but can also negatively affect relationship satisfaction. It is important for relationship partners to minimize the use of verbally aggressive messages during conflict episodes.

© Nicholas Sutcliffe, 2007, Shutterstock.

Loreen Olsen (2002) conducted a qualitative investigation of romantic couples' conflict episodes to study the relationship between communication competence and aggression. In her study, she found that partners felt that aggressive communication indicated a lack of communication competence. However, she also found there were times when individuals felt that use of aggressive communication was justifiable. For example, participants described the use of aggressive communication as a constructive way to clear the air, gain their partner's attention, and reach a resolution faster. Some participants felt aggression was appropriate in certain situations because it became a relationship-changing event and permanently altered the way the couple managed conflict episodes. Can you think of a time when an aggressive conflict episode ultimately changed the way relationship partners communicated in the future? Olsen points out that her results should be interpreted with caution because most of her participants were female European Americans and because the participants recalled a conflict event that got out of hand. Thus, while these findings might not extend to all conflict episodes, they identify descriptive accounts of when relationship partners might view aggression as appropriate. In other words, because this study had participants recall conflict events, these results suggest that in hindsight there might have been productive results from aggressive behaviors.

Are there times when aggressive communication is justifiable?

MANAGING CONFLICT

In the final sections of this chapter, we offer a number of useful suggestions for approaching conflict productively, regardless of the communication situation. First, when approaching a conflict situation, you should consider the advantages and disadvantages of using avoidance, competitive, or collaborative conflict management strategies. Each of these strategies requires a different set of communication behaviors and produces a variety of outcomes. From a relational perspective, collaboration is consistently viewed as the most competent way to manage conflict; often resulting in higher reported satisfaction for relationship partners. Conversely, avoidance and competition are regarded as less effective and appropriate strategies, often resulting in less relationship satisfaction.

Refusing to discuss problems is unproductive to conflict resolution.

© Fred Goldstein, 2007, Shutterstock.

Individuals should also consider the way they respond or react to problems in their relationships. Carl Rusbult and his colleagues (1982) found that when individuals experience problems in relationships, there are typically four different ways to react: exit, voice, loyalty, and neglect. These responses vary to the extent in which they are perceived as productive or unproductive and passive or active. **Exit** responses typically involve threats of physical separation between partners. Consider a time when you had a conflict with another person and one of you physically left the room during the episode. Did you view this as a productive way to respond to the situation? Probably not. Exit is a passive strategy that is unproductive to conflict resolution. Similarly, when relationship partners adopt a **neglect** response to conflict, they might avoid the relationship partner, refuse to discuss problems they are experiencing, and communicate with one another in a hostile or aggressive manner. This type of response is described as active and destructive. Rusbult and his colleagues (1982) found that college couples in satisfying relationships were less likely to use neglect and exit responses.

Couples reporting higher satisfaction in their relationships were more likely to use loyalty and voice responses as a response to conflict (Rusbult 1982). When individuals adopt a **loyalty** response, they remain loyal to one another by not addressing the conflict. They may decide to "wait it out" in the hopes that by doing so, the relationship will improve on its own. Loyalty is described as a passive strategy that could be viewed as productive or unproductive, depending on the situation. On the one hand, loyalty indicates that a partner is committed to the relationship and will stick with the other partner during both good and bad times. However, because the loyalty response is passive, and the partner adopting this response to a relationship problem is not actively addressing an issue, it could also be described as an unproductive response. As mentioned previously, avoiding conflict does little to bring it to a resolution.

A more productive response to problems in relationships is the **voice** response. When individuals adopt this response, they discuss relationship concerns openly and often offer suggestions for repairing the relationship transgression. Rusbult, Johnson and Morrow (1986) noted that adopting a voice response during mild relationship transgressions assisted in stabilizing the relationship's health. Use of the voice response has been positively associated with both relationship satisfaction and commitment. Interestingly, men and women differ in the extent to which they use voice and loyalty responses. Women, more so than men, use the voice response as a means of managing minor problems and use loyalty for a wide range of problems. Men were more likely to use neglect responses than women (Rusbult et al. 1986). These gender-based differences are interesting and offer some support for the notion that many women often feel they must be the "relationship experts" or the keeper of the relationship standards.

© 2007, JupiterImages, Inc.

How do men and women typically differ in their responses to relationship problems?

A final suggestion for managing conflict effectively and appropriately has to do with using **"fair fighting"** tactics in relationships. When we use the term fair fighting, we are not referring to physical fighting in relationships. Instead, we are referring to the use of productive or competent communication practices that promote problem solving, compromise and collaboration. Table 7.5 provides additional information regarding productive and unproductive communication responses to conflict.

Table 7.5 Managing Conflict Effectively

Productive Communication	Unproductive Communication
Active listening	Pseudo-listening, defensive listening
Use of empathy	Focus on self
Choosing the right time and place (e.g., private contexts) to discuss the problem	Choosing an inappropriate time and place (e.g., public contexts) to discuss issue
Communicating with respect	Being disrespectful
Describing the problem clearly	Being ambiguous
Using I statements. For example, "I feel ____ when you ____"	Starting statements with "You are . . .!"
Stay in the present	Bringing up the past
Focusing on relevant issues only	Kitchensinking—throwing everything into the argument [including?] the kitchen sink!

How can you show that you are making an effort to understand someone's concerns?

To manage conflict in a productive and healthy way, it is important to adopt communication patterns that create an environment in which individuals feel comfortable sharing their concerns without being belittled, embarrassed, or ridiculed. It is important to choose an appropriate time and place to discuss the problem, listen actively when the other person is talking, and refrain from using negative listening behaviors such as pseudo-listening or defensive listening. Also, it is important be empathetic when communicating with the other person. Make an attempt to understand the other person's feelings. Individuals often experience problems in their relationships because they do not really listen to one another. It is important to show individuals that you are listening by using active listening behaviors, paraphrasing their messages, and asking relevant questions to help understand their perspective.

SUMMARY

Relationships require work and effort! In this chapter we explored reasons for maintaining relationships, identified various maintenance strategies, and discussed the outcomes of strategy use. Because more people are using the Internet as a means of maintaining their relationships, we discussed the benefits and drawbacks of using CMC to maintain our relationships. In the last sections of this chapter, we focused on managing conflict effectively as a means of stabilizing our relationships. More specifically, we focused on the definition of conflict, different types of conflict management strategies, conflict responses, and using productive communication during conflict episodes.

APPLICATIONS

Discussion Questions

A. Relationship maintenance strategies are used in virtually all relationships. The research on relationship maintenance has focused primarily on strategies used in platonic and romantic relationships. However, it is likely that individuals use strategies to maintain their work or professional relationships. Identify several relationship maintenance strategies that you use to sustain your work relationships. Are they similar to those identified in the chapter?

B. Burleson and Samter state that maintaining relationships with others typically involves mastery of specific communication skills. Can you identify five or more skills needed to effectively maintain relationships with family members, friends, or romantic partners?

C. Reflect on a recent conflict that you may have experienced with a friend, roommate, or co-worker. What was your approach to this situation? What conflict management style did you use? What was the outcome of this situation? In retrospect, do you feel that you could have handled this situation more effectively? What would you have done differently?

REFERENCES

Ayres, J. 1983. Strategies to maintain relationships. *Communication Quarterly, 31,* 62–67.

Braiker, H. B., and H. H. Kelley. 1979. Conflict in the development of close relationships. In R. L. Burgess and T. L. Huston (Eds.), *Social Exchange in Developing Relationships.* New York: Academic Press.

Burgoon, J. K., and J. L. Hale. 1984. The fundamental topoi of relational communication. *Communication Monographs, 51,* 19–41.

Burleson, B., and W. Samter. 1994. A social skills approach to relationship maintenance: How individual differences in communication skills affect the achievement of relationship functions. In D. J. Canary and L. Stafford (Eds.), *Communication and relational maintenance* (61–90). New York: Academic Press.

Cahn, D. 1992. *Conflict in intimate relationships* (72–112). New York: The Guilford Press.

Canary, D. J., and B. H. Spitzberg. 1989. A model of perceived competence of conflict strategies. *Human Communication Research, 15,* 630–649.

Canary, D. J., and L. Stafford. 1992. Relational maintenance strategies and equity in marriage. *Communication Monographs, 59,* 243–267.

———. 1994. Maintaining relationships through strategic and routine interaction. In D. J. Canary and L. Stafford (Eds.), *Communication and relational maintenance* (pp. 3–22). San Diego, CA: Academic Press.

———. 2001. Equity in the preservation of personal relationships. In J. H. Harvey and A. Wenzel (Eds.), *Close romantic relationships: Maintenance and enhancement* (pp. 133–151). Mahwah, NJ: Lawrence Erlbaum Associates, Publishers.

Canary, D. J., and W. R. Cupach. 1988. Relational and episodic characteristics associated with conflict tactics. *Journal of Social and Personal Relationships, 5,* 305–325.

Canary, D. J., L. Stafford, K. S. Hause, and L. A. Wallace. 1993. An inductive analysis of relational maintenance strategies: Comparison among lovers, friends, relatives, and others. *Communication Research Reports, 10,* 5–14.

Canary, D. J., W. R. Cupach, and S. J. Messman. 1995. *Relationship conflict.* Thousand Oaks, CA: Sage Publications.

Cialdini, R. B. 2003. *Influence: Science and practice (4th ed.).* International Edition (country or state?): Allyn and Bacon.

Dainton, M. 2000. Maintenance behaviors, expectations for maintenance and satisfaction: Linking comparison levels to relational maintenance strategies. *Journal of Social and Personal Relationships, 17,* 827–842.

Dainton, M., and B. Aylor. 2002. A relational uncertainty analysis of jealousy, trust, and maintenance in long-distance versus geographically close relationships. *Communication Quarterly, 49,* 172–188.

Dainton, M., and L. Stafford. 1993. Routine maintenance behaviors: A comparison of relationship type, partner similarity, and sex differences. *Journal of Personal and Social Relationships, 10,* 255–272.

deTurck, M. A. 1987. When communication fails: Physical aggression as a compliance gaining strategy. *Communication Monographs, 51,* 106–112.

Diggs, R. C., and L. Stafford. 1998. Maintaining marital relationships: A comparison between African American and European American individuals. In V. J. Duncan (Ed.), *Towards achieving MAAT.* (192–292). Dubuque, IA: Kendall Hunt.

Dindia, K., and D. J. Canary. 1993. Definitions and theoretical perspectives on maintaining relationships. *Journal of Social and Personal Relationships, 10,* 163–173.

Dindia, K., and L. Baxter. 1987. Strategies for maintaining and repairing marital relationships. *Journal of Social and Personal Relationships, 4,* 143–158.

Duck, S. 1988. *Relating to others.* Buckingham, PA: Open University Press.

Eldrige, N. S., and L. A. Gilbert. 1990. Correlates of relationship satisfaction in lesbian couples. *Psychology of Women Quarterly, 14,* 43–62.

Fox, S., L. Rainie, E. Larsen, J. Horrigan, A. Lenhart, T. Spooner, and C. Carter. 2001. The Pew Internet and American life project. www.pewinternet.org/

Haas, S. M., and L. Stafford. 1998. An initial examination of maintenance behaviors in gay and lesbian relationships. *Journal of Social and Personal Relationships, 15,* 846–855.

Hocker, J. L., and W. W. Wilmot. 1991. *Interpersonal Conflict* (4–42, 103–144). Dubuque, IA: Wm C. Brown Publishers.

Infante, D. A., T. A. Chandler, and J. E. Rudd. 1989. Test of an argumentative skill deficiency model of interspousal violence. *Communication Monographs, 56,* 163–177.

Infante, D. A., T. C. Sabourin, J. E. Rudd, and E. A. Shannon. 1990. Verbal aggression in violent and nonviolent disputes. *Communication Quarterly, 38,* 361–371.

Jones, R. W., and J. E. Bates. 1978. Satisfaction in male homosexual couples. *Journal of Homosexuality, 3,* 217–224.

Messman, S. J., D. J. Canary, and K. S. Hause. 2000. Motives to remain platonic, equity, and the use of maintenance strategies in opposite-sex friendships. *Journal of Social and Personal Relationships, 17,* 67–94.

Myers, S. 2001. Relational maintenance behaviors in the sibling relationship. *Communication Quarterly, 49,* 19–37.

Myers, S., and K. Weber. 2004. Preliminary development of a measure of sibling relational maintenance behaviors: Scale development and initial findings. *Communication Quarterly, 52,* 334–347.

Olsen, L. 2002. "As ugly and as painful as it was, it was effective": Individuals' unique assessment of communication competence during aggressive conflict episodes. *Communication Studies, 53,* 171–188.

Punyanunt-Carter, N. M. 2006. Evaluating the effects of attachment styles on relationship maintenance behaviors in father-daughter relationships. *Family Journal, 14,* 135–143.

Ragsdale, J. D. 1996. Gender, satisfaction level, and the use of relational maintenance strategies in marriage. *Communication Monographs, 63,* 354–369.

Rands, M., G. Levinger, and G. D. Mellinger. 1981. Patterns of conflict resolution and marital satisfaction. *Journal of Family Issues, 2,* 297–321.

Rohlfing, M. 1995. "Doesn't anybody stay in the same place anymore?" An exploration of the understudied phenomenon of long-distance relationships. In J. Wood and S. Duck (Eds.) *Communication and relational maintenance* (23–44). New York: Academic Press.

Rusbult, C. E., D. J. Johnson, and G. D. Morrow. 1986. Determinants and consequences of exit, voice, loyalty, and neglect: Responses to dissatisfaction in adult romantic involvements. *Human Relations, 39,* 45–63.

Rusbult, C. E., I. M. Zembrodt, and L. K. Grunn. 1982. Exit, voice, loyalty, and neglect: Responses to dissatisfaction in romantic involvements. *Journal of Personality and Social Psychology, 43,* 1230–1242.

Sillars, A. L., and W. W. Wilmot. 1994. Communication strategies in conflict and mediation. In J. A. Daly and J. M. Wiemann (Eds.), *Strategic interpersonal communication* (163–190). Hillsdale, NJ: Lawrence Erlbaum.

Spitzberg, B. H., D. J. Canary, and W. R. Cupach. 1994. A competence based approach to the study of interpersonal conflict. In D. D. Cahn (Ed.), *Conflict in personal relationships* (183–202). Hillsdale, NJ: Lawrence Erlbaum.

Stafford, L., and D. J. Canary. 1991. Maintenance strategies and romantic relationship type, gender and relational characteristics. *Journal of Social and Personal Relationships, 8,* 217–242.

Ting-Toomey, S. 1983. An analysis of verbal communication patterns in high and low marital adjustment groups. *Human Communication Research, 9,* 306–319.

Wright, K. 2004. Online relational maintenance strategies and perceptions of partners within exclusively internet-based and primarily internet-based relationships. *Communication Studies, 55,* 239–253.

8

The Dark Side of Relationships
Deception, Embarrassment, Jealousy, Power, and Obsession

OBJECTIVES

- Understand what is meant by the "dark side" of communication
- Define *deception*
- Explain Interpersonal Deception Theory
- Discuss the three potential deceptive responses
- Describe five fundamental dimensions that deceivers use to manage information
- Discuss three possible methods of deception detection
- Identify three sets of key questions used to contemplate telling a lie
- Explain three reasons embarrassment occurs in social situations
- Identify three roles associated with embarrassment
- Provide three potential responses to embarrassing communication
- Define *jealousy* and identify the six types of jealousy
- Explain the six jealousy-related goals
- Distinguish between the five bases of power
- Describe the three levels of influence
- Distinguish between argumentativeness and aggressiveness
- Explain the four levels of aggression
- Define *Obsessive Relational Intrusion* (ORI)
- Recognize potential risks for ORI as a result of computer-mediated communication

© Marcin Balcerzak, 2007, Shutterstock.

KEY TERMS

dark side of
  communication
deception
Interpersonal
  Deception Theory
  (IDT)
falsification
concealment

equivocation
completeness
relevance/directness
clarity
personalization
veridicality
leakage cues

positive relational
  deceptive strategies
third-party
  information
solicited vs.
  unsolicited
  confessions

embarrassment
agent
recipients
observer
accounts
apologies
joking
jealousy
friend jealousy
family jealousy
romantic jealousy
power jealousy

activity jealousy
intimacy jealousy
compensatory
  restoration
power
reward power
coercive power
legitimate power
referent power
expert power
compliance
identification

internalization
dominance
argumentativeness
verbal aggression
low aggression
moderate aggression
high aggression
severe aggression
Employee Emotional
  Abuse (EEA)
obsessive relational
  intrusion

OVERVIEW

Yoda warns us in *Star Wars* about the symbolic dangers of the "dark side." He identifies anger, fear, and aggression as characteristics of this dark place. In the past two chapters we have discussed how we initiate and sustain relationships. But the stark reality is this—our interpersonal relationships can, and often *do*, experience a dark side. Friends and family members can deceive us, romantic partners may lie and cheat, and our colleagues and supervisors could attempt to abuse their power. As a result of these negative behaviors in our relation-

> *Beware of the dark side. Anger . . . fear . . . aggression. The dark side of the Force are they. Easily they flow, quick to join you in a fight.*
>
> *Star Wars: Episode V The Empire Strikes Back* directed by George Lucas, 2 hrs. 4 min., LucasFilm, 1980.

ships, we can become angry, fearful, and perhaps even aggressive towards others. Although most of the research in communication is devoted to discussing appropriate and effective behavior to foster positive communicative outcomes, William Cupach and Brian Spitzberg challenged academic scholars to tackle problematic and disruptive communication patterns in their 1994 book, *The Dark Side of Interpersonal Communication*. What exactly is the dark side of communication? The **dark side of communication** is defined as, "an integrative metaphor for a certain perspective toward the study of human folly, frailty and fallibility" (Cupach and Spitzberg 1994, 240). Some examples of **dark communication** that have been studied are: deception or lying, conflict, jealousy, intentionally hurtful messages, relationship termination, embarrassment, loneliness, co-dependency, and obsession, or stalking (Spitzberg 2006). This chapter recognizes that interpersonal relationships are not always filled with sunshine and smiles. People can, and do, lie, deceive, abuse power, and cheat in all types of relationships.

    The goal of this chapter is to recognize the dark side of communication and to understand the motivation behind these behaviors. Although we cannot possibly attempt to discuss all of the communication behaviors that have been identified as potentially negative or dark, we have selected a few which most students in interpersonal communication are likely to encounter. Specifically, we will explore the how and why individuals in romantic or platonic relationships deceive each other, become jealous, deal with social embarrassment, engage in aggressive behavior, and abuse relationships. Further, we will discuss the role that dark communication plays in online interactions. To assist you in understanding how these concepts have been examined, we will discuss various studies that provide a clearer picture of these destructive forms of communicating. We will also provide suggestions on how to cope if you encounter these circumstances.

DECEPTION AND INTERPERSONAL RELATIONSHIPS

In 2004, a study conducted by Britain's *That's Life!* magazine examined the prevalence of lies in relationships. The magazine surveyed 5,000 women and discovered that ninety-four percent of them admitted to lying. While thirty-four percent of them reported that they tell "white lies" daily, seventy-six percent of the women revealed to researchers that they have told life-changing lies (Knox, Schact, Holt, and Turner 1993). While your initial reaction may be one of shock at the high percentage of women who admitted to lying, stop for a minute and recall the last time that you failed to tell the complete and honest truth. Perhaps your significant other asked what you thought about a meal he had cooked or how she looked in an outfit. Or maybe you lied to your boss about why you called off work or needed to switch shifts. What do we lie about? Most people admit to lying about everything from what they ate for breakfast to why they were late for work. Married couples may even lie to one another about their finances. In 2006, the *New Zealand Herald* reported results of a poll taken by a bank which discovered that forty-two percent of women and thirty-five percent of men lie to their partners about their financial situation. **Deception** is defined as, "a message knowingly transmitted by a sender to foster a false belief or conclusion by a receiver" (Buller and Burgoon, 1996, 209). While we would like to believe that our relationships are built on truth and honesty, the reality is that friends, family members, and romantic partners deceive each other from time to time. Consider this scenario:

> Jack has been in love with Shawna since their freshman year of college. He was always extremely nervous about speaking with her and he came to terms with the fact that they would probably never be together. In the meantime, Jack started dating Shawna's roommate, Tina. After three months, Jack really started to fall for Tina. One evening, Shawna asked Jack for a ride to the library. He agreed. In the car, Shawna started expressing feelings for Jack. Jack was stunned. He just could not believe that this day had come. His heart raced as he tried to think of an appropriate reply. However, out of respect to his relationship with Tina, he reluctantly told Shawna that he did not have feelings for her.

In this example, Jack protects his current relationship with Tina by deceiving Shawna about his true feelings. Of course, we know that not all deception is done with such honorable intentions. David Buller and Judee Burgoon (1996) proposed **Interpersonal Deception Theory** (IDT) to explain the strategic choices made when engaging in deceptive communication (1996). While a person may attempt to be strategic in creating a deceptive message, there are cues that alert the other person that the individual is being less than honest. At the same time, the receiver of the message attempts to mask, or hide, his knowledge of the deception. Rather than directly accuse the person who is lying, the person may nod their head, offer verbal prompts ("I see!" or "So what else happened?"), and generally behave in ways designed to keep the source from seeing his suspicion. In essence, it is a back-

and-forth game between relational partners. The source tries to mask the deception and the receiver tries to hide his suspicion of the deception. Now, consider this example:

> Julie and Robbie have been dating for two years. During the fall semester of their junior year, Julie decided to study abroad in Scotland. Although, Robbie was not happy that Julie was leaving, he was excited for her. At first, Julie was extremely homesick and spoke with Robbie every evening. As time passed, she met several new friends in Scotland and enjoyed going out dancing every night. Some evenings she had a little too much to drink and would end up kissing other men on the dance floor. Robbie continued to call Julie each night. He was becoming increasingly suspicious of Julie's behavior abroad. One evening he asked Julie, "Have you been with anyone since you have been there?"

There are three potentially deceptive responses that Julie can give. She can tell an outright lie or resort to **falsification:** "No, I have been completely faithful." Oftentimes this requires the source to create a fictional story to explain the lie. Alternatively, Julie might partially tell the truth while leaving out important details. This refers to **concealment:** "Well, when I go out I do dance with other guys." We typically do this when we want to hide a secret. Or Julie could engage in **equivocation,** or be strategically vague: "Just because I go out dancing does not necessarily mean I have to hook up with someone." This type of response is used to avoid the issue altogether.

In addition to managing the deceptive responses discussed previously (falsification, concealment, equivocation), Interpersonal Deception Theory also suggests that deceivers manipulate their verbal and nonverbal behavior to appear more credible (Burgoon et al. 1996). This manipulation is accomplished by varying the message along five fundamental dimensions.

Completeness

First, deceivers may vary on the **completeness** or extent of message details. The deceiver knows that an appropriate amount of information needs to be provided in order to be perceived truthful by the receiver. The more practiced deceiver also realizes that specific details are probably best kept to a minimum; there is less for the receiver to challenge. When interpreting the completeness of a message, receivers may become suspicious if the information provided is too brief or vague.

Relevance/Directness

A second fundamental dimension on which deceptive messages are manipulated is its **relevance** or **directness.** This refers to the extent to which the deceiver produces messages that are logical in flow and sequence, and are pertinent to the conversation. The more direct and relevant the message, the more it is perceived as truthful. Two indicators of potential deception are when a person goes off on a tangent in response to a question or is cautious in his or her response.

Clarity

The extent to which the deceiver is clear, comprehensible, and concise is a third dimension of message manipulation. The **clarity** dimension varies along a continuum from very clear to completely ambiguous. The more evasive or vague a message is, the more cause there is for a receiver to probe for additional information and clarification.

Personalization

A fourth dimension involves the **personalization** of the information. The extent to which the deceiver takes ownership of the information may vary. If the deceiver relies on verbal distancing or non-immediate communication, he will be perceived as less truthful. For example, the suggestions "everyone goes out during the week here" and "I just miss you so much that I am just trying to keep myself busy," are two examples that disassociate the deceiver with the behavior.

Veridicality

The last dimension is the extent to which the deceiver appears to be truthful, or the **veridicality** of the message. This dimension is twofold. First, the message is constructed based on the objective truth value reported by the source. In other words, to what extent does the deceiver believe the message is truthful? Next, the believability of the message is judged by the receiver. In evaluating the truthfulness of a message, receivers often rely on nonverbal cues that are the result of our body language. Examples of behaviors believed to signal deception include increased blinking, speech errors, higher voice pitch and enlarged pupils (Zuckerman and Driver 1985). These unconscious behaviors are often referred to as **leakage cues,** and while deceptive individuals attempt to control these behaviors, others may be able to detect their dishonesty.

People often tell lies to make themselves seem more attractive to someone new.

© iofoto, 2007, Shutterstock.

WHY DO WE LIE?

Based on the high percentage of people who report engaging in deception, the question becomes, why are we so prone to lying? When asked, most people suggest that they lie to make themselves appear more admirable. In Chapter Six we discussed the role of physical attraction in initiating relationships. Thus, it comes as no surprise that one study revealed that we lie to attract an attractive date (Rowatt, Cunningham and Druen 1999). In the study, participants reported lying about their own personal attributes such as appearance, personality, income, career, grades and past relational outcomes in an attempt to attract another person. In fact, twenty-five percent of respondents indicated that they engage in this type of deception in initial encounters with someone they are attracted to.

Consider the following conversation from the *Friends* episode "The One the Morning After." Ross debates whether he should be honest with Rachel about sleeping with another woman during the time that he and Rachel were apart.

Ross tells Chandler and Joey that Rachel wants to work on their relationship and worries about how she will react to hearing that he slept with another woman. They can't believe Ross is even considering telling Rachel about it . . . how stupid can he be?

But Ross believes that he needs to be completely honest with Rachel if there is any hope to rebuild their relationship. Joey agrees that being honest is best, as long as it doesn't cause any problems! And Chandler points out that it will only hurt Rachel. There won't be anything left to save if Ross tells her.

Ross still isn't completely convinced that he should keep quiet. Chandler concedes, saying that at least Ross should wait until the time is right to tell Rachel . . . and that would be when he's on his deathbed.

According to the deception literature, there are three types of lies that people tell (Camden, Motley, and Wilson 1984; DePaulo, Kashy, Kirkendale, Wyer, and Epstein 1996). These include lies to: (1) harm others, (2) protect self, and (3) spare others.

Lying to Harm Others

The first type of deceptions, lying to harm others, is often the most damaging type of lie in interpersonal relationships. These types of lies are done to intentionally hurt others by distorting information, fabricating stories, or deliberately omitting important information. Perhaps the best example of lies designed to harm others are those seen during political campaign ads. Specific information about one's opponent is strategically distorted and manipulated in an attempt to damage their candidacy.

Lying to Protect Self

A more egotistical goal refers to lying to protect self. The goal of this type of lie is to make oneself look good. This can be accomplished by exaggerating praise and/or omitting weaknesses. In a study that examined sexual lies among college students, lying about the number of previous sexual partners emerged as the most frequently told lie (Knox et al. 1993). Regardless of whether the number of sexual partners was inflated to appear more experienced, or reduced to appear more "pure," the goal of the lie was to enhance one's image.

Spare Others

The most common type of lie is to spare others. In the movie *A Few Good Men*, Jack Nicholson's character, Colonel Nathan R. Jessep, states, "You can't handle the truth." In this situation, Col. Jessep emphasizes that sometimes we lie in order to spare or protect others from the truth. Perhaps we want to avoid hurting the other person's feelings or damaging his self-esteem. At other times we may "stretch the truth" or omit details for the good of the relationship.

Consider the earlier example of Ross' lie to Rachel. Joey and Chandler try to help justify the deception by pointing out that the truth would end up hurting Rachel and would eliminate any chance of a potential future together.

ARE THERE GOOD REASONS FOR LYING?

Have you ever lied about a friend's appearance to avoid hurt feelings?

© Simone van den Berg, 2007, Shutterstock.

While the definition of deception indicates that a source intentionally designs the message with the goal of instilling a false belief in the receiver, it is important to take a step back and consider the potential benefits of deception in relationships (Knapp and Vangelisti 2006). Dan O'Hair and Michael Cody (1994) distinguish between positive or negative deceptive strategies. They suggest that strategies that enhance, escalate, repair, and improve relationships can be considered **positive relational deceptive strategies.** These include responses to the inevitable questions, "How do you like my new outfit?" or "What do you think of my new haircut?" In these situations we often respond with a white lie in order to foster liking, or positive affect. In other words, we are motivated to deceive to preserve the relationship, to avoid hurting the other person's feelings, to avoid a conflict, or even to protect a third party. In other instances, we may decide that the deception is not worth the risk. Consider the following example when it was determined that the potential consequences of deception outweighed the benefits. In the film *The Pursuit of Happyness*, Will Smith portrays a homeless man who is seeking an internship with a stock brokerage firm. After spending the night in jail for unpaid parking tickets, Smith rushes to his interview at Dean Witter. As he enters the room in a t-shirt and jeans spattered with paint, he says, "I've been sitting outside trying to think up a good story of why I would show up for such an important interview dressed like this. And I couldn't think of a good story. So I finally decided it was probably best to just tell the truth." In the end, his character's honesty impresses the interviewers, and he is offered the internship.

DETECTING DECEPTION

Understanding the ways in which messages are manipulated is one way to enhance your ability to detect deception. Earlier we described some of the nonverbal cues associated with deception. But there are several verbal cues that can tip us off about lies as well. In a recent study on deceptive communication practices (Park et al. 2002), 202 college students were asked to recall a time when they had caught another person being deceptive. While a variety of discovery mechanisms were identified in the study, the three most prominent ones include the strategies labeled third party information, physical evidence, and confessions.

Third-Party Information

Third-party information involves information being revealed by a person outside the relationship. Suppose a teenager wants to go to a party while his parents are out of town, but he knows his parents would not approve. He lies to his parents and tells them that he is spending the night at his friend's house in case they call home while he is at the party. When his mother speaks with the friend's mother a few days later and thanks her for allowing him to stay at their house, the friend's mother reveals that he never spent the night. Thus the lie is revealed by an outside party.

Physical Evidence

Sometimes we are able to detect deception by doing our best Sherlock Holmes impression and looking for physical evidence. For instance, on an episode of *Grey's Anatomy*, Addison, Dr. Shepherd's wife, discovered a pair of black panties that clearly did not belong to her in her husband's tuxedo pocket. The physical evidence swiftly revealed Derek's betrayal and finally ended the fragile marriage. The classic lipstick-on-the-collar shtick is another familiar Hollywood portrayal of deception detection.

Confessions

Another method by which deception is detected is via confessions made by the deceiver. **Solicited confessions** are often offered as the result of direct questioning or confrontation. Suppose you heard that your best friend went on a ski trip with a group of people the same weekend that the two of you had planned to go to a professional hockey game. Initially, he told you that he could not go to the game because he was swamped with homework. When you follow up and tell him that you heard he had gone skiing that same weekend, he feels guilty and confesses his lie. While some confessions are solicited, at other times these declarations come from out of the blue. Suppose your significant other spontaneously confesses that she has been reading your emails without your knowledge. Nothing caused you to suspect that she was engaging in this behavior, yet she decided to make an **unsolicited confession.** An important point to note is that we are often able to detect deception using a combination of cues—in fact, many people report a combination of verbal and nonverbal signals as tipping them off about dishonesty.

TO LIE OR NOT TO LIE: THAT IS THE QUESTION

Deception and lying are multidimensional constructs. Key components to consider when analyzing a deceptive message include: the importance of the relationship, the importance of the information to the relationship, and the costs and rewards associated with the lie. When deciding whether it is to your benefit to tell a lie, consider the following three sets of questions posed by Knapp and Vangelisti (2006):

1. What is the potential outcome of the lie? Can it potentially benefit our relationship, or one of us, individually?
2. Based on the rules we have established for our relationship, is it reasonable and just for me to tell a lie? Or am I violating one of the spoken or unspoken expectancies that we have for our relationship? What lies would we agree upon that are acceptable versus unacceptable?

3. Am I telling a lie in an attempt to protect my partner from being harmed? If I were to be caught telling the lie, would my partner understand my justification for telling the lie?

What is the most important determinant in ending a relationship as a result of deception? Knapp and Vangelisti (2006) state that the more importance the receiver attaches to the information being lied about, the greater the chance that he or she will decide to end the relationship.

Now that you have a better understanding of the concept of deception and of the reasons why people lie, it is our hope that you will be strategic in your analysis of the appropriateness of deceptive messages.

EMBARRASSMENT: WHY DID I SAY THAT?

Can you remember a time when you had a huge crush on someone, and when you finally had the opportunity to talk to them and make that great first impression, something went horribly wrong and you ended up putting your foot in your mouth? Or have you ever told a joke at a party and nobody laughed? In these types of situations, we often experience social embarrassment. Recall our discussion in Chapter Two regarding the role of self-presentation in relationships. When we perceive that our self-esteem has been threatened or if we have presented what we perceive to be a negative view of the self to others, **embarrassment** occurs. Our sense of identity is at stake if the response to our behavior is not what we expected. Gross and Stone (1964) proposed that embarrassment emerges as the result of three factors that occur in social interactions. First, misrepresentations or cognitive shortcomings may cause us to feel embarrassment. Have you ever called someone by the wrong name or forgotten how you know someone? Losing confidence in our role or ability in a social situation can also cause us to experience discomfort. Sometimes we script out an interaction, such as the all-important first phone call to an attractive person, and the conversation does not turn out like we had anticipated. Finally, a loss of dignity, or composure, can cause us to become "red-faced." Examples of this may include tripping as you are making your big entrance into the campus hangout, or discovering that your pants are unzipped after you have just had a conversation with your boss.

Our Role in Embarrassment

It is easy to see why we would be embarrassed in any of these situations, even as we were in control of our own behavior. We can just as easily become uncomfortable in those situations where we are the silent observer. Sattler (1965) identified three roles that exist in embarrassing social situations: agent, recipient, and observer. As an **agent,** we are responsible for our own embarrassment, perhaps by accidentally swearing in front of your grandmother or unexpectedly burping during an important interview lunch. In other situations, we are the **recipients,** or targets, of embarrassing communication. Examples of this type of embarrassment might include your best friend revealing to your secret crush that you are attracted to him and your mother telling your friend about the time you ran naked around the neighborhood when you were three years old. Finally, it is likely that you can recall a situation where you were simply a bystander, or **observer,** of another's embarrassment and experienced feelings of discomfort yourself. In these situations, we often offer an awkward comment, express a reassuring remark, or simply attempt to ignore the situation.

Responding to Embarrassment

Building on Goffman's theory of face-saving and identity management, Edelmann (1985) identified three primary types of messages individuals use in response to embarrassing encounters. These include accounts, apologies, and jokes. **Accounts** provide a potential explanation for the cause of the embarrassing situation. Suppose you arrive at class only to discover that you forgot an important assignment that was due. You decide to speak with your instructor and explain that you have been overwhelmed with group projects in two other classes and with searching for a job. In some instances, we may feel the need to apologize for the embarrassing behavior. **Apologies** are attempts to identify the source of blame for the incident. Suppose you accidentally revealed to your friend that she has not been included in the group's plans for the weekend. As you stumble over your words, you might comment, "I'm sorry. I didn't realize until now that you weren't invited," or "I didn't make the plans. They invited me along and I just assumed you were included." These responses are made with the hope that your friend will forgive you for the non-invitation. **Joking** involves using humor to create a more light-hearted response to a situation. At the 2006 Academy Awards, Jennifer Garner tripped over her dress as she approached the podium. To cover her embarrassment, she joked, "I do all my own stunts." According to arousal relief theory (Berylne 1969), use of humor in embarrassing or difficult situations often evokes positive affective responses which can help individuals diffuse anxiety or stress.

The next time that you find yourself becoming embarrassed in a social situation, remember—everyone experiences this discomfort at one time or another. While at the time it may appear to be a black cloud that hangs over your head, it is likely that these feelings will be temporary and short-lived. However, there are other dark aspects of interpersonal communication whose impact may not be so minimal on our interactions and relationships.

© Andrew Taylor, 2007, Shutterstock.

Sometimes one embarrassing moment seems like it will last forever.

JEALOUSY IN INTERPERSONAL RELATIONSHIPS

Another aspect of interpersonal relationships that has received a lot of attention in the literature is jealousy. Chances are that you have heard jealousy described as the "green-eyed monster." In the movie *Terms of Endearment*, a mother's jealousy over her daughter's relationships wreaks havoc in their own relationship. Jealousy causes us to experience a variety of emotions and sometimes causes us to communicate or react in ways that we normally would not. Consider some of the things that can cause us to experience jealousy:

- Your best friend recently went away to college. He sends you text messages describing all the fun he is having with his new roommate and other friends he has made in the dorm.
- A co-worker talks about all the activities that she does with her young children. You wonder how she is able to find the time to finish her work and spend so much time with her kids, especially because you see yourself as a neglectful parent.
- Your relationship partner has been spending a great deal of time lately with a new friend and has expressed repeatedly how much he likes this friend.

In situations like those described in the scenarios above, it is normal to experience feelings of anger or sadness. Maybe we even feel a little bit envious or resentful. **Jealousy** has been defined as, "a protective reaction to a perceived threat to a valued relationship, arising from a situation in which the partner's involvement with an activity and/or another person is contrary to the jealous person's definition of their relationship" (Hansen 1985, 713). It is important to point out that this definition addresses the fact that jealousy can be experienced in various types of relationships, not just romantic, and can be induced by various issues or situations.

Types of Jealousy in Relationships

Jennifer Bevan and Wendy Samter (2004) used this definition as the foundation for their study, which examined six different types of jealousy, three that are experienced as a result of the type of the relationship, and three that are based on the issues experienced between partners. The types identified in this study include: (1) friend jealousy, (2) family jealousy, (3) romantic jealousy, (4) power jealousy, (5) intimacy jealousy, and (6) activity jealousy. The first two types, **friend jealousy** and **family jealousy,** are typically the result of an individual's relationship with another friend or family member. In this situation, we often become frustrated and perceive them as being "taken" away from us. **Romantic jealousy** is also the result of a partner's relationship with another person, and is associated with perceived intimacy between two people. Consider the following example:

Justin noticed that his wife, Nicole, had been spending more and more time at work. One evening, he decided to surprise her by taking dinner to her office. As he approached her office, he noticed that she was engrossed in a quiet conversation with an attractive man. Angry, Justin stormed out of the building without saying a word. For the next several days, Justin was very curt in his conversations with Nicole. Finally she asked him what was bothering him. Justin exploded, "So who is the new guy at work? And why didn't you tell me that you're spending so much time together?" Nicole was dumbfounded and responded, "I don't know what you're talking about." Justin mentioned that he had stopped by to bring her dinner and had seen them talking quietly in her office. Finally, Nicole understood who he was referring to and responded, "That was Marcus, the consultant who was brought in from Seattle to help with this project. He saw the picture of the kids on my desk and wanted to talk about how much he's missing his own kids since he's been away from them for the past two weeks."

In this scenario, romantic jealousy caused Justin to perceive a potential relationship between Nicole and her co-worker. It should come as no surprise that this type of jealousy has received the most attention in literature. Therefore, many of the studies discussed in this section will refer to romantic jealousy.

The last three types of jealousy examined by Bevan and Samter (2004) involve issues experienced by relational partners. **Power jealousy** is often associated with perceptions that a partner's other relationships or obligations are viewed as more important than your relationship with the person. If a friend changes plans and cannot spend time with you, or decides to invite others to go to the game with the two of you, you may question whether outside issues are more important to her than your relationship. **Activity jealousy** emerges when our relational partner dedicates time to various hobbies or interests. Have you ever become frustrated by the amount of attention that a friend dedicates to PlayStation, fraternity or sorority activities, or sports? In these instances, the activities are perceived as a threat to your relationship. Finally, **intimacy jealousy** is the result of the exchange of intimate or private information that a partner may share with a third party, someone not in the relationship. Suppose your significant other reveals to his best friend that he is undergoing a series of medical tests, but says nothing to you. Your discovery of the "concealed" information results in feelings of intimacy jealousy. Later, you may discover that your partner simply did not want you to worry, and decided not to tell you until the results of the test were returned.

Why Does Jealousy Occur?

What causes us to experience feelings of jealousy? Laura Guerrero and Peter Anderson (1998) suggest that there are at least six jealousy-related goals. An extensive body of research on this topic has concluded that individuals evoke or suppress feelings of jealousy to obtain a variety of goals or objectives in their personal relationships. In the next sections we examine the six jealousy-related goals identified by researchers.

An attempt to make yourself appear more "attractive" than the competition may just make you look insecure.

Maintain the Primary Relationship.   First, we become jealous in situations where we wish to maintain the primary relationship. Specifically, we are concerned with preserving the relationship. When individuals are interested in maintaining a current relationship, they will often compare themselves to a rival and try to appear more rewarding to their partner by compensating for any perceived shortcomings (Guerrero and Afifi 1999). Making oneself appear more "attractive" than the competition (also referred to as **compensatory restoration,** see table 8.1) may be an effective maintenance strategy—up to a point. Making incessant comparisons to rivals may cause your partner to perceive you as being desperate or insecure.

Preserving One's Self-Esteem.

A second goal associated with jealousy is focused on preserving one's self-esteem. This jealousy goal is concerned with maintaining one's pride, and with feeling good about oneself. Individuals who are concerned about protecting their self-esteem rarely seek out circumstances that may threaten how they view themselves (Kernis 1995). Therefore, it comes as no surprise that the more an individual is focused on preserving his or her self-esteem, the more likely he or she is to avoid or deny jealous situations (Guerrero and Afifi 1999). Since jealousy has a negative connotation in our culture and is related to perceptions of "weakness," it makes sense that these individuals are less likely to question or scrutinize their partners' behavior or to communicate jealous feelings.

Reducing Uncertainty about the Relationship.

Another goal of jealousy is to reduce uncertainty about the relationship. The purpose of this type of jealousy is to help an individual learn where one stands in the relationship, predict the future of the relationship, and understand how the other partner perceives the relationship. This was the only goal found to predict open and non-aggressive communication between partners (Guerrero and Afifi 1999). If the purpose of jealousy is to reduce uncertainty and learn more about the partner, it makes sense that open and direct communication are essential to accomplishing this goal.

Reducing Uncertainty about a Rival Relationship.

A fourth goal involves reducing uncertainty about a rival relationship. This jealousy goal determines the threat of the competition, or how serious the rival relationship is. Individuals who focus on this goal often resort to indirect strategies, such as spying, checking up on the partner, or questioning the rival about the situation (Guerrero and Afifi 1999). They may do this to save face with their partners so they are not perceived as "jealous" people.

Re-assess the Relationship.

When individuals are questioning the status of a relationship, they may use jealousy in an attempt to re-assess the relationship. This goal is concerned with comparing the cost with the benefits associated with the relationship. When analyzing this goal, Guerero and Afifi (1999) found that individuals typically engage in indirect strategies such as avoidance, distancing, or making the partner feel jealous. When we are evaluating a relationship, we typically step back to reconsider our own perceptions of autonomy (see our discussion of the relationship stages of coming apart in Chapter Ten). Therefore, it may make sense to give the relationship space.

Restoring Equity through Retaliation.

Do you know anyone who purposely evoked jealousy to get back at someone or to make his or her partner feel bad? The last goal of jealousy refers to this idea of restoring equity through retaliation. The purpose of evoking this type of jealousy response is to show the partner what it is like to experience negative emotions and to hurt the person as retribution for something the partner has done.

There are clearly a number of different reasons that relationship partners attempt to evoke jealousy responses from their partners. Not surprisingly, experiencing heightened amounts of jealousy in relationships negatively affects relationship satisfaction (Guerrero and Eloy 1992). Thus, it is important for you to understand the reasons why we evoke feelings of jealousy in others and, at the same time, to refrain from using tactics or strategies that cause others to feel jealous.

Characteristics Associated with Jealousy

Researchers have examined many questions associated with jealousy, including: How does someone become jealous? What types of relationships are more likely to evoke jealousy? What are the results of feeling jealous? Studies have revealed that psychological predictors of jealousy are low levels of self-esteem and feelings of insecurity (Mcintosh 1989). Another study found that jealousy is more likely to occur in relationships of shorter duration (for less than one year) than in those of longer duration (more than one year) (Knox, Zusman, Mabon, and Shriver 1999). What conditions are most likely to elicit jealous reactions? A 1999 study (Knox et al.) found that talking to or about a previous partner is the action or topic that is most likely to evoke jealousy. So are you guilty of attempting to make others feel jealous? Complete the Evoking Jealousy Scale on the next page to help you identify your own tendencies.

Gender Differences and Jealousy

Studies have found no significant differences between males and females with regard to one gender being more likely to emerge as a primary source of jealousy (Knox, Zusman, Mabon, and Shriver 1999). Further, no significant sex differences have been found with regard to the frequency, duration, or intensity of jealousy (Pines and Friedman 1998). However, while males and females do not necessarily differ in their amount of expressed jealousy, research has shown that they do experience jealousy for different reasons, or as the result of the specific characteristics associated with the threat. For example, males are more likely to become jealous as a result of sexual infidelity, whereas females become more jealous over emotional infidelity (Buss et al. 1992). Recent studies have found that, regardless of biological sex, the reactions to different types of jealousy are similar for males and females (Dijkstar and Buunk 2004). That is, emotional infidelity typically evoked responses of anxiety, worry, distrust, and suspicion, while responses to sexual infidelity were associated with feelings of sadness, rejection, anger, and betrayal. The physical or social attractiveness of the perceived competition also plays a role in determining the amount of jealousy experienced. Women experience more jealousy in response to a physically attractive threat, while men become more jealous when the threat is perceived as being more socially dominant (Dijkstra and Buunk 1998). Evolutionary psychologists argue the reason for this gender difference is due to the fact that our society typically rates a female's value in a relationship as determined by her physical attractiveness, whereas the relationship value of males is often evaluated by their status or dominance (Townsend and Levy 1990).

© vgstudio, 2007, Shutterstock.

The attractiveness of perceived competition plays a role in determining the amount of jealousy experienced.

Evoking Jealousy Scale

Directions: Rate how often you have attempted the following items using the scale below:

1 = Never
2 = Almost never
3 = Sometimes
4 = Neutral
5 = Often
6 = Almost always
7 = Always

"I have tried to make my partner jealous by . . ."

_____ 1. Dancing with someone else while he or she is around.

_____ 2. Dressing nicely when going out.

_____ 3. Telling him or her someone flirted with me.

_____ 4. Telling him or her I found a person attractive.

_____ 5. Acting like it does not matter what he or she does.

_____ 6. Pretending to be interested in another person.

_____ 7. Talking to an ex-boyfriend or ex-girlfriend.

_____ 8. Wearing clothing that highlights my features.

_____ 9. Spending time doing activities without him or her.

_____ 10. Talking about activities I have been involved in.

_____ 11. Doing things he or she wants to do, but cannot.

_____ 12. Going out and not inviting him or her.

_____ 13. Talking with his or her friends.

_____ 14. Talking about a person of the opposite sex.

_____ 15. Having a person of the opposite sex answer the phone.

_____ 16. Telling him or her how much fun I had with a person of the opposite sex.

_____ 17. Having an opposite sex friend stop by when he or she is there.

_____ 18. Flirting with members of the opposite sex.

Source: From "Relationship Orientation, Jealousy, and Equity: An Examination of Jealousy Evoking and Positive Communication Responses" by J.L. Cayanus and M. Booth-Butterfield, _Communication Quarterly,_ 2004, 52, 237–250. Reprinted by permission of Taylor & Francis Ltd., www.informaworld.com.

Coping with Jealousy

The way people initially express feelings of jealousy to a partner will ultimately influence how the partner responds. Stephen Yoshimura (2004) found that responses such as integrative communication and negative affect expression (e.g., crying) were perceived as evoking positive emotional responses by the partner (see Table 8.1). In other words, expressing your feelings openly and directly with your partner and appearing hurt by the threat produces positive emotional and behavior outcomes. This same study also found that negative emotional outcomes were more likely to produce violent behavior and manipulation attempts by the other partner. See Table 8.1 for a complete list of the ways people respond to feelings of jealousy.

Table 8.1 Communicative Responses to Jealousy

Strategy	Definition/Examples
1. Negative affect expression	Nonverbal expressions of jealousy-related affect that the partner can see. *Examples:* acting anxious when with the partner, appearing hurt, wearing "displeasure" on face, crying in front of the partner
2. Integrative communication	Direct, nonaggressive communication about jealousy with the partner. *Examples:* disclosing jealous feelings to the partner, asking the partner probing questions, trying to reach an understanding with the partner, reassuring the partner that we can "work it out"
3. Distributive communication	Direct, aggressive communication about jealousy with the partner. *Examples:* accusing the partner of being unfaithful, being sarcastic or rude toward the partner, arguing with the partner, bringing up the issue over and over again to "bombard" the partner
4. Active distancing	Indirect, aggressive means of communicating jealousy to the partner. *Examples:* giving the partner the "silent treatment," storming out of the room, giving the partner cold or dirty looks, withdrawing affection and sexual favors
5. Avoidance/denial	Indirect, nonagressive communication that focuses on avoiding the jealousy-invoking issue, situation, or partner. *Examples:* denying jealous feelings when confronted by the partner, pretending to be unaffected by the situation, decreasing contact with the partner, avoiding jealousy-evoking situations
6. Violent communication/threats	Threatening or actually engaging in physical violence against the partner. *Examples:* threatening to harm the partner if they continue to see the rival, scaring the partner by acting as if they were about to hit the partner, roughly pulling the partner away from the rival, pushing or slapping the partner

(continued)

Table 8.1 Communicative Responses to Jealousy

Strategy	Definition/Examples
7. Signs of possession	Publicly displaying the relationship to others so they know the partner is "taken." *Examples:* putting an arm around the partner and saying "he or she is taken," constantly introducing the partner as a "girl/boy friend," telling potential rival of plans to be married, kissing the partner in front of potential rival
8. Derogating competitors	Making negative comments about potential rivals to the partner and to others. *Examples:* "bad mouthing" the rival in front of the partner and his or her friends, expressing disbelief that anyone would be attracted to the rival
9. Relationship threats	Threatening to terminate or de-escalate the primary relationship or to be unfaithful. *Examples:* threatening to end the relationship if the partner continues to see the rival, threatening infidelity
10. Surveillance/restriction	Behavioral strategies designed to find out about or interfere with the rival relationship. *Examples:* spying or checking up on the partner, looking through the partner's belongings for evidence of a rival relationship, pressing the redial button to see who the partner called last, restricting the partner's access to rivals at parties
11. Compensatory restoration	Behavior aimed at improving the primary relationship and/or making oneself more desirable. *Examples:* sending the partner gifts or flowers, keeping the house cleaned and nice, trying to present oneself as better than the rival, trying to appear more physically attractive
12. Manipulation attempts	Moves to induce negative feelings in the partner and/or shift responsibility for communicating about the problem to the partner. *Examples:* flirting with others to make the partner jealous, inducing guilt, calling the partner's "bluff" by daring him to break-up and go off with the rival, bring the rival's name up in conversation to check for a reaction, asking a friend to talk to the partner about the situation
13. Rival contacts	Direct communication with the rival about the jealousy situation, rival relationship, or partner. *Examples:* telling the rival to stop seeing the partner, informing the rival that the partner is "already in a relationship," saying something "mean" to the rival, asking the rival about the relationship without revealing one's identity, making negative comments about the partner in order to discourage the rival from pursuing the partner
14. Violent behavior	Directing violence toward objects, either in private or in the presence of others. *Examples:* slamming doors, breaking dishes, throwing the partner's possessions

Source: Adapted from Guerrero and Anderson 1998; Guerrero, Anderson, Jorgensen, Spitzberg, and Eloy 1995.

While we have explored some of the reasons for becoming jealous and have proposed some methods for managing situations that cause the green-eyed monster to emerge, let us take a moment to consider the role that perceived influence and power can play in causing us to experience envy.

INTERPERSONAL POWER AND AGGRESSION

A possible factor contributing to our tendency to encounter jealousy in relationships may be explained by the interpersonal power perceived by relational partners. In this section, we will take a closer look at the potential implications of power in relationships and explore power's relationship to verbal aggression and violence. **Power** can be defined as one's ability to influence others to behave in ways they normally might not. Popular television shows such as *Super Nanny* and *Nanny 911* often identify power as the key issue affecting families. What types of power impact our relationships with others?

Types of Power

French and Raven (1960) identified five types of power that individuals typically use when they are attempting to influence others. The five classic power bases are explained below.

Reward Power.   **Reward power** is based on a person's perception that the source of power can provide rewards. Example: *I'll clean up the apartment and maybe my roommate will invite me to go with him on the ski trip with his family this weekend.*

Coercive Power.   **Coercive power** focuses on the perceived ability of the source to punish or to enact negative consequences. Example: *I have to finish this report today or I know my boss will make me come in this weekend.*

Legitimate Power.   **Legitimate power** is centered on the perception that the source has authority because of a particular role that she plays in the relationship or a title that she holds. Example: *Because I'm the mommy, and I said so.*

Referent Power.   **Referent power** is based on a person's respect, identification and attraction to the source. Example: *No matter how ridiculous I feel, I will dress up in a costume and go to this Halloween party because I am really attracted to you and want you to like me.*

Expert Power.   **Expert power** is grounded in the perception that the source possesses knowledge, expertise, or skills in a particular area. Example: *I will listen to what she says about our household budget because she is the financial wizard in the family.*

In the role of a parent, one holds legitimate power in the relationship.

French and Raven propose that it is the perception of the receiver of the message that is the key to analyzing power. Consider our earlier discussions about interpersonal communication in Chapters One and Two. We stated that effective interpersonal communication is receiver-based. Thus, it is important to consider the receiver's perception of the source to predict future interactions. But do individuals have power if we do not give it to them? Based on the important role that receiver perception plays in the communication process, probably not. Consider the following scenario:

Alan had very little respect for his mother. At thirteen years old, he was completely out of control. He skipped school, ignored his mother's rules, and even hit his mother on several occasions when she attempted to discipline him. Finally, his mother had reached the breaking point. One night she caught Alan doing drugs with his friends in the basement. She reported Alan to the authorities and hoped that it would help him get back on track. But his misbehavior continued.

In this instance, Alan's mother should have legitimate power over him. However, his behavior is an obvious indicator that he does not perceive her to have any power in the relationship. Even when his mother attempts to utilize coercive power by calling the police, it does nothing to change Alan's perception. His inability to view his mother as having reward, coercive, or legitimate power even results in Alan's occasional use of physical violence. If you do not perceive your relational partner as having the power, then it is unlikely that you would comply with any requests he or she makes.

In Chapter Six we discussed the role of attraction in interpersonal relationships. Understanding the relationship between attraction and power may help explain why some influence attempts are successful whereas others fail. Depending on the perceived power base, receivers will alter their perceptions of the source's attractiveness and determine the level of acceptance or resistance in response to the request. Suppose your best friend uses a threat, or coercive power, in an attempt to influence you. This will typically decrease your level of perceived attraction for your friend, and chances are that you will resist their request. On the other hand, if you perceive that the friend has the power to reward you as a result of the request, it is likely that you would find them more attractive and would have minimal resistance to the request. These same principles can be applied in a variety of relationships. What if your mother told you that if you cleaned your room she would reward you with $5.00 and a trip to the movies? You would be more willing to agree to her request and you would find her to be more interpersonally attractive than if she would have said, "If you don't clean your room, you will have to pay me $5.00 to do it for you, and you'll be grounded from the movies for the next week." Threats and coercive behavior typically breed resentment and result in higher levels of resistance.

Relationship between Power and Interpersonal Influence

To better understand the impact of power in our decisions of whether to comply with requests made in our interpersonal relationships, we look at the three levels of influence that can be achieved. These include compliance,

Table 8.2 Power and Impact on Levels of Influence

Types of Power	Levels of Influence		
	Compliance	Identification	Internalization
Reward	X		
Coercive	X		
Legitimate	X		
Referent	X	X	X
Expert	X	X	X

Source: Adapted from Kelman 1961; Richmond, McCroskey, and McCroskey 2005.

identification, and internalization (Kelman 1961). **Compliance** occurs when an individual agrees to a request because he can see a potential reward or punishment for doing so. This level of influence is likely to persuade someone to do something, but his motivation is typically low and the change in the behavior is usually quite temporary. When you tell your roommate that she can have your car for the weekend if she drives you to the airport and she later complies with your request, you have influenced her at the compliance level. In this example, the only reason the roommate complies with the request is to obtain a reward.

If a person decides to agree to an influence attempt because she recognizes the potential benefits of doing so, or perhaps she wishes to establish a relationship with the source, then **identification** has occurred. A student agrees to his teacher's recommendation that he take honors level courses next semester to help prepare him for college instead of "cruising" in the regular classes with his friends. In this instance, individuals are typically more motivated to comply because they agree with the source's goals, interests and values. The last level of influence, **internalization,** is employed when an individual adopts a behavior because it is internally rewarding. In other words, it feels like the right thing to do. This type of influence is successful because the person sees the requested behavior as fitting within his or her existing value system. The individual agrees to the behavior because he intrinsically believes it should be done, not just because someone told him to do so. An example of this might be a spouse who takes on the responsibility of extra household or childcare duties in order to assist a partner who is experiencing a difficult time at work. In this instance, the person agrees to the request because of the value placed on family and the level of commitment made to the relationship. Table 8.2 summarizes the level of influence that can be achieved as a result of each of the five types of power.

Power versus Dominance in Relationships

What is the difference between power and dominance? Burgoon and Dillman (1995) argue, "Because power is broadly defined as the ability to exercise influence by possessing one or more power bases, dominance is but one means of many for expressing power" (65). In other words, power is the potential to influence another's behavior, whereas **dominance** is a mechanism typically associated with attempts to express power and take control in a relationship. What is the relationship between talking and influence? One study found that the more an individual talks, the more opportunities he has to gain influence over others (Daly, McCroskey, and Richmond 1977). A separate study suggests that managing what individuals talk about and "controlling the floor" are perceived as forms of interpersonal dominance or control (Palmer 1989).

VERBAL AGGRESSION

Perhaps one of the most vivid examples of verbal aggression in action can be witnessed in the movie and book, *The Devil Wears Prada*. As she attempts to navigate her way in the fashion magazine industry, Andrea Sachs learns that dealing with verbal attacks from her boss and co-workers is part of the "game," and something she must endure if she wishes to pursue a career in the field. She encounters both direct and indirect influence attempts. Miranda, her boss, prefers an influence style that attacks Andy's self-esteem. She bluntly tells Andy that she has "no style" and publicly criticizes Andy's work in front of her colleagues. To make matters worse, Emily, a co-worker, refers to Andy as being "hopeless." Nigel, the photographer who befriends Andy, eventually convinces her that she needs to change in order to make it in the business. He provides her with logical facts and arguments containing tips to help her succeed in the industry. It becomes apparent that Nigel's approach of presenting arguments was much more effective in helping Andy comply, and ultimately succeed, than the aggressive approach used by Miranda and Emily.

Attempts to gain influence over others are often made in one of two ways. First, rational arguments can be presented for why compliance should occur. A second strategy is to attack the other person's self-esteem or character. As you can see, one of these strategies is positive, and the other is negative and potentially damaging to relationships. So why do some individuals choose to present rational arguments while others choose to attack? The explanation rests in the distinction between communication traits known as argumentativeness and verbal aggression. **Argumentativeness** refers to the extent to which an individual challenges a position or issue (Infante and Rancer 1982). A person can question or debate whether they should comply with a request without directly addressing the personal characteristics of the person making the request. When a request is addressed with a response that attacks the self-confidence, chararacter, and/or intelligence of another person, **verbal aggressiveness** is being used (Infante and Wigley 1986). Suppose your best friend asks you to let him borrow your car to drive to a concert, but you do not wish to comply with his request. An argumentative person might respond with statements such as, "It's probably not a good idea, since you aren't insured to drive my car. Besides, I don't want to rack up miles on it since it's a lease." The request is addressed with logical, rational points. An example of a verbally aggressive response might be, "Are you stupid? Why in the world would you be crazy enough to think that I would trust you with my car?" In this instance, the person's intelligence, sanity, and trustworthiness have been attacked. Examples of verbally aggressive messages might include attacks on one's character or competence, teasing or ridiculing, or even making threats or jokes about another's appearance.

Loreen Olson suggests that there are four levels of aggression that are experienced in our interpersonal encounters (2004). **Low aggression** is characterized by yelling, crying, refusing to talk, or stomping out of the room. **Moderate aggression** involves more intense acts of verbal aggression such as verbal insults, swearing at the other, and indirect physical displays of anger such as kicking, hitting, throwing inanimate objects, or threatening to engage in these behaviors. Next, **high aggression** refers to intensive face threatening, and verbal belittling, and direct physical contact with the other person in the form of slapping, shoving, or pushing. The most severe level, **severe aggression,** includes intense verbal abuse and threats and involves physical attacks that include kicking, biting, punching, hitting with an object, raping, and using a weapon. Not only can verbally aggressive acts occur before relational conflicts, they occur as a consequence to partner aggression and also serve to escalate the conflict. In relationships, struggles for power and control are often at the heart of reciprocated and escalating aggression between partners (Olson 2004).

While our first tendency is to assume that aggression and violence are often restricted to close relationships with romantic partners or family members, this is not the case. Researchers have examined their presence and impact in a variety of relational contexts.

Verbal Aggression in the Classroom

Since verbal aggression is perceived as a negative communication behavior, it should come as no surprise that researchers have identified several negative outcomes associated with teachers who use words to attack students in the classroom. Students who perceive their instructors as being verbally aggressive report that they are less motivated in that class (Myers and Rocca 2001). Also, they evaluate the teacher as being less competent and as behaving inappropriately (Martin, Weber, and Burant 1997). In an environment where a student fears becoming the target of verbal abuse, less learning occurs (Myers 2002) and the chances are greater that students will choose to avoid the situation by skipping class (Rocca 2004). When you consider that aggressiveness fosters a negative learning experience, the power of a teacher's communication becomes apparent. The same principles hold true in other instructional contexts. In the movie *Kicking and Screaming*, Phil (Will Farrell) volunteers to coach his son's soccer team. In the beginning of the film, Phil's coaching style and communication are patient and nurturing—he even goes so far as to bring the boys finches as rewards for their hard work. Eventually, Phil's competitive nature emerges, and his interactions with the boys and their parents become verbally aggressive. At one point he taunts a young player who misses a goal by screaming at him in front of the entire team, "You've just been served a plate of humiliation!" While the purpose of these athletic experiences is to provide training, the aggressive communication could have serious negative implications.

Workplace Bullying

Another context that has been the target of research on verbal aggression is the workplace. Because it is likely that all of you either have been employed,

The vast majority of workplace bullies are bosses.

© Jaimie Duplass, 2007, Shutterstock.

or will be at some point in your life, it is important to understand the potential for verbal aggression and emotional abuse to occur in this environment. Approximately ninety percent of adults report that they have been a victim of workplace bullying at some point during their professional career (Hornstein 1996). Workplace bullying, intimidation, employee humiliation and organizational manipulation are all considered to be **Employee Emotional Abuse (EEA).** EEA is defined as repeated, targeted, unwelcome, destructive communication by more powerful individuals toward less empowered individuals in the organization, which results in emotional harm (Lutgen-Sandvik 2003). In February 2006, a Vallejo, California high school teacher agreed to an out-of-court settlement after suing the state administrator and other district officials for alleged harassment and discrimination. The school district agreed to pay the teacher $225,000, to compensate her for the emotional distress she experienced at work.

So who is most likely to engage in bullying at work? The results may surprise you. According to the United States Hostile Workplace Survey in 2000:

- Women comprised fifty percent of the bullies.
- Women bullies target other women an overwhelming eighty-four percent of the time; men bullies target women in sixty-nine percent of the cases; women are the majority (seventy-seven percent) of targets.
- The vast majority of bullies are bosses (eighty-one percent); they have the power to terminate their targets at will.
- Approximately forty-one percent of targets were diagnosed with depression.
- More than eighty percent of targets reported effects that prevented them from being productive at work (severe anxiety, lost concentration, sleeplessness, etc.).
- Post-Traumatic Stress Disorder (PTSD) symptoms afflicted thirty-one percent of the women who experienced workplace bullying; twenty-one percent of the men who had been bullied reported PTSD symptoms.

OBSESSIVE RELATIONAL INTRUSION

In some cases, verbal aggression and violence have been linked to instances of obsessive relational intrusion (ORI). William Cupach and Brian Spitzberg (1998) developed the concept of ORI to address the interpersonal aspect of stalking. All of us have heard stories in the news of celebrities who have been stalked: prior to his death in 1980, John Lennon was stalked by Mark Chapman; tennis champion Monica Seles was stabbed by a stalker who was a fan of her opponent, Steffi Graf. Cupach and Spitzberg (1998) distinguish ORI from stalking in the sense that ORI occurs out of a desire to initiate a relationship, whereas stalking often has a purpose of harming, and possibly even destroying, another person. The communication that takes place in ORI is typical of most relationships, the exchange of messages via phone calls, letters, or gifts. Many of these communicative behaviors are an attempt to either initiate or escalate a relationship; however, one person often becomes jealous and sometimes even possessive.

Obsessive relational intrusion is defined as the "repeated and unwanted pursuit and invasion of one's sense of physical or symbolic privacy by another person, either stranger or acquaintance, who desires and/or presumes an intimate relationship" (Cupach and Spitzberg 1998, 235). In a study of 341 college students, nineteen percent of the men and ten percent of the women indicated that they had obsessively pursued another person using various methods and strategies. As far as gender differences in the types of tactics used to communicate an interest in another, there were no significant differences found. Examples of the most frequently reported tactics by both men and women include the following:

- Sending/communicating unwanted messages
- Expressing exaggerated affection
- Giving or sending unwanted gifts
- Monitoring the other person's actions
- Intruding in the interactions of the other person
- Intruding on the other person's friends and/or family
- Covertly obtaining information about the person

Perhaps as you read this description of ORI, you may discover that you or someone you know has experienced this dark aspect of interpersonal relationships. To understand how victims of ORI manage these unwanted advances, Spitzberg and Cupach (2001) conducted an analysis of the coping strategies identified across a variety of studies. A summary of these coping strategies is presented in Table 8.3 on page 232.

Unfortunately, relational obsession and stalking are not restricted to face-to-face interactions. As more and more people use the Internet as a forum for initiating and building relationships, it is important to understand the potential dangers associated with these types of relationships. Cyberstalking refers to harassment, or obsessive communication, via the Internet. Several television news shows have recently conducted in-depth investigations regarding this phenomenon, focusing on the use of online communication by pedophiles to form relationships with children and minors. It is important to note that cyberstalkers often obtain personal information about their targets that is disclosed on the Internet and may use this information to harm others.

While you may be thinking that obsessive relationships are the result of posting personal information to online dating sites, consider the information that is posted on a variety of social networking websites that are gaining in popularity. More than 100 million people engage in interactions via online social communities where personal information is exchanged. Two of the most popular sites among college students and teenagers are MySpace and Facebook. Why have these online sites gained so much popularity in recent years? A study conducted at Carnegie Mellon University by students revealed that individuals join Facebook for several reasons: (1) as a result of peer pressure by friends encouraging them to

© 6454881632, 2007, Shutterstock.

As more relationships are initiated via the Internet, it is important to understand the potential dangers.

Table 8.3	**Summary of Obsessive Relational Intrusion Coping Strategies**
Coping Strategy	**Examples**
Moving inward	Ignore or deny the problem and hope it goes away
	Blame yourself
	Engage in self-destructive means to escape (e.g., alcohol, drugs, suicide)
Moving outward	Seek sympathy from others
	Seek social support from friends and/or family
	Seek legal assistance (e.g., police, attorney)
Moving away	Control interactions with the person (e.g., maintain a closed body position, avoid eye contact)
	Use verbal avoidance or escape tactics (e.g., make excuses)
	Restrict accessibility (e.g., change schedule, switch work shifts, obtain caller ID, change email address, use pseudonyms online)
Moving toward	Diminish seriousness of the situation (e.g., joke or tease the pursuer)
	Employ problem-solving tactics or negotiation
	Mutually negotiate relationship definition (e.g., discuss your preferences for the type of relationship you would like with the other)
Moving against	Issue verbal warnings/threats
	Build a legal case (e.g., save emails, letters, keep a record of calls)
	Use protective responses (e.g., email blocker, restraining order)

Source: Reprinted from *Aggression and Violent Behavior, Volume 8*, B.H. Spitzberg and W.R. Cupach, "What Mad Pursuit? Obsessive Relational Intrusion and Stalking Related Phenomena", 345–375, Copyright 2003 with permission from Elsevier.

create an online profile, (2) to maintain relationships at a distance, (3) to form new relationships, or (4) to get assistance with classes (Govani and Pashley 2005). While students report that they turn to these sites to assist in initiating and maintaining relationships, the harsh reality is that online behaviors have actually damaged many relationships. Incidences of students posting pictures depicting themselves in sexually provocative ways, or while engaging in illegal or excessive drinking have prompted university officials to use sites such as Facebook to identify improper and illegal behavior. Table 8.4 highlights some of the ways in which colleges and universities have used the Facebook site to monitor and discipline students.

While it is important to be aware of the potential dangers and risks of exchanging and revealing personal information online, the more critical issue involves learning how to manage and use these new communication mediums appropriately. In Chapter Fourteen we present a detailed overview of computer-mediated communication (CMC) research and provide suggestions for using CMC effectively and appropriately as a means of social networking. It is important to be selective in the information that you choose to share via CMC. Also, realize that people can and do lie about themselves in both face to face and computer mediated contexts. These issues will be discussed in much greater depth in Chapter Fourteen.

Table 8.4	**Facebook in the News**
April 2005	University of Mississippi students were threatened with a civil lawsuit for leading a Facebook group that devoted their desire to sleep with a certain female professor. They made a public apology. (*www.dukechronicle.com* 03/08/2006)
May 2005	LSU swimmers were kicked off the team after athletics officials discovered they belonged to a Facebook group that posts disparaging comments about swim coaches (usa.com-athletes sound over athletes Facebook time, 03/08/2006)
September 2005	Northern Kentucky men's basketball coach found Facebook photos of his underage athletes with alcohol. They were let off with a warning. (usa.com-athletes sound over athletes Facebook time, 03/08/2006)
October 2005	North Carolina State University resident advisor reported nine of her students for underage drinking when she found evidence in one resident's Facebook photo album (*www.dukechronicle.com* 03/08/2006)
	Penn State University police used Facebook as a tool to identify students who rushed the football field after the Ohio University game. (*http://www.thepost.ohiou.edu*)
December 2005	Florida State athletes were given ten days to cleanse their profiles. (usa.com-athletes sound over athletes facebook time, 03/08/2006)
	Loyola University of Chicago athletic director forbids his athletes to join to protect them from gamblers or sexual predators who can learn more about them (usa.com-athletes sound over athletes facebook time, 03/08/2006)
	Colorado athletes were accused of sending a racially threatening Facebook message to a fellow athlete. Campus police issued tickets for harassment. (usa.com-athletes sound over athletes facebook time, 03/08/2006)
January 2006	Kentucky athletic director told athletes to scrub their profiles of anything that could shed a bad light on the school. (www.usatoday.com-athletes sound over athletes Facebook time, 03/08/2006)
February 2006	Students at the University of Kansas living in the scholarship hall were written up for pictures uploaded to Facebook.com that indicated a party violating the alcohol policy. (Kansan.com)

SUMMARY

While the topics discussed in this chapter may not be particularly pleasant, it is important to address their role in our communication with others. Not all relationships are enjoyable. To use the analogy of a roller coaster, virtually all relationships experience ups and downs. In this chapter we have discussed the concept of interpersonal deception and explored the potential impact of telling lies on the future of our relationships. In addition, we discussed the potential embarrassment that pops up from time to time and causes us to become "red-faced" in our interactions. In keeping with color analogies, relationships often encounter the "green-eyed monster" when jealousy emerges and causes us to respond in ways that we might not otherwise. We identified power and influence as a potential source of jealousy and as something that can affect our interactions with others. The distinction between argumentativeness and aggressiveness was made, as we offered a glimpse into the ugly side of power, when it results in verbal attack against others. Finally, we discussed the concept of obsession in relationships and presented the concept of obsessive relational intrusion. We concluded this discussion by addressing the dark side of relationships and computer mediated communication. While at first glance social networking sites like Facebook and Myspace may seem beneficial, there is a dark side to these as well.

Oftentimes we hear the phrase, "Communication is the key to success." The purpose of this chapter was to introduce a few communication situations in which communication was not part of the solution, but was, in fact, part of the problem. It is important to remember that communication is a tool that can be used for good or evil purposes. It is up to us to understand how to effectively use communication to accomplish our goals and to become more competent in our interactions with others. By offering you a glimpse into the "dark side" of communication, it is our hope that your relationships will encounter more "ups" than "downs."

APPLICATIONS

Discussion Questions

A. Most people would agree that there are times when it is okay to deceive a friend, family member, or romantic partner. Have you ever been in a particular situation where you felt it was okay to deceive someone? Describe the situation and your reasons.

B. What are some ways to make sure that your partner does not feel jealous in regard to your romantic relationship? What are some suggestions for dealing with someone that often reports jealous feelings?

C. What is the best way to influence a friend or family member to change a problematic behavior? What type of persuasion and social influence tactics could you employ to get the friend or family member to change? Describe the tactics that you would use and those that you would avoid.

D. Provide three examples of types of information that should not be disclosed on social networking sites such as Facebook and Myspace.

REFERENCES

Berlyne, D. E. 1969. Laughter, humor and play. In G. Lindzey and E. Aronson (Eds.), *Handbook of Social Psychology*, Vol. 3, (795–813). Reading, Mass.: Addison-Wesley.

Bevan, J. L., and Samter, W. 2004. Toward a broader conceptualization of jealousy in close relationships: Two exploratory studies. *Communication Studies, 55,* 14–28.

Buller, D. B., and J. K. Burgoon. 1996. Interpersonal deception theory. *Communication Theory, 6,* 203–242.

Burgoon, J. K., D. B. Buller, L. K. Guerrero, W. Afifi, and C. M. Feldman. 1996. Interpersonal deception XII: Information management dimensions underlying types of deceptive messages. *Communication Monographs, 63,* 50–69.

Burgoon, J. K., and L. Dillman. 1995. Gender, immediacy and nonverbal communication. In P. J. Kalbfleisch and M. J. Cody (Eds.), *Gender, power, and communication in human relationships.* (63–81). Hillsdale, NJ: Lawrence Erlbaum Associates.

Buss, D. M., R. J. Larsen, D. Westen, and J. Semmelroth. 1992. Sex differences in jealousy: Evolution, physiology, and psychology. *Psychological Science, 3,* 251–255.

Camden, C., M. T. Motley, and A. Wilson. 1984. White lies in interpersonal communication: A taxonomy and preliminary investigation of social motives. *The Western Journal of Speech Communication, 48,* 309–325.

Cayanus, J. L., and M. Booth-Butterfield. 2004. Relationship orientation, jealousy, and equity: An examination of jealousy evoking and positive communication responses. *Communication Quarterly, 52,* 237–250.

Cupach, W. R., and B. H. Spitzberg. 1994. *The dark side of interpersonal communication.* Hillsdale, NJ: Lawrence Erlbaum.

———. 1998. Obsessive relational intrusion and stalking. In B. H. Spitzberg, and W. R. Cupach (Eds.), *The dark side of close relationships* (233–263). Hillsdale, NJ: Erlbaum.

Daly, J. A., J. C. McCroskey, and V. P. Richmond. 1977. Relationship between vocal activity and perception of communicators in small group interaction. *Western Journal of Speech Communication, 41,* 175–187.

DePaulo, B. M., D. A. Kasy, S. E. Kirkendale, M. M. Wyer, and J. A. Epstein. 1996. Lying in everyday life. *Journal of Personality and Social Psychology, 70,* 979–995.

Dijkstra, P., and B. P. Buunk. 1998. Jealousy as a function of rival characteristics: An evolutionary perspective. *Personality and Social Psychology Bulletin, 24,* 1158–1166.

Edelmann, R. J. 1985. Social embarrassment: An analysis of the process. *Journal of Social and Personal Relationships, 2,* 195–213.

French, J. P. R., and B. Raven. 1960. The bases of social power. In D. Cartwright and A. Zander (Eds.), *Group Dynamics* (607–623). New York: Harper and Row.

Govani, T. and H. Pashley. November 21, 2006 Student awareness of the privacy implications when using Facebook. *<http://lorrie.cranor.org/courses/fa05/tubzhlp.pdf>*

Gross, E., and G. P. Stone. 1964. Embarrassment and the analysis of role requirements. *American Journal of Sociology, 70,* 1–15.

Guerrero, L. K., and W. A. Afifi. 1999. Toward a goal-oriented approach for understanding communicative responses to jealousy. *Western Journal of Communication, 63,* 216–248.

Guerrero, L. K., and P. A. Anderson.1998. Jealousy experience and expression in romantic relationships. In P. A. Anderson and L. K. Guerrero (Eds.), *Handbook of communication and emotion* (155–188). San Diego, CA: Academic Press.

Guerrero, L. K., P. A. Anderson, P. F. Jorgensen, B. H. Spitzberg, and S. V. Eloy. 1995. Coping with the green-eyed monster: Conceptualizing and measuring communicative responses to romantic jealousy. *Western Journal of Communication, 59*, 270–304.

Guerrero, L. K. and S. V. Eloy. 1992. Relationship satisfaction and jealousy across marital types. *Communication Reports, 5*, 23–41.

Hansen, G. L. 1985. Dating jealousy among college students. *Sex Roles. 12*, 713–721.

Hornstein, H. A. 1996. *Brutal bosses and their prey. How to overcome and identify abuse in the workplace.* New York: Riverhead Books.

Infante, D. A., and A. S. Rancer. 1982. A conceptualization and measure of argumentativeness. *Journal of Personality Assessment, 46*, 72–80.

Infante, D. A., and C. J. Wigley. 1986. Verbal aggression: An interpersonal model and measure. *Communication Monographs, 53*, 61–69.

Kelman, H. C. 1961. Processes of opinion change. *Public Opinion Quarterly, 25*, 58–78.

Kernis, M. H. 1995. *Efficacy, agency and self-esteem.* New York: Plenum Press.

Knapp, M. L., and A. L. Vangelisti. 2006. Lying. In K. M. Galvin and P. J. Cooper (Eds.), *Making connections* (247–252). Los Angeles, CA: Roxbury.

Knox, D., C. Schact, J. Holt, and J. Turner. 1993. Sexual lies among university students. *College Student Journal, 27*, 269–272.

Knox, D., M. E. Zusman, L. Mabon, and L. Shriver. 1999. Jealousy in college student relationships. *College Student Journal, 33*, 328.

Lutgen-Sandvik, P. 2003. The communicative cycle of employee emotional abuse. *Management Communication Quarterly, 16*, 471–502.

Martin, M. M., K. Weber, and P. A. Burant. 1997. *Students' perceptions of a teacher's use of slang and verbal aggressiveness in a lecture: An experiment.* Paper presented at the Eastern Communication Association Convention, Baltimore, MD.

McIntosh, E. G. 1989. An investigation of romantic jealousy among black undergraduates. *Social Behavior and Personality, 17*, 135–141.

Myers, S. A. 2002. Perceived aggressive instructor communication and student state motivation, learning and satisfaction. *Communication Reports, 15*, 113–121.

Myers, S. A., and K. A. Rocca. 2001. Perceived instructor argumentativeness and verbal aggressiveness in the college classroom: Effects on student perceptions of climate, apprehension, and state motivation. *Western Journal of Communication, 65*, 113–137.

O'Hair, H. D., and M. J. Cody. 1994. Everyday deception. In W. R. Cupach and B. Spitzberg (Ed.), *The dark side of interpersonal communication* (181–213). Hillsdale, NJ: Lawrence Erlbaum Associates.

Olson, L. N. 2004. Relational control-motivated aggression: A theoretically-based typology of intimate violence. *Journal of Family Communication, 4*, 209–233.

Palmer, M. T. 1989. Controlling conversations: Turns, topics and interpersonal control. *Communication Monographs, 56*, 1–18.

Park, H. S., T. R. Levine, S. A. McCornack, K. Morrison, and M. Ferrara. 2002. How people really detect lies. *Communication Monographs, 69*, 144–157.

Pines, A. M., and A. Friedman. 1998. Gender differences in romantic jealousy. *The Journal of Social Psychology, 138*, 54–71.

Richmond, V. P., J. C. McCroskey, and L. L. McCroskey. 2005. *Organizational communication for survival, making work, work.* Boston: Allyn and Bacon.

Rocca, K. A. 2004. College student attendance: Impact of instructor immediacy and verbal aggression. *Communication Education, 53*, 185–195.

Rowatt, W. C. 1999. Lying to get a date: The effectiveness of facial physical attractiveness on the willingness to deceive prospective dating partners. *Journal of Social and Personal Relationships, 16*, 209–223.

Sattler, J. M. 1965. A theoretical, developmental, and clinical investigation of embarrassment. *Clinical Psychology Monographs, 71*, 19–59.

Spitzberg, B. H. 2006. A struggle in the dark. In K. M. Galvin and P. J. Cooper (Eds.), *Making connections* (240–246). Los Angeles, CA: Roxbury.

Spitzberg, B. H., D. J. Canary, and W. R. Cupach. 1994. A competence based approach to the study of interpersonal conflict. In D. D. Cahn (Ed.), *Conflict in personal relationships* (183–202). Hillsdale, NJ: Lawrence Erlbaum.

Spitzberg, B. H., and W. R. Cupach. 2001. Paradoxes of pursuit: Toward a relational model of stalking-related phenomena. In J. Davis (Ed.), *Stalking, stalkers and their victims: Prevention, intervention, and threat assessment.* Boca Raton, FL: CRC Press.

———. 2003. What mad pursuit? Obsessive relational intrusion and stalking related phenomena. *Aggression and Violent Behavior, 8,* 345–375.

Townsend, J. M., and G. D. Levy. 1990. Effects of potential partners' costume and physical attractiveness on sexual and partner selection. *Journal of Psychology, 124,* 371–389.

Yoshiimura, S. M. 2004. Sex differences in the contexts of extreme jealousy. *Personal Relationships, 11,* 319–328.

Zuckerman, M., and R. Driver. 1985. Telling lies: verbal and nonverbal correlates of deception. In A. Siegman and S. Feldstein (Eds.), *Multichannel integrations of nonverbal behavior,* (129–148). Hillsdale, NJ: Lawrence Erlbaum.

9

Terminating Relationships
Knowing When to Throw in the Towel

© Alex Brosa, 2007, Shutterstock.

OBJECTIVES

- Recall common reasons platonic friendships terminate
- Discuss the strengths and weaknesses of using indirect versus direct methods of terminating relationships
- Identify four common reasons romantic relationships terminate
- Describe Duck's four phases of relationship termination
- Explain Knapp's model of relationship dissolution. Describe each stage of coming apart and offer an example of typical communication that occurs in each stage
- Explain the five tactics used during relationship disengagement
- Identify several strategies you can employ to "remain friends" with ex-romantic partners
- Offer examples of strategies individuals can use to survive relationship dissolution

KEY TERMS

social exchange theory	equity theory	positive tone messages
indirect methods	intrapsychic phase	de-escalation messages
direct methods	dyadic phase	withdrawal/avoidance
infidelity	social phase	tactics
commitment	grave dressing phase	justification tactics
dissimilarity	differentiating	negative identity
outside pressure	circumscribing	management
self determination	stagnating	closure
theory	avoiding	granting forgiveness
fundamental	terminating	self-forgiveness
attribution error		reframing

OVERVIEW

From the old "Greensleeves" (Alas, my love, you do me wrong to cast me off discourteously . . .) to gleeful songs like "Already Gone," from most of Garth Brooks' repertoire to rock songs like Hoobastank's "The Reason," we are as concerned with the end as with the beginning. Romantic relationships are hardly exclusive; throughout life, relationships of different forms will be left as closed books. How?

We have discussed how our interpersonal relationships are initiated, maintained, and, in some instances, how they turn dark. In this chapter, we turn to the process of relationship disengagement for all types of relationships. Not surprisingly, the research, like Neal Sedaka's song, notes that "Breaking up is hard to do," and usually results in pain for one or both partners. Throughout this chapter, we examine the most common reasons for ending both platonic and romantic relationships. We also take an in-depth look at research involving both potentially aggravating and mitigating strategies used by individuals in relationship termination. We then face the aftermath of relationship disengagement, exploring suggestions for surviving relationship disengagement and ultimately moving on.

TERMINATING FRIENDSHIPS

Friendships are some of the most enduring relationships we have. There are friendships that we have had since youth with a shelf life of "forever." There are other friends who tend to drift in and out of our lives like last season's shoes. Why do some friendships tend to outlast others? Often, friendships are forged from commonalities in our life. For example, we meet certain people in a class who live in the same dorm, have the same major, work at the same job, share the same religion or social group, or share the same enemy or mutual friend. Friendships may terminate because the very thing that brought them together no longer exists. People move away, change jobs, or move on to a different life stage (i.e., marriage, children, etc.) and no longer share the proximity and closeness that once protected the relationship. The *Friends* are all singles in New York; the *Desperate Housewives* share Wisteria Lane; the Dundler Mifflin employees on *The Office* work together, as do the *Grey's Anatomy* interns. Remove the binding element and friendships may fade. Consider how, when not killed off, characters are removed from shows, particularly the cast-rotating *ER*. Whether for career, love, or family, a resident leaves the hospital and Chicago and, as a result, is detached from the life of the colleagues previously seen daily. While employed as a plot device to remove a character, such occasions illustrate an aspect of reality.

Why do some friendships tend to outlast others?

There are a number of reasons individuals end friendships. The most common reasons reported for terminating a friendship were less affection (22.8 percent), friend or self changed (21 percent), no longer participate in activities or spend time together (15.4 percent), and increase in distance (13 percent). (Johnson, Wittenberg, Haigh, Wigley, Becker, Brown and Craig 2004). Additional findings suggest that male same-sex friendships tend to dissolve for different reasons than female same-sex friendships. Females were more likely to

When they graduate and go their separate ways, will this friendship end?

terminate friendships due to a conflict situation, whereas males were more likely to terminate friendships as a result of fewer common interests.

The way that someone ends a friendship depends on the intimacy, or closeness, experienced in the relationship. Another study compared the differences in dissolution between casual and best friends (Rose and Serafica 1986). Researchers found that proximity was a stronger predictor of dissolution in casual friends, while decreased affection was more important in best friends. One reason reported for best and close friendships dissolving was the interface from other relationships, such as romantic relationships. This plays a particularly detrimental role in female friendships. When one individual begins to spend more time interacting with her romantic partners' male friends than with her own friends, the neglected female friends are likely to become frustrated with her behavior.

A friendship reward is having fun when you're together.

© Jason Stitt, 2007, Shutterstock.

As a friendship grows apart, we can neglect the responsibilities of the relationship by choosing to provide less of our time, energy, trust, understanding, and support. When an individual is neglecting the responsibilities of the friendship, individuals may start weighing the costs and rewards of the relationship. Recall our discussion of Social Exchange Theory in Chapter Six. To review, **Social Exchange Theory** refers to an assessment of costs and rewards in determining the value of pursuing or continuing a relationship (Thibaut and Kelley 1959). Rewards consist of behaviors or aspects of the relationship that are desirable, and that the recipient perceives as enjoyable or fulfilling. In friendships, rewards are how much fun you have with the person, and the extent to which he or she is trustworthy, honest, sincere, helpful, and supportive. By contrast, costs are perceived as undesirable behaviors or outcomes. Costs in friendships may be characterized as "toxic" behaviors: the extent to which a friend may be controlling, demanding, depressing, self-absorbed, deceitful, and unfair. Also, friendships take time and energy, which may be perceived as costs when we have less time and energy to devote to them. According to Social Exchange Theory, when the costs of the relationship outweigh the rewards, we contemplate ending the friendship. We may use indirect or direct methods to end a friendship.

Using Indirect Methods to End a Friendship

Indirect methods work best if your goal is to decrease the intensity of the friendship by increasing the emotional and physical distance between you and your friend. Indirect methods reflect your intentions of gradually letting go of the relationship. Examples of indirect methods include calling the friend less, sending fewer emails, blocking the friend from your Buddy List or switching your screen name, and spending less time with the friend.

There are drawbacks to using indirect methods to gradually weaken relationship bonds. For example, giving excuses for not hanging out may backfire. Florence Isaacs, author of *Toxic Friends/True Friends: How Your Friends Can Make or Break Your Health, Happiness, Family, and Career* (1999), suggests that giving excuses allows the other person an opportunity to overcome your refusal; he or she may answer your "Oh, I can't afford the gas to get out there," with "That's okay, I can pick you up."

In addition, because indirect methods are not the most honest approach, the friend is often left confused about your true feelings. Often he or she will keep trying and will not understand your indirect attempts to slow down, or even end, the friendship. If this is the case, it may be time to move to more direct approaches of ending the relationship.

Using Direct Methods to End a Friendship

Direct methods work best if your friend does not recognize the intent of your indirect attempts or if you are interested in terminating the friendship abruptly (due to some hurtful circumstance). As you can imagine, direct approaches are specifically telling the friend how you honestly feel. Sometimes this is not an easy task, but there are some tools you can use to ease this uncomfortable situation. First, use "I" statements. For example, "I'm very busy with my new girlfriend and with work so I cannot hang out with you every weekend," or "I was really hurt by your comment at dinner the other night and I'm not interested in being friends with someone who doesn't respect me." Direct methods leave little room for misinterpretation. While they are effective, they can be hurtful and sometimes shocking to hear from the perspective of the receiver. If you choose to engage in this approach, be prepared to be assertive and provide a valid reason for why you are ending the friendship.

TERMINATING ROMANTIC RELATIONSHIPS

"There must be fifty ways to leave your lover," and though Paul Simon suggests mainly variations on "slipping out the back," some individuals prove highly creative in their personal spins on "it's not you, it's me." The common causes of relationship disengagement, however, are more limited. There are several significant reasons individuals have provided for terminating romantic relationships. Typically, the decision to leave a romantic partner is a difficult and arduous task. In this section, we examine four common reasons individuals leave romantic relationships (adapted from Cupach and Metts 1986). These include: (1) infidelity, (2) lack of commitment, (3) dissimilarity, and (4) outside pressures.

Infidelity

Infidelity can be defined as behaving in a way that crosses the perceived boundary and expectation of an exclusive relationship. Infidelity can take many forms, including physical (holding hands), sexual (kissing and other activities), and emotional (sharing intimate conversation) (Spitzberg and Tafoya 2005). Research suggests that men are more likely to be upset with a partner's sexual infidelity, while women tend to be more upset with a partners' emotional infidelity (Glass and Wright 1985). Studies have also shown that infidelity is more likely to exist inside marriages with marital instability, dishonesty, arguments about trust, narcissism, and time spent apart (Atkins, Yi, Baucom and Christensen 2005). While approximately ninety-nine percent of married persons expect sexual fidelity from their spouse (Treas and Giesen 2000), not many couples are meeting those expectations.

Although infidelity statistics are difficult to measure, we report some interesting findings that describe the pervasiveness of infidelity. Atwood and Schwartz (2002) estimate that fifty to sixty percent of married men and forty-five to fifty-five percent of married women engage in some form of extramarital affair at some point in their marriage. The *Washington Post* reported that, according to counselor Janis Abrahms Spring, author of *After the Affair*, affairs affect one of every 2.7 couples. Other interesting findings suggest that ten percent of extramarital affairs last one day. Of those that last more than one day:

- Ten percent last less than a month
- Fifty percent last more than a month but less than a year
- Forty percent last two or more years

According to Spring's statistics, few extramarital affairs last longer than four years.

Additionally, a longitudinal study found that infidelity is the most frequently cited cause of divorce (Amato and Rogers 1997). Another study found that forty percent of divorced individuals reported at least one extramarital sexual contact during their marriage (Janus and Janus 1993). These alarming statistics imply that although not many condone infidelity, there is a significant proportion of people engaging in these types of behaviors.

Our culture has both romanticized and rebuked infidelity. The archetypical story of Tristan and Isolde, wherein a young queen cheats on her kind husband with the knight she truly loves, was turned into a hit 2006 film of the same title by Ridley Scott. Guinevere and Lancelot's doomed love that betrays the noble King Arthur, whom they both care deeply for, is continually retold in musical form. *Walk the Line* was another recent movie dealing with the relationship between Johnny Cash and June Carter, which caused the dissolution of Cash's previous marriage. Movies like *Fatal Attraction* and *What Lies Beneath*, however, offer deadly punishment for adultery. According to research, relationships in which one or both individuals have potential alternative partners with highly attractive qualities are "particularly vulnerable" to dissolution (Simpson 1987), and when a relationship's rewards fall below the expected rewards of an alternative relationship, it is most likely to end (Thibaut and Kelley 1959). Hollywood, California, where attractive individuals live in extremely close proximity, seems to be a natural hub for infidelity in all three of its forms.

Lack of Commitment

Another reason individuals provide for terminating romantic relationships is a lack of commitment. Although infidelity is one way to demonstrate an individuals' lack of commitment, other ways include: not spending enough time together, not prioritizing the relationship, not valuing the other's opinion, experiencing power struggles, and not nurturing the maintenance and development of the relationship. Lack of **commitment** in a relationship can foster feelings of abandonment and loneliness. Some relationship experts argue that partners' commitment to the relationship is a stronger pre-dictor of relationship stability than feelings of love (Lund 1985). Researcher Mary Lund studied heterosexual dating relationships in an attempt to determine whether love or commitment served as a stronger predictor of relationship stability. She found that couples with higher levels of commitment were more likely to continue the relationship than those with high levels of love and low levels of commitment. In this study, couples' expectations of staying together proved to be more important to relationship sta-bility than their feelings of love for one another.

High commitment to a relationship is a strong predictor of its stability.

Lack of commitment to the relationship may be a catalyst for more damaging outcomes, such as infidelity; couples often attempt therapy to resolve these issues. One study found two characteristics that identified unsuccessful couples in therapy. They are "inability or unwillingness to change" and "lack of com-mitment" (Whisman, Dixon, and Johnson 1997). Another report found that the most significant problems for couples who attended therapy are a lack of loving feelings and lack of communication, power struggles, extramarital affairs, and unrealistic expectations (Whisman, Dixon, and John-son 1997).

Can previous relationship experiences affect an individual's willingness to commit to future relationships? Communication researchers explored how past relationship solidarity was related to current relationship commitment, satisfaction, and investment among college students in dating relationships. They found that an individual's past relationship experiences may be to blame for a current relationships' lack of commitment with, specifically, a negative relationship between participants' past relationship solidarity and current relationship commitment and satisfaction. It is important to note that these relationships were only significant for the female participants in the study. Researchers argue that these find-ings may be based on the different ways in which "men and women cope with break-ups and how these differences might have affected their retrospective reports of their past relation-ships" (Merolla Weber, Myers, and Booth-Butterfield 2004, 261). Women may be more in tune with their physical and emotional closeness in past relationships than males. Males, on the other hand, may be more inclined to employ emotional distraction techniques after break-ups to avoid dealing with their feelings (Merolla et al. 2004).

Dissimilarity

Scholars have identified similarity as one of two components that relationship dyads consider when deciding whether to stay together or to break up (Hill, Rubin, and Peplau 1976). A longitudinal study suggested that couples who were most similar in educational plans, intelligence, and attractiveness were most likely to remain together, whereas couples that were different in the levels of these aspects were more likely to break up. Some may say, "opposites attract," but the truth is, **dissimilarity** creates more problems than solutions.

Couples who share similar beliefs and interests are more likely to stay together.

Having differences in backgrounds (religion, family values), intelligence (educational goals, IQ), attitudes concerning family roles, ethics, and communicating about conflicts, and temperament (argumentativeness, assertiveness) can contribute to conflict situations and misinterpretations of behavior.

A communication concept that is strongly linked to similarity is interpersonal solidarity. Lawrence Wheeless defined interpersonal solidarity as feelings of closeness between people that develop as a result of shared sentiments, similarities and intimate behaviors (1978). With that in mind, it makes sense that solidarity increases as relationships become more intimate, and it decreases as relationships turn toward termination (Wheeless, Wheeless, and Baus 1984). As solidarity increases in romantic relationships, so do individuals' levels of trust, reciprocity, and self-disclosures (Wheeless 1976). Also, the closer we feel to our partner, the more likely we are to provide emotional support (Weber and Patterson 1996). It makes sense to say that if individuals in romantic relationships perceive differences between themselves, there will be less trust, reciprocity, and emotional support, and fewer self-disclosures will be shared.

Writers often use a lack of interpersonal solidarity as the basis to break up fictional couples, particularly in cases when infidelity would be seen as out of character. On *Gilmore Girls*, for instance, Rory Gilmore ultimately breaks up with her devoted boyfriend when his lack of interest in books and of drive to strive beyond the community college in their town runs contrary to her love for literature and dream to attend Harvard. The contrast is made acute by a boy friend of hers who shares her interests in intellectual debate and matches her fast-paced banter. This sense of a widening gap between two individuals will commonly terminate a relationship.

Outside Pressures

External or **outside pressure** from friends, family, or occupations may negatively impact relationship satisfaction. Family members may put pressure on romantic relationships when they ask questions like "When are you two getting married?" or make comments such as, "You should save your money for a house!" and "I want to be a grandparent!" Friends also may exert pressure on romantic relationships by hinting that not enough time is spent with them, pressuring you to do things without your significant other. For couples in the public eye, the paparazzi acts as the external pressure peering over the hedge, demanding details and pushing theories of engagement, pregnancy, etc., on the pair.

According to **self determination theory**, people have an innate psychological need to feel autonomous, or self-governing, in one's behavior (Deci and Ryan 1985, 2000, 2002). In other words, we want to feel free to choose our own path in relationships, rather than be coerced or pressured into certain behaviors. Ultimately, this self-initiated behavior will lead to better personal and social adjustment. Trait autonomy, or the extent to which we are self-determined, is related to feelings of well-being and security in relationships (La Guardia et al. 2000). Hence, those who report feeling responsible for, and in control of, their

Stressful career demands can impact the satisfaction in relationships.

own decisions are also more secure and positive about their relationships with others.

Work relationships or job stressors can impact the satisfaction in our romantic relationship. An increase in job demands, hours, and travel requirements are examples of significant occupational pressures that may affect relationship stability. The time-consuming career of a doctor, for instance, can be seen in the media as being a challenge to relationships lasting, particularly on shows like *ER*, wherein constant relationship disengagement occurs.

HOMOSEXUAL VERSUS HETEROSEXUAL RELATIONSHIP DISSOLUTION

Although scant research has addressed gay and lesbian relationship termination, Lawrence Kurdek has found that cohabitating gay or lesbian partners are more similar than different when compared to married heterosexual partners (Kurdek 1992; 1998). In his 1998 longitudinal study, he examined relationship satisfaction among partners from gay, lesbian, and heterosexual married couples over five annual assessments. He found that neither gay nor lesbian partners differed from heterosexual partners in both the trajectory of change and the level of relationship satisfaction over time and that all three groups showed a similar decrease in satisfaction over the five years. However, some differences were detected. Both gay and lesbian partners reported more frequent relationship dissolution compared to married spouses. Additionally, gay and lesbian partners reported more autonomy than married people. Furthermore, lesbian partners reported significantly more intimacy and equality than married individuals (Kurdek 1998).

ASSESSING RELATIONSHIP PROBLEMS

When considering whether to stay in a relationship or not, we often assess the trouble occurring in the relationship and the explanations for these problems. For example, we ask ourselves questions such as, Why does he act that way? Why did she say that to me? or Why would he or she hurt me? To address these questions, it is necessary to recall our discussion of attribution theory and the Fundamental Attribution Error from Chapter Five. These theories provide a framework for understanding how we explain our own and others' behaviors. Recall our discussion of the **fundamental attribution error** which holds that people tend to attribute others' behaviors to internal, rather than external, causes. Rather than consider external or situational causes for others' behavior, which are also not always readily available, we often tend to take the "easy" way out and attribute others' behaviors to internal, or stable, factors, such as personality traits.

Not surprisingly, appraisals of our relationship partner's intentions relate to how satisfied we are in the relationship. Researchers have identified a consistent link between the attributions, or explanations, about relationship partners' intentions and reported relationship satisfaction (Fincham 1994; Waldinger and Schulz 2006). Much of the research on attributions in romantic relationships has examined how an assessment of a partner's accountability for a relationship transgression affects relationship satisfaction (Waldinger et al. 2006).

It is natural to want to understand why our partner is acting a certain way, and eventually, these judgments influence our evaluation of our partner.

When relationship partners offer consistently negative attributions or explanations for a partner's behavior, they are more likely to report lower relationship satisfaction (Fincham and Bradbury 1993; Miller and Bradbury 1995). Thus, when a relationship partner forgets to buy a birthday present or forgets to recognize an important date, the offended partner may offer negative explanations for the behavior, especially if the negative behavior has been repeated over time. The offended partner may say, "He didn't get me a present because he is lazy," or "She didn't remember our anniversary because she is so self-absorbed." When individuals view a partner's behavior as selfishly motivated and intentional, they are more likely to view their partner in a negative way and to report decreased relationship satisfaction (Fincham, Harold, and Gano-Phillips 2000). Recent research indicates that relationship satisfaction can also affect the types of attributions partners make about each other's behavior, with less satisfied partners being more inclined to provide negative attributions for a partner's behaviors. Thus, the relationship between attribution processes and relationship satisfaction is described as a bidirectional one, which makes this somewhat challenging for researchers to study (Fincham et al. 2000).

Anita Vangelisti (1992) interviewed dating couples to determine the association between relationship problems and relational dissatisfaction. In her study, she recognized a problem as significant for relationship partners when it meets at least two of the following criteria: (1) the behavior must be negatively valenced on the relationship, (2) it must occur with some degree of frequency, and (3) it must be salient enough for one or both partners to remember it and recall it as a continuing source of dissatisfaction within the relationship. This makes sense, because if it is an annoying habit (such as not looking at your partner while listening) and it is consistent over time, it may reach the point where it becomes a relational problem. However, a salient behavior (such as kissing a colleague at happy hour) may only have to happen once, but is prominent enough to continually cause displeasure in the relationship, even though the behavior was never repeated. This study found that the most frequently reported communicative problem was withholding expression of negative feelings; the feelings of anger, fear, distress, disgust and shame.

Once we assess the relational problems, we may conclude that there is some form of inequity. **Equity theory** suggests that couples are happiest in relationships when there is a balance of inputs and outputs. If you perceive you are receiving too little from the relationship compared to what you are contributing, this will impact your satisfaction. Alternatively, if you are receiving more outputs from the relationship than you are contributing, you will feel a sense of guilt from the imbalance. However, this is highly subjective in terms of one's personal view of inputs, outputs, and fairness.

DECISION MAKING DURING RELATIONSHIP TERMINATION

Now we turn our attention to Duck's (1982) four-phase model of decision-making during relationship termination to understand how individuals determine whether or not to end a relationship.

Intrapsychic Phase

When one partner recognizes that something is wrong in a relationship and that he or she is no longer happy, feelings of frustration set in. The individual begins to consider the costs and rewards of the relationship and to explore the possibilities of alternative relationships. The "leaver" finds fault and places blame on the partner until finally, enough justification to withdraw from the relationship has accumulated. This initial phase in the relationship termination process is the **intrapsychic phase.** During this phase, the leaver spends considerable time contemplating whether the relationship is worth saving.

Dyadic Phase

When the leaver officially announces to the partner that he or she is leaving or thinking of leaving, the **dyadic phase** begins. This phase opens the flood gates for discussion and justifications. This often emotionally exhaustive phase is characterized by long talks and rationalizations of how the partnership "got to this place." During this phase, the other partner may make attempts to reconcile the relationship and to illustrate the costs of withdrawing. This phase typically continues until someone admits, "I have had enough."

Social Phase

If the relationship cannot be salvaged, the relationship termination then goes public. When the relationship termination is focused less on the relationship and more on the relationship partners' friends and family, it is a sign that we have moved to the **social phase.** For example, the question, What are we going to tell people? is often negotiated in this phase. Stories, blaming, and accounts of situations are articulated to friends and family. At this time, friends will often choose sides. In terms of the relationship partners, the rules and roles of their post break-up status are discussed. In other words, questions like, Can we still be friends? or Can I still call you? are negotiated.

Grave Dressing

The last phase is **grave dressing.** This phase is called grave dressing because partners typically "dress up" the dead relationship (or grave) by promoting a positive image of their role in their particular version of the relationship. Grave dressing also refers to "officially burying" the relationship. Partners are able to articulate the explanation of the termination and create their own versions of the relationship, whether truthful or not. Some people in this stage will have a ceremonial burying phase by burning pictures and returning, giving away, or selling items given to them by their "ex."

FIVE STAGES OF RELATIONSHIP DISSOLUTION

Knapp's model of relationship dissolution is both similar to and different from the model presented by Steve Duck (1982). Mark Knapp's model of relationship dissolution focuses more on what happens between the relationship partners and less on how the partners interact with their social circles (Vange-listi 2002). You may recall our discussion of Knapp's (1978) stages of coming together in Chapter Six; he also developed a five-stage model that depicts how relationships typically come apart, or dissolve. The five stages of dissolution are labeled: differentiating, circumscribing, stagnating, avoiding, and terminating. Remember our earlier discussion of stage models; it is possible that (1) partners are not in the same stage together, (2) some stages last longer than others do, and (3) partners often skip stages. It is important to note that this model seems to depict what actually happens when relationships deteriorate, not what should happen (Knapp 1978).

Differentiating

While in the stages of coming together, couples tend to emphasize hobbies, interests, and values that they have in common; in the **differentiating** stage, partners highlight their differences. Individuals accentuate their unique attributes and use more "I" and "me" statements. During this phase of relationship dissolution partners may engage in a great deal of conflict that often emphasizes all of the ways they differ from one another. For example, if someone says she likes eating out, the partner expresses a preference for cooking at home. If an individual tells his partner that he likes action movies, the partner immediately states her affinity for romantic comedies. One's independence from the relationship is the central focus of this stage, which has both positive and negative implications. On one hand, when individuals reassert their individual needs, they may choose to do things on their own, spend more time with friends, and reestablish their identity. This process can be healthy for a relationship. For example, let us say before two individuals entered into a relationship, he enjoyed playing hockey and she enjoyed participating in a yoga class. But as the relationship developed, there was less time for each person to enjoy his or her personal activity due to favoring more collaborative activities with the partner. In due course, these interests were neglected. In the differentiating stage, those roots may be returned to, with hockey or yoga classes being taken up again. This may provide a "spark" needed in the relationship and provide alternative topics for the partners to discuss. On the other hand, if the individual taking part in the activity excludes the significant other from his or her feelings and experiences, this independence may ultimately create more emotional distance in the relationship. If the partner is kept involved in emotional travels, this stage may have beneficial outcomes.

Circumscribing

When there is not a conscious decision to keep the partner involved, the relationship may drift apart. The next stage of relationship dissolution is labeled the **circumscribing** stage. During this stage, the communication between the relationship partners is often described as restricted, controlled, or constrained. Akin to the "don't talk about politics or religion" standard, relationship partners choose to talk about safe topics that will not lead to some type of argument (Vangelisti 2002). Both the quality and quantity of information exchanged between the relationship partners deteriorates as partners attempt to avoid sensitive subject matter. Relationship partners discuss "safe" topics such as plans for the day, current events, and the weather, which are barely deeper or warmer than material used in conversation with an acquaintance.

Stagnating

The third stage of relationship dissolution is the **stagnating** stage. This stage is often described as two people who are merely "going through the motions" in their relationship because their communication has come to a virtual standstill. There is very little interaction within the relationship and partners continue to do things separately. When they think of bringing up any issues regarding the relationship they tell themselves, "It will just turn into an argument," so they resort to holding things inside to avoid a conflict. They conserve their energy for their daily activities and do not exert any energy on preserving the relationship. Roommates, friends, and even family members may feel stagnant in their relationships with one another. Extended time in this stage can be particularly problematic as individuals may lose their motivation to fix the relationship. Over time, the thought of having to face the partner may become arduous. Therefore, it is often easier to just avoid the partner.

© iofoto, 2007, Shutterstock.

When couples resort to holding things inside to avoid conflict, communication is stagnant.

Avoiding

The fourth stage of coming apart is accurately labeled the **avoiding** stage. During this stage, relationship partners will actively fill their schedules to avoid seeing their partners. Vangelisti (2002) describes this stage as particularly difficult, noting that when the partners do talk to one another, "they make it clear that they are not interested in each other or in the relationship" (666). Relationship partners will arrive early to work and come home late in an effort to avoid one another. The idea of seeing the relationship partner is exhausting and any dialogue with this person is short, to the point, and often superficial. On the inside, individuals are exhausted from creating activities to avoid their partner and have increased disdain for him or her.

Termination

As we grow increasingly disappointed in a relationship and in our partner, we reach a threshold and we want to move on. This is when we reach the final stage of coming apart, the **termination** stage, which marks the end of the relationship. Relationship partners may choose to divorce the partner, move out, or call an end to any type of formal or contractual commitment with the partner. When relationship partners do communicate during this stage, they make attempts to put physical and/or psychological distance between themselves and their relationship partner. Relationship partners will also make attempts to disassociate themselves from their relationship partner. Some married individuals will disassociate themselves from their partners by using

Table 9.1	Typical Communications in Knapp's Stages of Coming Apart
Stage	**Communication Example**
Differentiating	*"You always stare at my sister!"* *"You are just so different from me!"* *"I hate when you don't wash the dishes!"*
Circumscribing	*"It's going to rain tomorrow."* *"Did you let the dog out yet?"* *"I am not going to answer that because it will just lead to a fight!"*
Stagnating	*"Oh, you're home."* *"What is the point of discussing this anymore?"* *"I know, I know. The usual."*
Avoiding	*"I have to work nights all this week."* *"I will not be home for dinner."* *"What time are you going?"*
Terminating	*"I don't want to be in this relationship."* *"Sorry, but we can't date anymore."* *"I'm moving out."*

their maiden names or explicitly stating to friends, co-workers, and family members, "We are not a couple anymore." See Table 9.1 for examples of typical communication that occur during the stages of coming apart.

STRATEGIES USED TO TERMINATE RELATIONSHIPS

Determining how one should end a relationship can be quite stressful. Whether you are terminating a relationship with a romantic partner, a roommate, or a neighbor it can create much anxiety. When we are stressed we often turn to easily accessible solutions that are not always effective. However, we recommend that you do not employ any of the romantic relationship break-up lines provided in Table 9.2 below.

Once the leaver decides to verbalize his or her intentions, he or she typically relies on relational disengagement tactics. During the relational disen-

Table 9.2	Worst Break-Up Lines

1. I think we both know this is not working out.
2. I think one of us knows this is not really working out.
3. I am trouble, baby, with a capital T.
4. My wife is having a bigger problem with us dating than I thought she would.
5. It is not you, it is me.
6. It is not me, it is you.
7. Buh-bye.

Source: Adapted from www.esquire.com/features/articles. Ted Allen and Scott Omelianuk

gagement period, there is obviously a great deal of conflict. Leavers will use different strategies, depending on the type of the relationship and the timing of the disengagement. For example, more polite and face-saving tactics are typically used in the beginning of the relationship termination phase. However, if the rejected partner does not respond to these tactics, or if the leaver is in a dangerous relationship and immediate action is needed, more forceful and direct tactics may be necessary. Researchers have studied what people specifically recall saying during a break-up (Baxter 1982; Cody 1982) and they have identified five tactics used during relational disengagement.

Positive Tone Messages

First, **positive tone messages** are created to ease the pain for the rejected partner. These messages have a strong emotional tone and usually imply that the leaver would like to see less of the other person, but not entirely end the relationship. When individuals employ this strategy they usually want to try to end the relationship in a positive and pleasant way. An example of a positive tone message would be, "I really like you as a person, but I do not feel as strongly about you, as you do me." In other words, the classic "It's not you, it's me." Here the leaver tries to ease the pain of the break-up by suggesting that he or she still likes the rejected partner and is interested in a friendship.

De-escalation Messages

The second tactic also involves reducing the amount of time spent with the partner. **De-escalation messages** are less emotional than positive tone messages and typically provide a rationale for wanting to see less of the rejected partner. For example, "I think we need a break," or "My feelings for you have changed since the start of this relationship," would both be de-escalation messages. This strategy may be problematic because it is only perceived as a partial or temporary type of relationship termination strategy. Individuals who want to end the relationship for good may want to follow up with a more direct strategy for ending the relationship.

Withdrawal or Avoidance

A third tactic, **withdrawal** or **avoidance,** refers to actively spending less time with the person. This includes dodging phone calls, blocking IMs, and rerouting daily activities in order to avoid the individual. When you do run into the person, conversations are kept brief and shallow. This strategy is very indirect and can affect the individuals' ability to maintain a friendship in the future.

© Alex Brosa, 2007, Shutterstock.

When the relationship is not working, you may feel justification to end it.

Justification Tactic

A fourth way to disengage from a relationship involves the **justification tactic.** This tactic has three important elements. First, the relationship partner states that he or she needs to stop seeing the other person. Next, the relationship partner provides a reason for ending the relationship with the other person. Finally, the relationship partner recognizes that the relationship is not salvageable and may even become worse if the relationship continues. An example of this tactic is, "This relationship is not giving me what I need so we need to stop seeing each other." A person might say to his roommate, "I cannot live with you anymore because all we do is fight and argue and I do not see things getting any better. I am worried that if we stay roommates, things will get even worse than they are now!"

The last tactic is typically used as a last resort to terminate a relationship or when relationship partners are in need of immediate disengagement.

Negative Identity Management Tactic

A strategy which is used to hurry the disengagement process and has little consideration for the rejected partner is called the **negative identity management** tactic. Manipulation is often part of this tactic. For example, the leaver may spark a disagreement with the partner to create an unpleasant situation and then suggest, "See, this isn't working . . . we should see other people."

REDEFINING THE RELATIONSHIP AFTER THE BREAK-UP: REMAINING "JUST FRIENDS"

After a break-up, we often want to remain friends with our "ex." This makes sense because we have self-disclosed personal information to each other, relied on this person for emotional support and guidance, and have a number of things in common. Think about everything that drew you two together in the first place. But what are the chances that this new definition of your relationship will be successful? Some research suggests that a couple is much more likely to stay friends when the man has been the one who precipitated the break-up (or when the break-up was mutual) than when the woman initiated the break-up (Hill, Rubin, Peplau 1976).

Other research studies suggest that if the romantic couple were friends prior to the romantic involvement, their chances of returning to a friendship is significantly higher than those who never maintained a friendship (Metts, Cupach, and Bejlovec 1989). Additionally, if the partners were still receiving rewards or resources from the relationship, these could influence the impact of a partner's satisfaction with the post break-up friendship (Busboom, Collins, and Givertz 2002).

Certain relationship disengagement strategies are more effective in creating a positive post break-up relationship. When we ask our students how they would prefer to end a romantic relationship, most agree that they would desire an honest and direct strategy. Negative disengagement strategies, such as withdrawal, neglecting, or avoidance have been identified as inhibiting post-dating relationship quality (Metts et. al. 1989; Banks et al. 1987; Busboom, Collins, and Givertz 2002). If relationship partners would like to remain friends, it is a good idea to use positive tone messages, direct strategies or other tactics that protect the other person's feelings.

Although it is certainly possible to remain friends after a break-up, it is important that both parties agree with the new relational "rules." Discuss the boundaries of the relationship and be open about what is appropriate and inappropriate behavior. It is not unusual for post break-up friendships to cross the friendship boundaries in times of distress due to the familiarity, comfortableness, and security of the relationship (think Ross and Rachel from the television show *Friends*). It is important to remember you broke up for a reason!

METHODS OF COPING WITH RELATIONSHIP DISSOLUTION

Scholars also note that the dissolution of a romantic relationship can be one of the most painful and stressful experiences people endure in their personal lives (Feeney and Noller 1992; Simpson 1987). This section will discuss methods of coping with relationship dissolution and creating closure.

After a break-up, keep yourself busy with family or friends you may have neglected during the relationships.

Because ending a relationship can be one of the most emotionally charged events we experience, often there is no easy or painless way. No two relationships are identical in nature and there are no scripts to terminate relationships. We are flooded with different emotions including sadness, anger, fear, denial, guilt, and confusion. Sometimes we are relieved that the relationship is over and we are anticipating more rewarding relationships. Here are some methods of coping with relationship dissolution:

1. Recognize that relationship dissolution is a process. Allow yourself time to feel a range of emotions. This is normal and healthy. Do not reject your feelings or hide them behind negative coping strategies such as binge eating (or refusing to eat), binge drinking, or drug use. Also, do not rush into another romantic relationship without properly healing from the past.
2. Rely on your support network. Discuss your feelings with friends and family. Engage in activities that were neglected during your romantic relationship. Stay busy and redirect your attention. For example, find a new hobby or go on vacation with some of your friends.
3. If you feel you are burdening your friends and family, or you continue to feel depressed or angry, talking with a professional can help. Often, counseling is covered by health insurance. Most university counseling services are provided free of charge to students; take advantage of resources that are included in your tuition. Discussing issues with a third party that has no personal involvement in your existing relationships can provide a fresh perspective.

CLOSURE AND FORGIVENESS

Closure refers to a level of understanding, or emotional conclusion, to a difficult life event, such as terminating a romantic relationship. In this situation, closure often includes the rationale for the break-up. Some research suggests that individuals need a certain level of closure of their break-up before they can effectively move on (Weber 1998). The purpose of closure is to discuss things that "worked" in the relationship as well as to discuss the challenges of the relationship in order to learn from them. Remember, the purpose of this discussion is to make future relationships more effective, and not to resurrect the terminated relationship. Therefore, blaming, accusations, and name-calling are anti-productive. If properly executed, closure is helpful in understanding what went wrong in the relationship, providing some direction for future relationships.

Granting forgiveness is one strategy used during closure. Forgiveness does not mean you forget, accept, understand, or excuse the behavior; it simply implies that you will not hold your partner in debt for his or her wrong-doing. Granting forgiveness is a powerful tool. When you forgive someone that you are terminating a relationship with, you set yourself and your partner free from harboring negative feelings toward each other and perceptions of the relationship.

Self-forgiveness refers to you giving yourself permission to heal and move forward. You give yourself permission to shed yourself of the burden, guilt, pain, and anger that is held inside of you. Once you grant yourself forgiveness you can focus on how to become a better person and make healthier choices in the future.

Creating closure optimally involves getting together with your "ex" face-to-face to discuss the good times and the bad. In most situations, this option is impossible because either it is too difficult to sit in the same room or a partner has physically moved away. Therefore, closure is often difficult and not easily attainable. One way to create an emotional conclusion to a relationship is to reframe the event. Frequently, this is a way individuals can create a sense of closure without relying on the ex-partner. **Reframing** is a psychological process in which you change the way you look at the romantic termination in order to foster a more productive resolution. For example, if you are angry and hurt that your partner cheated on you, you may reframe the event by thinking about how dishonest the partner was. Instead of focusing on your hurt and anger, you psychologically emphasize that untruthfulness is not a characteristic of a person you want to share a romantic relationship with. You focus on recognizing signs of the cheating behavior and predictors of his or her behavior so you can be more aware in future relationships. By reframing the event, you are looking at the event in a different light, which enables you to move forward.

SUMMARY

In Hoobastank's hit song "The Reason," the singer apologizes for the choices he made in their relationship. "I've found a reason for me/ To change who I used to be. . . . and the reason is you," he claims, suggesting he has learned from the mistakes made in the relationship and has grown as an individual. Although there are countless break-up songs, we deliberately chose this one because it demonstrates that relationship dissolution can be a learning experience. This chapter reviewed the indirect and direct ways individuals dissolve relationships. We reviewed the four-phase process of decision-making during relationship termination: intrapsychic phase, dyadic phase, social phase, and grave dressing phase, and also explored the five stages of relationship deterioration: differentiating, circumscribing, stagnating, avoiding, and terminating. Furthermore, we identified the five tactics used to terminate romantic relationships: positive tone messages, de-escalation messages, withdrawal tactics, justification tactics, and negative identity management tactics. Finally, we discussed consequences of relationship dissolution, including closure, forgiveness, and reframing the event.

APPLICATIONS

Exercise to Forgive Yourself

1. Write down with pen and paper all of the things that you have done wrong. It is imperative that you *write*. Word processing is not the same.

2. Read the list.

3. Now say "I did the best that I could with the knowledge that I had at the time. I now forgive myself and go free."

4. Destroy the list (burn, shred, do not eat).

5. Repeat the exercise for each of the other people who have hurt you.

6. Now begin anew to live your life without the burden of unforgiven pain.

Once you are able to talk about difficult subjects, you might try the following exercise.

From "Forgiveness as a Key to the Future" by Steven Martin & Catherine Martin, www.positive-way.com. Reprinted with permission of The Positive Way.

Exercise to Forgive a Partner

1. Set an agenda to work on one issue at a time. You both must agree that you are ready to talk about that issue.

2. Using active listening techniques and ground rules that you have agreed to, discuss the pain and concerns that you have about the issue. The object is to understand how you each *feel* about the issue. Do not point the finger and do not place blame, but try to understand the consequences of each other's actions. You must show respect and care for each other.

3. The offender asks for forgiveness. Apologies are extremely powerful. Understand the pain and feelings of the offended person.

4. The offended person agrees to forgive. Commit the issue to the past without getting even or holding the offender in debt. The issue will not be used as a weapon in future conflicts.

5. The offender agrees to change his or her behavior as appropriate.

6. You both move forward with a commitment to create a better future.

Source: Adapted from *http://www.positive-way.com/* Steven Martin and Catherine Martin.

REFERENCES

Abrahms Spring, J. 1997. *After the affair: Healing the pain and rebuilding trust when a partner has been unfaithful.* New York: Harper Collins.

Amato, P. R., and S. J. Rogers. 1997. A longitudinal study of marital problems and subsequent divorce. *Journal of Marriage and the Family, 59,* 612–624.

Atkins, D. C., J. Yi, D. H. Baucom, and A. Christensen. 2005. Infidelity in couples seeking marital therapy. *Journal of Family Psychology, 19,* 470–473.

Atwood, J. D., and L. Schwartz. 2002. Cyber-sex: The new affair treatment considerations. *Journal of Couple and Relationship Therapy, 1,* 37–56.

Banks, S. P., D. M. Altendorf, J. O. Green, and M. J. Cody. 1987. An examination of relationship disengagement: Perceptions, breakup strategies and outcomes. *The Western Journal of Speech Communication, 52,* 19–41.

Baxter, L. 1982. Strategies for ending relationships: Two studies. *Western Journal of Speech Communication, 46,* 233–242.

Busboom, A. L., D. M. Collins, and M. D. Givertz. 2002. Can we still be friends? Resources and barriers to friendship quality after romantic relationship dissolution. *Personal Relationships, 9,* 215–223.

Cody, M. 1982. A typology of disengagement strategies and an examination of the role intimacy reactions to inequity and relational problems play in strategy selection. *Communication Monographs, 49,* 148–170.

Cupach, W. R., and S. Metts. 1986. Accounts of relational dissolution: A comparison of marital and non-marital relationships. *Communication Monographs, 53,* 311–334.

Deci, E. L., and R. M. Ryan. 1985. *Intrinsic motivation and self determination in human behavior.* New York: Plenum Press.

———. 2000. The "what" and "why" of goal pursuits: Human needs and the self-determination of behavior. *Psychological Inquiry, 11,* 227–268.

————. 2002. Self-determination research: Reflections and future directions. In E. L. Deci and R. M. Ryan (Eds.), *Handbook of self-determination research* (431–441). Rochester, NY: University of Rochester Press.

Duck, S. W. 1982. A topography of relationship disengagement and dissolution. In S. W. Duck (Ed.), *Personal relationships 4: Dissolving personal relationships* (1–30). London: Academic Press.

Feemey, J. A., and P. Noller. 1992. Attachment style and romantic love: Relationship dissolution. *Australian Journal of Psychology, 44,* 69–74.

Fincham, F. D. 1994. Cognition in marriage: Current status and future challenges. *Applied and preventative psychology: Current scientific perspectives, 3,* 185–198.

Fincham, F. D., and T. N. Bradbury. 1993. Marital satisfaction, depression and attributions: A longitudinal analysis. *Journal of Personality and Social Psychology, 64,* 442–452

Fincham, F. D., G. T. Harold, and S. Gano-Phillips. 2000. The longitudinal association between attributions and marital satisfaction: Direction of effects and role of efficacy expectations. *Journal of Family Psychology, 14,* 267–285.

Glass, D. P., and T. L. Wright. 1985. Sex differences in type of extramarital involvement and marital dissatisfaction. *Sex Roles, 12,* 1101–1120.

Hill, C. T., Z. Rubin, and L. A. Peplau. 1976. Breakups before marriage: The end of 103 affairs. *Journal of Social Issues, 32,* 147–168.

Isaacs, F. 1999. *Toxic friends/true friends: How your friends can make or break your health, happiness, family and career.* Scranton: William Morrow & Co.

Janus, S. S., and C. L. Janus. 1993. *The Janus report on sexual behavior.* New York: Wiley.

Johnson, A. J., E. Wittenberg, M. Haigh, S. Wigley, J. Becker, K. Brown, and E. Craig. 2004. The process of relationship development and deterioration: Turning points in friendships that have terminated. *Communication Quarterly, 52,* 54–67.

Knapp, M. L. 1978. *Social intercourse: From greeting to goodbye.* Boston: Allyn & Bacon.

Kurdek, L. A. 1998. Relationship outcomes and their predictors: Longitudinal evidence from heterosexual married, gay cohabiting, and lesbian cohabiting couples. *Journal of Marriage and the Family, 60,* 553–568.

————. 1992. Relationship stability and relationship satisfaction in cohabiting gay and lesbian couples: A prospective longitudinal test of the contextual and interdependence models. *Journal of Social and Personal Relationships, 9,* 125–142.

La Guardia, J. G., R. M. Ryan, C. E. Couchman, and E. L. Deci. 2000. Within-person variation in security of attachment: A self-determination theory perspective on attachment, need fulfillment, and well-being. *Journal of Personality and Social Psychology, 79,* 367–384.

Lund, M. 1985. The development of investment and commitment scales for predicting continuity of personal relationships. *Journal of Social and Personal Relationships, 2,* 3–23.

Merolla, A. J., K. D. Weber, S. A. Myers, and M. B. Booth-Butterfield. 2004. The impact of past dating relationship solidarity on commitment, satisfaction, and investment in current relationships. *Communication Quarterly, 52,* 251–264.

Metts, S., W. R. Cupach, and R. A. Bejlovec. 1989. "I love you too much to ever start liking you": Redefining romantic relationships. *Journal of Social and Personal Relationships, 6,* 259–274.

Miller, G. E., and T. N. Bradbury. 1995. Refining the association between attributions and behavior in marital interaction. *Journal of Family Psychology, 9,* 196–208.

Rose, S., and F. C. Serafica. 1986. Keeping and ending casual, close, and best friendships. *Journal of Social and Personal Relationships, 3,* 275–288.

Simpson, J. A. 1987. The dissolution of romantic relationships: Factors involved in relationship stability and distress. *Journal of Personality and Social Psychology, 53,* 683–692.

Spitzberg, B., and M. Tafoya. 2005. Explorations in communicative infidelity: Jealousy, sociosexuality, and vengefulness. Paper presented at the International Communication Association annual meeting in New York, NY.

Thibault, J. W., and H. H. Kelley. 1959. *The Social Psychology of Groups.* New York: Wiley.

Treas, J., and D. Giesen. 2000. Sexual infidelity among married and cohabiting Americans. *Journal of Marriage and the Family, 62,* 48–60.

Vangelisti, A. L. 2002. Interpersonal processes in romantic relationships. In M. L. Knappand J. A. Daly. (Eds.), *Handbook of interpersonal communication* (643–679). Thousand Oaks, CA: Sage Publications.

————. 1992. Communicative problems in committed relationships: An attributional analysis. In J. H. Harvery, T. L. Orbuch, and A. L. Weber (Eds.), *Attributions, accounts, and close relationships* (144–164). New York: Springer-Verlag.

Waldinger, R. J., and M. S. Schulz. 2006. Linking hearts and minds in couple interactions: Intentions, attributions, and overriding sentiments. *Journal of Family Psychology, 20*, 494–504.

Weber, A. L. 1998. Losing, leaving, and letting go: Coping with nonmarital breakups. In B. H. Spitzberg and W. R. Cupach (Eds.), *The dark side of close relationships* (267–306). Mahwah, NJ: Erlbaum.

Weber, K., and B. R. Patterson. 1996. Construction and validation of a communication based emotional support scale. *Communication Research Reports, 13*(1), 68–76.

Wheeless, L. 1976. Self-disclosure and interpersonal solidarity: Measurement, validation, and relationships. *Human Communication Research, 3*(1), 47–61.

————. 1978. A follow-up study of the relationships among trust, disclosure, and interpersonal solidarity. *Human Communication Research, 4*(2), 143–157.

Wheeless, L. R., V. E. Wheeless, and R. Baus. 1984. Sexual communication, communication satisfaction, and solidarity in the developmental stages of intimate relationships. *Western Journal of Speech Communication, 48*, 217–230.

Whisman, M. A., A. E. Dixon, and B. Johnson. 1997. Therapists' perspectives of couple problems and treatment issues in couple therapy. *Journal of Family Psychology, 11*, 361–366.

Wilmont, W. W., D. A. Carbaugh, and L. A. Baxter. 1985. Communicative strategies used to terminate romantic relationships. *Western Journal of Speech Communication, 49*, 204–216.

IPC in Various Communication Contexts

part

3

Intercultural Communication
Variety Is the Spice of Life

OBJECTIVES

- Understand three reasons for studying the impact of diversity on interpersonal relationships
- Increase awareness of four basic core concepts: knowledge, understanding, acceptance, and skills
- Define culture
- Differentiate the co-cultural categories of ethnicity, race, region, and social class
- Identify three characteristics of culture
- Discuss factors which affect our perceptions of others: needs, beliefs, values, and attitudes
- Identify three steps in the process of forming stereotypes
- Recognize how stereotypes and prejudice influence interpersonal relationships
- Describe three forms of prejudice
- Explain the three functions that prejudices fulfill in our interpersonal relationships
- Evaluate the impact of Hofstede's four dimensions of cultural values on interpersonal communication
- Recognize five strategies to enhance effective interpersonal communication in diverse relationships

© 2007, JupiterImages Corporation.

KEY TERMS

knowledge	culture	personal orientation system
uncertainty reduction theory (URT)	diversity	needs
passive strategies	socialization	beliefs
active strategies	ethnicity	values
interactive strategies	race	attitudes
self-disclosure	regional differences	stereotyping
understanding	social class	racial profiling
acceptance	homophily	prejudice
ethnocentrism	explicit learning	racism
skills	implicit learning	race
	perception	

ageism   high/low context   power distance
sexism   cultures   masculine/feminine
verbal abuse   individualism/   cultures
discrimination   collectivism   uncertainty avoidance
violence
acceptance

On July 28, 2006, actor Mel Gibson was pulled over while speeding on Pacific Coast Highway in Malibu, California. As officers were questioning Gibson, he began yelling at them, making anti-Semitic and sexist comments toward the arresting officers.

In October 2006, *Grey's Anatomy* actor Isaiah Washington got into a fight with fellow actor Patrick Dempsey over an alleged gay slur that Washington made about their colleague, T. R. Knight. Even though the incident eventually faded from the spotlight, Washington publicly made an anti-gay comment at the 2007 Golden Globe awards a few months later as he attempted to defend his earlier actions to members of the press.

In November 2006, *Seinfeld* actor Michael Richards erupted into a series of racial epithets targeted toward two African American men attending his performance at the Laugh Factory in Los Angeles. Richards claimed that he was angry at the men for heckling him and allegedly disturbing his comedy routine.

What causes individuals to engage in such negative behavior? Why do people exchange such hurtful words and actions? One reason may be the inability to engage in effective interpersonal communication with those who are different. We make decisions on how to communicate with others based on our beliefs, our values, and our attitudes. As a result, if our beliefs or attitudes toward another individual or group are negative, our communication with them may be negative as well. Why is it that some people fear and apprehend communication with diverse others instead of embracing differences as the added "spice" of interpersonal relationships? In this chapter we will explore a variety of concepts that help explain how our attitudes, beliefs, and values both shape and are shaped by our interactions with others.

OVERVIEW

Throughout this text, we have discussed various aspects of interpersonal communication and the roles they play in initiating and sustaining relationships. As we approach the end of the journey of exploring the specifics of interpersonal communication, we would be remiss if we failed to discuss the one variable that *all* interpersonal relationships have in common—they are comprised of diverse individuals. Typically, discussions of diversity focus on things that we can see: race, ethnicity, and gender being the most commonly identified elements when defining diversity. Focusing attention on the obvious

Relationships are comprised of individuals who are diverse in many ways.

© Stephen Coburn, 2007, Shutterstock.

differences may cause us to fail to recognize that cultural attitudes, values, and norms also play a role in our interpersonal relationships. These are only a few of the less apparent factors that create challenges for relational partners when trying to achieve shared meaning. Consider friends who get upset with one another simply because they differ in their beliefs of how to spend their first weekend out of school. One might want to hang out with family members who were visiting from out of town instead of going out to the exclusive "Summer Kickoff Party" at the hot new nightclub that the other friend had received an exclusive invitation to attend. Differing values for family relationships and friendships contribute to the diversity encountered in this relationship. Maybe you have had a difficult time getting a teacher to understand that your questions are not intended to "challenge his authority," but are attempts to better understand the information being presented in class.

Diversity comes in many shapes and forms. While knowledge of the traditional views of cultural diversity can help you to understand the challenges you may encounter in your own relationships, it is important to focus on the source of many of our communication behaviors and to understand how cultural perceptions impact our view of relationships and communication. We can use the analogy of a coach and a team to understand the influence of diversity on interpersonal relationships and the role communication plays in the process. A good coach would not send a team out on the playing field without preparing them for the game. Plays are taught and rehearsed; team members know what to expect from one another. Practice sessions are conducted so that these preferred ways of acting and reacting can be learned and refined. Sure, there are times when the game plan does not work as planned. The coach and team may become frustrated. They regroup, communicate, and develop an alternate plan. However, if the team continues to run exactly the same play every single game, the chances for success will be slim. Becoming a competent communicator across cultures requires you to develop a similar game plan. You need to be aware of the characteristics that can lead to misunderstandings when communicating with people from diverse backgrounds. Knowing that each person's communication is guided by his unique set of values, beliefs, and attitudes will prepare you for differences in your approaches to conversations. Just as a team needs to study plays, people need to study and understand the various elements that create confusion and miscommunication in cross-cultural encounters. This chapter will help you to develop a personal game plan for becoming a competent communicator in diverse interpersonal relationships. Four core concepts which are essential to enhancing competence include: knowledge, understanding, skills, and acceptance. Let us examine each of these concepts more closely.

THE IMPACT OF CULTURAL DIVERSITY ON INTERPERSONAL RELATIONSHIPS

As buzz words such as "diversity" and "cultural sensitivity" continue to permeate discussions regarding relationships in the workplace, the classroom, and our personal lives, there is a need to increase the understanding of both diversity and communication, and their influence on personal relationships. This is an extremely exciting time in our history. Changes in political and social policy, evolving demographics, and technological advances have provided us with vast opportunities for forming relationships with diverse others. Three specific reasons for exploring the impact of cultural diversity on communication in interpersonal relationships are (1) increased awareness of self, (2) appreciation for technological transformations, and (3) understanding of demographic transitions.

© Laurence Gough, 2007, Shutterstock.

Now more than ever, we have opportunities to form relationships with many different people.

Understanding the Self

Perhaps the simplest and most overlooked reason for studying the impact of diversity on our relationships is the opportunity it provides for exploring and understanding our own cultural background and identity. By delving into the cultural factors which influence communication patterns, we begin to gain an awareness of our own reasons for thinking and behaving as we do.

> A woman had lived in a small town with a population of 350 all of her life. The population was entirely Caucasian, and the overwhelming majority was Methodist and middle-class. Upon moving to a large metropolitan area, she found the challenges of understanding the cultural differences to be phenomenal. Her knowledge of initiating relationships was limited to experiences in a small, cohesive community. Shortly after moving into her new apartment, she encountered her next door neighbor struggling to bring several bags of groceries from the parking lot to the building. While introducing herself, she attempted to take a couple of bags from her neighbor's car. She was quickly told that her assistance was not needed. She discussed the incident with a roommate. The roommate pointed out, "You have to understand that people in large cities don't just walk up and help one another. Don't be offended. City folks just don't trust people as easily as people you're accustomed to." As she found the first few weeks in the city to be frustrating, her focus was on how "strange" other people were, not on understanding how her own cultural background influenced her perceptions and expectations of others' behavior.

In Chapter Two, the impact of individual identity on our communication in relationships was discussed. When considering the impact they have on our identity formation, our first instinct may be to focus on interactions with family members and peers. Communication with significant others plays a large role in shaping our sense of self. However, it is essential that we examine the role that culture has played in the process as well. After all, it is likely that the rules and expectations that our family and friends have for our communication behaviors are derived from cultural expectations. Many unspoken guidelines are within different cultural influences.

How have cell phones impacted the way we communicate?

Technological Transformations

In the 1960s, Marshall McLuhan introduced the notion of a "global village" (McLuhan and Powers 1989). He predicted that mass media and technology would bring the world closer together, a notion considered to be farfetched at that time. But a quick inventory of today's technologies, which provide opportunities for forming diverse relationships, reveals that McLuhan's vision was quite accurate. Airline travel, television, cell phones, and the Internet are just a few of the technologies that have changed the way we communicate. Humans now have the capability to travel around the world in a matter of hours, simultaneously view events as they occur in other cities and countries, and concurrently interact with persons from around the globe.

Opportunities provided by technology for forming relationships with diverse persons have increased exponentially over the past twenty years. A 2005 survey revealed that nearly 1 billion people worldwide have access to the Internet (*http://www.internetworldstats.com/america.htm*). In the United States alone, nearly 250 million people use the World Wide Web to find information and to form relationships with others. Teenagers are forming and maintaining relationships via the computer at increasing rates due to social networking sites such as MySpace and Facebook. Some schools encourage students to communicate with intercultural email partners in a variety of subject areas. Internet chat rooms and discussion boards enable individuals to form friendships with others from almost anywhere. An examination of one teen chat site revealed that there were students communicating with one another from seven different states as well as from Canada, Great Britain, and Puerto Rico. As corporate America expands its boundaries to include many overseas partners, work teams will be comprised of members from diverse cultures. People come to the workplace with diverse beliefs, experiences, and expectations about the role of communication in relationships at work. Gergen (1991) emphasizes the fact that new technology has eliminated the barriers of space and time which previously inhibited relationships from forming with diverse individuals. Technology provides opportunities to communicate with persons who come from backgrounds entirely different than our own. Understanding the factors that influence communication will enhance our appreciation of these opportunities.

Influence of Demographic Transitions

Over the past twenty years, the demographic composition of the United States has changed dramatically. And predictions for the twenty-first century indicate that the life expectancy of the population will be longer and that the racial and ethnic composition will be more diverse than ever. Medical advancements have extended the life expectancy of Americans. Immigration patterns have changed dramatically since the 1960s, before then most immigrants came primarily from European countries. Today, nearly ninety percent of immigrants arrive from Latin American and Asian nations. By the middle of the twenty-first century, the majority of the U.S. population will be comprised of today's racial and ethnic minorities. Over the past decade, the number of interracial and interdenominational marriages has increased, and the U.S. workplace has seen a shift from the predominance of white male employees to a more diverse workforce that is also comprised of women and racial and ethnic groups. Opportunities to expand our linguistic, political, and social knowledge abound.

The demographic composition of the United States will continue to change and become more diverse.

However, not all intercultural encounters are viewed as opportunities. While these demographic shifts create opportunities for diverse relationships, it is important to recognize that they present communication challenges as well. Some intercultural encounters are approached with fear and apprehension. Uncertainty about other individuals creates tension. In July 2005, a series of bombs exploded on subways and a bus in London. Since that time, reporters have pointed to the mistrust, misunderstanding, and fear that have caused members of this city (which once prided itself on its racial, ethnic, and religious diversity), to be more cautious in their interactions with others.

Consequences of changing demographics are being felt in many social institutions. Schools are faced with issues such as bilingualism, differences in learning styles, and challenges of conflict among diverse groups. The Los Angeles school system reported that more than 100 different languages were spoken in classrooms across the county. Yet language is only one piece of a cultural code to be deciphered; other factors include understanding the perceptions and motivations that influence relationships in the home culture. Administrators at Taylor County High School in Georgia were faced with the challenge of how to address a group of students who wanted to host a "white-only" prom:

> Even after schools were integrated in the South, many rural areas still held separate proms for blacks and whites, and Taylor County High School was no exception. The first integrated prom in 31 years was organized by the school's Junior class because they collectively decided they all wanted to be together as a complete group. Every year before that, students and their parents planned separate dances. The proms weren't organized by the school itself, as school officials were concerned about potential interracial dating issues. The year after the first integrated prom, a small group of white students announced that they also wanted a separate dance. One of the students who had initiated the integrated dance said she was bitterly disappointed to hear that some students wanted to go back to the old ways after they had succeeded in bringing about such a change in the school.

Now more than ever, relationship success depends on the ability to demonstrate communication competence across cultures. Achieving communication competence is the ultimate goal in our interpersonal relationships. When the source and receiver are from diverse backgrounds and have unique expectations of communication, this goal may be perceived as difficult to achieve.

COMMUNICATION COMPETENCE: FOUR CORE CONCEPTS

Knowledge

Knowledge refers to the theoretical principles and concepts that explain behaviors occurring within a specific communication context. In other words, increasing your knowledge of communication theories and the concepts used to explain the challenges faced in intercultural relationships will enhance your ability to understand and accept those differences. In addition, knowledge will enhance your interpersonal skills when communicating with diverse others. You have already increased your knowledge base as a result of reading this textbook up to this point. Each of the concepts and theories that have been introduced has enhanced your understanding of the factors that impact communication in interpersonal relationships. Throughout this chapter we will take a second look at some of the theories introduced earlier in the text that have direct implications for intercultural encounters.

Uncertainty Reduction Theory.   Berger and Calabrese's **uncertainty reduction theory** (URT) helps us understand how knowledge can assist us in forming effective interpersonal relationships by predicting the attitudes, behaviors, and emotions of others. As we initiate new relationships, our goal is to reduce our level of uncertainty about the other person (Berger and Calabrese 1975). When crossing cultural lines, alleviating this ambiguity becomes a bit trickier. For example, the notion of what constitutes acceptable disclosures in interpersonal relationships in the U.S. might differ from what is considered proper in other cultures. Is it acceptable to ask about another person's occupation? About her family? How does the other person view status differentials and what rules does he or she adopt for communicating with someone of different status? Berger (1979) identified three primary communication strategies used to reduce uncertainty in relationships. These are: passive strategies, active strategies, and interactive strategies.

Passive strategies typically involve observation and social comparison. We observe members of other cultures and make assessments as to the differences that exist. When one of your authors arrived in Hong Kong to teach summer classes, she did not speak Chinese. She spent many hours during her first weekend there sitting at the busy harbor, browsing through shopping areas, and walking around campus to observe how people interacted with one another. Through her observations, she learned the cultural rules for personal space, noticed styles of dress and forms of nonverbal greetings, and became familiar with the protocol for communication between students and teachers on campus.

Active strategies require us to engage in interactions with others to learn additional information about the other person. Suppose your professor assigns you to have weekly conversations with an international partner during the semester. Prior to your first meeting, you may decide to ask other international students what they know about your conversation partner's culture, or you may go online and participate in chat rooms that have members from the conversation partner's culture.

Interactive strategies typically involve a face-to-face encounter between two individuals to reduce uncertainty. Typically, partners engage in **self-**

disclosure as a means of sharing information about themselves with others. When examining cultural differences in disclosure, it was found that American college students disclose about a much wider range of topics, and to more people outside the family, whereas college students in Korea self-disclose mostly to immediate family members (Ishii, Thomas and Klopf 1993). Consider the following example:

> Alicia was excited to learn that she had been selected to live with an international student in the dorm during her freshmen year. She had been fortunate enough to travel with her parents on business trips to various countries for the past several years and found learning about other cultures to be fascinating. Her new roommate, Kyon, was from Korea. As they were unpacking their things, Alicia told Kyon about her hometown, her summer vacation to Hilton Head Island, and about all of her friends from high school who were attending their college. She shared how frightened she was about the first day of classes, and she laughed as she told Kyon how she had taken her schedule and walked around campus to locate her classrooms for the first day of class. Eventually, Alicia noticed that she had been doing all the talking, so she began asking Kyon questions. While Kyon was willing to discuss the classes she would be taking and the plane trip from Korea, she seemed reluctant to talk about her family, friends, or even her fears about starting college.

Without knowledge of cultural differences in communication styles, Alicia may have become easily frustrated by Kyon's lack of disclosure. After all, in the United States it is common to engage in question-asking and self-disclosure to reduce our uncertainty about others. But understanding that expectations for self-disclosure in Korea are different from those held by Americans will help alleviate the potential frustration and hurt feelings that could occur otherwise.

Knowledge of one's own culture is learned. Cultures teach their members preferred perceptual and communication patterns just as a coach teaches a team the plays. Beginning at a very young age, this learning process instills knowledge about the culture's accepted behaviors. As children enter kindergarten in the U.S., they learn that they need to raise their hand to ask a question in class and to listen quietly while the teacher is speaking. Communication is the channel for teaching these lessons. Members of a culture practice the preferred behaviors and, if they deviate from the endorsed mannerisms they will probably find that they are unsuccessful in their communication. Consider the following example:

© PhotoCreate, 2007, Shutterstock.

Young children learn quickly that listening quietly to the teacher is the accepted behavior for school.

> A student from Ethiopia shared this story about his experiences in American classrooms. During his high school years, he lost class participation points because of his unwillingness to speak out in class. While he was confused about his low grade, he did not approach the teacher and ask for clarification. Rather, he accepted the teacher's evaluation of his performance. However, what the teacher did not know was that in his culture students are not active participants in class. The

teacher is viewed as the authority and the students are expected to listen and learn. Further, to question a teacher's authority would be viewed as extremely disrespectful.

As we engage in relationships with diverse persons, the knowledge of what constitutes competent communication behaviors is learned. Recent articles have focused on the need for cultural and social knowledge among U.S. armed service workers (McFate 2005; McFate and Jackson 2005). As U.S. military personnel travel overseas for service, it is important that they have a solid understanding of the cultural beliefs and norms that are expected. While the mission of the troops may be to restore order, respect for cultural expectations must still be demonstrated. Even the simple act of eating and drinking could be perceived as being offensive without proper knowledge of cultural norms. Soldiers training for duty in Iraq need to understand that members of Muslim cultures do not eat or drink during the day during the month of Ramadan. By refraining from eating or drinking in front of members of the Muslim culture during this period, U.S. soldiers can display respect for the Muslim culture. Studying the role of values, beliefs, attitudes, and needs in shaping and sustaining relationships can be invaluable. New knowledge can remove some of the barriers that can create communication challenges in relationships with diverse people. But knowledge in and of itself is insufficient for achieving competence. We also need to gain an understanding of why others communicate the way they do.

Understanding

Understanding involves applying knowledge to specific situations in an attempt to explain the behaviors that are occurring. While you may know how uncertainty reduction theory (URT) is defined, it is important to gain an understanding of how it impacts a particular interaction. Understanding involves exploring the roots, or sources of communication, rather than simply explaining the behavior. Imagine this scenario. You attend the funeral of the mother of your close friend who is Jewish. At the end of the ceremony, Jewish tradition calls for friends and family members to shovel dirt onto the coffin, but you are not aware of this tradition. This act makes you extremely uncomfortable, and you decide not to participate in the tradition; you end up offending your friend. Knowledge of the Jewish cultural customs would have assisted you in understanding the negative reaction that resulted from your refusal to participate in the ceremony.

As the twenty-first century opens, the cultural composition of the United States is becoming increasingly diverse. A recent Associated Press news article suggests that the term "minority" may no longer be an accurate descriptor for various U.S. co-cultures *(http://www.diversityinc.com/public/16722print.cfm)*. Non-Latino whites currently encompass less than fifty percent of the population of Texas, and it is predicted that more than one-third of all Americans will soon live in a state where groups formerly considered minority groups will outnumber Caucasians. Changes in demographics provide more opportunities for individuals to interact with individuals who are from diverse cultural backgrounds. Consider the various relationship contexts we have discussed in this text. The chances are greater than ever before that you will form relationships with teachers, physicians, and co-workers who are from diverse backgrounds.

Broadening our understanding of diversity to understand the influence of a variety of elements such as race, ethnicity, language differences, and religious beliefs is essential for relationship success. In many classrooms across the U.S., Caucasians are no longer the majority. On the surface, twenty-five students may appear to be similar, based on their racial or ethnic status, but it is quite possible that there are twenty-five different cultural backgrounds represented. One aspect of their diverse backgrounds may be seen in the language that is spoken in each of their homes. Nearly seventeen percent of elementary and secondary school students speak a language other than English in their homes (*http://www.census.gov/prod/2004pubs/04statab/educ.pdf*). Even where racial and ethnic diversity may be minimal, students come from different geographical locations and religious backgrounds and are impacted by their unique family backgrounds. Understanding how each of these elements impacts individual decisions to communicate in relationships is essential. For example, Jack was confused when he saw his friend Adam place a rock on the grave of a close friend who had recently passed away after a car accident. He did not understand that Adam's behavior was guided by an old Jewish custom of placing a rock on a loved one's grave as a sign of respect. According to tradition, the rocks were originally used as a way to mark gravesites. As more people visited the site, they added rocks to demonstrate how many people loved and respected the person.

© PhotoCreate, 2007, Shutterstock.

A room full of students appearing to be similar on the surface could have many different cultural backgrounds.

It is important to understand that what works in one relationship may not work in all. Consider our earlier example of the coach and his team. Just as it would be ineffective to run the same play over and over again in a game, communicating with diverse persons in the same manner would not result in satisfying relationships. While this chapter will assist you in building knowledge and understanding of communication differences, acceptance of differences is also key to interpersonal success.

Acceptance

Acceptance refers to our awareness of the feelings and emotions involved in diverse approaches to relationships and communication. It encompasses our willingness to understand the behavior of others. Accepting differences in behavior enables us to be less judgmental and to reject ethnocentric thinking. **Ethnocentrism** refers to the tendency to perceive our own ways of behaving and thinking as being correct, or acceptable, and judging the behaviors of others as being "strange," incorrect, or inferior. Challenges in our interactions are often attributed to external, rather than cultural factors. Consider two co-workers who attempt to influence one another on a project on which they are collaborating. Joe tries to persuade Maynae by directly disagreeing with her proposal and engaging in assertive communication. Maynae's cultural background is one that values saving face. Thus, she avoids directly disagreeing with Joe—rather, she nods her head and proceeds with the project as she planned. Both of them end up frustrated. Joe cannot understand why Maynae did not follow their game plan. Had she not nodded her head and agreed with him? Joe attributes Maynae's actions to her shyness. Maynae is frustrated by Joe's confusion. Did he not understand that she did not want to embarrass him in front of their colleagues? She deduces that he must be in a bad mood and was not paying attention. As they continue to disagree about how to proceed with the project, they attribute the communication difficulty to the other person's mood or to shyness, both reasons being external to cultural factors. In reality, they may have diverse cultural expectations for how to influence others.

Skills

We have discussed many of the specific skills that are central to interpersonal communication throughout this text. **Skills** are the specific communication behaviors which contribute to competent and effective interpersonal communication. Effective listening, assertiveness, responsiveness, nonverbal sensitivity, language comprehension, and conflict management are only a few of the many skills required when interacting in diverse relationships. It is important to note that there is a difference between knowing how to communicate effectively across cultures, and actually being able to engage in the appropriate behaviors. You might understand that the Chinese culture values silence, but because you are an extremely talkative person and are ineffective in practicing silence you may be perceived as being rude when interacting with members of the Chinese culture. While language is an important skill to enhance communication competence, practicing nonverbal skills can also assist in producing effective interpersonal encounters. For example, when dining with friends from Japan, it is appropriate to make loud slurping sounds while eating a meal. The act of slurping is a behavior that is considered to be a compliment to the cook in Japan as it communicates that the food is delicious. But what if you feel very uncomfortable and do not know how to demonstrate the proper slurping behavior because you have never been encouraged to do so? Remaining silent while eating is perceived as an insult in these cultures, but your lack of slurping skills inhibit your ability to communicate your appreciation for the meal.

CULTURE AND DIVERSITY DEFINED

Culture has been defined by scholars in a number of different ways. In fact, one book identified more than 200 different definitions of culture (Kroeber and Kluckhohn 1952). In the fifty years since these definitions were compiled, attention to the increasing diversity of our world has prompted scholars to create even more. Anthropologists have broadly defined culture as being comprised of perceptions, behaviors, and evaluations. This definition was expanded to include shared ideas of a group which incorporates ethical standards as well as other intellectual components. Other researchers have adopted a descriptive approach to explaining culture. Their definitions include characteristics such as knowledge, morals, beliefs, customs, art, music, law, and values. In this text, we define **culture** as shared perceptions which shape the communication patterns and expectations of a group of people.

Diversity refers to the unique qualities or characteristics that distinguish individuals and groups from one another. The following is a list of characteristics that contribute to diversity in our interpersonal relationships.

- Age
- Educational background
- Ethnicity
- Family status
- Gender
- Income
- Military experience
- National, regional, or other geographical areas of origin
- Ownership of property and assets
- Physical and mental ability
- Race
- Sexual orientation
- Social class
- Spiritual practice
- Work experience

Diversity takes into consideration specific elements that have tremendous potential for our relationships. Consider the characteristics that you share with your closest friend. Chances are that you formed a relationship based on similarities in some of the areas listed above. Perhaps you are close in age and have similar educational backgrounds. Stop for a moment and consider the relationship implications when there are differences across these characteristics. A couple with different spiritual backgrounds may need to negotiate whose religious beliefs will be followed in raising their children. A daughter who is a lesbian may find it difficult communicating her feelings about her relationship with her heterosexual parents. Or a soldier may be challenged to convey his beliefs about war and his value of freedom with his friends back home who have not served in the military. When considering the many charac-

© Michelle D. Milliman, 2007, Shutterstock.

What characteristics do close friends share?

teristics of diversity, it is easy to see why many relationships encounter stumbling blocks as individuals attempt to navigate differences in knowledge, experiences, beliefs, and values.

One of the first steps in becoming competent in our relationships involves recognizing the unique characteristics that each relationship partner possesses. Recall the discussion in Chapter Five about the role perception plays in shaping communication in our relationships. Our culture shapes our perception and society teaches us the preferred ways of behaving. The American value for democracy is shared by many members of this country. Beginning in elementary school, we are taught the meaning of democracy. As we grow up, we see people defending their rights to free speech. Thus, our culture begins shaping our perceptions at a very young age. Perception influences and forms our values, beliefs, and attitudes. These shared perceptions are both consciously taught and unconsciously learned. **Socialization** refers to the process of learning about one's cultural norms and expectations. This is critical for an individual to become a functioning member of society. Sources of socialization

Americans typically learn to value democracy at a young age.

include parents, peers, teachers, celebrities, political leaders, workplace colleagues, educational materials, and mass media. Perceptions are highly individualized, so much so that we may not realize that others see things differently. It may be easy to overlook the impact that diversity has on our communication patterns. Communication behaviors are often unique to a culture, allowing us to easily identify members of various cultural groups. For example, an employee from Georgia assigned to work on a project with a team from Ohio is likely to be identified by her accent. Forms of address, such as when a child refers to an adult as "Miss Sarah," may also indicate a southern background. Culture is not only reflected in our behavior, it also influences our expectations. We form assumptions about how individuals should behave and what we should expect in our relationships with them. Japan is considered to be a collectivistic culture which values and encourages the accomplishments of groups over individual achievement. A student from Japan may experience difficulty in the U.S. where individualism is valued. He may be uncomfortable in situations where he is "singled out" for his individual academic achievements, preferring to be acknowledged with his class.

While we each have diverse characteristics that make us unique, we also share some aspects in common with other members of our larger culture. These shared characteristics allow us to identify with various groups and help shape our identity.

CO-CULTURES WITHIN THE UNITED STATES

Within the larger cultural context, numerous co-cultures exist, each distinguishable by unique characteristics. It is important to note that individuals are members of more than one co-culture. Consider this. An employee may claim membership as a member of the organization, in addition to being an adult, male, African-American Texan with Republican views, and of the Methodist faith. A total of seven co-cultures are claimed. Multiple memberships may contribute to confusion and miscommunication that occurs in relationships. Suppose you assume that because a teammate on your soccer team likes sports, she would not be interested in classical music or the theatre. As you pass a poster announcing the upcoming cultural arts series on your campus, you make some negative comments about people who attend musical and theatrical events. What you do not know is that your teammate has been a student of classical music since a young age, and that her mother is a trained opera singer. While this scenario is an extremely simplified example, assuming that membership in one group precludes an individual from having interests in other groups can lead to embarrassing situations that can impact relationships. Some examples of co-cultural classifications follow.

Ethnicity

While the terms "race" and "ethnicity" have often been used synonymously, these two categories are unique. **Ethnicity** refers to the common heritage, or background, shared by a group of people. Categories may be established to identify the culture from which one's ancestors came. These include

Irish-American, Polish-American, or Mexican-American. While there has been some debate over the connotations associated with the labeling of some of these groups, the intention of naming is simply for identification purposes.

Race

Race is the term used to refer to genetically inherited biological characteristics such as hair texture and color, eye shape, skin color, and facial structure. Terms used to describe different racial categories include Caucasian, African American, and Asian. One situation which impacts our classification of groups results from the increasing number of intercultural marriages and relationships. Previously there were no categories on the U.S. census form to allow individuals to indicate their identification with more than one racial classification. This changed on the 2000 census with the addition of the category "other" to allow citizens to report their racial identification. As a result, individuals can now identify themselves as members of multiple racial groups rather than being restricted to only one racial identity.

Regional Differences

Within a given culture, speech patterns, attitudes, and values may differ significantly depending on the geographic location that an individual calls home. Northern Germans express values which are quite different from those of southern Germans. Those who reside in northern Brazil communicate using nonverbal gestures which are unrecognizable to those from southern Brazil. Accents within a culture also vary depending on the geographic region. Japanese spoken in Okinawa takes on different tones when spoken in Tokyo. English spoken by those who live in the Amish region of Pennsylvania is used differently by Texans. Dodd (1998) observed a variety of **regional differences** in communication styles within the boundaries of the United States. These include variety in the amount of animation, perceived openness, informal rapport, and rate of speech delivery. Even when examining the values of urban versus rural cultures, differences in values are obvious. Rural cultures appear to approach decisions more cautiously and simplistically. Members of urban cultures are more willing to take risks and reach decisions more quickly.

Social Class

Cultures often find that members stratify themselves on the basis of educational, occupational, or financial backgrounds, resulting in classifications and status differentials. Those whose careers produce high financial gain are usually awarded greater power and status in the American culture. Other cultures are more concerned with the amount of education that a person has completed. Stratification often occurs on the basis of **homophily,** the idea that we choose to be with people who are similar to us. Thus, when initiating relationships, we seek out those in similar careers, with similar educational experiences, and of similar financial status.

© digitalskillet, 2007, Shutterstock.

When we initiate relationships, we choose to be with people who share our common interests.

In some cultures, it is possible to move from one social class category to another. For example, a person in the U.S. can easily move from one category to another as a result of their economic or educational status. Graduating from college may enable a person to gain a more prestigious job, and thereby allow him to achieve a higher social standing. Other cultures adhere to a philosophy of ascribed roles in society; an individual is born into a particular social class and there is nothing that can be done to warrant movement to a higher level. The caste system in India is one that restricts members from gaining social status. Relationships in these cultures are restricted to those who are in the same social class.

CHARACTERISTICS OF CULTURE

In the next sections we explain the three primary characteristics of culture: 1) it is learned, 2) it is dynamic, and 3) it is pervasive.

Culture Is Learned

The preferred ways of behaving as a member of a society are learned at a young age. Consider the learning experiences of children. Adults teach them how to say words, which foods can be eaten with the fingers and which should be eaten with utensils, and songs and rituals that are part of the culture. They may be taught that profanity is not acceptable and they are rewarded for saying the Pledge of Allegiance. Children are even taught biases and prejudices. Expectations about the nature of relationships and communication are also learned at a young age. For example, in the United States it is viewed as unacceptable for male friends to hold hands. In some Arab cultures it is not uncommon to see two men engage in this behavior. Society teaches us the behaviors that are accepted by most members of the culture, and, at the same time, instills within us a response mechanism for reacting to violations of cultural norms.

What is acceptable behavior in a culture is learned both explicitly and implicitly. **Explicit learning** involves actual instructions regarding the preferred way of behaving. A school may print a brochure that specifies the dress code that is required of all students, or a teacher may instruct students to raise their hand before speaking in class. In our families, we learn expectations for communication in relationships. For example, a young girl whose mother has experienced negative relationships with former spouses might be taught to "never trust men" and may find it difficult to engage in disclosure and to form relationships with males. **Implicit learning** occurs via observation. We are not directly told what behaviors are preferred; rather they are learned by observing others. Our choices of what to wear for a first date or the first day of work are influenced by observing what others wear or by what we have learned from the media. We learn the preferred ways of dressing so as to be accepted by our peers.

Culture Is Dynamic

Over time, events occur that cause change; cultures do not remain static. Consider changes in relationships that occurred after the events of September 11th.

In the days and months following the tragedy, people reported that they engaged in more frequent communication with friends and family members. People were more willing to engage in open expressions of affection. Cultures and their members also change as a result of "borrowing" aspects from other cultures. It is quite common to open a fashion magazine and see examples of trends being borrowed from other cultures. For example, many stores and catalogues showcase Asian-inspired t-shirts and jewelry that include Chinese or Japanese writing. It is also quite common to see clothing adopting cultural styles such as the recent style of women in the U.S. wearing kimono style dresses.

Depending on a culture's approach to uncertainty, the encouragement and acceptance of change may occur at different rates. Within the last decade, change has occurred at a rapid rate within the United States. Technological advances make some computers obsolete a year or two after purchase. Food and exercise trends also appear to go through changes as new diet fads are constantly introduced to the culture. In 2003, the Atkins diet gained popularity in the United States and carbohydrates were declared to be taboo. Not only did people begin to alter their dietary habits, restaurants altered their menus by designing and promoting dishes that were "Atkins-friendly." Eventually, doctors began questioning the health issues associated with the Atkins diet, and in 2005, the U.S. Department of Agriculture revised the traditional food pyramid to include six dimensions recommended for a healthy diet. Not only do cultures change with regard to food and clothing styles, but popular culture also undergoes transitions. The popularity of television shows change as new shows are introduced. What is "hot" one season may be "out" the next.

While you may initially question what impact these changes in various cultural aspects has on our interpersonal relationships, consider the amount of time we spend discussing aspects of culture with others. Friends gather around the water cooler and in dorm rooms to discuss the previous night's episode of *Survivor* or *Desperate Housewives*. They analyze the reasons for changes in the cafeteria menu to accommodate society's low carb trend. Changes in our culture provide many topics for discussion and debate in our personal relationships. However, not all cultures embrace change. In fact, some cultures are reluctant to implement change. For example, Germany scores high on uncertainty avoidance. This high score is reflective of the culture's reluctance to change as well as the desire to have strict rules and guidelines in place to maintain order. Some countries, such as Argentina, may find that their members adopt similar religious beliefs. When the majority of a culture's members practice the same religion, there is very little uncertainty about the beliefs held by individuals.

Culture Is Pervasive

Culture is everywhere. Take a moment and look around you. Chances are that you see numerous examples of your culture's influence with one simple glance. Is there a computer on your desk? Perhaps there are posters, photos, or artwork on the walls. Is there a television turned on or music playing? Maybe you are on campus and there are other students nearby. Take a look at the style of their clothes and listen to the words that they are saying to one another. Each of these things demonstrates the pervasive nature of culture. It

Culture surrounds our lives and its influence is everywhere.

© mihaicalin, 2007, Shutterstock.

surrounds us—in fact, we cannot escape the influence of our culture. If one were to adopt a descriptive definition of culture, this prevalence could be seen as influencing everything: our expectations for relationships, the clothing we wear, the language we speak, the food we choose, and even our daily schedules. Culture is represented not only in our material possessions, but also in the values, beliefs, and attitudes that comprise our personal orientation system. It shapes virtually every aspect of our lives and influences our thoughts and actions. Culture also affects how we initiate and maintain our interpersonal relationships. In many European cultures, it is common for teenagers to go out on large "group" dates, while females in Australia may ask out males and offer to split the cost of a date. In China and Japan, dating is typically reserved for those who are older, typically in their twenties. Dating was discouraged in India until recently. Families were expected to introduce couples and help them get to know one another socially in preparation for marriage. While online dating has grown in popularity in the U.S. and many European countries, this method of initiating romantic relationships would be frowned upon in cultures that view dating as a time for getting to know one's potential future in-laws.

By taking a moment to consider the impact that culture has on our lives, it becomes clear that culture and communication are inseparable. Our verbal and nonverbal messages are shaped by our culture's influence, and we learn about our culture through the messages we receive from others. Given the level of influence that culture and communication have on one another, it should come as no surprise that the diversity that exists among members of a culture impacts the relationships that they form with one another.

HOW DIVERSITY IMPACTS INTERPERSONAL RELATIONSHIPS

Think about the first day in a new school or at a new job. Consider some of the thoughts that may go through your mind. Probably many expectations are formed about the people you see as you walk through the door. Some of the differences may be visible simply by looking at the other person, such as their gender, race, or age. In addition, many "hidden" differences also exist, such as their beliefs, values, and attitudes. Once the realization sets in that we are expected to communicate with someone whose cultural makeup is likely different from our own, we quickly search for any information, or cues, to help us make sense of how to interact in the particular situation. The process which helps us to organize the stimuli that bombards us in a potential communication encounter is known as perception.

In Chapter Five, we defined **perception** as the process of selecting, organizing, and interpreting stimuli into something that makes sense or is meaningful. Our perception causes us to view relationships and communicate in ways that are potentially different from the ways of others. The perception process may be explained in this way. Think about all the possible things that you could identify by using all five of your senses. Consider all the possible things that you could see, touch, feel, taste, and smell. Literally hundreds of stimuli compete for your attention at a given time! It would be virtually impossible to perceive all of the stimuli at the same time, so we pick and choose which things to pay attention to and ignore the others. Because individuals are selective in what they pay attention to and how they interpret it, each person forms their own perception of behaviors and events. As a result, we each have our own unique view of the world.

The role of selective interpretation was also discussed in Chapter Five. Because of our cultural influences, we may assign different meanings to behaviors. If we do not take the time or make the effort to see what is truly behind our interpretation, serious barriers to effective communication may occur. Imagine the reaction of a teacher who traveled to Hong Kong and, at a celebration dinner, was presented with an appetizer of chicken feet! She perceived the consumption of chicken feet to be disgusting, and her nonverbal behavior of wrinkling her nose and her refusal of the appetizer offended her hosts. The teacher regretted her reaction of obvious disgust, especially after she considered the fact that individuals of other cultures might view her favorite food (a cheeseburger), as disgusting due to their perception of the cow being sacred.

PERSONAL ORIENTATION SYSTEM

Each individual has a set of predispositions which serves as a guide for thoughts, actions, and behaviors. These predispositions are comprised of one's needs, beliefs, values, and attitudes and are commonly referred to as one's **personal orientation system.** Communication plans and relationship expectations are developed and organized based on these characteristics. Many of the components of the personal orientation system are learned within the cultural context. Messages are transmitted from parents, teachers, and friends who teach the younger members of society to perceive certain actions as good or bad, fair or unfair. For example, Chinese children are taught to value history and tradition, and stories of the past are viewed as lessons to guide their behavior. Children in the U.S. tend to view stories of the past as entertaining, but instead of following tradition, they are encouraged to find new and innovative ways of doing things. When faced with decisions regarding the proper way to respond in situations, our needs, beliefs, values, and attitudes assist us in guiding our perception of a situation.

Needs

All individuals have **needs,** strong feelings of discomfort or desire which motivate them to achieve satisfaction or comfort. A strong relationship exists between needs and interpersonal communication, with communication serving as the primary mechanism through which we satisfy needs. If a student needs to have an assignment explained more clearly, he or she must communicate that need to the instructor. If an employee needs assistance in obtaining a copy of a company report, communication with the human resources director or with a supervisor can satisfy the need.

Maslow's hierarchy of needs (1954) organizes the needs which humans must fulfill. A hierarchical structure helps us to understand the importance

Everyone has a need to love and be loved.

© Lee Morris, 2007, Shutterstock.

and priority of having some needs achieved before others. At the most basic level are the physiological needs of humans. These include the need for food, clothing, and shelter. While most cultures are able to devote adequate attention to meeting these needs, others cannot. The next level includes safety needs. Individuals possess a motivation to feel safe and secure in their surroundings. However, cultures differ in their methods for satisfying this need. At the middle of the hierarchy are affection needs. Schutz (1958) identified three basic needs across cultures: affection, control, and inclusion. We have a need to love and to be loved. Esteem needs are located at the next level of Maslow's hierarchy. Humans have a need to feel good about themselves. Interpersonal communication with others is one mechanism for meeting this need. Things that cultural members say and do impact the fulfillment of these needs. At the highest level of Maslow's hierarchy is self-actualization. This level is achieved when an individual feels that he or she has accomplished all that can be achieved in a lifetime. As the U.S. Army's motto implies, self-actualization is fulfilled when an individual feels that the goal "be all that you can be" has been met.

When applying Maslow's hierarchy to our interpersonal relationships, it becomes apparent that communication is the mechanism through which we meet some of our most basic needs, as well as fulfilling higher levels of need. Communication is the key to understanding individuals' needs and in comprehending the value placed on need fulfillment. Understanding what needs individuals have and their importance enables us to interact more effectively and to avoid misunderstandings. While one person may have a need for power and status, another may possess a strong need for friendship and affection. The intensity with which each of these needs is experienced may cause these two people to interact in very different ways.

Beliefs

A second component of culture which guides our thoughts and behaviors is our belief system. **Beliefs** are an important part of understanding our interactions with diverse others because they not only influence our conscious reactions to situations, but dominate our subconscious thoughts as well. We are constantly influenced by our beliefs. They are our personal convictions regarding the truth or existence of things. In Chapter Two we discussed how interactions with others shape our view of self. Through our interpersonal communication, we form beliefs about ourselves and our relationships. Based on positive interactions with your family members and teachers, you may believe that you are destined to succeed in college. Less supportive interactions might result in the belief that you will accomplish very little in life. Ultimately, these beliefs impact our communication with others. The formation of the central substance of our belief system begins at a very early age and continues to evolve as we grow and form relationships with others.

When crossing cultural borders, an examination of the beliefs possessed by a culture's members yields some fascinating differences. People from

Malaysia believe that it is bad luck to touch someone on the top of the head as it is believed to be the location of the center for spiritual energy. Hawaiians possess a number of beliefs about the messages indicated by the appearance of a rainbow. Consider the superstitious beliefs held by members of the American culture. Walking under a ladder, having a black cat cross your path, and the groom seeing the bride on the wedding day prior to the ceremony are all believed to be signs of bad luck. Our beliefs impact our interpersonal communication.

Because most people do not question social institutions, many of the beliefs of a culture are perpetuated from generation to generation without any thought being given to the reasons for the existence of the beliefs. Some individuals have reported that reactions to their questioning of beliefs have been so negative that they feared rejection in their relationships and simply adopted the accepted beliefs into their own personal orientation system.

Values

Values serve as the guide for an individual's behavior. They dictate what we should and should not do. Kluckhohn (1951) describes **values** as a personal philosophy, either explicitly or implicitly expressed, that influences the choice of alternative actions which may be available to an individual. This definition highlights the relationship between values and communication in that values are communicated both explicitly and implicitly through our behaviors. The majority of our actions are reflective of the values which are firmly established in our personal orientation system.

Values are often communicated explicitly through verbal communication. Some cultural values are evident in the proverbs shared among people. "A stitch in time saves nine" communicates the value placed on addressing issues or problems when they are small rather than waiting until they grow bigger. Practicality and being satisfied with what you have is expressed in the proverb, "A bird in the hand is worth two in the bush." The Swedish proverb, "Friendship doubles our joy and divides our grief" describes the value placed on friendships. In his book, *A Pirate Looks at Fifty*, Jimmy Buffett communicates his value for family relationships and friendships when he states, "I have always looked at life as a voyage, mostly wonderful, sometimes frightening. In my family and friends I have discovered treasure more valuable than gold."

Nonverbal communication may be a more subtle means for communicating values. Many Asian cultures practice the custom of giving a gift to demonstrate the value for reciprocity and friendship. It is not unusual for students to offer their teachers gifts in exchange for the lessons that are learned. In the American culture, many teachers would be extremely uncomfortable accepting these gifts, resulting in confusion in the student-teacher relationship, possibly making subsequent interactions uncomfortable. It is important to gain an understanding not only of the values held by a culture's members, but also the ways in which individuals communicate these values. By doing so, misunderstandings may be avoided.

© Galina Barskaya, 2007, Shutterstock.

Friendships are often the most valued things in peoples' lives.

Attitudes: Stereotyping and Prejudice

Throughout our lives, each of us develops learned predispositions to respond in favorable or unfavorable ways toward people or objects. These tendencies are known as **attitudes.** A primary goal of this chapter is to assist you in identifying your responses to differences as well as to help you to understand your internal orientations guiding these reactions. If ever we interpret another's cultural customs or actions as being wrong or offensive, it is important to understand our own attitudes and how our culture has influenced their formation. Failure to understand these tendencies can result in irrational attitude formation, producing negative results in interpersonal relationships with diverse others. Two attitude formations to avoid are stereotypes and prejudices.

Stereotyping.   Stereotyping results from the inability to see and appreciate the uniqueness of individuals. When generalizations about a group are made and are then attributed to any individuals who either associate with, or are members of, the group, the process of **stereotyping** is evolving. Three steps have been identified in the process of stereotyping.

The first step involves categorizing a group of people based on observable characteristics that they have in common. An international student from Scotland commented that she thought that all Americans would be like the people she saw on Beverly Hills 90210—tan, attractive, and extremely materialistic. As a result, she reported that she was initially apprehensive about forming relationships with many of her American classmates and socialized mainly with other international students.

The second step involves assigning characteristics to a group of people. An example of this step would be a popular magazine characterizing mothers who are employed outside the home as being less dedicated to their children.

Finally, we apply those characteristics to any individual that is a member of that group. An example would be the teacher who assumes that a student-athlete is not serious about academic studies. Following the events of 9/11, some members of Arab cultures have reported that they have been subjected to racial profiling. **Racial profiling** occurs when law enforcement or other officials use race as a basis for investigating a person of criminal involvement. This is a result of applying the single characteristic of race in determining whether a person should be viewed as threatening.

While stereotyping can be irrational, it is actually quite normal. Because humans are uncomfortable with uncertainty, stereotyping enables us to make predictions about our potential interactions with others. In order to become more competent in our interactions with diverse others, it is important to realize that stereotypes *can* and *do* impact our perceptions and our communication.

Prejudice.   Another form of attitude which involves negative reactions toward a group of people based on inflexible and inaccurate assumptions is commonly known as **prejudice.** In essence, prejudice involves "pre-judging" individuals. Some of the most common forms of prejudice in the U.S. include racism, sexism, and ageism.

Racism.   **Racism** refers to prejudice against an individual or group based on their racial composition. **Race** is a term used to refer to inherited biological characteristics such as skin color, eye color, hair texture, and facial structure.

> In her 1995 film entitled *Blue Eyed,* Jane Elliott shares with viewers a diversity training session conducted with adults of various racial and ethnic backgrounds in Kansas City. Blue-eyed members of the group are told that they are inferior to the rest of the group simply based on their eye color. As the film unfolds, it is amazing to watch the confusion, mistrust, lack of confidence, and fear of communication that emerges among members of the group. Elliott explains that while some may consider her decision to discriminate simply on the basis of eye color to be irrational, it is not much different than choosing to treat someone differently on the basis of skin color. She points out that the chemical which produces eye color is the same one that produces skin color.

Ageism.   Negative communication toward persons based on their age is referred to as **ageism.** In our culture, some people assume that senior citizens are incapable of making contributions to society and can be considered helpless. In 1967, Congress passed the ADEA (Age Discrimination in Employment Act) to protect older workers against age discrimination. According to the law, an employer cannot replace an employee over the age of forty with a younger person if the current employer is able to satisfactorily perform her or his job. Sue Sewell, age fifty-one, expresses her frustration of ageism in the workplace:

> "Society is missing out on the talent and a wealth of experience of the older worker. I have recently returned to the workplace after a spell at home and have noticed that some younger workers and management are not tolerant of the older worker. I think the older worker is stereotyped as being slow and less likely to be able to pick up new ideas and be able to use new technology. I, like many others in my age bracket, cannot give up work as we have mortgages, bills to pay, and dependents to support. I actually also enjoy being out in the world of work; it makes me feel more a part of society. If the retirement age is to be 70 and beyond as is being mooted at present, then we must have more opportunities for people to be employed whatever their age." (*http://www.maturityworks.co.uk/uploads/files/matwrksreport.qxd1.pdf*)

Ageism is also communicated when negative prejudices are harbored by adults against teenagers based on the attitude that teens are rude and unruly. While some equate college students on Spring Break with partying and drinking, recent programs have been developed on college campuses to provide students with opportunities to complete community service projects during their break from studies. In 2006, thousands of college students traveled to post-Hurricane Katrina Mississippi and New Orleans and spent their Spring Break vacations assisting in the clean-up process.

Sexism.   **Sexism** refers to negative communication directed toward persons of a particular sex. In the United States, sexist attitudes have traditionally been directed toward females. As a result, females have experienced discrimination in the workplace and in other walks of life. While stories of sexism frequently focus on the prejudices against females, men also are subject to sexist behaviors. Consider the father who stays at home and raises the children. As he shops for groceries with the children in the cart or plays with them at the park on a sunny weekday afternoon, he may hear a comment such as, "It's so nice that he's babysitting the children!" Not surprisingly, he may become offended because it is assumed that he is not capable of being the primary caregiver for his children.

COMMUNICATING PREJUDICE

There are three primary means for communicating prejudice. **Verbal abuse** refers to the process of engaging in comments or jokes that are insulting or demeaning to a targeted group. Consider the impressions that we form of people as a result of their negative verbal behaviors toward others. The racist comments made by *Seinfeld*'s Michael Richards may have caused some Kramer fans to question their positive attitudes toward the actor. **Discrimination** involves denying an individual or group of people their rights. While prejudice involves negative cognitions, or thoughts, discrimination is displayed when behaviors are used to express one's negative cognitions. Typically, discrimination is expressed through negative verbal comments made toward a group or an individual, with physical avoidance being the ultimate goal. The most severe form of prejudice is **violence.** On April 29, 1992, the verdict in the trial involving the 1991 beating of Rodney King by four Los Angeles police officers was read. Only one of the four officers was found guilty of using excessive force; the others were cleared of all charges against them. As word of the verdict was spread, riots erupted throughout Los Angeles. During the next three days, television viewers witnessed physical attacks, arson, and looting throughout the city. In the end, more than 4,000 people were injured, more than fifty were killed, and the city suffered over $1 billion in damages. This violence demonstrates the potentially extreme outcome of prejudice.

Fortunately, a 2004 study of 2,000 teens conducted by Teenage Research Unlimited (TRU) in Illinois points to changing trends among young Americans. Nearly sixty percent of teenagers reported that they have close friends of different races. Friendships of diverse religious or political beliefs and economic backgrounds are also prominent among today's teens. TRU President Michael Wood summarized the changing views of this generation as, "Teens still prefer to hang out with peers who share common ground with them. But that no longer means that their friends have to necessarily *look* the part. It's all about attitudes and actions—about *who* you are and what you *do*, not *what* you are" (*http://www.teenresearch.com/PRview. cfm?edit_id=278.*) Additional research points to the benefits of multicultural interactions that occur among college students. A 1997 study found that college students who have frequent interactions with students of different racial backgrounds and engage in positive discussions

Teens prefer to have friends who share their interests, regardless of their backgrounds.

© William Frederick Lawson, 2007, Shutterstock.

about race and ethnicity tend to have a higher self-concept and report that they are more satisfied with college (Smith and Associates, 1997).

Functions of Prejudice

While prejudice is often based on false, irrational, and inflexible generalizations, it is often considered "normal." Why do individuals form prejudice? Three primary reasons for forming prejudice have been identified.

Acceptance.   **Acceptance** is when a person communicates negative feelings toward a particular group in order to fit in within a desired group. An example of this is when a fraternity member expresses hatred for another fraternity's members. When asked why he has these strong feelings, the only reason offered is "because all Alpha Betas dislike them."

Defend the Ego.   Another reason for communicating prejudice is to defend the ego. By expressing negative feelings and attitudes toward a group of people, individuals create a scapegoat for their own misfortunes. An employee was overheard expressing his prejudice against women being selected for administrative positions. Upon further questioning, he admitted that he did not actually harbor any ill feelings toward women supervisors. Rather, he was frustrated by the fact that a woman had been offered the position rather than him.

Provide Information.   A final reason for prejudice is to provide information. As was stated earlier, humans have a need to reduce uncertainty. Unfortunately, many individuals form prejudice as a means for forming knowledge about a group of people with whom little or no contact has been made. Recall our earlier example of the student from Scotland who was reluctant to interact with American students because of the stereotypes formed as a result of watching *Beverly Hills 90210*. Because limited information was available, the student experienced high levels of uncertainty about how to interact with American college students. Prejudices were formed as a means to reduce the level of uncertainty and to provide a framework for building expectations. By forming these negative predispositions, an information base was constructed on which to form expectations about potential interactions.

Cultural Value Orientations

To understand the values shared by a culture's members, a number of scholars have developed models for studying value orientations. These models pose questions designed to measure the intensity with which a culture's members value specific characteristics.

Kluckhohn and Strodbeck (1961) developed one of the first models of cultural value orientation, and it is still being used in research today. Questions are designed to gain insight into such perceptions regarding relationships between humans and humans and nature. Sample questions include:

- What is the basic nature of human beings? Are they inherently evil and incapable of being trusted, or do most humans have a good heart?
- How are social relationships organized? Are relationships viewed as being hierarchical with divisions of power? Or should equal rights be present in all social relationships?

Hall's model of cultural values (1976) represents a continuum of characteristics associated with high-context and low-context cultures. These differences are characterized by distinct differences in communication styles. Cultures which fall at the **low-context** end of the continuum exhibit high verbal tendencies. This style is associated with a direct approach and verbal expressiveness. A philosophy of "say what you mean" is embraced. **High-context** cultures, on the other hand, prefer a more indirect style; cues about the intended message are interpreted through nonverbal channels. Whereas persons from a low-context culture expect messages to be direct, those from a high-context culture search the environment for cues. Rather than asking a person whether he or she is happy, high-context cultures would infer these feelings from other cues such as posture, facial expressions, and disposition. Consider the difficulties experienced by a couple who have different cultural backgrounds:

> Alec was confused. He and Miki had been living together for the past year and were engaged to be married in a few months. One evening, Miki was silent as they ate dinner. He knew something was upsetting her, but she kept insisting that things were fine. Miki was extremely frustrated as well. Why did Alec always insist that she tell him what was wrong? Did she always have to put her feelings into words? Why couldn't Alec be more in tune with her nonverbal behaviors and understand that things were not quite right?

This example illustrates the difference between the influence of the low-context approach of the U.S. on Alec's behavior and the high-context approach of Miki's Japanese upbringing. Miki expects Alec to be more aware of the messages that are being communicated via nonverbal channels, while Alec expects Miki to say what is bothering her.

A final model of cultural values is presented by Hofstede (1980). Four dimensions of values were identified by examining the attitudes of employees in more than forty cultures. These dimensions include individualism/collectivism, power distance, masculinity/femininity, and uncertainty avoidance.

Individualism/Collectivism.

Individualism/collectivism describes the relationship between the individual and the groups to which he or she belongs. **Individualistic** cultures, such as in the United States, focus on individual accomplishments and achievements. **Collectivism,** or value and concern for the group, is the primary value of many Asian cultures. Consider the cultural differences portrayed in the automobile manufacturing plant in the film *Gung Ho*. Asian managers took great pride in their work as their performance ultimately reflected on their group. They did not dream of taking time off for personal reasons. The American workers, on the other hand, whose behaviors reflected individualism, placed their individual needs over those of the company. Employees would take time off to be at the birth of a child or to keep a medical appointment. These differences in the values of the group versus the self had disastrous outcomes, with the company facing the risk of closing as a result of conflicting cultural values.

Power Distance.

Power distance refers to the distribution of power in personal relationships as well as within organizations. Low power distance cultures have a flat structure with most individuals being viewed as equals. The tendency to show favoritism to individuals based on their age, status, or gender is minimized. High power cultures are depicted by a tall hierarchical structure with distinct status differences. Imagine the frustration experienced by a young intercultural couple who had been married for only a few months. The husband, who was Hispanic, was raised in a culture that places the man as the head of the household (high power distance). His wife, who was raised by a single working mother in New York City, valued her independence. The power differential in her family of origin was low, thus she anticipated that her husband would view her as an equal partner in their relationship. As a result of their differing values for status and power based on their roles as husband and wife, the couple experienced many arguments.

Masculine/Feminine.   Prevalence of masculine and feminine traits in a culture characterizes Hofstede's (1980) dimensions of masculinity and femininity. **Masculine** cultures demonstrate a preference for assertiveness, ambition, and achievement. Characteristics of responsiveness, nurturance, and cooperation are associated with cultures at the **feminine** end of this dimension. Gender roles in these cultures are perceived to be more equal. Cultures such as those found in Japan and Mexico exhibit more masculine tendencies, while those found in Brazil, Sweden, and Taiwan are more feminine.

Uncertainty Avoidance.   **Uncertainty avoidance** refers to the willingness of a culture to approach or to avoid change. Cultures high in uncertainty avoidance demonstrate a preference for avoiding change. They embrace tradition and order. China and Germany are examples of countries with cultures that avoid uncertainty and embrace tradition. Cultures low in uncertainty avoidance welcome the possibility of change and are more willing to take risks. The United States and Finland are more open to change and are more tolerant of taking risks and adopting new and innovative approaches.

Understanding these dimensions can provide cues as to which values are promoted among members of a culture. This information is useful for determining the appropriate methods to approach interpersonal communication and for providing valuable information that assists in checking the accuracy of one's perceptions.

SUGGESTIONS FOR SUCCESSFUL INTERPERSONAL RELATIONSHIPS WITH DIVERSE OTHERS

As shown throughout this chapter, perceptions can be faulty. But there are strategies which can enhance accuracy in perception. Each of the suggestions below involves understanding and practicing better interpersonal communication.

- Engage in careful listening and clear communication. Focus on listening for what is really being said, not what you want to hear. Be clear and explicit in your communication. Refrain from using slang or idioms.
- Refrain from judging people based on observable differences such as race, ethnicity, or gender.
- Do not misjudge people based on verbal (e.g., accent or grammar) or nonverbal differences.

- Be patient with yourself. Remember that becoming an effective cross-cultural communicator requires skills and knowledge. It takes time to practice those skills. You may make mistakes, but there are lessons to be learned from those faux pas.
- Practice patience with others. Cultural influences are powerful, and making the transition from one culture's way of thinking and behaving to another's takes time.
- Check for understanding. Do not be afraid to ask for clarification or to ensure that you understood what was being communicated. One simple question now can save offending someone later.

SUMMARY

Throughout this chapter we have discussed the prevalence of diversity in *all* of our interpersonal relationships. While diversity is most frequently identified based on observable characteristics such as race, ethnicity, or sex, it is important to consider additional variables that influence our communication choices as we interact with others. Individual beliefs, attitudes, and values have a significant impact on the messages we send as well as on our reactions to the messages that we receive. At this point we would like to reiterate the importance of studying and understanding the impact of cultural diversity on our interpersonal interactions—by taking a moment to enhance your own knowledge and skills, you are better equipped to understand the reasons underlying your own communication preferences as well as the communication choices of others.

APPLICATIONS

Discussion Questions

1. Interview a friend, co-worker, or family member who has traveled to another country for an extended period of time. What did this individual learn about his own culture? Ask this individual to describe how our culture differs in attitudes, beliefs, values, and practices from the one that he or she visited.

2. Cite several examples of how intercultural communication competence is related to personal and professional success.

3. Discuss five ways that individuals are diverse and how these differences may lead to miscommunication.

4. Provide explicit and implicit examples of how you learned about your culture.

REFERENCES

Antonio, A. L., M. Chang, K. Hakuta, D. Kenny, S. Levin, and J. Milem. 2004. Effects of racial diversity on complex thinking in college students. *Psychological Science, 15*, 507–510.

Berger, C. 1979. Beyond initial interactions: In H. Giles and R. St. Clair (Eds.), *Language and social psychology* (122–144). Oxford: Basil Blackwell.

Berger, C., and R. Calabrese. 1975. Some explorations in initial interaction and beyond: Toward a developmental theory of interpersonal communication. *Human Communication Research, 1*, 99–112.

Buffet, Jimmy. *A Pirate Looks at Fifty.*

CNN.com May 2003. Georgia high school students plan white-only prom. Retrieved September 13, 2007 http://www.cnn.com/2003/EDUCATION/05/02/separate.proms.ap/

Dodd, C. 1998. *Dynamics of intercultural communication (5th ed.).* San Francisco, CA: McGraw-Hill.

Gergen, K. 1991. *The saturated self: Dilemmas of identity in contemporary life.* New York: Harper Collins Basic Books.

Hall, E. T. 1976. *Beyond culture.* Garden City, NY: Anchor.

Hofstede, G. 1980. Motivation, leadership, and organizations: Do American theories apply abroad? *Organizational Dynamics, Summer,* 42–63.

http://www.internetworldstats.com/america.htm

http://www.diversityinc.com/pbhz/16722pont.cfm

Ishii, S., C. Thomas, and D. Klopf. 1993. Self-disclosure among Japanese and Americans. *Otsuma Review, 26*, 51–57.

Kluckhohn, C. 1951. Values and value-orientation in the theory of action. In T. Parsons and E. Shils (Eds.), *Toward a general theory of action* (388–433). Cambridge, MA: Harvard University Press.

Kluckhohn, C., and F. Strodbeck. 1961. *Variations in value orientations.* Evanston, IL: Row, Peterson.

Kroeber, A. L., and C. Kluckhohn. 1952. *Culture: A critical review of concepts and definitions.* Cambridge, MA: Harvard University Press.

Maslow, A. 1954. *Motivation and personality.* New York: Harper.

McFate, M. 2005. The military utility of understanding adversary culture. *Joint Force Quarterly, 38*, 42–48.

McFate, M., and A. Jackson. 2005. An organizational solution for DOD's cultural knowledge needs. *Military Review, 85*, 18–21.

McLuhan, M., and B. Powers. 1989. *The global village: Transformations in world life and media in the 21st century.* New York: Oxford University Press.

Schutz, W. 1958. *FIRO: A three dimensional theory of interpersonal behavior.* New York, NY: Holt, Rinehart & Winston.

Smith, D. and Associates. 1997. *Diversity works: The emerging picture of how students benefit.* Washington, DC: Association of American Colleges and Universities.

The Maturity Works Report. June 2003. *The Social Impact of Workplace Ageism.* Retrieved June 3, 2007. http://www.maturityworks.co.uk/uploads/files/matwrksreport.qxd1.pdf.

Teen Research Unlimited. November 2004. *Diversity in Word and Deed: Most Teens Claim Multicultural Friends.* Retrieved July 29, 2007. http://www.teenresearch.com/PRview.cfm?edit_id=278.

11

Family Communication
It's All Relative

OBJECTIVES

- List three types of family relationships (marital, parent-child, sibling) and discuss communication issues experienced in each type of relationship
- Distinguish between content versus relational expectations as they relate to marital satisfaction
- Identify six sibling relational maintenance strategies
- Apply the central elements of systems theory to family interactions
- Explain family communication patterns theory
- List the four family types identified by Koerner and Fitzpatrick
- Recall the three underlying assumptions of symbolic interaction theory as it relates to families
- Discuss ways in which families form their own identity (stories, myths, metaphors, themes)
- Distinguish between confirmation, rejection, and disconfirming messages
- Discuss the ABCX model of stress as it applies to family interactions

© digitalskillet, 2007, Shutterstock.

KEY TERMS

voluntary and
  involuntary
  relationships
content expectations
relational expectations
traditional couples
separate couples
independent couples
launching stage
deidentification
family systems theory
wholeness
interdependence

hierarchy
boundaries
ambiguous boundaries
calibration
equifinality
family communication
  patterns theory
conversation
  orientation
conformity orientation
pluralistic families
consensual families
laissez-faire families

protective families
symbolic
  interactionism
family stories
birth stories
courtship stories
stories of survival
myths
metaphors
themes
confirmation
rejection
disconfirmation

intimacy
ABCX model
internal stressor
external stressor

normative stressor
non-normative
  stressor
voluntary stressor

involuntary stressor
chronic stressor
acute stressor

OVERVIEW

We begin this chapter by advancing an important question about family communication: What makes family relationships unique from the other types of interpersonal relationships we experience in a lifetime? Vangelisti (2004) describes the significance of the family by labeling it "the crucible of society" (p. ix). Family relationships are unique from other types of interpersonal relationships because they are described as both voluntary and involuntary and play a significant role in shaping self-perceptions. Our family relationships usually offer our first glimpse of what it means to form an intimate connection with another person.

> *"The family. We were a strange little band of characters trudging through life sharing diseases and toothpaste, coveting one another's desserts, hiding shampoo, borrowing money, locking each other out of our rooms, inflicting pain and kissing to heal it in the same instant, loving, laughing, defending, and trying to figure out the common thread that bound us all together."*
>
> Erma Bombeck. *Family: The Ties That Bind...And Gag!* New York: McGraw-Hill, 1987, p. 9.

Erma Bombeck wrote for three decades, chronicling absurdities encountered in life, such as families. Families contain unique communicative features. Each of us has a frame of reference for understanding communication in families since these are the first and often the longest-lasting relationships formed in our lives. Perhaps the best way to understand family relationships is to take a look at the role of interpersonal communication in the family and how it shapes our sense of identity and serves as a model for communication choices. Even in situations where relationships with family members have become strained, the bonds have likely shaped an individual's sense of self, served as a model for desirable or undesirable communication, and shaped expectations for future relationships. In this chapter we examine some of the classic and contemporary family communication research, theories and concepts. We will also address interpersonal communication concepts as they apply across the family life span, focusing on both the positive and challenging aspects of these interactions.

DEFINITION OF FAMILY

If you were asked to list the number of people you consider to be part of your family, would you include in-laws, close family friends, close personal friends, neighbors, siblings' spouses, stepfamilies, co-workers? Would you include only those relatives related by blood or marriage? When students are asked this question, they often include a wide range of individuals in their list of family members. Most family relationships are described as **involuntary** types because we do not get to choose our parents, siblings, cousins, aunts, uncles, grandparents, and so on. Some family relationships may be

Most family relationships are involuntary because we don't get choose who to include.

© Pascale Wowak, 2007, Shutterstock.

formed of **voluntary** members. For example, the television series *Friends* shows how non-biological relationships can fulfill family roles. As we grow older, our choices of who we include in our "family" expand. Voluntary families are created as a result of conscious decisions made to include others in the familial relationship. For example, we select our spouse or life partner. We all have experience with family relationships, but have you considered the unique nature of these bonds? A scene from the 2005 film *The Family Stone* illustrates this obligation. Sarah Jessica Parker portrays a young woman struggling to be accepted by her fiancé's close-knit family. At one point she becomes frustrated and asks her future mother-in-law, "What's so great about you guys?" Diane Keaton replies, "Uh, nothing . . . it's just that we're all that we've got." Each family member recognizes other family members' idiosyncrasies, but also realizes that the strength of the family bond surpasses all other relationships.

TYPES OF FAMILY RELATIONSHIPS

It is difficult to describe a "typical" family in the twenty-first century. Over the years, the structure of the typical American family has changed. The *Handbook of Family Communication* explores several different family forms such as intact families, divorced or single parent families, stepfamilies, and the families of lesbian women or gay men. But while the forms may have changed, core relationships continue to exist and have provided scholars with opportunities to take a glimpse into how communication develops in these relationships. While we do not have the space to discuss all family forms, three specific interpersonal relationships that exist in the family structure will be discussed: marital relationships, parent-child relationships, and sibling relationships.

Marital Relationships

Individuals in healthy marriages tend to be healthier and happier than others.

© sonya etchison, 2007, Shutterstock.

In a recent issue of *Psychology Today* anthropologist Helen Fisher wrote "I have long been captivated by one of the most striking characteristics of our species: We form enduring pair bonds. The vast majority of other mammals—some 97 percent—do not" (Fisher, 2007, 78). These enduring pair bonds, or marriages, often provide individuals with a great deal of social support, happiness, personal fulfillment and satisfaction. According to family communication researchers Turner and West (2002), "marriage is often seen as the most important intimate relationship two people can share" (232). Some research indicates that individuals in healthy marriages tend to be both healthier and happier than unmarried individuals or those in unhealthy relationships. The longstanding question posed by researchers from a variety of academic and professional fields has always been how to obtain and maintain an enduring marital relationship.

Each life partner brings his or her own set of expectations to the marital relationship. If you have ever tuned into a television talk show, you have probably seen a couple asking the host to solve their marital problems. It is not unusual for the host to identify differing expectations as the root of the problem. Earlier in this text, we mentioned that messages have both content and relational dimensions. The same is true of our expectations for relationships—couples hold content expectations and relational expectations for their partnership.

Content Expectations.

Content expectations focus on how the relationship is defined by the role each partner plays. Roles are defined by the expectations held for a position in family. The popular ABC television show *Wife Swap* focuses on the role expectations established for wives in two different types of families. In each episode, the wives switch families for two weeks. Clashes ensue over differing content expectations for husbands' and wives' roles in housekeeping and child-rearing. It is important to note that one of the difficult tasks involved in the marital relationship is ensuring that the two sets of expectations are congruent.

Relational Expectations.

Relational expectations refer to the similarity, or correspondence, of the emotional, or affective, expectations each partner has for defining the relationship. In one episode of *Wife Swap*, the Kraut and Hardin wives exchange households. One wife spends considerable time shopping and focusing on the current fashion trends, while her husband tends to the household duties. The other wife expects all family members to participate in household chores, and the couple has formed the expectation that the role of the wife will include being responsible for home schooling the children. When the two families swap wives for the two-week period, they discover that their relational expectations are incongruent in the new environment. This often causes the sparks to fly! When the wives are in their own homes, communication is more satisfying because their spouses and children have congruent expectations for the relationship. They understand what their family roles are, and they have become comfortable with the communication expectations associated with these roles. Marital satisfaction is greater in relationships where couples discuss their expectations for the relationship—failure to talk about expectancies is often equated to playing "guess what's inside my mind."

To explain the various expectations that couples have for communication and for the relationship, Fitzpatrick (1987) developed a model to distinguish each couple type and how they view role conventionality, interdependence, and approach to conflict. Three couple types were identified: traditionals, separates, and independents (see also Table 11.1).

Traditionals.

Those who exhibit a high level of interdependence and sharing are considered **traditional couples**. Conventional sex roles are adopted in traditional couples, with males performing tasks such as lawn care, automobile maintenance, and taking out the garbage. Women fulfill

© Losevsky Pavel, 2007, Shutterstock.

Traditional couples adopt conventional sex roles in their marriages.

Table 11.1	Description of Marital Types
Marital Type of Couples	**Characteristics**
Traditionals	Demonstrate a high amount of interdependence and sharing; adopt traditional or conventional sex roles
Separates	Emphasize each other's individual identity over relational maintenance; typically avoid conflict
Independents	Respect the need for autonomy; negotiate a high level of communication and sharing; adopt nonconventional sex roles (husband stays home and wife works outside of home)

the role of nurturing caregiver and are responsible for housekeeping and childcare duties. In her research, Fitzpatrick (1987) found that traditionals tend to be the most satisfied of the three couple types.

Separates.   **Separate couples** tend to emphasize each individual's identity and independence over maintaining the relationship. In addition to maintaining conventional sex roles in the relationship, this couple is characterized by their avoidance of conflict. As is evident, this couple type typically reports a low level of marital satisfaction.

Independents.   **Independent couples** simultaneously respect the need for autonomy and engage in a high level communication and sharing with one another. Sex roles in the independent relationship are nonconventional or nonexistent. While it may appear that independents enjoy a happily married relationship, research shows that many independent couples report low levels of satisfaction. By applying this model to our examination of marital communication, we see that one of the characteristics that distinguish the various couple types from one another is their expectations for sex roles and their approach to conflict situations.

Parent-Child Relationships

The first family relationship formed is between a parent and a child. As well as having a legal responsibility to care for and protect their children, parents are responsible for the moral and character development of their children—not an easy task. In his book, *Family First*, Dr. Phil McGraw (2004) discusses the role that parents play in preparing children for life's challenges, and points out that parents need to realize the influence they have as a result of the messages they communicate to their children. A parent's role is complicated; biological and emotional attachments create a special bond that makes communication both rewarding and frustrating at times. Television shows such as *Nanny 911* and *Super Nanny* provide parents with advice for managing interactions with their children. They also provide a glimpse into the parenting challenges experienced by others, offering support to parents who can see that others are enduring the same, or worse, situations.

Over the course of the family life cycle, communication between parents and children evolves as new events occur. It is during this time that the dialectical tensions between autonomy and connection are perhaps the strongest. In the beginning of their lives children are totally dependent on the parents to provide for them and look out for their best interests. In the United States, many parents begin teaching children at a young age to become independent. Children are encouraged to learn to eat by themselves, pick out their own clothes, and to explore their individual interests in sports and other extracurricular activities. But even while encouraging independence, many parents simultaneously reinforce the message that they are still connected to their children. Providing children with cellular telephones is one strategy currently used by parents to stay connected as their children explore autonomy.

In her article *"Putting Parents in Their Place: Outside Class,"* (see page 294) Valerie Strauss (2006) illustrates how "too much parent involvement can hinder students' independence" as she explains parent involvement with the "millennial generation."

Young children assert their independence as they "do it all by myself."

As children progress through adolescence, a new set of communication issues needs to be considered. Up to this point, children have been encouraged to become independent, but eventually the dialectical tension between autonomy and connection kicks in and parents may begin to feel that children are becoming too independent. Adolescence is often a difficult transition period for both children and parents alike, and it is not uncommon for conflicts to occur during this time in the family life cycle. A common communication issue during this period involves the negotiation of rules, with new guidelines for behavior being added on a regular basis as parents and children clash over preferences for clothes, manners, curfews, and activities. As the occurrence of parent-child conflict increases during adolescence, issues that once seemed unimportant now take on new relevance. Consider the issues you and your parents disagreed on during your adolescence. Why do you think communication surrounding these issues was so problematic?

As children grow up, identify their aspirations, and pursue their goals, families may find that their time is divided, and this provides yet another source of tension in the household. One recent study found that parents and their teenage children spend less than one hour per day talking to one another *(http://www.familycommunication.org/)* and the number of families who report that they share meals at the dinner table each day has dwindled over the years.

While many adult privileges are granted to children when they reach the age of eighteen, parents and children view and negotiate the transition to adulthood in different ways. The period when children begin the separation process from their parents is often referred to as the **"launching" stage.** However, this term is often misleading because many families continue to experience a sense of interdependence in their lives for a period of time after the child reaches legal age. For example, after returning to college after Christmas break, one student was overheard saying, "It was kind of nice being back home and knowing that my mom would stay up and wait for me to come in at

During adolescence, issues that once were insignificant can create conflict.

Putting Parents in Their Place: Outside Class

They are needy, overanxious and sometimes plain pesky—and schools at every level are trying to find ways to deal with them.

No, not students. Parents—specifically parents of today's "millennial generation" who, many educators are discovering, can't let their kids go.

They text message their children in middle school, use the cellphone like an umbilical cord to Harvard Yard and have no compunction about marching into kindergarten class and screaming at a teacher about a grade.

To handle the modern breed of micromanaging parent, educators are devising programs to help them separate from their kids—and they are taking a harder line on especially intrusive parents.

At seminars, such as one in Phoenix last year titled "Managing Millennial Parents," they swap strategies on how to handle the "hovercrafts" or "helicopter parents," so dubbed because of a propensity to swoop in at the slightest crisis.

Educators worry not only about how their school climates are affected by intrusive parents trying to set their own agendas but also about the ability of young people to become independent.

"As a child gets older, it is a real problem for a parent to work against their child's independent thought and action, and it is happening more often," said Ron Goldblatt, executive director of the Association of Independent Maryland Schools.

"Many young adults entering college have the academic skills they will need to succeed but are somewhat lacking in life skills like self-reliance, sharing, and conflict resolution," said Linda Walter, an administrator at Seton Hall University in New Jersey and co-chairman of the family portion of new-student orientation.

Educators say the shift in parental engagement coincides with the rise of the millennial generation, kids born after 1982.

"They have been the most protected and programmed children ever—car seats and safety helmets, play groups and soccer leagues, cellphones and e-mail," said Mark McCarthy, assistant vice president and dean of student development at Marquette University in Milwaukee. "The parents of this generation are used to close and constant contact with their children and vice versa."

Strauss, Valerie. 2006. Putting Parents in Their Place: Outside Class; Too Much Involvement Can Hinder Students' Independence, Experts Say. ***Washington Post,* March 21.**

DISCUSSION QUESTION

How is the "millennial generation" parent different in terms of parent-child communication than the parents of past generations?

From "Putting Parents in Their Place: Outside Class" by Valerie Strauss, *The Washington Post*, March 21, 2006. © 2006, The Washington Post, excerpted with permission.

night. I guess I have to admit that I missed that during my first semester at college." While some may find comfort in the old routines, others may find that new rules need to be negotiated during the launching stage. Adult children who live in their parent's home while getting started in their careers may find that while they are independent in terms of their professional life, they are still dependent on their parents for need fulfillment in their personal life. Daily chores, financial contributions, and respect for household rules often emerge as topics requiring negotiation.

Divorce and remarriage create additional issues to consider in parent-child interactions. Stepfamilies face unique challenges that revolve around issues relating to discipline, resources, and ties to the biological family unit. An estimated one-third of Americans are likely to experience life in a stepfamily (Bumpass et al. 1995). Should stepfamilies and stepchildren expect communication and relationships to be similar to those between biological parents and children? Family communication scholars describe the experience of entering a stepfamily as similar to starting a novel halfway through the book (Coleman, Ganong, and Fine 2004). One student recently described the experience of joining a stepfamily as similar to reading the description of a movie on the back of a DVD and then making a decision about whether or not you will like the movie. Based on the brief description, the movie seems like a good choice. However, once you begin watching the movie, you learn that it is not at all what you expected. Similarly, individuals enter stepfamily situations and often expect them to function like intact families when often this is not the case (Coleman et al. 2004).

Images of stepfamilies portrayed in stories and the media often depict these relationships as filled with challenges and negative communication. In the 1998 film *Stepmom*, a conversation between the biological mother (Jackie) and her daughter (Anna) about her stepmother (Isabel) illustrates one of many potential communication issues associated with stepfamily relationships.

Anna: I think Isabel's pretty.

Jackie: Yeah, I think she's pretty too . . . if you like big teeth.

Anna: Mom?

Jackie: Yes sweetie?

Anna: If you want me to hate her, I will. (*Stepmom* directed by Chris Columbus, 2hr. 4 min.,1492 Pictures, 1998.)

Anger or guilt can impact communication about the relationship, and both children and parents may find it difficult to be open about their true feelings. Another communication hurdle faced in the stepparent-stepchild relationship is the use of names to refer to the relationship. In a 2003 interview on Moviehole.net, Jada Pinkett Smith revealed that she refers to her stepson as her "bonus child," and Demi Moore's daughters refer to stepdad, Ashton Kutcher, as "MOD" which stands for "My Other Dad." (*http://people.aol. com/people/articles/0,19736,1090617,00.html*).

Maintenance in Parent-Child Relationships.   Parents and children often find the need to increase efforts in maintaining their relationship as children grow older and gain more autonomy. Activities, new friends, and, eventually, the process of starting a new family can detract from the time and energy available for relationships with parents. In some instances, the onset of these maintenance challenges begins much earlier when parents decide to divorce. Non-custodial parents are faced with identifying new strategies to maintain the relationship with their children in the absence of the close physical proximity they once shared. While many strategies used to maintain the relationship are similar to those found in other types of relationships, in a 1999 study Thomas-Maddox identified several strategies unique to this context. Non-custodial parents indicated that they depend on mediated communication (sending letters, emails, phone calls) and material/monetary offerings (sending gifts, taking children on "exciting" trips) to maintain their relationship. Responses from children revealed that there are additional strategies they initiate to maintain a relationship with their non-custodial parents. Strategies listed most frequently by children include mediated communication, proximity (living with non-custodial parent during summer vacations and breaks by choice), and suggesting joint activities (proposing ideas such as going to the movies). While being physically separated as a result of this difficult decision may not be easy for parents and children, there are communication strategies that are used to continue the relationship from a distance.

Sibling Relationships

During younger years, siblings often spend more time together than with their parents.

© Terrie L. Zeller, 2007, Shutterstock.

Relationships with siblings generally last the longest, given that our brothers and sisters are often still with us long after our parents are gone. Approximately eighty percent of individuals have siblings and, with the exception of first-born children, sibling relationships are simultaneously formed with parent relationships. In their younger years, siblings often spend more time playing and interacting with one another than they do with their parents. But that does not necessarily mean these relationships are always positive. One minute siblings may be collaborating to "team up" against their parents, and the next minute they may be fighting like cats and dogs.

Communication in the sibling relationship often reflects both negative and positive aspects. As family resources such as time, parent's attention, or physical objects are perceived to be scarce, siblings may engage in conflict or competition.

Studies have shown that same-sex siblings tend to be more competitive than opposite-sex siblings. In some instances, siblings may be expected to fulfill the role of teacher or "co-parent." If you have siblings, chances are you have probably been instructed to "Watch out for your brother (or sister)" at some point in time. Often this occurs in single-parent families or in families where both parents are employed outside the home.

As siblings approach adolescence, their relationship experiences new transformations. Perhaps the competition for resources may become more intense, or siblings experience frustration when they are compared to one another. In these instances, a sibling may seek deidentification from other siblings. **Deidentification** is defined as an individual's attempt to create a distinct identity that is separate from that of their siblings. Have you ever had a teacher compare you to an older sibling? Or perhaps you have had friends at school who point out how similar or different you are compared to your brother or sister. When siblings are constantly evaluated against one another, they may experience a desire to create a unique identity and sense of self. Perhaps your ability to play soccer was often compared to one of your siblings that also played soccer. In an effort to distinguish yourself from your sibling, you quit playing soccer and started wrestling instead.

Maintenance in Sibling Relationships

Recall our discussion of the importance of relationship maintenance in Chapter Seven. Relational maintenance is of particular importance in the sibling relationship as the relationship between brothers and sisters typically lasts longer than any other family relationship. In a study designed to investigate unique maintenance strategies employed by siblings, six behaviors were identified (Myers and Weber 2004). These include confirmation, humor, social support, family visits, escape, and verbal aggression.

Confirmation.   Confirmation strategies consist of messages used to communicate the importance or value of siblings in one's life. Statements such as, "I'm lucky to have you as my brother" or "I really appreciate having you here to support me" are often viewed as validating the relationship.

Humor.   Often siblings use humor as a way to bring amusement or enjoyment to their relationship. Sharing private jokes about family members or making fun of their behaviors are ways siblings use humor to strengthen their bond.

Social Support.   Siblings provide social support to one another by using verbal and nonverbal comforting strategies to assist one another through difficult times. Asking a sibling for advice or sharing information about difficulties in other relationships illustrates the trust that is present in the relationship.

Family Events.   Siblings often maintain and strengthen their relationships with each other and other family members through participation in family events. They may agree to visit their parents at the same time during the summer or holidays to spend time together.

Escape.   Sometimes we view our relationships with our siblings as an escape during difficult situations. Have you ever agreed to attend a family wedding or reunion only because your sibling agreed to attend? Doing so solidifies the bond by communicating the dependence that you have on one another to provide an outlet during difficult times.

Verbal Aggression.   While the final strategy, verbal aggression, may seem counterintuitive to maintaining a relationship, this maintenance mechanism allows siblings to vent their frustrations with one another. Over the years, they may have discovered that yelling at one another is the most effective method for having their concerns heard.

© Galina Barskaya, 2007, Shutterstock.

Siblings often maintain their connections through participation in family events.

FAMILY COMMUNICATION THEORIES

Several theories can be applied to the study of communication in family relationships. Recall the definition of interpersonal communication: a process which occurs in a specific context and involves an exchange of verbal or nonverbal messages between two connected individuals with the intent to achieve shared meaning. The family is one context of connected individuals in which these interactions occur. Scholars of family communication have applied a variety of interpersonal theories to explain these interactions. In essence, virtually any theory of interpersonal communication could be applied to the study of families. Three theories which have implications for the family relationship in particular are systems theory, family communication patterns theory, and symbolic interactionism.

Systems Theory

Systems theory has been employed by family scholars to explore a variety of interactions, including children's attitudes about their single parent dating (Marrow-Ferguson and Dickson 1995), family involvement in addressing children's problems at school (Walsh and Williams 1997), and adolescent abuse of their parents (Eckstein 2004). **Family systems theory** is one of the most frequently used theories in family communication scholarship (Stamp 2004). The basic premise behind this theory is that family relationships can be treated as systems and can include the study of systemic qualities such as wholeness, interdependence, hierarchy, boundaries, calibration, and equifinality (Stamp 2004). Each of the elements of systems theory is particularly relevant in explaining how and why family members relate to one another.

Wholeness.   **Wholeness** implies that a family creates its own personality or culture, and that this personality is unique from that of each family member. Many studies that have applied systems theory recognize that in order to understand the dynamics of families, the role of individual family members must be considered as well.

Typically the parents are responsible for taking care of children and maintaining the powerful roles in the family.

© HTuller, 2007, Shutterstock.

Interdependence.   **Interdependence** proposes that the family system is comprised of interrelated parts, or members. A change experienced by one family member is likely to result in changes that impact all other family members. Suppose a child catches the flu and cannot attend school for several days. If both parents work outside the home, one will have to make adjustments to his work schedule to stay at home with the child. To protect other family members from being exposed to the illness, family routines such as sharing dinner or watching television together may be altered.

Hierarchy.   All systems have levels, or a **hierarchy,** present. Typically, parents take on the powerful roles in the family and are responsible for seeing that children's needs are fulfilled and that discipline and control are maintained in the system. Perhaps the system element that has gained the most attention in family studies is boundaries.

Boundaries.   Families create **boundaries** to communicate to members who are to be considered part of the system. These boundaries are often flexible as the family expands to include friends and pets. **Ambiguous boundaries** often create confusion about who family members perceive as being part of the system. In the movie *While You Were Sleeping*, Lucy (Sandra Bullock) discovers that the man the family refers to as Uncle Saul (Jack Warden) is included in the family's boundaries due to their strong friendship. Uncle Saul says, "Lucy, the Callaghans, well, they took me in as part of their family. I'd never let anyone hurt them." Even though the family bonds are not biological, he communicates that he is dedicated to protecting the family and views them as an important part of his life.

Calibration.   The system element of **calibration** is the mechanism that allows the family to review their relationships and communication and decide if any adjustments need to be made to the system. Television shows such as *Nanny 911* provide examples of families that can be used as a basis for comparison. Feedback communicated through messages received from others can also be taken into consideration. While waiting in line at the grocery store, a mother might be complimented on how well-behaved her children are. This provides her with feedback to gauge her performance as a mother.

Equifinality.   The final systems element, **equifinality,** refers to families' abilities to achieve the same goal by following different paths or employing different communication behaviors. For example, one family may teach the children independence by communicating the expectation that the children are responsible for getting themselves up and getting ready for school in the morning. In another family, the mother might enter the bedroom and gently sing "Good Morning" to the children, lay out their school clothes, and have breakfast ready for them. Both families accomplish the same goal: working through the morning routine of getting to school on time. However, each family has a different method for accomplishing the goal.

Family Communication Patterns Theory

Perhaps one of the most complicated phenomena to factor into the family communication equation is the role that intrapersonal communication plays in the process. **Family communication patterns theory** is a comprehensive theory that focuses on the cognitive processes used to shape and guide our interpersonal interactions. Originally developed by McLeod and Chaffee (1972, 1973) as a way for explaining family members' interactions associated with television viewing, the goal of the theory was to explain how parents help children to understand messages received from multiple sources through mediated channels. But consider for a moment all of the different messages received from outside the family that are processed on a daily basis. Ritchie and Fitzpatrick (1990) expanded the focus of this theory beyond mediated messages to focus on how a variety of messages are processed and discussed within the family to create shared meaning. This revised theory identified two primary orientations used by families: conversation and conformity.

Conversation.   **Conversation orientation** refers to the level of openness and the frequency with which a variety of topics are discussed. Families who adopt a high conversation orientation encourage members to openly and frequently share their thoughts and feelings with one another on a wide variety of topics. It is rare that a topic is "off limits" for discussion in families who have a high conversation orientation. On the other hand, families with low conversation orientation experience less frequent or less open interactions, and sometimes there are limits with regard to what topics can be discussed.

Conformity.   The second dimension of the communication pattern analysis focuses on the family's conformity orientation. **Conformity** refers to the degree to which a family encourages autonomy in individual beliefs, values, and attitudes. Families who emphasize a high level of conformity in interactions encourage family members to adopt similar ways of thinking about topics, often with the goal of avoiding conflict and promoting harmony in the family. At the other end of the conformity continuum, family members are encouraged to form independent beliefs and attitudes, and these differing opinions are often perceived as having equal value in discussions and decision-making. To explain the interrelationship between conversation orientation and conformity orientation, Koerner and Fitzpatrick identified four different family types (2002). These include pluralistic, consensual, laissez-faire, and protective families. See Table 11.2 for an integration of the family types into the two family orientations.

Parents who encourage their children to form relationships outside the home and couples who believe that each partner should pursue his own network of friends typically do so in an effort to broaden the perspectives of individuals within the family. Use the scale in Table 11.3 to find out what you perceive your family orientation to be.

Pluralistic.   **Pluralistic families** adopt a high conversation orientation and a low conformity orientation. Almost anything goes in this family! A wide range of topics are discussed, and family members are encouraged to have

Table 11.2   Family Types as Identified by Family Communications Patterns Theory

	High Conformity	**Low Conformity**
HIGH CONVERSATION	CONSENSUAL Strong pressure toward agreement; encouragement to take interest in ideas without disturbing power in family hierarchy	PLURALISTIC Open communication and discussion of ideas is encouraged but with little emphasis on social constraint; fosters communication competence as well as independence of ideas
LOW CONVERSATION	LAISSEZ-FAIRE Little parent-child interaction; child relatively more influenced by external social settings (e.g., peer groups)	PROTECTIVE Obedience is prized; little concern for conceptual matters; child is not well-prepared for dealing with outside influences and is easily persuaded

Table 11.3 The Revised Family Communication Pattern Instrument

Respond to the following statements as they apply to your communication with your parents while you were growing up. Place a number on the line that best describes your agreement with the statements below, using the following scale:

5 = Strongly Agree, 4 = Agree, 3 = Neither Agree nor Disagree, 2 = Disagree, 1 = Strongly Disagree

_____ 1. My parents often said things like, "You'll know better when you grow up."

_____ 2. My parents often asked my opinion when the family was talking about something.

_____ 3. My parents often said things like, "My ideas are right and you should not question them."

_____ 4. My parents encouraged me to challenge their ideas and beliefs.

_____ 5. My parents often said things like, "A child should not argue with adults."

_____ 6. I usually told my parents what I was thinking about things.

_____ 7. My parents often said things like, "There are some things that are just not to be talked about."

_____ 8. I can tell my parents almost anything.

_____ 9. When anything really important was involved, my parents expected me to obey without question.

_____ 10. In our family we often talk about our feelings and emotions.

_____ 11. In our home, my parents usually had the last word.

_____ 12. My parents and I often had long, relaxed conversation about nothing in particular.

_____ 13. My parents felt that it was important to be the boss.

_____ 14. I really enjoyed talking with my parents, even when we disagreed.

_____ 15. My parents sometimes became irritated with my views if they were different from theirs.

_____ 16. My parents often say something like "you should always look at both sides of an issue."

_____ 17. If my parents don't approve of it, they don't want to know about it.

_____ 18. My parents like to hear my opinions, even when they don't agree with me.

_____ 19. When I am at home, I am expected to obey my parents' rules.

_____ 20. My parents encourage me to express my feelings.

_____ 21. My parents tended to be very open about their emotions.

_____ 22. We often talk as a family about things we have done during the day.

_____ 23. In our family we often talk about our plans and hopes for the future.

_____ 24. In our family we talk about topics like politics and religion where some persons disagree with others.

_____ 25. My parents often say something like "Every member of the family should have some say in family decisions."

_____ 26. My parents often say something like "You should give in on arguments rather than risk making people mad."

SCORING DIRECTIONS:

Items 1, 3, 5, 7, 9, 11, 13, 15, 17, 19, 26 represent the Conformity items.

Add these items and divide by 11 to determine your Conformity score.

Items 2, 4, 6, 8, 10, 12, 14, 16, 18, 20, 21, 22, 23, 24, 25 represent the Conversation items.

Add these items and divide by 15 to determine your Conversation score.

Scoring—Your scores will range from 1–5 and the higher score is more likely to be the perceived communication pattern in your family.

Source: "Revised Family Communication Pattern Instrument" by L.D. Ritchie from "Family Communication Patterns: Measuring Interpersonal Perceptions of Interpersonal Relationships" by Michael E. Roloff, 1990, _Communication Research,_ 17 (4), 523–544. Reprinted by Permission of Sage Publications Inc.

their own opinions without feeling the pressure to agree with one another. Children in pluralistic families are often encouraged to participate in decision-making on topics ranging from where the family should go for vacation to the establishment of family rules.

Consensual.   **Consensual families** adopt both a high conversation and a high conformity orientation. These families often encourage members to be open in their interactions with one another, but they expect that family members will adopt similar opinions and values. Parents in consensual families promote open conversations, but they still believe that they are the authority when it comes to decisions in the family.

Laissez-Faire.   **Laissez-faire families** adopt both a low conversation and low conformity orientation. Rarely will family members talk with one another, and when conversations do occur, they are focused on a limited number of topics. Children are encouraged to make their own decisions, often with little or no guidance or feedback from their parents in the laissez-faire family.

Protective.   **Protective families** score low on conversation orientation and high on conformity. The phrase "Children should be seen but not heard" is characteristic of this family type. Parents are considered to be the authority, and children are expected to obey the family rules without questioning them.

Identifying and understanding the approaches used to communicate and to promote autonomy and independence is beneficial to understanding how these interactions shape both individual and family identities.

Symbolic Interaction Theory

Symbolic interactionism is perhaps one of the most widely applied theories in the study of family life. In Chapter Three we discussed the role that symbols and messages play in assigning meaning to our experiences, others, and ourselves. Mead's (1934) five concepts of symbolic interactionism (mind, self, I, me, and roles) are particularly useful in understanding the impact that family interactions have on shaping one's identity. In his discussion of the concept of "mind," Mead explains the role that symbols play in creating shared meaning. Children interact with family members and learn language and social meanings associated with words. Similarly, Mead points out that one's sense of "self" is developed through interactions with others. Families are influential in shaping this view of self through the messages and reactions to one another. Family members gain a sense of how they are viewed by others from messages that are exchanged. Statements such as "You're such a good husband!" or "He's such a rotten kid" shape how individuals see themselves.

It is important to note that individual differences, such as personality traits or communication predispositions, may cause family members to view the same situation in very different ways. Consider the following scenario.

Kaija was quiet as Jay drove up the driveway. Jay smiled at her and said, "Trust me, they'll love you!" Kaija was meeting Jay's family for the first time since he had proposed. As they entered the front door, she was bombarded with hugs and kisses from various aunts, uncles, grandparents, and cousins. During dinner the talking never stopped! Kaija felt so left out—and nobody even seemed to care enough to ask her questions about herself. At one point, she slipped out on the back patio just to have a few moments of peace and quiet. As they drove back to campus, Jay commented, "Wasn't it a great evening! Everyone thought you were awesome!" Kaija couldn't believe what she had just heard. How could Jay have come to the conclusion that his family liked her? After all, they didn't take the time to find out anything about her. And the hugs and kisses were so intimidating. Kaija's family would have never shown such open displays of affection the first time they met Jay. She was confused—how could Jay have thought the evening went so great when she thought it had been horrible?

Who was correct in his or her assessment of the evening's events? Symbolic interactionism would indicate that both Jay and Kaija formed accurate perceptions. Each of them had formed his own meaning of the event based on his interpretation of the messages and behaviors. We learn in the scenario that Kaija's family would not have displayed affection so openly, while Jay's family background shaped his acceptance of effusive greetings. Our experiences in our family of origin shape our meanings of events, messages, and behaviors. The fact that Jay's family did not ask Kaija about herself caused her to perceive them as being uninterested. But suppose Jay had shared with his family that Kaija was an only child and tended to be shy around large groups. He may have asked them to refrain from bombarding her with questions that might cause her to feel uncomfortable. To better understand how symbolic interactionism applies to this scenario, it might be useful to examine the three underlying assumptions of the theory (LaRossa and Reitzes 1993).

First, *our interactions with family members influence the meanings we assign to behaviors and messages.* Children determine if they should evaluate experiences as being positive or negative by watching the reactions of family members to various events and messages. A child whose parents avoid conflict may believe that conflict is a negative behavior that should be avoided at all costs. Coming from a family that shows caring through conversation, Kaija assigned a negative meaning to Jay's family's failure to ask her questions about herself.

Next, *individuals create a sense of self which serves as a guide for selecting future behaviors.* We assess situations and take into consideration whether others will perceive behaviors and messages in a positive or negative way. This assumption goes beyond our own evaluation of events to include the perceptions of others. A child whose father has told him "You're a rotten kid" and "You'll never amount to anything" has learned to misbehave. As the negative messages are repeated, he comes to believe that others expect him to misbehave.

Finally, symbolic interactionism posits that the *behavior of family members is influenced by culture and society.* Perhaps this assumption sheds light on the reasons families are reluctant to admit that they experience conflict from time to time. Based on media portrayals of family life and from listening to the happy stories of other families, an expectation has been established that "normal" families do not fight.

CREATING A FAMILY IDENTITY

While individual family members form their own identities, the family as a unit also creates a collective identity. Communication is the primary mechanism for creating this family identity, with various messages and behaviors providing insight as to how the family views itself as a group. Four ways that families create and sustain an identity as a unit are through stories, myths, themes, and metaphors. As we discuss each of these elements, reflect on your own family of origin and how these communicative acts shaped your sense of what it means to be a part of your family.

Family Stories

Family stories are narratives recounting significant events that have been shared by members. In essence, family life is comprised of a series of stories. Because they are about shared experiences, these stories are often personal and emotional; they may evoke positive or negative feelings in family members. Individuals often use these stories to shape their own sense of identity. One of the authors of your text had a difficult time gaining confidence in her driving ability. Do you think it might be due in part to the fact that her family members enjoyed telling and retelling the story of how she was responsible for wrecking the family car when she was four years old?

Families share special stories of a child's birth to connect the child within the family.

© Vladimir Melnik, 2007, Shutterstock.

Three types of family stories that have been studied by family scholars in an attempt to explain how families define their experiences are birth stories, courtship stories, and stories of survival. **Birth stories** describe how each person entered the family and can define how members "fit" into the system. One woman shared a story of enduring a forty-two hour labor prior to the birth of her son. She stated, "I guess I should have known then that he would always be challenging me because he gave me such a difficult time from the beginning!" **Courtship stories** provide a timeline for tracing romance in the family. They are often used to describe how parents and grandparents met and how they decided that they were right for one another. A young woman who was engaged to be married asked her grandfather how he met her grandmother. He explained that she was working in the fields on her family farm and that it was love at first sight. He joked, "I knew she was a hard worker, so I asked her to marry me!" But he went on to explain that he knew she was devoted to helping her family and knew that she would be dedicated to her own family. **Stories of survival** are narratives used to explain how family members have overcome difficult times, and they are often told to help family members cope with challenges they face. Three sisters who, at a young age, were physically abused by their father, discussed sharing their stories with one another as well as with other young girls to assist them in coping with similar experiences. While some might perceive the retelling of these stories as being too painful, the sisters viewed the stories as therapeutic and reinforced the notion that if they could survive the abuse of their father, they were strong enough to face any situation.

Family Myths

Family **myths** are created to communicate the beliefs, values, and attitudes held by members to represent characteristics that are considered important to the family. These myths are often fictional as they are based on an ideal image the family wishes to convey to others. Consider the following example:

> "I couldn't believe what I was hearing! At my grandfather's funeral, my dad's family members were all talking about what a great man my grandfather was and how much they would miss him. My grand-mother sobbed as she whispered, 'He was such a loving and caring man. I don't know what I'll do without him.' After the service, I asked my father why they were all referring to my grandfather that way. For years I had heard stories of the physical abuse that had taken place in the family during my dad's childhood, and I had heard my grandfather yell at my grandmother on numerous occa-sions. My dad responded, 'It's just easier on your grandmother if we all remember him in a positive way.' "

In this scenario, the family creates a myth that portrays the grandfather as a loving, caring man. Doing so enables them to protect the grandmother and to perpetuate the belief that he was a good father and husband. In the movie, *Doing Time on Maple Drive*, a family goes to great lengths to portray the image of the "perfect family" to their friends and neighbors. At one point, the son reveals to his parents that he attempted to commit suicide because he would rather be dead than admit to them that he is gay. This scene illustrates the power of family myths and the tremendous amount of pressure placed on family members to live up to the expectations communicated in these myths.

Metaphors

Sometimes families create **metaphors** to assist in communicating how family life as a system is experienced by members. Family metaphors make reference to specific objects, events, or images to represent the family experience and a collective identity. The metaphor of a "three-ring circus" may be used to describe the chaos and disorganization that exists within one family, while the "well-oiled machine" can depict the emphasis on control and organiza-tion that is the norm for another family. Metaphors can provide those within the family and outside of the family with an understanding of what behaviors are valued as well as how family members are expected to behave. A person from a "well-oiled machine" family can use the metaphor to understand the expectations associated with being a member of the family.

Themes

Family **themes** represent important concerns regarding the expected relation-ship between family members and can assist family members in understand-ing how to direct their energy as a family unit. These themes often emerge from two primary sources—the background or experience of parents, and the dialectical pulls experienced by the family. Suppose Joe and Marnie are hav-ing a difficult time managing the tensions of autonomy and connection as their children grow older, begin dating, and spend more time with friends than with family members. In an attempt to communicate their concern for the growing independence of family members, they remind the children that "Blood is thicker than water" and "Friends may come and go, but family is forever." These themes are intended to remind the children that while they may form many relationships outside the unit, the strongest ties should be reserved for those in their family.

CONSEQUENCES OF FAMILY RELATIONSHIPS

Throughout this text, various communication variables have been identified as being both beneficial and harmful to our interpersonal relationships. Because families play such a vital role in the development of our self-identity, understanding how specific communication behaviors can enhance and damage our relationships and our sense of self is important.

Families can serve as the primary source of understanding and support for individuals. As we grow older, we receive messages that let us know that we are cared for and accepted. These perceptions are often shaped by the types of verbal and nonverbal cues we receive from others and are often linked to the formation of our sense of self. Three types of messages are often used to indicate whether family members view us in the same way we see ourselves.

Confirmation

Confirmation occurs when we treat and communicate with family members in a way that is consistent with how they see themselves. A child who perceives himself to be independent is confirmed when a parent gives him responsibility and allows him to make his own decisions.

Rejection

Rejection occurs when family members treat others in a manner that is inconsistent with how they see themselves. Can you recall a time when you felt like you were "grown up" but your parents treated you as though you were still a child? Perhaps you felt you were responsible enough to be left alone while your parents went out for the evening, but they hired a babysitter to stay with you. At times, family members communicate with one another in a way that is disconfirming.

Disconfirmation

© Galina Barskaya, 2007, Shutterstock.

Offering encouragement fosters development of a more intimate relationship.

Disconfirmation occurs when family members fail to offer any type of response. This behavior can be viewed as lack of acknowledgement for how they view other family members. We often get caught up in our busy schedules and fail to communicate with family members. Even though our response is neither positive nor negative, it can cause others to feel dissatisfied with the relationship. A parent who fails to comment on a child's report card, or a wife who fails to acknowledge the efforts of her husband's attempts at cooking dinner are examples of disconfirming responses. Understanding and supportive communication are related to family satisfaction. If we perceive family members as being there for us, we are more willing to exert energy toward developing a more intimate relationship.

COMMUNICATING INTIMACY

Earlier in this text we discussed the concept of intimacy in romantic and marital relationships. Our first experience in developing intimacy in relationships is often a result of our interactions with parents, siblings, and other family members. **Intimacy** refers to close relationships in which two or more people share personal and private information with one another. Young children are often more willing to disclose their fears and goals with family members than with others, and this is often the result of the perceived trust and affection associated with these relationships. How do you show affection for your family members? Chances are that the most basic way this is demonstrated is through our willingness to share disclosures. While we know that intimacy is fostered through our self-disclosures, these revelations are not necessarily exchanged equally between family members. Studies of disclosure in families have found that wives engage in disclosures more often than husbands, and both male and female children report disclosing more information to their mothers than to their fathers. As children grow older, their disclosure patterns often change. College students often disclose more to friends than to their parents. Consider the changes in your own disclosure patterns with your parents. As you get older, you may discover that you are more willing to share negative and honest information about yourself with your friends than you are with parents.

DIFFICULT COMMUNICATION

We have addressed the positive and supportive aspects of interpersonal communication in family relationships, but it is important to note that families are not immune to difficult communication. Just as romantic partners and friends experience highs and lows in relationships, so do families. Because families evolve as members grow and encounter new life experiences, additional communication challenges emerge. The key to effectively managing these issues and maintaining a positive relationship is to understand the role of communication in guiding us through the muddy waters.

Family Stress

Reuben Hill developed the **ABCX model** to study the stress experienced by families during war (1958). Each component of this model provides a glimpse into how different families cope with stress. To begin, "A" represents the stressor event and resulting hardship. "B" refers to the resources a family has available to manage the stress. Given that different families define stress in unique ways, "C" is used to explain how the family defines the stress. Depending on how a family defines "A" "B" and "C," the perception of an event as a crisis is represented by "X." The model is useful for understanding how and why families label situations as stressful and cope with stressors.

Consider the example below.

"Mommy?" My three-year old grandson bolted out of his bed, his hands stretched up to grab around the silhouetted figure in the hallway. I couldn't move fast enough to restrain him, but the kind woman gave my little grandson a hug anyway. "Mommy? My mommy?" He saw the figure, the outline of the hair, but not the face. His mommy, as we all knew, was still in Iraq and wouldn't be home until January. I gently pulled him from the woman's legs where he was holding on and still saying, "Mommy." The woman thought he was being friendly; I knew he believed for one heart-shattering moment that his mommy had finally come home. My tears flowed as I placed him back in bed and comforted him. He could not tell me of his terrible disappointment, his confusion, his sorrow. Instead, I soothed him with "Sweetheart, Mommy is still far, far away. She is still flying helicopters. She'll be home in many, many days." How do you draw "many, many days?" How do you draw "far, far away" to a three-year old? How do you explain war? Danger? Insurgents? People who are determined to kill her because she is a soldier? He got up and walked into the living room where his father slept on the couch, and crawled under the covers. I went to my bedroom, and through half the night, sobbed because I hurt for him, this little three-year old son of a soldier.

From *MSNBC Citizen Journalist Reports* by Margo Ungricht and Lehi Utah, www.msnbc.msn.com. Copyright © 2007 by MSNBC Interactive News, LLC. Reproduced with permission of MSNBC Interactive News LLC in the format textbook via Copyright Clearance Center.

"A" represents the stressor event of a young mother stationed with the U.S. military in Iraq. In this story, extended family members serve as resources to assist with the care of a three-year old child in the absence of his mother, in this case representing the "B." The confusion experienced by the grandmother as she tries to help her grandson cope with the separation causes her to define the stressor as emotionally draining (C). While the family knows that the daughter will return home eventually, they also understand that she chose to serve her country and realize the danger associated with this responsibility. This may keep the family from evaluating the stress as crisis (X). Take a look at Table 11.4 to review each step of the ABCX model.

Table 11.4   The ABCX Model of Family Stress

A	Event producing the stress	Parent of a small child stationed overseas in the military
B	Resources a family has available	Extended family members (grandparents) assist with child care back home in the U.S.
C	Meaning family assigns to the stress	Grandmother finds the child's questions to be emotionally draining, to cause sadness
X	Perception of ability to manage stress (crisis or manageable)	Knowledge that parent chose to go overseas to serve in military; knowledge that this situation will eventually end keeps family from perceiving this as a "crisis"

Stressor events can take many forms; Boss (1988) developed a typology of stressors that families face. These include stressors that are internal versus external, normative versus non-normative, voluntary versus involuntary, and chronic versus acute. **Internal stressors** are those that evolve from a family member. Examples might include a daughter's upcoming wedding or a teen who has tried to run away from home. **External stressors,** on the other hand, are often the result of an event that occurs outside the family, such as a hurricane destroying a family's home or even just an increase in the price of gasoline.

Normative stressors are those that are expected to occur at some point during the course of the family life cycle. The birth of a child or the death of an elderly parent is are events that families anticipate dealing with at some point in time. **Non-normative stressors** are unpredictable and often catch families "off guard." While most people think that winning the lottery would be a great stressor to experience, families do not typically anticipate coming into such a large sum of money and have difficulty dealing with new challenges posed by their good fortune.

Voluntary stressors are those events that family members seek out, such as changing careers and moving to a new city or deciding to run for political office. **Involuntary stressors** are events that simply occur—a family member being injured in a car accident or the announcement of an unplanned teen pregnancy.

Illnesses such as cancer or alcoholism are examples of **chronic stressor** events that require families to cope with the situation for an extended period of time. **Acute stressors** are relatively short-lived and include events such as a student getting suspended for misbehaving or losing the only set of keys to the family car.

Violence and Abuse in Families

Some of us learn at a young age that family is a source of caring and support and will be throughout our lives, but this is not always the case. Often family members encounter stress in their lives and turn to alcohol, drug abuse, or domestic violence as a means to escape from their problems. In these situations, the sad reality is that family members often hurt the ones they love the most. In 1998, nearly one million incidents of violence against a former spouses, boyfriends, or girlfriends were reported (U.S. Dept. of Justice 1998). Unfortunately, abusive behavior often follows a pattern in families, with fifty percent of men who admitted to assaulting their wives reporting that they also frequently abused their children (Strauss, Gellas, and Smith 1990). Abuse may come in the form of physical violence, or verbal and psychological mistreatment. While spousal or child abuse are the forms most often discussed, it is important to note that there are numerous occurrences of elder abuse as well as incidents of abuse in same-sex couples. Disclosures may serve as a mechanism through which family reports reveal abuse, but often the abuse goes unreported.

As children gain more power in the family, incidents of parental abuse by adolescent children have increased (Eckstein 2004). The parent-child relationship is not meant to be equal. Parents need to have control and authority in this dependent relationship. However, in some instances, the reverse is true, with children assuming power in the relationship. Three forms of parental abuse have been identified: physical, psychological, and financial. Physical abuse involves hitting, slapping, and pushing parents. In a 1989 study, nearly fourteen percent of parents reported being physically abused by their adolescent children at least once (Agnew and Huguley). Children may also engage in psychological forms of abuse. Examples of this type of abuse would be creating a sense of fear and include making threats to run away or hurt themselves, or name-calling. A final form of mistreatment is financial abuse. Children who steal from their parents, make demands for things beyond the family's budget, or damage the family's home or possessions are guilty of this type of abuse.

So what mechanisms are available to help family members through these damaging and harmful situations? Before any other step, family members need to admit abuse occurs and to seek assistance in dealing with the situation. Family members often feel ashamed or perceive that the family is a failure by admitting that there is physical or psychological abuse in the home. Seeking professional assistance is a crucial first step in resolving these potentially harmful issues.

SUMMARY

While we form countless interpersonal relationships throughout our lifetime, the relationships and interactions with family members are perhaps the most influential. Beginning at a young age, messages received from family members shape our identity and influence our own choice of communication behaviors. In addition to the individual identities that are shaped by these interactions, the family itself begins to create an identity that is shared by members. Throughout this chapter we have discussed the importance of interpersonal communication throughout the family life cycle. Various interpersonal theories can be applied to the study of family communication to illustrate the dynamic nature of these relationships. While we often assume that "family is forever," it is important to recognize that just as other types of interpersonal relationships experience a "dark side," family relationships can experience turbulent times as well. By exploring the role that interpersonal communication plays in families, we are better able to understand our own tendencies for interacting with others.

APPLICATIONS

Discussion Questions

A. Talk about the definition of the term **family** with several other students. Who would you include in your family? Explain why these individuals are included. What individual differences affect how you define this term (e.g., sex, culture, age, your family of origin, relationship experiences) and who you include in your family?

B. Identify a family from one of your favorite television shows. Use systems theory to analyze the characters' communication patterns and relationships with one another (e.g., interdependence, wholeness, etc). Would you describe the family members' communication and relationships as healthy or unhealthy? Defend your response to this question and be sure to use specific examples to support your arguments.

REFERENCES

Agnew, R., and S. Huguley. 1989. Adolescent violence toward parents. *Journal of Marriage and the Family, 51,* 699–711.

Boss, P. 1988. *Family stress management.* Newbury Park, CA: Sage.

Bumpass, L. L., R. K. Raley, and J. Sweet. 1995. The changing character of stepfamilies: Implications of cohabitation and nonmarital childbearing. *Demography, 32,* 425–436.

Coleman, M., L. Ganong, and M. Fine. 2004. Communication in stepfamilies. In A. Vangelisti (Ed.), *Handbook of family communication.* (215–232). Lawrence Erlbaum Associates: Mahwah, NJ.

Eckstein, N. 2004. Emergent issues in families experiencing adolescent to parent abuse. *Western Journal of Communication, 68,* 365–388.

Fisher, H. 2007. The laws of chemistry. *Psychology Today.* 76–81.

Fitzpatrick, M. A., 1987. Marital interaction. In C. Berger and S. Chaffee (Eds.), *Handbook of communication science* (564–618). Newbury Park, CA: Sage.

Hill, R. 1958. Generic features of families under stress. *Social Casework, 49,* 139–150.

Koerner, A. F., and M. A. Fitzpatrick. 2002. Toward a theory of family communication. *Communication Theory, 12,* 70–91.

LaRossa, R., and D. C. Reitzes. 1993. Symbolic interactionism and family studies. In P. G. Boss, W. J. Doherty, R. LaRossa, W. R. Schumm, and S. K. Steinmetz (Eds.), *Sourcebook of family theories and methods: A contextual approach* (135–163). New York, NY: Plenum Press.

Marrow-Ferguson, S., and F. Dickson. 1995. Children's expectations of their single-parent's dating behavior: A preliminary investigation of emergent themes relevant to single-parent dating. *Journal of Applied Communication Research, 23,* 1–17.

McGraw, P. 2004. *Family first: Your step-by-step plan for creating a phenomenal family.* New York, NY: Free Press.

McLeod, J. M., and S. H. Chaffee. 1972. The construction of social reality. In J. Tedeschi (Ed.), *The social influence process* (50–59). Chicago, IL: Aldine-Atherton.

———. 1973. Interpersonal approaches to communication research. *American Behavior Scientist, 16,* 469–499.

Mead, G. H. 1934. *Mind, self and society.* Chicago: University of Chicago Press.

Myers, S. A., and K. D. Weber. 2004. Preliminary development of a measure of sibling relational maintenance behaviors: Scale development and initial findings. *Communication Quarterly, 52,* 334–346.

Ritchie, L. D. 1990. Family communication patterns: Measuring interpersonal perceptions of interpersonal relationships. *Communication Research, 17*(4), 523–544.

Ritchie, L. D., and M. A. Fitzpatrick. 1990. Family communication patterns: Measuring interpersonal perceptions of interpersonal relationships. *Communication Research, 17,* 523–544.

Sansone, K. 2005. *Woman first, family always.* Des Moines, IA: Meredith Books.

Smith, P. B., and D. R. Pederson. 1988. Maternal sensitivity and patterns of infant-mother attachment. *Child Development, 59,* 1097–1101.

Stafford, L., and D. J. Canary. 1999. Maintenance strategies and romantic relationship type, gender, and relational characteristics. *Journal of Social and Personal Relationships, 8,* 217–242.

Stamp, G. H. 2004. Theories of family relationships and a family relationships theoretical model. In A. Vangelisti (Ed.), *Handbook of family communication.* (1–30). Lawrence Erlbaum Associates: Mahwah, NJ.

Strauss, M. A., R. J. Gelles, and C. Smith. 1990. *Physical violence in American families; Risk factors and adaptations to violence in 8,145 families.* New Brunswick: Transaction Publishers.

Thomas-Maddox, C. 1999. *Keeping the relationship alive: An analysis of relational maintenance strategies employed by non-custodial parents and their children following divorce.* Paper presented at the National Communication Association convention. Chicago, IL.

Turner, L. H., and West, R. 2002. *Perspectives on Family Communication.* McGraw-Hill: Boston, MA.

U.S. Department of Justice. 1998. *Violence by intimates: Analysis of data on crimes by current or former spouses, boyfriends, and girlfriends.* Washington, DC.

Ungricht, Margo. (2006, February 17) MSNBC Citizen Journalist Reports: Stories from front line families. Retrieved from http://msnbc.com/id/7012316/.

Vangelisti, A. 2004. *Handbook of family communication.* Lawrence Erlbaum Associates: Mahwah, NJ.

Walsh, W. M., and R. Williams. 1997. *School and family therapy: Using systems theory and family therapy in the resolution of school problems.* Springfield, IL: Charles C. Thomas.

12

Organizational Communication
Combining the Personal
with the Professional

OBJECTIVES

- Identify three characteristics which distinguish work relationships from other types of interpersonal relationships
- Distinguish among five types of work relationships (superior-subordinate, peer, friendships, mentoring, romantic) and discuss communication issues experienced in each type of relationship
- Explain three approaches to communication in organizations (classical, human relations, human resources) and identify how each addresses interpersonal communication
- Discuss the view of interpersonal communication in the Leader-member exchange theory (LMX)
- Identify four factors that influence the formation of peer relationships at work
- Discuss five dialectical tensions experienced by friends in organizations
- Describe the two types of mentor relationships
- Discuss the pros and cons of romantic relationships among co-workers
- Describe the two types of sexual harassment
- Identify communication characteristics that contribute to effective relationships in organizations
- Discuss the three stages of organization socialization. Explain the role of communication in each of these stages
- Identify contemporary issues impacting interpersonal communication in organizations
- Discuss strategies for balancing work and family relationships
- Describe the impact of technology on interpersonal communication at work

© Andrew Taylor, 2007, Shutterstock.

KEY TERMS

superior-subordinate
  relationship
co-worker (peer)
  relationships

classical theories
human relations
human resources

leader-member
  exchanges (LMX)
autonomy/connection

openness/closedness
equality/inequality
impartiality/favoritism
judgment/acceptance
mentor relationships
supportive mentor
parent mentor
cheerleader mentor
groom mentor
self-promoter
guilt-trip producer
sexual harassment

quid pro quo
hostile work
  environment
organizational
  orientation
upward mobiles
indifferents
ambivalents
organizational culture
anticipatory
  socialization phase

encounter phase
metamorphosis
routinizing actions
connecting
alternating
prepping
reciprocating
improvising
requesting assistance
trading off
evading

Brad was excited! He had been looking forward to his promotion as a new branch manager for Credit One Bank. Unlike most new managers, he felt comfortable about his new position. After all, he would still be working with the team of colleagues he had been working with for the past eight years.

From the outset, Brad quickly discovered that several changes would need to be implemented in the bank in order to accomplish new goals established by the Board of Directors. As he reviewed schedules, he discovered that some of Credit One's employees had been taking advantage of the system. It became apparent that a few of them often extended their lunch hours by an extra twenty to thirty minutes to run errands. Other employees were often caught gossiping about customers after they left the building. Further, the Board wanted to expand the bank's operating hours and to implement new Saturday hours to compete with other banks in the area. Brad called a meeting to discuss these changes and to address some of the issues he had witnessed during his first few weeks as manager. As he discussed the new changes in operating hours, many of his employees began to complain. Susan commented, "What's going on here? Have you become 'Mr. Big Shot' and forgotten that we all have commitments with our families? I'm not going to work on Saturday!" Others chimed in with similar comments. The atmosphere of the meeting went from bad to worse as Brad tried to address the need to treat customers with respect and to refrain from gossiping about them behind their backs. Frustrated, Brad ended the meeting by stating, "Look, I think you're trying to take advantage of the situation here! I'm your supervisor now, and you need to listen."

As he walked away from the meeting, Brad was dumbfounded. How could his colleagues turn on him like that? Had that much really changed just because of his promotion? Or had he been blind to the relationship between employees and management in the past? He was contemplating the situation and decided that the branch manager position might not be all that it was cracked up to be.

OVERVIEW

From popular television shows such as *The Office* and *The Apprentice,* to films such as *Office Space,* work relationships are depicted as everyday circumstances in our lives. Throughout this text, we have discussed the theoretical foundations and concepts central to understanding the role communication plays in interpersonal relationships. As we continue to examine how and why our relationships are impacted by contextual issues, it is important to take a closer look at one context where many adults spend the majority of their time interacting with others—workplace. Many Americans spend more than the average forty hours per week at their jobs. Consider the fact that many employees take work home with them, and the amount of time dedicated to work relationships increases. For some individuals, this may mean that they could potentially spend more time engaged in communication in their work relationships than in any other context.

This chapter addresses the unique aspects of interpersonal communication in relationships associated with one's professional career. In this chapter, we discuss how and why work relationships differ from other types of interpersonal bonds, and explore different types of work relationships, as well as diversity in the workplace. We explain how technology impacts our work relationships, and address the issues faced when exploring the link between work and family.

THE UNIQUE NATURE OF WORK RELATIONSHIPS

Each of our interpersonal relationships is characterized by unique features, and the bonds formed with others at work are no exception. As we begin our discussion of interactions at work, we first need to consider the characteristics of these relationships. How are work relationships different from relationships we form with friends, family, and at school? Work relationships can be described as voluntary, involuntary, and temporary, and are often impacted by the presence of a hierarchy or status differential.

Voluntary

Very few employees remain at their first job for their entire lives. A study conducted by the U.S. Bureau of Labor Statistics found that employees report an average of 9.6 different jobs from age eighteen to age thirty-six. Consider the fact that the majority of our work relationships are voluntary. Organizational relationships are voluntary in the sense that individuals have the choice to interview with the organization and, if offered a job, they have the choice to accept the position and to become a member or not. Deciding to become a member of an organization indicates that a person is interested in pursuing the relationships associated with being an employee. While the initial decision to join an organization is voluntary, some tasks assigned to an employee may result in the formation of involuntary relationships. Involuntary relationships exist between members who did not have any initial desire to initiate a relationship. If you have ever been appointed by your supervisor to work on a project or a team, the relationship between you and the new team members was likely involuntary.

Temporary

Work relationships are also often temporary in nature. While family bonds are long-lasting, employees have the option to continue the relationships with those at work or to seek employment and, therefore, new co-workers, elsewhere. Further, some of the relationships formed in the workplace may be temporary in nature due to the task associated with them. For example, if Martha is assigned to work on a project that is scheduled to be completed six months from now, chances are that the relationships formed during the term of this project are temporary in nature.

Hierarchy/Status Differential

A final characteristic of work relationships is that the interactions are often regulated by a hierarchy or status differential. Our relationships with others in the workplace are impacted by a hierarchy that implies status differentials between members in the organization. Some organizations are "tall" structures with many levels of supervisors, administrators, and employees, while others have relatively "flat" structures with few hierarchical levels separating supervisors

The relationships you form when working on projects may be temporary ones.

from employees. Within the workplace, both implicit and explicit rules and norms for communicating with those of different status exist. For example, persons of lower status understand that they are expected to wait for those of higher level status. Have you ever waited for your academic advisor or professor to show up for his office hours to discuss an assignment that is due? Chances are you are willing to wait ten or fifteen minutes if he is late. It is not likely that the professor would be willing to wait that amount of time for a student to show up for an appointment. Organizational hierarchies form the backbone and/or foundation for a company. Managers and their employees must form relationships in order to meet mutually agreed-upon goals, co-workers are required to interact with one another in order to accomplish tasks and fulfill the goals, and numerous relationships are formed with individuals and other organizations that the company depends upon for its success.

Consider the following example. Clear Mountain Bank is a small community bank with branch offices located in several surrounding communities. By examining this small organization, we can see a vast number of relationships. The bank's officers and branch managers must interact with one another to ensure that they fulfill the organization's goals. If the bank is to succeed, its tellers must establish satisfactory relationships with its customers. But let us take a look beyond the confines of the bank buildings. In order to attract new customers, the bank is required to form relationships with the local media. To ensure that the bank is complying with federal regulations, interactions must be held with those responsible for insuring that regulations are met. Given its presence in the community, Clear Mountain may also form relationships through sponsorship of the local elementary school, as well as several youth athletic teams. This is but a small glimpse of the vast number of relationships formed within a single small organization. Let us take a closer look at the types of relationships formed in organizations.

Have you ever stopped to consider the number of organizations that influence your life each and every day? Given that you are a student, you are obviously influenced by your school. To ensure your physical care, relationships have been formed with those in your doctor's and dentist's offices. If you work while going to school, chock up one more organization you may interact with on a daily basis. In essence, we all exist in an organizational world. As you reflect on the relationships that you have formed in organizations, chances are that many of the communication variables we have discussed in this text have been influential. Whether the task involves building trust, listening to colleagues, providing feedback to your manager or clients, or initiating and maintaining relationships, communication plays a pivotal role.

Co-worker relationships are those among people on the same status level.

© Stephen Coburn, 2007, Shutterstock.

TYPES OF RELATIONSHIPS AT WORK

As you can see from the Clear Mountain example, there are a variety of relationships that can be formed within a single organization. Research that has focused on communication in organizations has primarily focused on two types of work relationships: superior-subordinate relationships and co-worker relationships. **Superior-subordinate** interactions are characterized by a status differential between individuals, and focus on the interactions that take place between supervisors or managers and their employees or subordinates. **Co-worker,** or peer, relationships evolve as a result of interactions between members of an organization at the same status level. Regardless of the type of relationship, communication factors play a vital role in achieving interpersonal effectiveness. Factors such as trust, listening, and feedback are critical.

Superior-Subordinate Relationships

Superior-subordinate relationships differ from other types of interpersonal bonds because of the explicit status differential that is present. Factors impacting relationships between organizational leaders and members include channels of communication, emphasis on task versus relational needs, and communication flow. As we take a closer look at the relationships between supervisors and subordinates, it is important to trace the theoretical foundations that have guided managers in developing various styles of communication.

Early theories of organizational communication focused on information being communicated downward from supervisor to subordinate. **Classical theories** viewed communication as being primarily one-way. Managers sent information down the channels to employees, and messages were typically formal and focused exclusively on task issues. The notion of hierarchy in organizational relationships is demonstrated by Taylor's principles of scientific management. Taylor's theory (1911) asserts that there are distinct differences between managers and employees. The manager's role is to plan and direct the workers as they perform physical labor. Over time, researchers realized that something was missing from this communication model. Meeting the interpersonal needs of workers emerged as an essential element in achieving high productivity and worker satisfaction.

Abraham Maslow's (1943) Hierarchy of Needs was one of the first theories used to specifically acknowledge the higher level needs of organizational employees. While previous theories had acknowledged the presence of worker's physiological and safety needs, Maslow's theory addressed needs for affiliation, esteem, and self actualization. Affiliation needs are placed at the third level of Maslow's hierarchy. These needs are often fulfilled through interpersonal relationships with managers and co-workers. Maslow's theory paved the way for scholars to examine the relationship between work factors, employees' higher-order needs, job satisfaction, and productivity. While many of the **human relations** theories of management provided valuable insight into the value of social relationships at work, one weakness was the overemphasis on informal communication and the assumption that face-to-face interactions were most effective.

As organizational theories evolved, the importance of the superior-subordinate relationship became more evident. In the 1960s, researchers began to explore the impact that interactions between supervisors and subordinates had on organizational efficiency, effectiveness, and satisfaction. Many of the theories developed during this time period are classified as **human resources** approaches. What distinguishes these theories from their earlier counterparts in the Classical and Human Relations approaches is the attention focused on multi-directional communication and the appreciation for both formal and informal communication styles. Human Resources managers recognize that while relationships are an essential part of organizational success, in order to effectively operate as a team, task messages should be regarded as crucial to accomplishing goals. A unique feature of the Human Resources approach is its focus on teams in organizations. Communication is no longer viewed as being strictly upward or downward. After all, employees need to interact not only with their supervisors, but may rely on communication with leaders and members of other teams in the organization, or even their peers within their own teams. Multi-directional communication paved the way for contemporary theories of communication in organizations. See Table 12.1 for a summary of the three approaches to superior-subordinate relationships.

Table 12.1   Approaches to Communication and Relationships

Approaches to Management	Direction of Communication	Focus of Messages	Manager's Style of Communication
Classical	Downward	Task	Formal
Human relations	Upward and downward	Relational	Informal
Human resources	Upward, downward, across, and diagonal	Task relational	Informal, with formal as needed

Leader-member exchange theory, or LMX, explains the process of relationship development between superiors and subordinates (Graen 1976; Graen and Cashman 1975; Graen and Uhl-Bien 1995). In essence, this theory states that leaders in organizations develop relationships with all members and that there are qualitative differences in these bonds. These relationships exist on a continuum ranging from perceptions of "in-group" to "out-group" status. According to LMX, high quality, or "in-group," relationships are the result of subordinates receiving support from supervisors, having influence on decisions that are made in the organization, and being given greater responsibility. Communication in interactions in high LMX relationships is often characterized by trust, liking, and support by both members (Dansereau, Graen, and Haga 1975). The obvious outcome of these positive

© Lorraine Swanson, 2007, Shutterstock.

If you are particularly interested in a certain subject, you may develop a high quality LMX relationship with that instructor.

factors is greater amounts of interaction, and ultimately, higher levels of satisfaction. Low quality, or "out-group," relationships are characterized by little supervisory support and limited influence in decision-making. In this low LMX context, communication can be compared to that of a secret club—one in which information is only shared by those in control or power. Interactions are characterized by the roles and rules to be followed within the hierarchy and, as a result, members of the organization often report being less satisfied and the organization often experiences higher levels of employee turnover. It is quite possible that you have experienced high- or low-quality LMX relationships within educational organizations. Recall a teacher with whom you developed a high quality LMX relationship. If you demonstrated a high level of interest in the subject matter being taught by the teacher, chances are that the instructor engaged in several interactions with you on topics of common interest. You may have even been asked to take on additional responsibilities, such as tutoring peers. But suppose a teacher disagrees with a student's opinions, or views the student as being disinterested in the subject. Fewer attempts may be made to engage in interactions, and a low-quality LMX relationship may evolve.

So what factors contribute to the development of high-quality exchanges among superiors and subordinates? You might be surprised to discover that concepts we have been discussing throughout this text play an influential role in forming these relationships. The concepts include similarity, attraction, and trust. First, the more similar supervisors and subordinates perceive themselves to be, the more likely they are to communicate with one another and to develop a high-quality relationship (Turban and Jones 1988). Recall our discussion of similarity and attraction in Chapter Six. The more similar two people perceive themselves to be, the more attractive they are to one another. Task attraction, which is based on factors that have the potential to help accomplish a goal, is influential in the development of quality LMX. Similarity and task attraction result in increased interaction among leaders and members, thus contributing to the level of trust. Supervisors trust in-group subordinates and allow them to contribute to decision-making by delegating responsibility. On NBC's *The Office*, ambitious subordinates attempt to encourage in-group relationships with branch manager Michael Scott. For example, Andy, the transfer from the Stamford branch who hopes to rise in power, uses "personality mirroring" by imitating Michael. Also, Dwight Schrute is delegated the extra responsibility of assistant regional manager/assistant-to-the-regional-manager because he is in Michael's in-group and is trusted.

As organizations become increasingly diverse, cultural competence is critical for the development of high-quality LMX relationships. Both superiors and subordinates must engage in the process of perspective taking. To avoid falling into the trap of stereotyping one another, each party must be open-minded and committed to learning from the other's perspective. Doing so potentially increases the chances for high-quality LMX relationships to emerge. Suppose a manager from a U.S.-based organization was working with employees in Japan. It would be important for the manager to keep in mind that her Japanese employees are uncomfortable being "singled-out" from the group and prefer to adopt a collectivistic approach to problem-solving. By allowing the employees the opportunity to collaborate in the problem-solving process and by acknowledging the contributions of the group rather than of specific individuals, the manager will likely enhance the LMX relationship. The television show *The Office* has repeatedly lampooned political correctness in the office, particularly since manager Michael Scott is incredibly offensive, unintentionally but continuously stereotyping both the women and minorities in his office. In one episode, manager Michael Scott's version of "Diversity Day" had his employees wearing cards with the name of a race stuck to their foreheads. Employees were then told to treat each other according to the corresponding stereotype of each race and, as expected, managed to offend just about everyone. Not surprisingly, Michael has developed an exceptionally low-quality LMX relationship with a majority of his employees, continually getting even lower as he singles out individuals from the group and communicates inappropriately.

Peer Relationships at Work

Managers and scholars have recognized that perhaps the most influential relationships in the workplace are those that form among co-workers, or peers. Several types of peer relationships have been examined by communication scholars. These include friendships, mentoring relationships, and romantic relationships. Stop for a moment and consider the number of times you interact with peers in your workplace in a given day. These relationships are often a central focus for understanding organizational life because, in many cases, we interact with peers in the workplace more frequently than we do with supervisors.

To understand the evolution of peer interactions in organizations, it is important to consider the factors which cause these relationships to form and strengthen. As we take a closer look at various types of peer relationships, the impact of factors such as physical proximity, communication climate, task/goal dependence, and dual meanings on relationship development will become evident.

Physical Proximity.   First, physical proximity affects relationship development among co-workers. Several studies have found that proximity increases opportunities for interaction (Fine 1986, Monge and Kirste 1980). The more opportunities that exist for interactions, the greater the chance that peer relationships are formed. Colleagues whose cubicles are located next to each other are more likely to form relationships and interact with one another than with those who are located across the building. One employee who describes his office as a "rat maze" of cubicles illustrates the role of proximity by stating, "Sometimes I just roll my office chair into the next cubicle and blow off steam after a meeting. It's like having a neighbor you can vent to when things get rough." Remember that most employees report spending an average of forty hours per week at work. More time together provides greater opportunities to share.

Do you find you develop closer relationships with people whose work area is located near you?

Communication Climate.   A second factor influencing the development of peer relationships is the communication

© Diego Cervo, 2007, Shutterstock.

When you're frustrated at work, it's easier to commiserate with those who are in the same environment and understand it.

climate between superiors and subordinates. An inherent hierarchical structure often contributes to the development of an "us versus them" mentality. Studies have found that co-workers come together to provide social support in situations where managers are perceived to be unfair or untrustworthy (Odden and Sias 1997; Sias and Jablin 1995). High levels of employee cohesiveness often result from these negative communication climates. Consider a time when you have been frustrated by something that happened at work or at school. You probably chose to communicate your frustrations to a co-worker or classmate who could relate to the situation you were experiencing because he was familiar with the environment. While family members or friends outside the workplace could certainly listen and offer support, they may not be able to understand the climate as well as a colleague who has experienced the same things that you have. In December 2005, New York City transit workers organized a strike a few days before Christmas that shut down subway and bus service to thousands of workers and tourists. Employee strikes are just one example of the "us versus them" phenomenon that often leads to employees joining forces against the supervisors. This collaborative force is unavoidable, as employees spend more time interacting with one another than they do communicating with their supervisors.

Task/Goal Dependence.   Task or goal dependence is a third factor influencing the development of peer relationships. By their very definition, organizations exist for the purpose of accomplishing a specific task or goal. Its members must work together to carry out its mission. Peer influence is an essential factor in fulfilling these goals. As we discuss team relationships in organizations later in this chapter, you will learn how shared tasks bring organizational members together. Team members depend on one another to meet the goals. If one team member "drops the ball," other members may communicate pressure in an attempt to encourage compliance. In some instances, co-workers may even have more influence over peer behaviors than supervisors do. In essence, peer influence in organizations is not that different from peer influence witnessed among teens in today's society. Have you ever been a part of a student organization that was sponsoring an event on campus? Students at a small midwestern university were organizing a blood drive as a service project on their campus. One committee was responsible for promotion and publicity, another was responsible for signing up donors, and a third committee was responsible for assisting the American Red Cross workers on the day of the event. Strong interpersonal relationships between members of the student organization resulted in a successful event. Each of the colleagues understood their common goal and engaged in communication to accomplish the task.

Dual Meanings.   A final factor that plays a key role in understanding the formation of relationships in organizations is the dual meanings communicated in messages. Messages exchanged between peers often contain "clues" to help define the nature of the relationship in addition to communicating specific information. Recall the example of the blood drive. If the chairperson of the committee to sign up donors states to a member that, "We're going to have to put it in high gear if we hope to meet our goal for this project," she is sending a message that they perceive themselves as being in a position to evaluate the performance of the group. The content dimension is clear—the number of donors needs to increase in order to meet the group's goal, and an implied relational message is present as well. By referencing the group through the use of pronouns such as "we," the chairperson communicates to the members that there is a bond that links them together.

As stated earlier, there are three types of co-worker relationships that have gained the interest of communication scholars: friendships, mentoring relationships, and romantic relationships. Let us take a closer look at the communication dynamics in each of these relationships in organizations.

FRIENDSHIPS IN ORGANIZATIONS

Reflecting on the proximity principle of peer relationships, it should come as no surprise that many friendships are formed as a result of organizational affiliations. As we explore the prevalence of these relationships, consider the friendships you have formed as a result of your membership in work, education, volunteer, or social organizations. Some individuals even create labels to describe these relationships by identifying a person as "a friend from work" or "a friend from my church." Our decision to form friendships at work is voluntary. While you may not have any choice regarding those you form relationships with at work, you do have options when it comes to forming friendships.

Friendships provide organizational members with social support and assistance throughout the socialization process. Communication scholars have realized the prevalence of these types of relationships and have applied theories to explain the dynamics of friendships at work. Bridge and Baxter (1992) identified five tensions experienced by friends in organizations, three of which are new to the study of struggles experienced in relationships. They point out that friendships in the workplace are unique, due to the blending of "personal" and "role" expectations. Tensions emerge because of the struggle between the behaviors we expect of someone as a friend and behaviors expected of that same person in his or her role as co-worker. Have you ever been frustrated with a friend at work who failed to pull her weight to accomplish a task? Determining which expectations to use as a guide for behaviors can be difficult when friends work together. The familiar tensions of autonomy/

© Lisa Marzano, 2007, Shutterstock.

Tensions can arise when a friend doesn't accomplish work expectations.

connection and openness/closedness that are typically experienced in intimate relationships also occur as a result of friendships formed at work. New tensions identified in the study include struggles between equality/inequality, impartiality/favoritism, and judgment/acceptance (Bridge and Baxter 1992).

Autonomy/Connection

Tension between **autonomy** and **connection** is fueled by the fact that friends at work are together several hours each day. Working together in close proximity enables friends to form close bonds. Stories about things that happen in the organization are shared, and trust between friends develops as they may depend on one another for the successful completion of tasks. But this same closeness may sometimes cause persons to feel "too" close. In the social world outside the organization, friends may find that discussions revert back to events at work. Extreme connection can lead to the feeling of being "smothered." An employee at a major retail store described the tension she experienced. "My friends at work and I are so much alike! In fact, I would describe Jo as my best friend. But sometimes it gets rough because I want to be considered for promotions, but I don't want to compete against Jo and end up jeopardizing our friendship."

Openness/Closedness

Tensions that are also experienced between friends at work are **openness** and **closedness.** Disclosures are common between friends—sharing stories about events that happen inside the office and at home strengthens the friendship bond. However, organizations often have confidentiality guidelines that could potentially restrict topics of discussion among friends. Consider the following situation. Lisa and Alonzo had been friends ever since they met at their new employee orientation session. As a human resources associate, Lisa was privy to information regarding cuts in the sales force over the next three weeks. Unfortunately, Alonzo was a member of the sales department that was targeted for these cuts. Because of their friendship, Lisa struggled with the desire to share this information with Alonzo, and the obligation to keep this information private until management decided to announce the cutbacks.

Equality/Inequality

Another tension experienced by friends at work focuses on the contradictory struggle between **equality** versus **inequality.** Earlier, we discussed the fact that organizational relationships are characterized by status differentials created by the presence of a hierarchical structure. As friends, two employees may view themselves as being equal in their relationship status. However, when role status as an organizational member is factored into the equation, inherent inequalities may emerge. One person may be placed in the position of reviewing the performance of the friend, and the inequities in the relationship become evident.

Impartiality/Favoritism

Friends at work may struggle between being **impartial,** treating all members the same, and showing **favoritism** to friends. Furthermore, friends trust that each one will look out for the other's best interests. While an inherent characteristic of friendship is to provide support, ethical or moral codes may prescribe the equal treatment of all employees. Abbey's story of the employee review process at work illustrates this type of tension that can emerge among friends. As manager of the restaurant, she was responsible for providing feedback on the performance of servers. One of the servers, Janelle, had become friends with Abbey over the past several months. Janelle, a single-mother of two young children, had been a source of support when Abbey found herself in the midst of a divorce, wondering how she could juggle work and raise her children alone. Recently, Janelle's daughter had been having some problems at school. Janelle was often called to meet with teachers during the day, requiring her to call off from work at the last minute. Abbey knew that she had to assess Janelle's absences in the report, but she felt horrible about giving her a low evaluation because she knew all of the issues Janelle had been struggling with. In this instance, we see the struggle between treating all employees fairly and wanting to make accommodations for a friend.

Judgment/Acceptance

A final tension encountered at work is the struggle between **judgment** and **acceptance.** Friends are expected to provide support and understanding to one another without judgment. However, depending on the role expectations associated with one's position in an organization, colleagues may be required to assess one another's work or performance. Consider Abbey and Janelle's situation. As a manager, Abbey knows that she needs to address the attendance issues with Janelle. But as Janelle's friend, she is reluctant to say anything because she is sympathetic to her situation. Part of Abbey's position is to provide feedback and sometimes that feedback is negative. Providing and taking criticism from a performance review from a friend may form a tension that otherwise may not exist in the workplace.

In an attempt to understand how friendships evolve in the workplace, Sias and Cahill (1998) interviewed nineteen pairs of friends in organizations. Individuals were asked to indicate the changes that occurred in their friendships between the initial meeting and the present time. Results of the study support the notion that there are three distinct phases of friendship development at work. Phase one involves the transition from acquaintances to friends, and is often experienced as the result of two employees working in close proximity for a period of time. Employees in the study stated that their decision to transition to the friendship stage during this time was the result of similarities that were discovered through interactions with one another. The second phase, friend to close friend, is often the result of supportive messages exchanged as a result of either personal or professional experiences. During this phase, friends socialize more outside the workplace than before, and the increase in interactions provides opportunities for more personal information to be shared. A final phase involves the transition from close friends to "almost best" friend (Sias and Cahill 1998). As the level of intimacy in the relationship increases and as more personal information is disclosed, friends experience an intense level of trust and support.

MENTOR RELATIONSHIPS

Friendship is only one type of interpersonal relationship that provides organizational members with support. **Mentor relationships** are characterized by a more experienced member serving as a role model, teacher, or guide for a colleague who is less experienced. Establishing a relationship with a mentor has repeatedly been linked to an individual's career progress, organizational influence, and

© Arne Trautmann, 2007, Shutterstock.

Those who establish a relationship with a mentor often achieve greater career success.

upward mobility within an organization (Ragins and Cotton 1991). Examples of mentoring in today's workplace would be an experienced employee providing guidance for a new colleague and a successful woman being called upon to offer guidance and advice to female colleagues who aspire to leadership positions. Dr. Phil McGraw has credited Oprah Winfrey for mentoring him through the early stages of his career. In the film *Up Close and Personal*, Robert Redford's character served as a mentor to news anchor Tally Atwater, portrayed by Michelle Pfeiffer.

Mentoring partnerships may be formed on a voluntarily or involuntarily basis. When organizational members seek out mentors who possess qualities or characteristics they admire, they form a voluntary or informal mentoring relationship. Similarity in personality, goals, attitudes, or background is often a force that guides the decision to pursue voluntary mentor relationships. Other members may establish these relationships through formal or involuntary mentor programs available in their organization. These involuntary, or assigned, mentoring partnerships may involve formal, written agreements that address the expectations for each person. Regardless of the method for initiating the relationship, several communication characteristics are common. Just as other types of relationships involve highs and lows, so does the mentor relationship. Mentors and protégés may have different goals which need to be negotiated, and the differences have the potential to result in jealousy or conflict. Trust is an essential part of the relationship, as both parties expect the other to be honest and open in their assessment and advice. Due to the time invested in this relationship, the concept of social exchange may become an issue to be resolved.

In their study of organizational mentoring, DeWine, Casbolt and Bentley (1983) identified various types of mentors. While the relationship is generally perceived as being supportive and nurturing, organizational members should be aware of the fact that some mentors approach their responsibility in less sensitive ways. **Supportive mentors** help employees achieve their goals and include types labeled as the "parent," the "cheerleader," and the "groom." **Parent mentors** are those who are considered to be "older and wiser" as a result of their tenure in the organization. Protégés often describe the parent mentor as having significant influence on their career. The **cheerleader mentor** is one who provides encouragement, and the mentor often describes the pride resulting from the protégé's success. **Groom mentors** are those who hold positions of power in an organization and are viewed as "grooming" a protégé for specific responsibilities or roles. However, not all mentor relationships result in positive experiences for the protégé. **"Self-promoter" mentors** are described as those who want to work with the best new members in order to surround themselves with high quality colleagues. The **"guilt-trip producer"** is a mentor who motivates a protégé by communicating messages of disappointment when performance fails to meet expectations. Phrases such as "I expected more from you" or "You know you can do better than that" are often associated with this type of mentor.

The outcomes of mentoring relationships can be beneficial for the individuals involved as well as for the organization. Mentors report a sense of satisfaction in seeing protégés achieve their goals, and protégés often credit their career success to the advice provided by mentors. Studies have found that employees who are mentored report more desirable occupational outcomes and advance more quickly in their professions (Ragins and Cotton 1991). An obvious benefit for organizations is the job satisfaction that results from mentoring relationships. While many mentoring relationships evolve as a result of friendships at work, it is important to remember their purpose and refrain from confusing the roles of friend and mentor.

ROMANTIC RELATIONSHIPS AT WORK

With more women in the workplace and employees working longer hours, it should come as no surprise that romantic relationships have captured the attention of communication scholars in recent years. In a 2002 report, the U.S. Department of Labor found that women spend an average of 1,584 hours in the office each year. A female employee in a large corporate banking center provided this explanation for her decision to pursue romantic relationships at work, "How can I not help being attracted to men at my office? They're dressed for success and I know they're career-driven. It's just easier to date someone at work than to spend time hanging out at bars where everything is so uncertain." A 2005 survey by vault.com stated that fifty-eight percent of employees reported that they have been involved in an office romance. In his book *The Office Romance*, Dennis Powers (1998) states that eight million co-workers will discover romance at the office, with nearly half of these relationships resulting in marriage. However, for every "happily ever after" that is found at work, there is a horror story for employees whose organizations frown upon workplace romance.

The communication strategy often used to initiate romantic relationships is flirting. While some flirting behaviors may be innocently used to explore interest in pursuing a romantic relationship, these behaviors have also been used for more manipulative purposes in organizations. Employees may flirt with a co-worker for self-serving purposes such as seeking assistance on a project or even advancing one's career.

Of the fifty-eight percent of employees who reported that they have been involved in an office romance, only nineteen percent indicated that they had been open and honest about the relationship. While nearly half of the employees surveyed indicated that they were unaware of the company's policies regarding workplace romances, those who said that policies did exist in the workplace stated that the guidelines typically involved relationships between superiors and subordinates (vault.com). Policies restricting romance between superiors and subordinates are often designed to protect both parties—issues of perceived credibility and sexual harassment may result from status and power differentials. Supervisors engaged in romantic relationships with subordinates may run the risk of being accused of showing favoritism. The relationship between Michael Scott and his supervisor Jan is comedy fodder on *The Office*. In one episode of *The Office* the characters attempt to keep their relationship a secret from Human Resources but accidentally release compromising photos of their vacation in Jamaica in an email to all employees.

The Civil Rights Act of 1964 made sexual harassment illegal in the workplace. While the main goal of the act was to prevent organizations from discriminating against minorities and women, it also addressed the legalities associated with making sexual relationships a condition for employment. Berryman-Fink (1997) cites the Equal Employment Opportunity Commission's definition of **sexual harassment** as "any unwelcome sexual advances,

© Yuri Arcurs, 2007, Shutterstock.

Co-workers may flirt for romantic reasons or in an effort to advance their career.

requests for sexual favors, and other verbal or physical conduct of a sexual nature" (272). In 1986, the definition of sexual harassment was further refined to address behaviors that contributed to an unpleasant or uncomfortable work environment. Today, organizations recognize two types of sexual harassment which they typically label quid pro quo and hostile work environment. **Quid pro quo** is a Latin term that translates as "something for something." An example of this type of harassment might include a boss telling his subordinate that she will not receive a promotion, raise, or opportunity at work unless she engages in a sexual act with him. The second form of sexual harassment, **hostile work environment,** is less clearly defined and might include employees exchanging sexual jokes, stories, or materials in front of other employees, or ongoing unwanted sexual behavior from a co-worker. Sexual harassment is distinguished from flirting and other types of physical, verbal or sexual behavior because it is perceived as unwelcome by the recipient and is reoccurring (Berryman-Fink 1997). There is some data that indicates that sexual harassment appears to be on the decline. A 1995 Department of Defense survey of its employees found that the number of female employees who reported unwanted sexual advances dropped from sixty-four percent in 1988 to fifty-five percent in 1995. Reports from male employees experiencing sexual harassment at work decreased from seventeen percent to fourteen percent.

As scholars, practitioners, and employees debate over whether romance should be allowed in the workplace, several outcomes of these relationships should be taken into consideration. While workers may report higher levels of motivation and involvement in organizations where romance has bloomed, a study by love.com found that online interactions between employees trying to keep their relationship secret resulted in up to forty-two minutes of lost productivity per day. There is additional evidence that organizational romance can lead to favoritism and jealousy in the workplace, loss of colleagues' respect, damage to one's professional image, and loss of productivity (Quinn and Lees 1984; Lowndes 1993). For those employees watching the romance from the sidelines, the relationship may become a distraction, and time and energy is spent focusing on the relationship rather than on issues relevant to work. Consider the climate when relationships between co-workers are terminated. The emotional aftermath has the potential to impact not only those formerly involved in the romance, but also co-workers who are inclined to "take sides." *The Office*, particularly, deals with romantic relationships in an office in all of their forms; from the clandestine relationship of oddball couple Dwight and Angela and the stilted attraction between Michael Scott and Jan, to the captivating relationship of Jim and Pam, who teeter between the flirtation of "almost best" friends, unrequited love, and the awkwardness resulting from the disclosure of feelings. As an example of the potential pitfalls of office romances, Jim ends up transferring to a different branch. Very little work appears to get done at Dunder-Mifflin: time is spent in favor of more amusing activities and relationship woes. The close proximity of work relationships and the difficulty of both terminating them and moving on, though usually not as thoroughly dramatic as their television enactments, do demand having second thoughts when initiating romantic relationships in the workplace.

INTERPERSONAL EFFECTIVENESS: COMMUNICATION IN WORK RELATIONSHIPS

Throughout our discussion of superior-subordinate and peer relationships in organizations, you might have noticed that many of the communication concepts and theories discussed throughout this text could be applied. The study of relationships across communication contexts often requires scholars to apply fundamental concepts in new ways. Concepts such as similarity and attraction can be used to explain the initiation process between friends, colleagues, or romantic partners. Trust and disclosure are fundamental to strengthening relationships regardless of whether the relationships are between co-workers, family members, or friends. Persuasion, listening, and feedback are essential communication tools for organizational effectiveness. While an entire text could be dedicated to discussing the role of interpersonal relationships in organizations, we examine three of the communication variables that have attracted the attention of organizational communication scholars.

In Chapter Two, we addressed the impact of individual differences on relationships. Superiors are always seeking ways to enhance organizational effectiveness. While several studies have shown that cognitive ability is a strong predictor of job performance, communication scholars have realized the impact of addressing individual differences in achieving effectiveness. **Organizational orientation** theory identifies three approaches used by members to enact their work roles (McCroskey, Richmond, Johnson, and Smith 2004). **Upward mobiles** refer to those members who demonstrate a high level of dedication toward accomplishing the organization's goals. They are easily identified by their demonstrated respect for roles and rules and they are often described as giving "110 percent" to tasks and the organization. **Indifferents,** on the other hand, view work as a means to earn a living. They are motivated to work simply to obtain a paycheck, and dedication to the organization is low on their list of personal goals. You will recognize the indifferents in your organization by their reluctance to participate in organizational activities not directly related to their job, and topics of discussion typically revolve around their personal lives rather than work. It should come as no surprise that indifferents make up the majority of organizational orientations at work, and indeed a majority of the characters on *The Office.* Ryan, the temp, who is determined not to be drawn into the world of the Scranton branch and form bonds, is a classic indifferent. The third orientation, **ambivalents,** is often the most difficult to communicate with at work. It is fairly easy to identify this orientation type at work—simply listen for those who point out the "issues" that need to be changed. Often these individuals become frustrated with their jobs, suggest changes that need to be made, and if things fail to turn around, they often decide to seek employment elsewhere. In essence, the ambivalent can be described as the employee who is always looking for a better opportunity. The best advice for communicating with ambivalents is to focus on neutral topics to keep the conversation from turning into a gripe session about the organization's weaknesses.

ORGANIZATIONAL CULTURE

We introduced the concept of culture in Chapter Ten, focusing on how members share common beliefs, values, and attitudes. Organizations can be considered cultures as well; after all, organizations aspire for supervisors and subordinates to share a common vision which is guided by similarities in beliefs and values for the company. Scholars have begun exploring organizational cultures to understand how members construct their organizational realities. **Organizational culture** is defined as the shared systems of symbols and meanings created by members through their interactions with one another (Trethewey 1997). To better understand how this meaning is exchanged, researchers have focused their attention on how elements such as stories, language, and rituals are used to help members of organizations understand their role in the culture.

Stories

Organizational members exchange stories about events that have shaped the history of the organization and help provide a rationale for the beliefs and values shared by supervisors and subordinates. An administrative assistant at Wendy's corporate headquarters in Ohio told the following story shared by one of her colleagues to describe how the company's founder, Dave Thomas, interacted with his employees during office visits:

> "One day Mr. Thomas came into the office and I was swamped! As the phone was ringing off the hook I greeted him and asked if I could get him a cup of coffee. He smiled and stated that I was the one who was busy and he went to get me a cup of coffee."

The story was used to communicate the value that Dave Thomas had for employees, and how he viewed the organization as a team effort.

Language

Organizational culture is also shaped by the specialized language, or vocabulary, used by members. This shared language serves to strengthen the bonds between colleagues, sometimes creating a means for distinguishing between members and non-members. Students and faculty at Ohio University share a common language to refer to transcripts and the system used to register for classes. TRIPS (touch-tone registration and information processing system) is used to refer to the system students use to register for their classes, and when a faculty member asks a student to bring his DARS (degree audit reporting system) to an advisory meeting, the student knows that he should bring a copy of the transcript. This specialized language helps students, faculty, and staff communicate more efficiently.

© PhotoCreate, 2007, Shutterstock.

What kind of a daily ritual could be implemented to break up the monotony of assembly work?

Rituals

Rituals and routines are mechanisms used by organizational members to make sense of their membership. Daily coffee breaks, annual Christmas parties, quarterly employee recognition ceremonies, or even simple greetings used to acknowledge colleagues each morning provide insight as to how members of an organization define their place in the organization. Powerful messages are exchanged through these routine behaviors, and they serve the function of promoting relationships among organizational members. In a 1960s article, Donald Roy describes the strategic use of everyday rituals such as Coke breaks, banana breaks, and opening the window at a particular time to break up the monotony of assembly work. Because employees spend so much of their time at work, collective attempts are often made by managers or groups of employees to improve employee morale and job satisfaction. Incorporating humor into the workplace through shared humorous stories, language, and rituals is one way of improving organizational culture.

SOCIALIZATION

Just as new members of cultures must assimilate to the new environment, newcomers to an organization experience a similar introductory process to learn information about the expectations for organizational behavior. A story by an employee in a large consulting firm describes the value of socialization to her success in the organization. "I accepted the job offer two weeks before I graduated from college. Boy, was I in for a surprise! There was no syllabus to tell me what was expected and when things were due. I quickly learned that I better open my eyes and ears and start asking questions." Jablin (1984) describes the process of organizational assimilation as the means by which individuals learn role expectations and what it means to be a member of an organization. Employees may be formally or informally socialized on the expectations of membership. An organization that conducts formal orientation programs or assigns mentors to new employees applies more formal methods for ensuring that employees learn the ropes. Informal socialization may result from an employee joining colleagues for lunch and learning that the supervisor sets strict deadlines and gets angry with those who do not meet goals.

Socialization typically evolves through three stages: anticipatory socialization, organizational encounter, and metamorphosis (Jablin 2001). In the **anticipatory socialization phase** new members form expectations regarding their role in the organization. These expectations can be formed as early as childhood, as when a young girl creates beliefs about what it is like to be a lawyer by watching her mother, or they can evolve through research about organizations or through stories portrayed in the media. Once a newcomer enters the organization, the **encounter phase** begins. While technically an employee, the newcomer may find that she may not yet be considered part of the group. Organizations use a variety of methods to socialize members during this phase. Methods may be formal or informal in nature and can include orientation or training programs, mentoring, and opportunities for employees to seek information. In a study of first-year medical students, friendships with older students were identified as a means for assimilating into and navigating the medical school culture (Zorn and Gregory 2005). The final stage of socialization, **metamorphosis,** involves changes in the new employee's behavior to adapt to the role expectations in the new environment. At this point, the employee begins to be viewed as an "insider."

Unspoken expectations are often discovered during this phase. While a manager may say that attendance at weekly update meetings is optional, an employee may soon learn that important information is shared during these sessions and that managers actually expect employees to be present. In essence, socialization can be the key to a successful organizational experience or a negative one.

CONTEMPORARY ISSUES IN WORKPLACE RELATIONSHIPS

As we reflect on the changes that have evolved in the ways supervisors, subordinates, and peers communicate with one another in the workplace, several trends become apparent. Managers have come to value the contributions of employees in decision-making and solicit their opinions and advice in these situations. As the number of males and females in organizations become more equal and more time is spent at the office, romance at work has gained the attention of scholars. Interpersonal relationships are the key to organizational success in industries. As the demographics of our work population continue to change, so does our need to address issues which will demand the attention of communication scholars in the twenty-first century. Three areas for focus are: diversity in the workplace, balancing work and family, and the impact of technology on interactions at work.

DIVERSITY IN ORGANIZATIONS

Many organizations have found themselves faced with the task of conducting business with partners from around the world. Globalization has increased the potential for interactions with clients and colleagues from other countries and cultures. Effective communication requires an understanding of cultural differences, and those who understand these differences can avoid embarrassing or insulting others. In Chapter Ten we explored communication concepts designed to enhance interactions across cultural differences. Employers have realized the importance of these concepts as they address the changing face of the workplace.

As we consider cultural differences, it is important to note the role of organizational culture that was discussed earlier. As larger corporations buy out smaller organizations, employees from diverse organizational cultures are often expected to not only adapt to one another, but also to be satisfied and productive. In January 2004, J. P. Morgan Chase announced its acquisition of and merger with Bank One, making it the second largest bank in the nation and drawing on each organization's strengths in consumer and corporate business. But the "blending" of these two large organizations would take time. Countless hours of negotiation occurred before the deal was signed; eventually it was decided that the board membership would have equal representation from Bank One and J. P. Morgan. Careful communication was designed to communicate the organizational changes to employees and the public. In January 2006, two years after the new organizational structure was announced to the public, many banks still retained the name "Bank One," and will do so until the process of forming the new culture is complete.

Age diversity has created a new set of issues for organizations. Current trends have found that older employees are making the decision to postpone retirement, and many more have decided to return from retirement. The result is a wider age range among employees, often with older workers being supervised by those who are younger. This role reversal may produce an uncomfortable situation for employees, with younger managers experiencing reluctance to give orders to their elders.

Effective organizations will realize the value of addressing the contributions that diversity can offer. Those of diverse cultural backgrounds can be used as resources to assist in training others to do business in their native cultures. Managers should recognize the value of diverse backgrounds and viewpoints in brainstorming and decision-making, and encourage openness and respect. However, it is important to note that diverse opinions could potentially result in conflict, requiring organizations to explore new approaches to conflict management. As our opportunities for interacting with those around the world increases with the emergence of new technologies and globalization, an organization's success depends on its ability to manage diverse interpersonal relationships.

Increasingly there is a wider age range among employees working together in organizations.

Communication scholars argue that "training could be the key to unlocking the potential of diversity in the organization" (Gonzalez, Willis, and Young 1997, 290). During the last few years, diversity training has become a buzz word in many organizational circles. For this training to be truly effective at building effective interpersonal relationships in the workplace, three steps are required. First, members of organizations should be encouraged to explore the differences that do exist in the workplace. Rather than assume that everyone is similar based on the fact that they chose to become members of the same group, organizations could benefit from encouraging the exploration of differences among co-workers. For example, what are the specific diversity issues that this particular organization is facing? Next, diversity training should address the presence of differences in communication styles and address how these unique approaches impact the organization's goals. Finally, training should encourage individuals to identify ways in which cultural differences in communication can be integrated to create a work team that is both cohesive and satisfying.

BALANCING WORK AND FAMILY RELATIONSHIPS

We all strive to achieve balance in our work and family relationships. After all, achieving balance in our personal and professional lives contributes to our self-esteem and relational satisfaction. In Chapter Two, we explored the relationship between roles and one's identity. One's self-esteem is often linked to having well-established roles. When our resources for fulfilling personal roles are limited, stress results and we start to question our identity as a good parent or a productive employee. The struggle appears to be more prevalent among female employees. Studies examining role conflict experienced by employees have found that women report dividing their time between various household and work-related tasks, while men report that the majority of their time is focused on tasks relating to work. So what can organizations do? Employees who perceive their supervisors as being supportive of their efforts to balance work and family often report higher levels of job satisfaction. Some organizations are addressing these issues and providing resources to help employees achieve balance in their personal and professional lives. Child and elder care opportunities are provided at some work sites, and options are being made for flexible work schedules through job sharing, compressed work weeks, and telecommuting.

Communication scholars have realized the value of peer, or co-worker, relationships and are addressing strategies to assist organizational members in achieving balance in different areas of their lives. Farley-Lucas (2000) discovered that valuable social support can be offered to working mothers through conversations with co-workers about child rearing, and employers who encouraged these dialogues were perceived as being more supportive of working mothers. To understand the strategies used to manage the stress of balancing work and family, Medved (2004) interviewed thirty-four mothers and asked them to describe their "typical" day balancing work and family life. Medved discovered that two types of actions, routinizing and improvising, are used to balance work and family responsibilities and illustrate the role that interpersonal communication plays in managing multiple demands.

Women use routinizing and improvising to manage daily home and work responsibilities.

© Bartosz Ostrowski, 2007, Shutterstock.

Routinizing actions incorporate recurring patterns or interactions to accomplish daily routines. One communicative strategy used on a regular basis was **connecting**. Daily calls to coordinate schedules with a spouse, or contacting the child care facility to check in on the child are examples of this management strategy. **Alternating** involves interactions between spouses to negotiate "trade-offs" or exchange tasks in the daily routine. Occasionally, a mother is asked to stay late at work to complete a task or to travel out of town on business. In these instances, she may call her spouse and ask him to pick up the children at daycare since her routine has been disrupted. Or perhaps parents have developed a schedule: one parent is responsible for giving the children baths and getting them to bed on designated nights of the week, and the other parent assumes the responsibility for the remaining nights. **Prepping** is a nightly strategy used to maintain order in the routine. Children may be asked what homework needs to be accomplished each evening, school lunches may be packed in the evening, and coats and shoes may be lined up next to the door in anticipation of the morning rush to catch the bus. In some instances, working mothers may need to call on family members or friends to assist with childcare issues. **Reciprocating** strategies often involve conversations to coordinate the exchange of child care issues on a regular basis. Coordinating carpools to sports practice so that a working mother only has to leave work early one evening each week is an example of this strategy. While the answers to the family-work juggling act may seem easy, women still devote the majority of their time to childcare, housework, and shopping. Table 12.2 highlights the discrepancies between the time devoted to these tasks by fathers and by mothers. Regardless of their employment status, women contribute more time to these tasks than do fathers. Consider the fact that mothers who work 40+ hours per week report dedicating an additional 25 hours per week to the household tasks compared to the 14.5 hours spent by fathers.

Parents may set up a schedule so Dad gets the baby ready for bed part of the week, while Mom takes over the other days.

© Losevsky Pavel, 2007, Shutterstock.

As much as we like predictability in our lives, there are times when events occur that are beyond our control. During these times, working mothers may use **improvising** action messages to help coordinate the demands of work and family. **Requesting assistance** involves asking others for work accommodations or childcare assistance as a result of last-minute circumstances. A sin-

Table 12.2	**Ratio of Time Dedicated to Household Chores**	
	Males	Females
Time devoted to childcare, housework, or shopping by working parent	14.5 hours	25 hours
Time devoted to childcare, housework, or shopping by non-working parent	20 hours	39 hours

Source: Robinson, J. P., and G. Godbey. 1997. *Time for life: The surprising way Americans use their time.* State College, PA: Pennsylvania State University Press.

gle mother taking college classes may approach an instructor and ask for an extension on an assignment due to the illness of her children, or a neighbor may be asked to watch the children when mom is delayed by a traffic jam. **Trading off,** or alternating, is a strategy that involves negotiating responsibilities between spouses when unique situations arise. One spouse may agree to pick up a sick child from school one day with the agreement that the other parent assumes the responsibility the next time the situation arises. A final improvising strategy, **evading,** involves withholding information, or intentionally deceiving others, as a means for managing multiple demands. A mother may decide that it is easier just to call in sick to work rather than risk explaining to her supervisor that she needs to stay home to care for an ill child. As more women enter the workplace, there will be a greater need for communication scholars to explore how both men and women use communication to balance their relationships at work and at home.

THE IMPACT OF TECHNOLOGY ON WORK RELATIONSHIPS

There is no escaping the impact of technology on how we interact with others at work. Some organizations have replaced live humans at the switchboard with automated voice systems that answer and direct calls, and studies have shown that as many as seventy-five percent of business calls do not reach a person—instead, the game of "phone tag" ensues. Electronic mail (email) has alleviated some of the frustrations of calling on the phone by providing colleagues with the convenience of asking and answering questions at times that are convenient for them. Some organizations have limited the ability of applicants to interact with a human resources representative by requiring them to submit applications online. Our work lives have become so busy that many of us depend on electronic calendars to organize our schedules. Blackberry and the Palm Treo provide employees with the opportunity to engage in work-related tasks away from the office. Look around the next time you are having dinner at a busy restaurant: you will probably see someone using one of these technologies to send messages, and there is a good chance that he is communicating with a supervisor or co-worker.

While these technologies have enabled us to organize our work lives and to enhance our task efficiency, some may question their impact on interpersonal relationships. Indeed, technology has provided employees with the opportunity to telecommute, or to work from home. Individuals report that technology

Technology can keep people connected to their work wherever they go.

© Darren Green, 2007, Shutterstock.

has caused a "blurring of the lines" between their work and personal lives, and this has made the task of balancing these relationships more difficult. Employees report a struggle to establish boundaries between work time and personal time. A study of employees in an organization that implemented home-based telecommuting found that only fifteen percent of respondents reported having regular social contact with their co-workers (Harris 2003). Decreases in face-to-face contact pose new issues for researchers in understanding the role that technology plays in our interpersonal communication at work.

SUMMARY

Considering the fact that you may spend the majority of your adult life interacting with individuals at work, it is essential that you understand the various types of relationships that are present in the workplace and the accompanying expectations for communication. While we may all aspire to be "the boss" someday, the reality is that we have to pay our dues. Understanding the relationship dynamics between supervisors and subordinates is essential to our success in an organization. In addition, positive relationships with co-workers contribute to employee motivation and satisfaction. After all, we might not necessarily like our jobs, but if we enjoy our interactions with co-workers, often the task becomes a bit more bearable. It is the interpersonal relationships on *The Office* that make the show and the character's lives interesting, not the monotonous work of paper sales. Given that so much time is spent at work, it should come as no surprise that friendships evolve and grow in organizations. But like all of our interpersonal relationships, these friendships are not without issues that need to be addressed. Dialectical tensions can emerge and create a struggle between professionalism and friendship. As our workplaces become increasingly diverse, the communication issues to be addressed will change. Technology will continue to change the way that we work and the ways in which we interact with those at work. In essence, your ability to build effective interpersonal relationships at work just might make the difference between waking up and looking forward to your job each morning, or wishing that you could stay at home.

APPLICATIONS

Exercises

1. Interview a manager in either a large or mid-sized organization and ask some of the following questions: 1) how much of your day is devoted to dealing with relationship or communication problems or issues? 2) can you give an example of a typical relationship-type of issue that you had to manage and how you addressed this situation? 3) how important are peer relationships to your employees? 4) what does your organization do to help foster healthy peer relationships?

2. Conduct research on some of the ways that organizations are addressing the issues addressed in this chapter (e.g., sexual harassment, dating in the workplace, impact of technology on communication, diversity in the workplace and work life balance). What are the organization's policies, procedures and opinions on these issues? Do the organizations that are recognized as some of **"The Best Places to Work in the US"** (e.g., Wegmans) make attempts to address these issues?

REFERENCES

Berryman-Fink, (Initial?). 1997. Gender issues: Management style, mobility and harassment. In P. Y. Byers (Ed.), *Organizational communication: Theory and behavior* (259–283). Boston: Allyn and Bacon.

Bridge, K., and L. A. Baxter. 1992. Blended relationships: Friends as work associates. *Western Journal of Communication, 56,* 200–225.

Dansereau, F., G. B. Graen, and W. Haga. 1975. A vertical linkage dyad approach to leadership within formal organizations: A longitudinal investigation of the role making process. *Behavior and Human Performance, 13,* 46–78.

DeWine, S., Casebolt, D., and N. Bentley. 1983. Moving through the organization: A field study assessment of the patron system. Paper presented at the International Communication Association, Dallas, TX.

Farley-Lucas, B. 2000. Communicating the (in)visibility of motherhood: Family talk and the ties to motherhood within the workplace. *The Electronic Journal of Communication, 10.* Available: *http://www.cios.org/www.ejcrec2.htm.*

Fine, G. A. 1986. Friendships in the work place. In V. J. Derlega and B. A. Winstead (Eds.), *Friendship and social interaction* (185–206). New York: Springer-Verlag.

Gonzalez, A., J. Willis, and C. R. Young. 1997. Cultural diversity and organizations. In P. Y. Byers (Ed.), *Organizational communication: Theory and behavior.* (284–304). Boston: Allyn and Bacon.

Graen, G. B. 1976. Role-making processes within complex organizations. In M. D. Dunnette (Ed.), *Handbook of industrial and organizational psychology* (1201–1245). Chicago: Rand McNally.

Graen, G. B, and J. F. Cashman. 1975. A role making model in formal organizations: A developmental approach. In J. G. Hunt and L. L. Larson (Eds.), *Leadership frontiers* (143–165). Kent, OH: Kent State Press.

Graen, G. B., and M. Uhl. 1995. Relationship based approach to leadership: Development of leader-member exchange (LMX) theory of leadership over 25 years: Applying a multi-level multi-domain perspective. *Leadership Quarterly, 6,* 219–247.

Harris, L. 2003. Home-based teleworking and the employment relationship. *Personnel Review, 32,* 422–437.

Jablin, F. M. 1984. Assimilating new members into organizations. In R. N. Bostrom, (Ed.), *Communication yearbook 8.* Beverly Hills, CA: Sage Publications.

Jablin, F. M. 2001. Organizational entry, assimilation, and disengagement/exit. In F. M. Jablin and L. L. Putnam, (Eds.), *The new handbook of organizational communication* (732–818). Thousand Oaks, CA: Sage Publications.

Lowndes, L. 1993. Dangerous office liaisons. *Legal Assistant Today,* 64–70.

Maslow, A. H. 1943. A theory of human motivation. *Psychology Review, 50,* 370–396.

McCroskey, J. C., V. P. Richmond, A. D. Johnson, and H. T. Smith. 2004. Organizational orientations theory and measurement: Development of measures and preliminary investigations. *Communication Quarterly, 52,* 1–14.

Medved, C. 2004. The everyday accomplishment of work and family: Exploring practical actions in daily routines. *Communication Studies, 55,* 128–145.

Monge, P. R., and K. K. Kirste. 1980. Measuring proximity in human organizations. *Social Psychology Quarterly, 43,* 110–115.

Odden, C. M., and P. M. Sias. 1997. Peer communication relationships and psychological climate. *Communication Quarterly, 45,* 153–166.

Powers, D. M. 1998. *The office romance: Playing with fire without getting burned.* New York, NY: AMACOM.

Quinn, R. E., and P. L. Lees. 1984. Attraction and harassment: Dynamics of sexual politics in the workplace. *Organizational Dynamics, 13,* 35–46.

Ragins, B. R., and J. L. Cotton. 1991. Easier said than done: Gender differences in perceived barriers to gaining a mentor. *Academy of Management Journal, 34,* 939–951.

Roy, D. 1960. Banana time: Job satisfaction and informal interaction. *Human Organization, 18,* 158–168.

Sias, P. M., and D. J. Cahill. 1998. From co-workers to friends: The development of peer friendships in the workplace. *Western Journal of Communication, 62,* 279–299.

Sias, P. M., and F. M. Jablin. 1995. Differential superior-subordinate relations, perceptions of fairness, and coworker communication. *Human Communication Research, 22,* 5–38.

Taylor, F. W. 1911. *The principles of scientific management.* New York: Harper & Row.

Trethewey, A. 1997. Organizational culture. In P. Y. Byers (Ed.), *Organizational communication: Theory and behavior* (203–234). Boston: Allyn and Bacon.

Turban, D. B., and A. P. Jones. 1988. Supervisor-subordinate similarity: Types, effects and mechanisms. *Journal of Applied Psychology, 73,* 234–238.

Zorn, T. E., and K. W. Gregory. 2005. Learning the ropes together: Assimilation and friendship among first-year medical students. *Health Communication, 17,* 211–231.

13

Health Communication
Managing Interpersonal Interactions that Produce Anxiety

OBJECTIVES

© Zsolt Nyulaszi, 2007, Shutterstock.

- State three types of interactions that cause anxiety for most individuals: provide three reasons each interaction is labeled difficult/challenging for most people
- State the definition of health communication
- Provide several examples of what health communication researchers typically study
- Offer three explanations for physician-patient communication problems
- State several potential outcomes of ineffective physician-patient communication
- Offer at least five suggestions for improving physician- and health care provider-patient communication and relationships; what can patients do and what can health care providers do?
- Explain the components of an appropriately assertive response
- Define and distinguish between the two types of disabilities discussed in this chapter
- State the two main reasons for communication problems between nondisabled and disabled persons
- Provide at least three examples of how communication between two nondisabled persons differs from communication between a person with a disability and a nondisabled person
- Discuss three ways persons with disabilities manage unwanted assistance from nondisabled persons
- Advance four suggestions for improving communication between persons with disabilities and nondisabled persons
- State three reasons people feel uncomfortable discussing death and dying
- Explain the stages of death and dying and provide an example of typical communication for each stage
- Define the term comforting communication and describe the least and most effective types of comforting messages
- Offer at least two examples of individual differences related to one's ability to deliver comforting messages
- Discuss effective and ineffective ways to communicate with someone who is terminally ill or recently lost a loved one

KEY TERMS

health communication

assertive
  communication

empathy

rationale

action

disability

visible disabilities

hidden disabilities

real barriers

perceptual barriers

denial

anger

bargaining

depression

acceptance

comforting
  communication

person-centered
  comforting

cognitively complex

affective orientation

nonverbal comforting
  strategies

OVERVIEW

It is not unusual for people to seek out friends, family members, co-workers, or relationship partners during difficult times. Because we rely on our friends, family members, or relationship partners to support us in times of need, we rarely *avoid* conversations with these individuals. When, and under what conditions, are individuals most likely to avoid interactions? We suspect individuals avoid interactions with others because the topics of discussion are perceived as potentially stressful or uncomfortable for one or both partners. Situations labeled difficult that are often avoided among family members or friends might include discussions about sex, relationship issues, and negative life experiences such as death and dying (Afifi and Guerrero 1998; Goodwin 1989; Guerrero and Afifi 1995). In this chapter we take a close look at three different, yet related, types of health communication interactions individuals often label challenging, painful, or stressful for a variety of reasons. Specifically, we investigate communication between physicians and patients, communication between persons with disabilities and nondisabled individuals, and communication about death and dying.

To become a more competent communicator, it is important to learn more about why these types of interactions are difficult. Also, because we cannot always avoid these types of interactions, it is important to understand and control our fears to better manage these situations. In this chapter we present classic and contemporary research on these topics to help you understand why people avoid these interactions and how to improve communication in each of these situations. For each of the three challenging areas the following questions are addressed: (1) why do these situations produce anxiety for one or both of the interactants, (2) what are some typical responses or reactions to these situations, and (3) how can we improve communication in these situations?

COMMUNICATION BETWEEN PHYSICIANS AND PATIENTS

Researchers from a variety of academic fields are fascinated with physician-patient communication and have been studying it extensively for quite some time (see, for example, Ainsworth-Vaughn 1998; Burgoon et al. 1987; Burgoon et al. 1990a; Burgoon et al. 1990b; Kreps and Thorton 1992; Thompson 1986).

Interpersonal scholars interested in physician-patient communication study an area called **health communication,** "an area of study concerned with human interaction in the health care process" (Kreps and Thorton 1992, 2). Interpersonal researchers study communication in health care settings by examining verbal and nonverbal messages exchanged between health care providers and patients, and the outcomes of these interactions. Health communication scholars have been particularly interested in physician-patient communication and patient compliance (Burgoon et al. 1987; Burgoon et al. 1990a; Burgoon et al. 1990b), physician and health care provider communication practices as they relate to patient satisfaction (Wanzer, Booth-Butterfield, and Gruber 2004), and the impact of patient anxiety on physician-patient interactions (Richmond, Smith, Heisel, and McCroskey 2001).

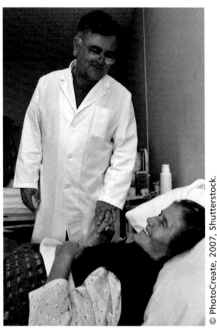

© PhotoCreate, 2007, Shutterstock.

If patients feel less anxious, they are more likely to have more satisfying relationships with their physicians.

Communication researchers study health care provider-patient interactions for a variety of reasons. By studying interactions between health care providers and patients, researchers learn more about why patients are anxious and can determine how to reduce this anxiety to improve communication and patient compliance (Thompson 1986). Patient anxiety often acts as a substantial barrier that can inhibit patients' communication with their health care providers. Booth-Butterfield (2006) and others (Richmond et al. 2001; Thompson 1986) noted that patients' communication anxiety can create serious problems for both the patient and physician/health care provider. Patients with high communication anxiety might avoid making appointments with their doctors even when they have symptoms of a problem. Also, when highly apprehensive patients finally do visit their physicians, they are more likely to rush through their appointments and to refrain from asking questions or seeking additional necessary information (Booth-Butterfield, Chory, and Benyon 1997). Not surprisingly, patients with higher communication apprehension tend to be less satisfied with their physicians and the medical care received (Richmond et al. 2001). When patients and physicians do not establish a "good doctor-patient relationship," patients are much more likely to sue their health care providers (Ostrum 2004).

There are often physiological signs which indicate that patients are anxious about visiting their physicians. While some medical professionals say there is no real explanation for the "white coat effect," also referred to as White Coat Hypertension (WCH), patients often experience surges in their blood pressure during visits to their doctor's office. According to Dr. Hong, a practicing physician that regularly provides medical advice on television, WCH is said to happen when a patient's blood pressure is 10mm Hg (millimeters of mercury) lower at home than in the doctor's office. Many medical professionals suspect that their white coats may trigger anxiety in patients, leading to increases in blood pressure. One of the textbook authors regularly experiences WCH, which her health care providers recognize as a somewhat "regular" occurrence with patient visits.

To determine your level of fear about visiting the physician, complete the scale in Table 13.1. Scores on this scale may help you determine just how anxious you are about visiting your health care provider. Read on to determine steps that you can take to make the most out of your doctor visits.

Table 13.1	**Measure Your Fear: Fear of Physician (FOP) Scale**

DIRECTIONS: There are five statements below which are common comments made by patients concerning their physicians. Please indicate how well each statement describes how you feel when communicating with your physician, employing the following scale:

1 = not at all; 2 = somewhat; 3 = moderately so; 4 = very much so

_____ 1. When communicating with my physician, I feel tense.

_____ 2. When communicating with my physician, I feel calm.

_____ 3. When communicating with my physician, I feel jittery.

_____ 4. When communicating with my physician, I feel nervous.

_____ 5. When communicating with my physician, I feel relaxed.

SCORING:

Step 1. Add the scores for items 1, 3, and 4.

Step 2. Add the scores for items 2 and 5.

Step 3. Complete the following formula: FOP = 15 + total for Step 1 – total for Step 2.

Scores above 13 indicate high fear of physician. Scores below 7 indicate low fear of physician. Scores between 7 and 13 indicate moderate fear of physician.

Source: From "The impact of communication apprehension and fear of talking with a physician and perceived medical outcomes" by V.P. Richmond, R.S. Smith, A.M. Heisel and J.C. McCroskey, *Communication Research Reports*, 1998, 15, 344–353. Reprinted by permission of the publisher Taylor & Francis Ltd., www.informaworld.com.

Problems with Physician Communication

Consider the following scenario:

> For at least two weeks, Roger, a college senior, was experiencing chest pains during basketball practices. After experiencing this problem for several weeks, the team trainer told Roger he could not play until he went to see his family physician to make sure his health was satisfactory. Roger was frustrated and at the same time extremely apprehensive about going to see his family doctor. His family physician, Dr. Smith, was unfriendly, rarely smiled or joked around, and always seemed in a hurry. As he sat in his doctor's office a week later, his mind was filled with a number of troublesome questions. What if he had to get more tests? What if he had to miss practice today or the next day? What if something was wrong with his heart? What if he had a problem that would prevent him from trying out for the NBA? After waiting for about an hour and a half to see his doctor, Roger finally went into an examining room. The doctor looked over his chart quickly and asked Roger when he first started having chest pains? Roger told her it that it had only been a week or so and the chest pains were not really that bad. The doctor asked a few more questions and then began talking about all of the possible health problems Roger could have, based on his current symptoms. She also told him that until the test results she ordered came back, he could not play. Roger

was furious about this news. When Dr. Smith asked if he had any questions, Roger said, "No!" and glared at her. He begged her to let him play, just this week. Dr. Smith did not seem to understand how important this next game was and instead stated in a matter-of-fact manner that she could not take the risk of allowing him to play, given his current symptoms. Roger stood up and stormed out of the room.

How would you describe this interaction? What could the doctor have done differently? What could Roger have done differently? How often do communication problems like the one described above occur between physicians and patients? After reading the following sections of this chapter, you should be able to answer the above questions.

Most individuals are like Roger and are reluctant to receive any type of health care. People often report experiencing a great deal of anxiety about visits to physicians. In one study, eighty-five percent of patients indicated feeling quite distressed when they had to visit their physician (Bertakis, Roter, and Putnam 1991). Why is this the case? Some reasons patients cite for not wanting to visit the physician are obvious ones: they might receive bad news about their health, be submitted to painful procedures or tests, or feel embarrassed. Other reasons patients might give for feeling embarrassed include: (1) patient did not adhere to the physician's recommendations (e.g., lose weight, quit smoking, etc.), (2) patient does not want to talk about private or personal issues (e.g., number of sexual partners, "gyn apprehension"), and (3) patient feels exposed during the examination when wearing the always popular and very attractive medical gowns.

Patient anxiety may also be explained by the physician's lack of supportive, patient-centered communication practices. In one study (Falvo and Tippy 1988) thirty-eight percent of the physicians did not specify the amount of medicine they prescribed and fifty percent did not indicate the length of the treatment. In a related study, physicians interrupted patients (Beckman and Frankel 1984) when patients were attempting to express concerns to physicians. Beckman and Frankel (1984) found that physicians, on average, gave patients eighteen seconds to express themselves and self-disclose information before interrupting them. In a recent article in the online version of the *Seattle Times*, patients stated that the main reason they sued their health care provider when problems occurred "was because their health professionals showed no concern, warmth, wouldn't listen, wouldn't talk or wouldn't answer questions" (Ostrum 2004, 2). Poor or inadequate communication between health care providers and patients can lead to lower patient satisfaction, poor patient health outcomes, and increases in patient lawsuits, (Ostrum 2004).

Today there is greater emphasis on communication between physicians and patients, with many physicians participating in communication skills training during medical school and beyond. Physicians and other health care providers desire better relationships with patients so they can increase patient compliance and cooperation, improve patient health outcomes and reduce malpractice lawsuits. While this news is promising, there are areas that still need to be addressed in order to achieve these outcomes. For example, while more medical students are receiving training today, the quality of their training should be evaluated. In a survey of primary care physicians, sixty percent indicated the current medical education curriculum did not provide sufficient communication skills training

(Gilbert 1997). The television show *Grey's Anatomy*, focusing on medical interns, has repeatedly shown the difficulty faced by its characters in communicating with their patients, from the poor reception of Dr. Christina Yang's detached professionalism to George's first fumbling that a loved one could not be saved. Even in fiction, preparation for how to relay such information seems to be lacking this crucial element. In targeting physicians' lack of communication skills, we are only addressing part of the problem. Researchers and health care providers agree that patients could also improve their communication practices during health care visits and, at the same time, make a greater effort to adhere to their health care provider requests as a means of improving relationships and patient outcomes (Cegala, Gade, Broz, and McClure 2004).

Patient Communication

As mentioned previously, interpersonal communication is described as a transaction that occurs between two individuals. The patient also has the potential to either contribute to or detract from the quality of the patient-physician relationship. One of the most significant and frequently cited ways the patient can affect the patient-physician relationship is by not complying with the physician's requests. Patient noncompliance and noncooperation are significant problems in health care (Thompson 1986). And while there are numerous reasons patients do not comply with physician requests, "patient cooperation depends on how the health care provider communicates more than on anything else" (Thompson 1986, 111). Kreps and Thorton (1992) identify common areas of patient noncompliance such as clients not keeping appointments, not following health care regimens, and not using prescribed drugs correctly. *Grey's Anatomy* highly dramatized an instance of noncompliance when a bypass surgery patient instructed to quit smoking proceeds to light up in his highly oxygenated room, causing an explosion.

Another problem linked to ineffective communication between patients and physicians is the unrealistic expectations some patients might have of their health care providers' abilities to cure the sick (Kreps and Thorton 1992). Patients might even expect their physicians to perform amazing miracles like those seen in soap operas or movies. Soap operas, particularly, regularly have characters slip into "hopeless" comas only to surface a few days later. Even *slightly* more reality-driven serials, like *ER* and *Grey's Anatomy*, produce highly unlikely expectations. Even though he regularly loses patients, *Grey's Anatomy's* Dr. McDreamy has also produced his share of neuro-surgery "miracles," including saving the dangling life of fellow surgeon Miranda Bailey's husband (while Dr. Bailey is in labor and the hospital under bomb threat, no less). It is not unusual for patients to expect too much from their health care providers and to view their own health care concerns as more significant or serious than the problems of other patients (Kreps and Thorton 1992).

Recently, patients have started bringing information they gather from the Internet to physician visits and questioning their providers' decisions based on the information (Ahmad, Hudak, Bercovitz, Hollenberg, and Levinson 2006). Physicians report feeling overburdened by this trend because they are expected to be familiar with, and receptive to, the Internet information. In a recent study of primary care physicians, the physicians expressed concern with patients self-diagnosing and self-treating based on Internet information

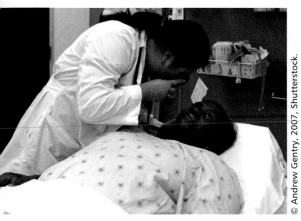

Being a patient in a hospital can be an especially overwhelming situation.

© Andrew Gentry, 2007, Shutterstock.

(Ahmad et al. 2006). Physicians may not react well to this trend and may even become defensive when patients question their treatment decisions. When these problems occur, patients are more likely to communicate ineffectively with their health care provider and establish poor relationships. As Kreps and Thorton (1992) point out, physician-patient miscommunication, lack of cooperation, and unrealistic expectations are all problematic and can lead to a tumultuous physician-patient relationship.

Many individuals experience difficulty performing their "patient" roles because they are often uncertain about what being a patient entails (Northouse and Northouse 1998). When they enter a health care setting, individuals shed the familiar roles (as wife, mother, father, employee) and assume the unfamiliar role of patient. Hospital settings are especially overwhelming for patients. When patients enter the hospital they encounter numerous health care professionals, each with a different role in providing patient care. These health care experiences cause anxiety for most patients.

Potential Responses or Reactions in these Situations

When physician-patient communication is ineffective, a variety of problems can occur. According to Kreps and Thorton (1992) "communication is also pragmatically important and can save the health care provider from malpractice suits" (2). Malpractice suits are a significant problem in health care that affect all of us in some way. Approximately seventy percent of malpractice claims linked in some way to health care providers' ineffective communication skills (Levinson 1994; Levinson, Roter, Mullooly, Dull, and Frankel 1997). As Levinson (1994) notes, while physician mistakes are not common, poor communication practices along with physician mistakes are perceived as a recipe for litigation.

A significant and expected outcome of communication problems in this context is widespread dissatisfaction for both the health care providers and the clients. What happens when patients are less than satisfied with their health care experiences? They avoid getting professional assistance, even when they really need it (Kreps and Thorton 1992). What happens when patients avoid visits to their physicians? This decision affects us all, either directly or indirectly. If a patient does not get regularly screened for certain types of diseases, then potentially curable diseases or illnesses persist undetected. Patients are not the only ones who are dissatisfied with the current state of our health care. Health care professionals, frustrated with the lack of patient compliance and other work-related stressors, are more likely to experience burnout and leave the profession (Kreps and Thorton 1992).

Ineffective, or poor, communication between physicians and patients affects patient compliance and cooperation. The research has indicated that both patient and physician behaviors can explain patient noncompliance and noncooperation. Rates of patient noncooperation have been estimated to be as high as seventy percent (Thompson 1986)! Patients might not comply with physician requests because they are lazy, apathetic, scared, ignorant, or defiant. On the other hand, physicians also contribute to patient noncompliance by employing either ineffective or negative tactics to gain patient compliance (Thompson 1986). Regardless of whether the patient, the physician, or both are to blame for problems with patient noncompliance, it is another significant problem that can potentially affect a patient's health and rate of recovery.

IMPROVING HEALTH CARE PROVIDER-PATIENT COMMUNICATION

While much of this chapter has focused on physician-patient studies and related information, we want to expand our discussion to include suggestions for improving communication between all types of health care providers (e.g., physicians, nurses, technicians, physical therapists, and pharmacists) and patients. In the following sections, we advance several suggestions for improving communication between care providers and patients to reduce the incidence of patient noncompliance, reduce the prevalence of lawsuits, and increase patient and health care provider satisfaction with communication and relationships. While this list of suggestions is certainly not exhaustive, a number of them can improve communication and relationships between care providers and patients.

Suggestions for Patients and Care Providers

While there is a great deal of information available for physicians and care providers who want to improve their communication with their patients (see, for example, Klingle, 2004), there is considerably less available for patients who want to improve communication with their physicians. Additionally, patients and physicians seem to have quite different views of what constitutes competent patient communication (Cegala, Gade, Broz, and McClure 2004). According to Booth-Butterfield (2006) one of the most important communication skills for a patient to possess is appropriate assertiveness. **Assertive communication** involves defending your own rights and wishes while still respecting the rights and wishes of others. In addition to using an appropriately assertive response, the style of delivery is also important. Booth-Butterfield (2006) feels individuals can maximize the effectiveness of their assertive communication by sending nonverbal messages that are consistent with the verbal. For example, individuals should strive to maintain eye contact and appear confident through one's facial expressions, use appropriately assertive gestures and a firm and confident tone of voice. Individuals can enhance their assertiveness and credibility by displaying confidence in their voice, gestures, posture, and facial expressions. Booth-Butterfield offers a model of an appropriately assertive response that includes three components: **empathy, rationale,** and **action** (ERA) as illustrated in Table 13.2.

© Dennis Sabo, 2007, Shutterstock.

A patient needs to possess appropriate assertiveness to help improve communication with a health care provider.

Table 13.2   Responding Assertively: ERA Model

Components	Examples
E Empathy—indicates to the other person that you understand his/her position or feelings. This statement illustrates your concern for the other person.	*"I know you must have a lot of patients to see today. . . ."*
R Rationale—the reason for bringing up the request. The rationale is the thesis or main concern you have and, without it, people will be left guessing what it is you want or need from the interaction.	*"However, I really need some extra time with you today to ask some questions about my treatment options."*
A Action—communicates specifically what you want done. Booth-Butterfield emphasizes the importance of providing specific information about what exactly it is that you would like to have done, changed, improved, etc., because of this interaction.	*"So in order to address all of my concerns, could we meet for an extra thirty minutes today?"*

© iofoto, 2007, Shutterstock.

Maintaining eye contact and projecting confidence maximize the effectiveness of assertive communication.

Don Cegala, another health communication researcher and communication professor (patcom.jcomm.ohio-state .edu), offers several helpful suggestions for patients preparing for medical interviews. One key piece of advice for patients is to *prepare* for medical interactions by writing down physical symptoms or questions prior to the appointment. His advice, expressed as the acronym **PACE**, is easy to remember and can help patients to communicate more effectively with their physicians. His suggestions are listed in the table below.

Health care providers can use a number of communication strategies to establish good relationships with their patients. For example, Levinson and her colleagues (1997) found that physicians who laughed and smiled more and used more facilitation statements (*First I am going to take your blood pressure . . .*) with their patients were less likely to be sued than those who used these behaviors less often. Wanzer and her colleagues (2004) tested a preliminary model of health care providers' use of patient-centered communication. The patient-centered communication model, **CHILE**, can be used by health care providers to

Table 13.3   Preparing Communication for Medical Interviews

P	Present detailed, descriptive information about how you are feeling to your health care provider. Be sure to describe your symptoms and any irregularities in your health. This information will help the care provider diagnose and treat you.
A	Ask questions if appropriate information is not provided by your health care provider. If you are confused about the information, seek clarification by *asking questions*.
C	Check your understanding of information that is given to you (e.g., paraphrasing information back to your health care provider, *"So what you are saying is . . ."*)
E	Express any concerns that you may have about the recommended treatment. If necessary be appropriately assertive (ERA)

Table 13.4	Suggestions for Health Care Providers: Increasing Communication Satisfaction

C	Clarity—communicate directions and explanations clearly
H	Humor—use appropriate humor to reduce stressful situations
I	Immediacy—be responsive to the patients
L	Listening—pay attention to the patient's needs, fears, and concerns.
E	Empathy—express understanding and sympathy

improve communication between care providers and patients and increase patient satisfaction. See Table 13.4 for an explanation of CHILE.

Wanzer and her colleagues found a significant positive correlation between health care providers' use of these behaviors and reported satisfaction with communication and medical care of parents' of child patients. It was especially important for physicians to be immediate, to listen, and to exhibit empathic messages with parents of child patients as a means of increasing satisfaction with communication. For more information on patient-centered communication, see research by Stewart 1995; and Stewart et al. 2000.

These suggestions should help both patients and care providers improve their interactions, leading to better relationships, increased patient compliance, and increased satisfaction for both physicians and patients.

© iofoto, 2007, Shutterstock.

Parents are more satisfied with pediatricians who are responsive, listen to them, and express empathy.

COMMUNICATION BETWEEN NONDISABLED PERSONS AND PERSONS WITH DISABILITIES

While there is a great deal of research regarding communication in health care settings, there is significantly less available on communication between nondisabled persons and persons with disabilities, especially from the perspective of the person with the disability (Braithwaite and Harter 2000, 17). A concern addressed by individuals conducting research in this area is that the available research often presents individuals with disabilities as passive and reactive during interpersonal encounters (Braithwaite 1996). To improve communication between nondisabled persons and persons with disabilities, it is important to learn more about how both interactants view communication in these situations. This section addresses the following questions: Why does communication between nondisabled persons and persons with disabilities cause anxiety for both interactants? What are some typical responses or reactions for individuals in these situations? Finally, how can individuals approach these situations and improve communication and relationships between persons with disabilities and persons without?

Consider this scenario:

Monique was a freshman at a large university. She was an excellent student who really enjoyed participating in class discussions. She typically sat in the front of class and raised her hand often when the instructor solicited feedback from students. As a freshman at a large university, Monique was having some difficulties making the transition from high school to college classroom situations. In her philosophy and math classes, she noticed her instructors often avoided eye contact with her and lectured on the opposite side of the room. She raised her hand often in both of these classes, but was rarely noticed or called upon. Monique wondered why she was not being called on in class. When she did interact with each of these professors, they seemed anxious around her and maintained a great amount of distance. Monique wondered whether her wheelchair made them anxious, because these professors did not seem as nervous around the nondisabled students.

Why did these professors act this way with Monique? Are the professors' reactions to Monique unusual? Why are people anxious in these situations? More importantly, what could be done to improve communication in these types of situations? All of these questions will be answered in the following sections of this chapter.

Disability Defined

Forty-three million Americans have some type of disability (Booth-Butterfield 1999). In order to be identified as someone with a **disability,** individuals must have either a mental or a physical condition that substantially limits one or more of their major life activities. Major life activities include caring for oneself, seeing, hearing, speaking and learning (Booth-Butterfield 1999). Individuals with disabilities may possess visible or invisible disabilities or, in some cases, both.

Visible disabilities are noticeable to others and might include physical deformities, deafness, or blindness and require the use of a wheelchair. Visible disabilities are readily perceived by others and make the individual with the disability seem more conspicuous and open to public scrutiny (Booth-Butterfield 1999; Harrington and Matthews 1997). Most of the research on communication between nondisabled individuals and persons with disabilities examines the impact of visible disabilities on social interaction from the nondisabled person's perspective (Grove and Werkman 1991; Thompson 1981; 1983). Individuals with visible disabilities may experience maltreatment from others because they are perceived as being different, or stigmatized. Falk (2001) defines a stigma as a "negative social meaning" (109). In his book, *Stigma: How We Treat Outsiders*, Falk includes those with developmental disabilities and mental retardation as part of the stigmatized population in the United States. In a culture that values good looks and intelligence, those with disabilities like mental illness are often rejected (Falk 2001). To negotiate interactions successfully in our society, it is common for the stigmatized individual to employ different types of strategies to maintain communication with non-stigmatized or nondisabled individuals (Harrington and Matthews 1997). Kyle Maynard, a quadruple amputee, wrestler, and motivational speaker, states that he often smiles and initiates conversations with non-disabled persons to make them feel more at ease about his disability.

The second type of disability individuals might have is labeled **hidden disabilities,** which are not typically noticed by the co-interactant except under unusual circumstances or if the individual with the disability discloses information about it (Matthews 1994). Learning disabilities, arthritis, diabetes, asthma, AIDS, and heart disease are all forms of invisible disabilities. While there is markedly less research available on communication between persons with invisible disabilities and nondisabled persons, the research indicates that there are challenges associated with these types of interactions as well (Frymier and Wanzer 2003). Those with invisible disabilities are often ashamed or embarrassed by their disability and worry about their disability being exposed to those around them. "The risk of shame is particularly great for those who are invisibly disabled precisely because of the hidden or concealed nature of their condition" (Harrington and Matthews 1997, 2). Thus, when individuals with invisible disabilities interact with nondisabled persons, they often experience anxiety that can affect the quality of their interactions.

Reasons for Communication Problems between Nondisabled Persons and Persons with Disabilities

It is for both simple and complex reasons that communication between nondisabled persons and persons with disabilities produces anxiety for one or both interactants. In some cases, nondisabled individuals may not be able to communicate with individuals with disabilities, or vice versa, because of **real barriers.** Some disabilities create more real obstacles, or barriers, to communication through regular channels. For example, a nondisabled individual attempting to communicate with someone who is deaf may not know sign language, or a deaf individual may not be able to read lips (Booth-Butterfield 1999).

More often than not, perceptual barriers are the real problem in communication between nondisabled individuals and individuals with disabilities. **Perceptual barriers** are those internal obstacles that often disrupt communication due to cognitive or emotional reactions located within the individual (Booth-Butterfield 1999). Perceptual barriers may be in the form of a stigma (Goffman 1963; Hebl and Kleck 2000) or may be the fears or worries about how the other person might react during the interaction (Booth-Butterfield 1999). Persons with and without disabilities might become excessively self-conscious about what they say or do during the interaction. Nondisabled persons might have inaccurate perceptions about the communication skills, or lack of skills, a person with a disability might possess. In addition, nondisabled persons might have unanswered questions about the disabled person that disrupt the flow of the conversation. For example, nondisabled individuals might wonder, Was it

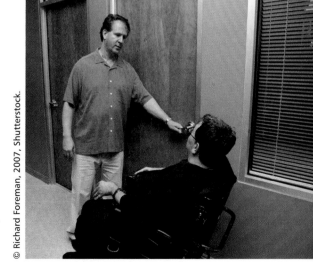

© Richard Foreman, 2007, Shutterstock.

Perceptual barriers are internal obstacles that often disrupt communication.

a serious accident that put her in the wheelchair? Can she understand me? Should I help her? These concerns are problematic and disrupt the conversation between the disabled and nondisabled person.

Nondisabled individuals may also form impressions of individuals with disabilities that are inaccurate and negative. Individuals with disabilities have been misrepresented in the research conducted on persons with disabilities as well as in the media. For example, persons with disabilities are often stereotyped as being dependent, socially withdrawn, emotionally unstable, and easily offended about their disability (Coleman and DePaulo 1991). Most of the early research on communication between nondisabled persons and persons with disabilities offered an unflattering and inaccurate picture of the communication skills of persons with disabilities (Braithwaite and Harter 2000). In a number of early studies in this area, persons with disabilities were often depicted as passive and reactive participants in the communication process, ineffective communicators and socially isolated (Braithwaite 1996; Thompson 1981). These inaccurate perceptions are problematic in that they can lead to anxiety for persons both with and without disabilities.

Persons with disabilities are also anxious about communicating with nondisabled persons. This anxiety can be partially explained by previous negative experiences had when communicating with nondisabled persons. While there is limited research from the perspective of persons with disabilities, most of it paints a negative picture of these interactions. For example, students with disabilities felt that most of their professors, who also happened to be nondisabled, held negative attitudes toward them (Worley 2000). Other research indicated students with disabilities "often encounter stigma, misunderstanding, social isolation, and attitudinal barriers in their interactions with nondisabled peers who are not friends" (Worley 2000, 134). In general, students with disabilities who attend college often experience more negative attitudes from peers and professors than nondisabled students (Fine and Asch 1988; Hart and Williams 1995; Worley 2000).

Recently, Frymier and Wanzer (2003) investigated differences between nondisabled and disabled students' perceptions of their professors' communication patterns. Additionally, differences in perceptions of student-teacher communication patterns were investigated between students with visible and hidden disabilities. Students with both visible and hidden disabilities felt less understood by their professors than nondisabled students. When the researchers compared perceptions of students with visible disabilities and students with hidden disabilities, students with hidden disabilities such as learning disabilities saw professors as less communicatively competent and reported less attitude similarity than those with visible disabilities. One explanation for this finding is that students with hidden disabilities, like learning disabilities, were more likely to experience misunderstandings about their disabilities with their professors than those with visible disabilities. Most professors understand the constraints associated with a physical limitation but they may not understand limitations associated with learning disabilities. This study and others (e.g., Hart and Williams 1995) illustrates the influence of negative attitudes and perceptions on both the quality and quantity of communication which occurs between nondisabled and disabled individuals.

Communication between Nondisabled Individuals and Persons with Disabilities: Common Responses to these Situations

What happens when nondisabled individuals communicate with persons with disabilities? Interactions between persons with visible disabilities and nondisabled persons tend to be shorter (Hebl and Kleck 2000; Kleck 1968) and gestures and body movements of nondisabled persons tend to be less natural, more rigid and stiff (Hebl and Kleck 2000; Kleck 1968). Additionally, nondisabled individuals tend to maintain much greater interpersonal distance from persons with visible disabilities (Worthington 1974). According to Thompson (1982a; 1982b), persons with disabilities receive less eye contact, increased stares, greater distance, and decreased conversational time during interaction with nondisabled individuals. Overall, nondisabled individuals display less receptivity during interactions with persons with disabilities.

How do persons with disabilities respond to interactions with nondisabled individuals? Much of the research on communication between persons with disabilities and nondisabled persons has examined how nondisabled persons provide assistance for persons with disabilities from the perspective of the disabled individual (Braithwaite and Eckstein 2003; Thompson and Cusella 1988). When examining communication situations in which nondisabled individuals offered assistance to persons with disabilities, there was very little interaction and persons with disabilities did not generally refuse assistance (Thompson and Cusella 1988). More recently, Braithwaite and Eckstein (2003) interviewed individuals with visible physical disabilities about their perceptions of receiving both solicited and unsolicited assistance from nondisabled individuals. They identified four main ways individuals managed instrumental support during interactions between disabled and nondisabled persons: (1) physical assistance, (2) assistance initiated by persons with disabilities, (3) assistance initiated by nondisabled persons, and (4) unwanted assistance managed by persons with disabilities. Most persons with disabilities indicated they preferred to be the one initiating assistance from others, and they preferred the help to come from acquaintances rather than from strangers. Persons with disabilities offered a number of reasons for not wanting assistance from nondisabled persons. Reasons indicated were: the nondisabled person was patronizing, was making too big a production about providing help, was giving too much assistance, was making the situation worse by helping, or was giving help without asking (Braithwaite and Eckstein 2003).

Persons with disabilities often report receiving unwanted assistance from nondisabled persons and manage these situations by employing a variety of tactics. In Braithwaite and Eckstein's (2003) research, persons with disabilities indicated using one of six different strategies to manage these situations. When offered unwanted assistance by nondisabled persons, persons with disabilities might accept the help even if it is not needed, or ignore the offers for help. Sometimes persons with disabilities would directly refuse the strategy by just saying, No, thank you, providing a direct refusal and then explaining why help was not needed or necessary. Another strategy some persons with disabilities indicated using to refuse assistance was humor. Use of humor varied greatly depending on the situation and was a way to refuse help while at the same time "sparing the nondisabled person embarrassment" (Braithwaite and Eckstein 2003, 17). The final strategy employed by persons with disabilities was refusals, which ranged between aggressive and assertive rejections of offered assistance. Aggressive strategies might include "telling someone off" or showing anger to indicate that the help is unwanted. Persons with disabilities who receive unwanted assistance from nondisabled persons might begin with assertive refusals for help that eventually escalate into verbally aggressive refusals.

Because persons with disabilities must interact daily with nondisabled strangers, family members, friends, co-workers, and relationship partners, they are often required to possess more sophisticated communication skills. Braithwaite and Harter (2000) support this claim and argue that persons with disabilities must often "develop a wider repertoire of communication abilities in a world where many people will misunderstand them, feel uncomfortable around them, and do not know how to talk to them" (19). Thus, as indicated by Braithwaite and Eckstein's (2003) recent investigation, persons with disabilities are well aware of the challenging nature of these interactions and, as a result, have developed strategies for effectively managing interactions with nondisabled persons.

What are some suggestions for improving communication between nondisabled persons and persons with disabilities? Here are some suggestions for improving communication between nondisabled and disabled persons:

- Nondisabled persons should wait for the person with the disability to ask for help. Research indicates that it is important for the person with disability to control their actions throughout the day (Braithwaite and Eckstein 2003)
- When nondisabled persons assist persons with disabilities they should use general types of questions such as Do you need anything? or May I help you? Again, asking these general questions allows the person with the disability to control, regulate, or guide the help he or she receives
- When offering help or communicating in other general situations, nondisabled persons should be sure to communicate in a casual and natural manner. Persons with disabilities often evaluate how the offer for assistance is communicated. The offer for assistance should be delivered in the same way you would ask any individual, disabled or not
- Nondisabled persons should always ask before acting, and should listen carefully to what the person with the disability needs
- Nondisabled persons should be willing to take no for an answer. Research indicates that persons with disabilities receive an overabundance of help from nondisabled individuals and do not always need or want assistance
- Persons with disabilities should try to use direct verbal strategies when asking for assistance as they are more easily interpreted than nonverbal signals
- Both persons with disabilities and persons without should engage in active listening practices and, when needed, seek clarification of unclear messages
- When possible, both persons with and without disabilities should refrain from sending verbally aggressive messages and instead communicate assertively—use ERA!

While interactions between persons with disabilities and nondisabled persons can be difficult for a variety of reasons, we feel these situations can be improved by adhering to the suggestions we have offered, and not by avoiding these interactions in the future. If individuals want to learn more about how to reduce anxiety in these situations and how to communicate more effectively, we suggest reading more of the scholarship that addresses some of these issues in detail (see, for example, Hebl and Kleck 2000).

DEATH AND DYING COMMUNICATION

Consider the following scenario:

> At the beginning of her senior year in college, Lacey found out that her father had lung cancer and would probably die in a few months. After learning more about his prognosis and speaking at length with her family members, Lacey called one of her closest friends to discuss her feelings about the news. While Lacey's friend was supportive during the initial conversation about her father's illness, as time went on Lacey realized her friend was consistently avoiding any discussion about this situation. One day Lacey decided to confront her friend about her behavior by making yet another attempt to talk to her friend about her fear of losing her father. As soon as Lacey began talking about her father, her friend glared at her and yelled, "Lacey, I just can't talk about your dad's death; it is way too difficult for me!" After this conversation, Lacey's relationship with her friend was never quite the same.

Why do you think Lacey's friend reacted this way? What would you do or say if someone close to you acted like Lacey's friend? The information presented in the last sections of this chapter will help you understand why it is so difficult to talk about death and dying and how to negotiate your way through similar difficult situations.

The topic of death and dying is an extremely difficult subject for most individuals, even professionals who deal with death and dying on a regular basis. In this section, we discuss the reasons individuals find this to be a difficult topic and the typical responses to situations involving death and dying. Suggestions for improving communication about death and dying from both the dying person's perspective and the family member's or loved one's perspective are offered in the final sections of this chapter. After reading this chapter, we hope that you will be able to manage conversations about this topic more effectively and provide appropriate comforting communication to individuals who are either ill or have recently experienced the death of a loved one.

Reasons for Anxiety when Discussing Death and Dying

There are a number of reasons individuals become anxious or uncomfortable when discussing death and dying. For many of us, we wonder how and when we will die. Will we die of old age? Will our death include suffering or pain? Will we die suddenly? Where do we go after we die? Another significant worry often triggered by discussions about death and dying is the potential loss of our loved ones. We fear losing the ones we love or leaving them behind when we die.

Another reason death, even aging, is not discussed is because it is a subject that is "evaded, ignored, and denied by our youth-worshipping, progress-oriented society" (Kubler-Ross 1975, x). Elisabeth Kubler-Ross (1975), also known as the "death and dying lady," discusses our culture's inability to approach aging and death as a natural part of life. Instead, she notes, we often treat death as an illness or disease we should be able to conquer. For a number of years Dr. Kubler-Ross interviewed terminally ill patients in front of medical students, physicians, nurses, social workers, and clergy, to provide care providers with greater insight into the perspective of the dying patient. As a result of her research and others' on this topic (e.g., Kastenbaum 1992), professionals who treat terminally ill patients now know more about the thoughts, feelings, and behaviors exhibited by the terminally ill and are better equipped to treat them and to help them make end-of-life decisions.

Despite the work by Kubler-Ross and others, it is not unusual for dying patients to continue to experience communication problems with their health care providers, often leading to poor care (Hines, Babrow, Badzek, and Moss 2001). Because approximately eighty percent of people die in institutional settings such as hospitals, nursing homes, or retirement facilities, it is likely that they will interact with health care professionals who are poorly equipped to discuss issues related to death and dying (Servaty, Krejci, and Hayslip 1996). Thus, health care providers, who deal with death on a regular basis, have become the focus of much of the more recent research (Servaty et al. 1996). Both doctors and patients are reluctant to talk about death for various reasons (Hines et al. 2001). Physicians are not typically trained to talk about death with patients, and even with training, are usually not willing to talk about death and dying due to reluctance on the patient's behalf. Even family members of the terminally ill are unwilling to talk about death with their loved ones. Hines and his colleagues note that family involvement with the terminally ill patient may often be counterproductive or even contradict the patients' needs (Hines et al. 2001). While family members can be a great source of support and comfort, they may also become overly emotional and agitated, hindering their ability to help their loved one make important end-of-life care decisions. Given our culture's reluctance to discuss death, it is not surprising that health care providers, patients, and patients' family members often avoid discussing end-of-life issues.

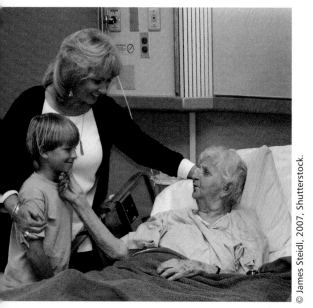

© James Steidl, 2007, Shutterstock.

Given our culture's reluctance to discuss death, it is not surprising that people often avoid the topic.

Responses to Death and Dying

How do people typically react when they are faced with death? According to Elisabeth Kubler-Ross, there seem to be several stages that both individuals who are dying and loved ones of terminally ill go through. The stages of death and dying are denial, anger, bargaining, depression, and acceptance (Kubler-Ross 1974; 1975). Kubler-Ross draws a number of important conclusions regarding the stages: (1) the stages do not always occur in the same order for every person, (2) some individuals might not go through every stage of the process, and (3) some patients exhibit two or three stages simultaneously. Kubler-Ross notes that, ideally, both the dying patient and the patient's family should reach the stage of acceptance before death occurs, although this is not always possible. Some individuals may stay in one stage throughout the process due to unique personality traits, emotional states, or individual coping styles. It is important to know what individuals experience during each of these stages to communicate more effectively with them throughout the process.

Denial Stage.　The first stage of death and dying is typically the **denial** stage. In the denial stage, the patient may "deny the bad news and continue to work as if he were as well and as strong as before" (Kubler-Ross 1975, 1). Family members or friends of the loved ones may deny that the individual is sick as well and continue to interact with the individual as if he or she is healthy. Denial is viewed as an unproductive stage for both the dying patient and loved ones because it may either prevent treatment of the illness, hasten death, or prevent the terminally ill person and loved one from talking about end-of-life issues and engaging in grief work.

Anger.　The next stage of death and dying is **anger.** During this stage individuals might ask Why me? and become angry at everyone around them. Individuals might lash out at loved ones, possibly resulting in isolation from the very people they need the most. Similar to denial, this stage is also unproductive and prevents individuals from enjoying the time they have left, engaging in grief work, and dealing with end-of-life issues. If the terminally ill person or loved one is in this stage for extended periods of time, social support from others may dwindle significantly.

Bargaining Stage.　During the **bargaining** stage of death and dying, individuals try to strike deals with others in order to recover from their illness. It is not unusual for people to bargain with God, promising good behavior or increased church attendance, for an extension of life or to escape pain and suffering. Similar to the other two stages, this phase is generally considered unproductive for both the terminally ill individual and the loved ones because it may prevent further treatment, create a sense of false hope, or prevent individuals from facing end-of-life issues. In addition, some terminally ill individuals and family members may be taken advantage of by those who promise miracle or quack cures.

Depression Stage.　During the **depression** stage the terminally ill individual or loved one may lose interest in the outside world and significantly reduce his or her contact with other people. It is difficult to observe the patient or loved one in this stage. Patients might abuse drugs or alcohol or contemplate suicide because they are depressed. It is important to help individuals move through this stage. Patient's family members or friends might consider recommending professional help or seeking other means of helping the patient manage his depression and begin the grieving process.

Acceptance.   According to Kubler-Ross, if the dying person is afforded the opportunity to grieve and his family members have learned to let go, then he will be able to die in a stage of **acceptance.** Patients would typically reach the acceptance stage of death and dying if it were not for members of the helping professions who are reluctant to admit defeat and family members who are reluctant to let go of their loved one (Kubler-Ross 1974). Kubler-Ross feels that the acceptance stage is the most realistic goal a dying person can work toward, since all of us have to die eventually. Once someone has reached this stage he has a much better chance to focus all of his energies on working with the physician and treatment team to prolong his life. The important question then becomes, how can we help individuals reach the acceptance stage of death and dying?

Suggestions for Improving Communication Related to Death and Dying

It is important for all of us to help our friends, relatives, co-workers, or relationship partners during difficult times. One way to help those we care about is by providing appropriate and effective comforting communication. Brant Burleson's (1984) definition of **comforting communication** is "the type of communication behavior having the intended function of alleviating, moderating, or salving the distressed emotional states of others" (64). Comforting communication can include verbal messages such as "I am really sorry this happened to you," or nonverbal behaviors such as eye contact, attentiveness, crying, hugs, or gestures (Dolin and Booth-Butterfield 1993). What types of messages are perceived as the most effective comforting strategies? Effective comforting messages are those that are described as more person-centered (Burleson and MacGeorge 2002). **Person-centered comforting** messages are strategies that help a person explain how he is feeling at the moment, recognize and validate the expressed feelings, and illustrate how those feelings fit in a broader social context. Person-centered messages are often perceived as the most effective means of helping others deal with difficult situations because they "tend to be more listener-centered, accepting, emotionally focused, and evaluatively neutral" (Burleson and MacGeorge 2002, 395). To illustrate the stark contrast between comforting messages that are high and low in person-centeredness, let us imagine that your friend's grandmother died recently in a car accident. An example of a comforting message that is high in person-centeredness would be, "How are you feeling right now? I can see why you would be upset. Anyone that has been through a situation as difficult as yours would probably feel like you do right now. Is there anything I can do to help you get through this difficult time?" By contrast, a comforting message that is low in person-centeredness would be, "Why are you so upset? Don't you think that you are overreacting right now? You really need to stop moping around and move on with your life. Let's just go out tonight and drink some beers!" These not-so-subtle examples illustrate the difference between comforting messages that help individuals feel better and messages that do not help, and may even make others feel worse.

Some people are better at providing comfort and social support than others. Interpersonal researchers have studied the relationship between individual differences and comforting abilities. For example, individuals described as **cognitively complex** possess more highly abstract and differentiated construct systems (e.g., schema) and are more likely to enact sophisticated comforting messages compared to individuals low in cognitive complexity (Burleson and Samter 1990). Individuals higher in cognitive complexity can access a variety of different comforting strategies and, as a result, are more likely to employ more sophisticated person-centered messages than those low in cognitive complexity. Are there other factors that impact one's ability to deliver effective comforting communication? Dolin and Booth-Butterfield (1993) studied how individual differences such as sex and **affective orientation** affect the types of nonverbal comforting individuals provide. They found that females tended to be more affectively oriented than males, which meant that they were more likely to use their emotions to guide communication decisions. In addition, females who were high in affective orientation employed more diverse nonverbal comforting strategies than individuals scoring low in affective orientation (Dolin and Booth-Butterfield 1993). Affectively oriented individuals also employed more diverse **nonverbal comforting strategies** (e.g., hugging, patting the person on the back, and showing concern through their voice), which seems to indicate greater cognitive complexity as well. Individual differences such as cognitive complexity and affective orientation affect peoples' abilities to provide verbal and nonverbal comforting communication.

Effective and Ineffective Death and Dying Communication

What are some of the best ways to provide comfort to individuals who are terminally ill? First and foremost, Kubler-Ross (1974; 1975) encourages those caring for the terminally ill to meet the individual's support needs by spending time with him or her, acknowledging that death is imminent, and addressing any needs or immediate concerns he or she may have. It seems most important to spend time with the terminally ill person, listening and allowing the person to express his or her feelings. Additionally, experts say, it is important to allow the individual to grieve and mourn on his own terms and to not force him to reach a particular stage of death and dying. While it is most beneficial to help him reach the acceptance stage, forcing the person to feel or think a certain way is not productive. It is extremely important to be supportive and to listen actively, always letting the person know you are available. Being available, listening, taking care of the person's needs, and nonverbal comforting strategies are all valuable ways of helping individuals manage this difficult time. From the patient's perspective, it is important for those caring for the dying individual to be honest and compassionate and, when necessary, to express fears about the situation.

What about after the terminally ill person has died—what is the *best* thing to say to someone who has lost a loved one? There are some support attempts that are recognized as unhelpful by the recipient; much of what people say after someone has died is not helpful and does not alleviate the pain associated with the loss. Davidowitz and Myrick (1984) found that eighty

It's important to comfort and support a grieving friend and validate feelings of loss.

© Darrell Young, 2007, Shutterstock.

percent of the statements made to individuals who had recently lost a loved one were not helpful. Commonly delivered statements such as, She led a full life, Be thankful you have another son, or Don't question God's will, are not comforting for the recipient. In similar research conducted by Lehman and his colleagues (1986), they asked recipients who had lost a spouse or a child in a motor vehicle accident in the last four to seven years to identify the least helpful support tactics. The top four strategies identified as the least helpful in providing comfort were: giving advice, encouragement of recovery, minimization/forced cheerfulness, and identification with feelings. From Lehman's research, the most helpful strategies included contact from a similar other, expressions of concern and caring, allowing the person to vent their feelings, involvement in social activities, and just being available. Range, Walston, and Pollard (1992) also identified a number of effective and ineffective verbal comforting strategies delivered to loved ones after a suicide, homicide, accident, or natural death. The most helpful statements were, If there is anything I can do, please let me know, and I am here if you need someone to talk to.

In death and dying situations, it is important to let the other person know that you are available for him or her and are willing to help if needed. When faced with death, individuals handle situations differently and experience varied emotions and feelings. It is important to support them and validate their feelings without minimizing their grief or concern. As validated by Lehman's research, a highly ineffective comforting strategy would be to state, I know exactly how you feel because my dog just died. Why is this statement an example of ineffective comforting communication? Because the source does not know *exactly* how the individual is feeling, and providing the example of losing a pet as being similar to losing a parent is not appropriate or reassuring. It is comforting to know that sophisticated communication strategies are not required in these situations. It is important for the person providing support to listen, allowing the other person time to vent, and to ask how he or she can help make the situation better. Effective comforting communication would not include the use of trite, or common, phrases such as Doesn't life seem unfair? God needed another angel, or Heaven is a nice place. Virtually everyone who has lost a loved one would agree that these statements are not usually helpful in death and dying situations.

SUMMARY

In this chapter, we outlined three situations identified as challenging for most individuals because they cause anxiety for either one or both of the interactants. Now that you are more aware of why these situations are difficult and the strategies available for effectively communicating in each of these situations, we hope you will approach these experiences with greater confidence. In addition, there is one final important piece of advice we would like to offer. Do not be afraid of making mistakes in these situations, because everyone does! If you say the wrong thing when interacting with your physician, with a person with a disability, or with someone who recently lost a loved one, provide a genuine apology for your mistake. Try to not make the same mistake again, but do not avoid these interactions in the future. As we mentioned in Chapter One, communication is a skill that individuals can improve upon over time. Now that you understand *why* these situations are challenging and *how* you can manage these difficult situations, we hope that you will make a conscious effort to employ some of the strategies recommended in this chapter.

APPLICATIONS

Exercises

A. Use ERA to respond to the following situations.

    1. In the last two visits to your health care provider, she has told you that she does not have time to answer your questions about alternative treatments for your asthma. You would like to talk about other options available for treating this chronic condition. What can you say?

    2. One of your closest friends died recently. Naturally, you are feeling sad about this and do not feel like going out with other friends. During a recent phone conversation one of your friends says, "You need to move on and stop feeling sorry for yourself." What can you say?

B. As mentioned in the chapter, people are using the internet more often to obtain health information. Interview a health care provider about informational sites that are viewed as credible. Ask the care provider to help you learn how to sift through all of the available sites to find useful and reliable information. Discuss these interviews in class.

C. For those students who have lost a family member or friend, discuss whether the stages of death and dying accurately depict what individuals go through during that time. Ask students to discuss comforting strategies that helped them get through this difficult time period.

REFERENCES

Afifi, W. A., and L. K. Guerrero. 1998. Some things are better left unsaid II: Topic avoidance in friendships. *Communication Quarterly, 46*, 231–249.

Ainsworth-Vaughn, N. 1998. *Claiming power in doctor-patient talk.* New York, NY: Oxford University Press.

Ahmad, F., P. L. Hudak, K. Bercovitz, E. Hollenberg, and W. Levinson. 2006. Are physicians ready for patients with Internet-based information? *Journal of Medical Internet Research, 8,* e22.

Beckman, H. B., and R. M. Frankel. 1984. The effect of physician behaviour on the collection of data. *Annals of Internal Medicine, 101,* 692–696.

Bertakis, K. D., D. Roter, and S. M. Putnam. 1991. The relationship of the physician's medical interviewing style to patient satisfaction. *Journal of Family Practice, 32,* 175–181.

Booth-Butterfield, M. 2006. *Influential health communication.* Littleton, MA: Tapestry Press.

———. 1999. *Communication in contemporary society.* Acton, MA: Tapestry Press.

Booth-Butterfield, S., R. Chory, and W. Beynon. 1997. Communication apprehension and health communication behaviors. *Communication Quarterly, 45,* 235–250.

Braithwaite, D. O. 1996. "I am a person first": Different perspectives on the communication of persons with disabilities. In E. B. Ray (Ed.), *Communication and disenfranchisement: Social health issues and implications*, (257–272). Mahwah, NJ: Lawrence Erlbaum Associates.

Braithwaite, D. O., and L. M. Harter. 2000. Communication and the management of dialectical tensions in the personal relationships of people with disabilities. In D. O. Braithwaite and T. L. Thompson (Eds.), *Handbook of communication and people with disabilities*. Mahwah, NJ: Lawrence Erlbaum Associates.

Braithwaite, D. O., and N. J. Eckstein. 2003. How people with disabilities manage assistance: Helping as instrumental social support. *Journal of Applied Communication Research, 31,* 1–26.

Bullis, C., and C. Horn. 1995. Get a little closer: Further examination of nonverbal comforting strategies. *Communication Reports, 8,* 10–17.

Burgoon, J. K., M. Pfau, R. Parrott, T. Birk, R. Coker., and M. Burgoon. 1987. Relational communication, satisfaction, compliance-gaining strategies, and compliance in communication between physicians and patients. *Communication Monographs, 54,* 307–324.

Burgoon, M., R. Parrott, J. K. Burgoon, T. Birk, M. Pfau, and R. Coker. 1990a. Primary care physicians' selection of verbal compliance gaining strategies. *Health Communication, 2,* 13–27.

———. 1990b. Patients' severity of illness, noncompliance, and locus of control and Physicians' compliance gaining messages. *Health Communication, 2,* 29–46.

Burleson, B. R. 1984. Comforting communication. In H. E. Sypher and J. L. Applegate (Eds.), *Communication by children and adults social cognitive and strategic processes* (63–105). Beverly Hills, CA: Sage Publications.

Burleson, B. R., and E. L. MacGeorge. 2002. Supportive communication. In M. L. Knapp and J. A. Daly (Eds.), *Handbook of interpersonal communication* (374–424.) Thousand Oaks, CA: Sage Publications.

Burleson, B. R., and W. Samter. 1990. Effects of cognitive complexity on the perceived importance of communication skills in friends. *Communication Research, 17,* 165–182.

Cegala, D., C. Gade, S. Broz, and L. McClure. 2004. Physicians' and patients' perceptions of patients' communication competence in a primary care medical interview. *Health Communication, 16,* 289–305.

Coleman, L. M., and B. M. DePaulo. 1991. Uncovering the humans spirit: Moving beyond disability and "missed" communications. In N. Coupland and H. Giles (Eds.), *Miscommunication and problem talk* (61–84).

Davidowitz, M., and R. D. Myrick. 1984. Responding to the bereaved: An analysis of "helping" statements. *Death Education, 8,* 1–10.

Dolin, D. J., and M. B. Booth-Butterfield. 1993. Reach out and touch someone: Nonverbal comforting communication. *Communication Quarterly, 41,* 383–393.

Falk, G. 2001. *Stigma: How we treat outsiders.* Amherst, NY: Prometheus Books.

Falvo, D., and P. Tippy. 1988. Communicating information to patients—Patient satisfaction and adherence as associated with resident skill. *Journal of Family Practice, 26,* 643–647.

Fine, M., and A. Asch. 1988. Disability beyond stigma: Social interaction, discrimination, and activism. *Journal of Social Issues, 44,* 3–21.

Frymier, A. B., and M. B. Wanzer. 2003. Examining differences in perceptions of students' communication with professors: A comparison of students with and without disabilities. *Communication Quarterly, 51,* 174–191.

Gilbert, S. 1997. Forget about bedside manners, some doctors have no manners. *New York Times,* p. F7.

Goffman, E. 1963. *Stigma: Notes on the management of spoiled identity.* New York: Simon & Schuster.

Goodwin, R. 1989. Taboo topics among close friends: A factor analytic investigation. *The Journal of Social Psychology, 130,* 691–692.

Grove, T. G., and D. L. Werkman. 1991. Conversations with able-bodied and visibly disabled strangers: An adversarial test of predicted outcome value and uncertainty reduction theories. *Human Communication Research, 17 (4),* 507–534.

Guerrero, L. K., and W. A. Afifi. 1995. Some things are better left unsaid: Topic avoidance in family relationships. *Communication Quarterly, 43,* 276–296.

Harrington, N. G., and C. K. Matthews. 1997. Shame-proneness among the invisibly disabled: Implications for communication with health care providers. Paper presented at the annual meeting of the National Communication Association in Chicago, IL.

Hart, R. D., and D. E. Williams. 1995. Able-bodied instructors and students with physical disabilities: A relationship handicapped by communication. *Communication Education, 44(2),* 140–153.

Hebl, M. R., and R. E. Kleck. 2000. The social consequences of physical disability. In T. F. Heatherton, R. E. Kleck, M. R. Hebl, and J. G. Hull, (Eds.), *The social psychology of stigma* (419–439). New York, NY: Guilford Press.

Hines, S., A. S. Babrow, L. Badzek, and A. Moss. 2001. From coping with life to coping with death: Problematic integration for the seriously ill elderly. *Health Communication, 13,* 327–342.

Kastenbaum, R. 1992. *The psychology of death (2nd ed)*. New York: Springer Publishing Company.

Kleck, R. 1968. Physical stigma and nonverbal cues emitted in face to face interaction. *Human Relations, 21*, 19–28.

Klingle, R. 2004. Compliance gaining in medical contexts. In Gass and Seiter (Eds.),*Perspectives in persuasion, social influence, and compliance gaining* (289–315). Boston, MA: Allyn & Bacon.

Kreps, G. L., and B. C. Thorton. 1992. *Health communication: Theory and practice (2nd ed)*. Prospect Heights, Illinois: Waveland Press.

Kubler-Ross, E. 1974. *Questions and answers on death and dying*. New York: Macmillan Publishing Co.

———. 1975. *Death: The final stage of growth*. Englewood Cliffs, New Jersey: Prentice Hall.

Lehman, D. R., J. H. Ellard, and C. B. Wortman. 1986. Social support for the bereaved: Recipients' and providers' perspectives on what is helpful. *Journal of Consulting and Clinical Psychology, 54*, 438–446.

Levinson, W. 1994. Physician-patient communication: A key to malpractice prevention. *Journal of the American Medical Association, 272*, 1619–1620.

Levinson, W., D. L. Roter, J. P. Mullooly, V. T. Dull, and R. M. Frankel. 1997. Physician-patient communication: The relationship with malpractice claim among primary care physicians and surgeons. *Journal of the American Medical Association, 227*, 553–559.

Matthews, C. K. 1994, February. To tell or not to tell: The management of privacy boundaries by the invisibly disabled. Paper presented at the annual meeting of the Western States Communication Association, San Jose, CA.

Northouse, L. L, and P. G. Northouse, 1998. *Health communication: Strategies for professionals (3rd ed.)*. Stamford, CT: Appleton & Lange.

Ostrum, C. M. 2004. Good medicine begins with good doctor-patient relationship. *The Seattle Times*. Retrieved 12/11/2006 from *http://archives.seattletimes.nwsource.com*

Range, L. M., A. S. Walston, and P. M. Pollard. 1992. Helpful and unhelpful comments after suicide, homicide, accident or natural death. *OMEGA, 25*, 25–31.

Richmond, V. P., R. S. Smith, A. D. Heisel, and J. C. McCroskey. 1998. The impact of communication apprehension and fear of talking with a physician and perceived medical outcomes. *Communication Research Reports, 15*, 344–353.

Richmond, V. P., R. S. Smith, A. D. Heisel, and J. C. McCroskey. 2001. Nonverbal immediacy in the physician/patient relationship. *Communication Research Reports, 18*, 211–216.

Servaty, H. L., Krejci, M. J., and B. Hayslip. 1996. Relationships among death anxiety, communication apprehension with the dying, and empathy in those seeking occupations as nurses and physicians. *Death Studies, 20*, 149–161.

Stewart, M. 1995. Effective physician-patient communication and health outcomes: A review. *Canadian Medical Association Journal, 152*, 1423–1433.

Stewart, M., J. B. Brown, A. Donner, I. R. McWhinney, J. Oates, W. W. Weston, et al. 2000. The impact of patient-centered care on outcomes. *Journal of Family Practice, 49*, 796–804.

Thompson, T. L. 1981. The development of communication skills in physically handicapped children. *Human Communication Research, 7(4)*, 312–324.

———. 1982a. Disclosure as a disability-management strategy: A review and conclusions. *Communication Quarterly, 30*, 196–204.

———. 1982b. The development of listener-adapted communication in physically handicapped children: A cross-sectional study. *Western Journal of Speech Communication, 46*, 32–44.

———. 1983. Communication with the handicapped: A three-year study of the effectiveness of mainstreaming. *Communication Education, 32*, 185–195.

———. 1986. *Communication for Health Professionals*. Lanham, MD: University Press of America.

Thompson, T. L., and L. P. Cusella. 1988. Help between disabled and ablebodied persons: An exploratory observational study of a feedback system. *Journal of Applied Communication Research, 16*, 51–68.

Wanzer, M. B., M. Booth-Butterfield, and K. Gruber. 2004. Perceptions of health care providers' communication: Relationships between patient-centered communication and satisfaction. *Health Communication, 16*, 363–384.

Worley, D. W. 2000. Communication and students with disabilities on college campuses. In D. O. Braithwaite and T. L. Thompson (Eds.), *Handbook of communication and people with disabilities* (125–137). Mahwah, NJ: Lawrence Erlbaum Associates.

Worthington, M. E. 1974. Personal space as a function of the stigma effect. *Environment and Behavior, 6*, 289–294.

14

From Face-to-Face to Cyberspace
Forming Relationships Online*

OBJECTIVES

- Discuss how relationships developed prior to the Internet
- Explain how the evolution of the Internet has changed the way people develop interpersonal relationships
- Discuss factors of online attraction
- Explain the differences between face-to-face and computer mediated communication
- Identify the benefits and drawbacks of forming relationships via CMC
- Identify and explain the two factors individuals should consider when forming online relationships
- Identify cues that may indicate deception in online communication

© Franz Pfluegl, 2007, Shutterstock.

KEY TERMS

social networking
self-disclosure
hyperpersonal model of CMC
active vs. passive communication activity

reduced social cues theory
flaming
detachment
informal vs. formal language style
synchronous
asynchronous

media richness theory
social presence theory
digital divide
gender-bending
coup de foudre
time and behavioral factors

OVERVIEW

The process of initiating relationships has evolved. Online social networks such as Facebook and MySpace have created opportunities for individuals to research other people and decide whether they want to pursue a relationship. Even dating practices have changed over the last few years. No longer do we have to count on friends to introduce us to someone they think is perfect for us or to frequent singles bars to look for love. Thanks to the Internet, we can find our perfect mate by posting a list of personal interests or by completing online personality profiles and allowing sites such as eHarmony and match.com to find a match.

Examples of the connection between Computer Mediated Communication (CMC) and relationship development are identified and discussed

---

*Chapter Contributions by Mary Mino

throughout this book. In Chapter Six we discussed the role of CMC in the initiating stages of relationship development. In Chapter Seven, we discussed how CMC is used to help us maintain relationships. In this chapter, we focus exclusively on research, theories, and constructs related to CMC and relationship development processes. In addition, we take a much closer look at how the use of this medium has altered interpersonal communication and the process of relationship development.

Online dating is one of the many ways in which people use online communication to build and sustain relationships. While mediated matchmaking is not necessarily a new phenomenon (Ellison, Heino, and Gibbs 2006) it certainly has changed and increased in popularity. Ellison and her colleagues describe the evolution of mediated matchmaking and note that as early as the mid-nineteenth century, singles placed ads in the newspaper to find a perfect mate (Ellison, Heino, and Gibbs 2006). Decades later, in the 1980s, singles used video dating services to meet potential mates. Today, a significant percentage of single persons turn to the Internet to help them find their "perfect match" (Lenhart and Madden 2006a). Nearly thirty-seven percent of single people state that they have visited Internet dating sites in the pursuit of romance.

A significant number of single people turn to the Internet to find their "perfect match."

Interpersonal scholars Mark Knapp and John Daly (2002) encourage researchers to study CMC because of its impact on face-to-face communication and relationship development processes. As we have stated throughout this text, communication competence is essential to building and maintaining effective relationships. Individuals require knowledge, skill, and motivation to communicate effectively and establish rewarding relationships. The same is true in the context of online communication.

This chapter addresses competent online communication by providing an overview of existing research on CMC that explains why online communication has become so prevalent and how to use it effectively and appropriately to establish relationships. The prospect of forming interpersonal relationships through CMC poses a multitude of questions. Will these relationships be similar to those formed via face-to-face interaction? What are the positive and negative aspects of forming a relationship through CMC? What are some suggestions for establishing successful online relationships? How has the Internet altered the way people establish, maintain and terminate relationships? In the first section of this chapter, we briefly discuss the methods used in the past in developing interpersonal relationships. Next, we focus on positive and negative aspects of interpersonal relationships formed through CMC. In the final section, we offer suggestions for using CMC as a means of developing interpersonal relationships.

Since the early 1990s, communication scholars have written about how online relationships are developed and maintained (see, specifically, Wildermuth 2001; Rumbough 2001; Parks and Roberts 1998; Parks and Floyd 1996; Walther 1996; Walther 1995; Walther, Anderson, and Park 1994; Walther 1993; Walther 1992; Walther and Burgoon 1992). However, communication researchers are not the only ones studying the development of online relationships. Researchers from academic fields such as computer science, behavioral science, psychology, sociology, and business have written about the impact of CMC on social interaction (see, for example, Nie 2001;

Conley and Bierman 1999; Capulet 1998; Gwinnell 1998; Tanner 1994). At the end of 2004, more than an estimated 945 million people worldwide were participating in some form of online communication (Cyber Atlas 2005), and that number continues to increase. In fact, due to the prevalence of CMC, Steve Jacobs, cofounder of Apple Computer, made the recommendation that "personal computers be renamed 'interpersonal computers'" (Adler and Towne 2003, 20).

To better understand the how and why of relationships initiated and maintained online, let us first look at some comparisons between relationships that form via face-to-face communication (hereafter referred to as FTF) and those that form through CMC.

METHODS OF DEVELOPING INTERPERSONAL RELATIONSHIPS

In previous chapters, we have explored the ways in which individuals initiate, maintain, and terminate all types of relationships. It is important to note that the majority of the research conducted to discover how and why people come together and grow apart in relationships was in FTF contexts. Because we know that the communication situation, or context, greatly affects how messages are sent and received, it is important to consider how communication and relationship development processes may differ when individuals use CMC as a primary means of interaction. Before we identify the differences between FTF and CMC, let us examine some of the ways relationships began prior to the introduction of CMC.

How would your personal relationships change if you couldn't use a cell phone?

ESTABLISHING RELATIONSHIPS: BEFORE THE INTERNET

Take a minute and imagine how your relationships with friends and family members would change if you did not have access to the Internet or a cellular phone. Would it be possible to establish and maintain relationships with others without this technology? Of course, it would be possible! But prior to the introduction of these technological advancements, the ways people communicated in relationships were very different. In the following sections, we discuss some of the different methods individuals used to establish and maintain their relationships prior to the development of the Internet.

Family and Community

Stated simply, **social networking** refers to the process of connecting with others to form different types of relationships. Before the Industrial Revolution in 1760, families functioned as independent economic units and served as the primary source of social networking for most individuals. People relied almost exclusively on FTF interactions with others in their community as the primary means of establishing relationships. The family played a significant role in the socialization of its members and was most likely to interact with other families that lived in close proximity. During this era, many relationships initially formed due to convenience. Relationships also developed through family members' involvement in church activities or arrangements made among families and friends (Rogers 1997).

Advances in Transportation

The Industrial Revolution, which occurred from 1760–1830, transformed the family and resulted in drastic changes in social network systems. Advances in transportation such as the rail system and automobiles increased options for the formation of interpersonal relationships. Individuals could now leave their hometowns and travel across the country to establish relationships with people hundreds of miles away. As society became more mobile, individuals were no longer restricted geographically in their choices of relationship partners. Individuals could establish and even maintain long distance relationships with greater ease (Rogers 1997).

Letter Writing and Telephone Use

Prior to the invention of the telephone, writing letters was the primary means of establishing and maintaining interpersonal relationships. Written correspondence provided a method of remaining faceless and allowed intimacy with a reduced amount of risk (Pratt et al. 1999). The number of couples who fell in love through written correspondence peaked during World War II as women began to write to soldiers overseas. Gwinell (1998) points out the significance of letter writing by noting that it served as a means of helping individuals with similar backgrounds communicate across greater geographic distances. While letter writing was an important means of communicating with friends, relatives, and relationship partners, the feedback from receivers was limited to textual information only and the rate of receiving feedback was extremely slow.

The telephone, created in 1876, drastically altered the way individuals communicated with one another on a day-to-day basis. Unlike letter writing, the telephone allowed individuals to send verbal and nonverbal messages and the feedback was immediate. Today we use cellular phones that provide us with the ability to communicate with virtually anyone, anywhere, and anytime! While cellular phones offer the convenience of being able to communicate with our friends, family, and significant others, they also can be a source of frustration and annoyance. In a recent *20/20* survey, eighty-seven percent of Americans indicated experiencing rude cell phone behavior that included people talking on cell phones in public places in loud voices (Cohen and Langer 2006).

Singles Clubs

During the last few decades, individuals have flocked to bars and singles clubs in order to meet the "right person." Not only has the singles scene replaced the family's influence on interpersonal relationships, but Rogers

(1997) also contends, "The singles scene replaced the church social as one of the chief places to meet a member of the opposite sex" (1). Many agree that even today bars and clubs remain a common place to meet people (DeGol 2003). Think about how relationship initiation is portrayed in many television shows. Aside from on *Seventh Heaven*, no relationships are forming at church socials. Rather, Dr. McDreamy and Meredith Grey begin their relationship over drinks at the local bar in *Grey's Anatomy*, and the main characters in sitcoms such as *How I Met Your Mother* and *30 Rock* vainly attempt to forge connections with other singles at bars or clubs.

Mediated Matchmaking

While mediated matchmaking "is certainly not a new phenomenon" (Ellison, Heino, and Gibbs 2006, 416) it has evolved and, more recently, has increased in popularity. Ellison and her colleagues describe the evolution of mediated matchmaking and note that as early as the mid-nineteenth century, singles placed ads in the newspaper to find a perfect mate (Ellison, Heino, and Gibbs 2006; Schaefer 2003). Later, in the 1980s, singles used video dating services to meet potential mates (Woll and Cosby 1987; Woll and Young 1989).

During the late 1970s and early 80s, some individuals used dating services to help them find the perfect match (Jedlicka 1981). These singles agencies typically advertised in magazines and promised to match individuals using sophisticated computer technology. Singles using these services typically paid between fifteen and thirty dollars and then completed a questionnaire that asked for a variety of information such as physical appearance, race, age, religion, and hobbies. Once individuals submitted this information to the agency, they were matched with someone who scored similarly or who was deemed a good match. Jedlicka (1981) notes that "the computer's ability to evaluate and suggest alternatives is limited" (374). At the time, research on this type of mediated matchmaking was significant because it illustrated both the potential and limitations of computers as a means of social networking in the early 1980s.

With advances in technology, individuals have been able to increase the ways in which individuals establish and maintain their relationships. While many of the communication channels and forms of social networking mentioned in this section are still used, the arrival of the Internet has had a significant impact on the way we communicate with one another and the methods used to develop and maintain our relationships.

ESTABLISHING RELATIONSHIPS: THE INTERNET ERA

The birth of the Internet in the late 1960s resulted in electronic mail, or email. Originally, researchers used email to correspond with one another, but this technology rapidly moved beyond the research setting and became available for the general population (Lerner Productions 2003). For example, from 1995 to 1998, the number of people using email increased by fifty percent and by the year 2000, seventy-eight percent of the people online reported using the Internet specifically for email. This statistic is staggering—nearly three-fourths of online users depend on the medium to communicate via email (Boneva, Kraut, and Frohlich 2001).

Because of its popularity and immediacy, email has evolved into a common form of CMC. In fact, many of today's interpersonal relationships are established through email. Friendships form in MySpace or Facebook communities instead of at local community socials and events. Romantic relationships form because of connections made through Match.com or Yahoo! Personals as opposed to meeting at church socials or in high school classes. As Pratt and his co-authors (1999) have contended, the use of CMC as a form of correspondence in interpersonal relationships is merely the natural evolution of interpersonal relationships beyond face-to-face interaction.

The Internet has become one of the most rapidly growing technologies in the world. In 1997, over 50 million people utilized Internet services and almost half of them described the Internet as an "indispensable" part of their day-to-day lives (Miller and Clemente 1997). Although defining the Internet as "indispensable" may seem extreme, this medium has certainly added convenience to communication. With the click of a mouse, individuals can access a multitude of services from email to stock quotes. One can simply go to eBay to purchase a car, a rare collector's issue of *Sports Illustrated,* or the latest Fendi purse that has sold out in all the stores. Co-workers can easily access databases from all over the world or have a video conference with a client on the other side of the globe. In fact, research has suggested that the Internet is replacing other more traditional media (La Ferle, Edwards, and Lee 2002; Althaus and Tewksbury 2000; Johnson and Kaye 1999).

With all of these services, it seems logical that people turn to the Internet as a source of social networking. Today, a significant percentage of single persons are turning to the Internet to help them find their "perfect match" (Lenhart and Madden 2006a). Nearly thirty-seven percent of single people state that they have visited Internet dating sites in the pursuit of romance (Lenhart and Madden 2006b). Specifically, some people choose to use the Internet as a source for seeking out and developing interpersonal relationships. Yet many romantic partners are reluctant to admit to others that they met online. Why does this stigma of online romance exist? Individuals may be reluctant to admit meeting a relationship partner online because the use of CMC as a means of establishing relationships continues to be somewhat of an anomaly. Because many individuals meet their relationships partners through FTF encounters, using CMC to establish relationships is often regarded as nontraditional (Emmers-Sommer 2005) or somewhat unusual. However, we speculate that meeting partners online will be viewed differently over time as more singles use Internet services to "shop" for the ideal mate. After all, individuals use the Internet to shop for everything from cars to clothes online (Conley and Bierman 1999), why not "shop" for relationship partners as well?

© Juriah Mosin, 2007, Shutterstock.

Have any of your current relationships been established through email?

© Andresr, 2007, Shutterstock.

In today's world, people can video conference with colleagues and clients across the globe.

Online Dating

Technological advancements such as cell phones and computers have certainly altered the way we communicate with others during the initial stages of relationship development. Recall our discussion of "silent dating" practices in Chapter Six. With the advent of cell phones, individuals can now send multiple text messages first to gauge whether the other party is interested in furthering the relationship. Today, individuals that are interested in establishing a relationship will often "text" and "IM" one another prior to advancing to that first phone call or going on that first date.

It is also more common today for individuals to use CMC to meet, maintain, and terminate romantic relationships. As interpersonal relationships form because of connections made via the Internet, numerous online dating sites assist people in their search for similar relationship partners. Recall our earlier discussion of the role that similarity plays in deciding whether to initiate a relationship with someone. In cyberspace, the search for similarities in age, cultural background, sexual orientation, religion, educational level, interests, and likes and dislikes is easier. Many sites, such as eHarmony, Match.com, or Yahoo! Personals provide users with the opportunity to enter preferences for a variety of demographic categories. Some sites have even targeted specific audiences: silversingles.com for seniors; eSPIN-the-Bottle for tweens and older; Jdate for singles of the Jewish faith, and a few off-the-garden-path varieties, including gothicmatch.com and several variations thereof. Books such as *The Complete Idiot's Guide to Online Dating and Relating* (Swartz 2000) offer popular Internet sites that fulfill a variety of interpersonal needs and requirements. Many of these sites are increasing in popularity when it comes to initiating relationships because they provide more information than can be included in a written personal ad and they allow people to correspond anonymously for longer periods of time (Scharlott and Christ 1995). Consider the popularity of the online dating service, match.com. The website was created in 1995 and advances "a simple mission: to take the lottery out of love" (www.match.com). The creators of this website boast that use of their site has resulted in over 250,000 marriages per year! With over 15 million members, match.com offers a significant amount of choices in potential relationship partners. Individuals simply log on to the site and begin viewing portraits and reading descriptive information about the members of this online community. If members are uncomfortable posting personal information, they can use the alternative online dating service known as chemistry.com. Individuals choosing to use this online dating service allow others to do the "searching and matching for them."

As the demand for online dating websites increases, the services offered by these sites have become more sophisticated and now cater more specifically to users' needs. If a person is concerned about the honesty of a potential date, there are even sites such as true.com that conduct background checks on its members. Criminal background investigations and public record screenings are conducted to ensure that members are not married and are free of criminal charges. If an online dater is still uneasy about a potential date, sites such as truedater.com allow him to read reviews posted by others who have met the potential date through a dating website. Truedater.com claims to provide an objective review of how honestly someone has portrayed himself in his online profile by allowing others to comment on experiences with the person.

Individuals also use CMC to maintain their relationships. As mentioned in Chapter Seven, individuals send emails and use IM (instant messenger) to correspond regularly with friends, family members, and relationship partners. One of the most frequently used relationship maintenance strategies, labeled "mediated communication," involves the use of computers to stay in touch with significant others and sustain the quality of the relationship.

Not surprisingly, CMC can also be used to terminate relationships with significant others. Individuals can use the Internet to learn more about how to end a relationship and they can use email and Instant Messenger (IM) as a means of terminating the relationship. For example, individuals can use Positively Passionate Inc. *(www.positively.biz)*, an Internet break-up service, to end an unwanted relationship. For $200 this company will call or send an email to your partner and terminate the relationship for you. This website also offers a variety of relationship-related information and services.

© Zsolt Nyulaszi, 2007, Shutterstock.

The convenience of CMC can help family members stay in touch more often.

Online Social Networks

Just as online dating sites have gained in popularity, so have online social networking sites. Online social networking sites provide people with a place to come together to identify and discuss common interests or causes. The network expands as users add or invite "friends" to the site. Currently, some of the more popular social networking sites are MySpace, Facebook, and Xanga. For those who wish to share audio or video files, sites such as YouTube and Flickr provide a forum for distributing personal recordings to online friends. Children with Internet savvy visit sites such as clubpenguin.com, which allow them to chat with other children from around the country. While the social aspects of these sites have broadened our opportunities for forming friendships with those who may live thousands of miles away, there are also new "uses" for these sites.

Not only are Harry Potter and Rolling Stones fans seeking one another in online social networks, marketers, scammers, predators, and even journalists are reviewing these sites to gain information about individuals. A 2006 study conducted by Purdue University found that many employers report using online social networks for background checks of potential employees. Nearly thirty-five percent of the employers surveyed reported that they use search engines such as Google to locate information on potential hires, thirteen percent check social networking sites such as Facebook and MySpace, and an additional fifteen percent search for personal blogs posted on the Internet.

© Jacek Chabraszewski, 2007, Shutterstock.

There are Internet sites available for children to chat with other kids from all over the country.

As the number of people forming relationships via online dating sites and social networking sites increases, so does the need to understand the appeal of these sites for connecting individuals.

WHAT ATTRACTS PEOPLE TO ONE ANOTHER ONLINE?

When answering the question "What attracts people to one another online?" we discover qualities and characteristics that are similar to those that attract us to others in FTF relationships. Physical attractiveness and social attractiveness are still paramount. Recall our discussion of the importance of physical and social attractiveness in Chapter Six. If you have ever glanced at an online profile, you probably noticed that most individuals highlight their physical characteristics. A unique aspect of initiating relationships online is that individuals also spotlight factors of social attractiveness in their list of desired qualities in a potential mate. Background, attitude, and demographic similarities—information that often requires extensive small talk on a first date—can easily be determined by browsing an online profile.

Earlier in the text, we discussed the importance of self-disclosure in achieving intimacy in relationships. **Self-disclosure** involves divulging personal information to another individual and is usually delivered through face-to-face or computer-mediated channels. Consider the rate at which self-disclosure occurs in FTF relationships compared to CMC. When scholars compare FTF with online relationship development processes, they note quite significant differences. Walther (1996) advances a **hyperpersonal model of CMC**, noting that online communication often facilitates relationship development and perceptions of intimacy. Walther further explains his hyperpersonal model of CMC based on the following factors:

1. *The sender's ability to construct a specific and desired image of him/herself.* The sender can create an image that reflects an "ideal" versus the "real" self if he or she chooses. Unlike in FTF interactions where physical flaws or idiosyncratic personality traits may be readily apparent, a person's weaknesses are not on display or are often omitted from the personal description in computer-mediated contexts.
2. *The sender's ability to alter any message content prior to sending them.* The sender can create messages, review them, and then alter them as needed when using computer-mediated channels of communication. This process may improve the quality of the information exchanged and elicit more favorable responses from receivers.
3. *The receiver's propensity to create positive impressions of the partner.* Because the sender has created an ideal or desired image and has carefully monitored and edited the information exchanged, the receiver is likely to form more favorable impressions via CMC than through FTF contexts.
4. *The increased depth and breadth of self-disclosure exchanged between the relationship partners.* Similar to FTF interactions, if the initial exchanges between individuals are positive, this leads to increased disclosure. In CMC the rate at which individuals exchange private information tends to be much faster than in FTF contexts (Walther 1996; Anderson and Emmers-Sommer 2006).

Walther (1996; 1997) and other scholars agree that greater levels of intimacy can be established through CMC than in similar types of FTF interactions. Follow-up research has substantiated this claim, noting that intimate relationships often develop in computer-mediated contexts faster than in FTF contexts because of the higher frequency of interaction (Hian, Chuan, Trevor, and Detenber 2004).

If you are one of the millions of students who have created an online social profile on a site such as MySpace, think about how much personal information you have disclosed on the Internet. A twenty-year old woman named Sami posted one profile on MySpace.com. Sami is a college graduate and is employed as a dental assistant. She enjoys wakeboarding, jet skiing, and going to the mall to hang out with her friends. She has a countdown on her profile that informs us how soon the day of her wedding to David will arrive. In case we might question how she and David feel about one another, she posts a video clip of the two of them locked in a passionate embrace. For those of us who want to know her likes and dislikes, Sami posts a survey that details this information. We know how many tattoos and piercings she has and that she is right-handed. After only five minutes, we learn Sami's full name, birth date, and hometown, her weight, her eye color, her weaknesses and goals, how many CDs she owns, where she wants to visit abroad, and that she wants to have children. We also know what high school and college she attended and where she works. Sami also blogs her daily itinerary as well as her current "mood" status, and everyone can learn where she and her friends will be on Friday night. In less than ten minutes, you may know more about Sami than you know about classmates you have known since first grade! As you can see from this example, individuals tend to open up in the online environment more quickly than they do in FTF interactions. Information that one might typically keep "private" until a friendship or romantic relationship develops is posted on a site for the entire world to see. What are the benefits of this online disclosure? It has made it easier for people to "cut to the chase" in identifying similarities. A simple glance at an online profile allows us to determine whether we have anything in common with the other person.

What are some of the pitfalls associated with Internet disclosure? Perhaps the biggest concern with online disclosure of information is safety. Not surprisingly, people differ in the amount and type of information they disclose on these Internet sites. In a 2006 study of 487 teenagers who reported having an online profile posted on a site, gender differences emerged when comparing the types of information boys and girls disclosed online. Table 14.1 on page 370 highlights these findings.

Boys and girls were similar in their willingness to share first names, school names, or IM screen names. However, females indicated a tendency to post more photos (both of themselves and of their friends) than males, while boys were more likely to post videos or to reveal their hometowns and last names in their online profile. Thus, there appears to be subtle gender differences in the type of information disclosed online.

How Do FTF and CMC Differ?

Now that we have examined the transformation in relationship development because of the introduction of the Internet, let us focus on the distinctions between FTF and CMC and how these differences affect relationship development. Table 14.2 highlights the distinctions between these two forms of communication.

Table 14.1   What Information Teens Disclose Online

Type of Information	Percent of Boys Who Disclosed Information	Percent of Girls Who Disclosed Information
First name	83	80
Name of school	51	48
IM screen name	39	42
Link to personal blog	36	42
Email address	29	29
Cell phone number	4	1
Photo of myself	74	83
Photos of my friends	58	72
Hometown	68	54
Audio or MP3 files	53	30
Last name	40	20
Videos	40	20

Source: "Teens, Privacy & Online Social Networks" by Amanda Lenhart and Mary Madden. Pew Internet & American Life Project, April 18, 2006, www.pewinternet.org. Used with permission.

Table 14.2   Comparisons of FTF and CMC Qualities

Qualities	Face-to-Face (FTF)	Computer-Mediated Communication (CMC)
Level of communication activity	Active	Passive (lurking, viewing) Active (source of message)
Nonverbal cues	Real	Artificial
Language style	Elaborate and more formal	Restricted and less formal
Synchronicity	Synchronous	Asynchronous and synchronous
Richness of interaction	High	Low
Social presence	High	Low

Level of Communication Activity.   The vast majority of our FTF interactions require us to be **active** participants in a conversation. Of course, there are times when someone may engage in **passive** communication behaviors (e.g., responding "uh-huh" to a question while watching a game on television), but our physical presence typically requires us to be engaged in an interaction. In the CMC environment, the level of communication activity can range from active to passive. Active participation occurs when one sends an instant message (IM) to a friend or posts a response to an online chat room. Examples of passive activity are often less obvious and include "lurking," or viewing posts made on a discussion board or chat forum without responding. Since there are often several people engaged in chat room discussions, many who are unknown to the "regulars" participating in the online conversation, this passive behavior often goes unnoticed. This behavior is in stark contrast to social expectations in the FTF environment. If one were to stand by and listen in on a conversation without respond-ing, others would perceive the behavior as strange or threat-ening. The person that was not participating in the conver-sation would probably be asked if he or she had something to contribute.

Nonverbal Cues.   In cyberspace, the rules for nonverbal communication are drastically different from the rules in face-to-face interactions. One theory developed to explain the absence of nonverbal cues in online interactions is **reduced social cues theory** (Sproull and Kiesler 1986). According to this theory, humans depend on social cues such as a person's appearance, attire, facial expressions, and gestures to help interpret received messages. Many of the social cues that we depend on in FTF interactions are absent in CMC. One look at another person's face reveals a myriad of cues about the mood or intent of a message. During FTF interactions, we often check to see whether the other person is smiling, whether he or she looks confused, or if the per-son is focused on the message. The absence of cues makes the process of managing and interpreting online interac-tions much more difficult. As a result, alternative forms of nonverbal cues compensate for the lack of social cues: Emoticons are used to communicate emotion, capital letters are used to indicate the severity of the message, and acronyms or abbreviations are inserted in messages to indi-cate a playful or informal tone. Examples of these artificially created nonverbal cues are included in Table 14.3.

Several outcomes are associated with the reduction in social cues. Because we cannot see the expressions or responses of others in the online world, the social norms and constraints that typically guide our behavior are modified. In essence, our interpersonal behavior becomes "deregulated." In the absence of cues, people have a greater tendency to use

© Romanchuck Dimitry, 2007, Shutterstock.

Passive behavior online often goes unnoticed by active participants.

© Galina Barskaya, 2007, Shutterstock.

In FTF interactions, one look at someone's face can tell you how that person is reacting to your message.

Table 14.3	**Examples of CMC Nonverbal Cues**	
Emoticons	Smiling	☺ or :-)
	Bad hair day	&:-)
	Laughing	:-D
	Kissing	:-*
	Giving a rose	@-}—
Capital Letters	I WISH YOU WOULD STOP POSTING MESSAGES TO MY BULLETIN BOARD!	
Acronyms	AWHFY	Are we having fun yet?
	ROTFL	Rolling on the floor laughing
	CYAL8R	See you later
	EMFJI	Excuse me for jumping in
	HAK	Hug and kiss

"flaming" in their online communication. **Flaming** refers to aggressive attacks made against another person. An example of flaming would be the excessive use of capital letters in an attempt to scold a person. Another consequence of reduced social cues is the tendency for **detachment.** In CMC environments, participants may perceive themselves to be less connected to the conversation. As a result, a person may exit a chat room discussion abruptly and without warning or they may deliberately ignore attempts by others to communicate. In an FTF conversation, most people would make some indication of their intention to leave a conversation rather than simply walking away.

Language Style. Think about the last email you sent to a close friend or family member. Chances are the style of language was less formal than language typically used in your FTF conversations. Due to the tedious nature of typing, it is often easier to take "short cuts" when composing written messages. As a result, our CMC messages are often more **informal** in terms of language style compared to the more elaborate and **formal** nature of FTF messages. For example, one friend might say to the other, "Are you okay? You seem to be upset about something," in an FTF conversation. If the same interaction occurred via email or text message, the interaction might look more like this: "RUOK? U seem 2B upset . . ." For some Internet users, this informal language style has found its way into their written communication. Some faculty members report that students who engage in frequent online communication tend to use poor grammar in their academic writing. Lee (2002) points out that teachers are frustrated by student papers that include shortened words, improper capitalization and punctuation, and the erratic use of characters such as & and @.

Synchronicity. Another notable distinction between FTF and CMC interactions involves the synchronicity, or the rate at which responses occur in the exchange of messages. In FTF interactions, the sending and receiving of messages is **synchronous,** or occurs in real time, or simultaneously. At the same time a source sends a message, feedback cues are being received to help interpret the receiver's response. When you ask a friend to comment on your outfit, and you notice an odd look on his face while you are asking the question, feedback is being received while the message is being communicated. The source and the receiver are sending cues to one another simultaneously, thus synchronous communication occurs. Online environments can provide opportunities for synchronous communication in forums such as chat rooms or via instant messaging. The expectation is that once a message is received, an immediate response will be provided.

Asynchronous communication involves a time lapse between when a message is received and when a response is made. Asynchronous CMC messages are typically in the form of emails or discussion board postings. We do not expect a friend to respond immediately to an email that we send and often several days may pass between the time when someone posts a message to an online discussion board and others post responses.

Richness of Interaction. **Media richness theory** (Daft and Lengel 1984) describes the capability of a communication channel to convey a variety of cues. By information richness, or media richness, we refer to the channel's level of synchrony, the availability of social cues, the ability to use natural language (as opposed to text or symbols), and the ability to convey emotions using the channel. As CMC lacks social cues and non-verbal expressions and uses text language instead of natural language, it is typically judged as being "less rich" on the media richness continuum although it spans across varying levels of richness. Emails are low in richness due to the lack of nonverbal cues. However, suppose you were to have a conversation with a friend using a web camera attached to your computer. The camera allows you to observe a number of your friend's nonverbal cues and increases the level of media richness.

FTF interactions are the richest communication channel on the continuum. Recall some of the cues you received in the last conversation you had with your best friend. Not only did you receive the actual words of the message, you could also sense the mood through tone of voice, facial expressions, and posture.

Social Presence.   Short, Williams, and Christie (1976) created **social presence theory** to describe the perceived psychological closeness that occurs during a FTF interaction. Earlier chapters have discussed the concept of immediacy. Social presence focuses on the immediacy that occurs when we communicate with others. In a FTF conversation, there are numerous cues that cause us to feel psychologically closer to the person. A lingering glance or a forward lean accompanied by a smile can make a person feel connected to the other. The absence of nonverbal cues in email or chat room interactions results in low levels of social presence.

© Supri Suharjoto, 2007, Shutterstock.

Using a web camera can heighten interactive richness because you can see the other person's nonverbal cues.

WHO IS ONLINE AND WHY?

Parks and Roberts (1998) found that the most desirable online relationships center on developing close friendships and finding romance. When seeking interpersonal relationships online, the majority of users interact more often with members of the opposite sex. However, even though men and women use the Internet equally, they use it for different reasons. Boneva and his colleagues (2001) concluded that women spend more time using email to correspond with relatives and close friends. On the other hand, Scharlott & Christ (1995) found men are more likely to "maximize the number of contacts, presumably to increase their chances of finding someone interested in a physically intimate relationship" (198). Interestingly, women and men achieve different levels of success with their online relationships goals. Women who are looking for friendship achieve their goal thirty-three percent more often than men who are seeking romantic and sexual relationships (Scharlott and Christ 1995). In some instances, individuals may initially use the Internet as a means of establishing friendships, but these relationships eventually transform into something different over time. Consider the following example:

Posted on December 1, 2003
Margaret wrote: Wanted to share my internet romance. Back in May of 2001 I went on to an over 40's chat out of curiosity. I was not looking for anybody. I met a man through the chat who also was not on the lookout. I guess in the way I was talking, it caught his eye and

© Tomasz Trojanowski, 2007, Shutterstock.

In a FTF conversation, when you see a smile it makes you feel more connected to the other person.

he asked if he could e-mail me as a friend. We both stated from the beginning that it was nothing more than friendship. The more we talked, the more things began to change.

He sent me his photo and I sent him mine. He expressed his feelings of love for me and I did the same in return. On September 20th he came to Canada to visit me (he is from the U.S.) and we knew even before the visit we would be attracted to each other. As soon as we met at the airport we knew it! We had such a great time together. He kept telling me how much he loved me, he held my hand constantly as we walked around seeing the sights and the kisses were certainly there as well. On the 23rd he told me that he had to have me and asked me to be his wife. I immediately responded with a yes.

For all you that may think we might be very young people, this is not the case. I'm 42 and he is 51. I work for a police agency and he is in state government. My son and I are now flying down to his state for the American Thanksgiving and to meet his family, friends, and co-workers. He has already started with the immigration papers (which we are truly hoping) will not become a big headache or a long wait. We speak to each other every day either by computer or by telephone expressing our love for each other. In the future, when I have been given permission by immigration to be married, I will then move to the States and we will be married in his home state. I never thought in my wildest dreams that this kind of situation would ever happen to me.

I have heard the negative feedback on internet dating but on the other hand, I've heard more positive coming out of it. I already know— 2 girls in my office are successfully internet dating—one with someone in Canada and the other with someone in the U.S. Good luck to everybody who goes this route.

—http://www.internetdatingstories.com/

This example illustrates how rapidly relationships can evolve through CMC as well as the variety of ways that individuals use the Internet. Margaret states that she initially used the Internet because she was "curious," not because she was looking for a mate. She mentions that her online relationship started out as platonic but then quickly transformed into a romantic connection. This example also illustrates the hyperpersonal model of CMC discussed earlier in the chapter.

In addition to sex differences in Internet use, Nie (2001) established a correlation between income and education and the use of the Internet. College graduates are more likely to use the Internet consistently. Furthermore, research indicates that the average age of Internet users is under forty and that these individuals have an average yearly income of $55,000 (Suler 2002). With regard to Internet use among persons of various ethnic and racial backgrounds, research has found that nearly eighty percent of English-speaking Latinos, seventy-four percent of Caucasians, and sixty-one percent of African-Americans use the Internet (Marriott 2006). These demographic statistics support the presence of a **digital divide,** or a gap, between those who have access to the Internet and those who do not. With so many people turning to the Internet as the primary channel for communication and information, the notion of a digital divide is one that demands attention by researchers. The question of "power" becomes an issue as we analyze the accessibility of CMC.

EFFECTS OF CMC RELATIONSHIPS

The social dynamics and venues created by the Internet generate both opportunities and risks for developing interpersonal relationships (Parks and Floyd 1996). Over the years, our students have shared both success and horror stories about friends, family members, co-workers, or acquaintances who have established romantic relationships and friendships online. Students often recount stories about individuals who travel across the country to meet a "true love," only to find that the person has completely misrepresented him- or herself online. We suspect that the media may also play a role in shaping our students' negative opinions of online relationships. Perhaps the stories of healthy relationships that have developed online are not as newsworthy as those that end in heartache or disappointment. While the media may depict a relatively one-sided view of online relationships, much of the literature on forming online relationships focuses on both positive and negative aspects of communicating online.

Positive Aspects

An article published in *Time* magazine (Kirn 2000) compared the initiation of online relationships to dating practices of the past. "In many ways this is courtship as it once was, before the advent of the singles bar. There is plenty of conversation but no touching" (73). Communicating online may allow people to gradually build their level of intimacy before they meet, which may result in more meaningful relationships.

Several authors have discussed other positive aspects of using CMC to form interpersonal relationships: less chance of face-to-face rejection, less geographic limitations, less confrontation with unwanted admirers, and more potential relationship prospects (Anderson and Emmers-Sommer 2006; Walther 1993; 1996). Rabin (1999) also feels that there are benefits associated with the use of CMC to establish relationships. Rabin (1999) claims:

> "The risks involved in making an impression in an appearance-obsessed world and the embarrassment of face-to-face rejection are perils that don't affect the cyberflirt . . . Flirting online frees you from a host of offline pitfalls, including shyness . . . incompatibility (Poof! Mr./Ms. Wrong is gone just like that!) and geographic limitations (Stuck in a small town? Not any more.)" (2).

Other positive aspects include developing an initial interest without a major emphasis on physical appearance and an increased level of familiarity. Cooper and Sportolari (1997) contend that

> "In FTF [face-to-face] interaction, people make quick judgments based on physical attributes. . . . People who may have FTF encounters unwittingly keep themselves from intimate relationships by being overly focused upon or critical of their or others' physical appearance are freed up online to develop connections" Furthermore, "frequent contact with others is possible with little inconvenience or cost from the comfort and safety of one's own home" (9).

The concept of the importance of frequent contact supports Hendrick and Hendrick's (1983) contention that individuals who communicate on a more consistent basis tend to develop a stronger attraction to each other.

Negative Aspects

Studies often describe the physical dangers involved in forming online relationships, but there is an equal amount of danger present during face-to-face interactions (Conley and Bierman 1999). However, there are other negative aspects of forming relationships online.

Lack of Technical Knowledge and Absence of Social Context Cues.   A lack of technical knowledge and the absence of social context cues may impede some individuals from using the Internet to communicate effectively. Rintel and Pittam (1997) contend, "users must not only come to terms with the basics of interaction management vis-à-vis the technical commands necessary to communicate, but also the curtailment of the social context cues that are used in managing interactions and establishing interpersonal relationships" (530–531). In other words, those who choose to communicate via the Internet have to learn not only the technological aspects of interaction, but also how to compensate for the lack of social cues available in electronic messages. If a friend sends you an email, there is some technical knowledge required to access that message. Not only do you have to know how to "log on" to your email, there are probably also passwords and user identification codes that have to be entered in order to access your online mailbox. Once the message is accessed, the next task involves interpreting the emoticons and language that is used to communicate emotions and feelings. Specifically, Parks and Floyd (1996) have asserted, "Relational cues emanating from the physical context are missing, as are nonverbal cues regarding vocal qualities, bodily movements, and physical appearance. Thus, CMC is judged to have a narrower bandwidth and less information richness than face-to-face communication" (81). In essence, there is a new level of knowledge and skill required to effectively communicate online. Unfortunately, some individuals lack online competence. Emails that fail to address the other person by name or that include one-word responses are often perceived as being rude. Given that many email addresses are abbreviations or codes, sending emails without signing your name can also be confusing. After all, how is a receiver supposed to know that js123456@ohiou.edu is Jane Smith if she fails to sign her email? Failure to employ proper online etiquette can result in potential communication breakdowns and misunderstandings.

Anonymity.   Anonymity when communicating online may also pose problems. Rintel and Pittam (1997) have shared Kiesler, Seigel, and McGuire's (1984) fears that "the increased anonymity [of] CMC leads to uninhibited behavior . . . by some users to try extreme and (risky) attention-getting strategies to initiate interactions . . ." (531). This anonymity or pseudonymity allows individuals to communicate more openly and, in some cases, individuals may feel that they can get away with using exaggerated, deceptive, manipulative, or abusive communication. These risky behaviors "fail to establish new relationships and sometimes result in retaliation rather than interaction" (Rintel and Pittam 1997, 531).

Deceptive Behavior.   Furthermore, online anonymity may lead to an increase in deceptive behavior. Deceptive behaviors include misrepresenting personal attributes, failing to share important personal information such as existing interpersonal relationships with a spouse, an over reliance on an "online" persona, or accelerated intimacy. Greenfield (1999) has discussed the misinformation often shared during online interactions. He has observed:

> There are some estimates that between thirty-three and fifty percent of individuals on the Internet are lying about some aspect of who and what they are. Some people have been found to represent themselves as members of the opposite sex! There is undoubtedly a considerable amount of lying about marital and financial status along with portraying one's personal characteristics as being more desirable than in reality. Everyone online weighs less than the real-time scale indicates! People become actors and actresses, allowing their innermost fantasies to become expressed online (30).

In addition, lying online allows individuals to create a new identity, an online persona. As Cooper and Sportolari (1997) have warned, "rather than using the net as a way to work on inhibited or conflictual aspects of the self, people may instead (consciously or not) use online relating to further split off unintegrated parts of themselves, leading to a compulsive and destructive reliance on their screen personae and relationships" (12). Individuals can create online personas that differ greatly from their real self-presentation. For example, those that want to experience what it is like to be the opposite sex may engage in a practice described as online **gender-bending** (Slagle 2006). This deceptive practice often involves presenting oneself as the opposite sex in chat rooms or online video games to experience what it is like to be a man or woman. One man interviewed about his gender-bending practices admitted to adopting a female superhero persona named Robotrixie when participating in online games. A female that participates in similar online games stated that she has figured out how to identify males that are engaging in online gender-bending: "The fact that they are scantily clad is a huge clue" and "often the bigger the breasts, the more likely it's a guy" (Slagle 2006).

Internet Addiction.   Although some psychologists believe that excessive reliance on the Internet should not be defined as an addiction because substance abuse is not involved, research has categorized what is considered an excessive amount of Internet use as Internet addiction. According to one study (Young 1998), Internet addiction is characterized by spending six hours or more online at a time, craving online interaction, and feelings of anxiousness and irritation when offline. Furthermore, Young (1998) has contended that Internet addiction can affect an individual's life in many areas, including family and relationships, as it often leads to individuals becoming more involved with their virtual life and less involved with reality.

Accelerated Intimacy.   If used effectively, CMC can allow a relationship to form gradually. However, Trafford (1982) and Greenfield (1999) have both called attention to a phenomenon they often observe in online relationships known as **coup de foudre** (bolt of lightning), or accelerated intimacy. When comparing individuals that establish relationships online to those that establish their relationships via FTF communication, those establishing relationships online often experience significant increases in the amount of intimate information exchanged. Trafford (1982) and Greenfield (1999) agree that the accelerated amount of intimacy experienced in online relationships may not always benefit individuals or relationships. Most interpersonal researchers agree that it takes a great deal of time and effort to establish trust and intimacy in relationships. Individuals may need time to process information about the relationship partner, observe the relationship partner for consistency in their behaviors, and then determine whether there is the potential for the relationship to move forward.

FORMING SAFE AND MEANINGFUL ONLINE RELATIONSHIPS

Books such as *Putting Your Heart Online* (Capulet 1998), which details the process involved in forming an online relationship, devote pages to developing effective interpersonal relationships online and emphasize that the Internet offers a new framework in which to create meaningful interpersonal relationships. With the emergence of the Internet as a popular social network, there is a need for students of interpersonal communication to examine this form of communication. Thus, we believe that it is important to offer suggestions for forming safe and meaningful relationships online. Two important areas to consider when developing online relationships are time factors and behavioral cues.

Time Factors

Researchers emphasize the importance of taking the necessary **time** to develop meaningful online relationships (Walther 1992; Rintel and Pittam 1997). Given that many individuals post in-depth personal information on social networking and dating sites, we may think we have achieved intimacy in an online relationship when in fact, it may not be as intimate as we imagine. The information is available—personal likes, dislikes, hopes, and aspirations are posted for all to see. Similar information would typically be revealed only after multiple face-to-face conversations. Ample time for forming CMC relationships and allowing for adequate impression formation is critical.

Walther, Anderson, and Park (1994) applied Walther's (1992) social information processing perspective to analyze the impact of time factors in CMC relationships. This perspective acknowledges that, due to cue limitations of CMC, the medium cannot possibly convey all the task-related information (or the social information) in as little time as multi-channel FTF communication. While the personal information posted in an online profile may cause us to feel like we know a person, it is important to take into consideration that the lack of nonverbal cues may inhibit accurate impression formation. Consider the following example:

> Angela was eagerly anticipating her first face-to-face meeting with Marin. The two had met on Facebook and exchanged emails for the past three weeks. Angela's friends laughed when she said she was "in love," and they pointed out that it wasn't possible to fall in love so quickly. But they just didn't understand. Through their countless emails, they had shared so much information—much more than Angela had ever shared in any of her previous relationships that she developed via FTF interactions. They finally decided to meet in person.

From the first awkward hug at the entrance to the coffee shop, Angela began to second-guess things. While they talked, she became annoyed when Marin kept glancing around the room while she was talking, causing Angela to feel as though she really wasn't listening to what she was saying. As the conversation continued, Angela found that she was bothered by the critical tone and negative facial expressions that Marin made when talking about things around campus. At the end of the evening, Angela was crushed—what had happened to the relationship? Things had gone so well when they communicated online, so why did everything fall apart when they finally had the chance to meet?

At the beginning of the example we learn that Angela has been exchanging emails with Marin for three weeks and feels that she may be "in love" with Marin. When Angela says that she has shared more information with Marin online than she has ever shared in her previous FTF relationships, she illustrates the hyperpersonal nature of CMC described earlier in the chapter. This example illustrates the tendency for some individuals to self-disclose at greater depths and at a faster rate in CMC contexts than in FTF contexts. Additionally, this scenario reinforces the importance of spending **time** with individuals in FTF interactions in order to form more accurate perceptions of their attitudes, beliefs, values and behaviors. Walther, Anderson, and Park (1994) agree that time is an important factor when forming accurate impressions in online relationships. Specifically, they believe that the critical difference between FTF and CMC relationship formation is the rate at which perceived intimacy is achieved. While they acknowledge that we are certainly capable of achieving intimacy in CMC relationships, time is a critical factor.

Based on this research, we encourage students that want to develop relationships online to pay thoughtful attention to time factors. Take time to get to know one another, and recognize the potential value of social cues that are sometimes are only available through a face-to-face meeting. Beebe, Beebe, and Redmond (2002) have asserted, "The key to success [when developing online relationships] is to apply the same skills that you would in a face-to-face relationship" (384). Think about the additional information obtained in a FTF conversation—the tone of voice, nonverbal behaviors, and other cues that offer additional insight about the other person. Just as you would devote a significant amount of time and energy to relationships developed via FTF communication, the same would hold true for relationships developed online.

While we are unable to pinpoint exactly how much time it should take to develop a successful online relationship, we can offer another suggestion related to time. Beware the **coup de foudre,** or being "struck" by the "lightning" pace of a relationship! If you feel that a relationship is moving along too quickly, it probably is.

Behavioral Cues

In addition to considering the time factor, understanding **behavioral cues** is essential when forming online relationships. Ellison, Heino, and Gibbs (2006) conducted a study of the self-presentation strategies, or behaviors, used by online dating participants. Ellison and her colleagues interviewed thirty-four individuals that were currently active on a large online dating site to learn more about how they managed their online impressions. Participants indicated that they often paid close attention to small or minute online cues that they and others sent. For example, one participant described the significance of profiles that were well-written, stating "I just think if they can't spell or . . . formulate a sentence, I would image that they are not that educated" (Ellison et al. 2006, 10). Another participant commented that she did not want to come across as at all sexual in her profile because she "didn't want to invite someone who thought I was going to go to bed with them [as soon as] I shook their hand" (Ellison et al. 2006, 10). Individuals indicated that they also tried to be brief when responding to potential partners so as not to appear "too desperate for conversation" (Ellison et al. 2006, 10). All of these examples illustrate how individuals monitor behavioral cues to display a certain image online. Individuals must not only understand how to use effective behavioral cues, but also how to assess the behavioral cues of others. When communicating online, there are several strategies to use to maximize effective online communication.

Being honest is the first guideline to follow for effective online communication. Conley and Bierman (1999) contend that honesty is a crucial component of successful online relationships. One should not exaggerate personal attributes and must always be specific about self-attributes and the desired attributes one is looking for in others. Ellison (2006) describes the tendency for people to describe their ideal self, not their actual self, when attempting to find a relationship partner. For example, one woman using online dating services noted that the picture she posted on her profile was from five years ago and that the picture depicted her as a thinner version of her current self (Ellison et al. 2006). Because the picture was dated and depicted her ideal, not actual self, the woman expressed a desire to lose weight so that her online and FTF personas were consistent. This example illustrates the relationship between online behavior, FTF interactions and the potential for relationship development. When individuals are deceptive online about aspects of their appearance, likes, dislikes, or hobbies, they risk being "caught" in a lie once actual FTF interactions occur. Inconsistencies between the ways that individuals present themselves online and in FTF contexts could affect the potential for the relationship to develop further.

Secondly, Swartz (2000) discusses the importance of safety when forming online interpersonal relationships. Specifically, it is important to maintain a degree of anonymity by revealing personal information gradually. He observes, "many times because of loneliness, sexual desire, or desperation we might go against our better judgment" and warns not to "jump headlong into a relationship using a rationalization along the lines of 'you've got to take risks to succeed'" (24).

Moreover, Gwinnell (1998) has emphasized the importance of being very inquisitive during online interactions and has strongly suggested asking the following questions:

1. Are you seeing anyone now?
2. How many online relationships have you had?
3. Why did your last relationship end?
4. How many times have you been married?
5. What would your ex tell me about you?

6. How do you deal with everyday life issues such as cleanliness, religious preference, and use of alcohol and drugs?

7. Is there someone I can contact who can offer his or her personal opinion of you? (78–81). (See also Capulet 1998, 121–127).

While these questions may seem somewhat intrusive, it is important to learn as much as you can about this individual prior to meeting FTF.

In addition to being inquisitive, one must be alert to the possibility of deception. Beebe, Beebe, and Redmond (2002) believe "the detection of deception in face-to-face encounters is aided by the presence of nonverbal cues. However, online such deception is almost as easy as simply typing the words" (389). Thus, one must "be cautious in forming relationships with Internet strangers" (Beebe et al., 2002. 389). Detecting the warning signs of deception is paramount. Swartz (2000) provides one of the most comprehensive discussions of "red flags" for detecting deception. Specifically, he advises one to look for signs of vagueness or non-responsiveness, which may indicate the person is hiding something. Swartz also recommends that individuals pay attention to whether or not the person goes offline or disappears for days or weeks at a time. Consider when the individual seems to be the most available to communicate. If he or she seems to be getting online at odd hours or odd times of the day, this may indicate that the person is concealing something from you. Another warning sign to consider is the individual's tendency to form quick online emotional attachments. Finally, Swartz encourages online users to focus on the other person's knowledge of current or historical events, which may indicate actual age or specific gender information. In the same way that we attempt to identify red flags during initial FTF encounters, we can use these guidelines to monitor the quality of online interactions.

SUMMARY

An article in *Newsweek* (Levy 1997) describes the surge of consistent Internet use as an "indelible feature of modern life" (52). Those who support forming relationships online also believe that CMC is not necessarily a replacement for face-to-face interactions; rather, CMC can provide an option that allows people to be more selective when searching for interpersonal relationships. However, before using CMC individuals must possess the knowledge, skills, and motivation needed to communicate effectively using this medium. This chapter offered an overview of how the Internet has changed the way we establish relationships with others.

In the past, FTF communication with family and community members was the primary means of networking with others to establish platonic and romantic relationships. Today, individuals can connect with others through CMC and establish romantic or platonic relationships with individuals from all over the world! Of course, there are both benefits and drawbacks associated with CMC. We hope that individuals will adopt the suggestions offered in this chapter for communicating effectively online. By following the experts' guidelines and paying attention to any red flags that may indicate deceptive online behavior, we hope that our students will establish safe and rewarding relationships.

APPLICATIONS
Discussion Questions

1. Discuss the different communication channels used to interact with your friends and family. On any given day, which communication channel do you use the most? Explain why.
2. Discuss the pros and cons of using social networking sites such as Myspace and Facebook. Why do you think college students use these sites so often?
3. Do you feel that individuals are more willing to self-disclose private information through computer mediated communication than FTF communication? Why do you feel that this is/is not the case? Support your position with specific examples.
4. How is the *coup de foudre* phenomenon that often results from developing relationships via CMC problematic for individuals? What suggestions could you offer someone that chooses to establish an online romantic relationship?

REFERENCES

Anderson, A. T., and T. M. Emmers-Sommer. 2006. Predictors of relationship satisfaction in online romantic relationships. *Communication Studies, 57,* 153–172.

Althaus, S. L., and D. Tewksbury. 2000. Patterns of Internet and traditional news media in a networked community. *Political Communication, 17* (1), 21–45.

Adler, R. B., and N. Towne. 2003 *Looking out, looking in.* (10th ed.).Belmont, CA: Wadsworth.

Beebe, S. A., S. J. Beebe, and M. V. Redmond. 2002. *Interpersonal communication: Relating to others.* (3rd ed.). MA: Allyn & Bacon.

Boneva, B., R. Kraut, and D. Frohlich. 2001. Using e-mail for personal relationships: The difference gender makes. *American Behavioral Scientist, 45,* 530–549.

Capulet, N. 1998. *Putting you heart online.* CA: Variable Symbols, Inc.

Cohen, J., and G. Langer. Poll: Rudeness in America, 2006. Retrieved from abcnews.go.com June 6, 2006.

Conley, L., and J. Bierman. 1999. *Meet me online: The #1 practical guide to Internet dating.* NC: Old Mountain Press, Inc.

Cooper, A., and L. Sportolari. 1997. Romance in cyberspace: Understanding online attraction. *Journal of Sex Education & Therapy, 22* (1), 7–14.

Cyber Atlas. 2005. Geographics: Population explosion http://cyberatlas.internet.com/big_picture/geographics/article.

Daft, R. L., and R. H. Lengel. 1984. Information richness: A new approach to managerial behavior and organization design. *Research in Organizational Behavior, 6,* 191–233.

DeGol, T. (Executive Producer). (2003, February 13). *WTAJ Channel 10 News* [Television broadcast]. Altoona, PA.

Ellison, N., R. Heino, and J. Gibbs. 2006. Managing impressions online: Self-presentation processes in the online dating environment. *Journal of Computer-Mediated Communication, 11,* 1–28. Retrieved online June 19, 2007 from *www.blackwell-synergy.com.*

Emmers-Sommer, T. M. 2005. Non-normative relationships: Is there a norm of (non) normativity? *Western Journal of Communication, 69,* 1–4.

Greenfield, D. N. 1999. *Virtual addiction: Help for netheads, cyberfreaks, and those who love them.* CA: New Harbinger Publications.

Gwinnell, E. 1998. *Online seductions: Falling in love with strangers on the internet.* NY: Kodansha America, Inc.

Hian, L. B., S. L. Chuan, T. M. K. Trevor, and B. H. Detenber. 2004. Getting to know you: Exploring the development of relationship intimacy in computer-mediated communication. *Journal of Computer-Mediated Communication, 9,* Retrieved June 24, 2007 from http://www.ascusc.org/jcm/vol9/issue3/detenber.html.

Hendrick, C., and S. Hendrick. 1983. *Liking, loving and relating.* CA: Brooks/Cole.

Jedlicka, D. 1981. Automated go-betweens: Mate selection of tomorrow? *Family Relations, 30,* 373–376.

Johnson, T. L., and B. K. Kaye. 1999. Cruising is believing? Comparing Internet and traditional sources on media credibility measures. *Journalism and Mass Media Quarterly, 75* (12), 325–340.

Kiesler, S., J. Seigel, and T. W. McGuire. 1984. Social and psychological aspects of computer mediated communication. *American Psychologist, 39,* 1123–1134.

Kirn, W. 2000. The love machines. *Time, 155,* 73.

Knapp, M. L., and J. A. Daly (Eds.). 2002. *Handbook of interpersonal communication.* (3rd ed.). CA: Sage.

La Ferle, C., S. M. Edwards, and W. N. Lee. 2000. Teens' use of traditional media and the Internet. *Journal of Advertising Research, 40* (3), 55–66.

Lee, J. 2002. I Think, Therefore IM. *New York Times,* September 19, p. G.1.

Lenhart, A., and M. Madden. 2006a. Teens, Privacy, and Online Social Networks, PEW Internet and American Life Project. http://www.pewinternet.org/report_display.asp?r=211. Accessed May 26, 2007.

———. 2006b. "Online activities and pursuits," PEW Internet and American Life Project. http://www.pewinternet .org/PPF/r/177/report_display.asp. Accessed May 28, 2007.

Lerner Productions. 2003. *Master the basics: Birth of the net.* http:// www.learnthenet.com.

Levy, S. 1996/1997. Breathing is also addictive. *Newsweek,* December/January, 52–53.

Marriott, M. 2006. Digital Divide Closing as Blacks Turn to Internet. *New York Times,* March 31.

Miller, T. E., and P. C. Clemente. The 1997 American internet user survey: Realities beyond the hype. NY: Find/Svp, Inc. [On-line]. Available: http://www.findsvp.com/.

Nie, N. H. 2001. Sociability, interpersonal relations, and the internet: Reconciling conflicting findings. *The American Behavioral Scientist, 45,* 420–435.

Parks, M. R., and K. Floyd. 1996. Making friends in cyberspace. *Journal of Computer Mediated Communication, 46* (1), 80–97.

Parks, M. R., and L. D. Roberts. 1998. 'Making MOOsic' The development of personal relationships on line and a comparison to their off-line counterparts. *Journal of Social and Personal Relationships, 15* (4), 517–537.

Pew Research Center. 2006. Pew Internet and American Life Project. http://www.pewinternet.org

Pratt, L., R. L. Wiseman, M. J. Cody, and P. F. Wendt. 1999. Interrogative strategies and information exchange in computer-mediated communication. *Communication Quarterly, 47* (1), 46–66.

Rabin, S. 1999. *Cyberflirt: How to attract anyone, anywhere on the world wide web.* NY: Penguin Putnam, Inc.

Rintel, S. E., and J. Pittam. 1997. Strangers in a strange land: Interaction management on internet relay chat. *Human Communication Research, 23* (4), 507–534.

Rogers, R. M. 1997. *Looking for love online: How to meet a woman using an online service.* NY: Simon & Schuster Macmillan Co.

Rumbough, T. 2001. The development and maintenance of interpersonal relationships through computer-mediated communication. *Communication Research Reports, 18,* (3), 223–229.

Scharlott, B. W., and W. G. Christ. 1995. Overcoming relationship-initiation barriers: The impact of a computer-dating system on sex role, shyness, and appearance inhibitions. *Computers in Human Behavior, 11* (2), 191–204.

Short, J. A., E. Wiliams, and B. Christie. 1976. *The social psychology of telecommunications.* New York, NY: John Wiley & Sons.

Slagle, M. August 2006. Gender-bending proves popular in online games. Retrieved July 16, 2007 from Hamptonroads.com http://content.hamptonroads.com/story.cfm?story=109533&ran121532

Sproull, L., and S. Kiesler. 1986. Reducing social context cues: Electronic mail in organizational communication. *Management Science, 32,* 1492–1512.

Swartz, J. 2000. *The complete idiot's guide to online dating and relating.* IN: Que Corporation.

Suler, J. 2002. Internet demographics. In *The Psychology of cyberspace,* www.rider.edu/suler/psycyber/basicfeat.html (article orig. pub.1999).

Trafford, A. 1982. *Crazy time: Surviving divorce.* NY: Bantom Books, Inc.

Tanner, W. 1994. Gender gap in cyberspace. *Newsweek,* May, 52–53.

Walther, J. B. 1992. Interpersonal effects in computer-mediated interaction: A relational perspective. *Communication Reports, 19,* 52–90.

———. 1993. Impression development in computer-mediated interaction. *Western Journal of Communication, 57,* 381–389.

———. 1995. Relational aspects of computer-mediated communication: Experimental observations over time. *Organization Science, 6,* 186–203.

———. 1996. Computer-mediated communication: Interpersonal, intrapersonal, and hyperpersonal interaction. *Communication Research, 19,* 52–90.

Walther, J. B., J. F. Anderson, and D. W. Park. 1994. Interpersonal effects in computer-mediated interaction: A meta-analysis of social and antisocial communication. *Communication Research, 21* (4), 460–487.

Walther, J. B., and J. K. Burgoon. 1992. Relational communication in computer-mediated communication. *Human Communication Research, 19,* 50–88.

Wildermuth, S. M. 2001. Love on the line: Participants' descriptions of computer-mediated close relationships. *Communication Quarterly, 49* (2), 89–96. Belmont, CA: Wadsworth.

Woll, S.B., and Cosby, P.C. (1987). Videodating and other alternatives to traditional methods of relationship initiation. In W.H. Jones and D. Perlman (Eds.), *Advances in Personal Relationships* (Vol. 1, pp. 69–108). Greenwich, CT: JAI Press.

Woll, S.B., and Young, P. (1989). Looking for Mr. or Ms. Right: Self-presentation in videodating. *Journal of Marriage and the Family,* 51(2), 483–488.

Young, K. S. 1998. *Caught in the net.* NY: John Wiley & Sons, Inc.

Glossary

A

ABCX Model The model is useful for understanding how and why families label situations as stressful and cope with stressors.

Accenting This is used when we want to stress or emphasize a particular word or phrase in our verbal message.

Acceptance Refers to our awareness of the feelings and emotions involved in diverse approaches to relationships and communication.

Accounts A potential explanation for the cause of the embarrassing situation.

Acronyms Text messaging shorthand that is used to express a variety of nonverbal cues, for example "LOL."

Action Communicates specifically what you want done.

Action-oriented listener Listeners that prefer error-free and concise messages and they get easily frustrated with speakers who do not clearly articulate their message in a straightforward manner.

Active communication activity Dynamically engaged in an interaction.

Active strategies Require us to engage in interactions with others to learn additional information about others.

Activity jealousy Emerges when our relational partner dedicates time to various hobbies or interests.

Acute stressor Stressors that are relatively short-lived and include events such as a student getting suspended for misbehaving.

Adaptors Body movements that are enacted at a low level of awareness that usually indicate nervousness, anxiety, or boredom.

Advice Involves disclosing personal information to the relationship partner or giving or seeking advice on some issue.

Affect displays Overt physical responses to our emotions that can be either positive or negative.

Affective orientation Refers to the extent to which an individual uses their emotions to guide communication decisions.

Affinity-seeking strategies Verbal and nonverbal communication behaviors that are often used strategically to gain liking from others.

Agent The role in which we are responsible for our own embarrassing situation.

Ambiguous boundaries Create confusion about who family members perceive as being part of the system.

Ambushing Type of listener who will listen for information that they can use to attack the speaker.

Anger During this stage individuals might ask Why me?

Antisocial behaviors Behaviors which might seem unfriendly or coercive.

Anxious-ambivalent This style develops as a result of inconsistent and irregular treatment from parents.

Anxious-avoidant This style often reports trauma or neglect from their parents and can exhibit significant developmental deficits.

Apologies Attempts to identify the source of blame for an embarrassing incident by expressing regret.

Appreciative listening This type of listening is for the pure enjoyment of listening to the stimuli.

Argumentativeness A generally stable trait which predisposes individuals in communication situations to advocate positions on controversial issues and to attack verbally the positions which other people hold on these issues.

Artifacts personal adornment such as tattoos, jewelry, branding, scarring and environmental adornment such as the artwork on the wall, the cleanliness, the type of objects on the dresser, and the clothes hanging in the closet.

Assertive communication Involves defending your own rights and wishes while still respecting the rights and wishes of others.

Assertiveness The ability to stand up for oneself and the ability to initiate, maintain, and terminate conversations to reach interpersonal goals.

Assurances Refer to the expression of love and commitment as well as making references to the future of the relationship.

Asynchronous Involves a time lapse between when a message is received and when a response is made.

Attachment security   Predicts that individuals will be most attracted to those who are secure.

Attachment security hypothesis   This states that individuals are attracted to and seek out peers and relationship partners that can provide them with a sense of security.

Attachment theory   An attempt to explain the strong bond children form with the primary caregiver and the stress which results from separation from one another.

Attitude similarity   Focuses on our perception of the attitudes, beliefs, and values that we hold in common.

Attitudes   Learned predispositions to respond in favorable or unfavorable ways toward people or objects.

Attribution theory   The dominant theory that explains how people explain their own and others' behavior.

Autonomy/connection   Tension that occurs in the workplace when friends struggle on how close to become.

Avoidance   Conflict management style used by partners who deny having a problem in the first place, or by someone who is uncomfortable at the prospect of engaging in conflict.

Avoidant   Avoidance of "sore," or difficult, subjects.

Avoiding   During this stage, relationship partners will actively fill their schedules to avoid seeing their partners.

B

Back-channeling cues   Used to regulate our conversations, specifically used by listeners to signal that they are motivated to listen to us, but they are not interested in "taking over the floor."

Background similarity   Refers to commonalities that we share as a result of our life experiences.

Bargaining   Individuals try to strike deals with others in order to recover from their illness.

Beliefs   Our personal convictions regarding the truth or existence of things.

Biased information search   Our propensity to seek out certain types of information and avoid others.

Birth stories   Narratives on how each person entered the family and can define how members "fit" into the system.

Bonding   This stage is viewed as a formal contractual agreement that declares to the world that the couple has made a serious commitment to one another.

Boundaries   Refers to who are to be considered part of the system.

C

Calibration   The mechanism that allows the family to review their relationships and communication and decide if any adjustments need to be made to the system.

Ceremonial behavior   Refers to the relationship maintenance strategies that focus on rituals.

Character   This refers to the extent to which you are trustworthy.

Chronemics   Refers to how we use and perceive time.

Chronic stressor   Stressing events that require families to cope with the situation for an extended period of time.

Circumscribing   In this stage, the communication between the relationship partners is often described as restricted, controlled, or constrained.

Clarity   The extent to which the deceiver is clear, comprehensible, and concise.

Clarity/Equivocation   A communication style that ranges from direct and succinct language to non-straightforward communication that appears ambiguous, contradictory, tangential, or obscure

Closure   Refers to a level of understanding, or emotional conclusion, to a difficult life event, such as terminating a romantic relationship.

Coercive power   Power base that focuses on the perceived ability of the source to punish or to enact negative consequences.

Cognitive arousal   The mental response an individual has when a violation occurs, according to nonverbal expectancy violation theory.

Cognitive complexity   Refers to the extent to which an individual possesses more highly abstract and differentiated construct systems.

Cognitive modification   A type of behavior modification that is used to reduce communication apprehension that suggests people have learned to think negatively about themselves and can be taught to think positively.

Collaboration/integrative   Conflict management style that uses productive means of managing conflict because it requires open and ongoing communication.

Comforting communication   The type of communication behavior having the intended function of alleviating, moderating, or salving the distressed emotional states of others.

Comforting skills   The ability to reduce another's emotional distress.

Commitment   The extent of our dedication to continue a relationship.

Communication apprehension   Refers to the level of fear or anxiety an individual has that is associated with real or anticipated communication with another person.

Communication behavior   Refers to the relationship maintenance strategies that focus on the exchange of open and honest information.

Communication competence   The ability to send messages that are perceived as appropriate and effective.

Communication Predicament of Aging Model   Suggests that when young people communicate with the elderly they often rely on negative stereotypes.

Compensatory restoration   Making oneself appear more "attractive" than the competition.

Competence   This refers to your knowledge or expertise.

Competition/distributive   Conflict management style that uses aggressive and uncooperative types of behaviors.

Complementarity   Explains the saying "opposites attract."

Complementing   A process by which our nonverbal communication is used in conjunction with the verbal portion of the message.

Completeness   The extent to which the information provided in the message is too brief or vague.

Compliance   Level of influence that occurs when an individual agrees to a request because he can see a potential reward or punishment for doing so.

Comprehensive listening   This type of listening involves mindfully receiving and remembering new information.

Computer-mediated communication (CMC)   Refers to the use of the Internet as a channel for communication.

Concealment   Partially tell the truth while leaving out important details.

Concrete   Refers to messages that are well-defined.

Concreteness   Refers to being able to communicate thoughts and ideas.

Confirmation   Occurs when we treat and communicate with family members in a way that is consistent with how they see themselves.

Confirming messages   Process in which individuals feel recognized, acknowledged, valued, and respected.

Conflict   An expressed struggle between at least two interdependent parties who perceive incompatible goals, scarce resources, and interference from the other party in achieving their goals.

Conflict management styles   Habitual responses to conflict situations.

Conflict metaphors   "Conflict is a trial," "conflict is an upward struggle," "conflict is a mess," and "conflict is a game."

Conformity orientation   Refers to the degree to which a family encourages autonomy in individual beliefs, values, and attitudes.

Connotative meaning   Refers to the personal meaning that the source has with that word.

Consensual families   These families adopt both a high conversation and a high conformity orientation.

Consensus   Considers whether the behavior is unique to the individual or if they are behaving in the way that would be typically expected of others.

Consistency   Refers to whether an individual behaves the same way across contexts and at various times.

Constitutive rules   These help define communication by identifying appropriate words and behaviors.

Constructive aggression   Forms of aggression that are more active than passive, such as assertiveness and argumentativeness.

Constructivism   Refers to the process we use to organize and interpret experiences by applying cognitive structures labeled schemata.

Content expectations   Focus on how the relationship is defined by the role each partner plays.

Content level of meaning   The informational component of a message is the verbal message you send/the words you choose. The subjective meaning that is primarily related to the topic at hand.

Content-oriented listener   Listeners that focus on the details of the message, and they pick up on the facts of the story and analyze it from a critical perspective.

Context   Refers to the environment, situation, or setting in which we use verbal communication.

Continuous   Unclear distinction when things begin and end.

Control mutuality   The extent to which couples agree on who has the right to influence the other and establish relational goals.

Conventional (MDL)   Individuals working within this message design logic suggest that communication is socially constructed, rule guided behavior.

Conversation orientation   Refers to the level of openness and the frequency with which a variety of topics are discussed.

Costs   Refers to the undesirable behaviors or outcomes of relationships.

Coup de foudre   Translated as "bolt of lightning" but refers to accelerated intimacy.

Courtship stories   Narratives that provide a timeline for tracing romance in the family.

Covariation theory   The idea that we decide whether peoples' behavior is based on either internal or external factors by using three different and important types of information: distinctiveness, consensus, and consistency.

Co-worker (peer) relationships   Peer relationships that evolve as a result of interactions between members of an organization at the same status level.

Credibility   This is defined as having three dimensions: competence, character, and goodwill.

Culturally bounded   Suggests that the rules we follow are socially constructed and are restricted to a specific culture.

Culture   Shared perceptions which shape the communication patterns and expectations of a group of people.

D

Dark side of communication   An integrative metaphor for a certain perspective toward the study of human folly, frailty, and fallibility.

Deception   A message knowingly transmitted by a sender to foster a false belief or conclusion by a receiver.

Decoding   Refers to the ability to accurately read and interpret messages.

De-escalation messages   Typically provide a rationale for wanting to see less of the rejected partner.

De-escalatory conflict spirals   Covert or indirect way of expressing conflict.

Defensive listening   This type of listener perceives a threatening environment.

Deidentification   An individual's attempt to create a distinct identity that is separate from that of their siblings.

Demographic similarity   Based on similar physical and social characteristics.

Denial   Stage where the patient may continue to work as if he were as well and as strong as before.

Denotative meaning   Refers to the universal meaning of the word, or the definition you would find in the dictionary.

Depression   The terminally ill individual or loved one may lose interest in the outside world and significantly reduce his or her contact with other people.

Destructive aggression   Forms of aggression that can potentially damage individual's self-esteem.

Detachment   Perceptions of being less connected which results in abrupt leaving online environments without warnings.

Differentiating   In this stage, partners highlight their differences.

Digital divide   A gap between those who have access to the Internet and those who do not.

Direct definitions   Descriptions, or labels, families assign to its members that affect the way we see and define ourselves.

Direct methods   Refers to specific and straightforward strategy used in telling the friend how you honestly feel.

Direct/indirect   A communication style that ranges from explicit inquiries and comments in a straightforward manner to a communication style that relies on a more roundabout or subtle method of communicating.

Disability   Individuals that have either a mental or a physical condition that substantially limits one or more of their major life activities.

Disconfirmation   Occurs when family members fail to offer any type of response.

Disconfirming   Listeners that deny the feelings of the speaker.

Disconfirming messages   Indifference, imperviousness, and disqualification of the message or speaker.

Discriminate listening   This type of listening helps us understand the meaning of the message.

Dissimilarity   The differences between relationship dyads such as backgrounds, intelligence, attitudes, ethics, and temperament.

Distinctiveness   Refers to whether or not a person typically behaves the same way with the target, or receiver, of the behavior.

Diversity   Refers to the unique qualities or characteristics that distinguish individuals and groups from one another.

Dominance   A mechanism typically associated with attempts to express power and take control in a relationship.

Dual perspective   Refers to the attempt to see things from the other person's point of view.

Duration   Used to describe the length of time we have known the other person.

Dyadic phase   This phase is when the leaver officially announces to the partner that he or she is leaving or thinking of leaving.

E

Ectomorph   A body type that is described as being tall, thin, and frail.

Ego support   The ability to make others feel positive about themselves.

Electronic paralanguage   A type of computer-mediated nonverbal communication that includes emoticons, acronyms, abbreviations, and flaming.

Embarrassment   Occurs when we perceive that our self-esteem has been threatened or if we have presented what we perceive to be a negative view of the self to others.

Emblems   Nonverbal gestures that have a particular translation, for example, extending your forefinger over your lips means to be quiet.

Emoticons   Symbols made up of combinations of keyboard keys that convey emotions. For example, :).

Emotions Subjective feelings such as happiness, anger, shame, fear, guilt, sadness, and excitement that produce positive or negative reactions that are physical, psychological, and physiological.

Empathetic listening This type of listening is used to help others.

Empathy Indicate to the other person that you understand his/her position or feelings.

Employee Emotional Abuse (EEA) Repeated, targeted, unwelcome, destructive communication by more powerful individuals toward less empowered individuals in the organization, which results in emotional harm.

Encoding Refers to an individual's ability to display messages.

Endomorph A body type that is described as being short, round, and soft.

Environmental adornment Refers to artifacts that we use in our surroundings to identify ourselves.

Environmental factors These are closely related to artifacts and refer to the context, room layout, lighting, and/or color.

Equality/inequality Tensions that occur in the workplace when friends struggle with hierarchical structures in the workplace.

Equifinality Refers to families' abilities to achieve the same goal by following different paths or employing different communication behaviors.

Equity theory This theory suggests a relationship is considered equitable when the ratio of inputs to outputs is equal for both individuals involved.

Equivocation Strategically vague.

Escalatory conflict spirals A heavy reliance on overt power manipulation, threats, coercion, and deception.

Ethnicity Refers to the common heritage, or background, shared by a group of people.

Ethnocentrism Refers to the tendency to perceive our own ways of behaving and thinking as being correct, or acceptable, and judging other behaviors as being "strange," incorrect, or inferior.

Evaluative listening This type of listening involves critically assessing messages.

Exclusively Internet-Based Relationships (EIB) Relationships that are developed without any face-to-face interaction or interaction through traditional media, such as the telephone, letters.

Exit Response to conflict that typically involves threats of physical separation between partners.

Experimenting In this stage communication involves excessive questions and discussions about topics such as classes, hobbies, or other demographic information.

Expert power Power base that is grounded in the perception that the source possesses knowledge, expertise, or skills in a particular area.

Explicit learning Learning that involves actual instructions regarding the preferred way of behaving.

Expressed struggle The communicative interchanges that make up the conflict episode.

Expressive (MDL) Individuals working within this message design logic believe that language is a medium used for expressing thoughts and feelings.

External attribution Situational factors.

External stressor Stressors often the result of an event that occurs outside the family, such as a hurricane destroying a family's home.

F

Face management Refers to skills that one possesses in order to maintain relationships by protecting an individuals' self-perception during communication.

Facial communication Any expression on the face that sends messages.

False homophily Refers to the presentation of a deceptive image of self that appears to be more similar than it actually is.

Falsification An outright lie.

Family communication patterns theory This theory focuses on how a variety of messages are processed and discussed within the family to create shared meaning.

Family jealousy Jealousy that is typically the result of an individual's relationship with another family member.

Family stories Narratives recounting significant events that have been shared by members.

Family systems theory This theory suggests family relationships can be treated as systems and can include the study of systemic qualities such as wholeness, interdependence, hierarchy, boundaries, calibration, and equifinality.

Flaming Refers to anti-social electronic behavior, such as swearing, firing insults, or shouting.

Formal language style When short cuts are not used and proper language rules are adhered to.

Formal/informal A communication style that ranges from language that is used to show respect and is typically used when you are communicating with someone of higher power to a communication style that is used in a relaxed, casual, and familiar style.

Friend jealousy Jealousy that is typically the result of an individual's relationship with another friend.

Friendship-warmth touch Touches that occur between extended family members, close business associates, and friendly neighbors that signal caring, concern, and interest.

Functional-professional touch Touches that occur while accomplishing a specific task which is performed by those working within a specific role.

Fundamental attribution error   When attempting to explain others' negative behaviors, we tend to overestimate the internal factors or causes and underestimate the external factors or causes.

G

Gender-bending   Deceptive practice that often involves presenting oneself as the opposite sex in chat rooms or online video games to experience what it is like to be a man or woman.

Goal incompatibility   When relationship partners want the same thing or different things.

Goals   Desired end states toward which persons strive.

Goodwill   This refers to your ability to care or feel concerned.

Granting forgiveness   A powerful tool used to set yourself and your partner free from harboring negative feelings toward each other and perceptions of the relationship.

Grave dressing phase   In this phase partners are able to articulate the explanation of the termination and create their own versions of the relationship, whether truthful or not.

H

Haptics   A type of nonverbal communication also known as touch.

Hate speech   Verbally attacking individuals on the basis of their race, ethnic background, religion, gender, or sexual orientation.

Health communication   An area of study concerned with human interaction in the health care process.

Hearing   Involves the physical process of sound waves traveling into the ear canal, vibrating the ear drum, and eventually sending signals to the brain.

Hidden disabilities   Learning disabilities, arthritis, diabetes, asthma, AIDS, and heart disease are all forms of this.

Hierarchy   Levels of the family system.

High aggression   Refers to intensive face threatening, verbal belittling, and direct physical contact with the other person in the form of slapping, shoving, or pushing.

Homophily   The idea that we choose to be with people who are similar to us.

Hostility   The use of symbols (verbal or nonverbal) to express irritability, negativism, resentment, and suspicion.

Humor   The use of jokes and sarcasm in either positive or negative ways.

Humor orientation   The extent to which people use humor as well as their self-perceived appropriateness of humor production.

Hyperpersonal model of CMC   The idea that online communication often facilitates relationship development and perceptions of intimacy.

I

Identification   Level of influence that occurs when one recognizes the potential benefits of agreeing to an influence attempt, or perhaps they wish to establish a relationship with the source.

Identity scripts   Rules for living and relating to one another in family contexts. Example: "money does not grow on trees," "people who live in glass houses should not throw stones," "remember the golden rule," or "a family that prays together stays together."

Illustrators   The label used to indicate when you use your body to help describe or visually depict something.

Immediacy   Refers to the psychological and physical closeness we have with one another. The process of using communication behaviors purposefully to reduce psychological and physical distance.

Impartiality/favoritism   Tensions that occur in the workplace when friends struggle with not showing preferential treatment.

Implicit learning   Learning that occurs via observation.

Impression management   The process of maintaining a positive image of self in the presence of others.

Independent-mindedness   Refers to the extent to which employees can openly express their own opinions.

Independents   Couples simultaneously respect the need for autonomy and engage in a high level communication and sharing with one another.

Indirect methods   Refers to a gradual strategy used to let go of a relationship such as, calling the friend less or sending fewer emails.

Infidelity   Behaving in a way that crosses the perceived boundary and expectation of an exclusive relationship.

Informal language style   Refers to short cuts used such as shortened words, improper capitalization, and punctuation in language construction of online messages (RUOK?).

Initiation   In this stage one party decides to initiate conversation with another person.

Inner self   The self that we keep private and that may reflect how we really feel about ourselves.

Integrating   This stage is marked by a merging of personalities and identities.

Intensifying   In this stage the information shared becomes more personal and private (depth).

Intentionality   Described as being stable or persistent and often refers to behaviors that are likely to be exhibited repeatedly across a variety of contexts.

Interactive strategies   Typically involve a face-to-face encounter between two individuals to reduce uncertainty.

Interdependence   Proposes that the family system is comprised of interrelated parts, or members.

Interdependent   The extent to which a partner relies on one another and is aware of how their decisions or behaviors affect one another.

Interference   Someone or something standing in our way of accomplishing a goal.

Internal attribution   Dispositional factors.

Internal stressor   Stressors that evolve from a family member.

Internalization   Level of influence that occurs when an individual adopts a behavior because it is internally rewarding.

Interpersonal attraction   Refers to a general feeling or desire that impacts our decision to approach and initiate a relationship with another person.

Interpersonal communication   A process which occurs in a specific context and involves an exchange of verbal or nonverbal messages between two connected individuals with the intent to achieve shared meaning.

Interpersonal Deception Theory   Proposed to explain the strategic choices made when engaging in deceptive communication.

Interpretation   The subjective process of making sense of our perceptions.

Intimacy   Refers to close relationships in which two or more people share personal and private information with one another.

Intimacy jealousy   The result of the exchange of intimate or private information that a partner may share with a third party.

Intrapersonal communication   Takes place inside one's head and is silent and repetitive.

Intrapsychic phase   This phase is when one partner recognizes that something is wrong in a relationship and that he or she is no longer happy.

Involuntary relationships   Relationships that we do not choose.

Involuntary stressor   Stressing events that simply occur—a family member being injured in a car accident or the announcement of an unplanned teen pregnancy.

Involuntary/obligatory relationships   Relationships that often occur by chance and not by choice.

J

Jargon   Defined as a specialized vocabulary that is socially constructed and regularly used by members of a particular trade, profession, or organization.

Jealousy   A protective reaction to a perceived threat to a valued relationship, arising from a situation in which the partner's involvement with an activity and/or another person is contrary to the jealous person's definition of their relationship.

Joint activities   Refer to those behaviors relationship partners do together.

Joking   Using humor to create a more light-hearted response to an embarrassing situation.

Judgment/acceptance   Tensions that occur in the workplace when friends struggle with providing and taking criticism.

Justification tactics   Stating that he or she needs to stop seeing the other person; provides a reason for ending the relationship and recognizes that the relationship is not salvageable.

K

Kinesics   The use of body movements and gestures as forms of communication.

Knowledge   Refers to the theoretical principles and concepts that explain behaviors occurring within a specific communication context. Also refers to understanding what reaction or action is best suited for a particular situation.

L

Laissez-faire families   These families adopt both a low conversation and low conformity orientation.

Leader-member exchanges (LMX)   This theory states that leaders in organizations develop relationships with all members and they exist on a continuum ranging from perceptions of "in-group" to "out-group" status.

Leakage cues   Behaviors believed to signal deception include increased blinking, speech errors, higher voice pitch, and enlarged pupils.

Legitimate power   Power base that is centered on the perception that the source has authority because of a particular role or title.

Liking   Defined as the level of positive affect, or affinity, we feel toward another person.

Liking or affinity   Expressed affect.

Limited capacity processors   We are described as this because we have innate limitations in our ability to process information.

Linguistic Determinism   A concept that suggests that "language determines thought."

Linguistic Relativity   A concept that suggests distinctions encoded in one language are unique to that language alone

Listening   Involves the physical process of hearing, but it also involves the psychological process of attending to the stimuli, creating meaning, and responding.

Listening styles   A set of attitudes, beliefs, and predispositions about the how, where, when, who, and what of the information reception and encoding process.

Love-intimacy touch   Touches that occur between family members and friends where there is affection and a deep level of caring such as extended hugs and holding hands.

Low aggression   Characterized by yelling, crying, refusing to talk, or stomping out of the room.

Loyalty   Response to conflict that occurs when a partner decides to "wait it out" in the hopes that by doing so, the relationship will improve on its own.

M

Markers   Refer to physical objects that are placed in between ourselves and others to claim personal space or territory.

Maslow's Hierarchy of Needs   Theory that suggests once the basic physiological and safety needs have been fulfilled, humans seek to fulfill the love and belonging needs.

Mass communication   Involves communicators that are typically separated in both space and time and who send and receive messages indirectly.

Media richness theory   Describes the capability of a communication channel to convey a variety of cues such as the channel's level of synchrony, the availability of social cues, the ability to use natural language (as opposed to text or symbols), and the ability to convey emotions using the channel.

Mediated communication   Exchange of email messages, letters, text messages, or phone calls.

Mentor relationships   Characterized by a more experienced member serving as a role model, teacher, or guide for a colleague who is less experienced.

Mesomorph   A body type that is described as being physically fit, muscular, average height and weight, and athletic.

Message Design Logics (MDL)   Theories individuals use to interpret how communication works.

Metacommunication   Communicating about communication.

Metaphors   Make reference to specific objects, events, or images to represent the family experience and a collective identity ("three ring circus").

Moderate aggression   Involves more intense acts of verbal aggression such as verbal insults, swearing at the other, and indirect physical displays of anger such as kicking, hitting, throwing inanimate objects, or threatening to engage in these behaviors.

Monochronic   This time orientation spans across a "time line," and we can schedule appointments one after another in an orderly fashion.

Monopolizing   Involves taking the focus off the speaker and redirecting the conversation and attention to themselves.

Motivation   Refers to one's desire to achieve results in a competent manner.

Multi-channeled   The use of several senses to communicate.

Myths   Created to communicate the beliefs, values, and attitudes held by members to represent characteristics that are considered important to the family.

N

Needs   Strong feelings of discomfort or desire which motivate to achieve satisfaction or comfort.

Negative feedback   Refers to verbal and nonverbal behaviors that are often discouraging to a source to continue communicating.

Negative identity management   Used as a last resort to terminate or when relationship partners are in need of immediate disengagement.

Neglect   Response to conflict that might avoid the relationship partner, refuse to discuss problems they are experiencing, and communicate with one another in a hostile or aggressive manner.

No flirting   The act of avoiding overly familiar flirtatious acts.

Noise   Refers to anything that interferes with the reception of a message.

Non-normative stressor   Stressors that are unpredictable and often catch families "off guard."

Nonverbal comforting strategies   Hugging, patting the person on the back, and showing concern through their voice.

Nonverbal communication   Refers to all aspects of communication other than the words we use, including but not limited to: facial expressions, body movements and gestures, physical appearance, and voice.

Nonverbal Expectancy Violation Theory   This theory suggests that individuals hold expectancies for nonverbal behavior and when these expectations are violated (or the rules are not abided by) there are two reactions.

Nonverbal messages   The portion of communicating that involves everything other than the words we use.

Normative stressor   Stressors that are expected to occur at some point during the course of the family life cycle.

Novelty   Refers to the tendency to pay attention to stimuli that new or different.

O

Observer   The role in which you were an innocent bystander of another's embarrassment.

Obsessive relational intrusion   The repeated and unwanted pursuit and invasion of one's sense of physical or symbolic privacy by another person, either stranger or acquaintance, who desires and/or presumes an intimate relationship.

Oculesics   The study of eye behavior.

Openness   Refers to the open and ongoing discussions that partners have about the status of the relationship.

Openness/closedness   Tensions that occur in the workplace when friends struggle with how much information to disclose.

Organization   Refers to the process of placing stimuli or information into categories in order to make sense of it.

Organizational communication   Takes place between members within a clear hierarchical structure; individuals are typically encouraged to adhere to roles and rules established within this structure.

Organizational orientation   A theory which identifies three approaches used by members to enact their work roles: upward mobiles, indifferents, and ambivalents.

Outside pressure   Stress that stems from a relationship as a result of people external of the relationship such as family, friends, or occupations.

P

Paralanguage   A nonverbal communication that includes everything beyond the words in the verbally communicated message such as pitch, rate, volume, pronunciation, inflection, tempo, accents, and vocal fillers.

Paraphrasing   Involves restating a message in your own words to see if the meaning you assigned was similar to that which was intended.

Passive communication activity   Responding "uh-huh" to a question while watching a game on television.

Passive strategies   Typically involve observation and social comparison to learn information about others.

People-oriented listener   Listeners that seek common interests with the speaker and are highly responsive; interested in the speaker's feelings and emotions.

Perceived shared resources   The perception of anything that an individual identifies as valuable or meaningful.

Perception   How we interpret and assign meaning to others' behaviors and messages based on our background and past experiences. The process of selecting, organizing, and interpreting stimuli into something that makes sense or is meaningful.

Perceptual barriers   Those internal obstacles that often disrupt communication due to cognitive or emotional reactions located within the individual.

Perpetual conflict   Disagreements between relationship partners that are often directly related to personality issues.

Personal adornment   Refers to how we use artifacts on our bodies such as tattoos, jewelry, branding, and scarring.

Personal constructs   Bipolar dimensions of meaning used to predict and evaluate how people behave.

Personal orientation system   Predispositions that are comprised of one's needs, beliefs, values, and attitudes.

Personality   Our predisposition to behave a certain way.

Personalization   The extent to which the deceiver takes ownership of the information.

Person-centered comforting communication   Strategies that help a person explain how he is feeling at the moment, recognize and validate the expressed feelings, and illustrate how those feelings fit in a broader social context.

Physical appearance   A type of nonverbal communication that includes our body, clothing, make-up, height, size, and hair.

Physical arousal   The bodily response an individual has when violation occurs, according to nonverbal expectancy violation theory.

Physical attractiveness   When characteristics such as body shape or size, hair color or length, and facial features are used in making a determination of whether to initiate a relationship.

Pluralistic families   These families adopt a high conversation orientation and a low conformity orientation.

Polychronic   This time orientation suggests that several things can be done at the same time.

Positive feedback   Refers to verbal and nonverbal behaviors that encourage the speaker to continue communicating.

Positive relational deceptive strategies   Refers to strategies that enhance, escalate, repair, and improve relationships.

Positive tone messages   Created to ease the pain for the rejected partner.

Positivity   Involves being polite, acting cheerful and upbeat, and avoiding criticism.

Power   One's ability to influence others to behave in ways they normally might not.

Power jealousy   Often associated with perceptions that a partner's other relationships or obligations are viewed as more important than your relationship with the person.

Powerful language   Associated with positive attributes such as assertiveness and importance and it can be influential, commanding, and authoritative.

Powerless language   Associated with negative attributes such as shyness, introversion, timidity, nervousness, and apprehension.

Predicted outcome value   This theory focuses on the perceived rewards or benefits associated with a new relationship.

Primacy and recency   Refers to arguments delivered first and last.

Primarily Internet-Based Relationships (PIB)   Relationships may initially be formed online or through face-to-face interaction, could include acquaintances, friends, co-workers, or family members and often communicate through emails or instant messaging.

Prosocial behavior   Refers to being polite and cooperative in the relationship, while avoiding face-threatening communication.

Protective families   These families score low on conversation orientation and high on conformity.

Prototypes   Refers to knowledge structures which represent the most common attributes of a phenomenon.

Proxemics   The study of how the role of space has shape and influences our interactions with others. A type of nonverbal communication that is known as space, which can refer to the invisible bubble we place around our bodies.

Proximity   Refers to the physical distance between two people.

Pseudo-listening   This type of listening is used when we are pretending to listen.

Public self   The self that we project during social interaction.

R

Race   The term used to refer to genetically inherited biological characteristics such as hair texture and color, eye shape, skin color, and facial structure.

Rapport talk   Analogous to small talk or phatic communication.

Rationale   The thesis or main concern you have.

Real barriers   Obstacles to communication through regular channels.

Recipients   The role in which someone has targeted you in an embarrassing situation.

Reciprocal self-disclosure   The notion that disclosure of information between two people is best when it is similar in terms of topics discussed and depth of disclosure.

Reduced social cues theory   Developed to explain the absence of nonverbal cues in online interactions.

Referent power   Power base that is based on a person's respect, identification, and attraction to the source.

Reflected appraisal   Refers to the tendency to view ourselves based on the appraisals of others.

Regional differences   Speech patterns, attitudes, and values may differ significantly depending on the geographic location.

Regulating   Refers to ways in which we control conversation.

Regulative rules   These control our communication by managing communication interaction.

Regulators   Type of body movement that is used in conversation to control the communication flow.

Reinforce   Refers to messages that are consistent with our views.

Rejection   Occurs when family members treat others in a manner that is inconsistent with how they see themselves.

Relational expectations   Refer to the similarity, or correspondence, of the emotional, or affective, expectations each partner has for defining the relationship.

Relational level of meaning   This includes nonverbal messages such as eye contact, gestures, and vocal inflection and tells the receiver how you would like the message to be interpreted.

Relationship   A connection between two individuals that results in mutual interaction with the intent of achieving shared meaning.

Relationship disengagement   The process of terminating a relationship.

Relationship level of meaning   The subjective meaning that is highly sensitive to the people involved in the conversation.

Relationship maintenance strategies   Behaviors and activities used strategically to sustain desired relational qualities or to sustain the current status of the relationship.

Relevance/directness   Refers to the extent to which the deceiver produces messages that are logical in flow and sequence, and are pertinent to the conversation.

Repetition   Refers to both verbal and nonverbal expressions made simultaneously to reinforce each other.

Report talk   Involves discussions about facts, events, and solutions. Refers to talking to accomplish goals.

Reward power   Power base that focuses on a person's perception that the source of power can provide rewards.

Rewards   Refers to the desirable behaviors or outcomes of relationships which the recipient perceives as enjoyable or fulfilling.

Rhetorical (MDL)   Individuals working within this message design logic believe communication is a function of co-constructing reality with the parties involved.

Role   Used to describe the nature of a relationship such as *mother, teacher, supervisor, colleague,* or *coach.*

Romantic jealousy   Jealousy that is the result of a partner's relationship with another person and is associated with perceived intimacy between two people.

Rules   Expectations for communication that may be explicit or implicit.

S

Sapir-Whorf hypothesis   Suggests that the language we learn, as well as the culture we are exposed to, is used to shape our entire reality.

Schemata   Refers to mental filing cabinets with several drawers or organized clusters of knowledge and information about particular topics.

Script theory   The idea that we often interact with others in a way that could be described as "automatic" or even "mindless."

Scripts   Knowledge structures that guide and influence how we process information.

Secure   This style is characterized by intense feelings of intimacy, emotional security, and physical safety when the infant is in the presence of the attachment figure.

Selection   We are continually making choices about the amount and type of information that we choose to notice.

Selective attention   Refers to the decision to pay attention to certain stimuli while simultaneously ignoring others.

Selective exposure   Refers to the choice to subject oneself to certain stimuli.

Selective listening   Type of listening that occurs when a listener focuses only on parts of the message.

Selective retention   Refers to the choice to save or delete information from one's long-term memory.

Self   A psychological entity consisting of an organized set of beliefs, feelings, and behaviors.

Self-complexity   Refers to the number of self-aspects, also known as Sub-selves.

Self-concept   Refers to the cognitions about the self.

Self-determination theory   People have an innate psychological need to feel autonomous, or self-governing, in one's behavior.

Self-disclosure   Involves divulging personal information to another individual and is often delivered through face-to-face or computer mediated channels.

Self-esteem   Refers to the subjective perception of one's self-worth, or the value one places on the self.

Self-forgiving   Refers to giving yourself permission to heal and move forward.

Self-fulfilling prophecy   A process in which people act to conform to the expectations of others.

Self-monitoring   A personality construct that causes a person to respond to social and interpersonal cues for appropriate communication behaviors in a variety of situations.

Self-regulation   Refers to the capacity to exercise choice and initiation.

Self-serving bias   States that we tend to manufacture, or construct, attributions which best serve our own self-interests.

Separates   Couples tend to emphasize each individual's identity and independence over maintaining the relationship.

Severe aggression   Includes intense verbal abuse and threats and involves physical attacks that include kicking, biting, punching, hitting with an object, raping, and using a weapon.

Sexist language   Refers to any speech that is degrading to males or females.

Sexual harassment   Any unwelcome sexual advances, requests for sexual favors, and other verbal or physical conduct of a sexual nature.

Sexual-arousal touch   Touch that occurs within sexual/erotic contexts such as kissing.

Shared meaning   The goal of our interpersonal communication interactions.

Sharing tasks   The extent to which partners share the chores and responsibilities associated with the relationship.

Similarity   Another word for homophily.

Similarity hypothesis   According to this theory we are attracted to individuals who exhibit an attachment style similar to our own.

Similarity to current self   Refers to the belief that individuals are attracted to those who are similar to themselves.

Similarity to ideal view of self   Refers to the belief that individuals are attracted to those who are similar to our view of how we would ultimately like to be.

Size   Refers to the magnitude of the stimuli.

Skill   Addresses one's ability to utilize the appropriate behaviors in a situation.

Skill similarity model   Similarity in the nature and level of partners' social skills.

Skills   Specific communication behaviors which contribute to competent and effective interpersonal communication.

Skills training   A type of behavior modification that suggests taking courses to help individuals learn how to communicate more effectively will help reduce communication apprehension.

Small group communication   Occurs between three or more people who are interdependent and working to achieve commonly recognized goals or objectives.

Social attractiveness   Common interests or similar patterns of communication that cause individuals to perceive one another as someone they would like to spend time with.

Social class   Stratification based on educational, occupational, or financial backgrounds, resulting in classifications and status differentials.

Social comparison theory   This theory suggests that most individuals have a basic need, or drive, to evaluate and compare themselves to those around them.

Social exchange theory   Refers to an assessment of costs and rewards in determining the value of pursuing or continuing a relationship.

Social goals   Refer to desired end states that fulfill the need for inclusion or affection.

Social identity theory   An explanation for our tendency to evaluate in-groups more positively than out-groups.

Social networking   Refers to the process of connecting with others to form different types of relationships.

Social networks   Mutual friends and family members.

Social penetration theory   This theory focuses on how self-disclosure changes as relationships move from one level to the next.

Social phase   This phase is when the relationship termination is focused less on the relationship and more on the relationship partners' friends and family.

Social presence theory   To describe the perceived psychological closeness that occurs during an FTF interaction.

Social referencing   Refers to the process by which individuals will rely on others around them to determine how to respond to unfamiliar stimuli.

Socialization   Refers to the process of learning about one's cultural norms and expectations.

Social-polite touch   Touches that occur between business partners, acquaintances, and strangers including greetings and salutations, such as a handshake.

Solicited confessions   Offered as the result of direct questioning or confrontation.

Stagnating   This stage is described as two people who are merely "going through the motions" in their relationship because their communication has come to a virtual standstill.

State approach   Examining how individuals communicate in a particular situation or context.

Status   Refers to the level of position an individual has when compared with others.

Stereotypes   Impressions and expectations based on one's knowledge or beliefs about a specific group of people which are then applied to all individuals who are members of that group.

Stories of survival   Narratives used to explain how family members have overcome difficult times, and they are often told to help family members cope with challenges they face.

Subjective   Influence by a particular bias of one's own point of view.

Superior-subordinate relationship   Differ from other types of interpersonal bonds because of the explicit status differential that is present.

Symbolic interactionism   Discusses the role that symbols and messages play in assigning meaning to our experiences, others, and ourselves.

Symbols   Socially agreed upon representations of phenomena and range between being concrete and abstract.

Synchronous   Occurs in real time, or simultaneously.

Systematic desensitization   A type of behavior modification used to reduce communication apprehension that suggests anxiety related to communication is learned and therefore it can be unlearned.

T

Task attractiveness   Refers to the characteristics or qualities that are perceived as appealing when initiating relationships in which the goal is to complete a task or assignment.

Task goals   Defined as desired end states that fulfill the need for the completion of a task.

Terminating   This stage marks the end of the relationship.

Themes   Represent important concerns regarding the expected relationship between family members and can assist family members in understanding how to direct their energy as a family unit ("Blood is thicker than water").

Theory   A set of statements about the way things work.

Third-party information   Information being revealed by a person outside the relationship.

Time-oriented listener   Listeners that are particularly interested in brief interactions with others. They direct the length of the conversation.

Togetherness behavior   Refers to the relationship maintenance strategies that focus on dedicating time and energy to a person.

Traditionals   Couples who exhibit a high level of interdependence and sharing.

Trait approach   Examining how individuals interact the majority of the time.

Transactional   When we are sending messages, we are also receiving messages.

Trust   To depend or have faith in.

Turn denying   Listeners use this cue when they are not interested in "taking over the floor" by increasing space between themselves and the speaker and/or avoiding direct eye contact with the speaker.

Turn-maintaining   Used to regulate our conversations, specifically to signal to the listener that we want to continue talking.

Turn-requesting   Used to regulate our conversations, specifically to signal to the speaker that they are interested in speaking.

Turn-yielding   Used to regulate our conversations, specifically to signal to the listener that we are going to stop talking.

U

Uncertainty Reduction Theory   Suggests that human communication is used to gain knowledge and create understanding by reducing uncertainty and, therefore, increasing predictability. Helps us understand how knowledge can assist us in forming effective interpersonal relationships by predicting the attitudes, behaviors, and emotions of others.

Understanding   Applying knowledge to specific situations in an attempt to explain the behaviors that are occurring.

Unintentionally   Refers to one's inability to predict whether the behaviors will be consistent in the future.

Unsolicited confessions   Spontaneous declarations made by a partner.

Utility   The perception that particular messages are immediately useful.

V

Value   A personal philosophy, either explicitly or implicitly expressed, that influences the choice of alternative actions which may be available to an individual.

Verbal aggression   Involves assaulting or criticizing another person's sense of self and typically involves attacks on one's character, competence, background, or appearance.

Verbal aggressiveness   The tendency to attack the self-concept of an individual instead of addressing the other person's arguments.

Verbal communication   Refers to the words we use during the communication process.

Verbal immediacy   Refers to using specific word choices and syntactic structures to increase perceptions of psychological closeness.

Verbal messages   The portion of communication that involves the words we use.

Veridicality   The extent to which the deceiver appears to be truthful.

Visible disabilities   Noticeable to others and might include physical deformities, deafness, or blindness and require the use of a wheelchair.

Voice   Response to conflict that involves discussing relationship concerns openly and often offers suggestions for repairing the relationship transgression.

Voluntary relationships   Relationships we enter into out of our own volition.

Voluntary stressor   Stressors that include events that family members seek out, such as changing careers and moving to a new city.

W

Wholeness   Implies that a family creates its own personality or culture, and that this personality is unique from that of each family member.

Willingness to communicate   An individual's propensity to avoid or approach communication with others.

Withdrawal tactics   These include dodging phone calls, blocking IMs, and rerouting daily activities in order to avoid the individual.

Index